Spanish Letter	Pronunciation
n	As in English.
ñ	Like English *ny* in *canyon*.
o	Approximately like English *o* in *vote*, but more clipped.
p	As in English.
qu	Like English *k*
r	Not at all like American English *r*; a quick flap of the tongue-tip on the roof of the mouth.
rr	A strongly "rolled" or trilled version of Spanish *r*.
s	Like English *s* in *lease*.
t	As in English.
u	Like English *oo* in *boot*, but more clipped. Before *e* or after another vowel, like English *w* (except when accented).
v	See *b* above.
x	Like English *x*; although before consonants many speakers pronounce it like Spanish *s*; like Spanish *j* (in Mexican Indian words).
y	Approximately like English *y* in *yes*.
z	Like English *th* in *thin* (in Northern Spain); like English *s* in *lease* (in Southern Spain and the Americas).

Spanish Accentuation

In a number of words spoken stress is marked by an accent ('): *nación, país, médico, día*.

Words which are not so marked are, generally speaking, stressed on the next-to-the-last syllable if they end in a vowel, *n*, or *s*; and on the last syllable if they end in a consonant other than *n* or *s*.

Note: An accent is placed over some words to distinguish them from others having the same spelling and pronunciation but differing in meaning.

The Random House Spanish Dictionary

SPANISH – ENGLISH

ENGLISH – SPANISH

Edited by Donald F. Solá
Cornell University

Under the General Editorship of
Professor Frederick B. Agard,
Cornell University

RANDOM HOUSE

NEW YORK

Latest Printing 1980

Concise Pronunciation Guide

Spanish
Letter   Pronunciation

a   Like English *a* in *father*.

b, v   At beginning of word group and after *m* or *n*, like English *b*.
Elsewhere, like English *v*, but pronounced with both lips instead of upper teeth and lower lip.

c   Before *e* or *i*, like English *th* in *thin* (in Northern Spain); like Spanish *s* (in Southern Spain and the Americas); elsewhere, like English *k* in *key*.

ch   Like English *ch* in *child*.

d   At beginning of word group and after *n* or *l*, like English *d*.
Elsewhere, like English *th* in *either*.

e   Like English *e* in *bet*.

f   As in English.

g   Before *e* or *i*, the same as Spanish *j*.
Elsewhere, like English *g* in *get*.

gu   Before *e* or *i*, like English *g* in *get*.
Elsewhere, like English *gw* in *Gwynn*.

gü   Like English *gw* in *Gwynn*.

h   Silent.

i   Like English *s* in *machine*, but more clipped. Before or after another vowel, like English *y* (except when accented).

j   Like English *h*, but more rasping.

k   Like English *k*.

l   Like English *l* in *like*, but with the tongue behind the upper front teeth.

ll   Like English *lli* in *million* (in Northern Spain); like Spanish *y* (in Southern Spain and the Americas).

m   As in English.

Spanish Letter	Pronunciation
n	As in English.
ñ	Like English *ny* in *canyon*.
o	Approximately like English *o* in *vote*, but more clipped.
p	As in English.
qu	Like English *k*.
r	Not at all like American English *r*; a quick flap of the tongue-tip on the roof of the mouth.
rr	A strongly "rolled" or trilled version of Spanish *r*.
s	Like English *s* in *lease*.
t	As in English.
u	Like English *oo* in *boot*, but more clipped. Before *e* or after another vowel, like English *w* (except when accented).
v	See *b* above.
x	Like English *x*; although before consonants many speakers pronounce it like Spanish *s*; like Spanish *j* (in Mexican Indian words).
y	Approximately like English *y* in *yes*.
z	Like English *th* in *thin* (in Northern Spain); like English *s* in *lease* (in Southern Spain and the Americas).

Spanish Accentuation

In a number of words spoken stress is marked by an accent ('): *nación, país, médico, día.*

Words which are not so marked are, generally speaking, stressed on the next-to-the-last syllable if they end in a vowel, *n*, or *s*; and on the last syllable if they end in a consonant other than *n* or *s*.

Note: An accent is placed over some words to distinguish them from others having the same spelling and pronunciation but differing in meaning.

Irregular Verbs

Infinitive	Present	Future	Preterit	Past Part.
andar	ando	andaré	anduve	andado
caber	quepo	cabré	cupe	cabido
caer	caigo	caeré	caí	caído
conducir	conduzco	conduciré	conduje	conducido
dar	doy	daré	dí	dado
decir	digo	diré	dije	dicho
estar	estoy	estaré	estuve	estado
haber	he	habré	hube	habido
hacer	hago	haré	hice	hecho
ir	voy	iré	fuí	ido
jugar	juego	jugaré	jugué	jugado
morir	muero	moriré	morí	muerto
oír	oigo	oiré	oí	oído
poder	puedo	podré	pude	podido
poner	pongo	pondré	puse	puesto
querer	quiero	querré	quise	querido
saber	sé	sabré	supe	sabido
salir	salgo	saldré	salí	salido
ser	soy	seré	fuí	sido
tener	tengo	tendré	tuve	tenido
traer	traigo	traeré	traje	traído
valer	valgo	valdré	valí	valido
venir	vengo	vendré	viue	venido
ver	veo	veré	ví	visto

Days of the Week

Sunday	domingo
Monday	lunes
Tuesday	martes
Wednesday	miércoles
Thursday	jueves
Friday	viernes
Saturday	sábado

Months

January	enero	July	julio
February	febrero	August	agosto
March	marzo	September	septiembre
April	abril	October	octubre
May	mayo	November	noviembre
June	junio	December	diciembre

Weights and Measures

The Spanish use the *Metric System* of weights and measures, which is a decimal system in which multiples are shown by the prefixes: deci- (one tenth); centi- (one hundredth); mili- (one thousandth); deca- (ten); hecto- (hundred); kilo- (thousand).

1 centímetro	=	.3937 inches
1 metro	=	39.37 inches
1 kilómetro	=	.621 mile
1 centigramo	=	.1543 grain
1 gramo	=	15.432 grains
1 kilogramo	=	2.2046 pounds
1 tonelada	=	2,204 pounds
1 centilitro	=	.338 ounces
1 litro	=	1.0567 quart (liquid); .908 quart (dry)
1 kilolitro	=	264.18 gallons

Money

	MONETARY UNIT
Spain	peseta
Argentina	peso
Bolivia	peso
Brazil	cruzeiro
Chile	escudo
Colombia	peso
Costa Rica	colón
Cuba	peso
Dominican Republic	peso
Ecuador	sucre
El Salvador	colón
Guatemala	quetzal
Haiti	gourde
Honduras	lempira
Mexico	peso
Nicaragua	córdoba
Panama	balboa
Paraguay	guaraní
Peru	sol
Uruguay	peso
Venezuela	bolívar

6

Numerals

Cardinal

1	uno, una	30	treinta
2	dos	31	treinta y uno
3	tres	32	treinta y dos
4	cuatro	40	cuarenta
5	cinco	50	cincuenta
6	seis	60	sesenta
7	siete	70	setenta
8	ocho	80	ochenta
9	nueve	90	noventa
10	diez	100	cien
11	once	101	ciento uno
12	doce	102	ciento dos
13	trece	200	doscientos, -as
14	catorce	300	trescientos, -as
15	quince	400	cuatrocientos, -as
16	dieciséis	500	quinientos, -as
17	diecisiete	600	seiscientos, -as
18	dieciocho	700	setecientos, -as
19	diecinueve	800	ochocientos, -as
20	veinte	900	novecientos, -as
21	veinte y uno (or veintiuno)	1,000	mil
		2,000	dos mil
22	veinte y dos (or veintidos)	100,000	cien mil
		1,000,000	un millón
		2,000,000	dos millones

Ordinal

1st	primero
2nd	segundo
3rd	tercero
4th	cuarto
5th	quinto
6th	sexto
7th	séptimo
8th	octavo
9th	noveno
10th	décimo

Abbreviations

a.	adjective
abbr.	abbreviation
adv.	adverb
aero.	aeronautical
agr.	agriculture
anat.	anatomy
art.	article
bot.	botany
chem.	chemistry
coll.	colloquial
com.	commercial
conj.	conjunction
dem.	demonstrative
f.	feminine
fin.	finance
geog.	geography
govt.	government
gram.	grammar
interj.	interjection
interrog.	interrogative
leg.	legal
m.	masculine
mech.	mechanics
med.	medicine
Mex.	Mexico
mus.	musical
n.	noun
naut.	nautical
pl.	plural
prep.	preposition
pron.	pronoun
punct.	punctuation
rel.	relative, religion
S.A.	Spanish America
v.	verb

SPANISH - ENGLISH

A

a, *prep.* to; at.
abacero, *m.* grocer.
abad, *m.* abbot.
abadía, *f.* abbey.
abajo, *adv.* down; downstairs.
abandonar, *v.* abandon.
abanico, *m.* fan. **—abani-car,** *v.*
abaratar, *v.* cheapen.
abarcar, *v.* comprise; clasp.
abastecer, *v.* supply, pro-vision.
abatido, *a.* dejected, de-spondent.
abatir, *v.* depress, dishearten.
abdicar, *v.* abdicate.
abdomen, *m.* abdomen.
abeja, *f.* bee.
abejarrón, *m.* bumblebee.
abertura, *f.* opening, aper-ture, slit.
abeto, *m.* fir.
abierto, *a.* open; overt.
abismo, *m.* abyss, chasm.
ablandar, *v.* soften.
abochornar, *v.* embarrass.
abogado, *m.* lawyer, attor-ney.
abolengo, *m.* ancestry.
abolición, *f.* abolition.
abolladura, *f.* dent. **—abo-llar,** *v.*
abominable, *a.* abominable.
abominar, *v.* abhor.
abonar, *v.* pay; fertilize.
abonarse, *v.* subscribe.
abono, *m.* fertilizer; sub-scription.
aborrecer, *v.* hate, loathe, abhor.
aborto, *m.* abortion.
abovedar, *v.* vault.
abrasar, *v.* burn.
abrazar, *v.* embrace; clasp.
abrazo, *m.* embrace.

abreviar, *v.* abbreviate, abridge, shorten.
abreviatura, *f.* abbreviation.
abrigar, *v.* harbor, shelter.
abrigarse, *v.* bundle up.
abrigo, *m.* overcoat; shelter; (pl.) wraps.
abril, *m.* April.
abrir, *v.* open; (med.) lance.
abrochar, *v.* clasp.
abrojo, *m.* thorn.
abrumar, *v.* overwhelm, crush, swamp.
absceso, *m.* abscess.
absolución, *f.* absolution; acquittal.
absoluto, *a.* absolute; down-right.
absolver, *v.* absolve, pardon.
absorbente, *a.* absorbent.
absorber, *v.* absorb.
absorción, *f.* absorption.
abstenerse, *v.* abstain; re-frain.
abstinencia, *f.* abstinence.
abstracción, *f.* abstraction.
abstraer, *v.* abstract.
absurdo, 1. *a.* absurd. **2.** *m.* absurdity.
abuela, *f.* grandmother.
abuelo, *m.* grandfather; (pl.) grandparents.
abultado, *a.* bulky.
abultamiento, *m.* bulge. **—abultar,** *v.*
abundancia, *f.* abundance, plenty.
abundante, *a.* abundant, plentiful.
abundar, *v.* abound.
aburrido, *a.* boring, tedious.
aburrimiento, *m.* boredom.
aburrir, *v.* bore.
abusar, *v.* abuse, misuse.
abusivo, *a.* abusive.

abuso, *m.* abuse.

abyecto, *a.* abject, low.

acá, *adv.* here.

acabar, *v.* finish. **a. de . . .,** to have just . . . .

academia, *f.* academy.

académico, *a.* academic.

acaecer, *v.* happen.

acanalar, *v.* groove.

acaparar, *v.* hoard; monopolize.

acariciar, *v.* caress, stroke.

acaso, *m.* chance. **por si a.,** just in case.

acceder, *v.* accede.

accesible, *a.* accessible.

acceso, *m.* access, approach.

accesorio, *a.* accessory.

accidental, *a.* accidental.

accidente, *m.* accident, wreck.

acción, *f.* action, act; (com.) share of stock.

acechar, *v.* ambush, spy on.

aceite, *m.* oil.

aceitoso, *a.* oily.

aceituna, *f.* olive.

aceleración, *f.* acceleration.

acelerar, *v.* accelerate, speed up.

acento, *m.* accent.

acentuar, *v.* accent, accentuate, stress.

acepillar, *v.* brush; plane (wood).

aceptable, *a.* acceptable.

aceptación, *f.* acceptance.

aceptar, *v.* accept.

acequía, *f.* ditch.

acera, *f.* sidewalk.

acerca de, *prep.* about, concerning.

acercar, *v.* bring near.

acercarse, *v.* approach, come near, go near.

acero, *m.* steel.

acertar, *v.* guess right. **a. en,** hit (a mark).

acertijo, *m.* puzzle, riddle.

acidez, *f.* acidity.

ácido, 1. *a.* sour. **2.** *m.* acid.

aclamación, *f.* acclamation.

aclamar, *v.* acclaim.

aclarar, *v.* brighten; clarify, clear up.

acoger, *v.* welcome, receive.

acogida, *f.* welcome, reception.

acometer, *v.* attack.

acomodador, *m.* usher.

acomodar, *v.* accommodate, fix up.

acompañamiento, *m.* accompaniment; following.

acompañar, *v.* accompany.

acondicionar, *v.* condition.

aconsejable, *a.* advisable.

aconsejar, *v.* advise.

acontecer, *v.* happen.

acontecimiento, *m.* event, happening.

acorazado, *m.* battleship.

acordarse, *v.* remember, recollect.

acortar, *v.* shorten.

acosar, *v.* beset, harry.

acostar, *v.* lay down; put to bed.

acostarse, *v.* lie down; go to bed.

acostumbrado, *a.* accustomed; customary.

acostumbrar, *v.* accustom.

acrecentar, *v.* increase.

acreditar, *v.* accredit.

acreedor -ra, *n.* creditor.

acróbata, *m.* acrobat.

actitud, *f.* attitude.

actividad, *f.* activity.

activo, *a.* active.

acto, *m.* act.

actor, *m.* actor.

actriz, *f.* actress.

actual, *a.* present.

actuar, *v.* act.

acuarela, *f.* water color.

acuario, *m.* aquarium.

acuático, *a.* aquatic.

acuchillar, *v.* slash, knife.

acudir, *v.* rally; hasten; be present.

acuerdo, *m.* accord, agreement; settlement. **de a.,** in agreement, agreed.

acumulación, *f.* accumulation.

acumular, *v.* accumulate.

acuñar, *v.* coin, mint.

acusación, *f.* accusation, charge.

For pronunciation, see the concise guide on pages 3 to 4.

acusado -da, *a. & n.* accused; defendant.

acusador -ra, *n.* accuser.

acusar, *v.* accuse; acknowledge.

achicar, *v.* diminish, dwarf; humble.

acústica, *f.* acoustics.

adaptación, *f.* adaptation.

adaptar, *v.* adapt.

adecuado, *a.* adequate.

adelantado, *a.* advanced; fast (clock).

adelantamiento, *m.* advancement, promotion.

adelantar, *v.* advance.

adelante, *adv.* ahead, forward, onward, on.

adelanto, *m.* advancement, progress, improvement.

adelgazar, *v.* make thin.

ademán, *m.* attitude; gesture.

además, *adv.* in addition, besides, also.

adentro, *adv.* in, inside.

adepto, *a.* adept.

aderezar, *v.* prepare; trim.

adherirse, *v.* adhere, stick.

adhesivo, *a.* adhesive.

adición, *f.* addition.

adicional, *a.* additional, extra.

adicto, *a. & m.* addicted; addict.

adiós, *m. & interj.* good-bye, farewell.

adivinar, *v.* guess.

adjetivo, *m.* adjective.

adjunto, *a.* enclosed.

administración, *f.* administration.

administrador, *m.* administrator.

administrar, *v.* administer; manage.

administrativo, *a.* administrative.

admirable, *a.* admirable.

admiración, *f.* admiration; wonder.

admirar, *v.* admire.

admisión, *f.* admission.

admitir, *v.* admit, acknowledge.

adolescencia, *f.* adolescence, youth.

adolescente, *a.* adolescent.

adónde, *adv.* where.

adondequiera, *conj.* wherever.

adopción, *f.* adoption.

adoptar, *v.* adopt.

adoración, *f.* worship, love, adoration. —**adorar,** *v.*

adormecer, *v.* drowse.

adornar, *v.* adorn; decorate.

adorno, *m.* adornment, trimming.

adquirir, *v.* acquire, obtain.

adquisición, *f.* acquisition, attainment.

aduana, *f.* custom house, customs.

adujada, *f.* (naut.) coil of rope.

adulación, *f.* flattery.

adular, *v.* flatter.

adulterar, *v.* adulterate.

adulterio, *m.* adultery.

adulto, *a. & m.* adult.

adusto, *a.* gloomy; austere.

adverbio, *m.* adverb.

adversario, *m.* adversary.

adversidad, *f.* adversity.

adverso, *a.* adverse.

advertencia, *f.* warning.

advertir, *v.* warn; notice.

adyacente, *a.* adjacent.

aéreo, *a.* aerial; air.

aeroplano, *m.* airplane.

aeropuerto, *m.* airport.

afable, *a.* affable, pleasant.

afanarse, *v.* toil.

afear, *v.* deface, mar, deform.

afectación, *f.* affectation.

afectar, *v.* affect.

afecto, *m.* affection, attachment.

afeitada, *f.* shave. —**afeitarse,** *v.*

afeminado, *a.* effeminate.

afición, *f.* fondness, liking; hobby.

aficionado, *a.* fond.

aficionado -da, *n.* fan, devotee; amateur.

aficionarse a, *v.* become fond of.

afilado, *a.* sharp.

For pronunciation, see the concise guide on pages 3 to 4.

afilar, v. sharpen.

afiliación, f. affiliation.

afiliado, m. affiliate. —**afiliar,** v.

afinar, v. polish, tune up.

afinidad, f. relationship.

afirmación, f. affirmation, statement.

afirmar, v. affirm, assert.

afirmativa, f. affirmative. —**afirmativo,** a.

aflicción, f. affliction; sorrow, grief.

afligido, a. sorrowful, grieved.

afligir, v. grieve, distress.

aflojar, v. loosen.

afortunado, a. fortunate, successful, lucky.

afrenta, f. insult, outrage, affront. —**afrentar,** v.

afrentoso, a. shameful.

africano -na, a. & n. African.

afuera, adv. out, outside.

afueras, f.pl. suburbs.

agacharse, v. squat, crouch, cower.

agarrar, v. seize, grasp, clutch.

agarro, m. clutch, grasp.

agencia, f. agency.

agente, m. agent, representative.

ágil, a. agile, spry.

agitación, f. agitation, ferment.

agitado, a. agitated; excited.

agitador, m. agitator.

agitar, v. shake, agitate, excite.

agobiar, v. oppress, burden.

agosto, m. August.

agotamiento, m. exhaustion.

agotar, v. exhaust, use up, sap.

agradable, a. agreeable, pleasant.

agradar, v. please.

agradecer, v. thank; appreciate, be grateful for.

agradecido, a. grateful, thankful.

agradecimiento, m. gratitude, thanks.

agravar, v. aggravate, make worse.

agravio, m. wrong. —**agraviar,** v.

agregado, a. & m. aggregate.

agregar, v. add; gather.

agresión, f. aggression; (leg.) battery.

agresivo, a. aggressive.

agresor, m. aggressor.

agrícola, a. agricultural.

agricultor, m. farmer.

agricultura, f. agriculture, farming.

agrio, a. sour.

agrupar, v. group.

agua, f. water. —**aguar,** v.

aguacate, m. avocado, alligator pear.

aguantar, v. endure, stand, put up with.

aguardar, v. await; expect.

aguardiente, m. brandy.

agudo, a. sharp, keen, shrill, acute.

agüero, m. omen.

águila, f. eagle.

aguja, f. needle.

agujero, m. hole.

aguzar, v. sharpen.

ahí, adv. there.

ahogar, v. drown; choke; suffocate.

ahondar, v. deepen.

ahora, adv. now.

ahorcar, v. hang (execute).

ahorrar, v. save, save up; spare.

ahorros, m.pl. savings.

ahumar, v. smoke.

airado, a. angry, indignant.

aire, m. air. —**airear,** v.

aislamiento, m. isolation.

aislar, v. isolate.

ajedrez, m. chess.

ajeno, a. alien; someone else's.

ají, m. chili.

ajo, m. garlic.

ajustado, a. adjusted; trim; exact.

ajustar, v. adjust.

ajuste, m. adjustment, settlement.

al, contr. of a + el.

ala, f. wing; brim (of hat).

For pronunciation, see the concise guide on pages 3 to 4.

alabanza, *f.* praise. —**alabar**, *v.*

alabear, *v.* warp.

alambique, *m.* still.

alambre, *m.* wire. **a. de púas**, barbed wire.

alarde, *m.* boasting, ostentation.

alargar, *v.* lengthen; stretch out.

alarma, *f.* alarm. —**alarmar**, *v.*

alba, *f.* daybreak, dawn.

albanega, *f.* hair net.

albañil, *m.* bricklayer; mason.

albaricoque, *m.* apricot.

albergue, *m.* shelter. —**albergar**, *v.*

alborotar, *v.* disturb, make noise, brawl, riot.

alboroto, *m.* brawl, disturbance, din, tumult.

álbum, *m.* album.

alcachofa, *f.* artichoke.

alcalde, *m.* mayor.

alcance, *m.* reach; range, scope.

alcanfor, *m.* camphor.

alcanzar, *v.* reach, overtake, catch.

alcayata, *f.* spike.

alce, *m.* elk.

alcoba, *f.* bedroom; alcove.

alcohol, *m.* alcohol.

alcohólico, *a.* alcoholic.

aldaba, *f.* latch.

aldea, *f.* village.

alegación, *f.* allegation.

alegar, *v.* allege.

alegrar, *v.* make happy, brighten.

alegrarse, *v.* be glad.

alegre, *a.* gay, cheerful, merry.

alegría, *f.* gaiety, cheer.

alejarse, *v.* move away, off.

alemán **-ana**, *a. & n.* German.

Alemania, *f.* Germany.

alentar, *v.* cheer up, encourage.

alergia, *f.* allergy.

alerta, *adv.* on the alert.

aleve, **alevoso**, *a.* treacherous.

alfabeto, *m.* alphabet.

alfalfa, *f.* alfalfa.

alfarería, *f.* pottery.

alférez, *m.* (naval) ensign.

alfil, *m.* (chess) bishop.

alfiler, *m.* pin.

alfombra, *f.* carpet, rug.

alforja, *f.* knapsack; saddlebag.

algarabía, *f.* jargon; din.

álgebra, *f.* algebra.

algo, *pron. & adv.* something, somewhat; anything.

algodón, *m.* cotton.

alguien, *pron.* somebody, someone; anybody, anyone.

algún **-no** **-na**, *a. & pron.* some; any.

alhaja, *f.* jewel.

aliado, *a. & m.* allied; ally. —**aliar**, *v.*

alianza, *f.* alliance.

alicates, *m.pl.* pliers.

aliento, *m.* breath. **dar a.**, encourage.

aligerar, *v.* lighten.

alimentar, *v.* feed, nourish.

alimento, *m.* nourishment, food.

alinear, *v.* line up.

alisar, *v.* smooth.

alistamiento, *m.* enlistment.

alistar, *v.* make ready, prime.

alistarse, *v.* get ready; (mil.) enlist.

aliviar, *v.* alleviate, relieve, ease.

alivio, *m.* relief.

alma, *f.* soul.

almacén, *m.* department store; storehouse.

almacenaje, *m.* storage.

almacenar, *v.* store.

almanaque, *m.* almanac.

almeja, *f.* clam.

almendra, *f.* almond.

almíbar, *m.* syrup.

almidón, *m.* starch. —**almidonar**, *v.*

almirante, *m.* admiral.

almohada, *f.* pillow.

almuerzo, *m.* lunch. —**almorzar**, *v.*

alojamiento, *m.* lodging, accommodations.

alojar, *v.* lodge, house.

alojarse, *v.* stay, room.

alquiler, *m.* rent. —**alquilar,** *v.*

alrededor, *adv.* around.

alrededores, *m.pl.* environs.

altanero, *a.* haughty.

altar, *m.* altar.

altavoz, *m.* loud-speaker.

alteración, *f.* alteration.

alterar, *v.* alter.

alternativa, *f.* alternative. —**alternativo,** *a.*

alterno, *a.* alternate. —**alternar,** *v.*

alteza, *f.* highness.

altivo, *a.* proud, haughty; lofty.

alto, 1. *a.* high, tall; loud. **2.** *m.* height, story (house).

altura, *f.* height, altitude.

alud, *m.* avalanche.

aludir, *v.* allude.

alumbrado, *m.* lighting.

alumbrar, *v.* light.

aluminio, *m.* aluminum.

alumno -na, *n.* student, pupil.

alusión, *f.* allusion.

alza, *f.* rise; boost.

alzar, *v.* raise, lift.

allá, *adv.* there. **más a.,** beyond, farther on.

allanar, *v.* flatten, smooth, plane.

allí, *adv.* there. **por a.,** that way.

ama, *f.* housewife, mistress (of house). **a. de llaves,** housekeeper.

amable, *a.* kind; pleasant, sweet.

amalgamar, *v.* amalgamate.

amamantar, *v.* suckle, nurse.

amanecer, 1. *m.* dawn, daybreak. **2.** *v.* dawn; awaken.

amante, *m.* lover.

amar, *v.* love.

amargo, *a.* bitter.

amargón, *m.* dandelion.

amargura, *f.* bitterness.

amarillo, *a.* yellow.

amarradero, *m.* mooring.

amarrar, *v.* hitch, moor, tie up.

amartillar, *v.* hammer; cock (a gun).

amasar, *v.* knead, mold.

ámbar, *m.* amber.

ambarino, *a.* amber.

ambición, *f.* ambition.

ambicionar, *v.* aspire to.

ambicioso, *a.* ambitious.

ambiente, *m.* environment, atmosphere.

ambigüedad, *f.* ambiguity.

ambiguo, *a.* ambiguous.

ambos, *a. & pron.* both.

ambulancia, *f.* ambulance.

amenaza, *f.* threat, menace.

amenazar, *v.* threaten, menace.

ameno, *a.* pleasant.

americana, *f.* suit coat.

americano -na, *a. & n.* American.

ametralladora, *f.* machine gun.

amigable, *a.* amicable, friendly.

amígdala, *f.* tonsil.

amigo -ga, *n.* friend.

amistad, *f.* friendship.

amistoso, *a.* friendly.

amo, *m.* master.

amonestaciones, *f.pl.* banns.

amonestar, *v.* admonish.

amoníaco, *m.* ammonia.

amontonar, *v.* amass, pile up.

amor, *m.* love. **a. propio,** self-esteem.

amorío, *m.* romance, love affair.

amoroso, *a.* amorous; loving.

amortecer, *v.* deaden.

amparar, *v.* aid, befriend; protect, shield.

amparo, *m.* protection.

ampliar, *v.* enlarge; elaborate.

amplificar, *v.* amplify.

amplio, *a.* ample, roomy.

ampolla, *f.* bubble; bulb; blister.

amputar, *v.* amputate.

amueblar, *v.* furnish.

analfabeto, *a. & m.* illiterate.

For pronunciation, see the concise guide on pages 3 to 4.

análisis, *m. or f.* analysis.

analizar, *v.* analyze.

analogía, *f.* analogy.

análogo, *a.* similar, analogous.

anarquía, *f.* anarchy.

anatomía, *f.* anatomy.

ancho, *a.* wide, broad.

anchoa, *f.* anchovy.

anchura, *f.* width, breadth.

anciano -na, *a. & m.* old, aged (person).

ancla, *f.* anchor. **—anclar,** *v.*

anclaje, *m.* anchorage.

andamio, *m.* scaffold.

andar, *v.* walk; move, go.

andén, *m.* (railroad) platform.

andrajoso, *a.* ragged, uneven.

anécdota, *f.* anecdote.

anegar, *v.* flood, drown.

anestesia, *f.* anesthetic.

anexar, *v.* annex.

anexión, *f.* annexation.

anfitrión, *m.* host.

ángel, *m.* angel.

angosto, *a.* narrow.

anguila, *f.* eel.

angular, *a.* angular.

ángulo, *m.* angle.

angustia, *f.* anguish, agony.

angustiar, *v.* distress.

anhelar, *v.* long for.

anidar, *v.* nest, nestle.

anillo, *m.* ring; circle.

animación, *f.* animation; bustle.

animado, *a.* animated, lively; animate.

animal, *a. & m.* animal.

ánimo, *m.* state of mind, spirits; courage.

aniquilar, *v.* annihilate, destroy.

aniversario, *m.* anniversary.

anoche, *adv.* last night.

anochecer, 1. *m.* twilight, nightfall. **2.** *v.* get dark.

anónimo, *a.* anonymous.

anormal, *a.* abnormal.

anotación, *f.* annotation.

anotar, *v.* annotate.

ansia, ansiedad, *f.* anxiety.

ansioso, *a.* anxious.

antagonismo, *m.* antagonism.

antagonista, *m. & f.* antagonist, opponent.

anteayer, *adv.* day before yesterday.

antebrazo, *m.* forearm.

antecedente, *a. & m.* antecedent.

anteceder, *v.* precede.

antecesor, *m.* ancestor.

antemano. de a., in advance.

antena, *f.* antenna.

anteojos, *m.pl.* eyeglasses.

antepasado, *m.* ancestor, forefather.

anterior, *a.* previous, former.

antes, *adv.* before; formerly.

anticipación, *f.* anticipation.

anticipar, *v.* anticipate; advance.

anticuado, *a.* antiquated, obsolete.

antídoto, *m.* antidote.

antigüedad, *f.* antiquity; antique.

antiguo, *a.* former; old; ancient, antique.

antílope, *m.* antelope.

antipatía, *f.* antipathy.

antipático, *a.* disagreeable, nasty.

antiséptico, *a. & m.* antiseptic.

antojarse, *v.* **se me antoja . . . etc.,** I desire . . ., take a fancy to . . ., etc.

antojo, *m.* whim, fancy.

antorcha, *f.* torch.

antracita, *f.* anthracite.

anual, *a.* annual, yearly.

anudar, *v.* knot; tie.

anular, *v.* annul, void.

anunciar, *v.* announce; proclaim, advertise.

anuncio, *m.* announcement; advertisement.

añadir, *v.* add.

añil, *m.* bluing.

año, *m.* year.

apacible, *a.* peaceful, peaceable.

apaciguamiento, m. appeasement.

apaciguar, v. appease; placate.

apagado, a. dull.

apagar, v. extinguish, quench, put out.

aparador, m. buffet, cupboard.

aparato, m. apparatus; machine; appliance, set.

aparecer, v. appear, show up.

aparejo, m. rig. —**aparejar,** v.

aparentar, v. pretend; profess.

aparente, a. apparent.

apariencia, aparición, f. appearance.

apartado, 1. a. aloof; separate. **2.** m. post-office box.

apartamento, m. apartment.

apartar, v. separate; remove.

aparte, adv. apart; aside.

apasionado, a. passionate.

apatía, f. apathy.

apearse, v. get off, alight.

apedrear, v. stone.

apelación, f. appeal. —**apelar,** v.

apellido, m. family name.

apenas, adv. scarcely, hardly.

apéndice, m. appendix.

apercibir, v. prepare, warn.

aperitivo, m. appetizer.

aperos, m.pl. implements.

apetecer, v. desire, have appetite for.

apetito, m. appetite.

ápice, m. apex.

apilar, v. stack.

apio, m. celery.

aplacar, v. appease; placate.

aplastar, v. crush, flatten.

aplaudir, v. applaud, cheer.

aplauso, m. applause.

aplazar, v. postpone, put off.

aplicable, a. applicable.

aplicado, a. industrious, diligent.

aplicar, v. apply.

aplomo, m. aplomb, poise.

apoderado, m. attorney.

apoderarse de, v. get hold of, seize.

apodo, m. nickname. —**apodar,** v.

apologético, a. apologetic.

apoplejía, f. apoplexy.

aposento, m. room, flat.

apostar, v. bet, wager.

apóstol, m. apostle.

apoyar, v. support, prop; lean.

apoyo, m. support; prop; aid; approval.

apreciable, a. appreciable.

apreciar, v. appreciate, prize.

aprecio, m. appreciation, regard.

apremio, m. pressure, compulsion.

aprender, v. learn.

aprendiz, m. apprentice.

aprensión, f. apprehension.

aprensivo, a. apprehensive.

apresurado, a. hasty, fast.

apresurar, v. hurry, speed up.

apretado, a. tight.

apretar, v. squeeze, press; tighten.

apretón, m. squeeze.

aprieto, m. plight, predicament.

aprobación, f. approbation, approval.

aprobar, v. approve.

apropiación, f. appropriation.

apropiado, a. appropriate. —**apropiar,** v.

aprovechar, v. profit by.

aprovecharse, v. take advantage.

aproximado, a. approximate.

aproximarse a, v. approach.

aptitud, f. aptitude.

apto, a. apt.

apuesta, f. bet, wager, stake.

apuntar, v. point, aim; prompt; write down.

apunte, m. annotation, note; promptings, cue.

apuñalar, v. stab.

apurar, v. hurry; worry.

apuro, m. predicament, scrape, trouble.

aquel, aquella, dem. a. that.

aquél, aquélla, dem. pron. that (one); the former.

For pronunciation, see the concise guide on pages 3 to 4.

aquello, *dem. pron.* that.
aqui, *adv.* here. **por a.,** this way.
aquietar, *v.* allay; lull, pacify.
ara, *f.* altar.
árabe, *a. & n.* Arab, Arabic.
arado, *m.* plow. — **arar,** *v.*
arándano, *m.* cranberry.
araña, *f.* spider. **a. de luces,** chandelier.
arbitración, *f.* arbitration.
arbitrador -ra, *n.* arbitrator.
arbitraje, *m.* arbitration.
arbitrar, *v.* arbitrate.
arbitrario, *a.* arbitrary.
árbitro, *m.* arbiter, umpire, referee.
árbol, *m.* tree; mast.
arbusto, *m.* bush, shrub.
arca, *f.* chest; ark.
arcada, *f.* arcade.
arcaico, *a.* archaic.
arce, *m.* maple.
archipiélago, *m.* archipelago.
archivo, *m.* archive; file. **archivar,** *v.*
arcilla, *f.* clay.
arco, *m.* arc; arch; (archer's) bow. **a. iris,** rainbow.
arder, *v.* burn.
ardid, *m.* stratagem, cunning.
ardiente, *a.* ardent, burning, fiery.
ardilla, *f.* squirrel.
ardor, *m.* ardor, fervor.
arduo, *a.* arduous.
área, *f.* area.
arena, *f.* sand; arena.
arenoso, *a.* sandy.
arenque, *m.* herring.
arete, *n.* earring.
argentino -na, *a. & n.* Argentine.
argüir, *v.* dispute, argue.
árido, *a.* arid.
aristocracia, *f.* aristocracy.
aristócrata, *f.* aristocrat.
aristocrático, *a.* aristocratic.
aritmética, *f.* arithmetic.
arma, *f.* weapon, arm.
armadura, *f.* armor; reinforcement; framework.
armamento, *m.* armament.
armar, *v.* arm.
armario, *m.* cabinet, bureau, wardrobe.

armazón, *m.* framework, frame.
armería, *f.* armory.
armisticio, *m.* armistice.
armonía, *f.* harmony.
armonioso, *a.* harmonious.
armonizar, *v.* harmonize.
arnés, *m.* harness.
aroma, *f.* aroma, fragrance.
aromático, *a.* aromatic.
arpa, *f.* harp.
arquear, *v.* arch.
arquitecto, *m.* architect.
arquitectura, *f.* architecture.
arquitectural, *a.* architectural.
arrabal, *m.* suburb.
arraigar, *v.* take root, settle.
arrancar, *v.* pull out, tear out; start up.
arranque, *m.* dash, sudden start; fit of anger.
arrastrar, *v.* drag.
arrebatar, *v.* snatch, grab.
arrebato, *m.* sudden attack, fit of anger.
arrecife, *m.* reef.
arreglar, *v.* arrange; repair; fix; adjust, settle.
arreglárselas, *v.* manage, shift for oneself.
arreglo, *m.* arrangement, settlement.
arremeter, *v.* attack.
arrendar, *v.* rent.
arrepentimiento, *m.* repentance.
arrepentirse, *v.* repent.
arrestar, *v.* arrest.
arriba, *adv.* up; upstairs.
arriendo, *m.* lease.
arriero, *m.* muleteer.
arriesgar, *v.* risk.
arrimarse, *v.* lean.
arrodillarse, *v.* kneel.
arrogancia, *f.* arrogance.
arrogante, *a.* arrogant.
arrojar, *v.* throw, hurl; shed.
arrollar, *v.* roll, coil.
arroyo, *m.* brook; gully; gutter.
arroz, *m.* rice.
arruga, *f.* ridge; wrinkle.
arrugar, *v.* wrinkle, crumple.
arruinar, *v.* ruin, destroy, wreck.

arsenal, *m.* arsenal; armory.

arsénico, *m.* arsenic.

arte, *m.* (*f.* in *pl.*) art, craft; wiliness.

arteria, *f.* artery.

artesa, *f.* trough.

artesano, *m.* artisan, craftsman.

ártico, *a.* arctic.

articulación, *f.* articulation; joint.

articular, *v.* articulate.

artículo, *m.* article.

artífice, *m. & f.* artisan.

artificial, *a.* artificial.

artificio, *m.* artifice, device.

artificioso, *a.* affected.

artillería, *f.* artillery.

artista, *m. & f.* artist.

artístico, *a.* artistic.

arzobispo, *m.* archbishop.

as, *m.* ace.

asado, *m.* roast.

asaltador, *m.* assailant.

asaltar, *v.* assail, attack.

asalto, *m.* assault. —**asaltar**, *v.*

asamblea, *f.* assembly.

asar, *v.* roast; broil, cook (meat).

asaz, *adv.* enough; quite.

ascender, *v.* ascend, go up; amount.

ascenso, *m.* ascent.

ascensor, *m.* elevator.

ascensorista, *m. & f.* (elevator) operator.

asco, *m.* nausea; disgusting thing. **qué a.**, how disgusting.

aseado, *a.* tidy. —**asear**, *v.*

asediar, *v.* besiege.

asedio, *m.* siege.

asegurar, *v.* assure; secure.

asegurarse, *v.* make sure.

asemejarse a, *v.* resemble.

asentar, *v.* settle; seat.

asentimiento, *m.* assent. —**asentir**, *v.*

aseo, *m.* neatness, tidiness.

aserción, *f.* assertion.

aserrar, *v.* saw.

asesinar, *v.* assassinate; murder, slay.

asesinato, *m.* assassination, murder.

asesino -na, *n.* murderer, assassin.

aseveración, *f.* assertion.

aseverar, *v.* assert.

asfalto, *m.* asphalt.

así, *adv.* so, thus, this way, that way. **a. como**, as well as. **a. que**, as soon as.

asiático -ca, *a. & n.* Asiatic.

asiduo, *a.* assiduous.

asiento, *m.* seat; chair; site.

asignar, *v.* assign; allot.

asilo, *m.* asylum, sanctuary.

asimilar, *v.* assimilate.

asir, *v.* grasp.

asistencia, *f.* attendance, presence.

asistir, *v.* be present, attend.

asno, *m.* donkey.

asociación, *f.* association.

asociado, *m.* associate, partner.

asociar, *v.* associate.

asolar, *v.* desolate; burn, parch.

asoleado, *a.* sunny.

asomar, *v.* appear, loom up, show up.

asombrar, *v.* astonish, amaze.

asombro, *m.* amazement, astonishment.

aspa, *f.* reel. —**aspar**, *v.*

aspecto, *m.* aspect.

aspereza, *f.* harshness.

áspero, *a.* rough, harsh.

aspiración, *f.* aspiration.

aspirador, *m.* vacuum cleaner.

aspirar, *v.* aspire.

aspirina, *f.* aspirin.

asqueroso, *a.* dirty, nasty, filthy.

asta, *f.* shaft.

asterisco, *m.* asterisk.

astilla, *f.* splinter, chip. —**astillar**, *v.*

astillero, *m.* dry dock.

astro, *m.* star.

astronomía, *f.* astronomy.

astucia, *f.* cunning.

astuto, *a.* astute, sly, shrewd.

asumir, *v.* assume.

asunto, *m.* matter, affair, business; subject.

asustar, *v.* frighten, scare, startle.

For pronunciation, see the concise guide on pages 3 to 4.

atacar, v. attack, charge.

atajo, m. short cut.

ataque, m. attack, charge; spell, stroke.

atar, v. tie, bind, fasten.

atareado, a. busy.

atascar, v. stall, stop, obstruct.

ataúd, m. casket, coffin.

atavío, m. dress; gear, equipment.

audacia, f. audacity.

atemorizar, v. frighten.

atención, f. attention.

atender, v. heed; attend to, wait on.

atenerse a, v. count on, depend on.

atentado, m. crime, offense.

atento, a. attentive, courteous.

ateo, m. atheist.

aterrizar, v. land.

atesorar, v. hoard.

atestar, v. witness.

atestiguar, v. attest, testify.

atinar, v. hit upon.

atisbar, v. scrutinize, pry.

Atlántico, m. Atlantic.

atlántico, a. Atlantic.

atlas, m. atlas.

atleta, m. athlete.

atlético, a. athletic.

atletismo, m. athletics.

atmósfera, f. atmosphere.

atmosférico, a. atmospheric.

atómico, a. atomic.

átomo, m. atom.

atormentar, v. torment, plague.

atornillar, v. screw.

atracción, f. attraction.

atractivo, 1. a. attractive. **2.** m. attraction.

atraer, v. attract; lure.

atrapar, v. trap, catch.

atrás, adv. back; behind.

atrasado, a. belated; backward; slow (clock).

atrasar, v. delay, retard; be slow.

atraso, m. delay; backwardness; (pl.) arrears.

atravesar, v. cross.

atreverse, v. dare.

atrevido, a. daring, bold.

atrevimiento, m. boldness.

atribuir, v. attribute, ascribe.

atributo, m. attribute.

atrincherar, v. entrench.

atrocidad, f. atrocity, outrage.

atronar, v. deafen.

atropellar, v. trample; fell.

atroz, a. atrocious.

aturdir, v. daze, stun, bewilder.

audacia, f. audacity.

audaz, a. audacious, bold.

audible, a. audible.

auditorio, m. audience.

aula, f. classroom, hall.

aullar, v. howl, bay.

aullido, m. howl.

aumentar, v. augment; increase, swell.

aun, aun, adv. still; even. **a. cuando,** even though, even if.

aunque, conj. although, though.

áureo, a. golden.

aureola, f. halo.

aurora, f. dawn.

ausencia, f. absence.

ausentarse, v. stay away.

ausente, a. absent.

auspicio, m. auspice.

austeridad, f. austerity.

austero, a. austere.

austriaco -ca, a. & n. Austrian.

auténtico, a. authentic.

auto, automóvil, m. auto, automobile.

autobús, m. bus.

automático, a. automatic.

autonomía, f. autonomy.

autor, m. author.

autoridad, f. authority.

autoritario, a. authoritative.

autorizar, v. authorize.

auxiliar, 1. a. auxiliary. **2.** v. assist, aid.

auxilio, m. aid, assistance.

avaluar, v. evaluate, appraise.

avance, m. advance. —**avanzar,** v.

avaricia, f. avarice.

avariento, a. miserly, greedy.

avaro -ra, a. & m. miser; miserly.

For pronunciation, see the concise guide on pages 3 to 4.

ave, *f.* bird.

avena, *f.* oat.

avenida, *f.* avenue; flood.

avenirse, *v.* compromise; agree.

aventajar, *v.* surpass, get ahead of.

aventar, *v.* fan; scatter.

aventura, *f.* adventure.

aventurar, *v.* venture, risk, gamble.

aventurero, *a. & m.* adventurous; adventurer.

avergonzado, *a.* ashamed, abashed.

avergonzar, *v.* shame, abash.

avería, *f.* damage. —**averiar,** *v.*

averiguar, *v.* ascertain, find out.

aversión, *f.* aversion.

avestruz, *m.* ostrich.

aviación, *f.* aviation.

aviador -ra, *n.* aviator.

ávido, *a.* avid; eager.

avión, *m.* airplane.

avisar, *v.* notify, let know; warn, advise.

aviso, *m.* notice, announcement; advertisement; warning.

avispa, *f.* wasp.

avivar, *v.* enliven, revive.

aya, *f.* governess.

ayer, *adv.* yesterday.

ayuda, *f.* help, aid. —**ayudar,** *v.*

ayudante, *a.* assistant, helper; adjutant.

ayuno, *m.* fast. —**ayunar,** *v.*

ayuntamiento, *m.* city hall.

azada, *f.*, **azadón,** *m.* hoe.

azar, *m.* hazard, chance. **al a.,** at random.

azotar, [*v.* whip, flog; belabor.

azote, *m.* scourge, lash.

azúcar, *m.* sugar.

azul, *a.* blue.

azulado, *a.* azure.

azulejo, *m.* tile; bluebird.

B

baba, *f.* drivel. —**babear,** *v.*

babador, *m.* bib.

babucha, *f.* slipper.

bacalao, *m.* codfish.

bacía, *f.* wash basin.

bacterias, *f.pl.* bacteria.

bacteriología, *f.* bacteriology.

bachiller -ra, *n.* bachelor (degree).

bahía, *f.* bay.

bailador -ra, *n.* dancer.

bailar, *v.* dance.

bailarín -ina, *n.* dancer.

baile, *m.* dancing, dance.

baja, *f.* fall (in price); (mil.) casualty.

bajar, *v.* lower; descend.

bajeza, *f.* baseness.

bajo, 1. *prep.* under, below. **2.** *a.* low; short; base.

bala, *f.* bullet; ball; bale.

balada, *f.* ballad.

balancear, *v.* balance; roll, swing, sway.

balanza, *f.* balance; scales.

balbuceo, *m.* stammer; babble. —**balbucear,** *v.*

balcón, *m.* balcony.

balde, *m.* bucket, pail. **de b.,** gratis. **en b.,** in vain.

balística, *f.* ballistics.

balompié, *m.* football.

balón, *m.* football; (auto.) balloon tire.

baloncesto, *m.* basketball.

balota, *f.* ballot, vote. —**balotar,** *v.*

balsa, *f.* raft.

For pronunciation, see the concise guide on pages 3 to 4.

bálsamo, *m.* balm.

baluarte, *m.* bulwark.

ballena, *f.* whale.

bambolearse, *v.* sway.

bambú, *n.* bamboo.

banal, *a.* banal, trite.

banana, *f.* banana.

banano, *m.* banana tree.

bancarrota, *f.* bankruptcy.

banco, *m.* bank; bench; school of fish.

banda, *f.* band.

bandada, *f.* covey; flock.

bandeja, *f.* tray.

bandera, *f.* flag; banner; ensign.

bandido, *m.* bandit.

bando, *m.* faction.

bandolero, *m.* bandit, robber.

banquero, *m.* banker.

banqueta, *f.* stool; (Mex.) sidewalk.

banquete, *m.* feast, banquet.

bañera, *f.* bathtub.

baño, *m.* bath; bathroom.

bañar, *v.* bathe.

banquillo, *m.* stool.

baraja, *f.* pack of cards; game of cards.

baranda, *f.* railing, banister.

barato, *a.* cheap.

barba, *f.* beard; chin.

barbacoa, *f.* barbecue; stretcher.

barbaridad, *f.* barbarity; (Am.) excess (in anything).

bárbaro, *a.* barbarous; crude.

barbería, *f.* barber-shop.

barbero, *m.* barber.

barca, *f.* (small) boat.

barcaza, *f.* barge.

barco, *m.* ship, boat.

barniz, *m.* varnish. **—barnizar,** *v.*

barómetro, *m.* barometer.

barón, *m.* baron.

barquilla, *f.* (naut.) log.

barra, *f.* bar.

barraca, *f.* hut shed.

barrear, *v.* bar, barricade.

barreno, *m.* blast, blasting. **—barrenar,** *v.*

barrer, *v.* sweep.

barrera, *f.* barrier.

barricada, *f.* barricade.

barriga, *f.* belly.

barril, *m.* barrel; cask.

barrio, *m.* district, ward, quarter.

barro, *m.* clay, mud.

base, *f.* base; basis. **—basar,** *v.*

bastante, 1. *a.* enough, plenty of. **2.** *adv.* enough; rather, quite.

bastar, *v.* suffice, be enough.

bastardo -a, *a. & n.* bastard.

bastear, *v.* baste.

bastidor, *m.* wing (in theater).

bastón, *m.* (walking) cane.

bastos, *m.pl.* clubs (cards).

basura, *f.* refuse, dirt; garbage; junk.

basurero, *m.* scavenger.

batalla, *f.* battle. **—batallar,** *v.*

batallón, *m.* battalion.

batata, *f.* sweet potato.

bate, *m.* bat. **—batear,** *v.*

batería, *f.* battery.

batido, *m.* (cooking) batter.

batir, *v.* beat; demolish; conquer.

baúl, *m.* trunk.

bautismo, *m.* baptism.

bautista, *m. & f.* Baptist.

bautizar, *v.* christen, baptize.

bautizo, *m.* baptism.

baya, *f.* berry.

bayoneta, *f.* bayonet.

beato, *a.* blessed.

bebé, *n.* baby.

beber, *v.* drink.

bebible, *a.* drinkable.

bebida, *f.* drink, beverage.

beca, *f.* grant, scholarship.

becado -da, *n.* scholar.

becerro, *m.* calf; calfskin.

beldad, *f.* beauty.

belga, *a. & n.* Belgian.

Bélgica, *f.* Belgium.

belicoso, *a.* warlike.

beligerante, *a. & n.* belligerent.

bellaco, 1. *a.* sly, roguish. **2.** *m.* rogue.

belleza, *f.* beauty.

bello, *a.* beautiful.

bellota, *f.* acorn.
bendecir, *v.* bless.
bendición, *f.* blessing, benediction.
bendito, *a.* blessed.
beneficio, *m.* benefit. **—beneficiar,** *v.*
beneficioso, *a.* beneficial.
benevolencia, *f.* benevolence.
benévolo, *a.* benevolent.
benigno, *a.* benign.
beodo, *a.* drunk.
berenjena, *f.* eggplant.
beso, *m.* kiss. **—besar,** *v.*
bestia, *f.* beast, brute.
betabel, *m.* beet.
Biblia, *f.* Bible.
bíblico, *a.* Biblical.
biblioteca, *f.* library.
bicarbonato, *m.* bicarbonate.
bicicleta, *f.* bicycle.
bien, 1. *adv.* well. **2.** *n.* good; (*pl.*) possessions.
bienestar, *m.* wellbeing, welfare.
bienhechor -ra, *n.* benefactor.
bienvenida, *f.* welcome.
bienvenido, *a.* welcome.
biftec, *m.* steak.
bifurcación, *f.* fork. **—bifurcar,** *v.*
bigamía, *f.* bigamy.
bígamo -a, *n.* bigamist.
bigotes, *m.pl.* mustache.
bilis, *f.* bile.
billar, *m.* billards.
billete, *m.* ticket; bank note, bill.
billón, *m.* billion.
biografía, *f.* biography.
biología, *f.* biology.
biombo, *m.* screen.
bisel, *m.* bevel. **—biselar,** *v.*
bisonte, *m.* bison.
bisté, bistec, *m.* steak.
bizarro, *a.* brave; generous; smart.
bizcocho, *m.* biscuit, cake.
blanco, 1. *a.* white; blank. **2.** *m.* white; target.
blandir, *v.* brandish, flourish.
blando, *a.* soft.
blanquear, *v.* whiten; bleach.

blasfemar, *v.* blaspheme, curse.
blasfemia, *f.* blasphemy.
blindado, *a.* armored.
blindaje, *m.* armor.
bloque, *m.* block. **—bloquear,** *v.*
bloqueo, *m.* blockade. **—bloquear,** *v.*
blusa, *f.* blouse.
bobo -ba, *a. & n.* fool; foolish.
boca, *f.* mouth.
bocado, *m.* bit; bite, mouthful, morsel.
bocanada, *f.* puff (of smoke); mouthful (of liquor).
bocina, *f.* horn.
bochorno, *m.* sultry weather; embarrassment.
boda, *f.* wedding.
bodega, *f.* wine cellar; (naut.) hold; grocery store.
bofetada, *f.* **bofetón,** *m.* slap.
boga, *f.* vogue; fad.
bogar, *v.* row (a boat).
bohemio -a, *a. & n.* Bohemian.
boicoteo, *m.* boycott. **—boicotear,** *v.*
boina, *f.* beret.
bola, *f.* ball.
bolera, *f.* bowling alley.
boletín, *m.* bulletin.
boleto, *m.* ticket.
boliche, *m.* bowling alley.
boliviano -a, *a. & n.* Bolivian.
bolos, *m.pl.* bowling.
bolsa, *f.* purse; stock exchange.
bolsillo, *m.* pocket.
bollo, *m.* bun, loaf.
bomba, *f.* pump; bomb; gas station.
bombardear, *v.* bomb; bombard, shell.
bombear, *v.* pump.
bombero, *m.* fireman.
bombilla, *f.* (light) bulb.
bonanza, *f.* prosperity; fair weather.
bondad, *f.* kindness; goodness.
bondadoso, *a.* kind, kindly.

bonito, a. pretty.

bono, m. bonus; (fin.) bond.

boqueada, f. gasp; gape. — **boquear,** v.

boquilla, f. cigarette holder.

bordado, m., **bordadura,** f. embroidery.

bordar, v. embroider.

borde, m. border, rim, edge, brink, ledge.

borla, f. tassel.

borracho, a. drunk.

borrachón, m. drunkard.

borrador, m. eraser.

borradura, f. erasure.

borrar, v. erase, rub out.

borrasca, f. squall, storm.

borrico, m. donkey.

bosque, m. forest, wood.

bostezo, m. yawn. — **bostezar,** v.

bota, f. boot.

botalón, m. (mar.) boom.

botánica, f. botany.

botar, v. throw out, throw away.

bote, m. boat; can, box.

botica, f. pharmacy, drug store.

boticario, m. pharmacist, druggist.

botín, m. booty, plunder, spoils.

boto, a. dull, stupid.

botón, m. button.

botones, m. bellboy (in a hotel).

bóveda, f. vault.

boxeador, m. boxer.

boxeo, m. boxing. — **boxear,** v.

boya, f. buoy.

boyante, a. buoyant.

bozal, m. muzzle.

bramido, m. roar, bellow. — **bramar,** v.

brasileño-, -ña, a. & n. Brazilian.

bravata, f. bravado.

bravear, v. bully.

braza, f. fathom.

brazada, f. (swimming) stroke.

brazalete, m. bracelet.

brazo, m. arm.

brea, f. tar, pitch.

brecha, f. gap, breach.

bregar, v. scramble.

breña, f. rough country with brambly shrubs.

Bretaña, f. Britain.

breve, a. brief, short. **en b.,** shortly, soon.

brevedad, f. brevity.

bribón, m. rogue, rascal.

brida, f. bridle.

brigada, f. brigade.

brillante, 1. a. brilliant, shiny. **2.** m. diamond.

brillo, m. shine, glitter. — **brillar,** v.

brinco, m. jump; bounce, skip. — **brincar,** v.

brindis, m. toast. — **brindar,** v.

brío, m. vigor.

brioso, a. vigorous, spirited

brisa, f. breeze.

británico, a. British.

brocado, m. brocade.

brocha, f. brush.

broche, m. brooch, clasp, pin.

broma, f. joke. — **bromear,** v.

bronce, m. bronze; brass.

bronquitis, f. bronchitis.

brotar, v. gush; sprout; bud.

brote, m. bud, shoot.

bruja, f. witch.

brújula, f. compass.

bruma, f. mist.

brumoso, a. misty.

brusco, a. brusque; abrupt, curt.

brutal, a. savage, brutal.

brutalidad, f. brutality.

bruto, 1. a. brutish; ignorant. **2.** m. blockhead.

bucear, v. dive.

bueno, a. good, fair; well (in health).

buey, m. ox, steer.

búfalo, m. buffalo.

bufanda, f. scarf.

bufón -ona, n. fool, buffoon, clown.

buho, m. owl.

buhonero, m. peddler, vender.

bujía, f. spark plug.

bulevar, m. boulevard.

bulto, m. bundle; lump.

---

bullicio, *m.* bustle, noise.
bullicioso, *a.* boisterous, noisy.
buñuelo, *m.* bun.
buque, *m.* ship.
burdo, *a.* coarse.
burgés -esa, *a. & n.* bourgeois.
burla, *f.* mockery; fun.
burlador, *m.* trickster, jokester.
burlar, *v.* mock, deride.

burlarse de, *v.* scoff at; make fun of.
burro, *m.* donkey.
busca, *f.* search, pursuit, quest.
buscar, *v.* seek, look for; look up.
busto, *m.* bust.
butaca, *f.* armchair; (theat.) orchestra seat.
buzo, *m.* diver.
buzón, *m.* mailbox.

C

cabal, *a.* exact; thorough.
cabalgar, *v.* ride horseback.
caballeresco, *a.* gentlemanly, chivalrous.
caballería, *f.* cavalry; chivalry.
caballeriza, *f.* stable.
caballero, *m.* gentleman; knight.
caballete, *m.* sawhorse; easel; ridge (of roof).
caballo, *m.* horse.
cabaña, *f.* cabin; booth.
cabecear, *v.* pitch (as a ship).
cabecera, *f.* head (of bed, table).
cabello, *m.* hair.
caber, *v.* fit into, be contained in. **no cabe duda,** there is no doubt.
cabeza, *f.* head.
cabildo, *m.* city hall.
cabizbajo, *a.* downcast.
cablegrama, *m.* cablegram.
cabo, *m.* end; (geog.) cape; (mil.) corporal. **llevar a c.,** carry out, accomplish.
cabra, *f.* goat.
cacahuete, *m.* peanut.
cacao, *m.* cocoa; chocolate.
cacerola, *f.* pan, casserole.
cachorro, *m.* cub; puppy.
cada, *a.* each, every.
cadáver, *m.* corpse.
cadena, *f.* chain.

cadera, *f.* hip.
cadete, *m.* cadet.
caer, *v.* fall.
café, *m.* coffee; café.
cafetal, *m.* coffee plantation.
cafetera, *f.* coffee pot.
caída, *f.* fall, drop; collapse.
caimán, *m.* alligator.
caja, *f.* box, case.
cajero -ra, *n.* cashier.
cajón, *m.* drawer.
cal, *f.* lime.
calabaza, *f.* calabash, pumpkin.
calabozo, *m.* jail, cell.
calambre, *m.* cramp.
calamidad, *f.* calamity, disaster.
calcetín, *m.* sock.
calcio, *m.* calcium.
calcular, *v.* calculate, figure.
cálculo, *m.* calculation, estimate.
caldera, *f.* kettle, caldron; boiler.
caldo, *m.* broth.
calefacción, *f.* heat, heating.
calendario, *m.* calendar.
calentar, *v.* heat, warm.
calidad, *f.* quality, grade.
caliente, *a.* hot, warm.
calificar, *v.* qualify.
calma, *f.* calm, quiet.
calmado, *a.* calm.

calmante, a. soothing, calming.

calmar, v. calm, quiet, lull, soothe.

calor, n. heat, warmth. **tener c.,** to be hot, warm; feel hot, warm. **hacer c.,** to be hot, warm (weather).

calorífero, m. radiator.

calumnia, f. slander. **—caluminar,** v.

caluroso, a. warm, hot.

calvario, m. Calvary.

calvo, a. bald.

calzado, m. footwear.

calzar, v. wear (as shoes).

calzoncillos, m.pl. shorts.

calzones, m.pl. trousers.

callado, a. silent, quiet.

callarse, v. quiet down; keep still; stop talking.

calle, f. street.

callejón, m. alley.

callo, m. callus, corn.

cama, f. bed.

cámara, f. chamber; camera.

camarada, m. & f. comrade.

camarera, f. chambermaid; waitress.

camarero, m. steward; waiter.

camarón, m. shrimp.

camarote, m. stateroom, berth.

cambiar, v. exchange, change, trade; cash.

cambio, m. change, exchange. **en c.,** on the other hand.

cambista, m. banker, broker.

cambur, m. banana.

camello, m. camel.

camilla, f. stretcher.

caminar, v. walk.

caminata, f. tramp, hike.

camino, m. road; way.

camión, m. truck.

camisa, f. shirt.

camisería, f. haberdashery.

camiseta, f. undershirt.

campamento, m. camp.

campana, f. bell.

campaña, f. campaign.

campanario, m. bell tower, steeple.

campaneo, m. chime.

campeón, m. champion.

campeonato, m. championship.

campesino -na, n. peasant.

campestre, a. country, rural.

campo, m. field; (the) country.

Canadá, m. Canada.

canadiense, a. & n. Canadian.

canal, m. canal; channel.

canalla, f. rabble.

canario, m. canary.

canasta, f. basket.

cáncer, m. cancer.

canciller, m. chancellor.

canción, f. song.

candado, m. padlock.

candela, f. fire; light; candle.

candelero, m. candlestick.

candidato -ta, n. candidate; applicant.

candidatura, f. candidacy.

canela, f. cinnamon.

cangrejo, m. crab.

caníbal, m. cannibal.

canje. m. exchange, trade. **—canjear,** v.

cano, a. gray.

canoa, f. canoe.

cansado, a. tired, weary.

cansancio, m. fatigue.

cansar, v. tire, fatigue, wear out.

cantante, m. & f. singer.

cantar, 1. m. song. **2.** v. sing.

canto, m. chant, song, singing; edge.

caña, f. cane, reed; sugar cane.

cañón, m. canyon; cannon; gun barrel.

caoba, f. mahogany.

caos, m. chaos.

caótico, a. chaotic.

capa, f. cape, cloak; coat (of paint).

capacidad, f. capacity; capability.

capacitar, v. enable.

capataz, m. foreman.

capaz, a. capable, able.

capellán, m. chaplain.

caperuza, f. hood.

capilla, f. chapel.

---

capital, m. capital. f. capital (city).
capitalista, a. & n. capitalist.
capitán, m. captain.
capitular, v. yield.
capítulo, m. chapter.
capota, f. hood.
capricho, m. caprice; fancy; whim.
caprichoso, a. capricious.
cápsula, f. capsule.
capturar, v. capture.
capucha, f. hood.
capullo, m. cocoon.
cara, f. face.
caracol, m. snail.
carácter, m. character.
característica, f. characteristic.
característico, a. characteristic.
caramba, mild exclamation.
caramelo, m. caramel; candy.
cántaro, m. pitcher.
cantera, f. (stone) quarry.
cantidad, f. quantity, amount.
cantina, f. bar, tavern; restaurant.
carátula, f. dial.
caravana, f. caravan
carbón, m. carbon; coal.
carbonizar, v. char.
carburador, m. carburetor.
carcajada, f. burst of laughter.
cárcel, f. prison, jail.
carcelero, m. jailer.
cardenal, m. cardinal.
cardinal, a. cardinal.
carecer, v. lack.
carestía, f. scarcity; famine.
carga, f. cargo; load, burden; freight.
cargar, v. carry; load; charge.
cargo, m. load; charge, office.
caricia, f. caress.
caridad, f. charity.
cariño, m. affection; fondness.
cariñoso, a. affectionate, fond.
caritativo, a. charitable.

carmesí, a. & m. crimson.
carnaval, m. carnival.
carne, f. meat, flesh; pulp.
carnero, m. ram; mutton.
carnicería, f. meat market; massacre.
carnicero, m. butcher.
carnívoro, a. carnivorous.
caro, a. dear, costly, expensive.
carpa, f. tent.
carpeta, f. folder; briefcase.
carpintero, m. carpenter.
carrera, f. race; career.
carreta, f. wagon, cart.
carrete, m. reel, spool.
carretera, f. road, highway.
carril, m. rail.
carro, m. car, automobile; cart.
carroza, f. chariot.
carruaje, m. carriage.
carta, f. letter; (pl.) cards.
cartel, m. placard, poster; cartel.
cartera, f. pocketbook, handbag, wallet; portfolio.
cartero, m. mailman, postman.
cartón, m. cardboard.
cartucho, m. cartridge.
casa, f. house, dwelling; home.
casaca, f. dress coat.
casado, a. married.
casamiento, m. marriage.
casar, v. marry, marry off.
casarse, v. get married. **c. con,** marry.
cascabel, m. jingle bell.
cascada, f. waterfall, cascade.
cascajo, m. gravel.
cascanueces, m. nutcracker.
cascar, v. crack, break, burst.
cáscara, f. shell, rind, husk.
casco, m. helmet; hull.
casera, f. landlady; housekeeper.
caserío, m. settlement.
casero, 1. a. homemade. **2.** m. landlord, superintendent.
caseta, f. cottage, hut.
casi, adv. almost, nearly.

casilla, *f.* booth; ticket office; pigeonhole.

casino, *m.* club; clubhouse.

caso, *m.* case. hacer c. a, pay attention to.

casorio, *m.* informal wedding.

caspa, *f.* dandruff.

casta, *f.* caste.

castaña, *f.* chestnut.

castaño, 1. *a.* brown. 2. *m.* chestnut tree.

castañuela, *f.* castanet.

castellano, *a. & m.* Castilian.

castidad, *f.* chastity.

castigar, *v.* punish.

castigo, *m.* punishment.

castillo, *m.* castle.

castizo, *a.* pure, genuine; noble.

casto, *a.* chaste.

castor, *m.* beaver.

casual, *adj.* accidental, coinciden al.

casualidad, *f.* coincidence. por c., by chance.

casuca, *f.* hut, shanty, hovel.

catadura, *f.* act of tasting; appearance.

catalán, *a. & m.* Catalonian.

catálogo, *m.* catalogue. —catalogar, *v.*

catar, *v.* taste; examine, try; bear in mind.

catarata, *f.* cataract, waterfall.

catarro, *m.* head cold.

catástrofe, *m.* catastrophe.

catecismo, *m.* catechism.

cátedra, *f.* professorship.

catedral, *f.* cathedral.

catedrático, *m.* professor.

categoría, *f.* category.

categórico, *a.* categorical.

catequizar, *v.* catechize.

catolicismo, *m.* Catholicism.

católico -ca, *a. & n.* Catholic.

catorce, *a. & pron.* fourteen.

catre, *m.* cot.

cauce, *m.* river bed; ditch.

caución, *f.* precaution; security, guarantee.

cauchal, *m.* rubber plantation.

caucho, *m.* rubber.

caudal, *m.* means, fortune; (pl.) holdings.

caudaloso, *a.* prosperous, rich.

caudillaje, *m.* leadership; tyranny.

caudillo, *m.* leader, chief.

causa, *f.* cause. —causar, *v.*

cautela, *f.* caution.

cauteloso, *m.* cautious.

cautivar, *v.* captivate.

cautiverio, *m.* captivity.

cautividad, *f.* captivity.

cautivo -va, *a. & n.* captive.

cauto, *a.* cautious.

cavar, *v.* dig.

caverna, *f.* cavern, cave.

cavernoso, *a.* cavernous.

cavidad, *f.* cavity, hollow.

cavilar, *v.* criticize, cavil.

cayado, *m.* shepherd's staff.

cayo, *m.* small rocky islet, key.

caza, *f.* hunting, pursuit, game.

cazador, *m.* hunter.

cazar, *v.* hunt.

cazatorpedero, *m.* destroyer.

cazo, *m.* ladle, dipper; pot.

cazuela, *f.* crock.

cebada, *f.* barley.

cebo, *m.* bait. —cebar, *v.*

cebolla, *f.* onion.

ceceo, *m.* lisp. —cecear, *v.*

cecina, *f.* dried beef.

cedazo, *m.* sieve, sifter.

ceder, *v.* cede; transfer; yield.

cedro, *m.* cedar.

cédula, *f.* decree. c. personal, identification card.

céfiro, *m.* zephyr.

cegar, *v.* blind.

ceguedad, ceguera, *f.* blindness.

ceja, *f.* eyebrow.

cejar, *v.* go backwards; yield, retreat.

celada, *f.* trap; ambush.

celaje, *m.* appearance of the sky.

celar, *v.* watch carefully; guard.

celda, *f.* cell.

celebración, *f.* celebration.

celebrante, *m.* officiating priest.

celebrar, *v.* celebrate, observe.

célebre, *a.* celebrated, noted, famous.

celebridad, *f.* fame; celebrity; pageant.

celeridad, *f.* speed, rapidity.

celeste, *a.* celestial.

celestial, *a.* heavenly.

célibe, 1. *a.* unmarried. **2.** *m. & f.* unmarried person.

celo, *m.* zeal; (*pl.*) jealousy.

celosía, *f.* Venetian blind.

celoso, *a.* jealous; zealous.

céltico, *a.* Celtic.

célula, *f.* (biol.) cell.

celuloide, *m.* celluloid.

cellisca, *f.* sleet. —**cellisquear,** *v.*

cementar, *v.* cement.

cementerio, *m.* cemetery.

cemento, *m.* cement.

cena, *f.* supper.

cenagal, *m.* swamp, marsh.

cenagoso, *a.* swampy, marshy, muddy.

cenar, *v.* dine, eat.

cencerro, *m.* cowbell.

cendal, *m.* thin, light cloth; gauze.

cenicero, *m.* ashtray.

ceniciento, *a.* ashen.

cenit, *m.* zenith.

ceniza, *f.* ash, ashes.

censo, *m.* census.

censor, *m.* critic.

censura, *f.* reproof, censure; censorship.

censurable, *a.* objectionable.

censurar, *v.* censure, criticize.

centavo, *m.* cent.

centella, *f.* thunderbolt, lightning.

centellear, *v.* twinkle, sparkle.

centelleo, *m.* sparkle.

centenar, *m.* (a) hundred.

centenario, *m.* centennial, centenary.

centeno, *m.* rye.

centígrado, *a.* centigrade.

centímetro, *m.* centimeter.

céntimo, *m.* cent.

centinela, *m.* sentry, guard.

central, *a.* central.

centrar, *v.* center.

céntrico, *a.* central.

centro, *m.* center.

centroamericano -na, *a. & n.* Central American.

ceñidor, *m.* belt, sash; girdle.

ceñir, *v.* gird.

ceño, *m.* frown.

ceñudo, *a.* frowning, grim.

cepa, *f.* stump.

cepillo, *m.* brush; plane. —**cepillar,** *v.*

cera, *f.* wax.

cerámica, *m.* ceramics.

cerca, 1. *adv.* near. **2.** *f.* fence, hedge.

cercado, *m.* enclosure; garden.

cercamiento, *m.* enclosure.

cercanía, *f.* proximity.

cercano, *a.* near, nearby.

cercar, *v.* surround.

cercenar, *v.* clip; lessen, reduce.

cerciorar, *v.* make sure; affirm.

cerco, *m.* hoop; siege.

cerda, *f.* bristle.

cerdo, *m.* hog.

cerdoso, *a.* bristly.

cereal, *a. & m.* cereal.

cerebro, *m.* brain.

ceremonia, *f.* ceremony.

ceremonial, *a. & m.* ceremonial, ritual.

ceremonioso, *a.* ceremonious.

cereza, *f.* cherry.

cerilla, *f.,* **cerillo,** *m.* match.

cerner, *v.* sift.

cero, *m.* zero.

cerrado, *a.* cloudy; obscure; stupid.

cerradura, *f.* lock.

cerrajero, *m.* locksmith.

cerrar, *v.* close, shut.

cerro, *m.* hill.

cerrojo, *m.* latch, bolt.

certamen, *m.* contest; competition.

certero, *a.* accurate, exact; certain, sure.

certeza, *f.* certainty.

certidumbre, *f.* certainty.

certificado, *m.* certificate.

certificar, *v.* certify; register (a letter).

cerúleo, *a.* cerulean, sky-blue.

cervecería, *f.* brewery; beer saloon.

cervecero, *m.* brewer.

cerveza, *f.* beer.

cesante, *a.* unemployed.

cesar, *v.* cease.

césped, *m.* sod, lawn.

cesta, *f.,* **cesto,** *m.* basket.

cetrino, *a.* yellow, lemon-colored.

cetro, *m.* scepter.

cicatero, *a.* stingy.

cicatriz, *f.* scar.

cicatrizar, *v.* heal.

ciclo, *m.* cycle.

ciclón, *m.* cyclone.

ciego -ga, **1.** *a.* blind. **2.** *n.* blind person.

cielo, *m.* heaven; sky, heavens; ceiling.

ciempiés, *m.* centipede.

cien, ciento, *a. & pron.* hundred. **por c.,** per cent.

ciénaga, *f.* swamp, marsh.

ciencia, *f.* science.

cieno, *m.* mud.

científico, **1.** *a.* scientific. **2.** *n.* scientist.

cierre, *m.* fastener, snap, clasp.

cierto, *a.* certain, sure, true.

ciervo, *m.* deer.

cierzo, *m.* northerly wind.

cifra, *f.* cipher, number. **—cifrar,** *v.*

cigarra, *f.* locust.

cigarrera, cigarrillera, *f.* cigarette case.

cigarrillo, *m.* cigarette.

cigarro, *m.* cigar; cigarette.

cilíndrico, *a.* cylindrical.

cilindro, *m.* cylinder.

cima, *f.* summit, peak.

cimarrón, **1.** *a.* wild, untamed. **2.** *m.* runaway slave.

címbalo, *m.* cymbal.

cimbrar, *v.* shake, brandish.

cimientos, *m.pl.* foundation.

cinc, *m.* zinc.

cincel, *m.* chisel. **—cincelar,** *v.*

cincha, *f.* (harness) cinch. **—cinchar,** *v.*

cinco, *a. & pron.* five.

cincuenta, *a. & pron.* fifty.

cine, *m.* movies; movie theater.

cíngulo, *m.* girdle.

cínico, *a. & n.* cynical; cynic.

cinta, *f.* ribbon, tape; (movie) film.

cintilar, *v.* glitter, sparkle.

cinto, *m.* belt; girdle.

cintura, *f.* waist.

cinturón, *m.* belt.

ciprés, *m.* cypress.

circo, *m.* circus.

circuito, *m.* circuit.

circulación, *f.* circulation.

circular, **1.** *a. & m.* circular. **2.** *v.* circulate.

círculo *m.* circle, club.

circundante, *a.* surrounding.

circundar, *v.* encircle, surround.

circunferencia, *f.* circumference.

circunlocución, *n.* circumlocution.

circunscribir, *v.* circumscribe.

circunspección, *n.* decorum, propriety.

circunspecto, *a.* circumspect.

circunstancia, *f.* circumstance.

circunstante, *m.* bystander.

circunvecino, *a.* neighboring, adjacent.

cirio, *m.* candle.

ciruela, *f.* plum; prune.

cirugía, *f.* surgery.

cirujano, *m.* surgeon.

cisne, *m.* swan.

cisterna, *f.* cistern.

cita, *f.* citation; appointment, date.

citación, *f.* citation; (legal) summons.

citar, *v.* cite, quote; summon; make an appointment with.

ciudad, *f.* city.

ciudadanía, *f.* citizenship.

ciudadano -na, *n.* citizen.

ciudadela, *f.* fortress, citadel.

cívico, *a.* civic.

civil, *a. & n.* civil; civilian.

civilidad, *f.* politeness, civility.

civilización, *f.* civilization.

civilizador, *a.* civilizing.

civilizar, *v.* civilize.

cizallas, *f.pl.* shears. — **cizallar,** *v.*

cizaña, *f.* weed; vice.

clamar, *v.* clamor.

clamor, *m.* clamor.

clamoreo, *m.* persistent clamor.

clamoroso, *a.* clamorous.

clandestino, *a.* secret, clandestine.

clara, *f.* white (of egg).

claraboya, *m.* skylight; bull's-eye.

clarear, *v.* clarify; become light, dawn.

claridad, *f.* clarity.

clarificar, *v.* clarify.

clarín, *m.* bugle, trumpet.

clarinete, *m.* clarinet.

clarividencia, *f.* clairvoyance.

claro, *a.* clear; bright; light (in color); of course.

clase, *f.* class; classroom; kind, sort.

clásico, *a.* classic, classical.

clasificar, *v.* classify, rank.

claustro, *m.* cloister.

cláusula, *f.* clause.

clausura, *f.* cloister; inner sanctum.

clavado, *m.* dive.

clavar, *v.* nail, peg, pin.

clave, *f.* code; (mus.) key.

clavel, *m.* carnation.

clavetear, *v.* nail.

clavija, *f.* pin, peg.

clavijero, *m.* hatrack.

clavo, *m.* nail, spike.

clemencia, *f.* clemency.

clemente, *a.* merciful.

clerecía, *f.* clergy.

clerical, *a.* clerical.

clérigo, *m.* clergyman.

clero, *m.* clergy.

cliente, *m. & f.* customer, client.

clientela, *f.* clientele, practice.

clima, *m.* climate.

clímax, *m.* climax.

clínica, *f.* clinic.

clíper, *m.* clipper ship.

cloaca, *f.* sewer.

cloquear, *v.* cluck, cackle.

cloqueo, *m.* cluck.

cloro, *m.* chlorine.

club, *m.* club, association.

clueca, *f.* brooding hen.

coacción, *n.* compulsion.

coagular, *v.* coagulate, clot.

coágulo, *m.* clot.

coalición, *f.* coalition.

coartar, *v.* limit.

cobarde, *a. & n.* cowardly; coward.

cobardía, *f.* cowardice.

cobertizo, *m.* shed.

cobertor, *m.,* **cobija,** *f.,* blanket.

cobertura, *f.* cover, wrapping.

cobijar, *v.* cover; protect.

cobrador, *m.* collector.

cobranza, *f.* collection or recovery of money.

cobrar, *v.* collect; charge; cash.

cobre, *m.* copper.

cobrizo, *a.* coppery.

cobro, *m.* collection or recovery of money.

coca, *f.* coca leaves.

cocaína, *f.* cocaine.

cocal, *m.* coconut plantation.

cocear, *v.* kick; resist.

cocer, *v.* cook, boil, bake.

cocido, *m.* stew.

cociente, *m.* quotient.

cocimiento, *m.* cooking.

cocina, *f.* kitchen.

cocinar, *v.* cook.

cocinero -ra, *n.* cook.

coco, *m.* coconut; coconut tree.

cocodrilo, *m.* crocodile.

coctel, *m.* cocktail.

coche, *m.* coach; car, automobile.

cochera, *f.* garage.

cochero, *m.* coachman; cab driver.

cochinada, *f.* filth; herd of swine.

cochino, *m.* pig, swine.

codazo, *m.* nudge with the elbow.

codicia, *f.* avarice, greed; lust.

codiciar, *v.* covet.

codicioso, *a.* covetous; greedy.

código, *m.* (law) code.

codo, *m.* elbow.

codorniz, *f.* quail.

coetáneo, *a.* contemporary.

cofrade, *m.* fellow member of a club, etc.

cofre, *m.* coffer; chest; trunk.

coger, *v.* catch; pick; take.

cogote, *m.* nape.

cohecho, *m.* bribe. **—cohechar,** *v.*

coheredero, *m.* co-heir.

coherente, *a.* coherent.

cohesión, *f.* cohesion.

cohete, *m.* fire cracker, rocket.

cohibición, *n.* restraint; repression.

cohibir, *v.* restrain; repress.

coincidencia, *f.* coincidence.

coincidir, *v.* coincide.

cojear, *v.* limp.

cojera, *f.* limp.

cojín, *m.* cushion.

cojinete, *m.* small cushion, pad.

cojo, *a.* lame.

col, *f.* cabbage.

cola, *f.* tail; glue; line, queue. **hacer c.,** stand in line.

colaboración, *f.* collaboration.

colaborar, *v.* collaborate.

coladera, *f.* strainer.

colador, *m.* colander, strainer.

colapso, *m.* collapse, prostration.

colar, *v.* strain; drain.

colateral, *a.* collateral.

colcha, *f.* bedspread, quilt.

colchón, *m.* mattress.

colear, *v.* wag the tail.

colección, *f.* collection, set.

coleccionar, *v.* collect.

colecta, *f.* collection (a prayer).

colectivo, *a.* collective.

colector, *m.* collector.

colega, *m. & f.* colleague.

colegial, *m.* college student.

colegiatura, *f.* college scholarship.

colegio, *m.* (private) school, college.

colegir, *v.* infer, deduce.

cólera, *f.* rage, wrath.

colérico, *adj.* angry, irritated.

coleto, *m.* leather jacket.

colgador, *m.* rack, hanger.

colgaduras, *f.pl.* drapery.

colgante, *a.* hanging.

colgar, *v.* hang up, suspend.

colibrí, *m.* hummingbird.

coliflor, *m.* cauliflower.

coligarse, *v.* band together, unite.

colilla, *f.* butt of a cigar or cigarette.

colina, *f.* hill, hillock.

colinabo, *m.* turnip.

colindante, *a.* neighboring, adjacent.

colindar, *v.* neighbor, abut.

coliseo, *m.* theater; coliseum.

colisión, *f.* collision.

colmar, *v.* heap up, fill liberally.

colmena, *f.* hive.

colmillo, *m.* eye-tooth; tusk; fang.

colmo, *m.* height, peak, extreme.

colocación, *f.* place, position; employment, job; arrangement.

colocar, *v.* place, locate, put, set.

colombiano -na, *a. & n.* Colombian.

colon, *m.* colon (of intestines).

colonia, *f.* colony.

colonial, *a.* colonial.

colonización, *f.* colonization.

colonizador, *m.* colonizer.

colonizar, *v.* colonize.

colono, *m.* colonist; tenant farmer.

coloquio, *m.* conversation, talk.

color, *m.* color. **—colorar,** *v.*

coloración, *f.* coloring.

colorado, *a.* red, ruddy.

colorar, *v.* color, paint; dye.

colorete, *m.* rouge.

colorido, *m.* color, coloring. —**colorir,** *v.*

colosal, *a.* colossal.

columbrar, *v.* discern.

columna, *f.* column, pillar, shaft.

columpiar, *v.* swing.

columpio, *m.* swing.

collado, *m.* hillock.

collar, *m.* necklace; collar.

coma, *f.* coma; comma.

comadre, *f.* midwife; gossip; close friend.

comadreja, *m.* weasel.

comandancia, *m.* command; command post.

comandante, *m.* commandant; commander; major.

comandar, *v.* command.

comandita, *f.* silent partnership.

comanditario, *m.* silent partner.

comando, *m.* command.

comarca, *f.* region; border, boundary.

comba, *f.* bulge.

combar, *v.* bend; bulge.

combate, *m.* combat. —**combatir,** *v.*

combatiente, *a. & m.* combatant.

combinación, *f.* combination; (lady's) slip.

combinar, *v.* combine

combustible, 1. *a.* combustible. **2.** *m.* fuel.

combustión, *f.* combustion.

comedero, *m.* trough.

comedia, *f.* comedy; play.

comediante, *m.* actor; comedian.

comedido, *a.* polite, courteous; obliging.

comedirse, *v.* to be polite or obliging.

comedor, *m.* dining-room. **coche c.,** dining-car.

comendador, *m.* commander.

comensal, *m.* member of a household.

comentador, *m.* commentator.

comentario, *m.* commentary.

comento, *m.* comment. —**comentar,** *v.*

comenzar, *v.* begin, start, commence.

comer, *v.* eat, dine.

comercial, *a.* commercial.

comerciante, *m.* merchant, trader, business man.

comerciar, *v.* trade, deal, do business.

comercio, *m.* commerce trade, business.

comestible, 1. *a.* edible. **2.** *m.* (*pl.*) groceries, provisions.

cometa, *m.* comet. *f.* kite.

cometer, *v.* commit.

cometido, *m.* commission; duty; task.

comezón, *f.* itch.

comicios, *m.pl.* primary elections.

cómico -ca, *a. & n.* comic, comical; comedian.

comida, *f.* food; dinner; meal.

comidilla, *f.* light meal; gossip.

comienzo, *m.* beginning.

comilitona, *f.* banquet.

comilón, *m.* glutton; heavy eater.

comillas, *f.pl.* quotation marks.

comisario, *m.* commisary.

comisión, *f.* commission. —**comisionar,** *v.*

comisionado, *m.* agent, commissioner.

comisionar, *v.* commission.

comiso, *m.* (law) confiscation of illegal goods.

comistrajo, *m.* mess, hodgepodge.

comité, *m.* committee.

comitiva, *f.* retinue.

como, *conj. & adv.* like. as.

cómo, *adv.* how.

cómoda, *f.* bureau, chest (of drawers).

cómodamente, *adv.* conveniently.

comodatario, *m.* pawn-broker.

comodato, *m.* loan.

comodidad, *f.* convenience, comfort; commodity.

cómodo, *a.* comfortable; convenient.

comodoro, *m.* commodore.

compacto, *a.* compact.

compadecer, *v.* be sorry for, pity.

compadraje, *m.* clique.

compadre, *m.* close friend.

compaginar, *v.* put in order; arrange.

companage, *m.* cold lunch.

compañerismo, *m.* companionship.

compañero -ra, *n.* companion, partner.

compañía, *f.* company.

comparable, *a.* comparable.

comparación, *f.* comparison.

comparar, *v.* compare.

comparativamente, *adv.* comparatively.

comparativo, *a.* comparative.

comparecer, *v.* appear.

comparendo, *m.* summons.

comparsa, *f.* carnival masquerade; retinue.

compartimiento, *m.* compartment.

compartir, *v.* share.

compás, *m.* compass; beat, rhythm.

compasar, *v.* measure exactly.

compasible, *a.* compassionate.

compasión, *f.* compassion.

compasivo, *a.* compassionate.

compatibilidad, *f.* compatibility.

compatible, *a.* compatible.

compatriota, *m. & f.* compatriot.

compeler, *v.* compel.

compendiar, *v.* summarize; abridge.

compendiariamente, *adv.* briefly.

compendio, *m.* summary; abridgment.

compendiosamente, *adv.* briefly.

compensación, *f.* compensation.

compensar, *v.* compensate.

competencia, *f.* competence; competition.

competente, *a.* competent.

competentemente, *adv.* competently.

competición, *f.* competition.

competidor, *a. & n.* competitive; competitor.

competir, *v.* compete.

compilación, *f.* compilation.

compilar, *v.* compile.

compinche, *m.* pal.

complacencia, *f.* complacency.

complacer, *v.* please, oblige, humor.

complaciente, *a.* pleasing, obliging.

complejidad, *f.* complexity.

complejo, *a. & n.* complex.

complemento, *m.* complement; (gram.) object.

completamente, *adv.* completely.

completamiento, *m.* completion, finish.

completar, *v.* complete.

completo, *a.* complete, full, perfect.

complexidad, *f.* complexity.

complexión, *f.* nature, temperament.

complexo, *a.* complex, intricate.

complicación, *f.* complication.

complicado, *a.* complicated.

complicar, *v.* complicate.

cómplice, *m. & f.* accomplice, accessory.

complicidad, *f.* complicity.

complot, *m.* conspiracy.

componedor, *m.* typesetter.

componenda, *f.* compromise; settlement.

componente, *a. & m.* component.

componer, *v.* compose; fix, repair.

componible, *a.* reparable.

comportable, *a.* endurable.

For pronunciation, see the concise guide on pages 3 to 4.

comportamiento, *m.* behavior.

comportarse, *v.* behave.

comporte, *m.* behavior.

composición, *f.* composition.

compositivo, *a.* synthetic; composite.

compositor -ra, *n.* composer.

compostura, *f.* composure; repair; neatness.

compota, *f.* (fruit) sauce.

compra, *f.* purchase. **ir de compras,** to go shopping.

comprador -ra, *n.* buyer, purchaser.

comprar, *v.* buy, purchase.

comprehensivo, *a.* comprehensive.

comprender, *v.* comprehend, understand; include, comprise.

comprensibilidad, *f.* comprehensibility.

comprensible, *a.* understandable.

comprensión, *f.* comprehension, understanding.

comprensivo, *m.* comprehensive.

compresa, *f.* medical compress.

compresión, *f.* compression.

comprimir, *v.* compress.

comprobación, *f.* proof.

comprobante, **1.** *a.* proving. **2.** *m.* proof.

comprobar, *v.* prove; verify, check.

comprometer, *v.* compromise.

comprometerse, *v.* become engaged.

compromiso, *m.* compromise; engagement.

compropietario, *m.* co-owner.

compuerta, *f.* floodgate.

compuesto, *m.* composition; compound.

compulsión, *f.* compulsion.

compulsivo, *a.* compulsive.

compunción, *f.* compunction.

compungirse, *v.* regret, feel remorse.

computación, *f.* computation.

computador, *m.* computer.

computar, *v.* compute.

cómputo, *m.* computation.

comulación, *f.* cumulation.

comulgar, *v.* take communion.

comulgatorio, *m.* communion altar.

común, *a.* common, usual.

comunal, *m.* common people.

comunero, *m.* commoner.

comunicable, *a.* communicable.

comunicación, *f.* communication.

comunicante, *m. & f.* communicant.

comunicar, *v.* communicate; convey.

comunicativo, *a.* communicative.

comunidad, *f.* community.

comunión, *f.* communion.

comunismo, *m.* communism.

comunista, *a. & n.* communistic; communist.

comúnmente, *adv.* commonly; usually; often.

con, *prep.* with.

concavidad, *f.* concavity.

cóncavo, 1. *a.* concave. **2.** *m.* concavity.

concebible, *a.* conceivable.

concebir, *v.* conceive.

conceder, *v.* concede.

concejal, *m.* councilman.

concejo, *m.* city council.

concento, *m.* harmony.

concentración, *f.* concentration.

concentrar, *v.* concentrate.

concepción, *f.* conception.

conceptible, *a.* conceivable.

concepto, *m.* concept; opinion.

concerniente, *a.* concerning.

concernir, *v.* concern.

concertar, *v.* arrange.

concertina, *f.* concertina.

concesión, *f.* concession.

conciencia, *f.* conscience; consciousness; conscientiousness.

concienzudo, a. conscientious.

concierto, m. concert.

conciliación, f. conciliation.

conciliador, m. conciliator.

conciliar, v. conciliate.

concilio, m. council.

concisión, f. conciseness.

conciso, a. concise.

concitar, v. instigate, stir up.

conciudadano, m. fellow citizen.

concluir, v. conclude.

conclusión, f. conclusion.

conclusivo, a. conclusive.

concluso, a. concluded; closed.

concluyentemente, adv. conclusively.

concomitante, a. concomitant, attendant.

concordador, m. moderator; conciliator.

concordancia, f. agreement, concord.

concordar, v. agree; put or be in accord.

concordia, f. concord, agreement.

concretamente, adv. concretely.

concretar, v. summarize.

concretarse, v. limit oneself to.

concreto, a. & m. concrete.

concubina, f. concubine, mistress.

concupiscente, a. lustful.

concurrencia, f. assembly; attendance; competition.

concurrente, a. concurrent.

concurrido, a. heavily attended or patronized.

concurrir, v. concur; attend.

concurso, m. contest, competition; meeting.

concha, f. (sea) shell.

conde, m. (title) count.

condecente, a. appropriate, proper.

condecoración, f. decoration; medal; badge.

condecorar, v. decorate with a medal.

condena, f. prison sentence.

condenación, f. condemnation.

condenar, v. condemn; damn; sentence.

condensación, f. condensation.

condensar, v. condense.

condesa, f. countess.

condescendencia, f. condescension.

condescender, v. condescend, deign.

condescendiente, a. condescending.

condición, f. condition.

condicional, a. conditional.

condicionalmente, adv. conditionally.

condimentar, v. season, flavor.

condimento, m. condiment, seasoning, dressing.

condiscípulo, m. schoolmate.

condolencia, f. condolence, sympathy.

condolerse de, v. sympathize with.

condómino, m. co-owner.

condonar, v. condone.

cóndor, m. condor (bird).

conducción, f. conveyance.

conducente, a. conducive.

conducir, v. conduct, escort, lead; drive.

conducta, f. conduct, behavior.

conducto, m. pipe, conduit; sewer.

conductor, m. driver; conductor.

conectar, v. connect.

conejera, f. rabbit warren; place of ill repute.

conejo, m. rabbit.

conexión, f. connection; coupling.

conexivo, a. connective.

conexo, a. connected, united.

confalón, m. ensign, standard.

confección, f. workmanship; ready-made article; concoction.

confeccionar, v. concoct.

confederación, f. confederation.

confederado, *a. & m.* confederate.

confederar, *v.* confederate, unite, ally.

conferencia, *f.* lecture; conference.

conferenciante, *m. & f.* lecturer, speaker.

conferenciar, *v.* confer.

conferencista, *m. & f.* lecturer, speaker.

conferir, *v.* confer.

confesar, *v.* confess.

confesión, *f.* confession.

confesionario, *m.* confessional.

confesor, *m.* confessor.

confetti, *m.pl.* confetti.

confiable, *a.* dependable.

confiado, *a.* confident; trusting.

confianza, *f.* confidence, trust, faith.

confiar, *v.* entrust; trust, rely.

confidencia, *f.* confidence, secret.

confidencial, *a.* confidential.

confidente, *m. & f.* confidant.

confidentemente, *adv.* confidently.

confín, *m.* confine.

confinamiento, *m.* confinement.

confinar, *v.* confine, imprison; border on.

confirmación, *f.* confirmation.

confirmar, *v.* confirm.

confiscación, *f.* confiscation.

confiscar, *v.* confiscate.

confitar, *v.* sweeten; make into candy or jam.

confite, *m.* candy.

confitería, *f.* confectionery; candy store.

confitura, *f.* confection.

conflagración, *f.* conflagration.

conflicto, *m.* conflict.

confluencia, *f.* confluence, junction.

confluir, *v.* flow into each other.

conformación, *f.* conformation.

conformar, *v.* conform.

conforme, 1. *a.* acceptable, right, as agreed; in accordance, in agreement. **2.** *conj.* according as

conformidad, *f.* conformity; agreement.

conformismo, *m.* conformism.

conformista, *m.* conformist.

confortar, *v.* comfort.

confraternidad, *m.* brotherhood, fraternity.

confricar, *v.* rub.

confrontación, *f.* confrontation.

confrontar, *v.* confront.

confucianismo, *m.* Confucianism.

confundir, *v.* confuse; puzzle, mix up.

confusamente, *adv.* confusedly.

confusión, *f.* confusion, mix-up; clutter.

confuso, *a.* confused; confusing.

confutación, *n.* disproof.

confutar, *v.* refute, disprove.

congelable, *a.* congealable.

congelación, *f.* congealment.

congelado, *a.* frozen, congealed.

congelar, *v.* congeal, freeze.

congenial, *a.* congenial; analogous.

congeniar, *v.* be congenial.

congestión, *f.* congestion.

conglomeración, *f.* conglomeration.

congoja, *f.* grief, anguish.

congraciamiento, *m.* flattery; ingratiation.

congraciar, *v.* flatter; ingratiate oneself.

congratulación, *f.* congratulation.

congratular, *v.* congratulate.

congregación, *f.* congregation.

congregar, *v.* congregate.

congresista, *m. & f.* congressional representative.

congreso, m. congress; conference.

conjetura, f. conjecture. — conjeturar, v.

conjetural, a. conjectural.

conjugación, f. conjugation.

conjugar, v. conjugate.

conjunción, f. union; conjunction.

conjuntamente, adv. together, jointly.

conjunto. 1. a. joint, unified. 2. m. whole.

conjuración, f. conspiracy, plot.

conjurado, m. conspirator, plotter.

conjurar, v. conjure.

conllevador, m. helper, aide.

conmemoración, f. commemoration; remembrance.

conmemorar, v. commemorate.

conmemorativo, a. commemorative, memorial.

conmensal, m. messmate.

conmigo, adv. with me.

conmilitón, m. fellow soldier.

conminación, f. threat, warning.

conminar, v. threaten.

conminatorio, a. threatening, warning.

conmiseración, f. sympathy.

conmoción, f. commotion, stir.

conmovedor, a. moving, touching.

conmover, v. move, affect, touch.

conmutación, f. commutation.

conmutador, m. electric switch.

conmutar, v. exchange.

connotación, f. connotation.

connotar, v. connote.

connubial, a. connubial.

connubio, m. matrimony.

cono, m. cone.

conocedor -ra, n. expert, connoisseur.

conocer, v. know, be acquainted with; meet, make the acquaintance of.

conocible, a. knowable.

conocido -da, 1. a. familiar, well known. 2. n. acquaintance, person known.

conocimiento, m. knowledge, acquaintance; consciousness.

conque, conj. so then; and so.

conquista, f. conquest.

conquistador, m. conqueror.

conquistar, v. conquer.

consabido, a. aforesaid.

consagración, f. consecration.

consagrado, a. consecrated.

consagrar, v. consecrate, dedicate, devote.

consanguinidad, f. consanguinity.

consciente, a. conscious, aware.

conscientemente, adv. consciously.

conscripción, f. conscription for military service.

consecución, f. attainment.

consecuencia, f. consequence.

consecuente, a. consequent; consistent.

consecuentemente, adv. consequently.

consecutivamente, adv. consecutively.

consecutivo, a. consecutive.

conseguir, v. obtain, get, secure; succeed in, manage to.

conseja, n. fable.

consejero -ra, n. adviser, counselor.

consejo, m. council; counsel, (piece of) advice.

consenso, m. consensus.

consentido, a. spoiled, bratty.

consentimiento, m. consent.

consentir, v. allow, permit.

conserje, m. superintendent, keeper.

conserva, f. conserve, preserve.

conservación, f. conservation.

conservador, a. & m. conservative.

conservar, v. conserve.

conservativo, a. conservative, preservative.

conservatorio, m. conservatory.

considerable, a. considerable, substantial.

considerablemente, adv. considerably.

consideración, f. consideration.

consideradamente, adv. considerably.

considerado, a. considerate.

considerando, conj. whereas.

considerar, v. consider.

consigna, f. watchword.

consignación, f. consignment.

consignar, v. consign.

consignatorio, m. consignee; trustee.

consigo, adv. with herself, with himself, with oneself, with themselves, with yourself, with yourselves.

consiguiente, 1. a. consequent. **2.** m. consequence.

consiguientemente, adv. consequently.

consistencia, f. consistency.

consistente, a. consistent.

consistir, v. consist.

consistorio, m. consistory.

consocio, m. associate; partner; comrade.

consola, f. console.

consolación, f. consolation.

consolar, v. console.

consolativo, a. consolatory.

consolidación, n. consolidation.

consolidado, a. consolidated.

consolidar, v. consolidate.

consonancia, f. agreement, accord, harmony.

consonante, a. & n. consonant.

consonar, v. rime.

consorte, m. & f. consort, mate.

conspicuo, a. conspicuous.

conspiración, f. conspiracy, plot.

conspirador -ra, n. conspirator.

conspirar, v. conspire, plot.

constancia, f. perseverance; record.

constante, c. constant.

constantemente, adv. constantly.

constar, v. consist; be clear, be on record.

constelación, f. constellation.

consternación, f. consternation.

consternar, v. dismay.

constipación, f. head cold.

constipado, a. having a head cold.

constitución, f. constitution.

constitucional, a. constitutional.

constitucionalidad, f. constitutionality.

constituir, v. constitute.

constitutivo, m. constituent.

constituyente, a. constituent.

constreñidamente, adv. compulsively; with constraint.

constreñimiento, m. compulsion; constraint.

constreñir, v. constrain.

constricción, f. constriction.

construcción, f. construction.

constructivo, a. constructive.

constructor, m. builder.

construir, v. construct, build.

consuelo, m. consolation.

cónsul, m. consul.

consulado, m. consulate.

consular, a. consular.

consulta, f. consultation.

consultación, f. consultation.

consultante, m. & f. consultant.

consultar, v. consult.

consultivo, a. consultative.

consultor, m. adviser.

consumación, f. consummation; end.

consumado, a. consummate, downright.

consumar, v. consummate.

consumidor, *m.* consumer.
consumir, *v.* consume.
consumo, *m.* consumption.
consunción, *m.* consumption, tuberculosis.
contabilidad, *f.* accounting, bookkeeping.
contabilista, contable, *m. & f.* accountant.
contacto, *m.* contact.
contado, *m.* al c., (for) cash.
contador -ra, *n.* accountant, bookkeeper.
contagiar, *v.* infect.
contagio, *m.* contagion.
contagioso, *a.* contagious.
contaminación, *f.* contamination.
contaminar, *v.* contaminate, pollute.
contar, *v.* count; relate, recount, tell. c. con, count on.
contemperar, *v.* moderate.
contemplación, *f.* contemplation.
contemplador -ra, *n.* thinker.
contemplar, *v.* contemplate.
contemplativamente, *adv.* thoughtfully.
contemplativo, *a.* contemplative.
contemporáneo -nea, *a. & n.* contemporary.
contención, *f.* contention.
contencioso, *a.* quarrelsome; argumentative.
contender, *v.* cope, contend; conflict.
contendiente, *m. & f.* contender.
contenedor -ra, *n.* tenant.
contener, *v.* contain; curb, control.
contenido, *m.* contents.
contenta, *f.* endorsement.
contentamiento, *m.* contentment.
contentar, *v.* content, satisfy.
contentible, *a.* contemptible.
contento, 1. *a.* contented, happy. 2. *m.* contentment, satisfaction, pleasure.
contérmino, *a.* adjacent, abutting.

contestable, *a.* disputable.
contestación, *f.* answer. —
contestar, *v.*
contextura, *f.* texture.
contienda, *f.* combat; match; strife.
contigo, *adv.* with you.
contiguamente, *adv.* closely.
contiguo, *a.* adjoining, next.
continencia, *f.* continence, moderation.
continental, *a.* continental.
continente, *m.* continent; mainland.
continentemente, *adv.* in moderation.
contingencia, *f.* contingency.
contingente, *a.* contingent; incidental.
continuación, *f.* continuation. a c., thereupon, hereupon.
continuamente, *adv.* continuously.
continuar, *v.* continue, keep on.
continuidad, *f.* continuity.
continuo, *a.* continual; continuous.
contorcerse, *v.* writhe, twist.
contorción, *f.* contortion.
contorno, *m.* contour; profile, outline; neighborhood.
contra, *prep.* against.
contraalmirante, *m.* rear admiral.
contraataque, *m.* counterattack.
contrabalancear, *v.* counterbalance.
contrabandear, *v.* smuggle.
contrabandista, *m.* smuggler.
contrabando, *m.* contraband, smuggling.
contracción, *f.* contraction.
contractual, *a.* contractual.
contradecir, *v.* contradict.
contradicción, *f.* contradiction.
contradictorio, *adj.* contradictory.
contraer, *v.* contract; shrink.
contrahacedor -ra, *n.* imitator.

contrahacer, v. forge.

contralor, m. comptroller.

contramandar, v. countermand.

contraorden, f. countermand.

contraparte, f. counterpart.

contrapesar, v. counterbalance, offset.

contrapeso, m. counterweight.

contrapunto, m. counterpoint.

contrariamente, adv. contrarily.

contrariar, v. contradict; vex; antagonize; counteract.

contrariedad, f. contrariness; opposition; contradiction; disappointment; trouble.

contrario, a. & m. contrary, opposite.

contrarrestar, v. resist; counteract.

contrasol, m. sunshade.

contraste, m. contrast. —**contrastar,** v.

contratar, v. engage, contract.

contratiempo, m. accident; misfortune.

contratista, m. contractor.

contrato, m. contract.

contribución, f. contribution; tax.

contribuir, v. contribute.

contribuyente, m. contributor; taxpayer.

contrición, f. contrition.

contristar, v. afflict.

contrito, a. contrite, remorseful.

control, m. control. —**controlar,** v.

controversia, f. controversy.

controversista, m. disputant.

controvertir, v. dispute.

contumacia, f. stubbornness.

contumaz, adj. stubborn.

contumelia, f. contumely; abuse.

conturbar, v. trouble, disturb.

contusión, f. contusion; bruise.

convalecencia, f. convalescence.

convalecer, v. convalesce.

convaleciente, a. convalescent.

convecino, adj. near, close.

convencedor, adj. convincing.

convencer, v. convince.

convencimiento, m. conviction, firm belief.

convención, f. convention.

convencional, a. conventional.

conveniencia, f. suitability; advantage, interest.

conveniente, a. suitable; advantageous, opportune.

convenio, m. pact, treaty; agreement.

convenir, v. assent, agree, concur; be suitable, fitting, convenient.

convento, m. convent.

convergencia, f. convergence.

convergir, v. converge.

conversación, f. conversation.

conversar, v. converse.

conversión, f. conversion.

convertible, a. convertible.

convertir, v. convert.

convexidad, f. convexity.

convexo, a. convex.

convicción, f. conviction.

convicto, adj. guilty.

convidado -da, n. guest.

convidar, v. invite.

convincente, a. convincing.

convite, m. invitation, treat.

convocación, f. convocation.

convocar, v. convoke, assemble.

convoy, m. convoy, escort.

convoyar, v. convey; escort.

convulsión, f. convulsion.

convulsivo, adj. convulsive.

conyugal, adj. conjugal.

cónyuge, n. spouse, mate.

coñac, m. cognac, brandy.

cooperación, f. coöperation.

cooperador, adj. coöperative.

cooperar, v. coöperate.

cooperativo, *a.* coöperative.
coordinación, *f.* coördination.
coordinar, *v.* coördinate.
copa, *f.* goblet.
copartícipe, *m.* partner.
copete, *m.* tuft; toupee.
copia, *f.* copy. —**copiar**, *v.*
copioso, *a.* copious.
copista, *m.* copyist.
copla, *f.* popular song.
coplero, *m.* poetaster.
cópula, *f.* connection.
coqueta, *f.* flirt. —**coquetear**, *v.*
coraje, *m.* courage, bravery; anger.
coral, **1.** *a.* choral. **2.** *m.* coral.
coralino, *a.* coral.
corazón, *m.* heart.
corazonada, *f.* foreboding.
corbata, *f.* necktie.
corbeta, *f.* corvette.
corcova, *f.* hump, hunch.
corcovado, *m.* hunchback.
corcho, *m.* cork.
cordaje, *m.* rigging.
cordel, *m.* string, cord.
cordero, *m.* lamb.
cordial, *a.* cordial, hearty.
cordialidad, *f.* cordiality.
cordillera, *f.* mountain range.
cordón, *m.* cord; (shoe) lace.
cordura, *f.* sanity.
coreografía, *f.* choreography.
corista, *f.* chorus girl.
corneja, *f.* crow.
córneo, *a.* horny.
corneta, *f.* bugle, horn, cornet.
corniforme, *a.* horn-shaped.
cornisa, *f.* cornice.
cornucopia, *f.* cornucopia.
coro, *m.* chorus; choir.
corola, *f.* corolla.
corolario, *m.* corollary.
corona, *f.* crown, halo, wreath.
coronación, *f.* coronation.
coronamiento, *f.* completion of a task.
coronar, *v.* crown.
coronel, *m.* colonel.
coronilla, *f.* small crown.
corporación, *f.* corporation.

corporal, *adj.* corporeal, bodily.
corpóreo, *a.* corporeal.
corpulencia, *f.* corpulence.
corpulento, *a.* corpulent, stout.
corpuscular, *a.* corpuscular.
corpúsculo, *m.* corpuscle.
corral, *m.* corral, pen, yard.
correa, *f.* belt, strap.
corrección, *f.* correction.
correcto, *a.* correct, proper, right.
corrector, *m.* corrector, proofreader.
corredera, *f.* race course.
corredizo, *a.* easily untied.
corredor, *m.* corridor; runner.
corregible, *a.* corrigible.
corregidor, *m.* corrector; magistrate, mayor.
corregir, *v.* correct.
correlación, *f.* correlation.
correlacionar, *v.* correlate.
correlativo, *a.* correlative.
correo, *m.* mail.
correoso, *a.* leathery.
correr, *v.* run.
correría, *f.* raid; escapade.
correspondencia, *f.* correspondence.
corresponder, *v.* correspond.
correspondiente, *a. & m.* corresponding; correspondent.
corresponsal, *m.* correspondent.
corretaje, *m.* brokerage.
correvedile, *m.* tale bearer; gossip.
corrida, *f.* race. **c. (de toros)**, bullfight.
corrido, *a.* abashed; expert.
corriente, **1.** *a.* current, standard. **2.** *f.* current, stream. *m.* **al c.**, informed, up to date.
corroboración, *f.* corroboration.
corroborar, *v.* corroborate.
corroer, *v.* corrode.
corromper, *v.* corrupt.
corrompido, *adj.* corrupt.
corrupción, *f.* corruption.

corruptela, *f.* corruption, vice.

corruptibilidad, *f.* corruptibility.

corruptor, *m.* corrupter.

corsario, *m.* corsair.

corsé, *m.* corset.

corso, *m.* piracy.

cortadillo, *m.* small glass.

cortado, *a.* cut.

cortadura, *f.* cut.

cortante, *a.* cutting, sharp, keen.

cortapisa, *f.* obstacle.

cortaplumas, *m.* penknife.

cortar, *v.* cut, cut off, cut out.

corte, *f.* court. *m.* cut.

cortedad, *f.* smallness; shyness.

cortejar, *v.* pay court to, woo.

cortejo, *m.* court, courtship; sweetheart.

cortés, *a.* civil, courteous, polite.

cortesana, *f.* courtesan.

cortesano, 1. *a.* courtly, courteous. 2. *m.* courtier.

cortesía, *f.* courtesy.

corteza, *f.* bark; rind; crust.

cortijo, *m.* farmhouse.

cortina, *f.* curtain.

corto, *a.* short.

corva, *f.* bend of the knee.

cosa, *f.* thing. **c. de,** a matter of, roughly.

cosecha, *f.* crop, harvest. — **cosechar,** *v.*

coser, *v.* sew, stitch.

cosmético, *a. & m.* cosmetic.

cosmopolita, *a. & n.* cosmopolitan.

coso, *m.* arena for bull fights.

cosquilla, *f.* tickle. — **cosquillar,** *v.*

cosquilloso, *a.* ticklish.

costa, *f.* coast; cost, expense.

costado, *m.* side.

costal, *m.* sack, bag.

costanero, *a.* coastal.

costar, *v.* cost.

costarricense, *a. & n.* Costa Rican.

coste, *m.* cost, price.

costear, *v.* defray, sponsor; sail along the coast of.

costilla, *f.* rib; chop.

costo, *m.* cost, price.

costoso, *a.* costly.

costra, *f.* crust.

costumbre, *f.* custom, practice, habit.

costura, *f.* sewing; seam.

costurera, *f.* seamstress, dressmaker.

cota de malla, coat of mail.

cotejar, *v.* compare.

coteleta, *f.* cutlet.

cotidiano, *a.* daily, everyday.

cotillón, *m.* cotillion.

cotización, *f.* quotation.

cotizar, *v.* quote (a price).

coto, *m.* enclosure; boundary.

cotón, *m.* printed cotton cloth.

cotufa, *f.* Jerusalem artichoke.

coturno, *m.* buskin.

covacha, *f.* small cave.

coxal, *a.* of the hip.

coy, *m.* hammock.

coyote, *m.* coyote.

coyuntura, *f.* joint; juncture.

coz, *f.* kick.

crac, *m.* failure.

cráneo, *m.* skull.

craniano, *a.* cranial.

crapuloso, *a.* drunken.

crasiento, *a.* greasy, oily.

craso, *a.* fat; gross.

cráter, *m.* crater.

craza, *f.* crucible.

creación, *f.* creation.

creador -ra, *a. & n.* creative; creator.

crear, *v.* create.

creativo, *a.* creative.

crébol, *m.* holly tree.

crecer, *v.* grow, grow up; increase.

creces, *f. pl.* increase, addition.

crecidamente, *adv.* abundantly.

crecido, *a.* increased, enlarged; swollen.

creciente, 1. *a.* growing. 2. *f.* crescent.

crecimiento, *m.* growth.

---

credenciales, f.pl. credentials.

credibilidad, f. credibility.

crédito, m. credit.

credo, m. creed, belief.

crédulamente, adv. credulously, gullibly.

credulidad, f. credulity.

crédulo, a. credulous.

creedero, a. credible.

creedor, a. credulous, believing.

creencia, f. belief.

creer, v. believe; think.

creíble, a. credible, believable.

crema, f. cream.

cremación, f. cremation.

cremar, v. cremate.

crémor tártaro, cream of tartar.

creosota, f. creosote.

crepitar, v. crackle.

crepuscular, a. of or like the dawn or dusk.

crepúsculo, m. dusk, twilight.

crescendo, m. crescendo.

crespo, a. crisp; curly.

crespón, m. crepe.

cresta, f. crest.

crestado, a. crested.

creta, f. chalk.

cretáceo, a. chalky.

cretinismo, m. cretinism.

cretino, n. & a. cretin.

cretona, f. cretonne.

creyente, 1. a. believing. 2. n. believer.

creyón, m. crayon.

cría, f. (stock) breeding; young (of an animal), litter.

criada, f. girl servant, maid.

criadero, m. (agr.) nursery.

criado -da, m. servant.

criador, a. fruitful, prolific.

crianza, f. breeding; upbringing.

criar, v. raise, rear, bring up; breed.

criatura, f. creature; infant.

criba, f. sieve; crib.

cribado, a. sifted.

cribar, v. sift.

crimen, m. crime.

criminal, a. & m. criminal.

criminalidad, f. criminality.

criminalmente, adv. criminally.

criminoso, a. criminal.

crin, f. mane of a horse.

crinolina, f. crinoline.

criollo -lla, a. & n. native; creole.

cripta, f. crypt.

criptografía, f. cryptography.

crisantemo, m. chrysanthemum.

crisis, f. crisis.

crisma, m. chrism.

crisol, m. crucible.

crispamiento, m. twitch, contraction.

crispar, v. contract (the muscles); twitch.

crista, f. heraldic crest.

cristal, m. crystal; lens.

cristalería, f. glassware.

cristalino, a. crystalline.

cristalización, f. crystallization.

cristalizar, v. crystallize.

cristianar, v. baptize.

cristiandad, f. Christendom.

cristianismo, m. Christianity.

cristiano -na, a. & n. Christian.

Cristo, m. Christ.

criterio, m. criterion; judgment.

crítica, f. criticism; critique.

criticable, a. blameworthy.

criticador, a. critical.

criticar, v. criticize.

crítico, a. & m. critical; critic.

croar, v. croak.

crocante, m. peanut brittle.

crocidar, v. crow.

crocodilo, m. crocodile.

cromático, a. chromatic.

cromo, m. chromium.

cromotipia, f. color printing.

crónica, f. chronicle.

crónico, a. chronic.

cronicón, m. concise chronicle.

cronista, m. chronicler.

cronología, f. chronology.

cronológicamente, *adv.* chronologically.

cronológico, *a.* chronologic.

cronometro, *m.* chronometer.

croqueta, *f.* croquette.

croquis, *m.* sketch; rough outline.

crótalo, *m.* rattlesnake; castanet.

cruce, *m.* crossing, crossroads, junction.

crucero, *m.* cruiser.

crucífero, *a.* cross-shaped.

crucificado, *a.* crucified.

crucificar, *v.* crucify.

crucifijo, *m.* crucifix.

crucifixión, *f.* crucifixion.

crudamente, *adv.* crudely.

crudeza, *f.* crudeness.

crudo, *a.* crude, raw.

cruel, *a.* cruel.

crueldad, *f.* cruelty.

cruelmente, *adv.* cruelly.

cruentamente, *adv.* bloodily.

cruento, *a.* bloody.

crujía, *f.* corridor.

crujido, *m.* creak.

crujir, *v.* crackle, creak; rustle.

cruórico, *a.* bloody.

crup, *m.* croup.

crustáceo, *n. & a.* crustacean.

cruz, *f.* cross.

cruzada, *f.* crusade.

cruzado -da, *n.* crusader.

cruzamiento, *m.* crossing.

cruzar, *v.* cross.

cruzarse con, *v.* to (meet and) pass.

cuaderno, *m.* notebook.

cuadra, *f.* block; (hospital) ward.

cuadradamente, *adv.* exactly, precisely; completely, in full.

cuadradillo, *m.* lump of sugar.

cuadrado, *a. & m.* square.

cuadragésima, *f.* Lent.

cuadragesimal, *a.* Lenten.

cuadrángulo, *m.* quadrangle.

cuadrante, *m.* quadrant; dial.

cuadrar, *v.* square; suit.

cuadricular, *a.* in squares.

cuadrilátero, *a.* quadrilateral.

cuadrilla, *f.* band, troop, gang.

cuadrinieto, *n.* great-grandchild.

cuadro, *m.* picture; painting; frame. **a cuadros,** checked, plaid.

cuadro de servicio, time-table.

cuadrupedal, *a.* quadruped.

cuádruplo, *a.* fourfold.

cuajada, *f.* curd.

cuajamiento, *m.* coagulation.

cuajar, *v.* coagulate; overdecorate.

cuajo, *m.* rennet; coagulation.

cuakerismo, *m.* Quakerism.

cuákero, *n. & a.* Quaker.

cual, *rel. pron.* which.

cual, *a. & pron.* what, which.

cualidad, *f.* quality.

cualitativo, *a.* qualitative.

cualquiera, *a. & pron.* whatever, any; anyone.

cuando, *conj.* when.

cuando, *adv.* when. **de cuando en cuando,** from time to time.

cuantía, *f.* quantity; amount.

cuantiar, *v.* estimate.

cuantidad, *f.* quantity.

cuantiosamente, *adv.* abundantly.

cuantioso, *a.* abundant.

cuantitativo, *a.* quantitative.

cuanto, *a., adv. & pron.* as much as, as many as; all that which. **en c.,** as soon as. **en c. a,** as for. **c. antes,** as soon as possible. **c. más . . . tanto más,** the more . . . the more. **unos cuantos,** a few.

cuánto, *a. & adv.* how much, how many.

cuaquerismo, *m.* Quakerism.

cuáquero, *n. & a.* Quaker.

cuarenta, *a. & pron.* forty.

cuarentena, *f.* quarantine.

cuaresma, *f.* Lent.

For pronunciation, see the concise guide on pages 3 to 4.

cuaresmal, *a.* Lenten.

cuarta, *f.* quarter; quadrant; quart.

cuartana, *f.* ague.

cuartear, *v.* divide into quarters.

cuartel, *m.* (mil.) quarters; barracks; (naut.) hatch. **c. general,** headquarters. **sin c.,** giving no quarter.

cuartelada, *f.* military uprising.

cuarterón, *n. & a.* quadroon.

cuarteto, *m.* quartet.

cuartillo, *m.* pint.

cuarto, 1. *a.* fourth. **2.** *m.* quarter; room.

cuarto de baño, bathroom.

cuarto de dormir, bedroom.

cuarzo, *m.* quartz.

cuasi, *adv.* almost, nearly.

cuate, *a. & n.* twin.

cuatrero, *m.* cattle rustler.

cuadrillón, *m.* quadrillion.

cuatro, *a. & pron.* four.

cuatrocientos, *a. & pron.* four hundred.

cuba, *f.* cask, tub, vat.

cubano -na, *f. & n.* Cuban.

cubero, *m.* cooper.

cubertura, *f.* cover.

cubeta, *f.* small barrel, keg.

cúbico, *a.* cubic.

cubierta, *f.* cover; envelope; wrapping; tread (of a tire); deck.

cubiertamente, *adv.* secretly, stealthily.

cubierto, *m.* place (at table).

cubil, *m.* lair.

cubo, *m.* cube; bucket.

cubrecama, *f.* bedspread.

cubrir, *v.* cover.

cubrirse, *v.* put on one's hat.

cucaracha, *f.* cockroach.

cuclillo, *m.* cuckoo.

cuco, *a.* sly.

cuculla, *f.* hood, cowl.

cuchara, *f.* spoon, tablespoon.

cucharada, *f.* spoonful.

cucharita, cucharilla, *f.* teaspoon.

cucharón, *m.* dipper, ladle.

cuchicheo, *m.* whisper. —

cuchichear, *v.*

cuchilla, *f.* cleaver.

cuchillada, *f.* slash.

cuchillería, *f.* cutlery.

cuchillo, *m.* knife.

cucho, *m.* fertilizer.

cuchufleta, *f.* jest.

cuelga, *f.* cluster, bunch.

cuelgacapas, *m.* coat rack.

cuello, *m.* neck; collar.

cuenca, *f.* socket; (river) basin; wooden bowl.

cuenco, *m.* earthen bowl.

cuenta, *f.* account; bill. **darse c.,** to realize. **tener en c.,** to keep in mind.

cuentagotas, *m.* dropper (for medicine).

cuentista, *m.* informer.

cuento, *m.* story, tale.

cuerda, *f.* cord; chord; rope; string; spring (of clock). **dar c. a,** to wind (clock).

cuerdamente, *adv.* sanely; prudently.

cuerdo, *a.* sane; prudent.

cuerno, *m.* horn.

cuero, *m.* leather; hide.

cuerpo, *m.* body; corps.

cuervo, *m.* crow, raven.

cuesco, *m.* pit, stone (of fruit).

cuesta, *f.* hill, slope. **llevar a cuestas,** to carry on one's back.

cuestación, *f.* solicitation for charity.

cuestión, *f.* question; affair; argument.

cuestionable, *a.* questionable.

cuestionar, *v.* question; discuss; argue.

cuestionario, *m.* questionnaire.

cuete, *m.* firecracker.

cuetzale, *m.* quetzal.

cueva, *f.* cave; cellar.

cugujada, *f.* lark.

cuidado, *m.* care, caution, worry. **tener c.,** to be careful.

cuidadosamente, *adv.* carefully.

cuidadoso, *a.* careful, painstaking.

cuidante, *n.* caretaker, custodian.

cuidar, *v.* take care of.

cuita, *f.* trouble, care, grief.

cuitado, *a.* unfortunate; shy, timid.

cuitamiento, *m.* timidity.

culata, *f.* haunch, buttock; butt of a gun.

culatada, *f.* recoil.

culatazo, *m.* blow with the butt of a gun; recoil.

culebra, *f.* snake.

culero, *a.* lazy, indolent.

culinario, *a.* culinary.

culminación, *f.* culmination.

culminar, *v.* culminate.

culpa, *f.* fault, guilt, blame. **tener la c.**, to be at fault. **echar la culpa a**, to blame.

culpabilidad, *f.* guilt, fault, blame.

culpable, *a.* at fault, guilty, to blame.

culpar, *v.* blame, accuse.

cultamente, *adv.* politely, elegantly.

cultivable, *a.* arable.

cultivación, *f.* cultivation.

cultivador, *m.* cultivator.

cultivar, *v.* cultivate.

cultivo, *m.* cultivation; (growing) crop.

culto, **1.** *a.* cultured, cultivated. **2.** *m.* cult; worship.

cultura, *f.* culture; refinement.

cultural, *a.* cultural.

culturar, *v.* cultivate.

cumbre, *f.* summit, peak.

cumpleaños, *m.pl.* birthday.

cumplidamente, *adv.* completely.

cumplido, *a.* polite, polished.

cumplimentar, *v.* compliment.

cumplimiento, *m.* fulfillment; compliment.

cumplir, *v.* comply; carry out, fulfill; reach (years of age).

cumular, *v.* accumulate.

cumulativo, *a.* cumulative.

cúmulo, *m.* heap, pile.

cuna, *f.* cradle.

cundir, *v.* spread; expand; propagate.

cuneiforme, *a.* cuneiform, wedge-shaped.

cuneo, *m.* rocking.

cuña, *f.* wedge.

cuñada, *f.* sister-in-law.

cuñado, *m.* brother-in-law.

cuñete, *m.* keg.

cuociente, *m.* quotient.

cuota, *f.* quota; dues.

cuotidiano, *a.* daily.

cupé, *m.* coupé.

cupido, *m.* lover.

cupo, *m.* share; assigned quota.

cupón, *m.* coupon.

cúpula, *f.* dome.

cura, *m.* priest. *f.* treatment, (medical) care. **c. de urgencia**, first aid.

curable, *a.* curable.

curación, *f.* healing; cure; (surgical) dressing.

curado, *a.* cured, healed.

curador, *m.* custodian; curator.

curandero, *m.* healer, medicine man.

curar, *v.* cure, heal, treat.

curativo, *a.* curative, healing.

curia, *f.* ecclesiastical court.

curiosear, *v.* snoop, pry, meddle.

curiosidad, *f.* curiosity.

curioso, *a.* curious.

curro, *a.* showy, loud, flashy.

cursante, *n.* student.

cursar, *v.* frequent; attend to.

cursi, *a.* vulgar, shoddy, in bad taste.

curso, *m.* course.

curtidor, *m.* tanner.

curtir, *v.* tan.

curva, *f.* curve; bend.

curvatura, *f.* curvature.

cúspide, *f.* top, peak.

custodia, *f.* custody.

custodiar, *v.* guard, watch.

custodio, *m.* custodian.

cutáneo, *a.* cutaneous.

cutícula, *f.* cuticle.

cutis, *m. or f.* skin, complexion.

cuyo, *a.* whose.

CH

chabancano, *a.* clumsy.
chacal, *m.* jackal.
chacó, *m.* shako.
chacona, *f.* chaconne.
chacota, *f.* fun, mirth.
chacotear, *v.* joke.
chacra, *f.* small farm.
chafallar *v.* mend badly.
chagra, *m.* rustic; rural person.
chal, *m.* shawl.
chalán, *m.* horse trader.
chaleco, *m.* vest.
chalet, *m.* chalet.
challí, *m.* challis.
chamada, *f.* brushwood.
chamarillero, *m.* gambler.
chamarra, *f.* coarse linen jacket.
chambelán, *m.* chamberlain.
champaña, *f.* champagne.
champú, *m.* shampoo.
chamuscar, *v.* scorch.
chancaco, *a.* brown.
chancear, *v.* jest, joke.
chanciller, *m.* chancellor.
chancillería, *f.* chancery.
chancla, *f.* old shoe.
chancleta, *f.* slipper.
chanclos, *m.pl.* galoshes.
chancro, *m.* chancre.
changador, *m.* porter, handyman.
chantaje, *m.* blackmail.
chantajista, *n.* blackmailer.
chanto, *m.* flagstone.
chantre, *m.* precentor.
chanza, *f.* joke, jest. — **chancear,** *v.*
chanzoneta, *f.* chansonette.
chapa, *f.* (metal) sheet, plate; lock.
chaparrada, *f.* shower.
chaparral, *m.* chaparral.
chaparreras, *f.pl.* chaps.
chaparrón, *m.* downpour.
chapear, *v.* veneer.
chapeo, *m.* hat.
chapitel, *m.* spire, steeple; (architecture) capital.

chapodar, *v.* lop.
chapón, *m.* ink blot.
chapotear, *v.* paddle or splash in the water.
chapoteo, *m.* splash.
chapucear, *v.* fumble, bungle.
chapucero, *a.* sloppy, bungling.
chapurrear, *v.* speak (a language) brokenly.
chapuz, *m.* dive; ducking.
chapuzar, *v.* dive, duck.
chaqueta, *f.* jacket, coat.
charada, *f.* charade.
charamusca, *f.* twisted candy stick.
charanga, *f.* military band.
charanguero, *m.* peddler.
charca, *f.* pool, pond.
charco, *m.* pool, puddle.
charla, *f.* chat; chatter, prattle. — **charlar,** *v.*
charladuría, *f.* chatter.
charlatán, *m.* charlatan.
charlatanismo, *m.* charlatanism.
charol, *m.* varnish.
charolar, *v.* varnish; polish
charquear, *v.* jerk (beef).
charqui, *m.* jerked beef.
charrán, *a.* roguish.
chascarrillo, *m.* risqué story.
chasco, *m.* disappointment, blow; practical joke.
chasis, *m.* chassis.
chasquear, *v.* fool, trick; disappoint; crack (a whip).
chasquido, *m.* crack (sound).
chata, *f.* bedpan.
chato, *a.* flat-nosed, pugnosed.
chauvinismo, *m.* chauvinism.
chauvinista, *n. & a.* chauvinist.
chelín, *m.* shilling.
cheque, *m.* (bank) check.
chica, *f.* girl.
chicana, *f.* chicanery.
chicle, *m.* chewing gum.

For pronunciation, see the concise guide on pages 3 to 4.

chico, 1. *a.* little. **2.** *m.* boy.

chicote, *m.* cigar; cigar butt.

chicotear, *v.* whip, flog.

chicha, *f.* an alcoholic drink.

chícharo, *f.* pea.

chicharra, *f.* cicada; talkative person.

chicharrón, *m.* crisp fried scrap of meat.

chichear, *v.* hiss in disapproval.

chichón, *m.* bump, bruise, lump.

chifladura, *f.* mania; whim; jest.

chiflar, *v.* whistle; become insane.

chiflido, *m.* shrill whistle.

chile, *m.* chili.

chileno -na, *a. & n.* Chilean.

chillido, *m.* shriek, scream, screech. —**chillar,** *v.*

chillón, *a.* shrill.

chimenea, *f.* chimney, smokestack; fireplace.

china, *f.* pebble; maid; Chinese woman.

chinarro, *m.* large pebble, stone.

chinche, *f.* bedbug; thumbtack.

chinchilla, *f.* chinchilla.

chinchorro, *m.* fishing net.

chinela, *f.* slipper.

chinero, *m.* china closet.

chino -na, *a. & n.* Chinese.

chiquero, *m.* pen for pigs, goats, etc.

chiquito, 1. *a.* small, tiny. **2.** *n.* small child.

chiribitil, *m.* small room, den.

chirimía, *f.* flageolet.

chiripa, *f.* stroke of good luck.

chirla, *f.* mussel.

chirle, *a.* insipid.

chirona, *f.* prison, jail.

chirrido, *m.* squeak, chirp. —**chirriar,** *v.*

chis, *interj.* hush!

chisgarabís, *n.* meddler; unimportant person.

chisguete, *m.* squirt, splash.

chisme, *m.* gossip. —**chismear,** *v.*

chismero, *m.* gossiper.

chismoso, *adj.* gossiping.

chispa, *f.* spark.

chispeante, *a.* sparkling.

chispear, *v.* sparkle.

chisporrotear, *v.* emit sparks.

chistar, *v.* mumble.

chiste, *m.* joke; witty saying.

chistera, *f.* fish basket; top hat.

chistoso, *a.* funny, comic, amusing.

chito, *interj.* hush!

chiva, *f.* female goat.

chivato, *m.* kid, young goat.

chivo, *m.* male goat.

chocante, *a.* striking; shocking; unpleasant.

chocar, *v.* collide, clash, crash; shock.

chocarrear, *v.* joke, jest.

choclo, *m.* clog; overshoe; ear of corn.

chocolate, *m.* chocolate.

chocolatería, *f.* chocolate shop.

chochear, *v.* be in one's dotage.

chochera, *f.* dotage, senility.

chofer, chófer, *m.* chauffeur, driver.

chofeta, *f.* chafing dish.

cholo, *m.* half-breed.

chopo, *m.* black poplar.

choque, *m.* collision, clash, crash; shock.

chorizo, *m.* sausage.

chorrear, *v.* spout; drip.

chorro, *m.* spout; spurt, jet. **llover a chorros,** to pour (rain).

choto, *m.* calf, kid.

choza, *f.* hut, cabin.

chozno, *m.* great-grandson.

chubasco, *m.* shower, squall.

chubascoso, *a.* squally.

chuchería, *f.* trinket, knick-knack.

chulería, *f.* pleasant manner.

chuleta, *f.* chop, cutlet.

chulo, *m.* rascal, rogue; joker.

chupa, *f.* jacket.

chupada, *f.* suction.

chupado, *a.* very thin.
chupaflor, *m.* hummingbird.
chupar, *v.* suck.
churrasco, *m.* roasted meat.

chuscada, *f.* joke, jest.
chusco, *a.* funny, humorous.
chusma, *f.* mob, rabble.
chuzo, *m.* pike.

D

dable, *a.* possible.
dactilógrafo, *m.* typewriter.
dádiva, *f.* gift.
dadivosamente, *adv.* generously.
dadivoso, *a.* generous, bountiful.
dador, *m.* giver.
dados, *m.pl.* dice.
daga, *f.* dagger.
dalia, *f.* dahlia.
daltonismo, *m.* color blindness.
dallador, *m.* lawn mower.
dallar, *v.* mow.
dama, *f.* lady.
damasco, *m.* apricot.
damisela, *f.* young lady, girl.
danés -esa, *a. & n.* Danish, Dane.
danza, *f.* (the) dance. —danzar, *v.*
danzante, *m.* dancer.
dañable, *a.* condemnable.
dañar, *v.* hurt, harm; damage.
dañino, dañoso, *a.* harmful.
daño, *m.* damage; harm.
dañoso, *a.* harmful.
dar, *v.* give; strike (clock). d. a, face, open on. d. con, find, locate.
dardo, *m.* dart.
dársena, *f.* dock.
datar, *v.* date.
dátil, *m.* date (fruit).
dativo, *m. & a.* dative.
datos, *m.pl.* data.
de, *prep.* of; from; than.
debajo, *adv.* underneath. d. de, under.
debate, *m.* debate.

debatir, *v.* debate, argue.
debe, *m.* debit.
debelación, *f.* conquest.
debelar, *v.* conquer.
deber, 1. *v.* owe; must; be to, be supposed to. 2. *m.* obligation.
debido, *a.* due.
débil, *a.* weak, faint.
debilidad, *f.* weakness.
debilitación, *f.* weakness.
debilitar, *v.* weaken.
débito, *m.* debit.
debutante, *f.* debutante.
debutar, *v.* make a debut.
década, *f.* decade.
decadencia, *f.* decadence, decline, decay.
decadente, *a.* decadent, declining, decaying.
decaer, *v.* decay; decline.
decalitro, *m.* decaliter.
decálogo, *m.* decalogue.
decámetro, *m.* decameter.
decano, *m.* dean.
decantado, *a.* much discussed; overexalted.
decapitación, *f.* beheading.
decapitar, *v.* behead.
decencia, *f.* decency.
decenio, *m.* decade.
decente, *a.* decent.
decentemente, *adv.* decently.
decepción, *f.* disappointment; delusion.
decepcionar, *v.* disappoint, disillusion.
decididamente, *adv.* decidedly.
decidir, *v.* decide.
decigramo, *m.* decigram.

decilitro, *m.* deciliter.
décima, *f.* ten-line stanza.
decimal, *a.* decimal.
décimo, *a.* tenth.
decir, *v.* tell, say. **es d.,** that is (to say).
decisión, *f.* decision.
decisivamente, *adv.* decisively.
decisivo, *a.* decisive.
declamación, *f.* declamation, speech.
declamar, *v.* declaim.
declaración, *f.* declaration; statement; plea.
declarar, *v.* declare, state.
declarativo, *a.* declarative.
declinación, *f.* descent; decay; decline; declension.
declinar, *v.* decline.
declive, *m.* declivity, slope.
decocción, *f.* decoction.
decomiso, *m.* seizure, confiscation.
decoración, *f.* decoration, trimming.
decorado, *m.* (theat.) scenery, set.
decorar, *v.* decorate, trim.
decorativo, *a.* decorative, ornamental.
decoro, *m.* decorum; decency.
decoroso, *a.* decorous.
decrecer, *v.* decrease.
decrépito, *a.* decrepit.
decreto, *m.* decree. **—decretar,** *v.*
dechado, *m.* model; sample; pattern; example.
dedal, *m.* thimble.
dédalo, *m.* labyrinth.
dedicación, *f.* dedication.
dedicar, *v.* devote; dedicate.
dedicatoria, *f.* dedication, inscription.
dedo, *m.* finger, toe.
deducción, *f.* deduction.
deducir, *v.* deduce; subtract.
defecto, *a.* defective.
defecto, *m.* defect, flaw.
defectuoso, *a.* defective, faulty.
defender, *v.* defend.
defensa, *f.* defense.
defensivo, *a.* defensive.
defensor, *m.* defender.

deferencia, *f.* deference.
deferir, *v.* defer.
deficiente, *a.* deficient.
déficit, *m.* deficit.
definición, *f.* definition.
definido, *a.* definite.
definir, *v.* define; establish.
definitivamente, *adv.* definitely.
definitivo, *a.* definite; definitive.
deformación, *f.* deformation.
deformar, *v.* deform.
deforme, *a.* deformed; ugly.
deformidad, *f.* deformity.
defraudar, *v.* defraud.
defunción, *f.* death.
degeneración, *f.* degeneration.
degenerado, *a.* degenerate. **—degenerar,** *v.*
deglutir, *v.* swallow.
degollar, *v.* behead.
degradación, *f.* degradation.
degradar, *v.* degrade, debase.
deidad, *f.* deity.
deificación, *f.* deification.
deificar, *v.* deify.
deífico, *a.* divine, deific.
deísmo, *m.* deism.
dejadez, *f.* neglect, untidiness; laziness.
dejado, *a.* untidy; lazy.
dejar, *v.* let, allow; leave. **d. de,** stop, leave off. **no d. de,** not fail to.
dejo, *m.* abandonment; negligence; aftertaste; accent.
del, *contr.* of **de + el.**
delantal, *m.* apron.
delante, *adv.* ahead, forward; in front.
delantero, *a.* forward, front, first.
delator, *m.* informer; accuser.
delegación, *f.* delegation.
delegado -da, *n.* delegate. **—delegar,** *v.*
deleite, *m.* delight. **—deleitar,** *v.*
deleitoso, *a.* delightful.
deletrear, *v.* spell; decipher.
delfín, *m.* dolphin; dauphin.

delgadez, f. thinness, slenderness.

delgado, a. thin, slender, slim, slight.

deliberación, f. deliberation.

deliberadamente, adv. deliberately.

deliberar, v. deliberate.

deliberativo, a. deliberative.

delicadamente, adv. delicately.

delicadeza, f. delicacy.

delicado, a. delicate, dainty.

delicia, f. delight; deliciousness.

delicioso, a. delicious.

delincuencia, f. delinquency.

delincuente, a. & m. delinquent; culprit, offender.

delineación, f. delineation, sketch.

delinear, v. delineate, sketch.

delirante, a. delirious.

delirar, v. rave, be delirious.

delirio, m. delirium; rapture, bliss.

delito, m. crime, offense.

delta, m. delta (of river).

demagogia, f. demagogy.

demagogo, n. demagogue.

demanda, f. demand, claim.

demandador -ra, n. plaintiff.

demandar, v. sue; demand.

demarcación, f. demarcation.

demarcar, v. demarcate, limit.

demás, a. & n. other; (the) rest (of). **por d.,** too much.

demasía, f. excess; audacity; iniquity.

demasiado, a. & adv. too; too much; too many.

demencia, f. dementia; insanity.

demente, a. demented.

democracia, f. democracy.

demócrata, m. & f. democrat.

democrático, a. democratic.

demoler, v. demolish, tear down.

demolición, f. demolition.

demonio, m. demon, devil.

demontre, m. devil.

demora, f. delay. **—demorar,** v.

demostración, f. demonstration.

demostrador, m. demonstrator.

demostrar, v. demonstrate, show.

demostrativo, a. demonstrative.

demudar, v. change; disguise, conceal.

denegación, f. denial, refusal.

denegar, v. deny, refuse.

dengue, m. prudishness; dengue.

denigración, f. defamation, disgrace.

denigrar, v. defame, disgrace.

denodado, a. brave, dauntless.

denominación, f. denomination.

denominar, v. name, call.

denotación, f. denotation.

denotar, v. denote, betoken, express.

densidad, f. density.

denso, a. dense.

dentado, a. toothed; serrated; cogged.

dentadura, f. set of teeth.

dental, a. dental.

dentífrico, m. dentifrice.

dentista, m. dentist.

dentistería, f. dentistry.

dentro, adv. within, inside. **d. de poco,** in a short while.

denuedo, m. bravery, courage.

denuesto, m. insult, offense.

denuncia, f. denunciation; declaration.

denunciación, f. denunciation.

denunciar, v. denounce.

deparar, v. offer; grant.

departamento, m. department, section.

departir, v. talk, chat.

dependencia, f. dependence; branch office.

depender, v. depend.

dependiente, a. & m. dependent; clerk.

For pronunciation, see the concise guide on pages 3 to 4.

depilatorio, *a.* depilatory.

deplorable, *a.* deplorable, wretched.

deplorablemente, *adv.* deplorably.

deplorar, *v.* deplore.

deponer, *v.* depose.

deportación, *f.* deportation; exile.

deportar, *v.* deport.

deporte, *m.* sport. **—deportivo,** *a.*

deposición, *f.* assertion, deposition; removal; movement.

depositante, *m. & f.* depositor.

depósito, *m.* deposit. **—depositar,** *v.*

depravación, *f.* depravation; depravity.

depravado, *a.* depraved, wicked.

depravar, *v.* deprave, corrupt, pervert.

depreciación, *f.* depreciation.

depreciar, *v.* depreciate.

depredación, *f.* depredation.

depredar, *v.* pillage, depredate.

depresión, *f.* depression.

depresivo, *a.* depressive.

deprimir, *v.* depress.

depurar, *v.* purify.

derecha, *f.* right (hand, side).

derechera, *f.* short cut.

derecho, 1. *a.* right; straight. **2.** *m.* right; (the) law.

derechura, *f.* straightness.

derelicto, *a.* abandoned, derelict.

deriva, *f.* (naut.) drift.

derivación, *f.* derivation.

derivar, *v.* derive.

derogar, *v.* derogate; repeal, abrogate.

derramamiento, *m.* overflow.

derramar, *v.* spill, pour, scatter.

derrame, *m.* overflow; discharge.

derretir, *v.* melt, dissolve.

derribar, *v.* demolish, knock down; bowl over, floor, fell.

derrocamiento, *m.* overthrow.

derrocar, *v.* overthrow; oust; demolish.

derrochar, *v.* waste.

derroche, *m.* waste.

derrota, *f.* rout, defeat. **—derrotar,** *v.*

derrumbamiento, **derrumbe,** *m.* collapse; landslide.

derrumbarse, *v.* collapse, tumble.

derviche, *m.* dervish.

desabotonar, *v.* unbutton.

desabrido, *a.* insipid, tasteless.

desabrigar, *v.* uncover.

desabrochar, *v.* unbutton, unclasp.

desacierto, *m.* error.

desacobardar, *v.* remove fear; embolden.

desacomodadamente, *adv.* inconveniently.

desacomodado, *a.* unemployed.

desacomodar, *v.* molest; inconvenience; dismiss.

desacomodo, *m.* loss of employment.

desaconsejado, *a.* imprudent, ill advised, rash.

desaconsejar, *v.* dissuade.

desacordadamente, *adv.* unadvisedly.

desacordar, *v.* differ, disagree; be forgetful.

desacorde, *a.* discordant.

desacostumbradamente, *adv.* unusually.

desacostumbrado, *a.* unusual, unaccustomed.

desacostumbrar, *v.* give up a habit or custom.

desacreditar, *v.* discredit.

desacuerdo, *m.* disagreement.

desadeudar, *v.* pay one's debts.

desadormecer, *v.* waken, rouse.

desadornar, *v.* divest of ornament.

desadvertidamente, *adv.* inadvertently.

For pronunciation, see the concise guide on pages 3 to 4.

desadvertido, a. imprudent.
desadvertimiento, m. imprudence, rashness.
desadvertir, v. act imprudently.
desafección, f. disaffection.
desafecto, a. disaffected.
desafiar, v. defy; challenge.
desafinar, v. be out of tune.
desafío, m. defiance; challenge.
desaforar, v. infringe one's rights; be outrageous.
desafortunado, a. unfortunate.
desafuero, m. violation of the law; outrage.
desagraciado, a. graceless.
desagradable, a. disagreeable, unpleasant.
desagradablemente, adv. disagreeably.
desagradecido, a. ungrateful.
desagradecimiento, m. ingratitude.
desagrado, m. displeasure.
desagraviar, v. make amends.
desagregar, v. separate, disintegrate.
desagriar, v. mollify, appease.
desaguadero, m. drain, outlet; cesspool; sink.
desaguador, m. water pipe.
desaguar, v. drain.
desaguisado, m. offense; injury.
desahogadamente, adv. impudently; brazenly.
desahogado, a. impudent, brazen; cheeky.
desahogar, v. relieve.
desahogo, m. relief; nerve, cheek.
desahuciar, v. give up hope for; despair of.
desairado, a. graceless.
desaire, m. slight; scorn. — **desairar,** v.
desajustar, v. mismatch, misfit; make unfit.
desalar, v. hurry, hasten.
desalentar, v. make out of breath; discourage.

desaliento, m. discouragement.
desaliñar, v. disarrange; make untidy.
desaliño, m. slovenliness, untidiness.
desalivar, v. salivate.
desalmadamente, adv. mercilessly.
desalmado, a. merciless.
desalojamiento, m. displacement; dislodging.
desalojar, v. dislodge.
desalquilado, a. vacant, unrented.
desamar, v. cease loving.
desamasado, a. dissolve, undo.
desamistarse, v. quarrel, disagree.
desamor, m. disaffection, dislike; hatred.
desamorado, a. cruel; harsh; rude.
desamparador, m. deserter.
desamparar, v. desert, abandon.
desamparo, m. desertion, abandonment.
desamueblar, v. dismantle.
desandrajado, a. shabby, ragged.
desanimadamente, adv. in a discouraged manner; spiritlessly.
desanimar, v. dishearten, discourage.
desánimo, m. discouragement.
desanudar, v. untie; loosen; disentangle.
desapacible, a. rough, harsh; unpleasant.
desaparecer, v. disappear.
desaparición, f. disappearance.
desapasionadamente, adv. dispassionately.
desapasionado, a. dispassionate.
desapego, m. impartiality.
desapercibido, adj. unprepared.
desapiadado, a. merciless, cruel.

For pronunciation, see the concise guide on pages **3** to **4**.

desaplicación, f. indolence; laziness; negligence.

desaplicado, a. indolent; lazy; negligent.

desaposesionar, v. dispossess.

desapreciar, v. depreciate.

desapretador, m. screwdriver.

desapretar, v. loosen; relieve, ease.

desaprisionar, v. set free, release.

desaprobación, f. disapproval.

desaprobar, v. disapprove.

desaprovechado, a. useless, profitless; backward.

desaprovechar, v. waste; be backward.

desarbolar, v. unmast.

desarmado, a. disarmed, defenseless.

desarmar, v. disarm.

desarme, m. disarmament.

desarraigar, v. uproot; eradicate; expel.

desarreglar, v. disarrange, mess up.

desarrollar, v. develop.

desarrollo, m. development.

desarropar, v. undress; uncover.

desarrugar, v. remove wrinkles from.

desaseado, a. dirty; disorderly.

desasear, v. make dirty or disorderly.

desaseo, m. dirtiness; disorder.

desasir, v. loosen; disengage.

desasociable, a. unsociable.

desasosegar, v. disturb.

desasosiego, m. uneasiness.

desastrado, a. ragged, wretched.

desastre, m. disaster.

desastroso, a. disastrous.

desatar, v. untie, undo.

desatención, f. inattention; disrespect; rudeness.

desatender, v. ignore; disregard.

desatentado, a. inconsiderate; imprudent.

desatinado, a. foolish; insane, wild.

desatino, m. blunder. — **desatinar,** v.

desautorizado, a. unauthorized.

desautorizar, v. deprive of authority.

desavenencia, f. disagreement, discord.

desaventajado, a. disadvantageous.

desayuno, m. breakfast. — **desayunarse,** v.

desazón, f. insipidity; uneasiness.

desazonado, a. insipid; uneasy.

desbandada, f. disbanding.

desbandarse, v. disband.

desbarajuste, m. disorder, confusion.

desbaratar, v. destroy.

desbastar, v. plane, smoothen.

desbocado, a. foul-spoken, indecent.

desbocarse, v. use obscene language.

desbordamiento, m. overflow; flood.

desbordar, v. overflow.

desbrozar, v. clear away rubbish.

descabal, a. incomplete.

descabalar, v. render incomplete; impair.

descabellado, a. absurd, preposterous.

descabezar, v. behead.

descaecimiento, m. weakness; dejection.

descalabrar, v. injure, wound (esp. the head).

descalabro, m. accident, misfortune.

descalzarse, v. take off one's shoes.

descalzo, a. shoeless; barefoot.

descaminado, a. wrong, misguided.

descaminar, v. mislead; lead into error.

descamisado, a. shirtless; shabby.

---

descanso, m. rest. —**descansar,** v.

descarado, a. saucy, fresh.

descarga, f. discharge.

descargar, v. discharge, unload, dump.

descargo, m. acquittal.

descarnar, v. skin.

descaro, m. gall, effrontery.

descarriar, v. lead or go astray.

descarrilamiento, m. derailment.

descarrillar, v. derail.

descartar, v. discard.

descascarar, v. peel; boast, brag.

descendencia, f. descent, origin; progeny.

descender, v. descend.

descendiente, m. & f. descendant.

descendimiento, m. descent.

descenso, m. descent.

descentralización, f. decentralizing.

descifrar, v. decipher, puzzle out.

descoco, m. boldness, brazenness.

descolgar, v. take down.

descolorar, v. discolor.

descolorido, a. pale, faded.

descollar, v. stand out; excel.

descomedido, a. disproportionate; rude.

descomedirse, v. be rude.

descomponer, v. decompose, break down, get out of order.

descomposición, f. discomposure; disorder, confusion.

descompuesto, a. impudent, rude.

descomulgar, v. excommunicate.

descomunal, a. extraordinary, huge.

desconcertar, v. disconcert, baffle.

desconcierto, m. confusion, disarray.

desconectar, v. disconnect.

desconfiado, a. distrustful.

desconfianza, f. distrust.

desconfiar, v. distrust, mistrust; suspect.

desconocer, v. ignore, fail to recognize.

desconocido -da, n. stranger.

desconocimiento, m. ingratitude; ignorance.

desconsolado, a. disconsolate, wretched.

desconsuelo, m. grief.

descontar, v. discount, subtract.

descontentar, v. dissatisfy.

descontento, m. discontent.

descontinuar, v. discontinue.

desconvenir, v. disagree.

descorazonar, v. dishearten.

descorchar, v. uncork.

descortés, a. discourteous, impolite, rude.

descortesía, f. discourtesy, rudeness.

descortezar, v. peel.

descoyuntar, v. dislocate.

descrédito, m. discredit.

describir, v. describe.

descripción, f. description.

descriptivo, a. descriptive.

descuartizar, v. dismember, disjoint.

descubridor, m. discoverer.

descubrimiento, m. discovery.

descubrir, v. discover; uncover; disclose.

descubrirse, v. take off one's hat.

descuento, m. discount.

descuidado, a. reckless, careless; slack.

descuido, m. neglect. —**descuidar,** v.

desde, pr. p. since; from. **d. luego,** of course.

desdén, m. disdain. —**desdeñar,** v.

desdeñoso, a. contemptuous, disdainful, scornful.

desdicha, f. misfortune.

deseable, a. desirable.

desear, v. desire, wish.

desecar, v. dry, desiccate.

desechar, v. scrap, reject.

desecho, m. remainder, residue; (pl.) waste.

desembalar, v. unpack.

desembarazado, *a.* free; unrestrained.

desembarazar, *v.* free, extricate; unburden.

desembarcar, *v.* disembark, go ashore.

desembocar, *v.* flow into.

desembolsar, *v.* disburse; expend.

desembolso, *m.* disbursement.

desemejante, *a.* unlike, dissimilar.

desempacar, *v.* unpack.

desempeñar, *v.* carry out; redeem.

desempeño, *m.* fulfillment.

desencajar, *v.* disjoint; disturb.

desencantar, *v.* disillusion.

desencanto, *m.* disillusion.

desencarcelar, *v.* set free; release.

desenfadado, *a.* free; unembarrassed; spacious.

desenfado, *m.* freedom; ease; calmness.

desengaño, *m.* disillusion. —**desengañar**, *v.*

desenlace, *m.* outcome, conclusion.

desenredar, *v.* disentangle.

desensartar, *v.* unthread.

desentenderse, *v.* overlook; avoid noticing.

desenterrar, *v.* disinter, exhume.

desenvainar, *v.* unsheath.

desenvoltura, *f.* impudence; boldness.

desenvolver, *v.* evolve, unfold.

deseo, *m.* wish, desire, urge.

deseoso, *a.* desirous.

deserción, *f.* desertion.

desertar, *v.* desert.

desertor, *m.* deserter.

desesperación, *f.* despair, desperation.

desesperado, *a.* desperate; hopeless.

desesperar, *v.* despair.

desfalcar, *v.* embezzle.

desfavorable, *a.* unfavorable.

desfigurar, *v.* disfigure; mar.

desfiladero, *m.* defile.

desfile, *m.* parade. —**desfilar**, *v.*

desgaire, *m.* slovenly appearance.

desgana, *f.* lack of appetite; repugnance.

desgarrar, *v.* tear, lacerate.

desgastar, *v.* wear away, waste, erode.

desgaste, *m.* wear; erosion.

desgracia, *f.* misfortune.

desgraciado, *a.* unfortunate.

desgranar, *v.* shell.

desgreñar, *v.* dishevel.

deshacer, *v.* undo, take apart, destroy.

deshacerse de, *v.* get rid of, dispose of.

deshecho, *a.* undone; wasted.

deshelar, *v.* thaw, melt.

desheredamiento, *m.* disinheriting.

desheredar, *v.* disinherit.

deshielo, *m.* thaw; melting.

deshinchar, *v.* reduce a swelling.

deshojar, *v.* shed (leaves).

deshonestidad, *f.* dishonesty.

deshonesto, *a.* dishonest.

deshonra, *f.* dishonor.

deshonrar, *v.* disgrace; dishonor.

deshonroso, *a.* dishonorable.

desierto, *m.* desert, wilderness.

designar, *v.* appoint, name.

designio, *m.* purpose, intent.

desigual, *a.* uneven, unequal.

desigualdad, *f.* inequality.

desilusión, *f.* disappointment.

desinfección, *f.* disinfection.

desinfectar, *v.* disinfect.

desinterés, *m.* indifference.

desinteresado, *a.* disinterested, unselfish.

desistir, *v.* desist, stop.

desleal, *a.* disloyal.

deslealtad, *f.* disloyalty.

desleir, *v.* dilute, dissolve.

desligar, *v.* untie, loosen; free, release.

deslindar, *v.* make the boundaries of.

deslinde, *m.* demarcation.

desliz, *m.* slip; false step; weakness.

deslizarse, *v.* slide; slip; glide; coast.

deslumbramiento, *m.* dazzling glare; confusion.

deslumbrar, *v.* dazzle; glare.

deslustre, *m.* tarnish. —**deslustrar,** *v.*

desmán, *m.* mishap; misbehavior; excess.

desmañado, *a.* awkward, clumsy.

desmantelar, *v.* dismantle.

desmayar, *v.* dismay, appall.

desmayo, *m.* faint. —**desmayarse,** *v.*

desmejorar, *v.* make worse; decline.

desmembrar, *v.* dismember.

desmemoria, *f.* forgetfulness.

desmemoriado, *a.* forgetful.

desmentir, *v.* contradict, disprove.

desmenuzable, *a.* crisp, crumbly.

desmenuzar, *v.* crumble, break into bits.

desmesurado, *a.* excessive.

desmonetización, *f.* demonetization.

desmonetizar, *v.* demonetize.

desmontado, *a.* dismounted.

desmoralización, *f.* demoralization.

desmoralizar, *v* demoralize.

desmoronar, *v.* crumble, decay.

desmovilizar, *v.* demobilize.

desnatar, *v.* skim.

desnaturalización, *f.* denaturalization.

desnaturalizar, *v.* denaturalize.

desnegamiento, *m.* denial, contradiction.

desnervar, *v.* enervate.

desnivel, *m.* unevenness or difference in elevation.

desnudamente, *adv.* nakedly.

desnudar, *v.* undress.

desnudez, *f.* bareness, nudity.

desnudo, *a.* bare, naked.

desnutrición, *f.* malnutrition.

desobedecer, *v.* disobey.

desobediencia, *f.* disobedience.

desobediente, *a.* disobedient.

desobedientemente, *adv.* disobediently.

desobligar, *v.* release from obligation; offend.

desocupado, *a.* idle, not busy; vacant.

desocupar, *v.* vacate.

desolación, *f.* desolation; ruin.

desolado, *a.* desolate. —**desolar,** *v.*

desollar, *v.* skin.

desorden, *m.* disorder.

desordenar, *v.* disarrange.

desorganización, *f.* disorganization.

desorganizar, *v.* disorganize.

despabilado, *a.* vigilant, watchful; lively.

despacio, *adv.* slowly.

despachar, *v.* dispatch, ship, send.

despacho, *m.* shipment; dispatch, promptness; office.

desparpajo, *m.* glibness; fluency of speech.

desparramar, *v.* scatter.

despavorido, *a.* terrified.

despecho, *m.* spite.

despedazar, *v.* tear up.

despedida, *f.* farewell; leave-taking; discharge.

despedir, *v.* dismiss, discharge; see off.

despedirse de, *v.* say good-bye to, take leave of.

despegar, *v.* unglue; separate.

despego, *m.* indifference; disinterest.

despejar, *v.* clear, clear up.

despejo, *m.* sprightly; clear; unobstructed.

despensa, *f.* pantry.

despensero, *m.* butler.

despeñar, *v.* throw down.

desperdicio, *m.* waste. —**desperdiciar,** *v.*

despertador, *m.* alarm clock.

despertar, *v.* wake, wake up.

despesar, *m.* dislike.

despicar, *v.* satisfy.

despedida, *f.* gutter.

despierto, *a.* awake; alert, wide-awake.

despilfarrado, *a.* wasteful, extravagant.

despilfarrar, *v.* waste, squander.

despilfarro, *m.* waste, extravagance.

despique, *m.* revenge.

desplazamiento, *m.* displacement.

desplegar, *v.* display; unfold.

desplome, *m.* collapse. — **desplomarse,** *v.*

desplumar, *v.* defeather, pluck.

despoblar, *v.* depopulate.

despojar, *v.* strip; despoil, plunder.

despojo, *m.* plunder, spoils; (*pl.*) remains, debris.

desposado, *a.* newly married.

desposar, *v.* marry.

desposeer, *v.* dispossess.

déspota, *m. & f.* despot.

despótico, *a.* despotic.

despotismo, *m.* despotism, tyranny.

despreciable, *a.* contemptible.

despreciar, *v.* spurn, despise, scorn.

desprecio, *m.* scorn, contempt.

desprender, *v.* detach, unfasten.

desprenderse, *v.* loosen, come apart. **d. de,** part with.

desprendido, *a.* disinterested.

despreocupado, *a.* unprejudiced.

desprevenido, *a.* unprepared, unready.

desproporción, *f.* disproportion.

despropósito, *m.* nonsense.

desprovisto, *a.* devoid.

después, *adv.* afterwards, later; then, next. **d. de, d. que,** after.

despuntar, *v.* blunt; remove the point of.

desquiciar, *v.* unhinge; disturb, unsettle.

desquitar, *v.* get revenge, retaliate.

desquite, *m.* revenge, retaliation.

destacamento, *m.* (mil.) detachment.

destacar, *v.* stand out, be prominent.

destapar, *v.* uncover.

destello, *m.* sparkle, gleam.

destemplar, *v.* change; soften.

desteñir, *v.* fade, discolor.

desterrado -da, *n.* exile.

desterrar, *v.* banish, exile.

destierro, *m.* banishment, exile.

destilación, *f.* distillation.

destilar, *v.* distill.

destilería, *f.* distillery.

destinación, *f.* destination.

destinar, *v.* destine, intend.

destinatorio -ria, *n.* addressee.

destino, *m.* destiny, fate; destination.

destitución, *f.* dismissal; abandonment.

destituido, *a.* destitute.

destorcer, *v.* undo, straighten out.

destornillado, *a.* reckless, careless.

destornillador, *m.* screwdriver.

destraillar, *v.* unleash; set loose.

destral, *m.* hatchet.

destreza, *f.* cleverness, dexterity, skill.

destripar, *v.* eviscerate, disembowel.

destrísimo, *a.* extremely dexterous.

destronamiento, *m.* dethronement.

destronar, *v.* dethrone.

destrozador, *m.* destroyer, wrecker.

destrozar, *v.* destroy, wreck.

destrozo, *m.* destruction, ruin.

destrucción, *f.* destruction.

---

destructibilidad, f. destructibility.

destructible, a. destructible.

destructivamente, adv. destructively.

destructivo, a. destructive.

destruir, v. destroy; wipe out.

desuello, m. impudence.

desunión, f. disunion; discord; separation.

desunir, v. disconnect, sever.

desusadamente, adv. unusually.

desusado, a. archaic; obsolete.

desuso, m. disuse.

desvalido, a. helpless, destitute.

desvalijador, m. highwayman.

desván, m. attic.

desvanecerse, v. vanish; faint.

desvariado, a. delirious; disorderly.

desvarío, m. raving. —**desvariar,** v.

desvedado, a. free; unrestrained.

desveladamente, adv. watchfully, alertly.

desvelado, a. watchful; alert.

desvelar, v. be watchful; keep awake.

desvelo, m. vigilance; uneasiness.

desventaja, f. disadvantage.

desventar, v. let air out of.

desventura, f. misfortune.

desventurado, a. unhappy; unlucky.

desvergonzado, a. shameless, brazen.

desvergüenza, f. shamelessness.

desvestir, v. undress.

desviación, f. deviation.

desviado, a. devious.

desviar, v. divert; deviate.

desvío, m. detour; side track; indifference.

desvirtuar, v. decrease the value of.

deszumar, v. remove the juice from.

detalle, m. detail. —**detallar,** v.

detective, m. detective.

detención, f. detention, arrest.

detenedor, m. stopper; catch.

detener, v. detain, stop; arrest.

detenidamente, adv. carefully, slowly.

detenido, adv. stingy; thorough.

detergente, a. detergent.

deterioración, f. deterioration.

deteriorar, v. deteriorate.

determinable, a. determinable.

determinación, f. determination.

determinar, v. determine.

determinismo, m. determinism.

determinista, n. & a. determinist.

detestable, a. detestable, hateful.

detestablemente, adv. detestably, hatefully, abhorrently.

detestación, f. detestation, hatefulness.

detestar, v. detest.

detonación, f. detonation.

detonar, v. detonate, explode.

detracción, f. detraction, defamation.

detractar, v. detract, defame, vilify.

detraer, v. detract.

detrás, adv. behind; in back.

detrimento, m. detriment, damage.

deuda, f. debt.

deudo -da, n. relative, kin

deudor -ra, n. debtor.

Deuteronomio, m. Deuteronomy.

devalar, v. drift.

devanar, v. to wind, as on a spool.

devanear, v. talk deliriously, rave.

devaneo, m. frivolity; idle pursuit; delirium.

---

devantal, m. apron.

devastación, f. devastation, ruin, havoc.

devastador, m. devastator.

devastar, v. devastate.

devenir, v. happen, occur; become.

devoción, f. devotion.

devocionario, m. prayer book.

devocionero, a. devotional.

devolver, v. return, give back.

devorar, v. devour.

devotamente, adv. devotedly, devoutly, piously.

devoto, a. devout; devoted.

deyección, f. depression, dejection.

día, m. day. **buenos días,** good morning.

diabetes, f. diabetes.

diabético, a. diabetic.

diablear, v. play pranks.

diablo, m. devil.

diablura, f. mischief.

diabólicamente, adv. diabolically.

diabólico, a. diabolic, devilish.

diaconado, m. deaconship.

diaconía, f. deaconry.

diácono, m. deacon.

diacrítico, a. diacritic.

diadema, f. diadem, crown.

diáfano, a. transparent.

diafragma, m. diaphragm.

diagnosticar, v. diagnose.

diagonal, f. diagonal.

diagonalmente, adv. diagonally.

diagrama, m. diagram.

dialectal, a. dialectal.

dialéctico, a. dialectic.

dialecto, m. dialect.

diálogo, m. dialogue.

diamante, m. diamond.

diamantista, m. diamond cutter; jeweler.

diametral, a. diametric.

diametralmente, adv. diametrically.

diámetro, m. diameter.

diana, f. reveille.

diapasón, m. pitch; tuning fork.

diaplejía, f. paralysis.

diariamente, adv. daily.

diario, a. & m. daily; daily paper; diary; journal.

diarrea, f. diarrhea.

diatriba, f. diatribe, harangue.

dibujo, m. drawing, sketch. —**dibujar,** v.

dicción, f. diction.

diccionario, m. dictionary.

diccionarista, n. lexicographer.

diciembre, m. December.

dicotomía, f. dichotomy.

dictado, m. dictation.

dictador, m. dictator.

dictadura, f. dictatorship.

dictamen, m. dictate.

dictar, v. dictate; direct.

dictatoría, a. dictatorial; tyrannic.

dicha, f. happiness.

dicho, m. saying.

dichoso, a. happy; fortunate.

didáctico, a. didactic.

diecinueve, a. & pron. nineteen.

dieciocho, a. & pron. eighteen.

dieciseis, a. & pron. sixteen.

diecisiete, a. & pron. seventeen.

diente, m. tooth.

diestramente, adv. skillfully, ably; ingeniously.

diestro, a. dexterous, skillful; clever.

dieta, f. diet; allowance.

dietética, f. dietetic.

diez, a. & pron. ten.

diezmal, a. decimal.

diezmar, v. decimate.

difamación, f. defamation, smear.

difamar, v. defame, smear, libel.

difamatorio, a. defamatory.

diferencia, f. difference.

diferencial, a. & f. differential.

diferenciar, v. differentiate, distinguish.

diferente, a. different.

diferentemente, adv. differently.

diferir, v. differ; defer; put off.

difícil, a. difficult, hard.

difícilmente, adv. with difficulty or hardship.

dificultad, f. difficulty.

dificultar, v. make difficult.

dificultoso, a. difficult, hard.

difidencia, f. diffidence.

difidente, a. diffident.

difteria, f. diphtheria.

difundir, v. diffuse, spread.

difunto, a. deceased, dead, late.

difusamente, adv. diffusely.

difusión, f. diffusion, spread.

digerible, a. digestible.

digerir, v. digest.

digestible, a. digestible.

digestión, f. digestion.

digestivo, a. digestive.

digesto, m. digest or code of laws.

digitado, a. digitate.

digital, 1. a. digital. 2. f. foxglove.

dignación, f. condescension; deigning.

dignamente, adv. with dignity.

dignarse, v. condescend, deign.

dignidad, f. dignity.

dignificar, v. dignify.

digno, a. worthy; dignified.

digresión, f. digression.

digresivo, a. digressive.

dij, dije, m. trinket, piece of jewelry.

dilación, f. delay.

dilapidación, f. dilapidation.

dilatación, f. dilatation, enlargement.

dilatar, v. dilate; delay; expand.

dilatoria, f. delay.

dilecto, a. loved.

dilema, m. dilemma.

diligencia, f. diligence, industriousness.

diligente, a. diligent, industrious.

diligentemente, adv. diligently.

dilogía, f. ambiguous meaning.

dilución, f. dilution.

diluir, v. dilute.

diluvial, a. diluvial.

diluvio, m. flood, deluge.

dimensión, f. dimension; measurement.

diminución, f. diminution.

diminuto, diminutivo, a. diminutive, little.

dimisión, f. resignation.

dimitir, v. resign.

Dinamarca, f. Denmark.

dinamarqués -esa, a. & n. Danish, Dane.

dinámico, a. dynamic.

dinamita, f. dynamite.

dinamitero, m. dynamiter.

dínamo, m. or f. dynamo.

dinasta, m. dynast, king, monarch.

dinastía, f. dynasty.

dinástico, a. dynastic.

dinero, m. money, currency.

dinosauro, m. dinosaur.

diócesi, f. diocese.

Dios, m. God.

dios -sa, n. god, goddess.

diploma, m. diploma.

diplomacia, f. diplomacy.

diplomado -da, m. graduate.

diplomarse, v. graduate (from a school).

diplomática, f. diplomacy.

diplomático, a. & m. diplomat; diplomatic.

dipsomanía, f. dipsomania.

diptongo, m. diphthong.

diputación, f. deputation, delegation.

diputado, m. deputy.

diputar, v. depute, delegate; empower.

dique, m. dike; dam.

dirección, f. direction; address; guidance; (com.) management.

directamente, adv. directly.

directo, a. direct.

director, m. director; manager.

dirigente, a. directing, controlling, managing.

dirigible, a. dirigible.

dirigir, v. direct; lead; manage.

dirigirse a, v. address; approach, turn to; head for.

dirruir, v. destroy, devastate.

disanto, m. holy day.

discantar, v. sing (esp. in counterpoint); discuss.

disceptación, f. argument, quarrel.

disceptar, v. argue, quarrel.

discernimiento, m. discernment.

discernir, v. discern.

disciplina, f. discipline.

disciplinable, a. disciplinable.

disciplinar, v. discipline, train, teach.

discípulo -la, n. disciple follower; pupil.

disco, m. disk; (phonograph) record.

discontinuación, f. discontinuation.

discontinuar, v. discontinue, break off, cease.

discordancia, f. discordance.

discordar, v. disagree, conflict.

discordia, f. discord.

discreción, f. discretion.

discrecional, a. optional.

discrecionalmente, adv. optionally.

discrepancia, f. discrepancy.

discretamente, adv. discreetly.

discreto, a. discreet.

discrimen, m. risk, hazard.

discriminar, v. discriminate.

disculpa, f. excuse; apology.

disculpar, v. excuse; exonerate.

disculparse, v. apologize.

discurrir, v. roam; flow; think; plan.

discursante, n. lecturer, speaker.

discursivo, a. discursive.

discurso, m. speech, talk.

discusión, f. discussion.

discutible, a. debatable.

discutir, v. discuss; debate; contest.

disecación, f. dissection.

disecar, v. dissect.

disección, f. dissection.

diseminación, f. dissemination.

diseminar, v. disseminate, spread.

disensión, f. dissension; dissent.

disenso, m. dissent.

disentería, f. dysentery.

disentir, v. disagree, dissent.

diseñador -ra, n. designer.

diseño, m. design. **—diseñar,** v.

disertación, f. dissertation.

disfamación, f. defamation.

disforme, a. deformed, monstrous, ugly.

disformidad, f. deformity.

disfraz, m. disguise. **—disfrazar,** v.

disfrutar, v. enjoy.

disfrute, m. enjoyment.

disgustar, v. displease; disappoint.

disgusto, m. displeasure; disappointment.

disidencia, f. dissidence.

disidente, a. & n. dissident.

disímil, a. unlike.

disimilitud, f. dissimilarity.

disimulación, f. dissimulation.

disimulado, a. dissembling, feigning; sly.

disimular, v. hide, dissemble.

disímulo, m. pretense.

disipación, f. dissipation.

disipado, a. dissipated; wasted; scattered.

disipar, v. waste; scatter.

dislocación, f. dislocation.

dislocar, v. dislocate; displace.

disminuir, v. diminish, lessen, reduce.

disociación, f. dissociation.

disociar, v. dissociate.

disolubilidad, f. dissolubility.

disoluble, a. dissoluble.

disolución, f. dissolution.

disolutamente, adv. dissolutely.

disoluto, a. dissolute.

disolver, v. dissolve.

disonancia, f. dissonance; discord.

disonante, a. dissonant; discordant.

disonar, v. be discordant; clash in sound.

dísono, a. dissonant.

dispar, a. unlike.

disparadamente, adv. hastily, hurriedly.

disparar, v. shoot, fire (a weapon).

disparatado, a. nonsensical.

disparatar, v. talk nonsense.

disparate, m. nonsense, tall tale.

disparejo, a. uneven, unequal.

disparidad, f. disparity.

disparo, m. shot.

dispendio, m. extravagance.

dispendioso, a. expensive; extravagant.

dispensa, dispensación, f. dispensation.

dispensable, a. dispensable; excusable.

dispensar, v. dispense, excuse; grant.

dispensario, m. dispensary.

dispepsia, f. dyspepsia.

dispéptico, a. dyspeptic.

dispersar, v. scatter; dispel; disband.

dispersión, f. dispersion, dispersal.

disperso, a. dispersed.

displicente, a. unpleasant.

disponer, v. dispose. **d. de,** have at one's disposal.

disponible, a. available.

disposición, f. disposition; disposal.

dispuesto, a. disposed, inclined; attractive.

disputa, f. dispute, argument.

disputable, a. disputable.

disputador, m. disputant.

disputar, v. argue; dispute.

disquisición, f. disquisition.

distancia, f. distance.

distante, a. distant.

distantemente, adv. distantly.

distar, v. be distant, be far.

distención, f. distension, swelling.

distender, v. distend, swell, enlarge.

dístico, m. couplet.

distinción, f. distinction, difference.

distingo, m. restriction.

distinguible, a. distinguishable.

distinguido, a. distinguished, prominent.

distinguir, v. distinguish; make out, spot.

distintamente, adv. distinctly, clearly; differently.

distintivo, a. distinctive.

distinto, a. distinct, different.

distracción, f. distraction, pastime; absent-mindedness.

distraer, v. distract.

distraídamente, adv. absent-mindedly, distractedly.

distraído, a. absent-minded; distracted.

distribución, f. distribution.

distribuidor -ra, n. distributor.

distribuir, v. distribute.

distributivo, a. distributive.

distribuidor, m. distributor.

distrito, m. district.

disturbar, v. disturb, trouble.

disturbio, m. disturbance, outbreak; turmoil.

disuadir, v. dissuade.

disuasión, f. dissuasion.

disuasivo, a. dissuasive.

disyunción, f. disjunction.

dityrambo, m. dithyramb.

diurno, a. diurnal.

diva, f. singer.

divagación, f. digression.

divagar, v. digress, ramble.

diván, m. couch.

divergencia, f. divergence.

divergente, a. divergent, differing.

divergir, v. diverge.

diversamente, adv. diversely.

diversidad, f. diversity.

diversificar, v. diversify, vary.

diversión, f. diversion, pas-time.

diverso, a. diverse, different; (pl.) various, several.

divertido, a. humorous, amusing.

divertimiento, m. diversion; amusement.

divertir, v. entertain, amuse.

divertirse, v. enjoy oneself, have a good time.

dividendo, m. dividend.

divididero, a. divisible.

dividir, v. divide, separate.

divieso, m. (med.) boil.

divinamente, adv. divinely.

divinidad, f. divinity.

divinizar, v. deify.

divino, a. divine; heavenly.

divisa, f. badge, emblem.

divisar, v. sight, make out.

divisibilidad, f. divisibility.

divisible, a. divisible.

división, f. division.

divisivo, a. divisive.

diviso, a. divided.

divo, m. god.

divorcio, m. divorce. —**di-vorciar,** v.

divulgable, a. divulgable.

divulgación, f. divulgation.

divulgar, v. divulge, reveal.

dobladamente, adv. doubly.

dobladillo, m. hem of a skirt or dress.

dobladura, f. fold, bend.

doblar, v. fold; bend.

doble, a. double.

doblegable, a. flexible, fold-able.

doblegar, v. fold, bend; yield.

doblez, m. fold; duplicity.

doblón, m. doubloon.

doce, a. & pron. twelve.

docena, f. dozen.

docente, a. educational.

dócil, a. docile.

docilidad, f. docility, tract-ableness.

dócilmente, adv. docilely, meekly.

doctamente, adv. learnedly, profoundly.

docto, a. learned, expert.

doctor, m. doctor.

doctorado, m. doctorate.

doctoral, a. doctoral.

doctrina, f. doctrine.

doctrinador, m. teacher.

doctrinal, m. catechism.

doctrinar, v. teach.

documentación, f. docu-mentation.

documental, a. documen-tary.

documento, m. document.

dogal, m. noose.

dogma, m. dogma.

dogmáticamente, adv. dog-matically.

dogmático, m. dogmatic.

dogmatismo, m. dogmatism.

dogmatista, m. dogmatist.

dogo, m. bulldog.

dolar, v. cut, chop, hew.

dólar, m. dollar.

dolencia, f. pain; disease.

doler, v. ache, hurt, be sore.

doliente, a. ill; aching.

dolor, m. pain; grief, sorrow, woe.

dolorido, a. painful, sorrow-ful.

dolorosamente, adv. pain-fully, sorrowfully.

doloroso, a. painful, sorrow-ful.

dolosamente, adv. deceit-fully.

doloso, a. deceitful.

domable, a. that can be tamed or managed.

domar, v. tame; subdue.

dombo, m. dome.

domesticable, a. that can be domesticated.

domesticación, f. domesti-cation.

domésticamente, adv. do-mestically.

domesticar, v. tame.

domesticidad, f. domestic-ity.

doméstico, a. domestic.

domicilio, m. dwelling, home, residence.

dominación, f. domination.

dominador, a. dominating.

dominante, a. dominant.

dominar, v. rule, dominate; master.

dómine, m. teacher.

domingo, *m.* Sunday.
dominio, *m.* domain; rule; power.
dominó, *m.* domino.
domo, *m.* dome.
Don, *title used before a man's first name.*
don, *m.* gift.
dona, *f.* woman.
donación, *f.* donation.
donador -ra, *f.* giver, donor.
donaire, *m.* grace.
donairosamente, *adv.* gracefully.
donairoso, *a.* graceful.
donante, *n.* giver, donor.
donar, *v.* donate.
donativo, *m.* donation, contribution; gift.
doncella, *f.* lass; maid.
donde, dónde, *conj. & adv.* where.
dondequiera, *adv.* wherever, anywhere.
donosamente, *adv.* gracefully; wittily.
donoso, *a.* graceful; witty.
donosura, *f.* gracefulness; wittiness.
Doña, *title used before a lady's first name.*
dorado, *a.* gilded.
dorador, *m.* gilder.
dorar, *v.* gild.
dórico, *a.* Doric.
dormidero, *a.* sleep-inducing; soporific.
dormido, *a.* asleep.
dormir, *v.* sleep.
dormirse, *v.* fall asleep, go to sleep.
dormitar, *v.* doze.
dormitorio, *m.* dormitory; bedroom.
dorsal, *a.* dorsal.
dorso, *m.* spine.
dos, *a. & pron.* two. **los d.,** both.
dosañal, *a.* biennial.
doscientos, *a. & pron.* two hundred.
dosel, *m.* canopy; platform; dais.
dosificación, *f.* dosage.
dosis, *f.* dose.

dotación, *f.* endowment; (naut.) crew.
dotador, *m.* donor.
dotar, *v.* endow; give a dowry to.
dote, *m.* dowry (*f.*) talents.
dragaminas, *m.* mine sweeper.
dragar, *v.* dredge; sweep.
dragón, *m.* dragon; dragoon.
dragonear, *v.* pretend to be.
drama, *m.* drama; play.
dramática, *f.* dramatics.
dramáticamente, *adv.* dramatically.
dramático, *a.* dramatic.
dramatizar, *v.* dramatize.
dramaturgo, *m.* playwright, dramatist.
drástico, *a.* drastic.
drenaje, *m.* drainage.
dríada, *f.* dryad.
driza, *f.* halyard.
droga, *f.* drug.
droguería, *f.* drugstore.
droguero, *m.* druggist.
dromedario, *m.* dromedary.
druida, *m.* Druid.
dualidad, *f.* duality.
dubitable, *a.* doubtful.
dubitación, *f.* doubt.
ducado, *m.* duchy.
ducal, *a.* ducal.
dúctil, *a.* ductile.
ductilidad, *f.* ductility.
ducha, *f.* shower (bath).
duda, *f.* doubt.
dudable, *a.* doubtful.
dudar, *v.* doubt; hesitate; question.
dudosamente, *adv.* doubtfully.
dudoso, *a.* dubious; doubtful.
duela, *f.* stave.
duelista, *m.* duelist.
duelo, *m.* duel; grief; mourning.
duende, *m.* elf, hobgoblin.
dueño -ña, *n.* owner; landlord, -lady; master, mistress.
dulce, 1. *a.* sweet. **agua d.,** fresh water. **2.** *m.* piece of candy; (*pl.*) candy.
dulcedumbre, *f.* sweetness.

dulcemente, *adv.* sweetly.

dulcería, *f.* confectionery; candy shop.

dulcificar, *v.* sweeten.

dulzura, *f.* sweetness; mildness.

duna, *f.* dune.

dúo, *m.* duet.

duodenal, *a.* duodenal.

duplicación, *f.* duplication; doubling.

duplicadamente, *adv.* doubly.

duplicado, *a. & m.* duplicate.

duplicar, *v.* double, duplicate, repeat.

duplicidad, *f.* duplicity.

duplo, *a.* double.

duque, *m.* duke.

duquesa, *f.* duchess.

durabilidad, *f.* durability.

durable, *a.* durable.

duración, *f.* duration.

duradero, *a.* lasting, durable.

duramente, *adv.* harshly, roughly.

durante, *prep.* during.

durar, *v.* last.

durazno, *m.* peach.

dureza, *f.* hardness.

durmiente, *a.* dormant.

duro, *a.* hard; stiff; stern; stale.

dux, *m.* doge.

E

e, *conj.* and.

ebanista, *m.* cabinet-maker.

ebanizar, *v.* give an ebony finish to,

ébano, *m.* ebony.

ebonita, *f.* ebonite.

ebrio, *a.* drunken, inebriated.

ebullición, *f.* boiling.

eclecticismo, *m.* eclecticism.

ecléctico, *n. & a.* eclectic.

eclesiástico, *a. & m.* ecclesiastic.

eclipse, *m.* eclipse. —eclipsar, *v.*

eclipsis, *f.* ellipsis.

écloga, *f.* eclogue.

eco, *m.* echo.

economía, *f.* economy; thrift. e. política, economics.

económicamente, *adv.* economically.

económico, *a.* economic, economical, thrifty.

economista, *f.* economist.

economizar, *v.* save, economize.

ecuación, *f.* equation.

ecuador, *m.* equator.

ecuanimidad, *f.* equanimity.

ecuatorial, *a.* equatorial.

ecuatoriano -na, *a. & n.* Ecuadorian.

ecuestre, *a.* equestrian.

echada, *f.* throw.

echadillo, *m.* foundling; orphan.

echar, *v.* throw, toss; pour. e. a, start to. e. a perder, spoil, ruin. e. de menos, miss.

echarse, *v.* lie down.

edad, *f.* age.

edecán, *m.* aide-de-camp.

Edén, *m.* Eden.

edición, *f.* edition; issue.

edicto, *m.* edict, decree.

edificación, *f.* construction.

edificador, *n.* constructor; builder.

edificar, *v.* build.

edificio, *m.* edifice, building.

editar, *v.* publish, issue.

editor, *m.* publisher.

editorial, *m.* editorial.

edredón, *m.* quilt.

educación, *f.* upbringing, breeding; education.

---

educador, *m.* educator.

educar, *v.* educate, bring up; train.

educativo, *a.* educational.

educción, *f.* deduction.

educir, *v.* educe.

efectivamente, *adv.* actually, really.

efectivo, *a.* effective; actual, real. **en e.,** (com.) in cash.

efecto, *m.* effect.

efectuar, *v.* effect; cash.

eferente, *a.* efferent.

efervescencia, *f.* effervescence; zeal.

eficacia, *f.* efficacy.

eficaz, *a.* efficient, effective.

eficazmente, *adv.* efficaciously.

eficiencia, *f.* efficiency.

eficiente, *a.* efficient.

efigie, *f.* effigy.

efímera, *f.* May fly.

efímero, *a.* ephemeral, passing.

efluvio, *m.* effluvium.

efundir, *v.* effuse; pour out.

efusión, *f.* effusion.

egipcio -cia, *a. & n.* Egyptian.

Egipto, *m.* Egypt.

égira, *f.* hegira.

écloga, *f.* eclogue.

egoísmo, *m.* egoism, egotism, selfishness.

egoísta, *a. & n.* selfish, egoistic; egoist.

egotismo, *m.* egotism.

egotista, *m.* egotist.

egreso, *m.* expense, outlay.

eje, *m.* axis; axle.

ejecución, *f.* execution; performance; enforcement.

ejecutar, *v.* execute; enforce; carry out.

ejecutivo, *a. & m.* executive.

ejecutor, *m.* executor.

ejemplar, 1. *a.* exemplary. **2.** *m.* copy.

ejemplificación, *f.* exemplification.

ejemplificar, *v.* illustrate.

ejemplo, *m.* example.

ejercer, *v.* exert; practice.

ejercicio, *m.* exercise, drill. —**ejercitar,** *v.*

ejercitación, *f.* exercise, training, drill.

ejercitar, *v.* exercise, train, drill.

ejército, *m.* army.

ejotes, *m.pl.* string beans.

el, *art. & pron.* the; the one.

él, *pron.* he, him; it.

elaboración, *f.* elaboration, working up.

elaborado, *a.* elaborate.

elaborador, *m.* manufacturer, maker.

elaborar, *v.* elaborate; manufacture; brew.

elación, *f.* elation; magnanimity; turgid style.

elasticidad, *f.* elasticity.

elástico, *m.* elastic.

elección, *f.* election; option, choice.

electivo, *a.* elective.

electo, *a.* elected, chosen, appointed.

electorado, *m.* electorate.

electoral, *a.* electoral.

electricidad, *f.* electricity.

electricista, *m.* electrician.

eléctrico, *a.* electric.

electrización, *f.* electrification.

electrocución, *f.* electrocution.

electrocutar, *v.* electrocute.

electrodo, *m.* electrode.

electroimán, *m.* electromagnet.

electrólisis, *f.* electrolysis.

electrólito, *m.* electrolyte.

electrón, *m.* electron.

elefante, *m.* elephant.

elegancia, *f.* elegance.

elegante, *a.* elegant, smart, stylish, fine.

elegantemente, *adv.* elegantly.

elegía, *f.* elegy.

elegibilidad, *f.* eligibility.

elegible, *a.* eligible.

elegir, *v.* select, choose; elect.

elemental, *a.* elementary.

elementalmente, *adv.* elementally; fundamentally.

elementar, *a.* elementary.

elemento, *m.* element.

For pronunciation, see the concise guide on pages 3 to 4.

elevación, f. elevation; height.

elevador, m. elevator.

elevamiento, m. elevation.

elevar, v. elevate; erect, raise.

elidir, v. elide.

eliminación, f. elimination.

eliminar, v. eliminate.

elipse, f. ellipse.

elipsis, f. ellipsis.

elíptico, a. elliptic.

elocuencia, f. eloquence.

elocuente, a. eloquent.

elocuentemente, adv. eloquently.

elogio, m. praise, compliment. **—elogiar,** v.

elucidación, f. elucidation.

elucidar, v. elucidate.

eludir, v. elude.

ella, pron. she, her; it.

ello, pron. it.

ellos -as, pron. pl. they, them.

emaciación, f. emaciation.

emanar, v. emanate, stem.

emancipación, f. emancipation, freeing.

emancipador, n. emancipator.

emancipar, v. emancipate, free.

embajada, f. embassy; legation; (coll.) errand.

embajador, m. ambassador.

embalar, v. pack, bale.

embaldosado, m. tile floor.

embalsamador, m. embalmer.

embalsamar, v. embalm.

embarazada, a. pregnant.

embarazadamente, adv. embarrassedly.

embarazar, v. embarrass.

embarazo, m. embarrassment; pregnancy.

embarbascado, a. difficult; complicated.

embarcación, f. boat; ship; embarkation.

embarcadero, m. wharf, pier, dock.

embarcador, m. shipper, loader, stevedore.

embarcar, v. ship.

embarcarse, v. embark; sail.

embargador, m. one who impedes; one who orders an embargo.

embargante, a. impeding, hindering.

embargar, v. impede, restrain; (leg.) seize, embargo.

embargo, m. seizure, embargo. **sin e.,** however, nevertheless.

embarnizar, v. varnish.

embarque, m. shipment.

embarrador, m. plasterer.

embarrancar, v. get stuck in mud.

embarrar, v. plaster; besmear with mud.

embasamiento, m. foundation of a building.

embastecer, v. get fat.

embaucador, m. imposter.

embaucar, v. deceive, trick, hoax.

embaular, v. pack in a trunk.

embausamiento, m. amazement.

embebecer, v. amaze, astonish; entertain.

embeber, v. absorb; incorporate; saturate.

embelecador, m. imposter.

embeleco, m. fraud, perpetration.

embeleñar, v. fascinate, charm.

embelesamiento, m. rapture.

embelesar, v. fascinate, charm.

embeleso, m. rapture, bliss.

embellecer, v. beautify, embellish.

embestida, f. violent assault; attack.

emblandecer, v. soften; moisten; move to pity.

emblema, m. emblem.

emblemático, a. emblematic.

embocadura, f. narrow entrance; mouth of a river.

embocar, v. eat hastily; gorge.

embolia, f. embolism.

embolsar, v. pocket.

embonar, v. improve, fix, repair.

emborrachador, a. intoxicating.

emborrachar, v. get drunk.

emboscada, f. ambush.

emboscar, v. put or lie in ambush.

embotado, a. blunt, dull (edged). —**embotar,** v.

embotadura, f. bluntness; dullness.

embotellar, v. put in bottles.

embozado, a. muzzled; muffled.

embozar, v. muzzle; muffle.

embozo, m. muffler.

embrague, m. (auto.) clutch.

embravecer, v. be or make angry.

embriagado, a. drunken, intoxicated.

embriagar, v. intoxicate.

embriaguez, f. drunkenness.

embrión, m. embryo.

embrionario, a. embryonic.

embrochado, a. embroidered.

embrollo, m. muddle. —**embrollar,** v.

embromar, v. tease; joke.

embuchado, m. pork sausage.

embudo, m. funnel.

embuste, m. lie, fib.

embustear, v. lie, fib.

embustero -ra, n. liar.

embutir, v. stuff, cram.

emendación, f. emendation, change, correction.

emergencia, f. emergency.

emérito, a. emeritus.

emético, m. & a. emetic.

emigración, f. emigration.

emigrante, a. & n. emigrant.

emigrar, v. emigrate.

eminencia, f. eminence, height.

eminente, a. eminent.

emisario, m. emissary, spy; outlet.

emisión, f. issue.

emisor, m. radio transmitter.

emitir, v. emit.

emoción, f. feeling, emotion, thrill.

emocional, a. emotional.

emocionante, a. exciting.

emocionar, v. touch, move, excite.

emolumento, m. emolument; perquisite.

empacar, v. pack.

empacho, m. shyness, timidity; embarrassment.

empadronamiento, m. census; list of taxpayers.

empalizada, f. palisade, stockade.

empanada, f. meat pie.

empañar, v. blur; soil, sully.

empapar, v. soak.

empaque, m. packing; appearance, mien.

empaquetar, v. pack, package.

emparejarse, v. match, pair off; level, even off.

emparentado, a. related by marriage.

emparrado, m. arbor.

empastadura, f. (dental) filling.

empastar, v. fill (a tooth).

empate, m. tie, draw. —**empatarse,** v.

empecer, v. hurt, harm, injure; prevent.

empedernir, v. harden.

empeine, m. groin; instep; hoof.

empellar, v. shove, jostle.

empellón, m. hard push, shove.

empeñar, v. pledge; pawn.

empeñarse en, v. persist in, be bent on.

empeño, m. persistence; pledge; pawning.

empeoramiento, m. deterioration.

empeorar, v. get worse.

emperador, m. emperor.

emperatriz, f. empress.

empernar, v. nail.

empero, conj. however.

emperramiento, m. stubbornness.

empezar, v. begin, start.

empinado, a. steep.

empinar, v. raise; exalt.

empíreo, a. celestial, heavenly; divine.

empíricamente, adv. empirically.

empírico, a. empirical.

empirismo, m. empiricism.

emplastarse, v. get smeared.

emplasto, m. salve.

emplazamiento, m. court summons.

emplazar, v. summon to court.

empleado -da, n. employee.

emplear, v. employ; use.

empleo, m. employment, job; use.

empobrecer, v. make or become impoverished.

empobrecimiento, m. impoverishment.

empolvado, a. dusty.

empolvar, v. powder.

empollador, m. incubator.

empollar, v. hatch.

emporcar, v. soil, make dirty.

emporio, m. emporium.

emprendedor, a. enterprising.

emprender, v. undertake.

empreñar, v. make pregnant; beget.

empresa, f. enterprise, undertaking.

empresario, m. impresario.

empréstito, m. loan.

empujón, m. push; shove. —empujar, v.

empuñar, v. grasp, sieze; wield.

emulación, f. emulation; envy; rivalry.

emulador, m. emulator; rival.

émulo, a. rival. —emular, v.

emulsión, f. emulsion.

emulsionar, v. emulsify.

en, prep. in, on, at.

enaguas, f.pl. petticoat; skirt.

enajenable, a. alienable.

enajenación, f. alienation; derangement, insanity.

enajenar, v. alienate.

enamoradamente, adv. lovingly.

enamorado, a. in love.

enamorador, m. wooer; suitor; lover.

enamorarse, v. fall in love.

enano -na, n. midget; dwarf.

enardecer, v. inflame.

enastado, a. horned.

encabestrar, v. halter.

encabezado, m. headline.

encabezador, m. reaping machine.

encabezamiento, m. title; census; tax roll.

encabezar, v. head.

encachar, v. hide.

encadenamiento, m. connection, linkage.

encadenar, v. chain; link, connect.

encajar, v. fit in, insert.

encaje, m. lace.

encalar, v. whitewash.

encalvecer, v. lose one's hair.

encallarse, v. be stranded.

encallecido, a. hardened; calloused.

encaminar, v. guide; direct; be on the way to.

encandilar, v. dazzle; daze.

encantación, f. incantation.

encantado, a. charmed, fascinated, enchanted.

encantador, a. charming, delightful.

encanto, m. charm, delight. —encantar, v.

encante, m. public auction.

encapillado, m. clothes one is wearing.

encapotar, v. cover, cloak; muffle.

encaramarse, v. perch; climb.

encararse con, v. face.

encarcelación, f. imprisonment.

encarcelar, v. jail, imprison.

encarecer, v. recommend; extol.

encarecidamente, adv. extremely; ardently.

encargado, m. agent; attorney; representative.

encargar, v. entrust.

encargarse, v. take charge. be in charge.

encargo, m. errand; assignment; (com.) order.

encarnación, f. incarnation.

encarnado, a. red.

encarnar, v. embody.

encarnecer, v. grow fat or heavy.

encarnizado, a. bloody, fierce.

encarrilar, v. set right; put on the track.

encartar, v. ban, outlaw; summon.

encastar, v. improve by crossbreeding.

encastillar, v. be obstinate or unyielding.

encatarrado, a. suffering from a cold.

encausar, v. prosecute; take legal action against.

encauzar, v. channel; direct.

encefalitis, f. encephalitis.

encelamiento, m. envy, jealousy.

encenagar, v. wallow in mud.

encendedor, m. lighter.

encender, v. light; set fire to, kindle; turn on.

encendido, m. ignition.

encerado, m. oilcloth; tarpaulin.

encerar, v. wax.

encerrar, v. enclose; confine, shut in.

encía, f. gum.

encíclico, 1. a. encyclic. **2.** f. encyclical.

enciclopedia, f. encyclopedia.

enciclopédico, a. encyclopedic.

encierro, m. confinement; enclosure.

encima, adv. on top. **e. de,** on. **por e. de,** above.

encina, f. oak.

encinta, a. pregnant.

enclavar, v. nail.

enclenque, a. frail, weak, sickly.

encogerse, v. shrink. **e. de hombros,** shrug the shoulders.

encogido, a. shy, bashful, timid.

encojar, v. make or become lame; cripple.

encolar, v. glue, paste, stick.

encolerizar, v. make or become angry.

encomendar, v. commend; recommend.

encomiar, v. praise, laud, extol.

encomienda, f. commission, charge; (postal) package.

encomio, m. encomium, eulogy.

enconar, v. irritate, annoy, anger.

encono, m. rancor, resentment.

enconoso, a. rancorous, resentful.

encontrado, a. opposite.

encontrar, v. find; meet.

encorajar, v. encourage; incite.

encorralar, v. corral.

encorvadura, f. bend, curvature.

encorvar, v. arch, bend.

encorvarse, v. stoop.

encrucijada, f. crossroads.

encuadrar, v. frame.

encubierta, a. secret, fraudulent.

encubrir, v. hide, conceal.

encuentro, m. encounter; match, bout.

encurtido, m. pickle.

enchapado, m. veneer.

enchufe, m. (elec.) plug, socket.

endeble, a. frail, weak, sickly.

enderezar, v. straighten; redress.

endiablado, a. devilish.

endibia, f. endive.

endiosar, v. deify.

endorso, endoso, m. endorsement.

endosador, m. endorser.

endosar, v. endorse.

endosatario, m. indorsee.

endulzar, v. sweeten; soothe.

endurar, v. harden; endure.

endurecer, v. harden.

enemigo -ga, *n.* foe, enemy.

enemistad, *f.* enmity.

éneo, *a.* brass.

energía, *f.* energy.

enérgicamente, *adv.* energetically.

enérgico, *a.* forceful; energetic.

enero, *m.* January.

enervación, *f.* enervation.

enfadado, *a.* angry.

enfadar, *v.* anger, vex.

enfado, *m.* anger, vexation.

énfasis, *m. or f.* emphasis, stress.

enfáticamente, *adv.* emphatically.

enfático, *a.* emphatic.

enfermar, *v.* make ill; fall ill.

enfermedad, *f.* illness, sickness, disease.

enfermera, *f.* nurse.

enfermería, *f.* sanitorium.

enfermo -ma, *a. & n.* ill, sick; sickly; patient.

enfilar, *v.* line up; put in a row.

enflaquecer, *v.* make thin; grow thin.

enfoque, *m.* focus. —**enfocar,** *v.*

enfrascamiento, *m.* entanglement.

enfrascar, *v.* entangle oneself.

enfrenar, *v.* bridle, curb; restrain.

enfrente, *adv.* across, opposite; in front.

enfriadera, *f.* ice box; cooler.

enfriar, *v.* chill, cool.

enfurecer, *v.* infuriate, enrage.

engalanar, *v.* adorn, trim.

enganchar, *v.* hook, hitch, attach.

engañar, *v.* deceive, cheat.

engaño, *m.* deceit; delusion.

engañoso, *a.* deceitful.

engarce, *m.* connection, link.

engastar, *v.* to put (gems) in a setting.

engaste, *m.* setting.

engatusar, *v.* deceive, trick.

engendrar, *v.* engender, beget, produce.

engendro, *m.* fetus, embryo.

engolfar, *v.* be deeply absorbed.

engolosinar, *v.* allure, charm, entice.

engomar, *v.* gum.

engordador, *a.* fattening.

engordar, *v.* fatten; grow fat.

engranaje, *m.* (mech.) gear.

engranar, *v.* gear; mesh together.

engrandecer, *v.* increase, enlarge; exalt; exaggerate.

engrasación, *f.* lubrication.

engrasar, *v.* grease, lubricate.

engreído, *a.* conceited.

engreimiento, *m.* conceit.

engullidor, *v.* devourer.

engullir, *v.* devour.

enhebrar, *v.* thread.

enhestadura, *f.* raising.

enhestar, *v.* raise, erect, set up.

enhiesto, *a.* erect, upright.

enhorabuena, *f.* congratulations.

enigma, *m.* enigma, puzzle.

enigmáticamente, *adv.* enigmatically.

enigmático, *a.* enigmatic.

enjabonar, *v.* soap, lather.

enjalbegar, *v.* whitewash.

enjambradera, *f.* queen bee.

enjambre, *m.* swarm. —**enjambrar,** *v.*

enjaular, *v.* cage, coop up.

enjebe, *m.* lye.

enjuagar, *v.* rinse.

enjugar, *v.* wipe, dry off.

enjutez, *f.* dryness.

enjuto, *a.* dried; lean, thin.

enlace, *m.* attachment; involvement; connection.

enladrillador, *m.* bricklayer.

enlardar, *v.* baste.

enlazar, *v.* lace; join, connect; wed.

enlodar, *v.* cover with mud.

enloquecer, *v.* go insane; drive crazy.

enloquecimiento, *m.* insanity.

enlustrecer, *v.* polish, brighten.

For pronunciation, see the concise guide on pages 3 to 4.

enmarañar, v. entangle.

enmendación, f. emendation.

enmendador, m. emender, reviser.

enmendar, v. amend, correct.

enmienda, f. amendment; correction.

enmohecer, v. rust; mold.

enmohecido, a. rusty; moldy.

enmudecer, v. silence; become silent.

ennegrecer, v. blacken.

ennoblecer, v. ennoble.

enodio, m. young deer.

enojado, a. angry, cross.

enojarse, v. get angry.

enojo, m. anger. **—enojar,** v.

enojosamente, adv. angrily.

enorme, a. enormous, huge.

enormemente, adv. enormously; hugely.

enormidad, f. enormity; hugeness.

enraizar, v. take root, sprout.

enramada, f. bower.

enredado, a. entangled, snarled.

enredar, v. entangle, snarl; mess up.

enredo, m. tangle, entanglement.

enriquecer, v. enrich.

enrojecerse, v. color; blush.

enrollar, v. wind, coil, roll up.

enromar, v. make dull, blunt.

enronquecimiento, m. hoarseness.

enroscar, v. twist, curl, wind.

ensacar, v. put in a bag.

ensalada, f. salad.

ensaladera, f. salad bowl.

ensalmo, m. charm, enchantment.

ensalzamiento, m. praise.

ensalzar, v. praise, laud, extol.

ensamblar, v. join; unite; connect.

ensanchamiento, m. widening, expansion, extension.

ensanchar, v. widen, expand, extend.

ensangrentado, a. bloody; bloodshot.

ensañar, v. enrage, infuriate; rage.

ensayar, v. try out; rehearse.

ensayista, n. essayist.

ensayo, m. attempt; trial; rehearsal.

ensenada, f. cove.

enseña, f. ensign, standard.

enseñador, m. teacher.

enseñanza, f. education; teaching.

enseñar, v. teach, train; show.

enseres, m.pl. household goods.

ensilaje, m. ensilage.

ensillar, v. saddle.

ensordecer, v. deafen.

ensordecimiento, m. deafness.

ensuciar, v. dirty, muddy, soil.

ensueño, m. illusion, dream.

entablar, v. board up; initiate, begin.

entallador, m. sculptor, carver.

entapizar, v. upholster.

ente, m. being.

entenada, f. stepdaughter.

entenado, m. stepson.

entender, v. understand.

entendimiento, m. undrestanding.

entenebrecer, v. darken.

enterado, a. aware, informed.

enteramente, adv. entirely, completely.

enterar, v. inform.

enterarse, v. find out.

entereza, f. entirety; integrity; firmness.

entero, a. entire, whole, total.

enterramiento, m. burial, interment.

enterrar, v. bury.

entestado, a. stubborn, willful.

entibiar, v. to cool; moderate.

entidad, f. entity.

entierro, m. interment, burial.

entonación, *f.* intonation.

entonamiento, *m.* intonation.

entonar, *v.* chant; harmonize.

entonces, *adv.* then.

entono, *m.* arrogance; affectation.

entortadura, *f.* crookedness.

entortar, *v.* make crooked; bend.

entrada, *f.* entrance; admission, admittance.

entrambos, *a. & pron.* both.

entrante, *a.* coming, next.

entrañas, *f.pl.* entrails, bowels; womb.

entrañable, *a.* affectionate.

entrar, *v.* enter, go in, come in.

entre, *prep.* among; between.

entreabierto, *a.* ajar, half-open.

entreabrir, *v.* set ajar.

entreacto, *m.* intermission.

entrecejo, *a.* frowning.

entrecuesto, *m.* spine, backbone.

entredicho, *m.* prohibition.

entrega, *f.* delivery.

entregar, *v.* deliver, hand; hand over.

entrelazar, *v.* intertwine, entwine.

entremedias, *adv.* meanwhile; halfway.

entremés, *m.* side dish.

entremeterse, *v.* meddle, intrude.

entremetido, *m.* meddler; intermediary.

entrenador, *m.* coach. **—entrenar,** *v.*

entrenarse, *v.* train.

entrepalado, *a.* variegated; spotted.

entrerenglonar, *v.* interline.

entresacar, *v.* select, choose; sift.

entretanto, *adv.* meanwhile.

entretenedor, *m.* entertainer.

entretener, *v.* entertain, amuse; delay.

entretenimiento, *m.* entertainment, amusement.

entrevista, *f.* interview. **—entrevistar,** *v.*

entristecedor, *a.* sad.

entristecer, *v.* sadden.

entronar, *v.* enthrone.

entroncar, *v.* be related or connected.

entronización, *f.* enthronement.

entronque, *m.* relationship; connection.

entumecer, *v.* become or be numb; swell.

entusiasmado, *a.* enthusiastic.

entusiasmo, *m.* enthusiasm.

entusiasta, *m. & f.* enthusiast.

entusiástico, *a.* enthusiastic.

enumeración, *f.* enumeration.

enumerar, *v.* enumerate.

enunciación, *f.* enunciation; statement.

enunciar, *v.* enunciate.

envainar, *v.* sheathe.

envalentonar, *v.* encourage, embolden.

envanecimiento, *m.* conceit, vanity.

envasar, *v.* put in a container; bottle.

envase, *m.* container.

envejecer, *v.* age, grow old.

envejecimiento, *m.* oldness, age.

envenenar, *v.* poison.

envés, *m.* wrong side; back.

envestir, *v.* put in office; invest.

enviada, *f.* shipment.

enviado, *m.* envoy.

enviar, *v.* send; ship.

envidia, *f.* envy. **—envidiar,** *v.*

envidiable, *a.* enviable.

envidioso, *a.* envious.

envilecer, *v.* vilify, debase, disgrace.

envío, *m.* shipment.

envión, *m.* shove.

envoltura, *f.* wrapping.

envolvedero, *v.* wrapping.

envolver, *v.* wrap, wrap up.

enyesar, *v.* plaster.

enyugar, *v.* yoke.

eperlano, *m.* smelt (fish).

épica, *f.* epic writing.

épico, *a.* epic.

epicureísmo, *m.* Epicureanism.

epicúreo, *n. & a.* epicurean.

epidemia, *f.* epidemic.

epidémico, *a.* epidemic.

epidermis, *f.* epidermis.

epigrama, *m.* epigram.

epigramático, *a.* epigrammatic.

epilepsia, *f.* epilepsy.

epiléptico, *n. & a.* epileptic.

epílogo, *m.* epilogue.

episcopado, *m.* bishopric; episcopate.

episcopal, *a.* episcopal.

episódico, *a.* episodic.

episodio, *m.* episode.

epístola, *f.* epistle, letter.

epitafio, *m.* epitaph.

epidomadamente, *adv.* concisely.

epitomar, *v.* epitomize, summarize.

época, *f.* epoch, age.

epopeya, *f.* epic.

epsomita, *f.* Epsom salts.

equidad, *f.* equity.

equilibrado, *a.* stable.

equilibrio, *m.* equilibrium, balance.

equinoccio, *m.* equinox.

equipaje, *m.* luggage, baggage.

equipar, *v.* equip.

equiparar, *v.* compare.

equipo, *m.* equipment; team.

equitación, *f.* horsemanship.

equitativo, *a.* fair, equitable.

equivalencia, *f.* equivalence.

equivalente, *a.* equivalent.

equivaler, *v.* equal, be equivalent.

equivocación, *f.* mistake.

equivocado, *a.* wrong, mistaken.

equivocarse, *v.* make a mistake, be wrong.

equívoco, *a.* equivocal, ambiguous.

era, *f.* era, age.

erario, *m.* exchequer.

erección, *f.* erection; elevation.

eremita, *m.* hermit.

erguir, *v.* erect; straighten up.

erigir, *v.* erect, build.

erisipela, *f.* erysipelas.

erizado, *a.* bristly.

erizarse, *v.* bristle.

erizo, *m.* hedgehog; sea urchin.

ermita, *f.* hermitage.

ermitaño, *m.* hermit.

erogación, *f.* expenditure. —erogar, *v.*

erosión, *f.* erosion.

erótico, *a.* erotic.

erradicación, *f.* eradication.

erradicar, *v.* eradicate.

errado, *a.* mistaken, erroneous.

errante, *a.* wandering, roving.

errar, *v.* be mistaken.

errata, *f.* erratum.

errático, *a.* erratic.

erróneamente, *adv.* erroneously.

erróneo, *a.* erroneous.

error, *m.* error, mistake.

eructo, *m.* belch. —eructar, *v.*

erudición, *f.* scholarship, learning.

eruditamente, *adv.* learnedly.

erudito, *m.* scholar.

erupción, *f.* eruption; rash.

eruptivo, *a.* eruptive.

esbozo, *m.* outline, sketch. —esbozar, *v.*

escabechar, *v.* pickle; preserve.

escabel, *m.* small stool or bench.

escabroso, *a.* rough, irregular; craggy; rude.

escabullirse, *v.* steal away, sneak away.

escala, *f.* scale; ladder. hacer e., to make a stop.

escalador, *m.* climber.

escalar, *v.* climb; scale.

escaldar, *v.* scald.

escalera, *f.* stairs, staircase; ladder.

escalfado, *a.* poached.

escalofriado, *a.* chilled.

For pronunciation, see the concise guide on pages 3 to 4.

escalofrío, *m.* chill.
escalón, *m.* step.
escaloña, *f.* scallion.
escalpar, *v.* scalp.
escalpelo, *m.* scalpel.
escama, *f.* (fish) scale. — **escamar,** *v.*
escamondar, *v.* trim; cut; prune.
escampada, *f.* stampede.
escandalizar, *v.* shock, scandalize.
escandalizativo, *a.* scandalous.
escándalo, *m.* scandal.
escandaloso, *a.* scandalous; disgraceful.
escandinavo, *n.* & *a.* Scandinavian.
escandir, *v.* scan.
escanilla, *f.* cradle.
escañuelo, *m.* small footstool.
escapada, *f.* escapade.
escapar, *v.* escape.
escape, *m.* escape; (auto.) exhaust.
escápula, *f.* scapula.
escarabajo, *m.* black beetle; scarab.
escaramucear, *v.* skirmish; dispute.
escarbadientes, *m.* toothpick.
escarbar, *v.* scratch; poke.
escarcha, *f.* frost.
escardar, *v.* weed.
escarlata, *f.* scarlet.
escarmentar, *v.* correct severely.
escarnecedor, *m.* scoffer; mocker.
escarnecer, *v.* mock, make fun of.
escarola, *f.* endive.
escarpado, 1. *a.* steep. **2.** *m.* bluff.
escarpe, *m.* escarpment.
escasamente, *adv.* scarcely; sparingly; barely.
escasear, *v.* be scarce.
escasez, *f.* shortage, scarcity.
escaso, *a.* scant; scarce.
escatimoso, *a.* malicious; sly, cunning.
escena, *f.* scene; stage.

escenario, *m.* stage (of theater).
escénico, *a.* scenic.
escépticamente, *adv.* skeptically.
escepticismo, *m.* skepticism.
escéptico -ca, *a.* & *n.* skeptic; skeptical.
esclarecer, *v.* clear up.
esclavitud, *f.* slavery; bondage.
esclavizar, *v.* enslave.
esclavo -va, *n.* slave.
escoba, *f.* broom.
escocés, *a.* & *n.* Scotch, Scottish; Scot.
Escocia, *f.* Scotland.
escofinar, *v.* rasp.
escoger, *v.* choose, select.
escogido, *a.* choice, select.
escogimiento, *m.* choice.
escolar, 1. *a.* scholastic, (of) school. **2.** *n.* student.
escolasticismo, *m.* scholasticism.
escolta, *f.* escort. — **escoltar,** *v.*
escollo, *m.* reef.
escombro, *m.* mackerel.
escombros, *m.pl.* debris, rubbish.
esconce, *m.* corner.
escondedero, *m.* hiding place.
esconder, *v.* hide, conceal.
escondidamente, *adv.* secretly.
escondimiento, *m.* concealment.
escopeta, *f.* shotgun.
escopetazo, *m.* gunshot.
escoplo, *m.* chisel.
escorbuto, *m.* scurvy.
escorpena, *f.* grouper.
escorpión, *m.* scorpion.
escorzón, *m.* toad.
escribiente, *m.* & *f.* clerk.
escribir, *v.* write.
escritor -ra, *n.* writer, author.
escritorio, *m.* desk.
escritura, *f.* writing, handwriting.
escrófula, *f.* scrofula.
escroto, *m.* scrotum.
escrúpulo, *m.* scruple.
escrupuloso, *a.* scrupulous.

escrutinio, m. scrutiny; examination.

escuadra, f. squad; fleet.

escuadrón, m. squadron.

escualidez, f. squalor; poverty.

escuálido, a. squalid.

escualo, m. shark.

escuchar, v. listen; listen to.

escudero, m. squire.

escudo, m. shield; protection; coin of certain countries.

escuela, f. school.

escuerzo, m. toad.

esculpir, v. carve, sculpture.

escultor, m. sculptor.

escultura, f. sculpture.

escupidera, m. cuspidor, strainer.

escupir, v. spit.

escurridor, m. colander, strainer.

escurrir, v. drain off; wring out.

escurrirse, v. slip; sneak away.

ese, esa, dem. a. that.

ése, ésa, dem. pron. that (one).

esencia, f. essence; perfume.

esencial, a. essential.

esencialmente, adv. essentially.

esfera, f. sphere.

esfinge, f. sphinx.

esforzar, v. strengthen.

esforzarse, v. strive, exert oneself.

esfuerzo, m. effort, attempt; vigor.

esgrima, f. fencing.

eslabón, m. link (of a chain).

eslabonar, v. link, join, connect.

eslavo, a. & n. Slavic; Slav.

esmalte, m. enamel. —esmaltar, v.

esmerado, a. careful, thorough.

esmeralda, f. emerald.

esmerarse, v. take pains, do one's best.

esmeril, m. emery.

eso, dem. pron. that.

esófago, m. esophagus.

esotérico, a. esoteric.

espacio, m. space. —espaciar, v.

espaciosidad, f. spaciousness.

espacioso, a. spacious.

espada, f. sword; spade (in cards).

espadarte, m. swordfish.

espalda, f. back.

espaldera, f. espalier.

espantar, v. frighten, scare; scare away.

espanto, m. fright.

espantoso, a. frightening, frightful.

España, f. Spain.

español -ola, a. & n. Spanish; Spaniard.

esparcir, v. scatter, disperse.

espárrago, m. asparagus.

espartano, n. & a. Spartan.

espasmo, m. spasm.

espasmódico, a. spasmodic.

espata, f. spathe.

espato, m. spar (mineral).

espátula, f. spatula.

especia, f. spice. —especiar, v.

especial, a. special, especial.

especialidad, f. specialty.

especialista, m. & f. specialist.

especialización, f. specialization.

especialmente, adv. especially.

especie, f. species; sort.

especiería, f. grocery store.

especiero, m. grocer.

especificar, v. specify.

específico, a. specific.

espécimen, m. specimen.

especioso, a. neat; polished; specious.

espectáculo, m. spectacle, show.

espectador -ra, n. spectator.

espectro, m. specter, ghost.

especulación, f. speculation.

especulador, m. speculator.

especular, v. speculate.

especulativo, a. speculative.

espejo, m. mirror.

espelunca, f. dark cave, cavern.

espera, f. wait.

For pronunciation, see the concise guide on pages 3 to 4.

esperanza, f. hope, expectation.

esperar, v. hope; expect; wait, wait for, watch for.

espesar, v. thicken.

espeso, a. thick, dense, bushy.

espesor, m. thickness, density.

espía, m. & f. spy. —**espiar,** v.

espigón, m. bee sting.

espina, f. thorn.

espinaca, f. spinach.

espinal, a. spinal.

espinazo, m. spine.

espineta, f. spinet.

espino, m. briar.

espinoso, a. spiny, thorny.

espión, m. spy.

espionaje, m. espionage.

espiración, f. expiration.

espiral, a. & m. spiral.

espirar, v. expire; breathe, exhale.

espíritu, m. spirit.

espiritual, a. spiritual.

espiritualidad, f. spirituality.

espiritualmente, adv. spiritually.

espita, f. faucet, spigot.

espléndido, a. splendid.

esplendor, m. splendor.

espolear, v. incite, urge on.

espoleta, f. wishbone.

esponja, f. sponge.

esponjoso, a. spongy.

esponsales, m.pl. engagement, betrothal.

esponsalicio, a. nuptial.

espontáneamente, adv. spontaneously.

espontaneidad, f. spontaneity.

espontáneo, a. spontaneous.

espora, f. spore.

esporádico, a. sporadic.

esposa, f. wife.

esposar, v. shackle.

esposo, m. husband.

espuela, f. spur. —**espolear,** v.

espuma, f. foam. —**espumar,** v.

espumadera, f. colander.

espumajear, v. foam at the mouth.

espumajo, m. foam.

espumar, v. foam, froth; skim.

espumoso, a. foamy; sparkling (wine).

espurio, a. spurious.

esputar, v. spit, expectorate.

esputo, m. spit, saliva.

esquela, f. note.

esqueleto, m. skeleton.

esquema, m. scheme; diagram.

esquero, m. leather sack or pouch.

esquiciar, v. outline, sketch roughly.

esquicio, m. rough sketch or outline.

esquife, m. skiff.

esquilar, v. fleece, shear.

esquilmo, m. harvest.

esquimal, n. & a. Eskimo.

esquina, f. corner.

esquivar, v. evade, shun.

estabilidad, f. stability.

estable, a. stable.

establecedor, m. founder, originator.

establecer, v. establish, set up.

establecimiento, m. establishment.

establero, m. groom.

establo, m. stable.

estaca, f. stake.

estación, f. station; season.

estacionar, v. station; park (a vehicle).

estacionario, a. stationary.

estadista, m. statesman.

estadística, f. statistics.

estadístico, a. statistical.

estado, m. state; condition; status.

estafa, f. swindle, fake. —**estafar,** v.

estafeta, f. post office.

estallar, v. explode; burst; break out.

estallido, m. crash; crack; explosion.

estampa, f. stamp. —**estampar,** v.

estampado, *m.* printed cotton cloth.

estampida, *f.* stampede.

estampilla, *f.* (postage) stamp.

estancado, *a.* stagnant.

estancar, *v.* stanch, stop, check.

estancia, *f.* stay; (S.A.) small farm.

estanciero -ra, *n.* small farmer.

estandarte, *m.* banner.

estanque, *m.* pool; pond.

estante, *m.* shelf.

estaño, *m.* tin. —**estañar,** *v.*

estar, *v.* be; stand; look.

estática, *f.* static.

estático, *a.* static.

estatua, *f.* statue.

estatura, *f.* stature.

estatuto, *m.* statute, law.

este, *m.* east.

este, esta, *dem. a.* this.

éste, ésta, *dem. pron.* this (one); the latter.

estelar, *a.* stellar.

estenografía, *f.* stenography.

estenógrafo -fa, *n.* stenographer.

estera, *f.* mat, matting.

estéril, *a.* barren; sterile.

esterilidad, *f.* sterility, fruitlessness.

esterilizar, *v.* sterilize.

estética, *f.* esthetics.

estético, *a.* esthetic.

estetoscopio, *m.* stethoscope.

estibador, *m.* stevedore.

estiércol, *m.* dung, manure.

estigma, *m.* stigma; disgrace.

estilo, *m.* style; sort.

estilográfica, *f.* (fountain) pen.

estima, *f.* esteem.

estimable, *a.* estimable, worthy.

estimación, *f.* estimation.

estimar, *v.* esteem; value; estimate; gauge.

estimular, *v.* stimulate.

estímulo, *m.* stimulus.

estío, *m.* summer.

estipulación, *f.* stipulation.

estipular, *v.* stipulate.

estirar, *v.* stretch.

estirpe, *m.* stock, lineage.

esto, *dem. pron.* this.

estocada, *f.* stab, thrust.

estofado, *m.* stew. —**estofar,** *v.*

estoicismo, *m.* stoicism.

estoico, *n. & a.* stoic.

estómago, *m.* stomach.

estorbar, *v.* bother, hinder, interfere with.

estorbo, *m.* hindrance.

estornudo, *m.* sneeze. —**estornudar,** *v.*

estrabismo, *m.* strabismus.

estrago, *m.* devastation, havoc.

estrangulación, *f.* strangulation.

estrangular, *v.* strangle.

estratagema, *f.* stratagem.

estrategia, *f.* strategy.

estratégico, *a.* strategic.

estrato, *m.* stratum.

estrechar, *v.* tighten; narrow.

estrechez, *f.* narrowness; tightness.

estrecho, 1. *a.* narrow, tight. **2.** *m.* strait.

estregar, *v.* scour, scrub.

estrella, *f.* star.

estrellamar, *f.* starfish.

estrellar, *v.* shatter, smash.

estremecimiento, *m.* shudder. —**estremecerse,** *v.*

estrenar, *v.* wear for the first time; open (a play).

estreno, *m.* debut, first performance.

estrenuo, *a.* strenuous.

estreptococo, *m.* streptococcus.

estría, *f.* groove.

estribillo, *m.* refrain.

estribo, *m.* stirrup.

estribor, *m.* starboard.

estrictamente, *adv.* strictly.

estrictez, *f.* strictness.

estricto, *a.* strict.

estrofa, *f.* stanza.

estropajo, *m.* mop.

estropear, *v.* cripple, damage, spoil.

estructura, *f.* structure.

estructural, *a.* structural.

estruendo, m. din, clatter.
estuario, m. estuary.
estuco, m. stucco.
estudiante -ta, n. student.
estudiar, v. study.
estudio, m. study; studio.
estudioso, a. studious.
estufa, f. stove.
estulto, a. foolish.
estupendo, a. wonderful, grand, fine.
estupidez, f. stupidity.
estúpido, a. stupid.
estupor, m. stupor.
estuque, m. stucco.
esturión, m. sturgeon.
etapa, f. stage.
éter, m. ether.
etéreo, a. ethereal.
eternal, a. eternal.
eternidad, f. eternity.
eterno, a. eternal.
ética, f. ethics.
ético, a. ethical.
etimología, f. etymology.
etiqueta, f. etiquette; tag, label.
étnico, a. ethnic.
etrusco, n. & a. Etruscan.
eucaristía, f. Eucharist.
eufemismo, m. euphemism.
eufonía, f. euphony.
Europa, f. Europe.
europeo -pea, a. & n. European.
eutanasia, f. euthanasia.
evacuación, f. evacuation.
evacuar, v. evacuate.
evadir, v. evade.
evangélico, a. evangelical.
evangelio, m. gospel.
evangelista, m. evangelist.
evaporación, f. evaporation.
evaporarse, v. evaporate.
evasión, f. evasion.
evasivamente, adv. evasively.
evasivo, a. evasive.
evento, m. event, occurrence.
eventual, a. eventual.
eventualidad, f. eventuality.
evicción, f. eviction.
evidencia, f. evidence.
evidenciar, v. prove, show.
evidente, a. evident.
evitación, f. avoidance.

evitar, v. avoid, shun.
evocación, f. evocation.
evocar, v. evoke.
evolución, f. evolution.
exacerbar, v. irritate deeply.
exactamente, adv. exactly.
exactitud, f. precision, accuracy.
exacto, a. exact, accurate.
exageración, f. exaggeration.
exagerar, v. exaggerate.
exagonal, a. hexagonal.
exaltación, f. exaltation.
exaltamiento, m. exaltation.
exaltar, v. exalt.
examen, m. test, examination.
examinar, v. test, examine.
exánime, a. spiritless, weak.
exasperación, f. exasperation.
exasperar, v. exasperate.
excavación, f. excavation.
excavar, v. excavate.
exceder, v. exceed, surpass; outrun.
excelencia, f. excellence.
excelente, a. excellent.
excéntrico, a. eccentric.
excepción, f. exception.
excepcional, a. exceptional.
excepto, prep. except, except for.
exceptuar, v. except.
excesivamente, adv. excessively.
excesivo, a. excessive.
exceso, m. excess.
excitabilidad, f. excitability.
excitación, f. excitement.
excitar, v. excite.
exclamación, f. exclamation.
exclamar, v. exclaim.
excluir, v. exclude, bar, shut out.
exclusión, f. exclusion.
exclusivamente, adv. exclusively.
exclusivo, a. exclusive.
excomulgar, v. excommunicate.
excomunión, f. excommunication.
excreción, f. excretion.
excremento, m. excrement.
excretar, v. excrete.

For pronunciation, see the concise guide on pages 3 to 4.

exculpar, v. exonerate.

excursión, f. excursion.

excursionista, n. excursionist.

excusa, f. excuse. —excusar, v.

excusado, m. toilet.

excusarse, v. apologize.

exención, f. exemption.

exento, a. exempt. —exentar, v.

exhalación, f. exhalation.

exhalar, v. exhale, breathe out.

exhausto, a. exhausted.

exhibición, f. exhibit, exhibition.

exhibir, v. exhibit, display.

exhortación, f. exhortation.

exhortar, v. exhort, admonish.

exhumación, f. exhumation.

exhumar, v. exhume.

exigencia, f. requirement, demand.

exigente, a. exacting, demanding.

exigir, v. require, exact, demand.

eximir, v. exempt.

existencia, f. existence; (econ.) supply.

existente, a. existent.

existir, v. exist.

éxito, m. success.

éxodo, m. exodus.

exoneración, f. exoneration.

exonerar, v. exonerate, acquit.

exorar, v. beg, implore.

exorbitancia, f. exorbitance.

exorbitante, a. exorbitant.

exorcismo, m. exorcism.

exornar, v. adorn, decorate.

exótico, a. exotic.

expansibilidad, f. expansibility.

expansión, f. expansion.

expansivo, a. expansive; effusive.

expatriación, f. expatriation.

expatriar, v. expatriate.

expectación, f. expectation.

expectorar, v. expectorate.

expedición, f. expedition.

expediente, m. expedient, means.

expedir, v. send off, ship; expedite.

expeditivo, a. speedy, prompt.

expedito, a. speedy, prompt.

expeler, v. expel, eject.

expendedor, m. dealer.

expender, v. expend.

expensas, f.pl. expenses, costs.

experiencia, f. experience.

experimentado, a. experienced.

experimental, a. experimental.

experimentar, v. experience

experimento, m. experiment.

expertamente, adv. expertly.

experto, a. & m. expert.

expiación, f. atonement.

expiar, v. atone for.

expiración, f. expiration.

expirar, v. expire.

explanación, f. explanation.

explanar, v. make level.

expletivo, n. & a. expletive.

explicable, a. explicable.

explicación, f. explanation.

explicar, v. explain.

explicativo, a. explanatory.

explícitamente, adv. explicitly.

explícito, adj. explicit.

exploración, f. exploration.

explorador, m. explorer; scout.

explorar, v. explore; scout.

exploratorio, a. exploratory.

explosión, f. explosion; outburst.

explosivo, a. explosive.

explotación, f. exploitation.

explotar, v. exploit.

exponer, v. expose; set forth.

exportación, f. exportation; export.

exportador, m. exporter.

exportar, v. export.

exposición, f. exhibit; exposition; exposure.

expósito, n. foundling; orphan.

expresado, a. aforesaid.

For pronunciation, see the concise guide on pages 3 to 4.

expresamente, *adv.* clearly, explicitly.
expresar, *v.* express.
expresión, *f.* expression.
expresivo, *a.* expressive; affectionate.
expreso, *a. & m.* express.
exprimir, *v.* squeeze.
expropiación, *f.* expropriation.
expropiar, *v.* expropriate.
expulsar, *v.* expel, eject; evict.
expulsión, *f.* expulsion.
expurgación, *f.* expurgation.
expurgar, *v.* expurgate.
exquisitamente, *adv.* exquisitely.
exquisito, *a.* exquisite.
éxtasi, *m.* ecstasy.
extemporáneo, *a.* extemporaneous, impromptu.
extender, *v.* extend; spread; widen; stretch.
extensamente, *adv.* extensively.
extensión, *f.* extension, spread, expanse.
extenso, *a.* extensive, widespread.
extenuación, *f.* weakening; emaciation.
extenuar, *v.* extenuate.
exterior, *a. & m.* exterior.
exterminar, *v.* exterminate.
exterminio, *m.* extermination, ruin.
extinción, *f.* extinction.
extinguir, *v.* extinguish.
extinto, *a.* extinct.
extintor, *m.* fire extinguisher.

extirpar, *v.* eradicate.
extorsión, *f.* extortion.
extra, *n.* extra.
extracción, *f.* extraction.
extractar, *v.* summarize.
extracto, *m.* extract; summary.
extradición, *f.* extradition.
extraer, *v.* extract.
extranjero -ra, **1.** *a.* foreign. **2.** *n.* foreigner; stranger.
extrañar, *v.* surprise; miss.
extraño, *a.* strange, queer.
extraordinariamente, *adv.* extraordinarily.
extraordinario, *a.* extraordinary.
extravagancia, *f.* extravagance.
extravagante, *a.* extravagant.
extraviado, *a.* lost, misplaced.
extraviarse, *v.* stray, get lost.
extravío, *m.* aberration, deviation.
extremadamente, *adv.* extremely.
extremado, *a.* extreme.
extramaunción, *f.* extreme unction.
extremidad, *f.* extremity.
extremista, *n. & a.* extremist.
extremo, *a. & m.* extreme, end.
extrínseco, *a.* extrinsic.
exuberancia, *f.* exuberance.
exuberante, *a.* exuberant.
exudación, *f.* exudation.
exudar, *v.* exude, ooze.
exultación, *f.* exultation.

F

fábrica, *f.* factory.
fabricación, *f.* manufacture, manufacturing.
fabricante, *m.* manufacturer, maker.

fabricar, *v.* manufacture, make.
fabril, *a.* making, building.
fábula, *f.* fable, myth.
fabuloso, *a.* fabulous.

For pronunciation, see the concise guide on pages 3 to 4.

facción, f. faction, party; (pl.) features.

faccioso, a. factious.

fácil, a. easy.

facilidad, f. facility, ease.

facilitar, v. facilitate, make easy.

fácilmente, adv. easily.

facsímil, m. facsimile.

factible, a. feasible.

factor, m. factor.

factótum, m. factotum; jack of all trades.

factura, f. invoice, bill.

facturar, v. check (baggage).

facultad, f. faculty; ability.

facultativo, a. optional.

fachada, f. façade, front.

faena, f. task; work.

faja, f. band; sash; zone.

falacia, f. fallacy; deceitfulness.

falda, f. skirt; lap.

falibilidad, f. fallibility.

falsear, v. falsify, counterfeit; forge.

falsedad, f. falsehood; lie; falseness.

falsificación, f. falsification; forgery.

falsificar, v. falsify, counterfeit, forge.

falso, a. false; wrong.

falta, f. error, mistake; fault; lack. **hacer f.,** to be lacking, to be necessary. **sin f.,** without fail.

faltar, v. be lacking, be missing; be absent.

faltriquera, f. pocket.

falla, f. failure, fault.

fallar, v. fail.

fallecer, v. pass away, die.

fallo, m. verdict.

fama, f. fame; reputation; glory.

familia, f. family; household.

familiar, a. familiar; domestic; (of) family.

familiaridad, f. familiarity, intimacy.

familiarizar, v. familiarize, acquaint.

famoso, a. famous.

fanal, m. lighthouse; lantern, lamp.

fanático -ca, a. & n. fanatic.

fanatismo, m. fanaticism.

fanfarria, f. bluster. **—fanfarrear,** v.

fango, m. mud.

fantasía, f. fantasy; fancy, whim.

fantasma, m. phantom; ghost.

fantástico, a. fantastic.

faquín, m. porter.

faquir, m. fakir.

farallón, m. cliff.

Faraón, m. Pharaoh.

fardel, m. bag; package.

fardo, m. bundle.

farináceo, a. farinaceous.

faringe, f. pharynx.

fariseo, m. pharisee, hypocrite.

farmacéutico, m. pharmacist.

farmacia, f. pharmacy.

faro, m. beacon; lighthouse; headlight.

farol, m. lantern; (street) light.

farra, f. spree.

fárrago, m. medley; hodgepodge.

farsa, f. farce.

fascinación, f. fascination.

fascinar, v. fascinate, bewitch.

fase, f. phase.

fastidiar, v. disgust; irk, annoy.

fastidio, m. disgust; annoyance.

fastidioso, a. annoying; tedious.

fatal, a. fatal.

fatalidad, f. fate; calamity, bad luck.

fatalismo, m. fatalism.

fatalista, n. & a. fatalist.

fatiga, f. fatigue. **—fatigar,** v.

fauno, m. faun.

favor, m. favor; behalf. **por f.,** please.

favorable, a. favorable.

favorablemente, adv. favorably.

For pronunciation, see the concise guide on pages 3 to 4.

favorecer, v. favor; flatter.
favoritismo, m. favoritism.
favorito -ta, a. & n. favorite.
faz, f. face.
fe, f. faith.
fealdad, f. ugliness, homeliness.
febrero, m. February.
febril, a. feverish.
fécula, f. starch.
fecundar, v. fertilize.
fecundidad, f. fecundity, fertility.
fecundo, a. fecund, fertile.
fecha, f. date. —**fechar,** v.
federación, f. confederacy.
federal, a. federal.
felicidad, f. happiness; bliss.
felicitación, f. congratulation.
felicitar, v. congratulate; compliment.
feligrés -esa, n. parishioner.
feliz, a. happy; fortunate.
felón, m. felon.
felonía, f. felony.
felpa, f. plush.
felpudo, m. doormat.
femenino, a. feminine.
feminismo, m. feminism.
feminista, n. feminist.
fenecer, v. conclude; die.
fénix, m. phoenix; model.
fenomenal, a. phenomenal.
fenómeno, m. phenomenon.
feo, a. ugly, homely.
feracidad, f. feracity, fertility.
feraz, a. fertile, fruitful; copious.
feria, f. fair; market.
feriado, a. **día f.,** holiday.
fermentación, f. fermentation.
fermento, m. ferment.
fermentar, v.
ferocidad, f. ferocity, fierceness.
feroz, a. ferocious, fierce.
férreo, a. of iron.
ferrería, f. ironworks.
ferretería, f. hardware; hardware store.
ferrocarril, m. railroad.
fértil, a. fertile.
fertilidad, f. fertility.

fertilizar, v. fertilize.
férvido, a. fervid, ardent.
ferviente, a. fervent.
fervor, m. fervor, zeal.
fervoroso, a. zealous, eager.
festejar, v. entertain, fete.
festejo, m. feast.
festín, m. feast.
festividad, f. festivity.
festivo, a. festive.
fétido, adj. fetid.
feudal, a. feudal.
feudo, m. feud.
fiado, adj. on trust, on credit.
fianza, f. bail.
fiar, v. trust, sell on credit; give credit.
fiarse de, v. trust (in), rely on.
fiasco, m. fiasco.
fibra, f. fiber; vigor.
fibroso, a. fibrous.
ficción, f. fiction.
ficticio, a. fictitious.
ficha, f. slip, card; chip.
fidedigno, a. trustworthy.
fideicomisario, m. trustee.
fideicomiso, m. trust.
fidelidad, f. fidelity.
fideo, m. noodle.
fiebre, f. fever.
fiel, a. faithful.
fieltro, m. felt.
fiera, f. wild animal.
fiereza, f. fierceness, wildness.
fiero, a. fierce; wild.
fiesta, f. festival, feast; party.
figura, f. figure. —**figurar,** v.
figurarse, v. imagine.
figurón, m. dummy.
fijar, v. fix; set, establish; post.
fijarse en, v. notice.
fijeza, f. firmness.
fijo, a. fixed. stationary, permanent, set.
fila, f. row, rank, file, line.
filantropía, f. philanthropy.
filete, m. fillet.
film, m. film. —**filmar,** v.
filo, m. (cutting) edge.
filón, m. vein (of ore).
filosofía, f. philosophy.
filosófico, a. philosophical.
filósofo, m. philosopher.

filtro, *m.* filter. **—filtrar.** *v.*

fin, *m.* end, purpose, goal.
  a f. de que, in order that.
  en f., in short. **por f.,**
  finally, at last.

final, 1. *a.* final. **2.** *m.* end.

finalidad, *f.* finality.

finalmente, *adv.* at last.

financiero, 1. *a.* financial.
  2. *m.* financier.

finca, *f.* real estate; estate;
  farm.

finés, *a.* Finnish.

fineza, *f.* courtesy, politeness; fineness.

fingimiento, *m.* pretense.

fingir, *v.* feign, pretend.

fino, *a.* fine; polite, courteous.

firma, *f.* signature; (com.)
  firm.

firmamento, *m.* firmament,
  heavens.

firmar, *v.* sign.

firme, *a.* firm, fast, steady,
  sound.

firmemente, *adv.* firmly.

firmeza, *f.* firmness.

fisco, *m.* exchequer, treasury.

física, *f.* physics.

físico, *a. & n.* physical; phys-
  icist.

fisiología, *f.* physiology.

fláccido, *a.* flaccid, soft.

flaco, *a.* thin, gaunt.

flagelación, *f.* flagellation.

flagelar, *v.* flagellate, whip.

flagrancia, *f.* flagrancy.

flagrante, *a.* flagrant.

flama, *f.* flame; ardor, zeal.

flamante, *a.* flaming.

flamenco, *m.* flamingo.

flan, *m.* custard.

flanco, *m.* side; (mil.) flank.

flanquear, *v.* flank.

flaqueza, *f.* thinness; weakness.

flauta, *f.* flute.

flautín, *m.* piccolo.

flautista, *m. & f.* flutist,
  piper.

fleco, *m.* fringe; flounce.

flecha, *f.* arrow.

flechero, *m.* archer.

flema, *f.* phlegm.

flete, *m.* freight. **—fletar.** *v.*

flexibilidad, *f.* flexibility.

flexible, *a.* flexible, pliable.

flirtear, *v.* flirt.

flojo, *a.* limp; loose, flabby,
  slack.

flor, *f.* flower; compliment.

flora, *f.* flora.

floral, *a.* floral.

florecer, *v.* flower, bloom;
  flourish.

floreo, *m.* flourish.

florero, *m.* flower pot; vase.

floresta, *f.* forest.

florido, *a.* flowery; flowering.

florista, *m. & f.* florist.

flota, *f.* fleet.

flotante, *a.* floating.

flotar, *v.* float.

flotilla, *f.* flotilla, fleet.

fluctuación, *f.* fluctuation.

fluctuar, *v.* fluctuate.

fluente, *a.* fluent.

fluidez, *f.* fluency.

fluido, *a. & m.* fluid, liquid.

fluir, *v.* flow.

flujo, *m.* flow, flux.

flúor, *m.* fluorine.

fluorescencia, *f.* fluorescence.

fluorescente, *a.* fluorescent.

fobia, *f.* phobia.

foca, *f.* seal.

foco, *m.* focus, center.

fogata, *f.* bonfire.

fogón, *m.* hearth, fireplace.

fogosidad, *f.* vehemence,
  ardor.

fogoso, *a.* vehement, ardent.

folklore, *m.* folklore.

follaje, *m.* foliage.

folleto, *m.* pamphlet, booklet.

fomentar, *v.* develop, promote, further, foster.

fomento, *m.* fomentation.

fonda, *f.* eating house, inn.

fondo, *m.* bottom; back
  (part); background; (pl.)
  funds; finances. **a f.,** thoroughly.

fonética, *f.* phonetics.

fonético, *a.* phonetic.

fonógrafo, *m.* phonograph.

forastero -ra, 1. *a.* foreign,
  exotic. **2.** *n.* stranger.

forjar, *v.* forge.

forma, *f.* form, shape.

formar, *v.*

For pronunciation, see the concise guide on pages 3 to 4.

formación, *f.* formation.

formal, *a.* formal.

formaldehido, *m.* formaldehyde.

formalidad, *f.* formality.

formalizar, *v.* finalize; formulate.

formidable, *a.* formidable.

formidablemente, *adv.* formidably.

formón, *m.* chisel.

fórmula, *f.* formula.

formular, *v.* formulate, draw up.

formulario, *m.* form.

foro, *m.* forum.

forraje, *m.* forage, fodder.

forrar, *v.* line.

forro, *m.* lining.

fortalecer, *v.* fortify.

fortaleza, *f.* fort, fortress; fortitude.

fortificación, *f.* fortification.

fortitud, *f.* fortitude.

fortuitamente, *adv.* fortuitously.

fortuito, *a.* fortuitous.

fortuna, *f.* fortune; luck.

forúnculo, *m.* boil.

forzar, *v.* force, compel, coerce.

forzosamente, *adv.* compulsorily; forcibly.

forzoso, *a.* compulsory; necessary. **paro f.,** unemployment.

forzudo, *a.* powerful, vigorous.

fosa, *f.* grave.

fósforo, *m.* match; phosphorus.

fósil, *m.* fossil.

foso, *m.* ditch, trench; moat.

fotografía, *f.* photograph. **—fotografiar,** *v.*

frac, *m.* dress coat.

fracasar, *v.* fail.

fracaso, *m.* failure.

fracción, *f.* fraction.

fractura, *f.* fracture, break.

fragancia, *f.* fragrance; perfume; aroma.

fragante, *a.* fragrant.

frágil, *a.* fragile, breakable.

fragilidad, *f.* fragility.

fragmentario, *a.* fragmentary.

fragmento, *m.* fragment, bit.

fragor, *m.* noise, clamor.

fragoso, *a.* noisy.

fragua, *f.* forge. **—fraguar,** *v.*

fraile, *m.* monk.

frambuesa, *f.* raspberry.

francamente, *adv.* frankly, candidly.

francés -esa, *a. & n.* French; Frenchman.

Francia, *f.* France.

franco, *a.* frank.

franela, *f.* flannel.

frangible, *a.* breakable.

franqueo, *m.* postage.

franqueza, *f.* frankness.

franquicia, *f.* franchise.

frasco, *m.* flask, bottle.

frase, *f.* phrase; sentence.

fraseología, *f.* phraseology; style.

fraternal, *a.* fraternal, brotherly.

fraternidad, *f.* fraternity, brotherhood.

fraude, *m.* fraud.

fraudulento, *a.* fraudulent.

frazada, *f.* blanket.

frecuencia, *f.* frequency.

frecuente, *a.* frequent.

frecuentemente, *adv.* frequently, often.

fregadero, *m.* sink.

fregadura, *f.* scouring, scrubbing.

fregar, *v.* scour, scrub, mop.

freir, *v.* fry.

fréjol, *m.* kidney bean.

frenesí, *m.* frenzy.

frenéticamente, *adv.* frantically.

frenético, *a.* frantic, frenzied.

freno, *m.* brake. **—frenar,** *v.*

frente, 1. *f.* forehead. **2.** *m.* front. **en f., al f.,** opposite, across. **f. a,** in front of.

fresa, *f.* strawberry.

fresca, *f.* fresh, cool air.

fresco, *a.* fresh; cool; crisp.

frescura, *f.* coolness, freshness.

fresno, *m.* ash tree.
fresquería, *f.* soda fountain.
friabilidad, *f.* brittleness.
friable, *a.* brittle
frialdad, *f.* coldness.
fríamente, *adv.* coldly; coolly.
fricandó, *m.* fricandeau.
fricar, *v.* rub together.
fricción, *f.* friction.
friccionar, *v.* rub.
friega, *f.* friction.
frigidez, *f.* frigidity.
frígido, *a.* frigid.
frijol, *m.* bean.
frío, *a. & n.* cold. **tener f.**, to be cold, feel cold. **hacer f.**, to be cold (weather).
friolento, friolero, *a.* chilly; sensitive to cold.
friolera, *f.* trifle, trinket.
friso, *m.* frieze.
fritillas, *f.pl.* fritters.
frito, *a.* fried.
fritura, *f.* fritter.
frívolamente, *adv.* frivolously.
frivolidad, *f.* frivolity.
frívolo, *a.* frivolous.
frondoso, *a.* leafy.
frontera, *f.* frontier; border.
frotar, *v.* rub.
fructífero, *a.* fruitful.
fructificar, *v.* bear fruit.
fructuosamente, *adv.* fruitfully.
fructuoso, *a.* fruitful.
frugal, *a.* frugal, thrifty.
frugalidad, *f.* frugality; thrift.
frugalmente, *adv.* frugally, thriftily.
fruncir, *v.* gather, contract. **f. el entrecejo**, frown.
fruslería, *f.* trinket.
frustrar, *v.* frustrate, thwart.
fruta, *f.* fruit.
fruto, *m.* fruit; product; profit.
fucsia, *f.* fuchsia.
fuego, *m.* fire.
fuelle, *m.* bellows.
fuente, *f.* fountain; source; platter.
fuera, *adv.* without, outside.

fuero, *m.* statute.
fuerte, **1.** *a.* strong; loud. **2.** *m.* fort.
fuertemente, *adv.* strongly; loudly.
fuerza, *f.* force, strength.
fuga, *f.* flight, escape.
fugarse, *v.* flee, escape.
fugaz, *a.* fugitive, passing.
fugitivo -va, *a. & n.* fugitive.
fulcro, *m.* fulcrum.
fulgor, *m.* gleam, glow. — **fulgurar**, *v.*
fulminante, *a.* explosive.
fumador, *m.* smoker.
fumar, *v.* smoke.
fumigación, *f.* fumigation.
fumigador, *m.* fumigator.
fumigar, *v.* fumigate.
fumoso, *a.* smoky.
función, *f.* function; performance, show.
funcionar, *v.* function, work, run.
funcionario, *m.* official, functionary.
funda, *f.* case, sheath, slipcover.
fundación, *f.* foundation.
fundador -ra, *n.* founder.
fundamental, *a.* fundamental, basic.
fundamentalmente, *adv.* fundamentally.
fundamento, *m.* base, basis, foundation.
fundar, *v.* found, establish.
fundición, *f.* foundry.
fundir, *v.* fuse; smelt.
fúnebre, *a.* dismal.
funeral, *m.* funeral.
funestamente, *adv.* sadly.
fungo, *m.* fungus.
furente, *a.* furious, enraged.
furia, *f.* fury.
furiosamente, *adv.* furiously.
furioso, *a.* furious.
furor, *m.* furor; fury.
furtivamente, *adv.* furtively.
furtivo, *a.* furtive, sly.
furúnculo, *m.* boil.
fusibilidad, *f.* fusibility.
fusible, *a.* fuse.
fusil, *m.* rifle, gun.

fusilar, v. shoot.
fusión, f. fusion; merger.
fusionar, v. unite, fuse, merge.

fútbol, m. football, soccer.
fútil, a. trivial.
futilidad, f. triviality.
futuro, a. & m. future.

G

gabán, m. overcoat.
gabinete, m. closet; cabinet; study.
gacela, f. gazelle.
gaceta, f. gazette, newspaper.
gacetilla, f. personal news section of a newspaper.
gaélico, a. Gaelic.
gafas, f.pl. eyeglasses.
gaguear, v. stutter, stammer.
gaita, f. bagpipe.
gaje, m. salary; fee.
gala, f. gala, ceremony; (pl.) regalia. **tener a g.**, be proud of.
galán, m. gallant.
galano, a. stylishly dressed; elegant.
galante, a. gallant.
galantería, f. gallantry, compliment.
galápago, m. fresh-water turtle.
galardón, m. prize; reward.
gáleo, m. swordfish.
galera, f. wagon; shed.
galería, f. gallery, (theat.) balcony.
galés, n. & a. Welsh.
galgo, m. greyhound.
galillo, m. uvula.
galocha, f. galosh.
galón, m. gallon; (mil.) stripe.
galope, m. gallop. —**galopar**, v.
gallardete, m. pennant.
galleta, f. cracker.
gallina, f. hen.
gallinero, m. chicken coop.
gallo, m. rooster.
gambito, m. gambit.

gamuza, f. chamois.
gana, f. desire, wish, mind (to). **de buena g.**, willingly. **tener ganas de**, to feel like.
ganado, m. cattle.
ganador -ra, n. winner
ganancia, f. gain, profit; (pl.) earnings.
ganapán, m. drudge.
ganar, v. earn; win; beat.
gancho, m. hook, hanger, clip, hairpin.
gandul -la, n. idler, tramp, hobo.
ganga, f. bargain.
gangrena, f. gangrene.
gansarón, m. gosling.
ganso, m. goose.
garabato, m. hook; scrawl, scribble.
garaje, m. garage.
garantía, f. guarantee; collateral, security.
garantizar, v. guarantee, secure, pledge.
garbanzo, m. chickpea.
garbo, m. grace.
garboso, a. graceful, sprightly.
gardenia, f. gardenia.
garfa, f. claw, talon.
garganta, f. throat.
gárgara, f. gargle. —**gargarizar**, v.
garita, f. sentry box.
garito, m. gambling house.
garlopa, f. carpenter's plane.
garra, f. claw.
garrafa, f. decanter, carafe.
garrideza, f. elegance, handsomeness.

For pronunciation, see the concise guide on pages 3 to 4.

garrido, *a.* elegant, handsome.
garrote, *m.* club, cudgel.
garrotillo, *m.* croup.
garrudo, *a.* powerful, brawny.
garza, *f.* heron.
gas, *m.* gas.
gasa, *f.* gauze.
gaseosa, *f.* carbonated water.
gaseoso, *a.* gaseous.
gasolina, *f.* gasoline.
gastar, *v.* spend; use up, wear out; waste.
gasto, *m.* expense, expenditure; waste.
gastritis, *f.* gastritis.
gastrómano, *m.* glutton.
gastrónomo -ma, *n.* gourmet, epicure.
gatear, *v.* creep.
gatillo, *m.* trigger.
gato -ta, *n.* cat.
gaucho, *m.* Argentine cowboy.
gaveta, *f.* drawer.
gavilla, *f.* sheaf.
gaviota, *f.* sea gull.
gayo, *a.* merry, gay.
gazapera, *f.* rabbit warren.
gazapo, *m.* rabbit.
gazmonado, *f.* prudishness.
gazmoño, *m.* prude.
gaznate, *m.* windpipe.
gelatina, *f.* gelatine.
gemelo -la, *n.* twin.
gemelos, *m.pl.* cuff links; opera glasses.
gemido, *m.* moan, groan, wail. —**gemir,** *v.*
genciana, *f.* gentian.
genealogía, *f.* genealogy, pedigree.
generación, *f.* generation.
generador, *m.* generator.
general, *a. & m.* general.
generalidad, *f.* generality.
generalización, *f.* generalization.
generalizar, *v.* generalize.
generalmente, *adv.* generally.
género, *m.* gender; kind; (pl.) goods, material.
generosidad, *f.* generosity.
generoso, *a.* generous.
génesis, *m.* genesis.
genial, *a.* genial; brilliant.

genio, *m.* genius; temper; disposition.
genitivo, *m.* genitive.
gente, *f.* people, folk.
gentil, *a.* gracious; graceful.
gentileza, *f.* grace, graciousness.
gentío, *m.* mob, crowd.
genuino, *a.* genuine.
geografía, *f.* geography.
geográfico, *a.* geographical.
geométrico, *a.* geometric.
geranio, *m.* geranium.
gerencia, *f.* management.
gerente, *m.* manager, director.
germen, *m.* germ.
germinar, *v.* germinate.
gerundio, *m.* gerund.
gesticulación, *f.* gesticulation.
gesticular, *v.* gesticulate, gesture.
gestión, *f.* conduct; effort.
gesto, *m.* gesture, facial expression.
gigante, *a. & m.* gigantic, giant.
gigantesco, *a.* gigantic, huge.
gimnasio, *m.* gymnasium.
gimnástica, *f.* gymnastics.
gimotear, *v.* whine.
ginebra, *f.* gin.
girado, *m.* (com.) drawee.
girador, *m.* (com.) drawer.
girar, *v.* revolve, turn, spin, whirl.
giratorio, *a.* rotary, revolving.
giro, *m.* whirl, turn, spin; (com.) draft. **g. postal,** money order.
gitano -na, *a. & n.* Gypsy.
glacial, *a.* glacial, icy.
gladiador, *m.* gladiator.
glándula, *f.* gland.
glasé, *m.* glacé.
glicerina, *f.* glycerine.
globo, *m.* globe; balloon.
gloria, *f.* glory.
glorieta, *f.* bower.
glorificación, *f.* glorification.
glorificar, *v.* glorify.
glorioso, *a.* glorious.
glosa, *f.* gloss. —**glosar,** *v.*
glosario, *m.* glossary.

For pronunciation, see the concise guide on pages 3 to 4

glotón -ona, *a. & n.* gluttonous; glutton.

glutin, *m.* gluten; glue.

gobernación, *f.* government.

gobernador, *m.* governor.

gobernalle, *m.* rudder, tiller, helm.

gobernante, *m.* ruler.

gobernar, *v.* govern.

gobierno, *m.* government.

goce, *m.* enjoyment.

gola, *f.* throat.

golfo, *m.* gulf.

golondrina, *f.* swallow.

golosina, *f.* delicacy.

golpe, *m.* blow, stroke. **de g.,** suddenly.

golpear, *v.* strike, beat, pound.

gollete, *m.* upper portion of one's throat.

goma, *f.* rubber; gum; glue; eraser.

gonce, *m.* hinge.

góndola, *f.* gondola.

gordo, *a.* fat.

gordura, *f.* fatness.

gorila, *m.* gorilla.

gorja, *f.* gorge.

gorjeo, *m.* warble, chirp. —**gorjear,** *v.*

gorrión, *m.* sparrow.

gorro, *m.* cap.

gota, *f.* drop (of liquid).

gotear, *v.* drip, leak.

goteo, *m.* leak.

gotera, *f.* leak; gutter.

gótico, *a.* Gothic.

gozar, *v.* enjoy.

gozne, *m.* hinge.

gozo, *m.* enjoyment, delight, joy.

gozoso, *a.* joyful, joyous.

grabado, *m.* engraving, cut, print.

grabador, *m.* engraver.

grabar, *v.* engrave; record.

gracia, *f.* grace; wit, charm. **hacer g.,** to amuse, strike as funny. **tener g.,** to be funny, to be witty.

gracias, *f.pl.* thanks, thank you.

gracioso, *a.* witty, funny.

grada, *f.* step.

gradación, *f.* gradation.

grado, *m.* grade; rank; degree.

graduado -da, *n.* graduate.

gradual, *a.* gradual.

graduar, *v.* grade, graduate.

gráfico, *a.* graphic, vivid.

grafito, *m.* graphite.

grajo, *m.* jackdaw.

gramática, *f.* grammar.

gramo, *m.* gram.

gran, grande, *a.* big, large; great.

granada, *f.* grenade; pomegranate.

granar, *v.* seed.

grandeza, *f.* greatness.

grandiosidad, *f.* grandeur.

grandioso, *a.* grand, magnificent.

grandor, *m.* size.

granero, *m.* barn; granary.

granito, *m.* granite.

granizada, *f.* hailstorm.

granizo, *m.* hail. —**granizar,** *v.*

granja, *f.* grange; farm; farmhouse.

granjear, *v.* earn, gain; get.

granjero, *m.* farmer.

grano, *m.* grain; kernel.

granuja, *m.* waif, urchin.

grapa, *f.* clamp, clip.

grasa, *f.* grease, fat.

grasiento, *a.* greasy.

gratificación, *f.* gratification; reward; tip.

gratificar, *v.* gratify; reward; tip.

gratis, *adv.* gratis, free.

gratitud, *f.* gratitude.

grato, *a.* grateful; pleasant.

gratuito, *a.* gratuitous.

gravamen, *m.* tax; burden; obligation.

grave, *a.* grave, serious, severe.

gravedad, *f.* gravity; seriousness.

gravitación, *f.* gravitation.

gravitar, *v.* gravitate.

gravoso, *a.* burdensome.

graznido, *m.* croak. —**graznar,** *v.*

Grecia, *f.* Greece.

greco, *a. & n.* Greek.

greda, *f.* clay.

gresca, f. revelry; quarrel.

griego -ga, a. & n. Greek.

grieta, f. opening; crevice, crack.

grifo, m. faucet.

grillo, m. cricket.

grima, f. fright.

gringo -ga, n. foreigner (usually North American).

gripa, gripe, f. grippe.

gris, a. gray.

grito, m. shout, scream, cry. **—gritar,** v.

grosella, f. currant.

grosería, f. grossness; coarseness.

grosero, a. coarse, vulgar, discourteous.

grotesco, a. grotesque.

grúa, f. crane.

gruesa, f. gross.

grueso, 1. a. bulky; stout; coarse, thick. **2.** m. bulk.

grulla, f. crane.

gruñido, m. growl, snarl, mutter. **—gruñir,** v.

grupo, m. group, party.

gruta, f. cavern.

guadaña, f. scythe. **—guadañar,** v.

guagua, f. (S.A.) baby; (Carib.) bus.

gualdo, a. yellow, golden.

guano, m. guano (fertilizer).

guante, m. glove.

guapo, a. handsome.

guarda, m. or f. guard.

guardabarros, m. fender.

guardacostas, m. revenue ship.

guardar, v. keep, store, put away; guard.

guardarropa, f. coat room.

guardarse de, v. beware of, avoid.

guardia, 1. f. guard; watch. **2.** m. policeman.

guardián, m. guardian, keeper, watchman.

guardilla, f. attic.

guarida, f. den.

guarismo, m. number, figure.

guarnecer, v. adorn.

guarnición, f. garrison; trimming.

guasa, f. joke, jest.

guayaba, f. guava.

gubernativo, a. governmental.

guerra, f. war.

guerrero, m. warrior.

guía, 1. m. & f. guide. **2.** f. guidebook, directory.

guiar, v. guide; steer, drive.

guija, f. pebble.

guillotina, f. guillotine.

guindar, v. hang.

guinga, f. gingham.

guiñada, f., **guiño,** m. wink. **—guiñar,** v.

guión, m. dash, hyphen.

guirnalda, f. garland, wreath.

guisa, f. guise, manner.

guisado, m. stew.

guisante, m. pea.

guisar, v. cook.

guita, f. twine.

guitarra, f. guitar.

guitarrista, n. guitarist.

gula, f. gluttony.

gusano, m. worm, caterpillar.

gustar, v. please; taste.

gusto, m. pleasure; taste; liking.

gustoso, a. pleasant; tasteful.

gutural, a. guttural.

H

haba, f. bean.

habanera, f. Cuban dance melody.

haber, v. have. **h. de,** be to, be supposed to.

haberes, m.pl. property; worldly goods.

habichuela, f. bean.

hábil, a. skillful; capable; clever.

For pronunciation, see the concise guide on pages 3 & 4.

habilidad, *f.* ability; skill; talent.
habilidoso, *a.* able, skillful, talented.
habilitado, *m.* paymaster.
habilitar, *v.* qualify; supply, equip.
habilmente, *adv.* ably.
habitación, *f.* dwelling; room.
habitante, *m. & f.* inhabitant.
habitar, *v.* inhabit; dwell.
hábito, *m.* habit; custom.
habitual, *a.* habitual.
habituar, *v.* accustom, habituate.
habla, *f.* speech.
hablador, *a.* talkative.
hablar, *v.* talk, speak.
haca, *f.* pony.
hacedor, *m.* maker.
hacendado, *m.* hacienda owner; farmer.
hacendoso, *a.* industrious.
hacer, *v.* do; make. **hace dos años,** etc., two years ago, etc.
hacerse, *v.* become, get to be.
hacia, *prep.* toward.
hacienda, *f.* property; estate; ranch; farm; (govt.) treasury.
hacha, *f.* ax, hatchet.
hada, *f.* fairy.
hado, *m.* fate.
halagar, *v.* flatter.
halar, *v.* haul, pull.
halcón, *m.* hawk, falcon.
haleche, *m.* anchovy.
hallado, *a.* found. **bien h.,** welcome. **mal h.,** uneasy.
hallar, *v.* find, locate.
hallarse, *v.* be, be located; happen to be.
hallazgo, *m.* find, thing found.
hamaca, *f.* hammock.
hambre, *f.* hunger. **tener h., estar con h.,** to be hungry.
hambrear, *v.* hunger; starve.
hambriento, *a.* starving, hungry.
haragán, *m.* idler, lazy person.

haraganear, *v.* loiter.
harapo, *m.* rag, tatter.
haraposo, *a.* ragged, shabby.
harem, *m.* harem.
harina, *f.* flour, meal.
harnero, *m.* sieve.
hartar, *v.* satiate.
harto, *a.* stuffed; fed up.
hartura, *f.* superabundance, glut.
hasta, 1. *prep.* until, till; as far as, up to. **h. luego,** good-bye, so long. **2.** *adv.* even.
hastío, *m.* distaste, loathing.
hato, *m.* herd.
hay, *v.* there is, there are. **h. que,** it is necessary to. **no h. de qué,** you're welcome, don't mention it.
haya, *f.* beech tree.
haz, *f.* bundle, sheaf; face.
hazaña, *f.* deed; exploit, feat.
hebdomadario, *a.* weekly.
hebilla, *f.* buckle.
hebra, *f.* thread, string.
hebreo -rea, *a. & n.* Hebrew.
hechicero -ra, *n.* wizard, witch.
hechizar, *v.* bewitch.
hechizo, *m.* spell.
hecho, *m.* fact; act; deed.
hechura, *f.* workmanship, make.
hediondez, *f.* stench.
helada, *f.* frost.
helado, *m.* ice cream.
helar, *v.* freeze.
helecho, *m.* fern.
hélice, *f.* propeller.
helicóptero, *m.* helicopter.
helio, *m.* helium.
hembra, *f.* female.
hemisferio, *m.* hemisphere.
hemoglobina, *f.* hemoglobin.
henchir, *v.* stuff.
hendedura, *f.* crevice, crack.
heno, *m.* hay.
hepática, *f.* liverwort.
heraldo, *m.* herald.
herbáceo, *a.* herbaceous.
herbívoro, *a.* herbivorous.
heredar, *v.* inherit.
heredero -ra, *n.* heir; successor.
hereditario, *a.* hereditary.

hereje, *m. & f.* heretic.
herejía, *f.* heresy.
herencia, *f.* inheritance; heritage.
herético, *a.* heretical.
herida, *f.* wound, injury
herir, *v.* wound, injure.
hermafrodita. *a. & m.* hermaphrodite.
hermana, *f.* sister.
hermano, *m.* brother.
hermético, *a.* airtight.
hermoso, *a.* beautiful, handsome.
hermosura, *f.* beauty.
hernia, *f.* hernia, rupture.
héroe, *m.* hero.
heroico, *a.* heroic.
heroína, *f.* heroine.
heroísmo, *m.* heroism.
herradura, *f.* horseshoe.
herramienta, *f.* tool; implement.
herrería, *f.* blacksmith's shop.
herrero, *m.* blacksmith.
herrumbre, *f.* rust.
hervir, *v.* boil.
hesitación, *f.* hesitation.
heterogéneo, *a.* heterogeneous.
hexágono, *m.* hexagon.
hez, *f.* dregs, sediment.
híbrido, *n. & a* hybrid.
hidalgo -ga, *n.* noble.
hidalguía, *f.* nobility; generosity.
hidráulico, *a.* hydraulic.
hidrofobia, *f.* rabies.
hidrógeno, *m.* hydrogen.
hidropesía, *f.* dropsy.
hiedra, *f.* ivy.
hiel, *f.* gall.
hielo, *m.* ice.
hiena, *f.* hyena.
hierba, *f.* grass; herb.
hierbabuena, *f.* mint.
hierro, *m.* iron.
hígado, *m.* liver.
higiene, *f.* hygiene.
higiénico, *a.* sanitary, hygienic.
higo, *m.* fig.
higuera, *f.* fig tree.
hija, *f.* daughter.
hijastro, *m.* stepchild.

hijo, *m.* son.
hila, *f.* line.
hilandero, *m.* spinner.
hilar, *v.* spin.
hilera, *f.* row, line, tier.
hilo, *m.* thread; string; wire; linen.
himno, *m.* hymn.
hincar, *v.* drive, thrust, sink.
hincarse, *v.* kneel down.
hinchar, *v.* swell.
hindú, *n. & a.* Hindu.
hinojo, *m.* knee.
hipnótico, *a.* hypnotic.
hipnotismo, *m.* hypnotism
hipnotizar, *v.* hypnotize.
hipo, *m.* hiccough.
hipocresía, *f.* hypocrisy.
hipócrita, *a. & n.* hypocritical; hypocrite.
hipódromo, *m.* race track.
hipoteca, *f.* mortgage. --**hipotecar,** *v.*
hipótesis, *f.* hypothesis.
hirsuto, *a.* hairy, hirsute.
Hispanoamérica, *f.* Spanish America.
hispanoamericano -na, *a. & n.* Spanish American.
histeria, *f.* hysteria.
histérico, *a.* hysterical.
historia, *f.* history; story.
historiador, *m.* historian.
histórico, *a.* historic, historical.
histrión, *m.* actor.
hocico, *m.* snout, muzzle.
hogar, *m.* hearth; home.
hoguera, *f.* bonfire, blaze.
hoja, *f.* leaf; sheet (of paper); pane; blade.
hojalata, *f.* tin.
hojalatero, *m.* tinsmith.
hojear, *v.* scan, skim through.
hola, *interj.* hello.
Holanda, *f.* Holland, Netherlands.
holandés -esa, *a. & n.* Dutch; Hollander.
holganza, *f.* leisure; diversion.
holgazán, 1. *a.* idle, lazy.
 2. *m.* idler, loiterer, tramp.
holgazanear, *v.* idle, loiter.
hollín, *m.* soot.
hombre, *m.* man.

For pronunciation, see the concise guide on pages 3 to 4.

hombría, f. manliness.

hombro, m. shoulder.

homenaje, m. homage.

homeópata, m. homeopath.

homicidio, m. homicide.

homilía, f. homily.

honda, f. sling.

hondo, a. deep.

hondonada, f. ravine.

hondura, f. depth.

honestidad, f. modesty, unpretentiousness.

honesto, a. honest; pure; just.

hongo, m. fungus; mushroom.

honor, m. honor.

honorable, a. honorable.

honorario, 1. a. honorary. **2.** m. honorarium, fee.

honorífico, a. honorary.

honra, f. honor. **—honrar,** v.

honradez, f. honesty.

honrado, a. honest, honorable.

hora, f. hour, time (of day).

horadar, v. perforate.

horario, m. timetable, schedule.

horca, f. gallows; pitchfork.

horda, f. horde.

horizontal, a. horizontal.

horizonte, m. horizon.

hormiga, f. ant.

hormiguear, v. itch.

hormiguero, m. ant hill.

hornero -ra, n. baker.

hornillo, m. stove.

horno, m. oven; kiln.

horóscopo, m. horoscope.

horrendo, a. dreadful, horrendous.

horrible, a. horrible, hideous, awful.

horrido, a. horrid.

horror, m. horror.

horrorizar, v. horrify.

horroroso, a. horrible, frightful.

hortelano, m. horticulturist.

hospedaje, m. lodging.

hospedar, v. give or take lodgings.

hospital, m. hospital.

hospitalario, a. hospitable.

hospitalidad, f. hospitality.

hospitalmente, adv. hospitably.

hostia, f. host.

hostil, a. hostile.

hostilidad, f. hostility.

hotel, m. hotel.

hoy, adv. today. **h. día,** **h. en día,** nowadays.

hoya, f. dale, valley.

hoyo, m. pit, hole.

hoyuelo, m. dimple.

hoz, f. sickle.

hucha, f. chest, money box; savings.

hueco, 1. a. hollow, empty. **2.** m. hole, hollow.

huelga, f. strike.

huella, f. track, trace; footprint.

huérfano -na, a. & n. orphan.

huero, a. empty.

huerta, f. (vegetable) garden.

huerto, m. orchard.

hueso, m. bone; fruit pit.

huésped, m. & f. guest.

huesudo, a. bony.

huevo, m. egg.

huída, f. flight, escape.

huir, v. flee.

hule, m. oilcloth.

humanidad, f. humanity, mankind; humaneness.

humanista, m. humanist.

humanitario, a. humane.

humano, a. human; humane.

humareda, f. dense cloud of smoke.

humedad, f. humidity, moisture, dampness.

humedecer, v. moisten, dampen.

húmedo, a. humid, moist, damp.

humildad, f. humility, meekness.

humilde, a. humble, meek.

humillación, f. humiliation.

humillar, v. humiliate.

humo, m. smoke; (pl.) airs, affectation.

humor, m. humor, mood.

humorista, m. humorist.

hundimiento, m. collapse.

hundir, v. sink; collapse.

For pronunciation, see the concise guide on pages 3 to 4.

húngaro -ra, *a. & n.* Hungarian.
Hungría, *f.* Hungary.
huracán, *m.* hurricane.
huraño, *a.* shy, bashful.
hurgar, *v.* stir.
hurón, *m.* ferret.
hurraca, *f.* magpie.

hurtadillas, *f.pl.* **a h.**, on the sly.
hurtador, *m.* thief.
hurtar, *v.* steal, rob of; hide.
hurtarse, *v.* hide; withdraw.
husmear, *v.* scent, smell.
huso, *m.* spindle; bobbin.

I

ibérico, *a.* Iberian.
iberoamericano -na, *a. & n.* Latin American.
ida, *f.* departure; trip out. **i. y vuelta**, round trip.
idea, *f.* idea.
ideal, *a. & m.* ideal.
idealismo, *m.* idealism.
idealista, *m. & f.* idealist.
idear, *v.* plan, conceive.
idéntico, *a.* identical.
identidad, *f.* identity; identification.
identificar, *v.* identify.
idilio, *m.* idyll.
idioma, *m.* language.
idiota, *a. & n.* idiotic; idiot.
idiotismo, *m.* idiom; idiocy.
idolatrar, *v.* idolize, adore.
ídolo, *m.* idol.
idóneo, *a.* suitable, fit, apt.
iglesia, *f.* church.
ignición, *f.* ignition.
ignominia, *f.* ignominy, shame.
ignominioso, *a.* ignominious, shameful.
ignorancia, *f.* ignorance.
ignorante, *a.* ignorant.
ignorar, *v.* be ignorant of, not know.
ignoto, *a.* unknown.
igual, **1.** *a.* equal; the same; (pl.) alike. **2.** *m.* equal.
igualar, *v.* equal; equalize; match.
igualdad, *f.* equality.
ijada, *f.* flank (of an animal).

ilegal, *a.* illegal.
ilegítimo, *a.* illegitimate.
ileso, *a.* unharmed.
ilícito, *a.* illicit, unlawful.
iluminación, *f.* illumination.
iluminar, *v.* illuminate.
ilusión, *f.* illusion.
ilusorio, *a.* illusive.
ilustración, *f.* illustration; learning.
ilustrador, *m.* illustrator.
ilustrar, *v.* illustrate.
ilustre, *a.* illustrious, honorable, distinguished.
imagen, *f.* image.
imaginación, *f.* imagination.
imaginar, *v.* imagine.
imaginario, *a.* imaginary.
imaginativo, *a.* imaginative.
imán, *m.* magnet.
imbécil, *a. & n.* imbecile; stupid, foolish; fool.
imbuir, *v.* imbue, instil.
imitación, *f.* imitation.
imitador, *m.* imitator.
imitar, *v.* imitate.
impaciencia, *f.* impatience.
impaciente, *a.* impatient.
impar, *a.* unequal, uneven, odd.
imparcial, *a.* impartial.
impasible, *a.* impassive, unmoved.
impávido, *adj.* fearless, intrepid.
impedimento, *m.* impediment, obstacle.

For pronunciation, see the concise guide on pages 3 to 4.

impedir, v. impede, hinder, stop, obstruct.

impeler, v. impel; incite.

impensado, a. unexpected.

imperar, v. reign; prevail.

imperativo, a. imperative.

imperceptible, a. imperceptible.

imperdible, n. safety pin.

imperecedero, a. imperishable.

imperfecto, a. imperfect, faulty.

imperial, a. imperial.

imperialismo, m. imperialism.

impericia, f. inexperience.

imperio, m. empire.

imperioso, a. imperious. domineering.

impermeable, 1. a. waterproof. **2.** m. raincoat.

impersonal, a. impersonal.

impertinencia, f. impertinence.

ímpetu, m. impulse; impetus.

impetuoso, a. impetuous.

impiedad, f. impiety.

impío, a. impious.

implacable, a. implacable, unrelenting.

implicar, v. implicate, involve.

implorar, v. implore.

imponente, a. impressive.

imponer, v. impose.

importación, f. import, importing.

importancia, f. importance.

importador, m. importer.

importante, a. important.

importar, v. be important, matter; import.

importe, m. value, amount.

importunar, v. beg, importune.

imposibilidad, f. impossibility.

imposibilitado, a. helpless.

imposible, a. impossible.

imposición, f. imposition.

impostor, m. imposter, faker.

impotencia, f. impotence.

impotente, a. impotent.

impreciso, adj. inexact.

imprecar, v. curse.

impregnar, v. impregnate.

imprenta, f. press; printing house.

imprescindible, a. essential.

impresión, f. impression.

impresionable, a. emotional.

impresionar, v. impress.

impresor, m. printer.

imprevisión, f. oversight, thoughtlessness.

imprevisto, a. unexpected, unforeseen.

imprimir, v. print; imprint.

improbable, a. improbable.

improbo, a. dishonest.

improductivo, a. unproductive.

improperio, m. insult.

impropio, a. improper.

improvisación, f. improvisation.

improvisar, v. improvise.

improviso, a. unforeseen.

imprudencia, f. imprudence.

imprudente, a. imprudent, reckless.

impuesto, m. tax.

impulsar, v. prompt, impel.

impulsivo, a. impulsive.

impulso, m. impulse.

impureza, f. impurity.

impuro, a. impure.

imputación, f. imputation.

imputar, v. impute, attribute.

inaccesible, a. inaccessible.

inacción, f. inaction; inactivity.

inaceptable, a. unacceptable.

inactivo, a. inactive; sluggish.

inadecuado, a. inadequate.

inadvertencia, f. oversight.

inadvertido, a. inadvertent, careless; unnoticed.

inagotable, a. inexhaustible.

inalterado, a. unchanged.

inanición, f. starvation.

inanimado, adj. inanimate.

inapetencia, f. lack of appetite.

inaplicable, a. inapplicable; unfit.

inaudito, a. unheard of.

inauguración, f. inauguration.

inaugurar, v. inaugurate, open.

incandescente, a. incandescent.

incansable, a. tireless.

incapacidad, f. incapacity.

incapacitar, v. incapacitate.

incapaz, a. incapable.

incauto, a. unwary.

incendiar, v. set on fire.

incendio, m. fire, conflagration.

incertidumbre, f. uncertainty, suspense.

incesante, a. continual, incessant.

incidente, m. incident, event.

incienso, m. incense.

incierto, a. uncertain, doubtful.

incisión, f. incision, cut.

incitamiento, m. incitement, motivation.

incitar, v. incite, instigate.

incivil, a. impolite, rude.

inclemencia, f. inclemency.

inclemente, a. inclement, merciless.

inclinación, f. inclination, bent; slope.

inclinar, v. incline; influence.

inclinarse, v. slope; lean, bend over; bow.

incluir, v. include; enclose.

inclusivo, a. inclusive.

incluso, prep. including.

incógnito, a. unknown.

incoherente, a. incoherent.

incombustible, a. fireproof.

incomodar, v. disturb, bother, inconvenience.

incomodidad, f. inconvenience.

incómodo, m. uncomfortable; cumbersome; inconvenient.

incomparable, a. incomparable.

incompatible, a. incompatible.

incompetencia, f. incompetence.

incompetente, a. incompetent.

incompleto, a. incomplete.

incondicional, a. unconditional.

inconexo, a. incoherent; unconnected.

incongruente, a. not suitable.

inconsciencia, f. unconsciousness.

inconsciente, a. unconscious.

inconsecuencia, f. inconsistency.

inconsecuente, a. inconsistent.

inconsiderado, a. inconsiderate.

inconstancia, f. changeableness.

inconstante, a. changeable.

inconveniencia, f. unsuitability.

inconveniente, 1. a. unsuitable. **2.** m. disadvantage; objection.

incorporar, v. incorporate, embody.

incorporarse, v. sit up.

incorrecto, a. incorrect, wrong.

incredulidad, f. incredulity.

incrédulo, a. incredulous.

increíble, a. incredible.

incremento, m. increase.

incubar, v. hatch.

inculto, a. uncultivated.

incurable, a. incurable.

incurrir, v. incur.

indagación, f. investigation, inquiry.

indagador, m. investigator.

indagar, v. investigate, inquire into.

indebido, a. undue.

indecencia, f. indecency.

indecente, a. indecent.

indeciso, a. undecided.

indefenso, a. defenseless.

indefinido, a. indefinite.

indeleble, a. indelible.

indemnizar, v. indemnify.

independencia, f. independence.

independiente, a. independent.

India, f. India.

indicación, f. indication.

indicar, v. indicate, point out.

indicativo, a. & m. indicative.

índice, m. index; forefinger.

indicio, m. hint, clue.

indiferencia, f. indifference.

indiferente, a. indifferent.

indígena, a. & n. native.

indigente, a. indigent, poor.

indignación, f. indignation.

indignado, a. indignant, incensed.

indignar, v. incense.

indigno, a. unworthy.

indio -dia, a. & n. Indian.

indirecto, a. indirect.

indiscreción, f. indiscretion.

indiscreto, a. indiscreet.

indiscutible, a. unquestionable.

indispensable, a. indispensable.

indisposición, f. indisposition, ailment; reluctance.

indistinto, a. indistinct, unclear.

individual, a. individual.

individualidad, f. individuality.

individuo, a. & m. individual.

indócil, a. headstrong, unruly.

índole, f. nature, character, disposition.

indolencia, f. indolence.

indolente, a. indolent.

indómito, a. untamed, wild; unruly.

inducir, v. induce, persuade.

indudable, a. certain, indubitable.

indulgencia, f. indulgence.

indulgente, a. indulgent.

indultar, v. free; pardon.

industria, f. industry.

industrial, a. industrial.

industrioso, a. industrious.

inédito, a. unpublished.

ineficaz, a. inefficient.

inepto, a. incompetent.

inequívoco, a. unmistakable.

inercia, f. inertia.

inerte, a. inert.

inesperado, a. unexpected.

inestable, a. unstable.

inevitable, a. inevitable.

inexacto, a. inexact.

inexperto, a. unskilled.

inexplicable, a. inexplicable. unexplainable.

infalible, a. infallible.

infame, a. infamous, bad.

infamia, f. infamy.

infancia, f. infancy; childhood.

infante, m. infant.

infantería, f. infantry.

infantil, a. infantile, childish.

infatigable, a. untiring.

infausto, a. unlucky.

infección, f. infection.

infeccioso, a. infectious.

infectar, v. infect.

infeliz, a. unhappy, miserable.

inferior, a. inferior; lower.

inferir, v. infer; inflict.

infernal, a. infernal.

infestar, v. infest.

infiel, a. unfaithful.

infierno, m. hell.

infiltrar, v. infiltrate.

infinidad, f. infinity.

infinito, a. infinite.

inflamación, f. inflammation.

inflamar, v. inflame, set on fire.

inflar, v. inflate, pump up, puff up.

inflexible, a. inflexible, rigid.

inflexión, f. inflection.

infligir, v. inflict.

influencia, f. influence.

influenza, f. influenza, flu.

influir, v. influence, sway.

influyente, a. influential.

información, f. information.

informal, a. informal.

informar, v. inform; report.

informe, m. report; (pl.) information, data.

infortunio, m. misfortune.

infracción, f. violation.

infrascrito, m. signer, undersigned.

infringir, v. infringe, violate.

infructuoso, a. fruitless.

infundir, v. instil, inspire with.

For pronunciation, see the concise guide on pages 3 to 4.

ingeniería, f. engineering.

ingeniero, m. engineer.

ingenio, m. wit; talent.

ingeniosidad, f. ingenuity.

ingenioso, a. witty, ingenious.

ingenuidad, f. candor; naïveté.

ingenuo, a. ingenuous, naïve, candid.

Inglaterra, f. England.

ingle, f. groin.

inglés -esa, a. & n. English; Englishman.

ingratitud, f. ingratitude.

ingrato, a. ungrateful.

ingrediente, m. ingredient.

ingresar en, v. enter; join.

ingreso, m. entrance; (pl.) earnings, income.

inhábil, a. unskilled, incapable.

inhabilitar, v. disqualify.

inherente, a. inherent.

inhibir, v. inhibit.

inhumano, a. cruel, inhuman.

iniciador, m. initiator.

inicial, a. initial.

iniciar, v. initiate, begin.

iniciativa, f. initiative.

inicuo, a. wicked.

iniquidad, f. iniquity; sin.

injuria, f. insult. —injuriar, v.

injusticia, f. injustice.

injusto, a. unjust, unfair.

inmaculado, a. immaculate; pure.

inmediato, a. immediate.

inmensidad, f. immensity.

inmenso, a. immense.

inmersión, f. immersion.

inmigración, f. immigration.

inmigrante, a. & n. immigrant.

inmigrar, v. immigrate.

inminente, a. imminent.

inmoderado, a. immoderate.

inmodesto, a. immodest.

inmoral, a. immoral.

inmoralidad, f. immorality.

inmortal, a. immortal.

inmortalidad, f. immortality.

inmóvil, a. immobile, motionless.

inmundicia, f. dirt, filth.

inmune, a. immune.

inmunidad, f. immunity.

innato, a. innate, inborn.

innecesario, a. unnecessary, needless.

innoble, a. ignoble.

innocuo, a. innocuous.

innovación, f. innovation.

innumerable, a. innumerable, countless.

inocencia, f. innocence.

inocente, a. innocent.

inocular, v. inoculate.

inodoro, m. toilet.

inofensivo, a. inoffensive, harmless.

inolvidable, a. unforgettable.

inoportuno, a. inopportune.

inquietar, v. disturb, worry, trouble.

inquieto, a. anxious, uneasy, worried; restless.

inquietud, f. concern, anxiety, worry; restlessness.

inquilino -na, n. occupant, tenant.

inquirir, v. inquire into, investigate.

inquisición, f. inquisition, investigation.

insaciable, a. insatiable.

insalubre, a. unhealthy.

insano, a. insane.

inscribir, v. inscribe; record.

inscribirse, v. register, enroll.

inscripción, f. inscription; registration.

insecto, m. insect.

inseguro, a. unsure, uncertain; insecure, unsafe.

insensato, a. stupid, senseless.

insensible, a. unfeeling, heartless.

inseparable, a. inseparable.

inserción, f. insertion.

insertar, v. insert.

insidioso, a. insidious, crafty.

insigne, a. famous, noted.

insignia, f. insignia, badge.

insignificante, a. insignificant, negligible.

insincero, *a.* insincere.
insinuación, *f.* insinuation; hint.
insinuar, *v.* insinuate, suggest, hint.
insipidez, *f.* insipidity.
insípido, *a.* insipid.
insistencia, *f.* insistence.
insistente, *a.* insistent.
insistir, *v.* insist.
insolación, *f.* sunstroke.
insolencia, *f.* insolence.
insolente, *a.* insolent.
insólito, *a.* unusual.
insolvente, *a.* insolvent.
insomnio, *m.* insomnia.
insoportable, *a.* unbearable.
inspección, *f.* inspection.
inspeccionar, *v.* inspect, examine.
inspector, *m.* inspector.
inspiración, *f.* inspiration
inspirar, *v.* inspire
instalación, *f.* installation, fixture.
instalar, *v.* install, set up.
instantánea, *f.* snapshot.
instantáneo, *a.* instantaneous.
instante, *a. & m.* instant.
al i., at once.
instar, *v.* coax, urge.
instigar, *v.* instigate, urge.
instintivo, *a.* instinctive.
instinto, *m.* instinct.
institución, *f.* institution.
instituir, *v.*
instituto, *m.* institute.
institutriz, *f.* governess.
instrucción, *f.* instruction; education.
instructivo, *a.* instructive.
instructor, *m.* instructor.
instruir, *v.* instruct, teach.
instrumento, *m.* instrument.
insuficiente, *a.* insufficient.
insufrible, *a.* intolerable.
insular, *a.* island, insular.
insulto, *m.* insult. **—insultar,** *v.*
insuperable, *a.* insuperable.
insurgente, *n. & a.* insurgent, rebel.
insurrección, *f.* insurrection, revolt.

insurrecto, *a. & m.* insurgent.
intacto, *a.* intact.
integral, *a.* integral.
integridad, *f.* integrity; entirety.
íntegro, *a.* entire; upright.
intelecto, *m.* intellect.
intelectual, *a. & n.* intellectual.
inteligencia, *f.* intelligence.
inteligente, *a.* intelligent.
inteligible, *a.* intelligible.
intemperie, *f.* bad weather.
intención, *f.* intention.
intendente, *m.* manager.
intensidad, *f.* intensity.
intensificar, *v.* intensify.
intensivo, *a.* intensive.
intenso, *a.* intense.
intentar, *v.* attempt, try.
intento, *m.* intent.
interceptar, *v.* intercept.
intercesión, *f.* intercession.
interés, *m.* interest; concern; appeal.
interesante, *a.* interesting.
interesar, *v.* interest, appeal to.
interferencia, *f.* interference.
interino, *a.* temporary.
interior, **1.** *a.* interior, inner; **2.** *m.* interior.
interjección, *f.* interjection.
intermedio, **1.** *a.* intermediate. **2.** *m.* intermediary; intermission.
interminable, *a.* interminable, endless.
intermisión, *f.* intermission.
intermitente, *a.* intermittent.
internacional, *a.* international.
internarse en, *v.* enter into, go into.
interno, *a.* internal.
interpelar, *v.* ask questions; quiz.
interponer, *v.* interpose.
interpretación, *f.* interpretation.
interpretar, *v.* interpret; construe.
intérprete, *m. & f.* interpreter.

interrogación, f. interrogation.

interrogar, v. question, interrogate.

interrogativo, a. interrogative.

interrumpir, v. interrupt.

interrupción, f. interruption.

intersección, f. intersection.

intervalo, m. interval.

intervención, f. intervention.

intervenir, v. intervene, interfere.

intestino, m. intestine.

intimación, f. intimation, hint.

intimar, v. suggest, hint.

intimidad, f. intimacy.

intimidar, v. intimidate.

íntimo -ma, a. & n. intimate.

intolerable, a. intolerable.

intolerancia, f. intolerance, bigotry.

intolerante, a. intolerant.

intranquilo, a. uneasy.

intravenoso, a. intravenous.

intrepidez, f. daring.

intrépido, a. intrepid.

intriga, f. intrigue, plot, scheme. —intrigar, v.

intrincado, a. intricate, involved.

introducción, f. introduction.

introducir, v. introduce.

intruso -sa, n. intruder.

intuición, f. intuition.

inundación, f. flood. —inundar, v.

inútil, a. useless.

invadir, v. invade.

inválido -da, a. & n. invalid.

invariable, a. constant.

invasión, f. invasion.

invasor, m. invader.

invencible, a. invincible.

invención, f. invention.

inventar, v. invent; devise.

inventario, m. inventory.

inventivo, a. inventive.

invento, m. invention.

inventor, m. inventor.

invernáculo, m. greenhouse.

invernal, a. wintry.

inverosímil, a. improbable, unlikely.

inversión, f. inversion; (com.) investment.

inverso, a. inverse, reverse.

invertir, v. invert; reverse; (com.) invest.

investigación, f. investigation.

investigador, m. investigator.

investigar, v. investigate.

invierno, m. winter.

invisible, a. invisible.

invitación, f. invitation.

invitar, v. invite.

invocar, v. invoke.

involuntario, a. involuntary.

inyección, f. injection.

inyectar, v. inject.

ir, v. go. irse, go away, leave.

ira, f. anger, ire.

iracundo, a. wrathful, irate.

iris, m. iris. arco i., rainbow.

Irlanda, f. Ireland.

irlandés -esa, a. & n. Irish; Irishman.

ironía, f. irony.

irónico, a. ironical.

irracional, a. irrational; insane.

irradiación, f. radiation.

irradiar, v. radiate.

irrazonable, a. unreasonable.

irregular, a. irregular.

irreligioso, a. irreligious.

irremediable, a. irremediable, hopeless.

irresistible, a. irresistible.

irresoluto, a. irresolute, wavering.

irrespectuoso, a. disrespectful.

irreverencia, f. irreverence.

irreverente, adj. irreverent.

irrigación, f. irrigation.

irrigar, v. irrigate.

irritación, f. irritation.

irritar, v. irritate.

irrupción, *f.* raid, attack.

isla, *f.* island.

isleño -ña, *n.* islander.

israelita, *n. & a.* Israelite.

Italia, *f.* Italy.

italiano -na, *a. & n.* Italian.

itinerario, *m.* itinerary; timetable.

izar, *v.* hoist.

izquierda, *f.* left (hand, side).

izquierdista, *n. & a.* leftist.

izquierdo, *a.* left.

J

jabalí, *m.* wild boar.

jabón, *m.* soap.

jabonar, *v.* soap.

jaca, *f.* nag.

jacinto, *m.* hyacinth.

jactancia, *f.* boast. —**jactarse**, *v.*

jactancioso, *a.* boastful.

jadear, *v.* pant, puff.

jaez, *m.* harness; kind.

jalar, *v.* haul, pull.

jalea, *f.* jelly.

jaletina, *f.* gelatin.

jamás, *adv.* never, ever.

jamón, *m.* ham.

Japón, *m.* Japan.

japonés -esa, *a. & n.* Japanese.

jaqueca, *f.* headache.

jarabe, *m.* syrup.

jaranear, *v.* jest; carouse.

jardín, *m.* garden.

jardinero -ra, *n.* gardener.

jarra, *f.* jar; pitcher.

jarro, *m.* jug, pitcher.

jaspe, *m.* jasper.

jaula, *f.* cage; coop.

jauría, *f.* pack of hounds.

jazmín, *m.* jasmine.

jefatura, *f.* headquarters.

jefe, *m.* chief, boss.

Jehová, *m.* Jehovah.

jengibre, *m.* ginger.

jerez, *m.* sherry.

jerga, *f.* slang.

jergón, *m.* straw bed.

jerigonza, *f.* jargon.

jeringa, *f.* syringe.

jeringar, *v.* inject; annoy.

jeroglífico, *m.* hieroglyph.

jesuita, *m.* Jesuit.

Jesús, *m.* Jesus.

jeta, *f.* snout.

jícara, *f.* cup.

jinete, *m.* horseman.

jingoísmo, *m.* jingoism.

jingoísta, *n. & a.* jingoist.

jira, *f.* tour, picnic, outing.

jirafa, *f.* giraffe.

jocundo, *a.* jovial.

jornada, *f.* journey; day's work.

jornal, *m.* day's wage.

jornalero, *m.* day laborer, workman.

joroba, *f.* hump.

jorobado, *a.* humpbacked.

joven, 1. *a.* young. 2. *m. & f.* young person.

jovial, *a.* jovial, jolly.

jovialidad, *f.* joviality.

joya, *f.* jewel, gem.

joyelero, *m.* jewel box.

joyería, *f.* jewelry; jewelry store.

joyero, *m.* jeweler.

juanete, *m.* bunion.

jubilación, *f.* retirement; pension.

jubilar, *v.* retire, pension.

jubileo, *m.* jubilee, public festivity.

júbilo, *m.* glee, rejoicing.

jubiloso, *a.* joyful, gay.

judaico, *a.* Jewish.

judaísmo, *m.* Judaism.

judía, *f.* bean, string bean.

judicial, *a.* judicial.

judío -día, *a. & n.* Jewish; Jew.

juego, *m.* game; play; gambling; set. **j. de damas,** checkers.

juerga, *f.* spree.

jueves, *m.* Thursday.

juez, *m.* judge.

jugador -ra, *n.* player.

jugar, *v.* play; gamble.

juglar, *m.* minstrel.

jugo, *m.* juice.

jugoso, *a.* juicy.

juguete, *m.* toy, plaything.

juguetear, *v.* trifle.

juguetón, *a.* playful.

juicio, *m.* sense, wisdom, judgment.

juicioso, *a.* wise, judicious.

julio, *m.* July.

jumento, *m.* donkey.

junco, *m.* reed, rush.

junio, *m.* June.

junípero, *m.* juniper.

junquillo, *m.* jonquil.

junta, *f.* board, council; joint, coupling.

juntamente, *adv.* jointly.

juntar, *v.* join; connect; assemble.

junto, *a.* together. **j. a,** next to.

juntura, *f.* joint, juncture.

jurado, *m.* jury.

juramento, *m.* oath.

jurar, *v.* swear.

jurisconsulto, *m.* jurist.

jurisdicción, *f.* jurisdiction; territory.

jurisprudencia, *f.* jurisprudence.

justa, *f.* joust. **—justar,** *v.*

justicia, *f.* justice, equity.

justiciero, *a.* just.

justificación, *f.* justification.

justificadamente, *adv.* justifiably.

justificar, *v.* justify, warrant.

justo, *a.* right; exact; just; righteous.

juvenil, *a.* youthful.

juventud, *f.* youth.

juzgado, *m.* court.

juzgar, *v.* judge, estimate.

K, L, LL

káiser, *m.* kaiser.

kepis, *m.* military cap.

kerosena, *f.* kerosene.

kilo, kilogramo, *m.* kilogram.

kilolitro, *m.* kiloliter.

kilómetro, *m.* kilometer.

kiosco, *m.* newsstand; pavilion.

la, 1. *art. & pron.* the; the one. **2.** *pron.* her, it, you; (pl.) them, you.

laberinto, *m.* labyrinth, maze.

labia, *f.* eloquence, fluency.

labio, *m.* lip.

labor, *f.* labor, work.

laborar, *v.* work; till.

laboratorio, *m.* laboratory.

laborioso, *a.* industrious.

labrador, *m.* farmer.

labranza, *f.* farming; farm land.

labrar, *v.* work, till.

labriego -ga, *n.* peasant.

laca, *f.* shellac.

lacio, *a.* withered; limp; straight.

lactar, *v.* nurse, suckle.

lácteo, *a.* milky.

ladear, *v.* tilt, tip; sway.

ladera, *f.* slope.

ladino, *a.* cunning, crafty.

lado, *m.* side. **al l. de,** beside. **de l.,** sideways.

ladra, *f.* barking. **—ladrar,** *v.*

ladrillo, *m.* brisk.

ladrón -ona, *n.* thief, robber.

For pronunciation, see the concise guide on pages 3 to 4

lagarto, *m.* lizard; (Mex.) alligator.

lago, *m.* lake.

lágrima, *f.* tear.

lagrimear, *v.* weep, cry.

laguna, *f.* lagoon; gap.

laico, *a.* lay.

laja, *f.* stone slab.

lamentable, *a.* lamentable.

lamentación, *f.* lamentation.

lamentar, *v.* lament; wail; regret, be sorry.

lamento, *m.* lament, wail.

lamer, *v.* lick; lap.

lámina, *f.* print, illustration

lámpara, *f.* lamp.

lampiño, *a.* beardless.

lana, *f.* wool.

lanar, *a.* woolen.

lance, *m.* throw; episode; quarrel.

lancha, *f.* launch; small boat.

lanchón, *m.* barge.

langosta, *f.* lobster; locust.

languidecer, *v.* languish, pine.

languidez, *f.* languidness.

lánguido, *a.* languid.

lanza, *f.* lance, spear.

lanzada, *f.* thrust, throw.

lanzar, *v.* throw, hurl; launch.

lañar, *v.* cramp; clamp.

lapicero, *m.* mechanical pencil.

lápida, *f.* stone; tombstone.

lápiz, *m.* pencil; crayon.

lapso, *m.* lapse.

lardo, *m.* lard.

largar, *v.* loosen; free.

largo, 1. *a.* long. **a lo l. de,** along. **2.** *m.* length.

largor, *m.* length.

largueza, *f.* generosity; length.

largura, *f.* length.

laringe, *f.* larynx.

larva, *f.* larva.

lascivia, *f.* lasciviousness.

lascivo, *a.* lascivious.

laso, *a.* weary.

lástima, *f.* pity. **ser l.,** to be a pity, to be too bad.

lastimar, *v.* hurt, injure.

lastimoso, *a.* pitiful.

lastre, *m.* ballast. **—lastrar,** *v.*

lata, *f.* tin can; tin (plate); (coll.) annoyance, bore.

latente, *a.* latent.

lateral, *a.* lateral, side.

latigazo, *m.* lash, whipping.

látigo, *m.* whip.

latín, *m.* Latin (language).

latino, *a.* Latin.

latir, *v.* beat, pulsate.

latitud, *f.* latitude.

latón, *m.* brass.

laúd, *m.* lute.

laudable, *a.* laudable.

láudano, *m.* laudanum.

laurel, *m.* laurel.

lava, *f.* lava.

lavabo, lavamanos, *m.* washroom, lavatory.

lavandera, *f.* washerwoman, laundress.

lavandería, *f.* laundry.

lavar, *v.* wash.

lavatorio, *m.* lavatory.

laya, *f.* spade. **—layar,** *v.*

lazar, *v.* lasso.

lazareto, *m.* hospital; quarantine.

lazo, *m.* tie, knot; bow; loop.

le, *pron.* him, her, you; (pl.) them, you

leal, *a.* loyal.

lealtad, *f.* loyalty, allegiance.

lebrel, *m.* greyhound.

lección, *f.* lesson.

lecito, *m.* yolk.

lector -ra, *n.* reader.

lectura, *f.* reading.

leche, *f.* milk.

lechería, *f.* dairy.

lechero, *m.* milkman.

lecho, *m.* bed, couch.

lechón, *m.* pig.

lechoso, *a.* milky.

lechuga, *f.* lettuce.

lechuza, *f.* owl.

leer, *v.* read.

legación, *f.* legation.

legado, *m.* bequest.

legal, *a.* legal, lawful.

legalizar, *v.* legalize.

legar, *v.* bequeath, leave, will.

legible, *a.* legible.

legión, *f.* legion.

legislación, *f.* legislation.

legislador, *m.* legislator.

legislar, *v.* legislate.

legislativo, *a.* legislative.
legislatura, *f.* legislature.
legítimo, *a.* legitimate.
lego, *m.* layman.
legua, *f.* league (measure).
legumbres, *f.pl.* vegetables.
lejano, *a.* distant, far-off.
lejía, *f.* lye.
lejos, *adv.* far. a lo l., in the distance.
lelo, *a.* stupid, foolish.
lema, *m.* theme; slogan.
lengua, *f.* tongue; language.
lenguado, *m.* sole, flounder.
lenguaje, *m.* speech, language.
lenguaraz, *a.* talkative.
lente, *m.* or *f.* lens. *m.pl.* eyeglasses.
lenteja, *f.* lentil.
lentitud, *f.* slowness.
lento, *a.* slow.
leña, *f.* wood, firewood.
león, *m.* lion.
leopardo, *m.* leopard.
lerdo, *a.* dull-witted.
lesión, *f.* wound; damage.
lesionar, *v.* wound; damage.
letanía, *f.* litany.
letárgico, *a.* lethargic.
letargo, *m.* lethargy.
letra, *f.* letter (of alphabet); print; words (of a song).
letrado, 1. *a.* learned. 2. *m.* lawyer.
letrero, *m.* sign, poster.
leva, *f.* (mil.) draft.
levadura, *f.* yeast, leavening, baking powder.
levantador, *m.* lifter; rebel, mutineer.
levantar, *v.* raise, lift.
levantarse, *v.* rise, get up; stand up.
levar, *v.* weigh (anchor).
leve, *a.* slight, light.
levita, *f.* frock coat.
léxico, *m.* lexicon, dictionary.
ley, *f.* law, statute.
leyenda, *f.* legend.
lezna, *f.* awl.
libación, *f.* libation.
libelo, *m.* libel.
libélula, *f.* dragon fly.
liberación, *f.* liberation, release.

liberal, *a.* liberal.
libertad, *f.* liberty, freedom.
libertador, *m.* liberator.
libertar, *v.* free, liberate.
libertinaje, *m.* licentiousness.
libertino, *m.* libertine.
libídine, *f.* licentiousness; lust.
libidinoso, *a.* libidinous; lustful.
libra, *f.* pound.
libranza, *f.* draft, bill of exchange.
librar, *v.* free, rid.
libre, *a.* free, unoccupied.
librería, *f.* bookstore.
librero, *m.* bookseller.
libreta, *f.* notebook; booklet.
libreto, *m.* libretto.
libro, *m.* book.
licencia, *f.* permission, license, leave; furlough.
licenciado -da, *n.* graduate.
licencioso, *a.* licentious.
lícito, *a.* lawful.
licor, *m.* liquor.
lid, *f.* fight. —lidiar, *v.*
líder, *m.* leader.
liebre, *f.* hare.
lienzo, *m.* linen.
liga, *f.* league, confederacy; garter.
ligadura, *f.* ligature.
ligar, *v.* tie, bind, join.
ligero, *a.* light; fast, nimble.
ligustro, *m.* privet.
lija, *f.* sandpaper.
lijar, *v.* sandpaper.
lima, *f.* file; lime.
limbo, *m.* limbo.
limitación, *f.* limitation.
límite, *m.* limit. —limitar, *v.*
limo, *m.* slime.
limón, *m.* lemon.
limonada, *f.* lemonade.
limonero, *m.* lemon tree.
limosna, *f.* alms.
limosnero -ra, *n.* beggar.
limpiabotas, *m.* bootblack.
limpiadientes, *m.* toothpick.
limpiar, *v.* clean, wash, wipe.
límpido, *a.* limpid, clear.
limpieza, *f.* cleanliness.
limpio, *a.* clean.
linaje, *m.* lineage, ancestry.
linaza, *f.* linseed.

lince, *a.* sharp-sighted, observing.
linchamiento, *m.* lynching.
linchar, *v.* lynch.
lindar, *v.* border, bound.
linde, *m.* boundary; landmark.
lindero, *m.* boundary.
lindo, *a.* pretty, lovely, nice.
línea, *f.* line.
lineal, *a.* lineal.
linfa, *f.* lymph.
lingüista, *m. & f.* linguist.
lingüístico, *a.* linguistic.
linimento, *m.* liniment.
lino, *m.* linen; flax.
linóleo, *m.* linoleum.
linterna, *f.* lantern; flashlight.
lío, *m.* pack, bundle; mess, scrape.
liquidación, *f.* liquidation.
liquidar, *v.* liquidate; settle up.
líquido, *a. & m.* liquid.
lira, *f.* lyre.
lírico, *a.* lyric.
lirio, *m.* lily.
lirismo, *m.* lyricism.
lis, *f.* lily.
lisiar, *v.* cripple, lame.
liso, *a.* smooth, even.
lisonja, *f.* flattery.
lisonjear, *v.* flatter.
lisonjero -ra, *n.* flatterer.
lista, *f.* list; stripe; menu.
listar, *v.* list; put on a list.
listo, *a.* ready; smart, clever.
listón, *m.* ribbon.
litera, *f.* litter, bunk, berth.
literal, *a.* literal.
literario, *a.* literary.
literato, *m.* literary person, writer.
literatura, *f.* literature.
litigación, *f.* litigation.
litigio, *m.* litigation; lawsuit.
litoral, *m.* coast.
litro, *m.* liter.
liturgia, *f.* liturgy.
liviano, *a.* light (in weight).
lívido, *a.* livid.
lo, *pron.* the; him, it, you; (pl.) them, you.
loar, *v.* praise, laud.
lobina, *f.* striped bass.

lobo, *m.* wolf.
lóbrego, *a.* murky; dismal.
local, 1. *a.* local. **2.** *m.* site.
localidad, *f.* locality, location; seat (in theater).
localizar, *v.* localize.
loción, *f.* lotion.
loco -ca, 1. *a.* crazy, insane, mad. **2.** *n.* lunatic.
locomotora, *f.* locomotive.
locuaz, *a.* loquacious.
locución, *f.* locution, expression.
locura, *f.* folly; madness, insanity.
lodo, *m.* mud.
lodoso, *a.* muddy.
lógica, *f.* logic.
lógico, *a.* logical.
lograr, *v.* achieve; succeed in.
logro, *m.* accomplishment.
lombriz, *f.* earthworm.
lomo, *m.* loin; back (of an animal).
lona, *f.* canvas.
longevidad, *f.* longevity.
longitud, *f.* longitude; length.
lonja, *f.* shop; market.
lontananza, *f.* distance.
loro, *m.* parrot.
losa, *f.* slab.
lote, *m.* lot, share.
lotería, *f.* lottery.
loza, *f.* china, crockery.
lozanía, *f.* freshness, vigor.
lozano, *a.* fresh, spirited.
lubricación, *f.* lubrication.
lubricar, *v.* lubricate.
lucero, *m.* (bright) star.
lúcido, *a.* lucid, clear.
luciente, *a.* shining, bright.
luciérnaga, *f.* firefly.
lucimiento, *m.* success; splendor.
lucir, *v.* shine, sparkle; show off.
lucrativo, *a.* lucrative, profitable.
lucha, *f.* fight, struggle; wrestling. **—luchar,** *v.*
luchador, *m.* fighter, wrestler.
luego, *adv.* right away; afterwards, next. **l. que,** as soon

For pronunciation, see the concise guide on pages 3 to 4.

as. desde l., of course.
hasta l., good-bye, so long.
lugar, *m.* place, spot; space, room.
lúgubre, *a.* gloomy; dismal.
lujo, *m.* luxury. **de l.,** de luxe.
lujoso, *a.* luxurious.
lumbre, *f.* fire; light.
luminoso, *a.* luminous.
luna, *f.* moon.
lunar, *m.* beauty mark, mole; polka dot.
lunático, *a. & n.* lunatic.
lunes, *m.* Monday.
luneta, *f.* (theat.) orchestra seat.
lustre, *m.* polish, shine.
lustrar, *v.*
lustroso, *a.* shiny.
luto, *m.* mourning.
luz, *f.* light. **dar a l.,** give birth to.
llaga, *f.* sore.
llama, *f.* flame; llama.
llamada, *f.* call; knock. —
llamar, *v.*
llamarse, *v.* be called, be named. **se llama . . .** etc., his name is **. . .** etc.
llamativo, *a.* gaudy, showy.

llamear, *v.* blaze.
llaneza, *f.* simplicity.
llano, 1. *a.* flat, level; plain. **2.** *m.* plain.
llanta, *f.* tire.
llanto, *m.* crying, weeping.
llanura, *f.* prairie, plain.
llave, *f.* key; wrench; faucet; (elec.) switch. **ll. inglesa,** monkey wrench.
llegada, *f.* arrival.
llegar, *v.* arrive; reach. **ll. a ser,** become, come to be.
llenar, *v.* fill.
lleno, *a.* full.
llenura, *f.* abundance.
llevadero, *a.* tolerable.
llevar, *v.* take, carry; bear; wear (clothes); **ll. a cabo,** carry out.
llevarse, *v.* take away, run away with. **ll. bien,** get along well.
llorar, *v.* cry, weep.
lloroso, *a.* sorrowful, tearful.
llover, *v.* rain.
llovido, *m.* stowaway.
llovizna, *f.* drizzle, sprinkle.
—**lloviznar,** *v.*
lluvia, *f.* rain.
lluvioso, *a.* rainy.

M

maca, *f.* blemish, flaw.
macaco, *a.* ugly, horrid.
macareno, *a.* boasting.
macarrones, *m.pl.* macaroni.
macear, *v.* molest, push around.
maceta, *f.* vase; mallet.
macizo, 1. *a.* solid. **2.** *m.* bulk; flower bed.
macular, *v.* stain.
machacar, *v.* pound; crush.
machina, *f.* derrick.
macho, *m.* male.
machucho, *a.* mature, wise.

madera, *f.* lumber; wood.
madero, *m.* beam, timber.
madrastra, *f.* stepmother.
madre, *f.* mother. **m. política,** mother-in-law.
madreperla, *f.* mother-of-pearl.
madriguera, *f.* burrow; lair, den.
madrina, *f.* godmother.
madroncillo, *m.* strawberry.
madrugada, *f.* daybreak.
madrugar, *v.* get up early.
madurar, *v.* ripen.
madurez, *f.* maturity.

maduro, *a.* ripe; mature.

maestría, *f.* mastery.

maestro, *m.* master; teacher.

maganto, *a.* lethargic, dull.

magia, *f.* magic.

mágico, *a. & m.* magic; magician.

magistrado, *m.* magistrate.

magnánimo, *a.* magnanimous.

magnético, *a.* magnetic.

magnetismo, *m.* magnetism.

magnificar, *v.* magnify.

magnificencia, *f.* magnificence.

magnífico, *a.* magnificent.

magnitud, *f.* magnitude.

magno, *a.* great, grand.

magnolia, *f.* magnolia.

mago, *m.* magician; wizard.

magosto, *m.* picnic, outing.

magro, *a.* meager; thin.

magullar, *v.* bruise.

mahometano, *n. & a.* Mohammedan.

mahometismo, *m.* Mohammedanism.

maíz, *m.* corn.

majadero, *a. & m.* foolish; fool.

majar, *v.* mash.

majestad, *f.* majesty.

majestuoso, *a.* majestic.

mal, 1. *adv.* badly; wrong. **2.** *m.* evil, ill; illness.

mala, *f.* mail.

malacate, *m.* hoist.

malandanza, *f.* misfortune.

malaventura, *f.* misfortune.

malcomido, *a.* underfed; malnourished.

malcontento, *a.* dissatisfied.

maldad, *f.* badness; wickedness.

maldecir, *v.* curse, damn.

maldición, *f.* curse.

maldito, *a.* accursed, damned.

malecón, *m.* embankment.

maledicencia, *f.* slander.

maleficio, *m.* spell, charm.

malestar, *m.* indisposition.

maleta, *f.* suitcase, valise.

malévolo, *a.* malevolent.

maleza, *f.* weeds; underbrush.

malgastar, *v.* squander.

malhechor, *m.* malefactor, evildoer.

malhumorado, *a.* morose ill-humored.

malicia, *f.* malice.

maliciar, *v.* suspect.

malicioso, *a.* malicious.

maligno, *a.* malignant, evil.

malo, *a.* bad; evil, wicked; naughty; ill.

malograr, *v.* miss, lose.

malparto, *m.* abortion, miscarriage.

malquerencia, *f.* hatred.

malquerer, *v.* dislike; bear ill will.

malsano, *a.* unhealthy; unwholesome.

malsín, *m.* malicious gossip.

malta, *f.* malt.

maltratar, *v.* mistreat.

malvado, 1. *a.* wicked. **2.** *m.* villain.

malviz, *m.* redwing.

malla, *f.* mesh, net.

mallete, *m.* mallet.

mamá, *f.* mamma, mother.

mamar, *v.* suckle; suck.

mamífero, *m.* mammal.

mampara, *f.* screen.

mampostería, *f.* masonry.

mamut, *m.* mammoth.

manada, *f.* flock, herd, drove.

manantial, *m.* spring (of water).

manar, *v.* gush, flow out.

mancebo, *m.* young man.

mancilla, *f.* stain; blemish.

manco, *a.* armless; one-armed.

mancha, *f.* stain, smear, blemish, spot. **—manchar,** *v.*

mandadero, *m.* messenger.

mandado, *m.* order, command.

mandamiento, *m.* commandment; command.

mandar, *v.* send; order, command.

mandatario, *m.* attorney; representative.

mandato, *m.* mandate, command.

mandíbula, f. jaw; jawbone.

mando, m. command, order; leadership.

mandón, a. domineering.

mandril m. baboon.

manejar, v. handle, manage; drive (a car).

manejo, m. management; horsemanship.

manera, f. way, manner, means. **de m. que,** so, as a result.

manga, f. sleeve.

mangana, f. lariat, lasso.

manganeso, m. manganese.

mango, m. handle; mango (fruit).

mangosta, f. mongoose.

manguera, f. hose.

manguito, m. muff.

maní, m. peanut.

manía, f. mania, madness; hobby.

maníaco, maniático, a. & m. maniac.

manicomio, m. insane asylum.

manicura, f. manicure.

manifactura, f. manufacture.

manifestación, f. manifestation.

manifestar, v. manifest, show.

manifiesto, a. & m. manifest.

manija f. handle; crank.

maniobra, f. maneuver. — **maniobrar,** v.

manipulación, f. manipulation.

manipular, v. manipulate.

maniquí, m. mannequin.

manivela, f. (mech.) crank.

manjar, m. food, dish.

manlieve, m. swindle.

mano, f. hand.

manojo, m. handful; bunch.

manómetro, m. gauge.

manopla, f. gauntlet.

manosear, v. handle, feel, touch.

manotada, f. slap, smack. — **manotear,** v.

mansedumbre, f. meekness, tameness.

mansión, f. mansion; abode.

manso, a. tame, gentle.

manta, f. blanket.

manteca, f. fat, lard; butter.

mantecado, m. ice cream.

mantecoso, a. buttery.

mantel, m. tablecloth.

mantener, v. maintain, keep; sustain; support.

mantenimiento, m. maintenance.

mantequera, f. butter dish; churn.

mantequilla, f. butter.

mantilla, f. mantilla; baby clothes.

mantillo, m. humus; manure.

manto, m. mantle, cloak.

manual, a. & m. manual.

manubrio, m. handle; crank.

manufacturar, v. manufacture; make.

manuscrito, m. manuscript.

manzana, f. apple; block (of street).

manzano, m. apple tree.

maña, f. skill; cunning; trick.

mañana, 1. adv. tomorrow. **2.** f. morning.

mañanear, v. rise early in the morning.

mañero, a. clever; skillful; lazy.

mapa, m. map, chart.

mapache, m. raccoon.

mapurito, m. skunk.

máquina, f. machine.

maquinación, f. machination; plot.

maquinador, m. plotter, schemer.

maquinal, a. mechanical.

maquinar, v. scheme, plot.

maquinaria, f. machinery.

maquinista, m. machinist; engineer.

mar, m. or f. sea.

marabú, m. marabou.

maraña, f. tangle; maze; snarl; plot.

maravilla, f. marvel, wonder. — **maravillarse,** v.

maravilloso, a. marvelous, wonderful.

marbete, m. tag, label; check.

For pronunciation, see the concise guide on pages 3 to 4.

marca, *f.* mark, sign; brand, make.

marcar, *v.* mark; observe, note.

marcial, *a.* martial.

marco, *m.* frame.

marcha, *f.* march, progress. —**marchar,** *v.*

marchante, *m.* merchant; customer.

marcharse, *v.* go away, depart.

marchitable, *a.* perishable.

marchitar, *v.* fade, wilt, wither.

marchito, *a.* faded, withered.

marea, *f.* tide.

mareado, *a.* seasick.

marearse, *v.* get dizzy; be seasick.

mareo, *m.* dizziness, seasickness.

marfil, *m.* ivory.

margarita, *f.* pearl; daisy.

margen, *m. or f.* margin, edge, rim.

marido, *m.* husband.

marimba, *f.* marimba.

marina, *f.* navy; seascape.

marinero, *m.* sailor, seaman.

marino, *a. & m.* marine, (of) sea; mariner, seaman.

marión, *m.* sturgeon.

mariposa, *f.* butterfly

mariquita, *f.* ladybird.

mariscal, *m.* marshal.

marisco, *m.* shellfish; mollusk.

marital, *a.* marital.

marítimo, *a.* maritime.

marmita, *f.* pot, kettle.

mármol, *m.* marble.

marmóreo, *a.* marble.

maroma, *f.* rope.

marqués, *m.* marquis.

marquesa, *f.* marquise.

Marte, *m.* Mars.

martes, *m.* Tuesday.

martillo, *m.* hammer. —**martillar,** *v.*

mártir, *m. & f.* martyr.

martirio, *m.* martyrdom.

martirizar, *v.* martyrize.

marzo, *m.* March.

mas, *conj.* but.

más, *a. & adv.* more, most; plus. **no m.,** only.

masa, *f.* mass; dough.

masaje, *m.* massage.

mascar, *v.* chew.

máscara, *f.* mask.

mascarada, *f.* masquerade.

mascota, *f.* mascot; good-luck charm.

masculino, *a.* masculine.

mascullar, *v.* mumble.

masón, *m.* freemason.

masticar, *v.* chew.

mástil, *m.* mast; post.

mastín, *m.* mastiff.

mastuerzo, *m.* fool, ninny.

mata, *f.* plant; bush.

matadero, *m.* slaughterhouse.

matador, *m.* matador.

matanza, *f.* killing, bloodshed, slaughter.

matar, *v.* kill, slay; slaughter

matasanos, *m.* quack.

mate, *m.* checkmate; Paraguayan tea.

matemáticas, *f.pl.* mathematics.

matemático, *a.* mathematical.

materia, *f.* material; subject (matter)

material, *a. & m.* material.

materialismo, *m.* materialism.

materializar, *v.* materialize.

maternal, materno, *a.* maternal.

maternidad, *f.* maternity.

matiné, *f.* matinee.

matiz, *m.* hue, shade.

matizar, *v.* blend; tint.

matón, *m.* bully.

matorral, *m.* thicket.

matoso, *a.* weedy.

matraca, *f.* rattle. —**matraquear,** *v.*

matrícula, *f.* registration; tuition.

matricularse, *v.* enroll, register.

matrimonio, *m.* matrimony, marriage; married couple.

matriz, *f.* womb; (mech.) die, mold.

matrona, *f.* matron.

maullar, v. mew.

máxima, f. maxim.

máxime, a. principally.

máximo, a. & m. maximum.

maya, f. daisy.

mayo, m. May.

mayonesa, f. mayonnaise.

mayor, 1. a. larger, largest; greater, greatest; elder, eldest, senior. **m. de edad,** major, of age. **al por m.,** at wholesale. **2.** m. major.

mayoral, m. head shepherd; boss; foreman.

mayordomo, m. manager; butler, steward.

mayoría, f. majority, bulk.

mazmorra, f. dungeon.

mazorca, f. ear of corn.

me, pron. me; myself.

mecánico, a. & m. mechanical; mechanic.

mecanismo, m. mechanism.

mecanizar, v. mechanize.

mecanografía, f. typewriting.

mecanógrafo -fa, n. typist.

mecedor, m. swing.

mecedora, f. rocking chair.

mecer, v. rock; swing, sway.

mecha, f. wick; fuse.

mechón, m. lock (of hair).

medalla, f. medal.

médano, m. sand dune.

media, f. stocking.

mediación, f. mediation.

mediador, m. mediator.

mediados, m.pl. **a m. de,** about the middle of (a period of time).

medianero), m. mediator.

medianía, f. mediocrity.

mediano, a. medium; moderate; mediocre.

medianoche, f. midnight.

mediante, prep. by means of.

mediar, v. mediate.

medicamento, m. medicine, drug.

medicastro, m. quack.

medicina, f. medicine.

medicinar, v. treat (as a doctor).

médico, 1. a. medical. **2.** m. doctor, physician.

medida, f. measure, step.

medidor, m. meter.

medio, 1, a. half; mid, middle of. **2.** m. middle; means.

mediocre, a. mediocre.

mediocridad, f. mediocrity.

mediodía, m. midday, noon.

medioeval, a. medieval.

medir, v. measure, gauge.

meditación, f. meditation.

meditar, v. meditate.

mediterráneo, a. Mediterranean.

medrar, v. thrive.

medroso, a. fearful, cowardly.

megáfono, m. megaphone.

mejicano, a. & m. Mexican.

mejilla, f. cheek.

mejor, a. & adv. better; best. **a lo m.,** perhaps.

mejora, f., **mejoramiento,** m. improvement.

mejorar, v. improve, better.

mejoría, f. improvement; superiority.

melancolía, f. melancholy.

melancólico, a. melancholy.

melaza, f. molasses.

melena, f. mane; long or loose hair.

melindroso, a. fussy.

melocotón, m. peach.

melodía, f. melody.

melodioso, a. melodious.

melón, m. melon.

meloso, a. like honey.

mella, f. notch; dent. —**mellar,** v.

mellizo -za, n. & a. twin.

membrana, f. membrane.

membrete, m. memorandum; letterhead.

membrillo, m. quince.

membrudo, a. strong, muscular.

memorable, a. memorable.

memorándum, m. memorandum; notebook.

memoria, f. memory; memoir; memorandum.

mención, f. mention, **mencionar,** v.

mendigar, v. beg (for alms).

mendigo -a, n. beggar.

mendrugo, m. crumb, bit.

menear, v. shake, wag; stir.

menester, m. need, want; duty, task. **ser m.**, to be necessary.

menesteroso, a. needy.

mengua, f. decrease; lack; poverty.

menguar, v. abate, decrease.

menor, a. smaller, smallest; lesser, least; younger, youngest, junior. **m. de edad**, minor, under age. **al por m.**, at retail.

menos, a. & adv. less, least; minus. **a m. que**, unless. **echar de m.**, to miss.

menospreciar, v. cheapen; despise; slight.

mensaje, m. message.

mensajero -ra, n. messenger.

menstruar, v. menstruate.

mensual, a. monthly.

mensualidad, f. monthly income or allowance; monthly payment.

menta, f. mint, peppermint.

mentado, a. famous.

mental, a. mental.

mentalidad, f. mentality.

mente, f. mind.

mentecato, a. foolish, stupid.

mentir, v. lie, tell a lie.

mentira, f. lie, falsehood. **parece m.**, it seems impossible.

mentiroso, a. lying, untruthful.

mentol, m. menthol.

menú, m. menu.

menudeo, m. retail.

menudo, a. small, minute. **a m.**, often.

meñique, a. tiny.

meple, m. maple.

merca, f. purchase.

mercader, m. merchant.

mercaderías, f. pl. merchandise, commodities.

mercado, m. market.

mercancía, f. merchandise. (pl.) wares.

mercante, a. merchant.

mercantil, a. mercantile.

merced, f. mercy, grace.

mercenario -ria, a. & m. mercenary.

mercurio, m. mercury.

merecedor, a. worthy.

merecer, v. merit, deserve.

merecimiento, m. merit.

merendar, v. eat lunch.

merendero, m. lunchroom.

meridional, a. southern.

merienda, f. mid-day meal, lunch.

mérito, m. merit, worth.

meritorio, a. meritorious.

merla, f. blackbird.

merluza, f. haddock.

mermelada, f. marmalade.

mero, a. mere.

mes, m. month.

mesa, f. table.

meseta, f. plateau.

mesón, m. inn.

mesonero, m. innkeeper.

mestizo -za, a. & n. half-caste.

meta, f. goal, objective.

metabolismo, m. metabolism.

metafísica, f. metaphysics.

metáfora, f. metaphor.

metal, m. metal.

metálico, a. metallic.

metalurgia, f. metallurgy.

meteoro, m. meteor.

meteorología, f. meteorology.

meter, v. put (in).

meterse, v. interfere, meddle.

metódico, a. methodic.

método, m. method, approach.

metralla, f. shrapnel.

métrico, a. metric.

metro, m. meter (measure); subway.

metrópoli, f. metropolis.

mexicano -na, a. & n. Mexican.

mezcla, f. mixture; blend.

mezclar, v. mix; blend.

mezcolanza, f. mixture; hodge-podge.

mezquino, a. stingy; petty.

mi, a. my.

mí, pron. me; myself.

microbio, m. microbe, germ.

micrófono, m. microphone.

microscópico, a. microscopic.

microscopio, *m.* microscope.

miedo, *m.* fear. **tener m.,** fear, be afraid.

miedoso, *a.* fearful.

miel, *f.* honey.

miembro, *m.* member; limb.

mientras, *conj.* while. **m. tanto,** meanwhile. **m.más . . . más,** the more . . . the more.

miércoles, *m.* Wednesday.

miga, migaja, *f.* scrap, crumb

migración, *f.* migration.

migratorio, *a.* migratory.

mil, *a. & pron.* thousand.

milagro, *m.* miracle.

milagroso, *a.* miraculous.

milicia, *f.* militia.

militante, *a.* militant.

militar, 1. *a.* military. **2.** *m.* military man.

militarismo, *m.* militarism.

milla, *f.* mile.

millar, *m.* (a) thousand.

millón, *m.* million.

millonario -ria, *n.* millionaire.

mimar, *v.* pamper, spoil (a child).

mimbre, *m.* willow; wicker.

mímico, *a.* mimic.

mimo, *m.* mime. —mimic.

mina, *f.* mine. —**minar,** *v.*

mineral, *a. & m.* mineral.

minero, *m.* miner.

miniatura, *f.* miniature.

mínimo, *a. & m.* minimum.

ministerio, *m.* ministry; cabinet.

ministro, *m.* (govt.) minister, secretary.

minoría, *f.* minority.

minoridad, *f.* minority; nonage.

minucioso, *a.* minute; thorough.

minué, *m.* minuet.

minuta, *f.* minute; draft.

mío, *a.* mine.

miopía, *f.* myopia.

mira, *f.* gunsight.

mirada, *f.* look; gaze, glance.

miramiento, *m.* consideration; respect.

mirar, *v.* look, look at; watch. **m. a,** face.

miríada, *f.* myriad.

mirlo, *m.* blackbird.

mirón, *m.* bystander, observer.

mirra, *f.* myrrh.

mirto, *m.* myrtle.

misa, *f.* mass, church service.

misceláneo, *a.* miscellaneous.

miserable, *a.* miserable, wretched.

miseria, *f.* misery.

misericordia, *f.* mercy.

misericordioso, *a.* merciful.

misión, *f.* assignment; mission.

misionario -ria, misionero -ra, *n.* missionary.

mismo, 1. *a. & pron.* same; -self, -selves. **2.** *adv.* right, exactly.

misterio, *m.* mystery.

misterioso, *a.* mysterious, weird.

místico, *a. & m.* mystical, mystic.

mitad, *f.* half.

mítico, *a.* mythical.

mitigar, *v.* mitigate.

mitin, *m.* meeting.

mito, *m.* myth.

mitón, *m.* mitten.

mitra, *f.* miter (bishop's).

mixto, *a.* mixed.

mixtura, *f.* mixture.

mobiliario, *m.* household goods.

mocasín, *m.* moccasin.

mocedad, *f.* youthfulness.

moción, *f.* motion.

mocoso -sa, *n.* brat.

mochila, *f.* knapsack.

mocho, *a.* cropped, trimmed, shorn.

moda, *f.* mode, fashion, style.

modales, *m.pl.* manners.

modelo, *m.* model, pattern.

moderación, *f.* moderation.

moderado, *a.* moderate. —**moderar,** *v.*

modernizar, *v.* modernize.

moderno, *a.* modern.

modestia, *f.* modesty.

modesto, *a.* modest.

módico, *a.* reasonable, moderate.

modificación, *f.* modification.

modificar, *v.* modify.

modismo, *m.* (gram.) idiom.

modista, *f.* dressmaker; milliner.

modo, *m.* way, means.

modular, *v.* modulate.

mofarse, *v.* scoff, sneer.

mofletudo, *a.* fat-cheeked.

mohín, *m.* grimace.

moho, *m.* mold, mildew.

mohoso, *a.* moldy.

mojar, *v.* wet.

mojón, *m.* landmark; heap.

molde, *a.* mold, form.

molécula, *f.* molecule.

moler, *v.* grind, mill.

molestar, *v.* molest, bother, disturb, annoy, trouble.

molestia, *f.* bother, annoyance, trouble.

molesto, *a.* bothersome; annoyed; uncomfortable.

molicie, *f.* softness.

molinero, *m.* miller.

molino, *m.* mill.

molusco, *m.* mollusk.

mollera, *f.* top of the head.

momentáneo, *a.* momentary.

momento, *m.* moment.

mona, *f.* female monkey.

monarca, *m.* monarch.

monarquía, *f.* monarchy.

monarquista, *n. & a.* monarchist.

monasterio, *m.* monastery.

mondadientes, *m.* toothpick.

moneda, *f.* coin; money.

monetario, *a.* monetary.

monición, *m.* warning.

monigote, *m.* puppet.

monja, *f.* nun.

monje, *m.* monk.

mono -na, 1. *a.* (coll.) cute. **2.** *m. & f.* monkey.

monólogo, *m.* monologue.

monopolio, *m.* monopoly.

monopolizar, *v.* monopolize.

monosílabo, *m.* monosyllable.

monotonía, *f.* monotony.

monótono, *a.* monotonous, dreary.

monstruo, *m.* monster.

monstruosidad, *f.* monstrosity.

monstruoso, *a.* monstrous.

monta, *f.* amount; price.

montaña, *f.* mountain.

montañoso, *a.* mountainous.

montar, *v.* mount, climb; amount; (mech.) assemble. **m. a caballo,** ride horseback.

montaraz, *a.* wild, barbaric.

monte, *m.* mountain; forest.

montón, *m.* heap, pile.

montuoso, *a.* mountainous.

montura, *f.* riding horse, mount.

monumental, *a.* monumental.

monumento, *m.* monument.

mora, *f.* blackberry.

morada, *f.* residence, dwelling.

morado, *a.* purple.

moral, 1. *a.* moral. **2.** *f.* morale.

moraleja, *f.* moral.

moralidad, *f.* morality, morals.

moralista, *m. & f.* moralist.

morar, *v.* dwell, live, reside.

mórbido, *a.* morbid.

mordaz, *a.* caustic; sarcastic.

mordedura, *f.* bite.

morder, *v.* bite.

moreno -na, *a. & n.* brown; dark-skinned; dark-haired; brunette.

morfina, *f.* morphine.

moribundo, *a.* dying.

morir, *v.* die.

morisco -ca, moro -ra, *a. & n.* Moorish; Moor.

morro, *m.* bluff.

morriña, *f.* sadness.

mortaja, *f.* shroud.

mortal, *a. & m.* mortal.

mortalidad, *f.* mortality.

mortero, *m.* mortar.

mortífero, *a.* fatal, mortal.

mortificar, *v.* mortify.

mortuario, *a.* funereal.

mosaico, *a. & m.* mosaic.

mosca, *f.* fly.

For pronunciation, see the concise guide on pages 3 to 4.

mosquito, *m.* mosquito.
mostacho, *m.* mustache.
mostaza, *f.* mustard.
mostrador, *m.* counter; show-case.
mostrar, *v.* show, display.
mote, *m.* nickname; alias.
motín, *m.* mutiny; riot.
motivo, *m.* motive, reason.
motocicleta, *f.* motorcycle.
motor, *m.* motor.
motorista, *m.* motorist.
movedizo, *a.* movable; shaky.
mover, *v.* move; stir.
movible, *a.* movable.
móvil, *a.* mobile.
movilización, *f.* mobilization.
movilizar, *v.* mobilize.
movimiento, *m.* movement, motion.
mozo, *m.* boy; servant, waiter, porter.
muaré, *m.* moiré.
mucoso, *a.* mucous.
muchacha, *f.* girl; maid (servant).
muchachez, *m.* boyhood, girlhood.
muchacho, *m.* boy.
muchedumbre, *f.* crowd, mob.
mucho, 1. *a.* much, many. **2.** *adv.* much.
muda, *f.* change.
mudanza, *f.* change; change of residence.
mudar, *v.* change, shift.
mudarse, *v.* change residence, move.
mudo -da, *a.* & *n.* mute.
mueble, *m.* piece of furniture; (pl.) furniture.
mueca, *f.* grimace.
muela, *f.* (back) tooth.
muelle, *m.* pier, wharf; (mech.) spring.
muerte, *f.* death.
muerto -ta, 1. *a.* dead. **2.** *n.* dead person.
muesca, *f.* notch; groove.
muestra, *f.* sample, specimen; sign.
mugido, *m.* lowing; mooing.
mugir, *v.* low, moo.

mugre, *f.* filth, dirt.
mugriento, *a.* dirty.
mujer, *f.* woman; wife.
mujeril, *a.* womanly, feminine.
mula, *f.* mule.
mulato, *a.* & *m.* mulatto.
muleta, *f.* crutch; prop.
mulo, *m.* mule.
multa, *f.* fine, penalty.
multicolor, *a.* many-colored.
múltiple, *a.* multiple.
multiplicación, *f.* multiplication.
multiplicar, *v.* multiply.
multiplicidad, *f.* multiplicity.
multitud, *f.* multitude, crowd.
mundanal, *a.* worldly.
mundano, *a.* worldly, mundane.
mundial, *a.* world-wide; (of the) world.
mundo, *m.* world.
munición, *f.* ammunition.
municipal, *a.* municipal.
muñeca, *f.* doll; wrist.
muñeco, *m.* doll; puppet.
mural, *a.* & *m.* mural.
muralla, *f.* wall.
murciélago, *m.* bat.
murga, *f.* musical band.
murmullo, *m.* murmur; rustle.
murmurar, *v.* murmur; rustle; grumble.
murta, *f.* myrtle.
musa, *f.* muse.
muscular, *a.* muscular.
músculo, *m.* muscle.
muselina, *f.* muslin.
museo, *m.* museum.
música, *f.* music.
musical, *a.* musical.
músico, *a.* & *m.* musical; musician.
muslo, *m.* thigh.
mustio, *a.* sad.
muta, *f.* pack of hounds.
mutabilidad, *f.* mutability.
mutación, *f.* mutation.
mutilación, *f.* mutilation.
mutilar, *v.* mutilate; mangle.
mutuo, *a.* mutual.
muy, *adv.* very.

For pronunciation, see the concise guide on pages 3 to 4.

N, Ñ

nabo, m. turnip.

nacar, m. mother-of-pearl.

nacarado, a. pearly.

nacer, v. be born.

naciente, a. rising.

nacimiento, m. birth.

nación, f. nation.

nacional, a. national.

nacionalidad, f. nationality.

nacionalismo, m. nationalism.

nacionalista, n. & a. nationalist.

nacionalización, f. nationalization.

nacionalizar, v. nationalize.

nada, 1. pron. nothing; anything. **de n.,** you're welcome. **2.** adv. at all.

nadador, m. swimmer.

nadar, v. swim.

nadie, pron. no one, nobody; anyone, anybody.

nafta, f. naphtha.

naipe, m. (playing) card.

naranja, f. orange.

naranjada, f. orangeade.

naranjo, m. orange tree.

narciso, m. daffodil; narcissus.

narcótico, a. & m. narcotic.

nardo, m. spikenard.

nariz, f. nose; (pl.) nostrils.

narración, f. account.

narrador, m. narrator.

narrar, v. narrate.

narrativo, f. narrative.

nata, f. cream.

natal, a. native, natal.

natalicio, m. birthplace.

natalidad, f. birth rate.

natilla, f. custard.

nativo, a. native; innate.

natural, 1. a. natural. **2.** m. & f. native. m. nature, disposition.

naturaleza, f. nature.

naturalidad, f. naturalness; nationality.

naturalista, a. & m. naturalistic; naturalist.

naturalización, f. naturalization.

naturalizar, v. naturalize, accustom.

naufragar, v. be shipwrecked; fail.

naufragio, m. shipwreck; disaster.

náufrago -ga, a. & n. shipwrecked (person).

náusea, f. nausea.

nausear, v. feel nauseous.

náutico, a. nautical.

navaja, f. razor; pen knife.

naval, a. naval.

nave, f. ship.

navegable, a. navigable.

navegación, f. navigation.

navegador, m. navigator.

navegante, m. navigator.

navegar, v. sail; navigate.

Navidad, f. Christmas.

navío, m. ship.

neblina, f. mist, fog.

nebuloso, a. misty; nebulous.

necedad, f. stupidity; nonsense.

necesario, a. necessary.

necesidad, f. necessity, need, want.

necesitado, a. needy, poor.

necesitar, v. need.

necio -cia, 1. a. stupid, silly. **2.** n. fool.

néctar, m. nectar.

nefando, a. nefarious.

negable, a. deniable.

negación, f. denial, negation.

negar, v. deny.

negarse, v. refuse, decline.

negativa, f. negative, refusal.

negativamente, adv. negatively.

negativo, a. negative.

negligencia, f. negligence, neglect.

negligente, a. negligent.

For pronunciation, see the concise guide on pages 3 to 4.

negociación, f. negotiation, deal.

negociador, m. negotiator.

negociante, m. businessman.

negociar, v. negotiate, trade.

negocio, m. trade; business.

negro -gra, 1. a. black. m. Negro.

nene -na, n. baby.

neo, neón, m. neon.

nervio, m. nerve.

nervioso, a. nervous.

nerviosamente, adv. nervously.

nesciencia, f. ignorance.

nesciente, a. ignorant.

neto, a. net.

neumático, 1. a. pneumatic. **2.** m. (pneumatic) tire.

neumonía, f. pneumonia.

neurótico, a. neurotic.

neutral, a. neutral.

neutralidad, f. neutrality.

neutro, a. neuter; neutral.

nevada, f. snowfall.

nevado, a. snow-white; snow-capped.

nevar, v. snow.

nevera, f. icebox.

nevoso, a. snowy.

ni, 1. conj. nor. **ni . . . ni,** neither . . . nor. **2.** adv. not even.

nicho, m. recess.

nido, m. nest.

niebla, f. fog; mist.

nieto -ta, n. grandchild.

nieve, f. snow.

nilón, m. nylon.

nimio, adj. stingy.

ninfa, f. nymph.

ningún -no -na, a. & pron. no, none, neither (one); any, either (one).

niñera, f. nursemaid.

niñez, f. childhood.

niño -ña, 1. a. young; childish; childlike. **2.** n. child.

níquel, m. nickel.

niquelado, a. nickel-plated.

nítido, a. neat, clean, bright.

nitrato, m. nitrate.

nitro, m. niter.

nitrógeno, m. nitrogen.

nivel, m. level; grade. **—nivelar,** v.

no, 1. adv. not. **no más,** only. **2.** interj. no.

noble, a. & v. noble; nobleman.

nobleza, f. nobility; nobleness.

noción, f. notion, idea.

nocivo, a. harmful.

noctiluca, f. glowworm.

nocturno, a. nocturnal.

noche, f. night; evening. **Nochebuena,** f. Christmas Eve.

nodriza, f. wet nurse.

nogal, m. walnut.

nombradía, f. fame.

nombramiento, m. appointment, nomination.

nombrar, v. name, appoint, nominate; mention.

nombre, m. name; noun.

nómina, f. list; payroll.

nominación, f. nomination.

nominal, a. nominal.

nominar, v. name.

non, a. uneven, odd.

nonada, f. trifle.

nordeste, m. northeast.

nórdico, a. Nordic.

norma, f. norm, standard.

normal, a. normal, standard.

normalidad, f. normality.

normalizar, v. normalize; standardize.

noroeste, m. northwest.

norte, m. north.

norteamericano -na, a. & n. North American.

Noruega, f. Norway.

noruego -ga, a. & n. Norwegian.

nos, pron. us; ourselves.

nosotros -as, pron. we, us; ourselves.

nostalgia, f. nostalgia, homesickness.

nostálgico, a. nostalgic.

nota, f. note; grade, mark.

notable, a. notable, remarkable.

notación, f. notation; note.

notar, v. note, notice.

notario, m. notary.

noticia, *f.* notice; piece of news; (pl.) news.
notificación, *f.* notification.
notificar, *v.* notify.
notorio, *a.* well-known.
novato -ta, *n.* novice.
novecientos, *a. & pron.* nine hundred.
novedad, *f.* novelty; piece of news.
novel, *a.* new, inexperienced.
novela, *f.* novel.
novelista, *m. & f.* novelist.
novena, *f.* novena.
noveno, *a.* ninth.
noventa, *a. & pron.* ninety.
novia, *f.* bride; sweetheart, fiancée.
noviazgo, *m.* engagement, match.
novicio -cia, *n.* novice, beginner.
noviembre, *m.* November.
novilla, *f.* heifer.
novio, *m.* bridegroom; sweetheart, fiancé.
nube, *f.* cloud.
nubile, *a.* marriageable.
nublado, *a.* cloudy.
núcleo, *m.* nucleus.
nudo, *m.* knot.

nuera, *f.* daughter-in-law.
nuestro, *a.* our, ours.
nueva, *f.* news.
nueve, *a. & pron.* nine.
nuevo, *a.* new. **de n.,** again, anew.
nuez, *f.* nut; walnut.
nulidad, *f.* nonentity.
nulo, *a.* null, void.
numeración, *f.* numeration.
numerar, *v.* number.
numérico, *a.* numerical.
número, *m.* number; size (of shoe, etc.)
numeroso, *a.* numerous.
numismática, *f.* numismatics.
nunca, *adv.* never; ever.
nupcial, *a.* nuptial.
nupcias, *f.pl.* nuptials, wedding.
nutrición, *f.* nutrition.
nutrimento, *m.* nourishment.
nutrir, *v.* nourish.
nutritivo, *a.* nutritious.
ñame, *m.* yam.
ñapa, *f.* something extra.
ñoñería, *f.* dotage.
ñoño, *a.* feeble-minded, senile.

O

o, *conj.* or. **o . . . o,** either . . . or.
oasis, *m.* oasis.
obedecer, *v.* obey, mind.
obediencia, *f.* obedience.
obediente, *a.* obedient.
obelisco, *m.* obelisk.
obertura, *f.* overture.
obeso, *a.* obese.
obispo, *m.* bishop.
obituario, *m.* obituary.
objeción, *f.* objection.
objetivo, *a. & m.* objective.
objeto, *m.* object. **—objetar,** *v.*

oblicuo, *a.* oblique.
obligación, *f.* obligation, duty.
obligar, *v.* oblige, require, compel; obligate.
obligatorio, *a.* obligatory, compulsory.
oblongo, *a.* oblong.
oboe, *m.* oboe.
obra, *f.* work. **—obrar,** *v.*
obrero -ra, *n.* worker, laborer.
obscenidad, *f.* obscenity.
obsceno, *a.* obscene.
obscurecer, *v.* obscure; darken.

For pronunciation, see the concise guide on pages 3 to 4.

obscuridad, *f.* obscurity; darkness.

obscuro, *a.* obscure; dark.

obsequiar, *v.* court; make presents to, fete.

obsequio, *m.* obsequiousness; gift; attention.

observación, *f.* observation.

observador, *m.* observer.

observancia, *f.* observance.

observar, *v.* observe, watch.

observatorio, *m.* observatory.

obsesión, *f.* obsession.

obstáculo, *m.* obstacle.

obstante, *adv.* **no o.,** however, yet, nevertheless.

obstar, *v.* hinder, obstruct.

obstetricia, *f.* obstetrics.

obstinación, *f.* obstinacy.

obstinado, *a.* obstinate, stubborn.

obstinarse, *v.* persist, insist.

obstrucción, *f.* obstruction.

obstruir, *v.* obstruct, clog, block.

obtener, *v.* obtain, get, secure.

obtuso, *a.* obtuse.

obvio, *a.* obvious.

ocasión, *f.* occasion; opportunity, chance. **de o.,** second-hand.

ocasional, *a.* occasional.

ocasionalmente, *adv.* occasionally.

ocasionar, *v.* cause, occasion.

occidental, *a.* western.

occidente, *m.* west.

océano, *m.* ocean.

ocelote, *m.* ocelot.

ocio, *m.* idleness, leisure.

ociosidad, *f.* idleness, laziness.

ocioso, *a.* idle, lazy.

ocre, *m.* ochre.

octava, *f.* octave.

octavo, *a.* eighth.

octogonal, *a.* octagonal.

octubre, *m.* October.

oculista, *m.* oculist.

ocultación, *f.* concealment.

ocultar, *v.* hide, conceal.

oculto, *a.* hidden.

ocupación, *f.* occupation.

ocupado, *a.* occupied; busy.

ocupante, *m.* occupant.

ocupar, *v.* occupy.

ocuparse de, *v.* take care of, take charge of.

ocurrencia, *f.* occurrence; witticism.

ocurrir, *v.* occur, happen.

ochenta, *a. & pron.* eighty.

ocho, *a. & pron.* eight.

ochocientos, *a. & pron.* eight hundred.

oda, *f.* ode.

odio, *m.* hate. **—odiar,** *v.*

odiosidad, *f.* odiousness; hatred.

odioso, *a.* obnoxious, odious.

odisea, *f.* odyssey.

oeste, *m.* west.

ofender, *v.* offend, wrong.

ofenderse, *v.* be offended, take offense.

ofensa, *f.* offense.

ofensiva, *f.* offensive.

ofensivo, *a.* offensive.

ofensor -ra, *n.* offender.

oferta, *f.* offer, proposal.

ofertorio, *m.* offertory.

oficial, *a. & m.* official; officer

oficialmente, *adv.* officially.

oficiar, *v.* officiate.

oficina, *f.* office.

oficio, *m.* office; trade; church service.

oficioso, *a.* officious.

ofrecer, *v.* offer.

ofrecimiento, *m.* offer, offering.

ofrenda, *f.* offering.

oftalmia, *f.* ophthalmia.

ofuscamiento, *m.* obfuscation; bewilderment.

ofuscar, *v.* obfuscate; bewilder.

ogro, *m.* ogre.

oído, *m.* ear; hearing.

oír, *v.* hear; listen.

ojal, *m.* buttonhole.

ojalá, *interj. expressing wish or hope.* **o. que...** would that ...

ojeada, *f.* glance; peep; look.

ojear, *v.* eye, look at, glance at, stare at.

ojeriza, *f.* spite; grudge.

ojiva, *f.* pointed arch; ogive.

ojo, *m.* eye. **¡Ojo!** Look out!

ola, *f.* wave.

olaje, *m.* surge of waves.

oleada, *f.* swell.

oleo, *m.* oil; holy oil; extreme unction.

oleomargarina, *f.* oleomargarine.

oleoso, *a.* oily.

oler, *v.* smell.

olfatear, *v.* smell.

olfato, *m.* scent, smell.

oliva, *f.* olive.

olivar, *m.* olive grove.

olivo, *m.* olive tree.

olmo, *m.* elm.

olor, *m.* odor, smell, scent.

oloroso, *a.* fragrant, scented.

olvidadizo, *a.* forgetful.

olvidar, *v.* forget.

olvido, *m.* omission; forgetfulness.

olla, *f.* pot, kettle. **o. podrida,** stew.

ombligo, *m.* navel.

ominar, *v.* foretell.

ominoso, *a.* ominous.

omisión, *f.* omission.

omitir, *v.* omit, leave out.

ómnibus, *m.* bus.

omnipotencia, *f.* omnipotence.

omnipotente, *a.* almighty.

omnipresencia, *f.* omnipresence.

omnisciencia, *f.* omniscience.

omnívoro, *a.* omnivorous.

once, *a. & pron.* eleven.

onda, *f.* wave, ripple.

ondear, *v.* ripple.

ondulación, *f.* wave, undulation.

ondular, *v.* undulate, ripple.

onza, *f.* ounce.

opaco, *a.* opaque.

ópalo, *m.* opal.

opción, *f.* option.

ópera, *f.* opera.

operación, *f.* operation.

operar, *v.* operate; operate on.

operario -ria, *n.* operator; (skilled) worker.

operarse, *v.* have an operation.

operativo, *a.* operative.

opereta, *f.* operetta.

opiato, *m.* opiate.

opinar, *v.* opine.

opinión, *f.* opinion, view.

opio, *m.* opium.

oponer, *v.* oppose.

oporto, *m.* port (wine).

oportunidad, *f.* opportunity.

oportunismo, *m.* opportunism.

oportunista, *n. & a.* opportunist.

oportuno, *a.* opportune, expedient.

oposición, *f.* opposition.

opresión, *f.* oppression.

opresivo, *a.* oppressive.

oprimir, *v.* oppress.

oprobio, *m.* infamy.

optar, *v.* select, choose.

óptica, *f.* optics.

óptico, *a.* optic.

optimismo, *m.* optimism.

optimista, *a. & n.* optimistic; optimist.

óptimo, *a.* best.

opuesto, *a.* opposite; opposed.

opugnar, *v.* attack.

opulencia, *f.* opulence, wealth.

opulento, *a.* opulent, wealthy.

oración, *f.* sentence; prayer; oration.

oráculo, *m.* oracle.

orador, *m.* orator, speaker.

oral, *a.* oral.

orangután, *m.* orangutan.

orar, *v.* pray.

oratoria, *f.* oratory.

oratorio, *a.* oratorical.

orbe, *m.* orb; globe.

órbita, *f.* orbit.

orden, *m. or f.* order.

ordenanza, *f.* ordinance.

ordenar, *v.* order; put in order; ordain.

ordeñar, *v.* milk.

ordinal, *n. & a.* ordinal.

ordinario, *a.* ordinary; common, usual.

oreja, *f.* ear.

orejera, f. ear muff.

orfanato, m. orphanage.

organdí, m. organdy.

orgánico, a. organic.

organismo, m. organism.

organista, m. & f. organist.

organización, f. organization.

organizar, v. organize.

órgano, m. organ.

orgía, f. orgy, revel.

orgullo, m. pride.

orgulloso, a. proud.

orientación, f. orientation.

oriental, a. Oriental; eastern.

orientar, v. orient.

oriente, m. orient, east.

orificación, f. gold filling (for tooth).

origen, m. origin; parentage, descent.

original, a. original.

originalidad, f. originality.

originalmente, adv. originally.

originar, v. originate.

orilla, f. shore; bank; edge.

orín, m. rust.

orina, f. urine.

orinar, v. urinate.

orines, n.pl. urine.

oriol, m. oriole.

orla, f. border; edging.

ornado, a. ornate.

ornamentación, f. ornamentation.

ornamento, m. ornament. —ornamentar, v.

ornar, v. ornament, adorn.

oro, m. gold.

oropel, m. tinsel.

orquesta, f. orchestra.

ortiga, f. nettle.

ortodoxo, a. orthodox.

ortografía, f. orthography, spelling.

ortóptero, a. orthopterous.

oruga, f. caterpillar.

orzuelo, m. sty.

os, pron. you (pl.); yourselves.

osadía, f. daring.

osar, v. dare.

oscilación, f. oscillation.

oscilar, v. oscillate, rock.

ósculo, m. kiss.

oscurecer, oscuridad, oscuro = obscur-

oso, osa, n. bear.

ostentación, f. ostentation, showiness.

ostentar, v. show off.

ostentoso, a. ostentatious, flashy.

ostra, f. oyster.

ostracismo, m. ostracism.

otalgia, f. earache.

otero, m. hill, knoll.

otoño, m. autumn, fall.

otorgar, v. grant, award.

otro, a. & pron. other, another. o. vez, again. el uno al o., one another, each other.

ovación, f. ovation.

oval, ovalado, a. oval.

óvalo, m. oval.

ovario, m. ovary.

oveja, f. sheep.

ovejero, m. shepherd.

ovillo, m. ball of yarn.

oxidación, f. oxidation.

oxidar, v. oxidize; rust.

óxido, m. oxide.

oxígeno, m. oxygen.

oyente, m. hearer; (pl.) audience.

ozono, m. ozone.

P

pabellón m. pavilion.

pabilo, m. wick.

paciencia, f. patience.

paciente, a. & n. patient.

pacificar, v. pacify.

pacífico, a. pacific.

pacifismo, m. pacifism.

pacifista, n. & a. pacifist.

pacto, *m.* pact, treaty.

padecer, *v.* suffer.

padrasto, *m.* stepfather.

padre, *m.* father; priest; (pl.) parents.

padrenuestro, *m.* paternoster.

padrino, *m.* godfather; sponsor.

paella, *f.* dish of rice with meat or chicken.

paga, *f.* pay, wages.

pagadero, *a.* payable.

pagador, *m.* payer.

paganismo, *m.* paganism.

pagano -na, *a. & n.* heathen, pagan.

pagar, *v.* pay, pay for.

página, *f.* page.

pago, *m.* pay, payment.

país, *m.* country, nation.

paisaje, *m.* landscape, scenery, countryside.

paisano -na, *n.* countryman; compatriot; civilian.

paja, *f.* straw.

pajar, *m.* barn.

pájaro, *m.* bird.

paje, *m.* page (person).

pala, *f.* shovel, spade.

palabra, *f.* word.

palabrero, *a.* talkative.

palabrista, *m.* talkative person.

palacio, *m.* palace.

paladar, *m.* palate.

paladear, *v.* taste; relish.

palanca, *f.* lever.

palangana, *f.* wash basin.

palco, *m.* theater box.

palenque, *m.* palisade.

palidecer, *v.* turn pale.

palidez, *f.* paleness.

pálido, *a.* pale.

paliza, *f.* beating.

palizada, *m.* palisade.

palma, palmera, *f.* palm (tree).

palmada, *f.* slap, clap.

palmear, *v.* applaud.

palo, *m.* pole, stick; suit (in cards); (naut.) mast.

paloma, *f.* dove, pigeon.

palpar, *v.* touch, feel.

palpitación, *f.* palpitation.

palpitar, *v.* palpitate.

paludismo, *m.* malaria.

palleta, *f.* mat, pallet.

pampa, *f.* (South Amer.) prairie, plain.

pan, *m.* bread; loaf.

pana, *f.* corduroy.

panacea, *f.* panacea.

panadería, *f.* bakery.

panadero -ra, *n.* baker.

panameño -ña, *a. & n.* Panamanian, of Panama.

panamericano, *a.* Pan-American.

páncreas, *m.* pancreas.

pandeo, *m.* bulge.

pandilla, *f.* band, gang.

panecillo, *m.* roll, muffin.

panegírico, *m.* panegyric.

pánico, *m.* panic.

panocha, *f.* ear of corn.

panorámico, *a.* panoramic.

pantalones, *m.pl.* trousers, pants.

pantalla, *f.* (movie) screen; lamp shade.

pantano, *m.* bog, marsh, swamp.

pantanoso, *a.* swampy, marshy.

pantera, *f.* panther.

pantomima, *f.* pantomime.

panza, *f.* belly, paunch.

pañal, *m.* diaper.

paño, *m.* piece of cloth.

pañuelo, *m.* handkerchief.

Papa, *m.* Pope.

papa, *f.* potato.

papá, *m.* papa, father.

papado, *m.* papacy.

papagayo, *m.* parrot.

papal, *a.* papal.

papel, *m.* paper; role, part.

papelera, *f.* file or folder for papers.

papelería, *f.* stationery store.

papera, *f.* mumps.

paquete, *m.* package.

par, 1. *a.* even, equal. **2.** *m.* pair; equal, peer. **abierto de p. en p.,** wide open.

para, *prep.* for; in order to. **p. que,** in order that. **estar p.,** to be about to.

parabién, *m.* greeting; congratulation.

parabrisa, *m.* windshield.

paracaídas, *m.* parachute.
parachoques, *m.* (auto.) bumper.
parada, *f.* stop, halt; parade. stopping place.
paradero, *m.* whereabouts; stopping place.
paradigma, *m.* paradigm.
paradoja, *f.* paradox.
parafina, *f.* paraffin.
parafrasear, *v.* paraphrase.
paraguas, *m.* umbrella.
paraguayano -na, *n. & a.* Paraguayan.
paraíso, *m.* paradise.
paralelo, *a. & m.* parallel.
parálisis, *f.* paralysis.
paralizar, *v.* paralyze.
parapeto, *m.* parapet.
parar, *v.* stop, stem, ward off; stay.
pararse, *v.* stop; stand up.
parasismo, *m.* paroxysm.
parasítico, *a.* parasitic.
parásito, *m.* parasite.
parcela, *f.* plot of ground.
parcial, *a.* partial.
parcialidad, *f.* partiality; bias.
parcialmente, *adv.* partially.
pardo, *a.* brown.
parear, *v.* pair, match, mate.
parecer, 1. *m.* opinion. 2. *v.* seem, appear, look.
parecerse, *v.* look alike. **p. a,** look like.
parecido, *a.* similar.
pared, *f.* wall.
pareja, *f.* pair, couple; (dancing) partner.
parentela, *f.* kinfolk.
parentesco, *m.* parentage; lineage; kin.
paréntesis, *m.* parenthesis.
paria, *m.* outcast.
paridad, *f.* parity.
pariente, *m. & f.* relative.
parir, *v.* give birth to young.
parisiense, *n. & a.* Parisian.
parlamentario, *a.* parliamentary.
parlamento, *m.* parliament.
paro, *m.* stoppage; strike. **p. forzoso,** unemployment.
parodia, *f.* parody.
parodista, *m.* parodist.
paroxismo, *m.* paroxysm.

párpado, *m.* eyelid.
parque, *m.* park.
parra, *f.* grapevine.
párrafo, *m.* paragraph.
parranda, *f.* spree.
parrandear, *v.* carouse.
parrilla, *f.* grill.
párroco, *m.* parish priest.
parroquia, *f.* parish.
parroquial, *a.* parochial.
parsimonia, *f.* economy, thrift.
parsimonioso, *a.* economical, thrifty.
parte, *f.* part. **de p. de,** on behalf of. **alguna p.,** somewhere. **por otra p.,** on the other hand. **dar p. a,** to notify.
partera, *f.* midwife.
partición, *f.* distribution.
participación, *f.* participation.
participante, *m. & f.* participant.
participar, *v.* participate; announce.
participio, *m.* participle.
partícula, *f.* particle.
particular, 1. *a.* particular; private. 2. *m.* particular, detail; individual.
particularmente, *adv.* particularly.
partida, *f.* departure; (mil.) party; (sport) game.
partidario -ria, *n.* partisan.
partido, *m.* side, party, faction; game, match.
partir, *v.* leave, depart; part, cleave, split.
parto, *m.* delivery, childbirth.
pasa, *f.* raisin.
pasado, 1. *a.* past; last. 2. *m.* past.
pasaje, *m.* passage, fare.
pasajero -ra, 1. *a.* passing, transient. 2. *m.* passenger.
pasamano, *m.* banister.
pasaporte, *m.* passport.
pasar, *v.* pass; happen; spend (time). **p. por alto,** overlook. **p. lista,** call the roll. **p. sin,** do without.

For pronunciation, see the concise guide on pages 3 to 4.

pasatiempo, *m.* pastime, hobby.

pascua *f.* religious holiday; (pl.) Christmas (season). **P. Florida,** Easter.

paseo, *m.* walk, stroll; drive. **—pasear,** *v.*

pasillo, *m.* aisle; hallway.

pasión *f.* passion.

pasivo, *a.* passive.

pasmar, *v.* astonish, astound, stun.

pasmo, *m.* spasm; wonder.

paso, 1. *a.* dried (fruit). **2.** *m.* pace, step; (mountain) pass.

pasta, *f.* paste; batter; plastic.

pastar, *v.* graze.

pastel, *m.* pastry; pie.

pastelería, *f.* pastry; pastry shop.

pasteurización, *f.* pasteurization.

pasteurizar, *v.* pasteurize.

pastilla, *f.* tablet, lozenge, drop.

pasto, *m.* pasture; grass.

pastor, *m.* pastor, shepherd.

pastorear, *v.* pasture, tend (a flock).

pastura, *f.* pasture.

pata, *f.* foot (of animal).

patada, *f.* kick.

patán, *m.* boor.

patanada, *f.* rudeness.

patata, *f.* potato.

patear, *v.* stamp, tramp, kick.

patente, *a. & m.* patent. **—patentar,** *v.*

paternal, paterno, *a.* paternal.

paternidad, *f.* paternity, fatherhood.

patético, *a.* pathetic.

patíbulo, *m.* scaffold, gallows.

patín, *m.* skate. **—patinar,** *v.*

patio, *m.* yard, court, patio.

pato, *m.* duck.

patria, *f.* native land.

patriarca, *m.* patriarch.

patrimonio, *m.* inheritance.

patriota, *m. & f.* patriot.

patriótico, *a.* patriotic.

patriotismo, *m.* patriotism.

patrocinar, *v.* patronize, sponsor.

patrón, *m.* patron; boss; (dress) pattern.

patrulla, *f.* patrol. **—patrullar,** *v.*

pausa, *f.* pause. **—pausar,** *v.*

pavesa, *f.* embers.

pavimentar, *v.* pave.

pavimento, *m.* pavement.

pavo, *m.* turkey. **p. real,** peacock.

payaso, *m.* clown.

paz, *f.* peace.

peatón -na, *n.* pedestrian.

peca, *f.* freckle.

pecado, *m.* sin. **—pecar,** *v.*

pecador -ra, *a. & n.* sinful; sinner.

pecera, *f.* aquarium, fish bowl.

peculiar, *a.* peculiar.

peculiaridad, *f.* peculiarity.

pechera, *f.* shirt front.

pecho, *m.* chest; breast; bosom.

pedagogía, *f.* pedagogy.

pedagogo, *m.* pedagogue, teacher.

pedal, *m.* pedal.

pedantesco, *a.* pedantic.

pedazo, *m.* piece.

pedernal, *m.* flint.

pedestal, *m.* pedestal.

pediatría, *f.* pediatrics.

pedicuro, *m.* chiropodist.

pedir, *v.* ask, ask for, request; apply for; order.

pedregoso, *a.* rocky.

pegajoso, *a.* sticky.

pegar, *v.* beat, strike; adhere, fasten, stick.

peinado, *m.* coiffure, hair-do.

peine, *m.* comb. **—peinar,** *v.*

peineta, *f.* (ornamental) comb.

pelagra, *f.* pellagra.

pelar, *v.* skin, pare, peel.

pelea, *f.* fight, row. **—pelearse,** *v.*

pelícano, *m.* pelican.

película, *f.* movie, motion picture, film.

peligrar, *v.* be in danger.

peligro, *m.* peril, danger.
peligroso, *a.* perilous, dangerous.
pelo, *m.* hair.
pelota, *f.* ball.
peltre, *m.* pewter.
peluca, *f.* wig.
peludo, *a.* hairy.
peluquería, *f.* hairdresser's shop, beauty parlor.
peluquero, *m.* hairdresser.
pellejo, *m.* skin, peel (of fruit).
pellizco, *m.* pinch. —**pellizcar,** *v.*
pena, *f.* pain, grief, trouble, woe; penalty. **valer la p.,** to be worthwhile.
penacho, *m.* plume.
penalidad, *f.* trouble; penalty.
pender, *v.* hang, dangle; be pending.
pendiente, 1. *a.* hanging; pending. **2.** *m.* incline, slope; earring, pendant.
pendón, *m.* pennant, flag.
penetración, *f.* penetration.
penetrar, *v.* penetrate, pierce.
penicilina, *f.* penicillin.
península, *f.* peninsula.
penitencia, *f.* penitence, penance.
penitenciaría, *f.* penitentiary.
penoso, *a.* painful, troublesome, grievous.
pensador -ra, *n.* thinker.
pensamiento, *m.* thought.
pensar, *v.* think; intend, plan.
pensativo, *a.* pensive, thoughtful.
pensión, *f.* pension; boarding house.
pensionista, *m. & f.* boarder.
pentagonal, *a.* pentagonal.
penuria, *f.* penury, poverty.
peña, *f.* rock.
peñascoso, *a.* rocky.
peón, *m.* unskilled laborer; infantryman.
peonada, *f.* group of labor ers.
peonia, *f.* peony.
peor, *a.* worse, worst.

pepino, *m.* cucumber.
pepita, *f.* seed (in fruit).
pequeñez, *f.* smallness; trifle.
pequeño -ña, 1. *a.* small, little, short, slight. **2.** *n.* child.
pera, *f.* pear.
peral, *m.* pear tree.
perca, *f.* perch (fish).
percal, *m.* calico, percale.
percentaje, *m.* percentage.
percepción, *f.* perception.
perceptivo, *a.* perceptive.
percibir, *v.* perceive, sense; collect.
percha, *f.* perch; clothes hanger, rack.
perder, *v.* lose; miss; waste. **echar a p.,** spoil.
perdición, *f.* perdition, downfall.
pérdida, *f.* loss.
perdiz, *f.* partridge.
perdón, *m.* pardon, forgiveness.
perdonar, *v.* forgive, pardon; spare.
perdurable, *a.* enduring, everlasting.
perdurar, *v.* endure, last.
perecedero, *a.* perishable.
perecer, *v.* perish.
peregrinación, *f.* peregrination; pilgrimage.
peregrino -na, *n.* pilgrim.
perejil, *m.* parsley.
perenne, *a.* perennial.
pereza, *f.* laziness.
perezoso, *a.* lazy, sluggish.
perfección, *f.* perfection.
perfeccionar, *v.* perfect.
perfectamente, *adv.* perfectly.
perfecto, *a.* perfect.
perfidia, *f.* falseness, perfidy.
pérfido, *a.* perfidious.
perfil, *m.* profile.
perforación, *f.* perforation.
perforar, *v.* pierce, perforate.
perfume, *m.* perfume, scent. —**perfumar,** *v.*
pergamino, *m.* parchment.
pericia, *f.* skill, expertness.
perico, *m.* parakeet.
perímetro, *m.* perimeter.

periódico, 1. *a.* periodic. **2.** *m.* newspaper.

periodista, *m.* journalist.

período, *m.* period.

periscopio, *m.* periscope.

perito -ta, *a. & n.* experienced; expert, connoisseur.

perjudicar, *v.* damage, hurt; impair.

perjudicial, *a.* harmful, injurious.

perjuicio, *m.* injury, damage.

perjurar, *v.* commit perjury.

perjurio, *m.* perjury.

perla, *f.* pearl.

permanecer, *v.* remain, stay.

permanencia, *f.* permanence; stay.

permanente, *a.* permanent.

permiso, *m.* permission; per- n it; furlough.

permitir, *v.* permit, enable, let, allow.

permuta, *f.* exchange; barter.

pernicioso, *a.* pernicious.

perno, *m.* bolt.

pero, *conj.* but.

peróxido, *m.* peroxide.

perpendicular, *m. & a.* perpendicular.

perpetración, *f.* perpetration.

perpetrar, *v.* perpetrate.

perpetuar, *v.* perpetuate.

perpetuidad, *f.* perpetuity.

perpetuo, *a.* perpetual.

perplejo, *a.* perplexed, puzzled.

perro -rra, *n.* dog.

persecución, *f.* persecution.

perseguir, *v.* pursue; persecute.

perseverancia, *f.* perseverance.

perseverar, *v.* persevere.

persiana, *f.* shutter, Venetian blind.

persistente, *a.* persistent.

persistir, *v.* persist.

persona, *f.* person.

personaje, *m.* personage; (theat.) character.

personal, 1. *a.* personal. **2.** *m.* personnel, staff.

personalidad, *f.* personality.

personalmente, *adv.* personally.

perspectiva, *f.* perspective; prospect.

perspicaz, *a.* perspicacious, acute.

persuadir, *v.* persuade.

persuasión, *f.* persuasion.

persuasivo, *a.* persuasive.

pertenecer, *v.* pertain, belong.

pertinencia, *f.* pertinence.

pertinente, *a.* pertinent; relevant.

perturbar, *v.* perturb, disturb.

peruano -na, *a. & n.* Peruvian.

perversidad, *f.* perversity.

perverso, *a.* perverse.

pesadez, *f.* dullness, importunity.

pesadilla, *f.* nightmare.

pesado, *a.* heavy; dull, dreary, boring.

pésame, *m.* condolence.

pesar, 1. *m.* sorrow; regret. **a p. de,** in spite of. **2.** *v.* weigh.

pesca, *f.* fishing; catch (of fish).

pescado, *m.* fish. **—pescar,** *v.*

pescador, *m.* fisherman.

pesebre, *m.* stall, manger, crib.

peseta, *f.* monetary unit of Spain.

pesimismo, *m.* pessimism.

pesimista, *a. & n.* pessimistic; pessimist.

peso, *m.* weight; load; peso (monetary unit).

pesquera, *f.* fishery.

pesquisa, *f.* investigation.

pestaña, *f.* eyelash.

pestañeo, *m.* wink; blink. **— pestañear,** *v.*

peste, *f.* plague.

pestilencia, *f.* pestilence.

pétalo, *m.* petal.

petición, *f.* petition.

petirrojo, *m.* robin.

petrel, *m.* petrel.

pétreo, *a.* rocky.

petrificar, *v.* petrify.

petróleo, *m.* petroleum.

petunia, *f.* petunia.

pez, *m.* fish (in the water). *f.* pitch, tar.

pezuña, *f.* hoof.

piadoso, *a.* pious.

pianista, *m.* & *f.* pianist.

piano, *m.* piano.

picadura, *f.* sting, bite, prick.

picamaderos, *m.* woodpecker.

picante, *a.* hot, spicy.

picaporte, *m.* latch.

picar, *v.* sting, bite, prick; itch; chop up, grind up.

pícaro -ra, 1. *a.* knavish, mischievous. **2.** *n.* rogue, rascal.

picarse, *v.* be offended, piqued.

picazón, *f.* itch.

pícea, *f.* spruce.

pico, *m.* peak; pick; beak; spout; small amount.

picotazo, *m.* peck. **—picotear,** *v.*

pictórico, *a.* pictorial.

pichón, *m.* pigeon, squab.

pie, *m.* foot. **al p. de la letra,** literally; thoroughly.

piedad, *f.* piety; pity, mercy.

piedra, *f.* stone.

piel, *f.* skin, hide; fur.

pierna, *f.* leg.

pieza, *f.* piece; room; (theat.) play.

pijamas, *m. or f. pl.* pajamas.

pila, *f.* pile, stack; battery; sink.

pilar, *m.* pillar, column.

píldora, *f.* pill.

piloto, *m.* pilot.

pillo, *m.* thief; rascal.

pimienta, *f.* pepper (spice).

pimiento, *m.* pepper (vegetable).

pináculo, *m.* pinnacle.

pincel, *m.* (artist's) brush.

pinchazo, *m.* puncture. **—pinchar,** *v.*

pingajo, *m.* rag, tatter.

pino, *m.* pine.

pinta, *f.* pint.

pintar, *v.* paint; portray, depict.

pintor -ra, *n.* painter.

pintoresco, *a.* picturesque.

pintura, *f.* paint; painting.

pinzas, *f.pl.* pincers, tweezers; claws.

piña, *f.* pineapple.

pío, *a.* pious; merciful.

piojo, *m.* louse.

pionero -ra, *n.* pioneer.

pipa, *f.* tobacco pipe.

pique, *m.* resentment, pique. **echar a p.,** sink (ship).

pira, *f.* pyre.

pirámide, *f.* pyramid.

pirata, *m.* pirate.

pisada, *f.* tread, step. **—pisar,** *v.*

piscina, *f.* fishpond; swimming pool.

piso, *m.* floor.

pista, *f.* trace, clue, track; race track.

pistola, *f.* pistol

pistón, *m.* piston.

pitillo, *m.* cigarette.

pito, *m.* whistle. **—pitar,** *v.*

pizarra, *f.* slate; blackboard.

pizca, *f.* bit, speck; pinch.

placentero, *a.* pleasant.

placer, 1. *m.* pleasure. **2.** *v.* please.

plácido, *a.* placid.

plaga, *f.* plague, scourge.

plagio, *m.* plagiarism; (S.A.) kidnapping.

plan, *m.* plan. **—planear,** *v.*

plancha, *f.* plate, slab, flat-iron.

planchar, *v.* iron, press.

planeta, *m.* planet.

plano, 1. *a.* level, flat. **2.** *m.* plan; plane.

planta, *f.* plant; sole (of foot).

plantación, *f.* plantation.

plantar, *v.* plant.

plantear, *v.* pose, present.

plantel, *m.* educational institution; (agr.) nursery.

plasma, *m.* plasma.

plástico, *a.* & *m.* plastic.

plata, *f.* silver; (coll.) money.

plataforma, *f.* platform.

plátano, *m.* plantain, cooking banana.

platel, *m.* platter.

plática, *f.* chat, talk. —
  platicar, *v.*
platillo, *m.* saucer.
plato, *m.* plate, dish.
playa, *f.* beach, shore.
plaza, *f.* square. **p. de toros,**
  bull ring.
plazo, *m.* term, deadline; installment.
plebe, *f.* common people;
  masses.
plebiscito, *m.* plebiscite.
plegadura, *f.* fold, pleat. —
  plegar, *v.*
pleito, *m.* lawsuit; dispute.
plenitud, *f.* fullness; abundance.
pleno, *a.* full. **en pleno . . .**
  in the middle of . . .
pliego, *m.* sheet of paper.
pliegue, *m.* fold, pleat, crease.
plomería, *f.* plumbing.
plomero, *m.* plumber.
plomizo, *a.* leaden.
plomo, *m.* lead; fuse.
pluma, *f.* feather; (writing)
  pen.
plumafuente, *f.* fountain
  pen.
plumaje, *m.* plumage.
plumero, *m.* feather duster;
  plume.
plumoso, *a.* feathery.
plural, *a. & m.* plural.
población, *f.* population;
  town.
poblador -ra, *n.* settler.
poblar, *v.* populate; settle.
pobre, *a. & n.* poor; poor
  person.
pobreza, *f.* poverty, need.
pocilga, *f.* pigpen.
poción, *f.* drink; potion.
poco, **1.** *a. & adv.* little, not
  much, (pl.) few. **por p.,**
  almost, nearly. **2.** *m.* **un p.**
  (de). a little, a bit (of).
poder, 1. *m.* power. **2.** *v.*
  be able to; can; be able;
  may, might. **no p. más,** be
  all in. **no p. menos de,** not
  be able to help.
poderío, *m.* power, might.
poderoso, *a.* powerful,
  mighty, potent.
podrido, *a.* rotten.

poema, *m.* poem.
poesía, *f.* poetry; poem.
poeta, *m.* poet.
poético, *a.* poetic.
polaco -ca, *a. & n.* Polish;
  Pole.
polar, *a.* polar.
polaridad, *f.* polarity.
polea, *f.* pulley
polen, *m.* pollen.
policía, *f.* police. **m.** policeman.
poligamia, *f.* polygamy.
poligloto -ta, *n.* polyglot.
polilla, *f.* moth.
política, *f.* politics; policy.
político, *a. & m.* politic;
  political; politician.
póliza, *f.* (insurance) policy;
  permit. ticket.
polizonte, *m.* policeman.
polo, *m.* pole; polo.
polonés, *a.* Polish.
Polonia, *f.* Poland.
polvera, *f.* powder box;
  powder puff.
polvo, *m.* powder; dust.
pólvora, *f.* powder, gunpowder.
pollada, *f.* brood.
pollería, *f.* poultry shop.
pollino, *m.* donkey.
pollo, *m.* chicken.
pompa, *f.* pomp.
pomposo, *a.* pompous.
ponche, *m.* punch (beverage).
ponchera, *f.* punch bowl.
ponderar, *v.* ponder.
ponderoso, *a.* ponderous.
poner, *v.* put. set. lay place.
ponerse, *v.* put on; become;
  get; set (sun). **p. a,** start
  to.
poniente, *m.* west.
pontífice, *m.* pontiff.
popa, *f.* stern.
popular, *a.* popular.
popularidad, *f.* popularity.
populazo, *m.* populace; masses.
por, *prep.* by, through, for,
  because of; via; for. **p. qué,**
  why?
porcelana, *f.* porcelain, china-
  ware.
porcentaje, *m.* percentage.

porción, f. portion, lot.
porche, m. porch; portico.
porfiar, v. persist; argue.
pormenor, m. detail.
pornografía, f. pornography.
poro, m. pore.
poroso, a. porous.
porque, conj. because.
porqué, m. reason, motive.
porra, f. stick, club.
porrazo, m. blow.
portaaviones, m. aircraft carrier.
portador -ra, n. bearer.
portal, m. portal.
portar, v. carry.
portarse, v. behave, act.
portátil, a. portable.
portavoz, m. megaphone.
porte, m. bearing; behavior; postage.
portero, m. porter; janitor.
pórtico, m. porch.
portorriqueño -ña, n. & a. Puerto Rican.
portugués -esa, a. & n. Portuguese.
posada, f. lodge, inn.
posar, v. pose.
posdata, f. postscript.
poseer, v. possess, own.
posesión, f. possession.
posibilidad, f. possibility.
posible, a. possible.
posiblemente, adv. possibly.
posición, f. position, stand.
positivo, a. positive.
posponer, v. postpone.
postal, a. postal.
poste, m. post, pillar.
posteridad, f. posterity.
posterior, a. posterior, rear.
postizo, a. false, artificial.
postrado, a. prostrate. — **postrar,** v.
postre, m. dessert.
póstumo, a. posthumous.
postura, f. posture, pose; bet.
potable, a. drinkable.
potaje, m. porridge; pot stew.
potasa, f. potash.
potasio, m. potassium.
pote, m. pot, jar.
potencia, f. potency, power.
potencial, a. & f. potential.

potentado, m. potentate.
potente, a. potent, powerful.
potestad, f. power.
potro, m. colt.
pozo, m. well.
práctica, f. practice. —**practicar,** v.
práctico, a. practical.
pradera, f. prairie, meadow.
prado, m. meadow; lawn.
pragmátismo, m. pragmatism.
preámbulo, m. preamble.
precario, a. precarious
precaución, f. precaution.
precaverse, v. beware.
precavido, a. cautious, guarded, wary.
precedencia, f. precedence, priority.
precedente, a. & m. preceding; precedent.
preceder, v. precede.
precepto, m. precept.
preciar, v. value, prize.
preciarse de, v. take pride in.
precio, m. price.
precioso, a. precious; beautiful, gorgeous.
precipicio, m. precipice, cliff
precipitación, f. precipitation.
precipitar, v. precipitate, rush; throw headlong.
precipitoso, a. precipitous; rash.
precisar, v. fix, specify; be necessary.
precisión, f. precision; necessity.
preciso, a. precise; necessary.
precocidad, f. precocity.
precoz, a. precocious.
precursor -ra, **1.** a. preceding. **2.** n. precursor, forerunner.
predecesor, -ra, a. & n. predecessor.
predecir, v. predict, foretell.
predicación, f. sermon.
predicador, m. preacher.
predicar, v. preach; publish.
predicción, f. prediction.
predilecto, a. favorite, preferred.
predisponer, v. predispose.

predisposición, f. predisposition; bias.

predominante, a. prevailing, prevalent, predominant.

predominar, v. prevail, predominate.

predominio, m. predominance, sway.

prefacio, m. preface.

preferencia, f. preference.

preferentemente, adv. preferably.

preferible, a. preferable.

preferir, v. prefer.

prefijo, m. prefix. —**prefijar,** v.

pregón, m. proclamation, cry.

pregonar, v. proclaim, cry out.

pregunta, f. question, inquiry. **hacer una p.,** to ask a question.

preguntar, v. ask, inquire.

preguntarse, v. wonder.

prehistórico, a. prehistoric.

prejuicio, m. prejudice.

prelacía, f. prelacy.

preliminar, a. & m. preliminary.

preludio, m. prelude.

prematuro, a. premature.

premeditación, f. premeditation.

premeditar, v. premeditate.

premiar, v. reward; award a prize to.

premio, m. prize, award; reward.

premisa, f. premise.

premura, f. pressure; urgency.

prenda, f. jewel; (personal) quality. **p. de vestir,** garment.

prender, v. seize, arrest, catch; attack, pin, clip. **p. fuego a,** set fire to.

prensa, f. printing press; (the) press.

prensar, v. press, compress.

preñado, a. pregnant.

preocupación, f. worry, preoccupation.

preocupar, v. worry, preoccupy.

preparación, f. preparation.

preparar, v. prepare.

preparativo, m. preparation.

preparatorio, a. preparatory.

preponderante, a. preponderant.

preposición, f. preposition.

prerrogativa, f. prerogative, privilege.

presa, f. capture; prey; (water) dam.

presagiar, v. presage, forebode.

presbiteriano -na, n. & a. Presbyterian.

presbítero, m. priest.

prescindir de, v. dispense with; omit.

prescribir, v. prescribe.

prescripción, f. prescription.

presencia, f. presence.

presenciar, v. witness, be present at.

presentable, a. presentable.

presentación, f. presentation; introduction.

presentar, v. present; introduce.

presente, a. & m. present.

preservación, f. preservation.

preservar, v. preserve, keep.

preservativo, a. & m. preservative.

presidencia, f. presidency.

presidencial, a. presidential.

presidente -ta, n. president.

presidio, m. prison; garrison.

presidir, v. preside.

presión, f. pressure.

preso, m. prisoner.

presta, f. mint (plant).

prestador, m. lender.

prestamista, m. & f. money lender.

préstamo, m. loan.

prestar, v. lend.

presteza, f. haste, promptness.

prestidigitación, f. sleight of hand.

prestigio, m. prestige.

presto, 1. a. quick, prompt; ready. **2.** adv. quickly; at once.

presumido, a. conceited, presumptuous.

presumir, v. presume; boast; claim; be conceited.

presunción, f. presumption; conceit.

presunto, a. presumed; prospective.

presuntuoso, a. presumptuous.

presupuesto, m. motive, pretext; budget.

pretender, v. pretend; intend; aspire.

pretendiente, m. suitor; pretender (to throne).

pretensión, f. pretension; claim.

pretérito, a. & m. preterit, past (tense).

pretexto, m. pretext.

prevalecer, v. prevail.

prevención, f. prevention.

prevenir, v. prevent; forewarn; prearrange.

preventivo, a. preventive.

prever, v. foresee.

previamente, adv. previously.

previo, a. previous.

previsión, f. foresight. **p. social,** social security.

prieto, a. blackish, very dark.

primacía, f. primacy.

primario, a. primary.

primavera, f. spring (season).

primero, a. & adv. first.

primitivo, a. primitive.

primo -ma, n. cousin.

primor, m. beauty; excellence; lovely thing.

primoroso, a. exquisite, elegant; graceful.

princesa, f. princess.

principal, 1. a. principal, main. **2.** m. chief, head, principal.

principalmente, adv. principally.

príncipe, m. prince.

principiar, v. begin, initiate.

principio, m. beginning, start; principle.

prioridad, f. priority.

prisa, f. hurry, haste. **darse p.,** hurry, hasten. **tener p.,** be in a hurry.

prisión, f. prison; imprisonment.

prisionero -ra, n. captive, prisoner.

prisma, m. prism.

prismático, a. prismatic.

privación, f. privation, want.

privado, a. private, secret; deprived.

privar, v. deprive.

privilegio, m. privilege.

pro, m. or f. benefit, advantage. **en p. de,** in behalf of. **en p. y en contra,** pro and con.

proa, f. prow, bow.

probabilidad, f. probability.

probable, a. probable, likely.

probablemente, adv. probably.

probar, v. try, sample; taste; test; prove.

probarse, v. try on.

probidad, f. honesty, integrity.

problema, m. problem.

probo, a. honest.

procaz, a. impudent, saucy.

proceder, v. proceed.

procedimiento, m. procedure.

procesar, v. prosecute; sue.

procesión, f. procession.

proceso, m. process; (court) trial.

proclama, proclamación, f. proclamation.

proclamar, v. proclaim.

procreación, f. procreation.

procrear, v. procreate.

procurar, v. try; see to it; get, procure.

prodigalidad, f. prodigality.

prodigar, v. lavish, squander, waste.

prodigio, m. prodigy.

pródigo, a. prodigal, profuse, lavish.

producción, f. production.

producir, v. produce.

productivo, a. productive.

producto, m. product.

proeza, f. prowess.

profanación, f. profanation.

profanar, v. defile, desecrate.

profanidad, f. profanity.

profano, a. profane.
profecía, f. prophecy.
proferir, v. utter, express.
profesar, v. profess.
profesión, f. profession.
profesional, a. professional.
profesor -ra, n. professor, teacher.
profeta, m. prophet.
profético, a. prophetic.
profetizar, v. prophesy.
proficiente, a. proficient.
profundamente, adv. profoundly, deeply.
profundidad, f. profundity, depth.
profundizar, v. deepen.
profundo, a. profound, deep.
profuso, a. profuse.
progenie, f. progeny, offspring.
programa, m. program; schedule.
progresar, v. progress, advance.
progresión, f. progression.
progresista, progresivo, a. progressive.
progreso, m. progress
prohibición, f. prohibition.
prohibir, v. prohibit, forbid.
prohibitivo, a. prohibitive.
prole, f. progeny
proletariado, m. proletariat.
prolijo, a. prolix, tedious; long-winded.
prólogo, m. prologue; preface.
prolongar, v. prolong.
promedio, m. average.
promesa, f. promise.
prometer, v. promise.
prometido, a. promised; engaged (to marry).
prominencia, f. prominence.
promiscuamente, adv. promiscuously.
promiscuo, a. promiscuous.
promisorio, a. promissory.
promoción, f. promotion.
promover, v. promote, further.
promulgación, f. promulgation.
promulgar, v. promulgate.
pronombre, m. pronoun.

pronosticación, f. prediction, forecast.
pronosticar, v. predict, forecast.
pronóstico, m. prediction.
prontamente, adv. promptly.
prontitud, f. promptness.
pronto, 1. a. prompt; ready. **2.** adv. soon; quickly. **de p.** abruptly.
pronunciación, f. pronunciation.
pronunciar, v. pronounce.
propagación, f. propagation.
propaganda, f. propaganda.
propagandista, n. propagandist.
propagar, v. propagate.
propicio, a. propitious, auspicious, favorable.
propiedad, f. property.
propietario -ria, n. proprietor; owner; landlord, landlady.
propina, f. gratuity, tip.
propio, a. proper, suitable; typical; (one's) own; -self.
proponer, v. propose.
proporción, f. proportion.
proporcionado, a. proportionate.
proporcionar, v. provide with, supply, afford.
proposición, f. proposition, offer; proposal.
propósito, m. purpose; plan; **a p.,** by the way, apropos; on purpose.
propuesta, f. proposal, motion.
prorrata, f. quota.
prórroga, f. renewal, extension.
prorrogar, v. renew, extend.
prosa, f. prose.
prosaico, a. prosaic.
proscribir, v. prohibit, proscribe, ban.
prosecución, f. prosecution.
proseguir, v. pursue; proceed, go on.
prosélito, m. proselyte.
prospecto, m. prospectus.
prosperar, v. prosper, thrive, flourish.

For pronunciation, see the concise guide on pages 3 to 4.

prosperidad, *f.* prosperity.

próspero, *a.* prosperous, successful.

prosternado, *a.* prostrate.

prostitución, *f.* prostitution.

prostituir, *v.* prostitute; debase.

prostituta, *f.* prostitute.

protagonista, *m. & f.* protagonist, hero, heroine.

protección, *f.* protection.

protector -ra, *a. & n.* protective; protector.

proteger, *v.* protect, safeguard.

protegido -da, *n.* protégé.

proteína, *f.* protein.

protesta, *f.* protest. **—protestar,** *v.*

protestante, *a. & n.* Protestant.

protocolo, *m.* protocol.

protuberancia, *f.* protuberance, lump.

provecho, *m.* profit, gain, benefit. **¡ Buen provecho!** May you enjoy your meal!

provechoso, *a.* beneficial, advantageous, profitable.

proveer, *v.* provide, furnish.

provenir de, *v.* originate in, be due to, come from.

proverbial, *a.* proverbial.

proverbio, *m.* proverb.

providencia, *f.* providence.

providente, *a.* provident.

provincia, *f.* province.

provincial, *a.* provincial.

provinciano -na, *a. & n.* provincial.

provisión, *f.* provision, supply, stock.

provisional, *a.* provisional.

provocación, *f.* provocation.

provocador, *m.* provoker.

provocar, *v.* provoke, excite.

provocativo, *a.* provocative.

proximidad, *f.* proximity, vicinity.

próximo, *a.* next; near.

proyección, *f.* projection.

proyectar, *v.* plan, project.

proyectil, *m.* projectile, missile, shell.

proyecto, *m.* plan, project, scheme.

proyector, *m.* projector.

prudencia, *f.* prudence.

prudente, *a.* prudent.

prueba, *f.* proof; trial; test.

psicoanálisis, *m. or f.* psychoanalysis.

psicología, *f.* psychology.

psicológico, *a.* psychological.

psicólogo, *m.* psychologist.

psiquiatra, *m.* psychiatrist.

psiquiatría, *f.* psychiatry.

publicación, *f.* publication.

publicar, *v.* publish.

publicidad, *f.* publicity.

público, *a. & m.* public.

puchero, *m.* pot.

pudiente, *a.* powerful; wealthy.

pudín, *m.* pudding.

pudor, *m.* modesty.

pudoroso, *a.* modest.

pudrirse, *v.* rot.

pueblo, *m.* town, village; (the) people.

puente, *m.* bridge.

puerco -ca, *n.* pig.

pueril, *a.* childish.

puerilidad, *f.* puerility.

puerta, *f.* door; gate.

puerto, *m.* port, harbor.

puertorriqueño -ña, *a. & n.* Puerto Rican.

pues, 1. *adv.* well . . . **2.** *conj.* as, since, for.

puesto, *m.* appointment, post, job; place; stand. **p. que,** since.

pugilato, *m.* boxing.

pugna, *f.* conflict.

pugnacidad, *f.* pugnacity.

pugnar, *v.* fight; oppose.

pulcritud, *f.* beauty.

pulga, *f.* flea.

pulgada, *f.* inch.

pulgar, *m.* thumb.

pulir, *v.* polish; beautify.

pulmón, *m.* lung.

pulmonía, *f.* pneumonia.

pulpa, *f.* pulp.

púlpito, *m.* pulpit.

pulque, *m.* pulque (fermented maguey juice).

pulsación, *f.* pulsation, beat.

pulsar, *v.* pulsate, beat.

pulsera, *f.* wristband; bracelet; wristwatch.

pulso, *m.* pulse.

pulverizar, *v.* pulverize.

puma, *m.* puma.

pundonor, *m.* point of honor.

punta, *f.* point, tip, end.

puntada, *f.* stitch.

puntapié, *m.* kick.

puntería, *f.* (marksman's) aim.

puntiagudo, *a.* sharp-pointed.

puntillas, *f.pl.* **de p., en p.,** on tiptoe.

punto, *m.* point; period; spot, dot. **dos puntos,** (punct.) colon. **a p. de,** about to. **al p.,** instantly.

puntuación, *f.* punctuation.

puntual, *a.* punctual, prompt.

puntuar, *v.* punctuate.

puñada, *f.* fist, blow.

puñado, *m.* handful.

puñal, *m.* dagger.

puñalada, *f.* stab.

puñetazo, *m.* punch, fist blow.

puño, *m.* fist; cuff; handle.

pupila, *f.* pupil (of eye).

pupitre, *m.* writing desk school desk.

pureza, *f.* purity; chastity.

purgante, *m.* laxative.

purgar, *v.* purge, cleanse.

purgatorio, *m.* purgatory.

puridad, *f.* purity.

purificación, *f.* purification.

purificar, *v.* purify.

purismo, *m.* purism.

purista, *n.* purist.

puritanismo, *m.* puritanism.

puro, 1. *a.* pure. **2.** *m.* cigar.

púrpura, *f.* purple.

purpúreo, *a.* purple.

purulencia, *f.* purulence.

purulento, *a.* purulent.

pus, *m.* pus.

pusilánime, *a.* pusillanimous.

puta, *f.* prostitute.

putrefacción, *f.* putrefaction, rot.

putrefacto, *a.* putrid, rotten.

pútrido, *a.* putrid.

puya, *f.* goad.

Q

que, 1. *rel. pron.* who, whom; that, which. **2.** *conj.* than.

qué, 1. *a. & pron.* what. **por q., para q.,** why? **2.** *adv.* how.

quebrada, *f.* ravine, gully, gulch; stream.

quebradizo, *a.* fragile, brittle.

quebrar, *v.* break.

queda, *f.* curfew.

quedar, *v.* remain, be located; be left. **q. bien a,** be becoming to.

quedarse, *v.* stay, remain. **q. con,** keep, hold on to.

quedo, *a.* quiet; gentle.

quehacer, *m.* task; chore.

queja, *f.* complaint.

quejarse, *v.* complain, grumble.

quejido, *m.* moan.

quejoso, *a.* complaining.

quema, *f.* burning.

quemadura, *f.* burn.

quemar, *v.* burn.

querella, *f.* quarrel; complaint.

querencia, *f.* affection, liking.

querer, *v.* want, wish; will; love (a person). **q. decir,** mean. **sin q.,** without meaning to; unwillingly.

querido, *a.* dear, loved, beloved.

quesería, f. dairy.
queso, m. cheese.
quiebra, f. break, fracture; damage; bankruptcy.
quien, rel. pron. who, whom.
quien, interrog. pron. who, whom.
quienquiera, pron. whoever, whomever.
quietamente, adv. quietly.
quieto, a. quiet, still.
quietud, f. quiet, quietude.
quijada, f. jaw.
quijotesco, a. quixotic.
quilate, m. carat.
quilla, f. keel.
quimera, f. chimera, vision; quarrel.
química, f. chemistry.
químico, a. & m. chemical; chemist.

quincallería, f. hardware store.
quince, a. & pron. fifteen.
quinientos, a. & pron. five hundred.
quintana, f. country home.
quinto, a. fifth.
quirúrgico, m. surgeon.
quiste, m. cyst.
quitamanchas, m. stain remover.
quitanieves, m. snowplow.
quitar, v. take away, remove.
quitarse, v. take off; get rid of.
quitasol, m. parasol, umbrella.
quizá, quizás, adv. perhaps, maybe.
quórum, m. quorum.

R

rábano, m. radish.
rabí, rabino, m. rabbi.
rabia, f. rage; grudge; rabies.
rabiar, v. rage, be furious.
rabieta, f. tantrum.
rabioso, a. furious; rabid.
rabo, m. tail.
racimo, m. bunch, cluster.
ración, f. ration. **—racionar,** v.
racionabilidad, f. rationality.
racional, a. rational.
racionalismo, m. rationalism.
racionalmente, adv. rationally.
racha, f. streak.
radar, m. radar.
radiación, f. radiation.
radiador, m. radiator.
radiante, a. radiant.
radical, a. & m. radical.
radicalismo, m. radicalism.
radicoso, a. radical.

radio, m. or f. radio.
radioactividad, f. radioactivity.
radioactivo, a. radioactive.
radiodifundir, v. broadcast.
radiodifusión, f. (radio) broadcasting.
ráfaga, f. gust (of wind).
raíz, f. root.
raja, f. rip; split, crack. **—rajar,** v.
ralea, f. stock, breed.
ralo, a. thin, scattered.
rama, f. branch, bough.
ramillete, m. bouquet.
ramo, m. branch, bough.
ramonear, v. browse.
rampa, f. ramp.
rana, f. frog.
rancidez, f. rancidity.
rancio, a. rancid, rank, stale, sour.
ranchero -ra, n. small farmer.
rancho, m. ranch.

For pronunciation, see the concise guide on pages 3 to 4.

rango, *m.* rank.

ranúnculo, *m.* ranunculus; buttercup.

ranura, *f.* slot.

rapacidad, *f.* rapacity.

rapaz, 1. *a.* rapacious. **2.** *m.* young boy.

rapé, *m.* snuff.

rápidamente, *adv.* rapidly.

rapidez, *f.* rapidity, speed.

rápido, 1. *a.* rapid, fast, speedy. **2.** *m.* express (train).

rapiña, *f.* robbery, plundering.

rapsodia, *f.* rhapsody.

raqueta, *f.* (tennis) racket.

rareza, *f.* rarity, freak.

raridad, *f.* rarity.

raro, *a.* rare, strange, unusual, odd, queer.

rasar, *v.* skim.

rascar, *v.* scrape; scratch.

rasgadura, *f.* tear, rip. —**rasgar,** *v.*

rasgo, *m.* trait.

rasgón, *m.* tear.

rasguño, *m.* scratch. —**rasguñar,** *v.*

raso, 1. *a.* plain. **soldado r.,** (mil.) private. **2.** *m.* satin.

raspar, *v.* scrape; erase.

rastra, *f.* trail, track. —**rastrear,** *v.*

rastrillar, *v.* rake.

rastro, *m.* track, trail, trace; rake.

rata, *f.* rat.

ratificación, *f.* ratification.

ratificar, *v.* ratify.

rato, *m.* while, spell, short time.

ratón, *m.* mouse.

ratonera, *f.* mousetrap.

raya, *f.* dash, line, streak, stripe.

rayar, *v.* rule, stripe; scratch; cross out.

rayo, *m.* lightning bolt; ray; flash.

rayón, *m.* rayon.

raza, *f.* race; breed, stock.

razón, *f.* reason; ratio. **a r. de,** at the rate of. **tener r.,** to be right.

razonable, *a.* reasonable, sensible.

razonamiento, *m.* argument.

razonar, *v.* reason.

reacción, *f.* reaction.

reaccionar, *v.* react.

reaccionario, *m.* reactionary.

reacondicionar, *v.* recondition.

reactivo, *a. & m.* reactive; (chem.) reagent.

real, *a.* royal, regal; real, actual.

realdad, *f.* royal authority.

realeza, *f.* royalty.

realidad, *f.* reality.

realista, *a. & n.* realistic; realist.

realización, *f.* achievement, accomplishment.

realizar, *v.* accomplish; fulfill; effect; (com.) realize.

realmente, *adv.* in reality.

realzar, *v.* enhance.

reata, *f.* rope; lasso, lariat.

rebaja, *f.* reduction.

rebajar, *v.* cheapen; reduce (in price); lower.

rebanada, *f.* slice. —**rebanar,** *v.*

rebaño, *m.* flock, herd.

rebato, *m.* alarm; sudden attack.

rebelarse, *v.* rebel, revolt.

rebelde, *a. & n.* rebellious; rebel.

rebelión, *f.* rebellion, revolt.

reborde, *m.* border.

rebotar, *v.* rebound.

rebozo, *m.* shawl.

rebuscar, *v.* search thoroughly.

rebuznar, *v.* bray.

recado, *m.* message; errand.

recaída, *f.* relapse. —**recaer,** *v.*

recalcar, *v.* stress, emphasize.

recámara, *f.* (Mex.) bedroom.

recapitulación, *f.* recapitulation.

recapitular, *v.* recapitulate.

recatado, *m.* coy; prudent.

recelar, *v.* fear, distrust.

receloso, *a.* distrustful.

recepción, f. reception.
receptáculo, m. receptacle.
receptividad, f. receptivity.
receptivo, a. receptive.
receptor, m. receiver.
receta, f. recipe; prescription.
recetar, v. prescribe.
recibimiento, m. reception; cordiality.
recibir, v. receive.
recibo, m. receipt.
recidiva, f. relapse.
recién, adv. recently, newly, just.
reciente, a. recent.
recinto, m. enclosure.
recipiente, m. recipient.
reciprocación, f. reciprocation.
recíprocamente, adv. reciprocally.
reciprocar, v. reciprocate.
reciprocidad, f. reciprocity.
recitación, f. recitation.
recitar, v. recite.
reclamación, f. claim; complaint.
reclamar, v. claim; complain.
reclamo, m. claim; advertisement, advertising; decoy.
reclinar, v. recline, repose, lean.
recluta, m. recruit.
reclutar, v. recruit, draft.
recobrar, v. recover, salvage, regain.
recobro, m. recovery.
recoger, v. gather; collect; pick up.
recogerse, v. retire (for night).
recolectar, v. gather, assemble; harvest.
recomendación, f. recommendation; commendation.
recomendar, v. recommend; commend.
recompensa, f. recompense; compensation.
recompensar, v. reward; compensate.
reconciliación, f. reconciliation.
reconciliar, v. reconcile.
reconocer, v. recognize; acknowledge; inspect, examine; (mil.) reconnoiter.
reconocimiento, m. recognition; appreciation, gratitude.
reconstituir, v. reconstitute.
reconstruir, v. reconstruct, rebuild.
record, m. (sports) record.
recordar, v. recall, recollect; remind.
recorrer, v. go over; read over; cover (distance).
recorte, m. clipping, cutting.
recostarse, v. recline, lean back, rest.
recreación, f. recreation.
recreo, m. recreation.
recriminación, f. recrimination.
rectangular, a. rectangular.
rectángulo, m. rectangle.
rectificación, f. rectification.
rectificar, v. rectify.
recto, a. straight; just, fair. **ángulo r.,** right angle.
recuento, m. recount.
recuerdo, m. memory, souvenir, remembrance; (pl.) regards.
reculada, f. recoil. **—recular,** v.
recuperación, f. recuperation.
recuperar, v. recuperate.
recurrir, v. revert; resort; have recourse.
recurso, m. resource; recourse.
rechazar, v. reject, spurn, discard.
rechinar, v. chatter.
red, f. net; trap.
redacción, f. (editorial) staff; composition (of written material).
redactar, v. draft, draw up; edit.
redactor, m. editor.
redada, f. netful, catch, haul.
redargución, f. retort. **—redargüir,** v.
redención, f. redemption, salvation.
redentor, m. redeemer.
redimir, v. redeem.

For pronunciation, see the concise guide on pages 3 to 4.

redoblante, *m.* drummer.

redonda, *f.* neighborhood, vicinity.

redondo, *a.* round, circular.

reducción, *f.* reduction.

reducir, *v.* reduce.

reembolso, *m.* refund. —**reembolsar,** *v.*

reemplazar, *v.* replace, supersede.

reencarnación, *f.* reincarnation.

reexaminar, *v.* reëxamine.

reexpedir, *v.* forward (mail).

referencia, *f.* reference.

referéndum, *m.* referendum.

referir, *v.* relate, report on.

referirse, *v.* refer.

refinamiento, *m.* refinement.

refinar, *v.* refine.

refinería, *f.* refinery.

reflejar, *v.* reflect; think, ponder.

reflejo, *m.* reflection; glare.

reflexión, *f.* reflection, thought.

reflexionar, *v.* reflect, think.

reflujo, *m.* ebb; ebbtide.

reforma, *f.* reform. —**reformar,** *v.*

reformación, *f.* reformation.

reformador, *m.* reformer.

reforzar, *v.* reinforce, strengthen; encourage.

refractario, *a.* refractory.

refrán, *m.* proverb, saying.

refrenar, *v.* curb, rein; restrain.

refrescar, *v.* refresh, freshen, cool.

refresco, *m.* refreshment; cold drink.

refrigeración, *f.* refrigeration.

refrigerador, *m.* refrigerator.

refrigerar, *v.* refrigerate.

refuerzo, *m.* reinforcement.

refugiado -da, refugee.

refugiarse, *v.* take refuge.

refugio, *m.* refuge, asylum, shelter.

refulgencia, *f.* refulgence.

refulgente, *a.* refulgent.

refulgir, *v.* shine.

refunfuñar, *v.* mutter, grumble, growl.

refutación, *f.* refutation; rebuttal.

refutar, *v.* refute.

regadizo, *a.* irrigable.

regadura, *f.* irrigation.

regalar, *v.* give (a gift), give away.

regalo, *m.* gift, present. **con r.,** in luxury.

regañar, *v.* reprove; scold.

regaño, *m.* reprimand, scolding.

regar, *v.* water, irrigate.

regatear, *v.* haggle.

regateo, *m.* bargaining, haggling.

regazo, *m.* lap.

regencia, *f.* regency.

regeneración, *f.* regeneration.

regenerar, *v.* regenerate.

regente, *m.* regent.

régimen, *m.* regime; diet.

regimentar, *v.* regiment.

regimiento, *m.* regiment.

región, *f.* region.

regional, *a.* regional, sectional.

regir, *v.* rule; be in effect.

registrar, *v.* register; record; search.

registro, *m.* register; record; search.

regla, *f.* rule, regulation. **en r.,** in order.

reglamento, *m.* code of regulations.

regocijarse, *v.* rejoice, exult.

regocijo, *m.* rejoicing; merriment, joy.

regordete, *a.* chubby, plump.

regresar, *v.* go back, return.

regresión, *f.* regression.

regresivo, *a.* regressive.

regreso, *m.* return.

regulación, *f.* regulation.

regular, 1. *a.* regular; fair, middling. **2.** *v.* regulate.

regularidad, *f.* regularity.

regularmente, *adv.* regularly.

rehabilitación, *f.* rehabilitation.

rehabilitar, *v.* rehabilitate.

rehén, *m.* hostage.

rehusar, *v.* refuse; decline.

reina, f. queen.
reinado, m. reign. —reinar, v.
reino, m. kingdom; realm; reign.
reír, v. laugh.
reiteración, f. reiteration.
reiterar, v. reiterate.
reja, f. grating, grillwork.
relación, f. relation; account, report.
relacionar, v. relate, connect.
relajamiento, m. laxity, laxness.
relajar, v. relax, slacken.
relámpago, m. lightning; flash (of lightning).
relatador, m. teller.
relatar, v. relate, recount.
relativamente, adv. relatively.
relatividad, f. relativity.
relativo, a. relative.
relato, m. account, story.
relegación, f. relegation.
relegar, v. relegate.
relevar, v. relieve.
relicario, m. reliquary; locket.
relieve, m. (sculpture) relief.
religión, f. religion.
religiosidad, f. religiosity.
religioso -sa, 1. a. religious. 2. m. member of a religious order.
reliquia, f. relic.
reloj, m. clock; watch.
relojería, f. watchmaker's shop.
relojero, m. watchmaker.
relucir, v. glow, shine; excel.
relumbrar, v. glitter, sparkle.
rellenar, v. refill; fill up, stuff.
relleno, m. filling; stuffing.
remache, m. rivet. —remachar, v.
remar, v. row (a boat).
rematado, a. finished; sold.
remate, m. end, finish; auction. de r., utterly.
remedador, m. imitator.
remedar, v. imitate.
remedio, m. remedy. —remediar, v.
remendar, v. mend, patch.
remesa, f. shipment; remittance.

remiendo, m. patch.
remilgado, a. prudish; affected.
reminiscencia, f. reminiscence.
remitir, v. remit.
remo, m. oar.
remolacha, f. beet.
remolcador, m. tug (boat).
remolino, m. whirl; whirlpool; whirlwind.
remolque, m. tow. —remolcar, v.
remontar, v. ascend, go up.
remontarse, v. get excited; soar. r. a, date from; go back to (in time).
remordimiento, m. remorse.
remotamente, adv. remotely.
remoto, a. remote.
remover, v. remove; stir; shake; loosen.
rempujar, v. jostle.
remuneración, f. remuneration.
remunerar, v. remunerate.
renacimiento, m. rebirth; renaissance.
rencor, m. rancor, bitterness, animosity; grudge.
rencoroso, a. rancorous, bitter.
rendición, f. surrender.
rendido, a. weary, worn out.
rendir, v. yield; surrender; give up; win over.
renegado, m. renegade.
renglón, m. line; (com.) item.
reno, m. reindeer.
renombre, m. renown.
renovación, f. renovation, renewal.
renovar, v. renew; renovate.
renta, f. income; rent.
rentar, v. yield; rent for.
renuencia, f. reluctance.
renuente, a. reluctant.
renuncia, f. resignation; renunciation.
renunciar, v. resign; renounce, give up.
reñir, v. scold, berate; quarrel, wrangle.

reo, *a.* & *n.* criminal; convict.

reorganizar, *v.* reorganize.

reparación, *f.* reparation, atonement; repair.

reparar, *v.* repair; mend; stop, stay over. **r. en,** notice; consider.

reparo, *m.* repair; remark; difficulty; objection.

repartición, *f.,* **repartimiento, reparto,** *m.* division, distribution.

repartir, *v.* divide, apportion, distribute; (theat.) cast.

repaso, *m.* review. —**repasar,** *v.*

repatriación, *f.* repatriation.

repatriar, *v.* repatriate.

repeler, *v.* repel.

repente, *m.* **de r.,** suddenly; unexpectedly.

repentinamente, *adv.* suddenly.

repentino, *a.* sudden.

repercusión, *f.* repercussion.

repertorio, *m.* repertoire.

repetición, *f.* repetition.

repetidamente, *adv.* repeatedly.

repetir, *v.* repeat.

repisa, *f.* shelf.

réplica, *f.* reply; objection.

replicar, *v.* reply; answer back.

repollo, *m.* cabbage.

reponer, *v.* replace; repair.

reponerse, *v.* recover, get well.

reporte, *m.* report; news.

repórter, reportero, *m.* reporter.

reposado, *a.* tranquil, peaceful, quiet.

reposo, *m.* repose, rest. —**reposar,** *v.*

reposte, *f.* pantry.

represalia, *f.* reprisal.

representación, *f.* representation; (theat.) performance.

representante, *m.* representative, agent.

representar, *v.* represent, depict; (theat.) perform.

representativo, *a.* representative.

represión, *f.* repression.

represivo, *a.* repressive.

reprimenda, *f.* reprimand.

reprimir, *v.* repress, quell.

reproche, *m.* reproach. —**reprochar,** *v.*

reproducción, *f.* reproduction.

reproducir, *v.* reproduce.

reptil, *m.* reptile.

república, *f.* republic.

republicano -na, *a.* & *n.* republican.

repudiación, *f.* repudiation.

repudiar, *v.* repudiate; disown.

repuesto, *m.* spare part. **de r.,** spare.

repugnancia, *f.* repugnance.

repugnante, *a.* repugnant, repulsive.

repugnar, *v.* disgust.

repulsa, *f.* refusal; repulse.

repulsar, *v.* refuse; repulse.

repulsivo, *a.* repulsive.

reputación, *f.* reputation.

reputar, *v.* repute; appreciate.

requerir, *v.* require.

requesón, *m.* cottage cheese.

requisición, *f.* requisition.

requisito, *m.* requisite, requirement.

res, *f.* head of cattle.

resbalar, *v.* slide; slip.

resbaloso, *a.* slippery.

rescate, *m.* rescue, ransom. —**rescatar,** *v.*

rescindir, *v.* rescind.

resentimiento, *m.* resentment.

resentirse, *v.* resent. —**reserva,** *f.* reserve. —**reservar,** *v.*

reservación, *f.* reservation.

resfriado, *m.* (med.) cold.

resfriarse, *v.* catch cold.

resguardar, *v.* guard, protect.

residencia, *f.* residence, seat.

residente, *a.* & *n.* resident.

residir, *v.* reside.

residuo, *m.* remainder.

resignación, *f.* resignation.

resignar, *v.* resign.

resina, *f.* resin; rosin.

resistencia, f. resistance.

resistir, v. resist; endure.

resolución, f. resolution.

resolutivamente, adv. resolutely.

resolver, v. resolve; solve.

resonante, a. resonant.

resonar, v. resound.

resorte, m. (mech.) spring.

respaldar, v. indorse; back.

respaldo, m. back (of a seat).

respectivo, a. respective.

respecto, m. relation, proportion; **r. a,** concerning, regarding.

respetabilidad, f. respectability.

respetable, a. respectable.

respeto, m. respect. —**respetar,** v.

respetuosamente, adv. respectfully.

respetuoso, a. respectful.

respiración, f. respiration, breath.

respirar, v. breathe.

resplandeciente, a. resplendent.

resplandor, m. brightness, glitter.

responder, v. respond, answer.

responsabilidad, f. responsibility.

responsable, a. responsible.

respuesta, f. answer, response, reply.

resquicio, m. crack, slit.

resta, f. subtraction, remainder.

restablecer, v. restore, reëstablish.

restablecerse, v. recover, get well.

restar, v. remain; subtract.

restauración, f. restoration.

restaurante, m. restaurant.

restaurar, v. restore.

restitución, f. restitution.

restituir, v. restore, give back.

resto, m. remainder, rest; (pl.) remains.

restorán, m. restaurant.

restregar, v. scrape.

restricción, f. restriction.

restrictivo, a. restrictive.

restringir, v. restrict, curtail.

resucitar, v. resuscitate; resurrect.

resuelto, a. resolute.

resultado, m. result.

resultar, v. result; turn out; ensue.

resumen, m. résumé, summary. **en r.,** in brief.

resumir, v. sum up.

resurgir, v. resurge, reappear.

resurrección, f. resurrection.

retaguardia, f. rear guard.

retal, m. remnant.

retardar, v. retard, show.

retardo, m. delay.

retención, f. retention.

retener, v. retain, keep, withhold.

reticencia, f. reticence.

reticente, a. reticent.

retirada, f. retreat, retirement.

retirar, v. retire, retreat, withdraw.

retiro, m. retirement.

retorcer, v. wring.

retórica, f. rhetoric.

retórico, a. rhetorical.

retorno, m. return.

retozo, m. frolic, romp. —**retozar,** v.

retozón, a. frisky.

retracción, f. retraction.

retractor, v. retract.

retrasar, v. delay, set back; be slow.

retraso, m. delay, lag, slowness.

retratar, v. portray; photograph.

retrato, m. portrait, picture; photograph.

retreta, f. (mil.) retreat.

retrete, m. alcove; toilet.

retribución, f. retribution.

retroactivo, a. retroactive.

retroceder, v. recede, go back, draw back, back up.

retumbar, v. resound, rumble.

reumático, a. rheumatic.

reumatismo, m. rheumatism.

reunión, f. gathering, meeting, party; reunion.

reunir, v. gather, collect, bring together.

reunirse, v. meet, assemble, get together.

revelación, f. revelation.

revelar, v. reveal, betray; (phot.) develop.

reventa, f. resale.

reventar, v. burst; split apart.

reventón, m. blowout (of tire).

reverencia, f. reverence.

reverendo, a. reverend.

reverente, a. reverent.

revertir, v. revert.

revés, m. reverse; back, wrong side. **al r.,** just the opposite; inside out.

revisar, v. revise; review.

revisión, f. revision.

revista, f. magazine, periodical; review.

revivir, v. revive.

revocación, f. revocation.

revocar, v. revoke, reverse.

revolotear, v. hover.

revolución, f. revolution.

revolucionario -ria, a. & n. revolutionary.

revolver, v. revolve; stir, agitate.

revólver, m. revolver, pistol.

revuelta, f. revolt; turn.

rey, m. king.

reyerta, f. quarrel, wrangle.

rezar, v. pray.

rezongar, v. grumble; mutter.

ría, f. estuary.

riachuelo, m. creek.

riba, f. embankment.

rico, a. rich, wealthy; delicious.

ridículamente, adv. ridiculously.

ridiculizar, v. ridicule.

ridículo, a. & m. ridiculous; ridicule.

riego, m. irrigation.

rienda, f. rein.

riesgo, m. risk, gamble.

rifa, f. raffle; lottery; scuffle.

rifle, m. rifle.

rígidamente, adv. rigidly.

rigidez, f. rigidity.

rígido, a. rigid, stiff.

rigor, m. rigor.

riguroso, a. rigorous, strict.

rima, f. rhyme. —**rimar,** v.

rincón, m. corner, nook.

rinoceronte, m. rhinoceros.

riña, f. quarrel, feud.

riñón, m. kidney.

río, m. river.

ripio, m. debris.

riqueza, f. wealth.

risa, f. laugh; laughter.

risco, m. cliff.

risibilidad, f. risibility.

risotada, f. peal of laughter.

risueño, a. cheerful, smiling.

rítmico, a. rhythmical.

ritmo, m. rhythm.

rito, m. rite.

ritual, a. & m. ritual.

rival, m. & f. rival.

rivalidad, f. rivalry.

rivera, f. brook.

rizado, a. curly.

rizo, m. curl. —**rizar,** v.

robar, v. rob, steal.

roble, m. oak.

roblón, m. rivet. —**roblar,** v.

robo, m. robbery, theft.

robustamente, adv. robustly.

robusto, a. robust.

roca, f. rock; cliff.

rociada, f. spray, sprinkle. — **rociar,** v.

rocío, m. dew.

rodar, v. roll; roam.

rodear, v. surround, encircle.

rodeo, m. turn, winding; round-up.

rodilla, f. knee.

rodillo, m. roller.

rodio, m. rhodium.

rododendro, m. rhododendron.

roedor, m. rodent.

roer, v. gnaw.

rogación, f. request, entreaty.

rogar, v. beg, plead with, supplicate.

rojizo, a. reddish.

rojo, a. red.

For **pronunciation,** see the concise guide on pages 3 to 4.

rollo, *m.* roll; coil.

romadizo, *m.* head cold.

romance, *m.* romance, ballad.

románico, *a.* Romance.

romano -na, *a. & n.* Roman.

romántico, *a.* Romantic.

romería, *f.* pilgrimage; picnic.

romero -ra, *n.* pilgrim.

rompecabezas, *m.* puzzle (pastime).

romper, *v.* break, smash, shatter; sever; tear.

rompible, *a.* breakable.

ron, *m.* rum.

roncar, *v.* snore.

ronco, *a.* hoarse.

ronda, *f.* round.

rondar, *v.* prowl.

ronquido, *m.* snore.

ronzal, *m.* halter.

roña, *f.* scab; filth.

ropa, *f.* clothes, clothing. **r. blanca,** linen. **r. interior,** underwear.

ropero, *m.* closet.

rosa, *f.* rose. **r. náutica,** compass.

rosado, *a.* pink, rosy.

rosal, *m.* rose bush.

rosario, *m.* rosary.

rosbif, *m.* roast beef.

rosca, *f.* thread (of screw).

róseo, *a.* rosy.

rostro, *m.* face, countenance.

rota, *f.* defeat; (naut.) course.

rotación, *f.* rotation.

rotatorio, *a.* rotary.

rótulo, *m.* label. —**rotular,** *v.*

rotundo, *a.* round; sonorous.

rotura, *f.* break, fracture, rupture.

rozar, *v.* rub against, chafe; graze.

rubí, *m.* ruby.

rubio -bia, *a. & n.* blond.

rubor, *m.* blush; bashfulness.

rúbrica, *f.* caption; scroll.

rucho, *m.* donkey.

rudeza, *f.* rudeness; roughness.

rudimento, *m.* rudiment.

rudo, *a.* rude, rough.

rueda, *f.* wheel.

ruego, *m.* plea; entreaty.

rufián, *m.* ruffian.

rufo, *a.* sandy (colored).

rugir, *v.* bellow, roar.

rugoso, *a.* wrinkled.

ruibarbo, *m.* rhubarb.

ruido, *m.* noise.

ruidoso, *a.* noisy.

ruina, *f.* ruin, wreck.

ruinar, *v.* ruin, destroy.

ruinoso, *a.* ruinous.

ruiseñor, *m.* nightingale.

ruleta, *f.* roulette.

rumba, *f.* rumba (dance or music).

rumbo, *m.* course, direction.

rumor, *m.* rumor; murmur.

runrún, *m.* rumor.

ruptura, *f.* rupture, break.

rural, *a.* rural.

Rusia, *f.* Russia.

ruso -sa, *a. & n.* Russian.

rústico -ca, *a. & n.* rustic.

ruta, *f.* route.

rutina, *f.* routine.

rutinario, *a.* routine.

S

sábado, *m.* Saturday.

sábalo, *m.* shad.

sábana, *f.* sheet.

sabañón, *m.* chilblain.

saber, 1. *n.* knowledge. **2.** *v.* know; learn, find out; know how to; taste. **a s.,** namely, to wit.

sabiduría, f. wisdom; learning.

sabio, 1. a. wise; scholarly. **2.** m. sage; scholar.

sable, m. saber.

sabor, m. flavor, taste, savor.

saborear, v. savor, relish.

sabotaje, m. sabotage.

sabroso, a. savory, tasty.

sabueso, m. hound.

sacacorchos, m. corkscrew.

sacar, v. draw out; take out; take.

sacerdocio, m. priesthood.

sacerdote, m. priest.

saciar, v. satiate.

saco, m. sack, bag, pouch; suit coat, jacket.

sacramento, m. sacrament.

sacrificio, m. sacrifice. — **sacrificar,** v.

sacrilegio, m. sacrilege.

sacristán, m. sexton.

sacro, a. sacred, holy.

sacrosanto, a. sacrosanct.

sacudir, v. shake, jerk, jolt.

sádico, a. sadistic.

sadismo, m. sadism.

sagacidad, f. sagacity.

sagaz, a. sagacious, sage.

sagrado, a. sacred, holy.

sal, f. salt; (coll.) wit.

sala, f. room; living room, parlor; hall, auditorium.

salado, a. salted, salty; (coll.) witty.

salar, v. salt; steep in brine.

salario, m. salary, wages.

salchicha, f. sausage.

saldo, m. remainder, balance; (bargain) sale.

salero, m. salt shaker.

salida, f. exit, outlet; departure.

salir, v. go out, come out; set out, leave, start; turn out, result.

salirse de, v. get out of. **s. con la suya,** have one's own way.

salitre, m. saltpetre.

saliva, f. saliva.

salmo, m. psalm.

salmón, m. salmon.

salmuera, f. pickle; brine.

salobre, a. salty.

salón, m. parlor, living room; hall.

salpicar, v. spatter, splash.

salpullido, m. rash.

salsa, f. sauce; gravy.

saltamontes, m. grasshopper.

salteador, m. highwayman.

salto, m. jump, leap, spring. — **saltar,** v.

saltón, m. grasshopper.

salubre, a. salubrious, healthful.

salubridad, f. health.

salud, f. health.

saludable, a. healthful, wholesome.

saludar, v. greet; salute.

saludo, m. greeting; salutation; salute.

salutación, f. salutation.

salva, f. salvo.

salvación, f. salvation; deliverance.

salvador -ra, n. savior; rescuer.

salvaguardia, m. safeguard.

salvaje, a. & m. savage, wild (man).

salvamento, m. salvation; rescue.

salvar, v. save; salvage; rescue; jump over.

salvavidas, m. life preserver.

salvia, f. sage (plant).

salvo, 1. a. safe. **2.** prep. except, save (for). **s. que,** unless.

San, title. Saint.

sanar, v. heal, cure.

sanatorio, m. sanatorium.

sanción, f. sanction. — **sancionar,** v.

sandalia, f. sandal.

sandez, f. stupidity.

sandía, f. watermelon.

saneamiento, m. sanitation.

sangrar, v. bleed.

sangre, f. blood.

sangriento, a. bloody.

sanguinario, a. bloodthirsty.

sanidad, f. health.

sanitario, a. sanitary.

sano, a. healthy, sound, sane; healthful, wholesome.

santidad, *f.* sanctity, holiness.

santificar, *v.* sanctify.

santo -ta. 1. *a.* holy, saintly. **2.** *m.* saint.

Santo -ta, *title.* Saint.

santuario, *m.* sanctuary, shrine.

saña, *f.* rage, anger.

sapiente, *a.* wise.

sapo, *m.* toad.

saquear, *v.* sack, ransack, plunder.

sarampión, *m.* measles.

sarape, *m.* (Mex.) woven blanket; shawl.

sarcasmo, *m.* sarcasm.

sarcástico, *a.* sarcastic.

sardina, *f.* sardine.

sargento, *m.* sergeant.

sarna, *f.* itch.

sartén, *f.* frying pan.

sastre, *m.* tailor.

satánico, *a.* satanic.

satélite, *m.* satellite.

sátira, *f.* satire.

satírico, *a. & m.* satirical; satirist.

satirizar, *v.* satirize.

sátiro, *m.* satyr.

satisfacción, *f.* satisfaction.

satisfacer, *v.* satisfy.

satisfactorio, *a.* satisfactory.

saturación, *f.* saturation.

saturar, *v.* saturate.

sauce, *m.* willow.

savia, *f.* sap.

saxófono, *m.* saxophone.

saya, *f.* skirt.

sazón, *f.* season; seasoning. **a la s.,** at that time.

sazonar, *v.* flavor, season.

se, *pron.* -self, -selves.

seca, *f.* drought.

secante, *a.* **papel s.,** blotting paper.

secar, *v.* dry.

sección, *f.* section.

seco, *a.* dry; curt.

secreción, *f.* secretion.

secretar, *v.* secrete.

secretaría, *f.* secretary's office; secretariat.

secretario -ra, *n.* secretary.

secreto, *a. & m.* secret.

secta, *f.* denomination, sect.

secuela, *f.* result; sequel.

secuestrar, *v.* abduct, kidnap.

secuestro, *m.* abduction, kidnapping.

secular, *a.* secular.

secundario, *a.* secondary.

sed, *f.* thirst. **tener s., estar con s.,** to be thirsty.

seda, *f.* silk.

sedar, *v.* quiet, allay.

sedativo, *a. & m.* sedative.

sede, *f.* seat, headquarters.

sedentario, *a.* sedentary.

sedición, *f.* sedition.

sedicioso, *a.* seditious.

sediento, *a.* thirsty.

sedimento, *m.* sediment.

sedoso, *a.* silky.

seducir, *v.* seduce.

seductivo, *a.* seductive, alluring.

segar, *v.* reap, harvest; mow.

seglar, *m.* layman.

segmento, *m.* segment.

segregar, *v.* segregate.

seguida, *f.* succession. **en s.,** right away, at once.

seguido, *a.* consecutive.

seguir, *v.* follow; continue, keep on, go on.

según, 1. *prep.* according to. **2.** *conj.* as.

segundo, *a. & m.* second. — **segundar,** *v.*

seguridad, *f.* safety, security; assurance.

seguro, 1. *a.* safe, secure; sure, certain. **2.** *m.* insurance.

seis, *a. & pron.* six.

seiscientos, *a. & pron.* six hundred.

selección, *f.* selection, choice.

seleccionar, *v.* select, choose.

selecto, *a.* select, choice, elite.

selva, *f.* forest; jungle.

selvoso, *a.* sylvan.

sello, *m.* seal; stamp. —**sellar,** *v.*

semáforo, *m.* semaphore.

semana, *f.* week.

semanal, *a.* weekly.

semántica, *f.* semantics.

For pronunciation, see the concise guide on pages 3 to 4.

semblante, *m.* look, expression.

sembrado, *m.* sown field.

sembrar, *v.* sow, seed.

semejante. 1. *a.* like, similiar; such (a). **2.** *m.* fellow-man.

semejanza, *f.* similarity, likeness.

semejar, *v.* resemble.

semilla, *f.* seed.

seminario, *m.* seminary.

senado, *m.* senate.

senador -ra, *n.* senator.

sencillez, *f.* simplicity; naturalness.

sencillo, *a.* simple, natural; single.

senda, *f.* **sendero,** *m.* path.

senectud, *f.* old age.

senil, *a.* senile.

seno, *m.* breast, bosom.

sensación, *f.* sensation.

sensacional, *a.* sensational.

sensato, *a.* sensible, wise.

sensibilidad, *f.* sensibility; sensitiveness.

sensible, *a.* sensitive; emotional.

sensitivo, *a.* sensitive.

sensual, *a.* sensual.

sensualidad, *f.* sensuality.

sentar, *v.* seat. **s. bien,** fit well, be becoming.

sentarse, *v.* sit, sit down.

sentencia, *f.* (court) sentence.

sentidamente, *adv.* feelingly.

sentido, *m.* meaning; sense; consciousness.

sentimental, *a.* sentimental.

sentimiento, *m.* sentiment, feeling.

sentir, *v.* feel, sense; hear; regret, be sorry.

seña, *f.* sign, indication; (pl.) address.

señal, *f.* sign, signal; mark.

señalar, *v.* designate, point out; mark.

señor, *m.* gentleman; lord; (title) Mr., Sir.

señora, *f.* lady; wife; (title) Mrs., Madam.

señorita, *f.* young lady; (title) Miss.

sépalo, *m.* sepal.

separación, *f.* separation, parting.

separadamente, *adv.* separately.

separado, *a.* separate. **—separar,** *v.*

septentrional, *a.* northern.

septiembre, *m.* September.

séptimo, *a.* seventh.

sepulcro, *m.* sepulcher.

sepultar, *v.* bury, entomb.

sepultura, *f.* grave.

sequedad, *f.* dryness.

sequía, *f.* drought.

ser, *v.* be.

serenata, *f.* serenade.

serenidad, *f.* serenity.

sereno, *a.* **1.** *a.* serene, calm. **2.** *m.* dew; watchman.

serie, *f.* series, sequence.

seriedad, *f.* seriousness.

serio, *a.* serious. **en s.,** seriously.

sermón, *m.* sermon.

seroso, *a.* watery.

serpiente, *f.* serpent, snake.

serrano, *m.* mountaineer.

serrar, *v.* saw.

serrín, *m.* sawdust.

servicial, *a.* helpful, of service.

servicio, *m.* service; toilet.

servidor -ra, *n.* servant.

servidumbre, *f.* bondage; staff of servants.

servil, *a.* servile, menial.

servilleta, *f.* napkin.

servir, *v.* serve. **s. para,** be good for.

servirse, *v.* help oneself.

sesenta, *a. & pron.* sixty.

sesgo, *m.* slant. **—sesgar,** *v.*

sesión, *f.* session; sitting.

seso, *m.* brain.

seta, *f.* mushroom.

setecientos, *a. & pron.* seven hundred.

setenta, *a. & pron.* seventy.

seto, *m.* hedge.

severamente, *adv.* severely.

severidad, *f.* severity.

severo, *a.* severe, strict, stern.

sexo, *m.* sex.

sexto, *a.* sixth.

sexual, *a.* sexual.

si, *conj.* if; whether.

sí, **1.** *pron.* -self, -selves. **2.** *interj.* yes.

sicómoro, *m.* sycamore.

sidra, *f.* cider.

siempre, *adv.* always. **para s.,** forever. **s. que,** whenever; provided that.

sierra, *f.* saw; mountain range.

siervo, *m.* slave; serf.

siesta, *f.* (afternoon) nap.

siete, *a. & pron.* seven.

sifón, *m.* siphon; siphon bottle.

siglo, *m.* century.

signatura, *f.* signature.

significación, *f.* significance.

significado, *m.* meaning.

significante, *a.* significant.

significar, *v.* signify, mean.

significativo, *a.* significant.

signo, *m.* sign, symbol; mark.

siguiente, *a.* following, next.

sílaba, *f.* syllable.

silbar, *v.* whistle; hiss, boo.

silbato, silbido, *m.* whistle.

silencio, *m.* silence, stillness.

silenciosamente, *adv.* silently.

silencioso, *a.* silent, still.

silicato, *m.* silicate.

silicio, *m.* silicon.

silueta, *f.* silhouette.

silla, *f.* chair; saddle.

sillón, *m.* armchair.

sima, *f.* chasm; cavern.

simbólico, *a.* symbolic.

símbolo, *m.* symbol.

simetría, *f.* symmetry.

simétrico, *a.* symmetrical.

símil, similar, *a.* similar, alike.

similitud, *f.* similarity.

simpatía, *f.* congeniality; friendly feeling.

simpático, *a.* likeable, nice, congenial.

simple, *a.* simple.

simpleza, *f.* silliness; trifle.

simplicidad, *f.* simplicity.

simplificación, *f.* simplification.

simplificar, *v.* simplify.

simular, *v.* simulate.

simultáneo, *a.* simultaneous.

sin, *prep.* without.

sinagoga, *f.* synagogue.

sinceridad, *f.* sincerity.

sincero, *a.* sincere.

sincronizar, *v.* synchronize.

sindicato, *m.* syndicate; labor union.

sinfonía, *f.* symphony.

sinfónico, *a.* symphonic.

singular, *a. & m.* singular.

siniestro, *a.* sinister, ominous.

sino, *conj.* but.

sinónimo, *m.* synonym.

sinrazón, *f.* wrong, injustice.

sinsabor, *m.* displeasure, distaste.

sintaxis, *f.* syntax.

síntesis, *f.* synthesis.

sintético, *a.* synthetic.

síntoma, *m.* symptom.

siquiera, *adv.* **ni s.,** not even.

sirena, *f.* siren.

sirviente -ta, *n.* servant.

sistema, *m.* system.

sistemático, *a.* systematic.

sistematizar, *v.* systematize.

sitiar, *v.* besiege.

sitio, *m.* site, location, place, spot.

situación, *f.* situation; location.

situar, *v.* situate; locate.

smoking, *m.* tuxedo, dinner jacket.

so, *prep.* under.

soba, *f.* massage. **—sobar,** *v.*

sobaco, *m.* armpit.

sobaquero, *f.* armhole.

soberano -na, *a. & m.* sovereign.

soberbia, *f.* arrogance.

soberbio, *a.* superb; arrogant.

soborno, *m.* bribe. **—sobornar,** *v.*

sobra, *f.* excess, surplus. **de sobra,** to spare.

sobrado, *m.* attic.

sobrante, *a. & m.* surplus.

sobre, **1.** *prep.* about; above, over. **2.** *m.* envelope.

sobrecama, *f.* bedspread.

sobrecargo, *m.* supercargo.

sobredicho, *a.* aforesaid.

sobrehumano, *a.* superhuman.

sobrenatural, *a.* supernatural, weird.

sobrepasar, *v.* surpass.

sobresalir, *v.* excel.

sobretodo, *m.* overcoat.

sobrevivir, *v.* survive, outlive.

sobriedad, *f.* sobriety; moderation.

sobrina, *f.* niece.

sobrino, *m.* nephew.

sobrio, *a.* sober, temperate.

socarrén, *m.* eaves.

sociable, *a.* sociable.

social, *a.* social.

socialismo, *m.* socialism.

socialista, *a. & m.* socialistic; socialist.

sociedad, *f.* society; association.

socio -cia, *n.* associate, partner; member.

sociología, *f.* sociology.

socorro, *m.* help, aid. **—socorrer,** *v.*

soda, *f.* soda.

sodio, *m.* sodium.

sofá, *m.* sofa, couch.

sofisma, *m.* sophism.

sofista, *m.* sophist.

sofocación, *f.* suffocation.

sofocar, *v.* smother, suffocate, stifle, choke.

soga, *f.* rope.

soja, *f.* soy bean.

sol, *m.* sun.

solada, *f.* dregs.

solanera, *f.* sun bath.

solapa, *f.* lapel.

solar, 1. *a.* solar. **2.** *m.* building lot.

solaz, *m.* solace, comfort. **—solazar,** *v.*

soldado, *m.* soldier.

soldar, *v.* solder, weld.

soledad, *f.* solitude, privacy.

solemne, *a.* solemn.

solemnemente, *adv.* solemnly.

solemnidad, *f.* solemnity.

soler, *v.* be in the habit of.

solicitador, *m.* solicitor.

solicitar, *v.* solicit; apply for.

solícito, *a.* solicitous.

solicitud, *f.* solicitude; application.

sólidamente, *adv.* solidly.

solidaridad, *f.* solidarity.

solidez, *f.* solidity.

solidificar, *v.* solidify.

sólido, *a. & m.* solid.

soliloquio, *m.* soliloquy.

solitario, *a.* solitary, lone.

solo, 1, *a* only; single; alone; lonely. **a solas,** alone. **2.** *m.* solo.

sólo, *adv.* only, just.

soltar, *v.* release; loosen.

soltero -ra, *a. & n.* single, unmarried (person).

soltura, *f.* poise, ease, facility.

solubilidad, *f.* solubility.

solución, *f.* solution.

solucionar, *v.* solve, settle.

solvente, *a.* solvent.

sollozo, *m.* sob. **—sollozar,** *v.*

sombra, *f.* shade; shadow. **—sombrear,** *v.*

sombrero, *m.* hat.

sombrilla, *f.* parasol.

sombrío, *a.* somber, bleak, gloomy.

sombroso, *a.* shady.

someter, *v.* subject; submit.

somnolencia, *f.* drowsiness.

son, *m.* sound. **—sonar,** *v.*

sonata, *f.* sonata.

sondar, *v.* sound, fathom.

sonido, *m.* sound.

sonoridad, *f.* sonority.

sonoro, *a.* sonorous.

sonrisa, *f.* smile. **—sonreír,** *v.*

sonrojo, *m.* flush, blush. **—sonrojarse,** *v.*

soñador -ra, *a. & n.* dreamy; dreamer.

soñar, *v.* dream.

soñoliento, *a.* sleepy.

sopa, *f.* soup.

soplar, *v.* blow.

soplete, *m.* blow torch.

soplo, *m.* breath; puff, gust.

soportar, *v.* abide, bear, stand.

soprano, *m. & f.* soprano.

sorbete, *m.* sherbet.

sorbo, *m.* sip. **—sorber,** *v.*

sordera, *f.* deafness.

sórdidamente, *adv.* sordidly.

For pronunciation, see the concise guide on pages 3 to 4.

sordidez, f. sordidness.
sórdido, a. sordid.
sordo, a. deaf; muffled, dull.
sordomudo -da, a. & n. deaf-mute.
sorpresa, f. surprise. —**sorprender,** v.
sorteo, m. drawing lots; raffle.
sortija, f. ring.
sosa, f. (chem.) soda.
soso, a. dull, insipid, tasteless.
sospecha, f. suspicion.
sospechar, v. suspect.
sospechoso, a. suspicious.
sostén, m. support; brassière.
sostener, v. hold, support; maintain.
sostenimiento, m. sustenance.
sota, f. jack (in cards).
sótano, m. basement, cellar.
soto, m. grove.
soviet, m. soviet.
soya, f. soy bean.
su, a. his, her, its, their, your.
suave, a. smooth; gentle, soft, mild.
suavidad, f. smoothness; gentleness, softness, mildness.
suavizar, v. soften.
subalterno, a. & m. subordinate.
subasta, f. auction.
subconsciencia, f. subconscious.
súbdito -ta, n. subject.
subida, f. ascent, rise.
subilla, f. awl.
subir, v. rise, climb, ascend, mount. **s. a,** amount to.
súbito, a. sudden.
subjetivo, a. subjective.
subjuntivo, a. & m. subjunctive.
sublimación, f. sublimation.
sublimar, v. elevate; sublimate.
sublime, a. sublime.
submarino, a. & m. submarine.
subordinación, f. subordination.

subordinado, a. & m. subordinate. —**subordinar,** v.
subrayar, v. underline.
subscribirse, v. subscribe; sign one's name.
subscripción, f. subscription.
subsecuente, a. subsequent.
subsidiario, a. subsidiary.
subsiguiente, a. subsequent.
substancia, f. substance.
substancial, a. substantial.
substantivo, m. substantive, noun.
substitución, f. substitution.
substituir, v. replace; substitute.
substitutivo, a. substitute.
substituto -ta, n. substitute.
substraer, v. subtract.
subterfugio, m. subterfuge.
subterráneo, 1. a. subterranean, underground. **2.** m. place underground; subway.
suburbio, m. suburb.
subvención, f. subsidy, grant.
subversión, f. subversion.
subversivo, a. subversive.
subvertir, v. subvert.
subyugación, f. subjugation.
subyugar, v. subjugate, quell.
succión, f. suction.
suceder, v. happen, occur, befall. **s. a,** succeed, follow.
sucesión, f. succession.
sucesivo, a. successive. **en lo s.,** in the future.
suceso, m. event.
sucesor -ra, n. successor.
suciedad, f. filth, dirt.
sucio, a. filthy, dirty.
suculento, a. succulent.
sucumbir, v. succumb.
sud, m. south.
sudamericano -na, a. & n. South American.
sudar, v. perspire, sweat.
sudeste, m. southeast.
sudoeste, m. southwest.
sudor, m. perspiration, sweat.
Suecia, f. Sweden.
sueco -ca, a. & n. Swedish; Swede.
suegra, f. mother-in-law.

For pronunciation, see the concise guide on pages 3 to 4.

suegro, *m.* father-in-law.

suela, *f.* sole.

sueldo, *m.* salary, wages.

suelo, *m.* soil; floor; ground.

suelto, *a.* loose; free; odd, separate.

sueño, *m.* sleep; sleepiness; dream. **tener s.,** to be sleepy.

suero, *m.* serum.

suerte, *f.* luck; chance; lot.

suéter, *m.* sweater.

suficiente, *a.* sufficient.

sufragio, *m.* suffrage.

sufrimiento, *m.* suffering, agony.

sufrir, *v.* suffer; undergo; endure.

sugerencia, *f.* suggestion.

sugerir, *v.* suggest.

sugestión, *f.* suggestion.

sugestionar, *v.* influence; hypnotize.

suicida, *m. & f.* suicide (person).

suicidarse, *v.* commit suicide.

suicidio, *m.* (act of) suicide.

Suiza, *f.* Switzerland.

suizo -za, *a. & n.* Swiss.

sujeción, *f.* subjection.

sujetar, *v.* hold, fasten, clip.

sujeto, 1. *a.* subject, liable. **2.** *m.* (gram.) subject.

sulfato, *m.* sulphate.

sulfuro, *m.* sulphide.

sultán, *m.* sultan.

suma, 1. *f.* sum, amount. **en s.,** in short.

sumar, *v.* add up.

sumaria, *f.* indictment.

sumario, *m. & a.* summary.

sumergir, *v.* submerge.

sumersión, *f.* submersion.

sumisión, *f.* submission.

sumiso, *a.* submissive.

sumo, *a.* great, high, utmost.

suntuoso, *a.* sumptuous.

superar, *v.* overcome, surpass.

superficial, *a.* superficial, shallow.

superficie, *f.* surface.

superfluo, *a.* superfluous.

superhombre, *m.* superman.

superintendente, *m.* superintendent.

superior, 1. *a.* superior; upper, higher. **2.** *m.* superior.

superioridad, *f.* superiority.

superlativo, *m. & a.* superlative.

superstición, *f.* superstition.

supersticioso, *a.* superstitious.

supervisar, *v.* supervise.

supervivencia, *f.* survival.

suplantar, *v.* supplant.

suplementario, *a.* supplementary.

suplemento, *m.* supplement. **—suplementar,** *v.*

suplente, *a. & m.* substitute.

súplica, *f.* request, entreaty, plea.

suplicación, *f.* supplication; request, entreaty.

suplicar, *v.* request, entreat; implore.

suplicio, *m.* torture, ordeal.

suplir, *v.* supply.

suponer, *v.* suppose, presume, assume.

suposición, *f.* supposition, assumption.

supremacía, *f.* supremacy.

supremo, *a.* supreme.

supresión, *f.* suppression.

suprimir, *v.* suppress; abolish.

supuesto, *a.* supposed. **por s.,** of course.

sur, *m.* south.

surco, *m.* furrow. **—surcar,** *v.*

surgir, *v.* arise; appear suddenly.

surtido, *m.* assortment; supply, stock.

surtir, *v.* furnish, supply.

susceptibilidad, *f.* susceptibility.

susceptible, *a.* susceptible.

suscitar, *v.* stir up.

suscri- = subscri-

suspender, *v.* withhold; suspend; fail (in a course).

suspensión, *f.* suspension.

suspenso, *m.* failing grade. **en s.,** in suspense.

suspicacia, *f.* suspicion, distrust.

suspicaz, *a.* suspicious.

suspicazmente, *adv.* suspiciously.

suspiro, *m.* sigh. —**suspirar,** *v.*

sustan- = **substan-**

sustentar, *v.* sustain, support.

sustento, *m.* sustenance, support, living.

susti- = **substi-**

susto, *m.* fright, scare.

sustraer = **substraer.**

susurro, *m.* rustle; whisper. —**susurrar,** *v.*

sutil, *a.* subtle.

sutileza, sutilidad, *f.* subtlety.

sutura, *f.* suture.

suyo, *a.* his, hers, theirs, yours.

T

tabaco, *m.* tobacco.

tábano, *m.* horsefly.

taberna, *f.* tavern, bar.

tabernáculo, *m.* tabernacle.

tabique, *m.* dividing wall, partition.

tabla, *f.* board, plank; table, list.

tablado, *m.* stage, platform.

tablero, *m.* panel.

tableta, *f.* tablet.

tablilla, *f.* bulletin board.

tabú, *m.* taboo.

tabular, *a.* tabular.

tacaño, *a.* stingy.

tácitamente, *adv.* tacitly.

tácito, *a.* tacit.

taciturno, *a.* taciturn.

taco, *m.* heel (of shoe); billiard cue.

tacón, *m.* heel (of shoe).

táctico, *a.* tactical.

tacto, *m.* (sense of) touch; tact.

tacha, *f.* fault, defect.

tachar, *v.* find fault with; cross out.

tachuela, *f.* tack.

tafetán, *m.* taffeta.

taimado, *a.* sly.

tajada, *n.* cut, slice, chop. —**tajar,** *v.*

tajea, *f.* channel.

tal, *a.* such. **con t. que,** provided that. **t. vez,** perhaps.

taladrar, *v.* drill.

taladro, *m.* (mech.) drill.

talante, *m.* humor, disposition.

talco, *m.* talc.

talega, *f.* bag, sack.

talento, *m.* talent.

talón, *m.* heel (of foot); (baggage) check, stub.

talla, *f.* engraving; stature; size (of suit).

tallador -ra, *n.* engraver; dealer (at cards).

talle, *m.* figure; waist; fit.

taller, *m.* workshop, factory.

tallo, *m.* stem, stalk.

tamal, *m.* tamale.

tamaño, *m.* size.

tambalear, *v.* stagger, totter.

también, *adv.* also, too.

tambor, *m.* drum.

tamiz, *m.* sieve, sifter.

tampoco, *adv.* neither, either.

tan, *adv.* so.

tanda, *f.* turn, relay.

tándem, *m.* tandem bicycle.

tangencia, *f.* tangency.

tangible, *a.* tangible.

tango, *m.* tango (dance or music).

tanque, *m.* tank.

tanteo, *m.* estimate. —**tantear,** *v.*

tanto, 1. *a. & pron.* so much, so many; as much, as many. **entre t., mientras t.,** meanwhile. **por lo t.,**

For pronunciation, see the concise guide on pages 3 to 4.

therefore. **un t.,** somewhat. a bit. **2.** *m.* point (in games); (pl.) score. **estar al t.,** to be up to date.

tañer, *v.* play (an instrument); ring (bells).

tapa, *f.* cap, cover. **—tapar,** *v.*

tapadero, *m.* stopper, lid.

tápara, *f.* caper.

tapete, *m.* small rug, mat, cover.

tapia, *f.* wall.

tapicería, *f.* tapestry.

tapioca, *f.* tapioca.

tapiz, *m.* tapestry; carpet.

tapón, *m.* plug; cork.

taquigrafía, *f.* shorthand.

taquilla, *f.* ticket office; ticket window.

tarántula, *f.* tarantula.

tararear, *v.* hum.

tardanza, *f.* delay; lateness.

tardar, *v.* delay; be late; take (of time). **a más t.,** at the latest.

tarde, 1. *adv.* late. **2.** *f.* afternoon; early evening.

tardío, *a.* late, belated.

tarea, *f.* task, assignment.

tarifa, *f.* rate; tariff; price list.

tarjeta, *f.* card.

tarta, *f.* tart.

tartamudear, *v.* stammer, falter.

tasa, *f.* rate.

tasación, *f.* valuation.

tasar, *v.* assess, appraise.

tasugo, *m.* badger.

tautología, *f.* tautology.

taxi, taxímetro, *m.* taxi.

taxonomía, *f.* taxonomy.

taza, *f.* cup.

te, *pron.* you; yourself.

té, *m.* tea.

teátrico, *a.* theatrical.

teatro, *m.* theater.

tecla, *f.* key (of a piano, etc.).

técnica, *f.* technique.

téenicamente, *adv.* technically.

técnico, *a.* technical.

tecnología, *f.* technology.

techo, *m.* roof. **—techar,** *v.*

tedio, *m.* tedium, boredom.

tedioso, *a.* tedious.

teísmo, *m.* theism.

teja, *f.* tile.

tejado, *m.* roof.

tejer, *v.* weave; knit.

tejido, *m.* fabric; weaving.

tejón, *m.* badger.

tela, *f.* cloth, fabric, web. **t. metálica,** screen; screening.

telar, *m.* loom.

telaraña, *f.* cobweb.

telefonista, *m. & f.* (telephone) operator.

teléfono, *m.* telephone. **—telefonear,** *v.*

telégrafo, *m.* telegraph. **—telegrafiar,** *v.*

telegrama, *m.* telegram.

telescopio, *m.* telescope.

televisión, *f.* television.

telón, *m.* (theat.) curtain.

telurio, *m.* tellurium.

tema, *m.* theme, subject.

temblar, *v.* tremble, quake; shake, shiver.

temblor, *m.* tremor; shiver.

temer, *v.* fear, be afraid of, dread.

temerario, *a.* rash.

temeridad, *f.* temerity.

temerosamente, *adv.* timorously.

temeroso, *a.* fearful.

temor, *m.* fear.

témpano, *m.* kettledrum; iceberg.

temperamento, *m.* temperament.

temperancia, *f.* temperance.

temperatura, *f.* temperature.

tempestad, *f.* tempest, storm.

tempestuoso, *a.* tempestuous, stormy.

templado, *a.* temperate, mild, moderate.

templanza, *f.* temperance; mildness.

templar, *v.* temper; tune (an instrument)

templo, *m.* temple.

temporada, *f.* season, time, spell.

temporal, temporáneo, *a.* temporary.

temprano, *a. & adv.* early.

tenacidad, *f.* tenacity.

tenaz, *a.* tenacious, stubborn.

tenazmente, *adv.* tenaciously.

tendencia, *f.* tendency, trend.

tender, *v.* stretch, stretch out.

tendero -ra, *n.* shopkeeper, storekeeper.

tendón, *m.* tendon, sinew.

tenebrosidad, *f.* gloom.

tenebroso, *a.* dark, gloomy.

tenedor, *m.* keeper; holder; fork.

tener, *v.* have; own; hold. **t. que,** have to, must.

teniente, *m.* lieutenant.

tenis, *m.* tennis.

tenor, *m.* tenor.

tensión, *f.* tension, stress, strain.

tenso, *a.* tense.

tentación, *f.* temptation.

tentáculo, *m.* tentacle.

tentador, *a.* alluring, tempting.

tentar, *v.* tempt, lure; grope, probe.

tentativa, *f.* attempt.

tentativo, *a.* tentative.

teñir, *v.* tint, dye.

teología, *f.* theology.

teológico, *a.* theological.

teoría, *f.* theory.

teórico, *a.* theoretical.

terapéutico, *a.* therapeutic.

tercero, *a.* third.

tercio, *m.* third.

terciopelo, *m.* velvet.

terco, *a.* obstinate, stubborn.

termal, *a.* thermal.

terminación, *f.* termination, completion.

terminar, *v.* terminate, finish.

término, *m.* term; end.

terminología, *f.* terminology.

termómetro, *m.* thermometer.

termos, *m.* thermos.

ternero -ra, *n.* calf.

ternura, *f.* tenderness.

terquedad, *f.* stubbornness.

terraza, *f.* terrace.

terremoto, *m.* earthquake.

terreno, 1. *a.* earthly, terrestrial. **2.** *m.* ground, terrain; lot, plot.

terrible, *a.* terrible, awful.

terrífico, *a.* terrific.

territorio, *m.* territory.

terrón, *m.* clod, lump; mound.

terror, *m.* terror.

terso, *a.* smooth, glossy; terse.

tertulia, *f.* social gathering party.

tesis, *f.* thesis.

tesorería, *f.* treasury.

tesorero -ra, *n.* treasurer.

tesoro, *m.* treasure.

testamento, *m.* will, testament.

testarudo, *a.* stubborn.

testificar, *v.* testify.

testigo, *m.* witness; testimony.

testimonial, *a.* testimonial.

testimonio, *m.* testimony.

teta, *f.* teat.

tetera, *f.* teapot.

tétrico, *a.* sad; gloomy.

texto, *m.* text.

textura, *f.* texture.

tez, *f.* complexion.

ti, *pron.* you; yourself.

tía, *f.* aunt.

tibio, *a.* lukewarm.

tiburón, *m.* shark.

tiemblo, *m.* aspen.

tiempo, *m.* time; weather; (gram.) tense.

tienda, *f.* shop, store; tent.

tientas *f.pl.* **andar a t.,** to grope (in the dark).

tierno, *a.* tender.

tierra, *f.* land; ground; earth, dirt, soil.

tieso, *a.* taut, stiff, hard, strong.

tiesto, *m.* flower pot.

tiesura, *f.* stiffness; harshness.

tifo, *m.* typhus.

tifoideo, *f.* typhoid fever.

tigre, *m.* tiger.

tijeras, *f.pl.* scissors.

tila, *f.* linden.

timbre, *m.* seal, stamp; tone; (electric) bell.
timidamente, *adv.* timidly.
timidez, *f.* timidity.
tímido, *a.* timid, shy.
timón, *m.* rudder, helm.
tímpano, *m.* kettledrum; eardrum.
tina, *f.* tub, vat.
tinaja, *f.* jar.
tinta, *f.* ink.
tinte, *m.* tint, shade.
tintero, *m.* inkwell.
tinto, *a.* wine-colored; red (of wine).
tintorería, *f.* dry cleaning shop.
tintorero -ra, *n.* dyer; dry cleaner.
tintura, *f.* tincture; dye.
tiñoso, *a.* scabby; stingy.
tío, *m.* uncle.
tíovivo, *m.* merry-go-round.
típico, *a.* typical.
tipo, *m.* type, sort; (interest) rate; (coll.) guy, fellow.
tira, *f.* strip.
tirabuzón, *m.* corkscrew.
tirada, *f.* edition.
tiranía, *f.* tyranny.
tiránico, *m.* tyrannical; domineering.
tirano, *m.* tyrant.
tirante, **1.** *a.* tight, taut; tense. **2.** *m.* (pl.) suspenders.
tirar, *v.* throw; draw; pull; fire (a weapon).
tiritar, *v.* shiver.
tiro, *m.* throw; shot.
tirón, *m.* pull. **de un t.**, at a stretch, at one stroke.
tísico, *n. & a.* consumptive.
tisis, *f.* consumption, tuberculosis.
titania, *m.* titanium.
títere, *m.* puppet.
titilación, *f.* twinkle.
titubear, *v.* stagger; totter; waver.
titulado, *a.* entitled; so-called.
titular, **1,** *a.* titular. **2.** *v.* entitle.
título, *m.* title; headline.
tiza, *f.* chalk.

tiznar, *v.* smudge; stain.
toalla, *f.* towel.
toalleta, *f.* small towel.
tobillo, *m.* ankle.
tocado, *m.* hairdo.
tocador, *m.* boudoir; dressing table.
tocante, *a.* touching. **t. a,** concerning, relative to.
tocar, *v.* touch; play (an instrument). **t. a uno**, be one's turn; be up to one.
tocayo, *m.* namesake.
tocino, *m.* bacon.
todavía, *adv.* yet, still.
todo, **1.** *a.* all; whole. **todos los**, every. **2.** *pron.* all, everything. **con t.**, still, however. **del t.**, wholly; at all.
todopoderoso, *a.* almighty.
toldo, *m.* awning.
tolerancia, *f.* tolerance.
tolerante, *a.* tolerant.
tolerar, *v.* tolerate.
toma, *f.* taking, capture, seizure.
tomaína, *f.* ptomaine.
tomar, *v.* take; drink.
tomate, *m.* tomato.
tomillo, *m.* thyme.
tomo, *m.* volume.
tonada, *f.* tune.
tonel, *m.* barrel, cask.
tonelada, *f.* ton.
tonelaje, *m.* tonnage.
tónico, *a. & m.* tonic.
tono, *m.* tone, pitch, shade. **darse t.**, to put on airs.
tonsila, *f.* tonsil.
tonsilitis, *f.* tonsilitis.
tontería, *f.* nonsense, foolishness.
tonto -ta, *a. & n.* foolish, silly; fool.
topacio, *m.* topaz.
topar, *v.* run into. **t. con,** come upon.
tópico, **1.** *a.* topical. **2.** *m.* topic.
topo, *m.* mole (animal).
toque, *m.* touch.
tórax, *m.* thorax.
torbellino, *m.* whirlwind.
torcer, *v.* twist; wind; distort.

For pronunciation, see the concise guide on pages 3 to 4.

toreador, *m.* toreador.

torero, *m.* bull fighter.

torio, *m.* thorium.

tormenta, *f.* storm.

tormento, *m.* torment.

tornado, *m.* tornado.

tornar, *v.* return; turn.

tornarse en, *v.* turn into, become.

torneo, *m.* tournament.

tornillo, *m.* screw.

toro, *m.* bull.

toronja, *f.* grapefruit.

torpe, *a.* awkward, clumsy; sluggish.

torpedero, *m.* torpedo boat.

torpedo, *m.* torpedo.

torre, *f.* tower.

torrente, *m.* torrent.

tórrido, *a.* torrid.

torta, *f.* cake; loaf.

tortilla, *f.* omelet; (Mex.) tortilla, pancake.

tórtola, *f.* dove.

tortuga, *f.* turtle.

tortuoso, *a.* tortuous.

tortura, *f.* torture. **—torturar,** *v.*

tos, *m.* cough. **—toser,** *v.*

tosco, *a.* coarse, rough, uncouth.

tosquedad, *f.* coarseness, roughness.

tostar, *v.* toast; tan.

total, *a. & m.* total.

totalidad, *f.* totality, entirety, whole.

totalitario, *a.* totalitarian.

totalmente, *adv.* totally; entirely.

tótem, *m.* totem.

tóxico, *a.* toxic.

trabajador -ra, **1.** *a.* hard-working. **2.** *n.* worker.

trabajo, *m.* work; labor. **—trabajar,** *v.*

trabar, *v.* fasten, shackle; grasp; strike up.

tracción, *f.* traction.

tracto, *m.* tract.

tractor, *m.* tractor.

tradición, *f.* tradition.

tradicional, *a.* traditional.

traducción, *f.* translation.

traducir, *v.* translate.

traductor, *m.* translater.

traer, *v.* bring; carry; wear.

tráfico, *m.* traffic. **—traficar,** *v.*

tragar, *v.* swallow.

tragedia, *f.* tragedy.

trágicamente, *adv.* tragically.

trágico -ca, **1.** *a.* tragic. **2.** *n.* tragedian.

trago, *m.* swallow; drink.

traición, *f.* treason, betrayal.

traicionar, *v.* betray.

traidor -ra, *a. & n.* traitorous; traitor.

traje, *m.* suit; dress; garb, apparel.

trama, *v.* plot (of a story).

tramador, *m.* weaver; plotter.

tramar, *v.* weave; plot, scheme.

trámite, *m.* (business) deal, transaction.

tramo, *m.* span, stretch, section.

trampa, *f.* trap, snare.

trampista, *m.* cheater; swindler.

trance, *m.* critical moment or stage. **a todo t.,** at any cost.

tranco, *m.* stride.

tranquilidad, *f.* tranquility, calm, quiet.

tranquilizar, *v.* quiet, calm down.

tranquilo, *a.* tranquil, calm, quiet.

transacción, *f.* transaction.

transbordador, *m.* ferry.

transcribir, *v.* transcribe.

transcripción, *f.* transcription.

transcurrir, *v.* elapse.

transeúnte, *a. & n.* transient; passerby.

transferencia, *f.* transference.

transferir, *v.* transfer.

transformación, *f.* transformation.

transformar, *v.* transform.

transfusión, *f.* transfusion.

transgresión, *f.* transgression.

transgresor, *m.* transgressor.

transición, *f.* transition.

transigir, *v.* compromise, settle; agree.

transitivo, *a.* transitive.

tránsito, *m.* transit, passage.

transitorio, *a.* transitory.

transmisión, *f.* transmission; broadcast.

transmisora, *f.* broadcasting station.

transmitir, *v.* transmit; broadcast.

transparencia, *f.* transparency.

transparente, 1. *a.* transparent. 2. *m.* (window) shade.

transportación, *f.* transportation.

transportar, *v.* transport, convey.

transporte, *m.* transportation; transport.

tranvía, *m.* streetcar, trolley.

trapacero, *n.* cheat; swindler.

trapo, *m.* rag.

tráquea, *f.* trachea.

tras, *prep.* after; behind.

trasegar, *v.* upset, overturn.

trasero, *a.* rear, back.

traslado, *m.* transfer.—**trasladar**, *v.*

traslapo, *m.* overlap.—**traslapar**, *v.*

trasnochar, *v.* sit up all night.

traspalar, *v.* shovel.

traspasar, *v.* go beyond; cross; violate; pierce.

trasquilar, *v.* shear; clip.

trastornar, *v.* overturn, overthrow, upset.

trastorno, *m.* overthrow; upheaval.

tratado, *m.* treaty; treatise.

tratamiento, *m.* treatment.

tratar, *v.* treat, handle. **tratar de**, deal with; try to; call (a name).

tratarse de, *v.* be a question of.

trato, *m.* treatment; manners; (com.) deal.

través, *adv.* **a t. de**, through, across. **de t.**, sideways.

travesía, *f.* crossing; voyage.

travestido, *a.* disguised.

travesura, *f.* prank; mischief.

travieso, *a.* naughty, mischievous.

trayectoria, *f.* trajectory.

trazar, *v.* plan, devise; trace; draw.

trazo, *n.* plan, outline; line, stroke.

trébol, *m.* clover.

trece, *a. & pron.* thirteen.

trecho, *m.* space, distance, stretch.

tregua, *f.* truce, respite, lull.

treinta, *a. & pron.* thirty.

tremendo, *a.* tremendous.

tremer, *v.* tremble.

tren, *m.* train.

trenza, *f.* braid.—**trenzar**, *v.*

trepar, *v.* climb, mount.

trepidación, *f.* trepidation.

tres, *a. & pron.* three.

trescientos, *a. & pron.* three hundred.

triángulo, *m.* triangle.

tribu, *f.* tribe.

tribulación, *f.* tribulation.

tribuna, *f.* rostrum, stand; (pl.) grandstand.

tribunal, *m.* court, tribunal.

tributario, *a. & m.* tributary.

tributo, *m.* tribute.

triciclo, *m.* tricycle.

trigo, *m.* wheat.

trigonometría, *f.* trigonometry.

trigueño, *a.* swarthy, dark.

trilogía, *f.* trilogy.

trimestral, *a.* quarterly.

trinchar, *v.* carve (meat).

trinchera, *f.* trench, ditch.

trineo, *m.* sled; sleigh.

trinidad, *f.* trinity.

tripa, *f.* tripe, entrails.

triple, *a.* triple.—**triplicar**, *v.*

tripulación, *f.* (ship's) crew.

triste, *a.* sad, sorrowful; dreary.

tristemente, *adv.* sadly.

tristeza, *f.* sadness; gloom.

triunfal, *a.* triumphal.

triunfante, *a.* triumphant.

triunfo, *m.* triumph; trump.
— **triunfar,** *v.*

trivial, *a.* trivial, commonplace.

trivialidad, *f.* triviality.

trocar, *v.* exchange, switch; barter.

trofeo, *m.* trophy.

trombón, *m.* trombone.

trompa, trompeta, *f.* trumpet, horn.

tronada, *f.* thunderstorm.

tronar, *v.* thunder.

tronco, *m.* trunk, stump.

trono, *m.* throne.

tropa, *f.* troop.

tropel, *m.* crowd, throng.

tropezar, *v.* trip, stumble. **t. con,** come upon, run into.

trópico, *a.* & *m.* tropical; tropics.

tropiezo, *m.* stumble; obstacle; slip, error.

trote, *m.* trot. — **trotar,** *v.*

trovador, *m.* troubadour.

trozo, *m.* piece, portion, fragment, selection, passage.

trucha, *f.* trout.

trueco, trueque, *m.* exchange, barter.

trueno, *m.* thunder.

tu, *a.* your.

tú, *pron.* you.

tuberculosis, *f.* tuberculosis.

tubo, *m.* tube, pipe.

tuerca, *f.* (mech.) nut.

tulipán, *m.* tulip.

tumba, *f.* tomb, grave.

tumbar, *v.* knock down.

tumbarse, *v.* tumble.

tumbo, *m.* tumble; somersault.

tumor, *m.* tumor; growth.

tumulto, *m.* tumult, commotion.

tumultuoso, *a.* tumultuous, boisterous.

tunante, *m.* rascal, rogue.

tunda, *f.* spanking, whipping.

túnel, *m.* tunnel.

tungsteno, *m.* tungsten.

túnica, *f.* tunic, robe.

tupir, *v.* pack tight, stuff; stop up.

turbación, *f.* confusion, turmoil.

turbamulta, *f.* mob; crowd.

turbar, *v.* disturb, upset; embarrass.

turbina, *f.* turbine.

turbio, *a.* turbid; muddy.

turco -ca, *a.* & *n.* Turkish; Turk.

turismo, *m.* touring, (foreign) travel.

turista, *m.* & *f.* tourist.

turno, *m.* turn; (work) shift.

turquesa, *f.* turquoise.

Turquía, *f.* Turkey.

turrón, *m.* nougat.

tusa, *f.* corncob; corn.

tutear, *v.* use the pronoun **tú,** etc., in addressing a person.

tutela, *f.* guardianship; aegis.

tutor, *m.* tutor; guardian.

tuyo, *a.* your, yours.

U

u, *conj.* or.

ubre, *f.* udder.

ufano, *a.* proud, haughty.

úlcera, *f.* ulcer.

ulterior, *a.* ulterior.

último, *a.* last, final; ultimate; latest. **por ú.,** finally.

ultraje, *m.* outrage. — **ultrajar,** *v.*

umbral, *m.* threshold.

umbroso, *a.* shady.

For pronunciation, see the concise guide on pages 3 to 4.

un, una, *art. & a.* a, an; one; (pl.) some.

unánime, *a.* unanimous.

unanimidad, *f.* unanimity.

unción, *f.* unction.

ungüento, *m.* ointment, salve.

único, *a.* only, sole; unique.

unicornio, *m.* unicorn.

unidad, *f.* unit; unity.

unificar, *v.* unify.

uniforme, *a. & m.* uniform.

uniformidad, *f.* uniformity.

unión, *f.* union; joining.

unir, *v.* unite, join.

universal, *a.* universal.

universalidad, *f.* universality.

universidad, *f.* university; college.

universo, *m.* universe.

uno, una, *pron.* one; (pl.) some.

untar, *v.* spread; grease; anoint.

uña, *f.* fingernail.

urbanidad, *f.* urbanity; good breeding.

urbano, *a.* urban; urbane; well-bred.

urbe, *f.* large city.

urgencia, *f.* urgency.

urgente, *a.* urgent, pressing. **entrega u.,** special delivery.

urgir, *v.* be urgent.

urna, *f.* urn; ballot box; (pl.) polls.

usanza, *f.* usage, custom.

usar, *v.* use; wear.

uso, *m.* use; usage; wear.

usted, *pron.* you.

usual, *a.* usual.

usualmente, *adv.* usually.

usura, *f.* usury.

usurero, *m.* usurer.

usurpación, *f.* usurpation.

usurpar, *v.* usurp.

utensilio, *m.* utensil.

útero, *m.* uterus.

útil, *a.* useful, handy.

utilidad, *f.* utility, usefulness.

utilizar, *v.* use, utilize.

útilmente, *adv.* usefully.

utópico, *a.* utopian.

uva, *f.* grape.

V

vaca, *f.* cow; beef.

vacaciones, *f.pl.* vacation, holidays.

vacancia, *f.* vacancy.

vacante, 1. *a.* vacant. **2.** *f.* vacancy.

vaciar, *v.* empty; pour out.

vacilación, *f.* vacillation, hesitation.

vacilante, *a.* vacillating.

vacilar, *v.* falter, hesitate; waver; stagger.

vacío, 1. *a.* empty. **2.** *m.* void, empty space.

vacuna, *f.* vaccine.

vacunación, *f.* vaccination.

vacunar, *v.* vaccinate.

vacuo, 1. *a.* empty, vacant. **2.** *m.* vacuum.

vadear, *v.* wade through, ford.

vado, *m.* ford.

vagabundo, *a. & m.* vagabond.

vagar, *v.* wander, rove, roam; loiter.

vago -ga, 1. *a.* vague, hazy; wandering, vagrant. **2.** *m.* vagrant, tramp.

vagón, *m.* railroad car.

vahído, *m.* dizziness.

vaina, *f.* sheath; pod.

vainilla, *f.* vanilla.

vaivén, *m.* vibration, sway.

vajilla, *f.* (dinner) dishes.

valentía, f. valor, courage.

valer, 1. m. worth. **2.** v. be worth.

valerse de, v. make use of, avail oneself of.

valía, f. value.

validez, f. validity.

válido, a. valid.

valiente, a. valiant, brave, courageous.

valija, f. valise.

valioso, a. valuable.

valor, m. value, worth; bravery; (pl., com.) securities.

valoración, f. appraisal.

valorar, v. value, appraise.

vals, m. waltz.

valsar, v. waltz.

valuación, f. valuation.

valuar, v. value; rate.

válvula, f. valve.

valla, f. fence, barrier.

valle, m. valley.

vándalo, m. vandal.

vanidad, f. vanity.

vanidoso, a. vain, conceited.

vano, a., vain; inane.

vapor, m., vapor; steam; steamer, steamship.

vaquero, m. cowboy.

vara, f. wand, stick, switch.

varadero, m. shipyard.

varar, v. launch; be stranded; run aground.

variable, a. variable.

variación, f. variation.

variar, v. vary.

variedad, f. variety.

varios, a.& pron.pl. various; several.

varón, m. man; male.

varonil, a. manly, virile.

vasallo, m. vassal.

vasija, f. bowl, container (for liquids).

vaso, m. water glass; vase.

vástago, m. bud, shoot; twig; offspring.

vasto, a. vast.

vecindad, f. **vecindario,** m. neighborhood, vicinity.

vecino -na, a. & n. neighboring; neighbor.

vedar, v. forbid; impede.

vega, f. meadow.

vegetación, f. vegetation.

vegetal, m. vegetable.

vehemente, a. vehement.

vehículo, m. vehicle; conveyance.

veinte, a. & pron. twenty.

vejez, f. old age.

vejiga, f. bladder.

vela, f. vigil, watch; candle; sail.

velar, v. stay up, sit up; watch over.

velo, m. veil.

velocidad, f. velocity, speed; rate.

veloz, a. speedy, fast, swift.

vellón, m. fleece.

velloso, a. hairy; fuzzy.

velludo, a. downy.

vena, f. vein.

venado, m. deer.

vencedor -ra, n. victor.

vencer, v. defeat, overcome, conquer; (com.) become due, expire.

vencimiento, m. defeat.

venda, f. **vendaje,** m., bandage. —**vendar,** v.

vendedor -ra, n. seller, trader; sales clerk.

vender, v. sell.

vendimia, f. vintage.

veneno, m. poison.

venenoso, a. poisonous.

veneración, f. veneration.

venerar, v. venerate, revere.

venero, m. spring, origin.

véneto, a. Venetian.

venezolano, a. & n. Venezuelan.

vengador, m. avenger.

venganza, f. venegeance, revenge.

vengar, v. avenge.

venida, f. arrival, advent, coming.

venidero, a. future; coming.

venir, v. come.

venta, f. sale; sales.

ventaja, f. advantage; profit.

ventajoso, a. advantageous; profitable.

ventana, f. window.

ventero, m. innkeeper.

ventilación, m. ventilation.

ventilador, *m.* ventilator. fan.

ventilar, *v.* ventilate, air.

ventoso, *a.* windy.

ventura, *f.* venture; happiness; luck.

ver, *v.* see. **tener que v. con,** have to do with.

vera, *f.* edge.

veracidad, *f.* truthfulness, veracity.

verano, *m.* summer. **—veranear,** *v.*

veras, *f.pl.* **de v.,** really, truly.

veraz, *a.* truthful.

verbigracia, *adv.* for example.

verbo, *m.* verb.

verboso, *a.* verbose.

verdad, *f.* truth. **ser v.,** to be true.

verdadero, *a.* true, real.

verde, *a.* green; risqué, off-color.

verdor, *m.* greenness, verdure.

verdugo, *m.* hangman.

verdura, *f.* verdure, vegetation; (pl.) vegetables.

vereda, *f.* path.

veredicto, *m.* verdict.

vergonzoso, *a.* shameful, embarrassing; shy, bashful.

vergüenza, *f.* shame; disgrace; embarrassment.

verificar, *v.* verify, check.

verja, *f.* grating, railing.

verosímil, *a.* likely, plausible.

verraco, *m.* boar.

verruga, *f.* wart.

versátil, *a.* versatile.

verse, *v.* look, appear.

versión, *f.* version.

verso, *m.* verse, stanza; line (of poetry).

verter, *v.* pour, spill; shed; empty.

vertical, *a.* vertical.

vertiente, *f.* slope; watershed.

vertiginoso, *a.* dizzy.

vértigo, *m.* vertigo, dizziness.

vestíbulo, *m.* vestibule, lobby.

vestido, *m.* dress; clothing.

vestigio, *m.* vestige, trace.

vestir, *v.* dress, clothe.

veterano -na, *a. & n.* veteran.

veterinario, *m.* veterinary.

veto, *m.* veto.

vetusto, *a.* ancient, very old.

vez, *f.* time; turn. **tal v.,** perhaps. **a la v.,** at the same time. **en v. de,** instead of. **una v.,** once. **otra v.,** again.

vía, *f.* track; route, way.

viaducto, *m.* viaduct.

viajante, *a. & n.* traveling; traveler.

viajar, *v.* travel; journey, tour.

viaje, *m.* trip, journey, voyage; (pl.) travels.

viajero -ra, *n.* traveler; passenger.

viandas, *f.pl.* victuals, food.

víbora, *f.* viper.

vibración, *f.* vibration.

vibrar, *v.* vibrate.

vicepresidente, *m.* vice president.

vicio, *m.* vice.

vicioso, *a.* vicious; licentious.

víctima, *f.* victim.

victoria, *f.* victory.

victorioso, *a.* victorious.

vid, *f.* grapevine.

vida, *f.* life; living.

vidrio, *m.* glass.

viejo -ja, *a. & n.* old; old person.

viento, *m.* wind. **hacer v.,** to be windy.

vientre, *m.* belly.

viernes, *m.* Friday.

viga, *f.* beam, rafter.

vigente, *a.* in effect (prices etc.).

vigilante, *a. & m.* vigilant, watchful; watchman.

vigilar, *v.* guard, watch over.

vigilia, *f.* vigil, watchfulness; (rel.) fast.

vigor, *m.* vigor. **en v.,** in effect, in force.

vil, *a.* vile, low, contemptible.

vileza, *f.* baseness; vileness.

villa, *f.* town; countryhouse.

For pronunciation, see the concise guide on pages 3 to 4.

villancico, *m.* Christmas carol.
villanía, *f.* villainy.
villano, *m.* boor.
vinagre, *m.* vinegar.
vínculo, *m.* link. **—vincular,** *v.*
vindicar, *v.* vindicate.
vino, *m.* wine.
viña, *f.* vineyard.
violación, *f.* violation.
violar, *v.* violate.
violencia, *f.* violence.
violento, *a.* violent; impulsive.
violeta, *f.* violet.
violín, *m.* violin.
violón, *m.* bass viol.
virar, *v.* veer, change course.
virgen, *f.* virgin.
viril, *a.* virile, manly.
virilidad, *f.* virility; manhood.
virtual, *a.* virtual.
virtud, *f.* virtue; efficacy, power.
virtuoso, *a.* virtuous.
viruela, *f.* smallpox.
visa, *f.* visa.
visaje, *m.* grimace.
visera, *f.* visor.
visible, *a.* visible.
visión, *f.* vision.
visionario -ria, *a. & n.* visionary.
visita, *f.* visit; visitor, caller.
visitación, *f.* visitation.
visitante, *a. & n.* visiting; visitor.
visitar, *v.* visit; inspect, examine.
vislumbre, *m.* glimpse.
viso, *m.* looks; outlook.
víspera, *f.* eve, day before.
vista, *f.* view; scene; sight.
vistazo, *m.* glance, glimpse.
vistoso, *a.* beautiful; showy.
visual, *a.* visual.
vital, *a.* vital.
vitalidad, *f.* vitality.
vitamina, *f.* vitamin.
vitando, *a.* hateful.
vituperar, *v.* vituperate; revile.
viuda, *f.* widow.
viudo, *m.* widower.

vivaz, *a.* vivacious, buoyant; clever.
víveres, *m.pl.* provisions.
viveza, *f.* animation, liveliness.
vívido, *a.* vivid, bright.
vivienda, *f.* (living) quarters, dwelling.
vivificar, *v.* vivify, enliven.
vivir, *v.* live.
vivo, *a.* live, alive, living; vivid; animated, brisk.
vocablo, *m.* word.
vocabulario, *m.* vocabulary.
vocación, *f.* vocation, calling.
vocal, 1. *a.* vocal. **2.** *f.* vowel.
vocear, *v.* vociferate.
vodevil, *m.* vaudeville.
volante, 1. *a.* flying. **2.** *m.* memorandum; (steering) wheel.
volar, *v.* fly; explode.
volcán, *m.* volcano.
volcar, *v.* upset, capsize.
voltear, *v.* turn, whirl; overturn.
voltio, *m.* volt.
volumen, *m.* volume.
voluminoso, *a.* voluminous.
voluntad, *f.* will.
voluntario -ria, *a. & n.* voluntary; volunteer.
voluntarioso, *a.* wilful.
volver, *v.* turn; return, go back, come back. **v. a hacer** (etc.), do (etc.) again.
volverse, *v.* turn around; turn, become.
vómito, *m.* vomit. **—vomitar,** *v.*
voracidad, *f.* voracity; agreed.
voraz, *a.* greedy, ravenous.
vórtice, *m.* whirlpool.
vosotros -as, *pron.pl.* you; yourselves.
votación, *f.* voting, vote.
voto, *m.* vote; vow.**—votar,** *v.*
voz, *f.* voice; word. **a voces,** by shouting. **en v. alta,** aloud.
vuelco, *m.* upset.
vuelo, *m.* flight.
vuelta, *f.* turn, bend; return.

For pronunciation, see the concise guide on pages 3 to 4.

a la v. de, around. **dar una v.**, to take a walk.
vuestro, *a.* your, yours.
vulgar, *a.* vulgar, common.

vulgaridad, *f.* vulgarity.
vulgo, *m.* (the) masses, (the) common people.
vulnerable, *a.* vulnerable.

Y, Z

y, *conj.* and.
ya, *adv.* already; now; at once. **y. no**, no longer, any more. **y. que**, since.
yacer, *v.* lie.
yanqui, *a. & n.* North American.
yate, *m.* yacht.
yegua, *f.* mare.
yelmo, *m.* helmet.
yema, *f.* yolk (of an egg).
yerba, *f.* grass; herb.
yerno, *m.* son-in-law.
yerro, *m.* error, mistake.
yeso, *m.* plaster.
yo, *pron.* I.
yodo, *m.* iodine.
yoduro, *m.* iodide.
yugo, *m.* yoke.
yunque, *m.* anvil.
yunta, *f.* team (of animals).
zafarse, *v.* run away, escape. **z. de**, get rid of.
zafio, *a.* coarse, uncivil.
zafiro, *m.* sapphire.
zaguán, *m.* vestibule, hall.
zalamero -ra, *n.* flatterer, wheedler.

zambullir, *v.* plunge, dive.
zanahoria, *f.* carrot.
zanja, *f.* ditch, trench.
zapatería, *f.* shoe store; shoemaker's shop.
zapatero, *m.* shoemaker.
zapato, *m.* shoe.
zar, *m.* czar.
zaraza, *f.* calico; chintz.
zarza, *f.* bramble.
zarzuela, *f.* musical comedy.
zodíaco, *m.* zodiac.
zona, *f.* zone.
zoología, *f.* zoölogy.
zoológico, *a.* zoölogical.
zorro -rra, *n.* fox.
zozobra, *f.* worry, anxiety; capsizing.
zozobrar, *v.* capsize.
zumba, *f.* spanking.
zumbido, *m.* buzz, hum. — **zumbar**, *v.*
zumo, *m.* juice, sap.
zurcir, *v.* darn, mend.
zurdo, *a.* left-handed.
zurrar, *v.* flog, drub.

For pronunciation, see the concise guide on pages 3 to 4.

ENGLISH - SPANISH

A

a, *art.* un, una.

abacus, *n.* ábaco *m.*

abandon, 1. *n.* desenfreno, abandono *m.* **2.** *v.* abandonar, desamparar.

abandoned, *a.* abandonado.

abandonment, *n.* abandono, desamparo *m.*

abase, *v.* degradar, humillar.

abasement, *n.* degradación, humillación *f.*

abash, *v.* avergonzar

abate, *v.* menguar, moderarse.

abatement, *n.* disminución *f.*

abbess, *n.* abadesa *f.*

abbey, *n.* abadía *f.*

abbot, *n.* abad *m.*

abbreviate, *v.* abreviar.

abbreviation, *n.* abreviatura *f.*

abdicate, *v.* abdicar.

abdication, *n.* abdicación *f.*

abdomen, *n.* abdomen *m.*

abdominal, *a.* abdominal.

abduct, *v.* secuestrar.

abduction, *n.* secuestración *f.*

abductor, *n.* secuestrador *m.*

aberrant, *a.* extraviado.

aberration, *n.* error, extravío *m.*

abet, *v.* apoyar, favorecer.

abetment, *n.* apoyo *m.*

abettor, *n.* cómplice *m. & f.*

abeyance, *n.* suspensión *f.*

abhor, *v.* abominar, odiar.

abhorrence, *n.* detestación *f.*; aborrecimiento *m.*

abhorrent, *a.* detestable, aborrecible.

abide, *v.* soportar. **to a. by,** cumplir con.

abiding, *a.* perdurable.

ability, *n.* habilidad *f.*

abject, *a.* abyecto; desanimado.

abjuration, *n.* renuncia *f.*

abjure, *v.* renunciar.

ablative, *a. & n.* (gram.) ablativo *m.*

ablaze, *a.* en llamas.

able, *a.* capaz; competente. **to be a.,** poder.

able-bodied, *a.* robusto.

ablution, *n.* ablución *f.*

ably, *adv.* hábilmente.

abnegate, *v.* repudiar; negar.

abnegation, *n.* abnegación; repudiación *f.*

abnormal, *a.* anormal.

abnormality, *n.* anormalidad, deformidad *f.*

abnormally, *adv.* anormalmente.

aboard, *adv.* a bordo.

abode, *n.* residencia *f.*

abolish, *v.* suprimir.

abolishment, *n.* abolición *f.*

abolition, *n.* abolición *f.*

abominable, *a.* abominable.

abominate, *v.* abominar, detestar.

abomination, *n.* abominación; enormidad *f.*

aboriginal, *a.* primitivo.

abortion, *n.* aborto *m.*

abortive, *a.* abortivo.

abound, *v.* abundar.

about, 1. *adv.* como. **about to,** para; a punto de. **2.** *prep.* de, sobre, acerca de.

about-face, *n.* (mil.) media vuelta.

above, 1. *adv.* arriba. **2.** *prep.* sobre; por encima de.

aboveboard, *a. & adv.* sincero, franco.

abrasion, *n.* raspadura *f.*; (med.) abrasión *f.*

abrasive, 1. *a.* raspante. **2.** *n.* abrasivo *m.*

abreast, *adv.* de frente.

abridge, *v.* abreviar.

abridgment, *n.* abreviación *f.*; compendio *m.*

abroad, *adv.* en el extranjero, al extranjero.

abrogate, *v.* abrogar, revocar.

abrogation, *n.* abrogación, revocación *f.*

abrupt, *a.* repentino; brusco.

abruptly, *adv.* bruscamente, precipitadamente.

abruptness, *n.* precipitación; brusquedad *f.*

abscess, *n.* absceso *m.*

abscond, *v.* fugarse.

absence, *n.* ausencia, falta *f.*

absent, *a.* ausente.

absentee, *a. & n.* ausente *m.*

absent-minded, *a.* distraído.

absinthe, *n.* absenta *f.*

absolute, *a.* absoluto.

absolutely, *adv.* absolutamente.

absoluteness, *n.* absolutismo *m.*

absolution, *n.* absolución *f.*

absolutism, *n.* absolutismo despotismo *m.*

absolve, *v.* absolver.

absorb, *v.* absorber; preocupar.

absorbed, *a.* absorbido; absorto.

absorbent, *a.* absorbente.

absorbing, *a.* interesante.

absorption, *n.* absorción; preocupación *f.*

abstain, *v.* abstenerse.

abstemious, *a.* abstemio, sobrio.

abstinence, *n.* abstinencia *f.*

abstract, 1. *n.* resumen *f.* **2.** *v.* abstraer.

abstracted, *a.* distraído.

abstraction, *n.* abstracción *f.*

abstruse, *a.* abstruso.

absurd, *a.* absurdo, ridículo.

absurdity, *n.* absurdo *m.*

absurdly, *adv.* absurdamente.

abundance, *n.* abundancia *f.*

abundant, *a.* abundante.

abundantly, *adv.* abundantemente.

abuse, 1. *n.* abuso *m.* **2.** *v.* abusar de; maltratar.

abusive, *a.* abusivo.

abusively, *adv.* abusivamente, ofensivamente.

abut (on), *v.* terminar (en); lindar (con).

abutment, *n.* (constr.) estribo, contrafuerte *m.*

abyss, *n.* abismo *m.*

Abyssinian, *a. & n.* abisinio -nia.

academic, *a.* académico.

academy, *n.* academia *f.*

acanthus, *n.* (bot.) acanto *m.*

accede, *v.* acceder; consentir.

accelerate, *v.* acelerar.

acceleration, *n.* aceleración *f.*

accelerator, *n.* (auto.) acelerador *m.*

accent, 1. *n.* acento *m.* **2.** *v.* acentuar.

accentuate, *v.* acentuar.

accept, *v.* aceptar.

acceptability, *n.* aceptabilidad *f.*

acceptable, *a.* aceptable.

acceptably, *adv.* aceptablemente.

acceptance, *n.* aceptación *f.*

access, *n.* acceso *m.*, entrada *f.*

accessible, *a.* accesible.

accessory, 1. *a.* accesorio. **2.** *n.* cómplice *m. & f.*

accident, *n.* accidente *m.* **by a.,** por casualidad.

accidental, *a.* accidental.

accidentally, *adv.* accidentalmente, casualmente.

acclaim, *v.* aclamar.

acclamation, *n.* aclamación *f.*

acclimate, *v.* aclimatar.

acclivity, *n.* subida *f.*

accolade, *n.* acolada *f.*

accommodate, *v.* acomodar.

accommodating, *a.* bondadoso, complaciente.

accommodation, *n.* servicio *m.* (pl.) alojamiento *m.*

accompaniment, *n.* acompañamiento *m.*

accompanist, *n.* acompañador *m.*

accompany, *v.* acompañar.

accomplice. *n.* cómplice *m. & f.*

accomplish, *v.* llevar a cabo; realizar.

accomplished, *a.* acabado, cumplido; culto.

accomplishment, *n.* realización *f.*; logro *m.*

accord, 1. *n.* acuerdo *m.* **2.** *v.* otorgar.

accordance, *n.*: **in a. with,** de acuerdo con.

accordingly, *adv.* en conformidad.

according to, *prep.* según.

accordion, *n.* (mus.) acordeón *m.*

accost, *v.* dirigirse a.

account, 1. *n.* relato *m.*; (com.) cuenta *f.* **on a. of,** a causa de. **on no a.,** de ninguna manera. **2.** *v. a. for,** explicar.

accountable, *a.* responsable.

accountant, *n.* contador -ra.

accounting, *n.* contabilidad *f.*

accouter, *v.* equipar, ataviar.

accouterments, *n.* equipo, atavío *m.*

accredit, *v.* acreditar.

accretion, *n.* aumento *m.*

accrual, *n.* aumento, incremento *m.*

accrue, *v.* provenir; acumularse.

accumulate, *v.* acumular.

accumulation, *n.* acumulación *f.*

accumulative, *a.* acumulativo.

accumulator, *n.* acumulador *m.*

accuracy, *n.* exactitud, precisión *f.*

accurate, *a.* exacto.

accursed, *a.* maldito.

accusation, *n.* acusación *f.*; cargo *m.*

accusative, *a. & n.* acusativo *m.*

accuse, *v.* acusar.

accused, *a. & n.* acusado, procesado *m.*

accuser, *n.* acusador -ra.

accustom, *v.* acostumbrar.

accustomed, *a.* acostumbrado.

ace, 1. *a.* sobresaliente. **2.** *n.* as *m.*

acerbity, *n.* acerbidad, amargura *f.*

acetate, *n.* (chem.) acetato *m.*

acetic, *a.* acético.

acetylene, 1. *a.* acetilénico. **2.** *n.* (chem.) acetileno *m.*

ache, 1. *n.* dolor *m.* **2.** *v.* doler.

achieve, *v.* lograr, llevar a cabo.

achievement, *n.* realización *f.*; hecho notable.

acid, *a. & n.* ácido *m.*

acidify, *v.* acidificar.

acidity, *n.* acidez *f.*

acidosis, *n.* (med.) acidismo *m.*

acid test, prueba decisiva.

acidulous, *a.* agrio, acídulo.

acknowledge, *v.* admitir. (receipt) acusar.

acme, *n.* apogeo, colmo *m.*

acne, *n.* (med.) acne *m. & f.*; barros *m.pl.*

acolyte, *n.* acólito *m.*

acorn, *n.* bellota *f.*

acoustics, *n.* acústica *f.*

acquaint, *v.* familiarizar. **to be acquainted with,** conocer.

acquaintance, *n.* conocimiento *m.* (person known) conocido -da. **to make the a. of,** conocer.

acquainted, be acquainted with, *v.* conocer.

acquiesce, *v.* consentir.

acquiescence, *n.* consentimiento *m.*

acquire, *v.* adquirir.

acquirement, *n.* adquisición *f.*; *pl.* conocimientos *m.pl.*

acquisition, *n.* adquisición *f.*

acquisitive, *a.* adquisitivo.

acquit, *v.* exonerar, absolver.

acquittal, *n.* absolución *f.*

acre, *n.* acre *m.*

acreage, número de acres.

acrid, *a.* acre, picante.

acrimonious, *a.* acrimonioso, mordaz.

acrimony, *n.* acrimonia, aspereza *f.*

acrobat, n. acróbata m.

across, 1. adv. a través, al otro lado. **2.** prep. al otro lado de, a través de.

acrostic, n. acróstico m.

act, 1. n. acción f.; acto m. **2.** v. actuar, portarse. **act as,** hacer de. **act on,** decidir sobre.

acting, 1. a. interino. **2.** n. acción f.; (theat.) representación f

actinism, n. actinismo m.

actinium, n. (chem.) actinio m.

action, n. acción f. **take a.,** tomar medidas.

activate, v. activar.

activation, n. activación f.

activator, n. (chem.) activador m.

active, a. activo.

activity, n. actividad f.

actor, n. actor m.

actress, n. actriz f.

actual, a. real, efectivo.

actuality, n. realidad, actualidad f.

actually, adv. en realidad.

actuary, n. actuario m.

actuate, v. impulsar, mover.

acumen, n. cacumen m., perspicacia f.

acute, a. agudo; perspicaz.

acutely, adv. agudamente.

acuteness, n. agudeza f.

adage, n. refrán, proverbio m.

adamant, a. firme.

Adam's apple, nuez de la garganta.

adapt, v. adaptar.

adaptable, a. adaptable.

adaptability, n. adaptabilidad f.

adaptation, n. adaptación f.

adapter, n. (tech.) adaptador m.; (mech.) ajustador m.

adaptive, a. adaptable, acomodable.

add, v. agregar, añadir. **a. up,** sumar.

adder, n. víbora f.; serpiente m.

addict, n. adicto m.; ('fan') aficionado m.

addition, n. adición f. **in a. to,** además de.

additional, a. adicional.

addle, v. confundir.

address, 1. n. dirección f.; señas f.pl. (speech) discurso. **2.** v. dirigirse a.

addressee, n. destinatorio -ia. f.

adduce, v. aducir.

adenoid, a. adenoideo.

adept, a. adepto.

adeptly, adv. diestramente.

adeptness, n. destreza f.

adequacy, n. suficiencia f.

adequate, a. adecuado.

adequately, adv. adecuadamente.

adhere, v. adherirse, pegarse.

adherence, n. adhesión f.; apego m.

adherent, n. adherente, partidario m.

adhesion, n. adhesión f.

adhesive, a. adhesivo. **a. tape,** esparadrapo m.

adhesiveness, n. adhesividad f.

adieu, 1. interj. adiós. **2.** n. despedida f.

adjacent, a. adyacente.

adjective, n. adjetivo m.

adjoin, v. lindar (con).

adjoining, a. contiguo.

adjourn, v. suspender, levantar.

adjournment, n. suspensión f.; (leg.) espera f.

adjunct, n. adjunto m.; (gram.) atributo m.

adjust, v. ajustar, acomodar; arreglar.

adjuster, n. ajustador m.

adjustment, n. ajuste; arreglo m.

adjutant, n. (mil.) ayudante m.

administer, v. administrar.

administration, n. administración f.; gobierno m.

administrative, a. administrativo.

administrator, n. administrador m.

admirable, a. admirable.

admirably, adv. admirablemente.

admiral, n. almirante m.

admiralty, n. ministerio de marina.

admiration, n. admiración f.

admire, v. admirar.

admirer, *n.* admirador -ra; enamorado -da.

admiringly, *adv.* admirativamente.

admissible, *a.* admisible, aceptable.

admission, *n.* admisión; entrada *f.*

admit, *v.* admitir.

admittance, *n.* entrada *f.*

admittedly, *adv.* reconocidamente.

admixture, *n.* mezcla *f.*

admonish, *v.* amonestar.

admonition, *n.* admonición *f.*

adolescence, *n.* adolescencia *f.*

adolescent, *n. & a.* adolescente.

adopt, *v.* adoptar.

adoption, *n.* adopción *f.*

adorable, *a.* adorable.

adoration, *n.* adoración *f.*

adore, *v.* adorar.

adorn, *v.* adornar.

adornment, *n.* adorno *m.*

adrenalin, *n.* adrenalina *f.*

adrift, *adv.* a la ventura.

adroit, *a.* diestro.

adulate, *v.* adular.

adulation, *n.* adulación *f.*

adult, *a. & n.* adulto *m.*

adulterant, *a. & n.* adulterante *m.*

adulterate, *v.* adulterar.

adulterer, *n.* adúltero *m.*

adulteress, *n.* adúltera *f.*

adultery, *n.* adulterio *m.*

advance, 1. *n.* avance; adelanto *m.* **in a.**, de antemano, antes. 2. *v.* avanzar, adelantar.

advanced, *a.* avanzado, adelantado.

advancement, *n.* adelantamiento *m.*; promoción *f.*

advantage, *n.* ventaja *f.* **take a. of**, aprovecharse de.

advantageous, *a.* provechoso, ventajoso.

advantageously, *adv.* ventajosamente.

advent, *n.* venida, llegada *f.*

adventitious, *a.* adventicio, espontáneo.

adventure, *n.* aventura *f.*

adventurer, *n.* aventurero *m.*

adventurous, *a.* aventurero, intrépido.

adventurously, *adv.* arriesgadamente.

adverb, *n.* adverbio *m.*

adverbial, *a.* adverbial.

adversary, *n.* adversario *m.*

adverse, *a.* adverso.

adversely, *adv.* adversamente.

adversity, *n.* adversidad *f.*

advert, *v.* hacer referencia a.

advertise, *v.* avisar, anunciar.

advertisement, *n.* aviso, anuncio *m.*

advertiser, *n.* anunciante, avisador *m.*

advertising, *n.* publicidad *f.*

advice, *n.* consejos *m.pl.*

advisability, *n.* prudencia, propiedad *f.*

advisable, *a.* aconsejable, prudente.

advisably, *adv.* prudentemente.

advise, *v.* aconsejar.

advisedly, *adv.* avisadamente, prudentemente.

advisement, *n.* consideración *f.*; **take under a.**, someter a estudio.

adviser, *n.* consejero *m.*

advocacy, *n.* abogacía; defensa *f.*

advocate, 1. *n.* abogado *m.* 2. *v.* apoyar.

aegis, *n.* amparo *m.*

aerate, *v.* airear, ventilar.

aeration, *n.* aeración, ventilación *f.*

aerial, *a.* aéreo.

aerie, *n.* nido de águila.

aeronautics, *n.* aeronáutica *f.*

aerosol bomb, *n.* bomba insecticida.

afar, *adv.* lejos. **from a.**, de lejos, desde lejos.

affability, *n.* afabilidad, amabilidad *f.*

affable, *a.* afable.

affably, *adv.* afablemente.

affair, *n.* asunto *m.* **love a.**, aventura amorosa.

affect, *v.* afectar; (emotionally) conmover.

affectation, *n.* afectación *f.*

affected, *a.* artificioso.

affecting, *a.* conmovedor.

affection, *n.* cariño *m.*

affectionate, *a.* afectuoso, cariñoso.

affectionately, *adv.* afectuosamente, con cariño.

affiance, *v.* dar palabra de casamiento; **become affianced,** comprometerse.

affidavit, *n.* (leg.) declaración, deposición *f.*

affiliate, 1. *n.* afiliado *m.* **2.** *v.* afiliar.

affiliation, *n.* afiliación *f.*

affinity, *n.* afinidad *f.*

affirm, *v.* afirmar.

affirmation, *n.* afirmación *f.*, aserción *f.*

affirmative, 1. *n.* afirmativa *f.* **2.** *a.* afirmativo.

affirmatively, *adv.* afirmativamente, aseveradamente.

affix, 1. *n.* (gram.) afijo *m.* **2.** *v.* fijar, pegar, poner.

afflict, *v.* afligir.

affliction, *n.* aflicción *f.*; mal *m.*

affluence, *n.* abundancia, opulencia *f.*

affluent, *a.* opulento, afluente.

afford, *v.* proporcionar. **be able to a.,** tener con que comprar.

affront, 1. *n.* afrenta *f.* **2.** *v.* afrentar, insultar.

afield, *adv.* lejos de casa; lejos del camino; lejos del asunto.

afire, *adv.* ardiendo.

afloat, *adv.* (naut.) a flote.

aforementioned, aforesaid, *a.* dicho, susodicho.

afraid, *a.* **to be a.,** tener miedo, temer.

African, *n. & a.* africano -na.

aft, *adv.* (naut.) a popa, en popa.

after, 1. *prep.* después de. **2.** *conj.* después que.

aftermath, *n.* resultados *m.pl.*, consecuencias *f.pl.*

afternoon, *n.* tarde *f.* **good a.,** buenas tardes.

afterthought, *n.* idea tardía.

afterward(s), *adv.* después.

again, *adv.* otra vez, de nuevo. **to do a.,** volver a hacer.

against, *prep.* contra; en contra de.

agape, *adv.* con la boca abierta.

agate, *n.* ágata *f.*

age, 1. *n.* edad *f.* **of a.,** mayor de edad. **old a.,** vejez *f.* **2.** *v.* envejecer.

aged, *a.* viejo, anciano, añejo.

ageless, *a.* sempiterno.

agency, *n.* agencia *f.*

agenda, *n.* agenda *f.*, orden *m.*

agent, *n.* agente; representante *m.*

agglutinate, *v.* aglutinar.

agglutination, *n.* aglutinación *f.*

aggrandize, *v.* agrandar; elevar.

aggrandizement, *n.* engrandecimiento *m.*

aggravate, *v.* agravar; irritar.

aggravation, *n.* agravamiento; empeoramiento *m.*

aggregate, *a. & n.* agregado *m.*

aggregation, *n.* agregación *f.*

aggression, *n.* agresión *f.*

aggressive, *n.* agresivo.

aggressively, *adv.* agresivamente.

aggressiveness, *n.* agresividad *f.*

aggressor, *n.* agresor *m.*

aghast, *a.* horrorizado.

agile, *a.* ágil.

agility, *n.* agilidad, ligereza, prontitud *f.*

agitate, *v.* agitar.

agitation, *n.* agitación *f.*

agitator, *n.* agitador *m.*

agnostic, *a. & n.* agnóstico *m.*

ago, *adv.* hace. **two days a.,** hace dos días.

agonized, *a.* angustioso.

agony, *n.* sufrimiento *m.*; angustia *f.*

agrarian, *a.* agrario.

agree, *v.* estar de acuerdo; convenir. **a. with one,** sentar bien.

agreeable, *a.* agradable.

agreeably, *adv.* agradablemente.

agreement, *n.* acuerdo *m.*

agriculture, *n.* agricultura *f.*

ahead, *adv.* adelante.

aid, 1. *n.* ayuda *f.* **2.** *v.* ayudar.

aide, *n.* ayudante *m.*

ailing, *adj.* enfermo.

ailment, *n.* enfermedad *f.*

aim, 1. *n.* puntería *f.*; (purpose) propósito *m.* **2.** *v.* apuntar.

aimless, *a.* sin objeto.

air, *n.* aire *m.* **by a. by** avión. **2.** *v.* ventilar, airear.

air-conditioned, *a.* enfriado por aire.

air conditioning, acondicionamiento del aire.

aircraft, *n.* máquina de volar.

aircraft carrier, *n.* portaaviones *m.*

airing, *n.* ventilación *f.*

air line, línea aérea.

air liner, avión de transporte.

air mail, correo aéreo.

airplane, *n.* avión, aeroplano *m.*

airport, *n.* aeropuerto *m.*

air pressure, presión atmosférica.

air raid, ataque aéreo.

airsick, *a.* mareado.

airtight, *a.* hermético.

aisle, *n.* pasillo *m.*

ajar, *a.* entreabierto.

akin, *a.* emparentado, semejante.

alacrity, *n.* alacridad, presteza *f.*

alarm, 1. *n.* alarma *f.* **2.** *v.* alarmar.

alarmist, *n.* alarmista *m. & f.*

albino, *n.* albino -na.

album, *n.* album *m.*

alcohol, *n.* alcohol *m.*

alcoholic, *a.* alcohólico.

alcove, *n.* alcoba *f.*

ale, *n.* cerveza inglesa.

alert, 1. *n.* alarma *f.* **on the a.,** alerta. sobre aviso. **2.** *a.* listo, vivo. **3.** *v.* poner sobre aviso.

alfalfa, *n.* alfalfa *f.*

algebra, *n.* álgebra *f.*

alias, *n.* alias *m.*

alibi, *n.* excusa *f.*; (leg.) coartada *f.*

alien, 1. *a.* ajeno, extranjero. **2.** *n.* extranjero -ra.

alienate, *v.* enajenar.

alight, *v.* bajar, apearse.

align, *v.* alinear.

alike, 1. *a.* semejante, igual. **2.** *adv.* del mismo modo, igualmente.

alimentary canal, tubo digestivo.

alive, *a.* vivo; animado.

alkali, *n.* (chem.) álcali, cali *m.*

alkaline, *a.* alcalino.

all, *a. & pron.* todo. **not at a.,** de ninguna manera, nada.

allay, *v.* aquietar.

allegation, *n.* alegación *f.*

allege, *v.* alegar; pretender.

allegiance, *n.* lealtad *f.*; (to country) homenaje *m.*

allegory, *n.* alegoría *f.*

allergy, *n.* alergia *f.*

alleviate, *v.* aliviar.

alley, *n.* callejón *m.* **bowling a.,** bolera *f.*, boliche *m.*

alliance, *n.* alianza *f.*

allied, *a.* aliado.

alligator, *n.* caimán *m.* (Mex.) lagarto *m.* **a. pear,** aguacate *m.*

allocate, *v.* colocar, asignar.

allot, *v.* asignar.

allotment, *n.* lote, porción *f.*

allow, *v.* permitir, dejar.

allowance, *n.* abono *m.*; dieta *f.* **make a. for,** tener en cuenta.

alloy, *n.* mezcla *f.* (metal) aleación *f.*

all right, está bien.

allude, *v.* aludir.

allure, 1. *n.* atracción *f.* **2.** *v.* atraer, tentar.

alluring, *a.* tentador, seductivo.

allusion, *n.* alusión *f.*

ally, 1. *n.* aliado *m.* **2.** *v.* aliar.

almanac, *n.* almanaque *m.*

almighty, a. todopoderoso.

almond, n. almendra f.

almost, adv. casi.

alms, n. limosna f.

aloft, adv. arriba, en alto.

alone, adv. solo, a solas. **to leave a.,** dejar en paz.

along, prep. por; a lo largo de. **a. with,** junto con.

alongside, 1. adv. al lado. **2.** prep. junto a.

aloof, a. apartado.

aloud, adv. en voz alta.

alpaca, n. alpaca f.

alphabet, n. alfabeto m.

alphabetical, a. alfabético.

alphabetize, v. alfabetizar.

already, adv. ya.

also, adv. también.

altar, n. altar m.

alter, v. alterar.

alteration, n. alteración f.

alternate, 1. a. alterno. n. substituto -ta. **3.** v. alternar.

alternative, 1. a. alternativo. **2.** n. alternativa f.

although, conj. aunque.

altitude, n. altura f.

alto, n. contralto m.

altogether, adv. en junto; enteramente.

altruism, n. altruismo m.

alum, n. alumbre m.

aluminum, n. aluminio m.

always, adv. siempre.

amalgam, n. amalgama f.

amalgamate, v. amalgamar.

amass, v. amontonar.

amateur, n. aficionado -da.

amaze, v. asombrar; sorprender.

amazement, n. asombro m.

amazing, a. asombroso, pasmoso.

ambassador, n. embajador m.

amber, 1. a. ambarino. **2.** n. ámbar m.

ambidextrous, a. ambidextro.

ambiguity, n. ambigüedad f.

ambiguous, a. ambiguo.

ambition, n. ambición f.

ambitious, a. ambicioso.

ambulance, n. ambulancia f.

ambush, 1. n. emboscada f. **2.** v. acechar.

ameliorate, v. mejorar.

amenable, a. tratable, dócil.

amend, v. enmendar.

amendment, n. enmienda f.

amenity, n. amenidad f.

American, a. & n. americano -na, norteamericano -na.

amethyst, n. amatista f.

amiable, a. amable.

amicable, a. amigable.

amid, prep. entre, en medio de.

amidships, adv. (naut.) en medio del navío.

amiss, adv. mal. **to take a.,** llevar a mal.

amity, n. amistad, armonía f.

ammonia, n. amoníaco m.

ammunition, n. munición f.

amnesia, n. (med.) amnesia f.

amnesty, n. amnistía f., indulto m.

amoeba, n. amiba f.

among, prep. entre.

amoral, a. amoral.

amorous, a. amoroso.

amorphous, a. amorfo.

amortize, v. (com.) amortizar.

amount, 1. n. cantidad, suma f. **2.** v. **a. to,** subir a.

ampere, n. (elec.) amperio m.

amphibian, a. & n. anfibio m.

amphibious, a. anfibio.

amphitheater, n. anfiteatro, circo m.

ample, a. amplio; suficiente.

amplify, v. amplificar.

amputate, v. amputar.

amuse, v. entretener, divertir.

amusement, n. diversión f.

an, art. un, una.

anachronism, n. anacronismo m.

analogous, a. análogo, parecido.

analogy, n. analogía f.

analysis, n. análisis m. & f.

analyst, n. analizador m.

analytic, a. analítico.

analyze, v. analizar.

anarchy, n. anarquía f.

anatomy, n. anatomía f.

ancestor, n. antepasado m.

ancestral, a. de los antepasados, hereditario.

ancestry, n. linaje, abolengo m.

anchor, 1. n. ancla f. to weigh a., levar el ancla. 2. v. anclar.

anchorage, n. (naut.) ancladero, anclaje m.

anchovy, n. anchoa f.

ancient, a. & n. antiguo.

and, conj. y, (before i-, hi-) e.

anecdote, n. anécdota f.

anemia, n. (med.) anemia f.

anesthetic, n. anestesia f.

anew, adv. de nuevo.

angel, n. ángel m.

anger, 1. n. ira f., enojo m. 2. v. enfadar, enojar.

angle, n. ángulo m.

angry, a. enojado, enfadado.

anguish, n. angustia f.

angular, a. angular.

aniline, n. (chem.) anilina f.

animal, a. & n. animal m.

animate, 1. adj. animado. 2. v. animar.

animated, a. vivo, animado.

animation, n. animación, viveza f.

animosity, n. rencor m.

anise, n. anís m.

ankle, n. tobillo m.

annals, n.pl. anales m.pl.

annex, 1. n. anexo m., adición f. 2. v. anexar.

annexation, n. anexión, adición f.

annihilate, v. aniquilar, destruir.

anniversary, n. aniversario m.

annotate, v. anotar.

annotation, n. anotación f., apunte m.

announce, v. anunciar.

announcement, n. anuncio, aviso m.

announcer, n. anunciador m.; (radio) anunciador, noticiador m.

annoy, v. molestar.

annoyance, n. molestia, incomodidad f.

annual, a. anual.

annuity, n. anualidad, pensión f.

annul, v. anular, invalidar.

anode, n. (elec.) ánodo m.

anoint, v. untar; (rel.) ungir.

anomalous, a. anómalo, irregular.

anonymous, a. anónimo.

another, a. & pron. otro.

answer, 1. n. contestación, respuesta f. 2. v. contestar, responder. a. for, ser responsable de.

answerable, a. discutible, refutable.

ant, n. hormiga f.

antacid, a. & n. antiácido m.

antagonism, n. antagonismo m.

antagonist, n. antagonista m.

antagonistic, a. antagónico, hostil.

antagonize, v. contrariar.

antarctic, a. & n. antártico m.

antecedent, a. & n. antecedente m.

antedate, v. antedatar.

antelope, n. antílope m., gacela f.

antenna, n. antena f.

anterior, a anterior.

anteroom, n. antecámara f.

anthem, n. himno m.; (religious) antífona f.

anthology, n. antología f.

anthracite, n. antracita f.

anthrax, n. (med.) ántrax m.

anthropology, n. antropología f.

antiaircraft, a. antiaéreo.

antibody n. anticuerpo m.

anticipate, v. esperar, anticipar.

anticipation, n. anticipación f.

anticlerical, a. anticlerical.

anticlimax, n. anticlímax m.

antidote, n. antídoto m.

antimony, n. antimonio m.

antipathy, n. antipatía f.

antiquated, a. anticuado.

antique, 1. a. antiguo. 2. n. antigüedad f.

antiquity, n. antigüedad f.

antiseptic, a. & n. antiséptico m.

antisocial, *a.* antisocial.

antitoxin, *n.* (med.) antitoxina *f.*

antler, *n.* asta *f.*

anvil, *n.* yunque *m.*

anxiety, *n.* ansia, ansiedad *f.*

anxious, *a.* inquieto, ansioso.

any, *a.* alguno; (at all) cualquiera; (after *not*) ninguno.

anybody, *pron.* alguien; (at all) cualquiera; (after *not*) nadie.

anyhow, *adv.* de todos modos; en todo caso.

anyone, *pron.* = anybody

anything, *pron.* algo; (at all) cualquier cosa; (after *not*) nada.

anyway, *adv.* = anyhow

anywhere, *adv.* en alguna parte; (at all) dondequiera; (after *not*) en ninguna parte.

apart, *n.* aparte. **to take a.**, deshacer.

apartment, *n.* apartamento, piso *m.*

apathetic, *a.* apático.

apathy, *n.* apatía *f.*

ape, 1. *n.* mono *m.* **2.** *-v.* imitar.

aperture, *n.* abertura *f.*

apex, *n.* ápice *m.*

aphorism, *n.* aforismo *m.*

apiary, *n.* apiario, abejar *m.*

apiece, *adv.* por persona; cada uno.

apologetic, *a.* apologético.

apologist, *n.* apologista *m. & f.*

apologize, *v.* excusarse, disculparse.

apology, *n.* excusa; apología *f.*

apoplectic, *a.* apoplético.

apoplexy, *n.* apoplejía *f.*

apostate, *n.* apóstata *m. & f.*

apostle, *n.* apóstol *m.*

apostolic, *a.* apostólico.

appall, *v.* espantar; desmayar.

apparatus, *n.* aparato *m.*

apparel, *n.* ropa *f.*

apparent, *a.* aparente; claro.

apparition, *n.* fantasma *f.*

appeal, 1. *n.* súplica *f.*; interés *m.*; (legal) apelación *f.* **2.** *v.* apelar, suplicar; interesar.

appear, *v.* aparecer, asomar; (seem) parecer; (leg.) comparecer.

appearance, *n.* apariencia *f.*, aspecto *m.*

appease, *v.* aplacar, apaciguar.

appeasement, *n.* apaciguamiento *m.*

appeaser, *n.* apaciguador, pacificador *m.*

appellant, *n.* apelante, demandante *m.*

appellate, *a.* (leg.) de apelación.

appendage, *n.* pertenencia *f.*

appendectomy, *n.* (med.) apendectomía *f.*

appendicitis, *n.* (med.) apendicitis *m.*

appendix, *n.* apéndice *m.*

appetite, *n.* apetito *m.*

appetizer, *n.* apertivo *m.*

appetizing, *a.* apetitivo.

applaud, *v.* aplaudir.

applause, *n.* aplauso *m.*

apple, *n.* manzana *f.* **a. tree**, manzano *m.*

applesauce, *n.* compota de manzana.

appliance, *n.* utensilio, aparato *m.*

applicable, *a.* aplicable.

applicant, *n.* suplicante *m. & f.*; candidato -ta.

application, *n.* solicitud *f.*

applied, *a.* aplicado. **a. for**, pedido.

appliqué, *n.* (sew.) aplicación *f.*

apply, *v.* aplicar. **a. for**, solicitar, pedir.

appoint, *v.* nombrar.

appointment, *n.* nombramiento, puesto *m.*

apportion, *v.* repartir.

apposition, *n.* (gram.) aposición *f.*

appraisal, *n.* valoración *f.*; apremio *m.*

appraise, *v.* avaluar, tasar; estimar.

appreciable, *a.* apreciable; notable.

appreciate, *v.* apreciar, estimar.

appreciation, *n.* aprecio; reconocimiento *m.*

apprehend, v. prender, capturar.

apprehension, n. aprensión f.

apprehensive, a. aprensivo.

apprentice, n. aprendiz m.

apprise, v. informar.

approach, 1. n. acceso; método m. **2.** v. acercarse.

approachable, a. accesible.

approbation, n. aprobación f.

appropriate, 1. a. apropiado. **2.** v. apropiar.

appropriation, n. apropiación f.

approval, n. aprobación f.

approve, v. aprobar.

approximate, 1. a. aproximado. **2.** v. aproximar.

approximately, adv. aproximadamente.

approximation, n. aproximación f.

appurtenance, n. pertenencia f.

apricot, n. albaricoque, damasco m.

April, n. abril m.

apron, n. delantal m.

apropos, adv. a propósito.

apt, a. apto; capaz.

aptitude, n. aptitud; facilidad f.

aquarium, n. acuario m., pecera f.

aquatic, a. acuático.

aqueduct, n. acueducto m.

aqueous, a. ácueo, acuoso, aguoso.

aquiline, a. aquilino, aguileño.

Arab, a. & n. árabe m. & f.

arable, a. cultivable.

arbitrary, a. arbitrario.

arbitrate, v. arbitrar.

arbitration, n. arbitraje m., arbitración f.

arbitrator, n. arbitrador -ra.

arbor, n. emparrado m.

arboreal, a. arbóreo.

arc, n. arco m.

arch, 1. n. arco m. **2.** v. arquear, encorvar.

archaeology, n. arqueología f.

archaic, a. arcaico.

archbishop, n. arzobispo m.

archdiocese, n. archidiócesis m.

archduke, n. archiduque m.

archer, n. arquero m.

archery, n. ballestería f.

archipelago, n. archipiélago m.

architect, n. arquitecto m.

architectural, a. arquitectural.

architecture, n. arquitectura f.

archive, n. archivo m.

archway, n. arcada f.

arctic, a. ártico.

ardent, a. ardiente.

ardor, n. ardor m., pasión f.

arduous, a. arduo, difícil.

area, n. área; extensión f.

arena, n. arena f.

Argentine, a. & n. argentino -na.

argue, v. disputar; sostener.

argument, n. disputa f.; razonamiento m.

argumentative, a. argumentoso.

aria, n. (mus.) aria f.

arid, a. árido, seco.

arise, v. surgir.

aristocracy, n. aristocracia f.

aristocrat, n. aristócrata m.

aristocratic, a. aristocrático.

arithmetic, n. aritmética f.

ark, n. arca f.

arm, 1. n. brazo m.; (weapon) arma f. **2.** v. armar.

armament, n. armamento m.

armchair, n. sillón m., butaca f.

armed forces, fuerzas militares.

armful, n. brazada f.

armhole, n. (sew.) sobaquera f.

armistice, n. armisticio m.

armor, n. armadura f., blindaje m.

armored, a. blindado.

armory, n. armería f., arsenal m.

armpit, n. sobaco m.

army, n. ejército m.

arnica, n. árnica f.

aroma, n. fragancia f.

aromatic, a. aromático.

around, prep. alrededor de, a la vuelta de; cerca de. **a.**

here, por aquí.

arouse, v. despertar; excitar.

arraign, v. (leg.) procesar criminalmente.

arrange, v. arreglar; concertar; (mus.) adaptar.

arrangement, n. arreglo; orden m.

array, 1. n. orden; adorno m. **2.** v. adornar.

arrears, n. atrasos m.pl.

arrest, 1. n. detención f. **2.** v. detener, arrestar.

arrival, n. llegada f.

arrive, v. llegar.

arrogance, n. arrogancia f.

arrogant, a. arrogante.

arrogate, v. arrogarse, usurpar.

arrow, n. flecha f.

arrowhead, n. punta de flecha.

arsenal, n. arsenal m.

arsenic, n. arsénico m.

arson, n. incendio premeditado.

art, arte m. (f. in pl.); (skill) maña f.

arterial, a. arterial.

arteriosclerosis, n. arteriosclerosis m.

artery, n. arteria f.

artesian well, pozo artesiano.

artful, a. astuto.

arthritis, n. artritis f.

artichoke, n. alcachofa f.

article, n. artículo m.

articulate, v. articular.

articulation, n. articulación f.

artifice, n. artificio m.

artificial, a. artificial.

artificially, adv. artificialmente.

artillery, n. artillería f.

artisan, n. artesano m.

artist, n. artista m. & f.

artistic, a. artístico.

artistry, n. arte m. & f.

artless, a. natural, cándido.

as, adv. & conj. como; **as . . . as . . .** tan . . . como.

asbestos, n. asbesto m.

ascend, v. ascender.

ascendancy, n. ascen diente m.

ascendant, a. ascendente.

ascent, n. subida f., ascenso m.

ascertain, v. averiguar.

ascetic, 1. a. ascético. **2.** n. asceta m. & f.

ascribe, v. atribuir.

ash, n. ceniza f.

ashamed, a. avergonzado.

ashen, a. pálido.

ashore, adv. a tierra. **go a.,** desembarcar.

ashtray, n. cenicero m.

Asiatic, a. & n. asiático -ca.

aside, adv. al lado. **a. from,** aparte de.

ask, v. preguntar; invitar; (request) pedir. **a. for,** pedir. **a. a question,** hacer una pregunta.

askance, adv. de soslayo; con recelo.

asleep, a. dormido. **to fall a.,** dormirse.

asparagus, n. espárrago m.

aspect, n. aspecto m., apariencia f.

asperity, n. aspereza f.

aspersion, n. calumnia f.

asphalt, n. asfalto m.

asphyxia, n. asfixia f.

asphyxiate, v. asfixiar, sofocar.

aspirant, a. & n. aspirante.

aspirate, v. aspirar.

aspiration, n. aspiración f.

aspirator, n. aspirador m.

aspire, v. aspirar. **a. to,** ambicionar.

aspirin, n. aspirina f.

ass, n. asno, burro m.

assail, v. asaltar, acometer.

assailant, n. asaltador m.

assassin, n. asesino m.

assassinate, v. asesinar.

assassination, n. asesinato m.

assault, 1. n. asalto m. **2.** v. asaltar, atacar.

assay, v. examinar; ensayar.

assemblage, n. asamblea f.

assemble, v. juntar, convocar; (mechanism) montar.

assembly, n. asamblea, concurrencia f.

assent, 1. n. asentimiento m. **2.** v. asentir, convenir.

assert, v. afirmar, aseverar. **a. oneself,** hacerse sentir.

assertion, *n.* aserción, aseveración *f.*

assertive, *a.* asertivo.

assess, *v.* tasar, avaluar.

assessor, *n.* asesor *m.*

asset, *n.* ventaja *f.* **assets,** (commercial) capital *m.*

asseverate, *v.* aseverar, afirmar.

asseveration, *n.* aseveración *f.*

assiduous, *a.* asiduo.

assiduously, *adv.* asiduamente.

assign, *v.* asignar; destinar.

assignable, *a.* asignable, transferible.

assignation, *n.* asignación *f.*

assignment, *n.* misión; tarea *f.*

assimilate, *v.* asimilar.

assimilation, *n.* asimilación *f.*

assimilative, *a.* asimilativo.

assist, *v.* ayudar, auxiliar.

assistance, *n.* ayuda *f.*, auxilio *m.*

assistant, *n.* ayudante, asistente *m.*

associate, 1. *n.* socio *m.* **2.** *v.* asociar.

association, *n.* asociación; sociedad *f.*

assonance, *n.* asonancia *f.*

assort, *v.* surtir con variedad.

assorted, *a.* variado, surtido.

assortment, *n.* surtido *m.*

assuage, *v.* mitigar, aliviar.

assume, *v.* suponer; asumir.

assuming, *a.* presuntuoso. **a. that,** dado que.

assumption, *n.* suposición; (rel.) asunción *f.*

assurance, *n.* seguridad; confianza *f.*

assure, *v.* asegurar; dar confianza.

assured, 1. *a.* seguro. **2.** *a.* & *n.* (com.) asegurado *m.*

assuredly, *adv.* ciertamente.

aster, *n.* (bot.) aster *m.*

asterisk, *n.* asterisco *m.*

astern, *adv.* (naut.) a popa.

asteroid, *n.* asteroide *m.*

asthma, *n.* (med.) asma *f.*

astigmatism, *n.* astigmatismo *m.*

astir, *adv.* en movimiento.

astonish, *v.* asombrar, pasmar.

astonishment, *n.* asombro *m.*, sorpresa *f.*

astound, *v.* pasmar, sorprender.

astral, *a.* astral, estelar.

astray, *a.* desviado.

astride, *adv.* a horcajadas.

astringent, *a.* & *n.* astringente *m.*

astrology, *n.* astrología *f.*

astronomy, *n.* astronomía *f.*

astute, *a.* astuto; agudo.

asunder, *adv.* en dos.

asylum, *n.* asilo, refugio *m.*

asymmetry, *n.* asimetría *f.*

at, *prep.* a, en; cerca de.

ataxia, *n.* (med.) ataxia *f.*

atheist, *n.* ateo *m.*

athlete, *n.* atleta *m.*

athletic, *a.* atlético.

athletics, *n.* atletismo *m.*, deportes *m.pl.*

athwart, *prep.* á través de.

Atlantic, 1. *a.* atlántico. **2.** *n.* Atlántico *m.*

Atlantic Ocean, el mar atlántico.

atlas, *n.* atlas *m.*

atmosphere, *n.* atmósfera *f.*; (fig.) ambiente *m.*

atmospheric, *a.* atmosférico.

atoll, *n.* atolón *m.*

atom, *n.* átomo *m.*

atomic, *a.* atómico.

atomic bomb, bomba atómica.

atomic energy, energía atómica.

atomic theory, teoría atómica.

atomic weight, peso atómico.

atonal, *a.* (mus.) atonal.

atone, *v.* expiar, compensar.

atonement, *n.* expiación; reparación *f.*

atrocious, *a.* atroz.

atrocity, *n.* atrocidad *f.*

atrophy, 1. *n.* (med.) atrofia *f.* **2.** *v.* atrofiar.

atropine, *n.* (chem.) atropina *f.*

attach, *v.* juntar; prender; (hook) enganchar; (figurative) atribuir.

attaché, *n.* agregado *m.*

attachment, 1. *n.* enlace *m.;* accesorio *m.;* (emotional) afecto, cariño *m.*

attack, 1. *n.* ataque *m.* **2.** *v.* atacar.

attacker, *n.* asaltador *m.*

attain, *v.* lograr, alcanzar.

attainable, *a.* accesible, realizable.

attainment, *n.* logro; (pl.) dotes *f.pl.*

attempt, 1. *n.* ensayo; esfuerzo *m.;* tentativa *f.* **2.** *v.* ensayar, intentar.

attend, *v.* atender; (a meeting) asistir a.

attendance, *n.* asistencia; presencia *f.*

attendant, 1. *a.* concomitante. **2.** *n.* servidor -ra.

attention, *n.* atención *f.;* obsequio *m.* **to pay a. to,** hacer caso a.

attentive, *a.* atento.

attentively, *adv.* atentamente.

attenuate, *v.* atenuar, adelgazar.

attest, *v.* confirmar, atestiguar.

attic, *n.* desván *m.,* guardilla *f.*

attire, 1. *n.* traje *m.* **2.** *v.* vestir.

attitude, *n.* actitud *f.,* ademán *m.*

attorney, *n.* abogado, apoderado *m.*

attract, *v.* atraer. **a. attention,** llamar la atención.

attraction, *n.* atracción *f.,* atractivo *m.*

attractive, *a.* atractivo; simpático.

attributable, *a.* atribuible, imputable.

attribute, 1. *n.* atributo *m.* **2.** *v.* atribuir.

attrition, *n.* roce, desgaste *m.;* atrición *f.*

attune, *v.* armonizar.

auction, *n.* subasta *f.,* (S.A.) venduta *f.*

auctioneer, *n.* subastador *m.,* (S.A.) martillero *m.*

audacious, *a.* audaz.

audacity, *n.* audacia *f.*

audible, *a.* audible.

audience, *n.* auditorio, público *m.;* entrevista *f.*

audit, *v.* revisar cuentas.

audition, *n.* audición *f.*

auditor, *n.* interventor, revisor *m.*

auditorium, *n.* sala *f.;* teatro *m.*

auditory, *a. & n.* auditorio *m.*

augment, *v.* aumentar.

augur, *v.* augurar, pronosticar.

August, *n.* agosto *m.*

aunt, *n.* tía *f.*

auspice, *n.* auspicio *m.*

auspicious, *a.* favorable; propicio.

austere, *a.* austero.

austerity, *n.* austeridad; severidad *f.*

Austrian, *a. & n.* austríaco -ca.

authentic, *a.* auténtico.

authenticate, *v.* autenticar.

authenticity, *n.* autenticidad *f.*

author, *n.* autor, escritor *m.*

authoritarian, *a. & n.* autoritario *m.*

authoritative, *a.* autoritario; autorizado.

authoritatively, *adv.* autorizadamente.

authority, *n.* autoridad *f.*

authorization, *n.* autorización *f.*

authorize, *v.* autorizar.

auto, *n.* auto, automóvil *m.*

autobiography, *n.* autobiografía *f.*

autocracy, *n.* autocracia *f.*

autocrat *n.* autócrata *m. & f.*

autograph, *n.* autógrafo *m.*

automatic, *a.* automático.

automatically, *adv.* automáticamente.

automobile, *n.* automóvil, coche *m.*

automotive, *a.* automotriz.

autonomy, *n.* autonomía *f.*

autopsy, *n.* autopsia *f.*

autumn, *n.* otoño *m.*

auxiliary, *a.* auxiliar.

avail, 1. *n.* **of no a.,** en vano.

2. *v.* **a. oneself of,** aprovechar.

available, *a.* disponible.

avalanche, *n.* alud *m.*

avarice, *n.* avaricia, codicia *f.*

avariciously, *adv.* avaramente.

avenge, *v.* vengar.

avenger, *n.* vengador -ra.

avenue, *n.* avenida *f.*

average, 1. *a.* medio; común. **2.** *n.* promedio, término medio *m.* **3.** *v.* calcular el promedio.

averse, *a.* adverso.

aversion, *n.* aversión *f.*

avert, *v.* desviar; impedir.

aviary, *n.* pajarera, avería *f.*

aviation, *n.* aviación *f.*

aviator, *n.* aviador -ra.

aviatrix, *n.* aviatriz *f.*

avid, *a.* ávido.

avocation, *n.* pasatiempo *f.*

avoid, *v.* evitar.

avoidable, *a.* evitable.

avoidance, *n.* evitación *f.*; (leg.) anulación *f.*

avow, *v.* declarar; admitir.

avowal, *n.* admisión *f.*

avowed, *a.* reconocido; admitido.

avowedly, *adv.* reconocidamente; confesadamente.

await, *v.* esperar, aguardar.

awake, *a.* despierto.

awaken, *v.* despertar.

award, 1. *n.* premio *m.* **2.** *v.* otorgar.

aware, *a.* enterado, consciente.

awash, *a. & adv.* (naut.) a flor de agua.

away, *adv.* see under verb: **go away, put away, take away,** etc.)

awe, *n.* pavor *m.*

awesome, *a.* pavoroso; aterrador.

awful, *a.* horrible, terrible, muy malo.

awhile, *adv.* por un rato.

awkward, *a.* torpe, desmañado; (figurative) delicado, embarazoso.

awning, *n.* toldo *m.*

awry, *a.* oblicuo, torcido.

ax, axe, *n.* hacha *f.*

axiom, *n.* axioma *m.*

axis, *n.* eje *m.*

axle, *n.* eje *m.*

azure, *a.* azulado.

B

babble, 1. *n.* balbuceo; murmullo *m.* **2.** *v.* balbucear.

babbler, *n.* hablador -ra, charlador -ra.

baboon, *n.* mandril *m.*

baby, *n.* nene, bebé *m.*

babyish, *a.* infantil.

bachelor, *n.* soltero *m.*

bacillus, *n.* bacilo, microbio *m.*

back, 1. *adv.* atrás. **to be b.,** estar de vuelta. **b. of,** detrás de. **2.** *n.* espalda *f.*; (of animal) lomo *m.*

backbone, *n.* espinazo *m.*; (figurative) firmeza *f.*

backer, *n.* sostenedor -ra.

background, *n.* fondo *m.*, antecedentes *m.pl.*

backing, *n.* apoyo *m.*, garantía *f.*

backlog, *n.* rezago *m.*

backstage, *n.* entre bastidores *m.*

backward, 1. *a.* atrasado. **2.** *adv.* hacia atrás.

backwardness, *n.* atraso *m.*

backwater, *n.* remolino *m.*; contracorriente *f.*

backwoods, *n.* monte *m.*; región apartada.

bacon, *n.* tocino *m.*

bacteria, *n.* bacterias *f.pl.*

bacteriologist, n. bacteriólogo m.

bacteriology, n. bacteriología f.

bad, a. malo.

badge, n. insignia, divisa f.

badger, 1. n. tejón m. **2.** v. atormentar.

badly, adv. mal.

badness, n. maldad f.

bad-tempered, a. de mal humor.

baffle, v. desconcertar.

bafflement, n. contrariedad; confusión f.

bag, 1. n. saco m.; bolsa f. **2.** v. ensacar, cazar.

baggage, n. equipaje m. **b. check,** talón m.

baggy, a. abotagado; bolsudo; hinchado.

bagpipe, n. gaita f.

bail, 1. n. fianza f. **2.** v. desaguar.

bailiff, n. alguacil m.

bait, 1. n. cebo m. **2.** v. cebar.

bake, v. cocer en horno.

baker, n. panadero, hornero m.

bakery, n. panadería f.

baking, 1. n. hornada f. **b. powder,** levadura f.

balance, n. balanza f.; equilibrio m.; (com.) saldo m.

balcony, n. balcón m.; (theater) galería f.

bald, a. calvo.

baldness, n. calvicie f.

bale, 1. n. bala f. **2.** v. embalar.

balk, v. frustrar; rebelarse.

balky, a. rebelón.

ball, n. bola, pelota f.; (dance) baile m.

ballad, n. romance m.; balada f.

ballast, 1. n. lastre m. **2.** v. lastrar.

ball bearing, n. cojinete de bolas m.

ballerina, n. bailarina f.

ballet, n. danza f.; ballet m.

ballistics, n. balística f.

balloon, n. globo m. **b. tire,** neumático de balón.

ballot, 1. n. balota f., voto m. **2.** v. balotar, votar.

ballroom, n. salón de baile m.

balm, n. bálsamo; ungüento m.

balmy, a. fragante; reparador; calmante.

balsa, n. bálsamo m.

balsam, n. bálsamo m.

balustrade, n. barandilla f.

bamboo, n. bambú m., caña f.

ban, 1. n. prohibición. f. **2.** v. prohibir; proscribir.

banal, a. trivial; vulgar.

banana, n. banana f., cambur m. **b. tree,** banano, plátano m.

band, 1. n. venda f.; (of men) banda, cuadrilla, partida f. **2.** v. asociarse.

bandage, 1. n. vendaje m. **2.** v. vendar.

bandanna, n. pañuelo (grande) m.; bandana f.

bandbox, n. caja de cartón.

bandit, n. bandido -da.

bandmaster, n. músico mayor m.

bandstand, n. kiosco de música m.

bang, 1. int. ¡pum! **2.** n. ruido de un golpe. **3.** v. golpear ruidosamente.

banish, v. desterrar.

banishment, n. destierro m.

banister, n. pasamano m.

bank, 1. n. banco m.; (of a river) margen m. or f. **2.** v. depositar.

bankbook, n. libreta de depósitos f.

banker, n. banquero m.

banking, 1. a. bancaria. **2.** n. banca f.

bank note, n. billete de banco m.

bankrupt, a. insolvente.

bankruptcy, n. bancarrota f.

banner, n. bandera f.; estandarte m.

banquet, n. banquete m.

banter, 1. n. choteo m.; zumba; burla f. **2.** v. chotear; zumbar; burlarse.

baptism, n. bautismo, bautizo m.

baptismal, a. bautismal.

Baptist, n. bautista m.

baptize, v. bautizar.

bar, 1. n. barra f.; obstáculo m.; (tavern) taberna f., bar m. **2.** v. barrear; prohibir, excluir.

barbarian, 1. a. bárbaro. **2.** n. bárbaro -ra.

barbarism, n. barbarismo m., barbarie f.

barbarous, a. bárbaro, cruel.

barbecue, n. animal asado entero; (Mex.) barbacoa f.

barber, n. barbero m. **b. shop,** barbería f.

barbiturate, n. barbitúrico m.

bare, 1. a. desnudo; descubierto. **2.** v. desnudar; descubrir.

bareback, adv. sin silla.

barefoot(ed), a. descalzo.

barely, adv. escasamente, apenas.

bareness, 1. n. desnudez f.; pobreza f.

bargain, 1. n. ganga f., compra ventajosa f.; contrato m. **2.** v. regatear; negociar.

barge, n. lanchón m., barcaza f.

baritone, n. barítono m.

barium, n. bario m.

bark, 1. n. corteza f.; (of dog) ladra f. **2.** v. ladrar.

barley, n. cebada f.

barn, n. granero m.

barnacle, n. lapa f.

barnyard, n. corral m.

barometer, n. barómetro m.

barometric, a. barométrico.

baron, n. barón m.

baroness, n. baronesa f.

baronial, a. baronial.

baroque, a. barroco.

barracks, n. cuartel m.

barrage, n. cortina de fuego f.

barred, a. excluido; prohibido.

barrel, n. barril m.; (of gun) cañón m.

barren, a. estéril.

barrenness, n. esterilidad f.

barricade, n. barricada, barrera f.

barrier, n. barrera f.; obstáculo m.

barroom, n. cantina f.

bartender, n. tabernero; cantinero m.

barter, 1. n. cambio, trueque m. **2.** v. cambiar, trocar.

base, 1. a. bajo, vil. **2.** n. base f. **3.** v. basar.

baseball, n. beisbol m.

baseboard, n. tabla de resguardo.

baseness, n. bajeza, vileza f.

basement, n. sótano m.

bashful, a. vergonzoso, tímido.

bashfully, adv. timidamente; vergonzosamente.

bashfulness, n. vergüenza; timidez f.

basic, a. fundamental, básico.

basin, n. bacía f.; (of river) cuenca f.

basis, n. base f.

bask, v. tomar el sol.

basket, n. cesta, canasta f.

bass, n. (fish) lobina f.; (music) bajo profundo m. **b. viol,** violón m.

bassinet, n. bacinete m.

bassoon, n. bajón m.

bastard, a. & n. bastardo; hijo natural m.

baste, v. (sew.) bastear; (cook.) pringar.

bat, 1. n. (animal) murciélago m.; (baseball) bate m. **2.** v. batear.

batch, n. cantidad de cosas.

bath, n. baño m.

bathe, v. bañar.

bather, n. bañista m.

bathing resort, n. balneario m.

bathrobe, n. bata de baña f., peinador m.

bathroom, n. cuarto de baño.

bathtub, n. bañera f.

baton, n. bastón m.; (mus.) batuta f.

battalion, n. batallón m.

batter, 1. n. (cook.) batido m.; (baseball) voleador m. **2.** v. batir; derribar.

battery, n. batería f.; (elec.) pila f.

batting, n. agramaje, moldeaje m.

battle, 1. n. batalla f.; combate m. **2.** v. batallar.

battlefield

battlefield, *n.* campo de batalla.

battleship, *n.* acorazado *m.*

bauxite, *n.* bauxita *f.*

bawl, *v.* gritar; vocear.

bay, **1.** *n.* bahía *f.* **2.** *v.* aullar.

bayonet, *n.* bayoneta *f.*

bazaar, *n.* bazar *m.*, feria *f.*

be, *v. ser;* estar. (See **hacer; hay; tener** in Sp.-Eng. section).

beach, *n.* playa *f.*

beacon, *n.* faro *m.*

bead, *n.* cuenta *f.*; *pl.* (rel.) rosario *m.*

beading, *n.* abalorio *m.*

beady, *a.* globuloso; burbujoso.

beak, *n.* pico *m.*

beaker, *n.* vaso con pico *m.*

beam, *n.* viga *f.*; (of wood) madero *m.*; (of light) rayo *m.*

beaming, *a.* radiante.

bean, *n.* haba, habichuela *f.*, frijol *m.*

bear, **1.** *n.* oso -sa. **2.** *v.* llevar; (endure) aguantar.

bearable, *a.* sufrible; suportable.

beard, *n.* barba *f.*

bearded, *a.* barbado; barbudo.

beardless, *a.* lampiño; imberbe.

bearer, *n.* portador -ra.

bearing, *n.* porte, aguante *m.*

bearskin, *n.* piel de oso *f.*

beast, *n.* bestia *f.*; bruto *m.*

beat, *v.* golpear; batir; pulsar; (in games) ganar, vencer.

beaten, *a.* vencido; batido.

beatify, *v.* beatificar.

beating, *n.* paliza *f.*

beau, *n.* novio *m.*

beautiful, *a.* hermoso, bello.

beautifully, *adv.* bellamente.

beautify, *v.* embellecer.

beauty, *n.* hermosura, belleza *f.*

beaver, *n.* castor *m.*

becalm, *v.* calmar; sosegar; encalmarse.

because, *conj.* porque. **b. of**, a causa de.

beckon, *v.* hacer señas.

become, *v.* hacerse; ponerse.

becoming, *a.* propio, correc-

to; **be b.**, quedar bien, sentar bien.

bed, *n.* cama *f.*; lecho *m.*; (of river) cauce *m.*

bedbug, *n.* chinche *m.*

bedclothes, *n.* ropa de cama.

bedding, *n.* colchones *m.pl.*

bedfellow, *n.* compañero de cama *m.*

bedizen, *v.* adornar; aderezar.

bedridden, *a.* postrado (en cama).

bedrock, *n.* (mining) lecho de roca *m.*; (fig.) fundamento *m.*

bedroom, *n.* alcoba *f.*; (Mex.) recámara *f.*

bedside, *n.* lado de cama *m.*

bedspread, *n.* cubrecama, sobrecama *f.*

bedstead, *n.* armadura de cama *f.*

bedtime, *n.* hora de acostarse.

bee, *n.* abeja *f.*

beef, *n.* carne de vaca.

beefsteak, *n.* bistec, bisté *f.*

beehive, *n.* colmena *f.*

beer, *n.* cerveza *f.*

beeswax, *n.* cera de abejas

beet, *n.* remolacha *f.*; (Mex.) betabel *m.*

beetle, *n.* escarabajo *m.*

befall, *v.* suceder, sobrevenir.

befitting, *a.* conveniente; propio; digno.

before, **1.** *adv.* antes. **2.** *prep.* antes de; (in front of) delante de. **3.** *conj.* antes que.

beforehand, *adv.* de antemano.

befriend, *v.* amparar.

befuddle, *v.* confundir; aturdir.

beg, *v.* rogar, suplicar; (for alms) mendigar.

beget, *v.* engendrar; producir.

beggar, *n.* mendigo -ga; (Sp. Am.) limosnero -ra.

beggarly, *a.* pobre, miserable.

begin, *v.* empezar, comenzar, principiar.

beginner, *n.* principiante *m.*

beginning, *n.* principio, comienzo *m.*

begrudge, v. envidiar.

behalf; in, on b. of, a favor de, en pro de.

behave, v. portarse ,comportarse.

behavior, n. conducta f.; comportamiento m.

behead, v. decapitar.

behind, 1. adv. atrás, detrás. **2.** prep. detrás de.

behold, v. contemplar.

beige, a. crema.

being, n. existencia f.; (person) ser m.

bejewel, v. adornar con joyas.

belated, a. atrasado, tardío.

belch, 1. n. eructo m. **2.** v. vomitar; eructar.

belfry, n. campanario m.

Belgian, 1. a. belga. **2.** n. belga m. & f.

Belgium, n. Bélgica f.

belie, v. desmentir.

belief, n. creencia f.; parecer m.

believable, a. creíble.

believe, v. creer.

believer, n. creyente m.

belittle, v. dar poca importancia a.

bell, n. campana f.; (of house) campanilla f.; (electric) timbre m.

bellboy, n. mozo, botones m.

bellicose, a. guerrero.

belligerence n. beligerancia f.

belligerent, a. & n. beligerante.

belligerently, adv. belicosamente.

bellow, v. bramar, rugir.

bellows, n. fuelle m.

belly, n. vientre m.; panza, barriga f.

belong, v. pertenecer.

belongings, n. propiedad f.

beloved, a. querido, amado.

below, 1. adv. debajo, abajo. **2.** prep. debajo de.

belt, n. cinturón m.

bench, n. banco m.

bend, 1. n. vuelta; curva f. **2.** v. encorvar, doblar.

beneath, 1. adv. debajo, abajo. **2.** prep. debajo de.

benediction, n. bendición f.

benefactor, n. bienhechor -ra.

benefactress, n. bienhechora f.

beneficial, a. provechoso, beneficioso.

beneficiary, n. beneficiario, beneficiado m.

benefit, 1. n. provecho, beneficio m. **2.** v. beneficiar.

benevolence n. benevolencia f.

benevolent, a. benévolo.

benevolently, adv. benignamente.

benign, a. benigno.

benignity, n. benignidad; bondad f.

bent, 1. a. encorvado. **b. on,** resuelto a. **2.** n. inclinación f.

benzene, n. bencina f.

bequeath, v. legar.

bequest, n. legado m.

berate, v. reñir, regañar.

bereave, v. despojar; desolar.

bereavement, n. privación f.; despojo m.

berry, n. baya f.

berth, n. camarote m.; (mar.) litera f.; (for vessel) amarradero m.

beseech, v. suplicar; implorar.

beseechingly, adv. suplicantemente.

beset, v. acosar; rodear.

beside, prep. al lado de.

besides, adv. además, por otra parte.

besiege, v. sitiar; asediar.

besieged, a. sitiado.

besieger, n. sitiador m.

besmirch, v. manchar; deshonrar.

best, a. & adv. mejor. **at b.,** a lo más.

bestial, a. bestial; brutal.

bestir, v. incitar; intrigar.

best man, n. padrino de boda.

bestow, v. conferir.

bestowal, n. dádiva; presentación f.

bet, 1. n. apuesta f. **2.** v. apostar.

betoken, v. denotar, significar.

betray, v. traicionar; revelar.

betrayal, n. traición f.

betroth, v. contraer esponsales; prometer.

betrothal, n. esponsales m.pl.

better, 1. a. & adv. mejor. **2.** v. mejorar.

between, prep. entre, en medio de.

bevel, 1. n. cartabón m. **2.** v. cortar al sesgo.

beverage, n. bebida f.; (cold) refresco m.

bewail, v. llorar; lamentar.

beware, v. guardarse, precaverse.

bewilder, v. aturdir.

bewildered, a. descarriado.

bewildering, a. aturdente.

bewilderment, n. aturdimiento m.; perplejidad f.

bewitch, v. hechizar; embrujar.

beyond, prep. más allá de.

biannual, a. semianual; semestral.

bias, 1. n. parcialidad f.; prejuicio m. **on the b.,** al sesgo. **2.** v. predisponer influir.

bib, n. babador m.

Bible, n. Biblia f.

Biblical, a. bíblico.

bibliography, n. bibliografía f.

bicarbonate, n. bicarbonato m.

bicentennial, a. & n. bicentenario m.

biceps, n. biceps m.

bicker, v. altercar.

bicycle, n. bicicleta f.

bicyclist, n. biciclista m.

bid, 1. n. proposición, oferta f. **2.** v. mandar; ofrecer.

bidder, n. postor m.

bide, v. aguardar; esperar.

bier, n. ataúd m.

bifocal, a. bifocal.

big, a. grande.

bigamist, n. bígamo -ma.

bigamy, n. bigamia f.

bigot, n. persona intolerante.

bigotry, n. intolerancia f.

bilateral, a. bilateral.

bile, n. bilis f.

bilingual, a. bilingüe.

bilious, a. bilioso.

bill, 1. n. cuenta, factura f.; (money) billete m.; (of bird) pico m. **2.** v. facturar.

billet, n. billete m.; (mil.) boleta f. **2.** v. aposentar.

billfold, n. cartera f.

billiard balls, n. bolas de billar.

billiards, n. billar m.

billion, n. billón m.

bill of health, n. certificado de sanidad.

bill of lading, n. conocimiento de embarque.

bill of sale, n. escritura de venta.

billow, n. ola; oleada f.

bimetallic, a. bimetálico.

bimonthly, a. & adv. bimestral.

bin, n. hucha f.; depósito m.

bind, v. atar; obligar; (book) encuadernar.

bindery, n. taller de encuadernación m.

binding, n. encuadernación f.

binocular, 1. a. binocular. **2.** n.pl. gemelos m.pl.

biochemistry, n. bioquímica f.

biographer, n. biógrafo m.

biographical, a. biográfico.

biography, n. biografía f.

biological, a. biológico.

biologically, adv. biológicamente.

biology, n. biología f.

bipartisan, a. bipartito.

biped, n. bípedo m.

bird, n. pájaro m.; ave f.

bird of prey, n. ave de rapiña m.

birth, n. nacimiento m. **give b. to,** dar a luz.

birthday, n. cumpleaños m.

birthmark, n. estigma f., marca de nacimiento.

birthplace, n. natalicio m.

birth rate, n. natalidad f.

birthright, n. primogenitura f.

biscuit, n. bizcocho m.

bisect, v. bisecar.

bishop, n. obispo m.; (chess) alfil m.

bishopric, n. obispado m.

bismuth, n. bismuto m.

bison, n. bisonte m.

bit, *n.* pedacito *m.*; (mech.) taladro *m.*; (for horse) bocado *m.*

bitch, *n.* perra *f.*

bite, 1. *n.* bocado *m.*; picada *f.* **2.** *v.* morder; picar.

biting, *a.* penetrante; mordaz.

bitter, *a.* amargo.

bitterly, *adv.* amargamente; agriamente.

bitterness, *n.* amargura *f.*; rencor *m.*

bivouac, 1. *n.* vivaque *m.* **2.** *v.* vivaquear.

biweekly, *a.* quincenal.

black, *a.* negro.

blackberry, *n.* mora *f.*

blackbird, *n.* mirlo *m.*

blackboard, *n.* pizarra *f.*

blacken, *v.* ennegrecer.

black eye, *n.* ojo amoratado.

blackguard, *n.* tunante; pillo *m.*

blackmail, 1. *n.* chantaje *m.* **2.** *v.* amenazar con chantaje.

black market, *n.* mercado negro.

blackout, *n.* oscurecimiento, apagamiento *m.*

blacksmith, *n.* herrero *m.*

bladder, *n.* vejiga *f.*

blade, *n.* (sword) hoja *f.*; (oar) pala *f.*; (grass) brizna *f.*

blame, *v.* culpar, echar la culpa a.

blameless, *a.* inculpable.

blanch, *v.* blanquear; escaldar.

bland, *a.* blando.

blank, *a. & n.* blanco.

blanket, *n.* manta *f.*; cobertor *m.*

blare, 1. *n.* sonido de trompeta. **2.** *v.* sonar como trompeta.

blaspheme, *v.* blasfemar.

blasphemer, *n.* blasfemo; blasfemador *m.*

blasphemous, *a.* blasfemo, impío.

blasphemy, *n.* blasfemia *f.*

blast, 1. *n.* barreno *m.*; (wind) ráfaga *f.* **2.** *v.* barrenar.

blatant, *a.* bramante.

blaze, 1. *n.* llama, hoguera *f.* **2.** *v.* encenderse en llama.

blazing, *a.* flameante.

bleach, *v.* blanquear.

bleachers, *n.* asientos al aire libre.

bleak, *a.* frío y sombrío.

bleakness, *n.* intemperie *f.*

bleed, *v.* sangrar.

blemish, 1. *n.* mancha *f.*; lunar *m.* **2.** *v.* manchar.

blend, 1. *n.* mezcla *f.* **2.** *v.* mezclar, combinar.

blended, *a.* mezclado.

bless, *v.* bendecir.

blessed, *a.* bendito.

blessing, *n.* bendición *f.*

blight, 1. *n.* plaga *f.*; tizón *m.* **2.** *v.* atizonar.

blind, *a.* ciego.

blindfold, *v.* vendar los ojos.

blinding, *a.* deslumbrante; ofuscante.

blindly, *adv.* ciegamente.

blindness, *n.* ceguedad, ceguera *f.*

blink, 1. *n.* guiñada *f.* **2.** *v.* guiñar.

bliss, *n.* felicidad *f.*

blissful, *a.* dichoso; bienaventurado.

blissfully, *adv.* felizmente.

blister, *n.* ampolla *f.*

blithe, *a.* alegre; jovial; gozoso.

blizzard, *n.* chubasco de nieve.

bloat, *v.* hinchar.

bloc, *n.* grupo (político); bloc.

block, 1. *n.* bloque *m.*; (street) manzana, cuadra *f.* **2.** *v.* bloquear.

blockade, 1. *n.* bloqueo *m.* **2.** *v.* bloquear.

blond, *a. & n.* rubio -ia.

blood, *n.* sangre *f.*; parentesco, linaje *m.*

bloodhound, *n.* sabueso *m.*

bloodless, *a.* exangüe; desangrado.

blood poisoning, *n.* envenenamiento de sangre.

blood pressure, *n.* presión arterial.

bloodshed, *n.* matanza *f.*

bloodthirsty, *a.* cruel, sanguinario.

bloody, *a.* ensangrentado, sangriento.

bloom, 1. *n.* flor *f.* **2.** *v.* florecer.

blooming, *a.* lozano; fresco.

blossom, 1. *n.* flor *f.* **2.** *v.* florecer.

blot, 1. *n.* mancha *f.* **2.** *v.* manchar.

blotch, 1. *n.* mancha, roncha *f.* **2.** *v.* manchar.

blotter, *n.* papel secante.

blouse, *n.* blusa *f.*

blow, 1. *n.* golpe *m.*; (fig.) chasco *m.* **2.** *v.* soplar.

blowout, *n.* reventón de neumático.

blubber, *n.* grasa de ballena.

bludgeon, *n.* porra *f.*

blue, *a.* azul; triste, melancólico.

bluebird, *n.* azulejo *m.*

blueprint, *n.* heliografía *f.*

bluff, 1. *n.* risco *m.* **2.** *v.* alardear; baladronar.

bluing, *n.* añil *m.*

blunder, 1. *n.* desatino *m.* **2.** *v.* desatinar.

blunderer, *n.* desatinado *m.*

blunt, 1. *a.* embotado; descortés. **2.** *v.* embotar.

bluntly, *a.* bruscamente.

bluntness, *n.* grosería *f.*

blur, 1. *n.* trazo confuso. **2.** *v.* hacer indistinto.

blush, 1. *n.* rubor, sonrojo *m.* **2.** *v.* sonrojarse.

bluster, 1. *n.* fanfarria *f.* **2.** *v.* fanfarrear.

boar, *n.* verraco *m.* **wild b.,** jabalí *m.*

board, 1. *n.* tabla; (govt.) consejo *m.*; junta *f.* **b. and room,** cuarto y comida, casa y comida. **2.** *v.* (ship) abordar.

boarder, *n.* pensionista *m. & f.*

boarding house, pensión *f.*, casa de huéspedes.

boast, 1. *n.* jactancia *f.* **2.** *v.* jactarse.

boaster, *n.* fanfarrón *m.*

boastful, *a.* jactancioso.

boastfulness, *n.* jactancia *f.*

boat, *n.* barco, buque, bote *m.*

boathouse, *n.* casilla de botes *f.*

boatswain, *n.* contramaestre *m.*

bob, *v.* menear.

bobbin, *n.* bobina *f.*

bobby pin, *n.* invisible *f.*, gancho *m.*

bodice, *n.* corpiño *m.*

bodily, *a.* corporal.

body, *n.* cuerpo *m.*

bodyguard, *n.* guardia de corps.

bog, *n.* pantano *m.*

Bohemian, *a. & n.* bohemio -mia.

boil, 1. *n.* (med.) divieso *m.* **2.** *v.* hervir.

boiler, *n.* marmita; caldera *f.*

boisterous, *a.* tumultuoso.

boisterously, *adv.* tumultuosamente.

bold, *a.* atrevido, audaz.

bold faced type, (*print.*) letra negra.

boldly, *adv.* audazmente; descaradamente.

boldness, *n.* atrevimiento *m.*; osadía *f.*

Bolivian, *a. & n.* boliviano -na.

bologna, *n.* salchicha *f.*

bolster, 1. *n.* travesero, cojín *m.* **2.** *v.* apoyar, sostener.

bolt, 1. *n.* perno *m.*; (of door) cerrojo *m.*; (lightning) rayo *m.* **2.** *v.* acerrojar.

bomb, 1. *n.* bomba *f.* **2.** *v.* bombardear.

bombard, *v.* bombardear.

bombardier, *n.* bombardero *m.*

bombardment, *n.* bombardeo *m.*

bomber, *n.* avión de bombardeo.

bombproof, *a.* a prueba de granadas.

bombshell, *n.* bomba *f.*

bonbon, *n.* dulce, bombón *m.*

bond, *n.* lazo *m.*; (commercial) bono *m.*

bondage, *n.* esclavitud, servidumbre *f.*

bonded, *a.* garantizado.

bone, *n.* hueso *m.*

boneless, *a.* sin huesos.

bonfire, *n.* hoguera, fogata *f.*

bonnet, *n.* gorra *f.*

bonus, *n.* bono *m.*

bony, *a.* huesudo.

book, *n.* libro *m.*

bookbinder, *n.* encuadernador *m.*

bookcase, *n.* armario para libros.

bookkeeper, *n.* tenedor de libros.

bookkeeping, *n.* contabilidad *f.*

booklet, *n.* folleto *m.*, libreta *f.*

bookseller, *n.* librero *m.*

bookstore, *n.* librería *f.*

boom, *n.* (mar.) botalón *m.*; prosperidad repentina.

boon, *n.* dádiva *f.*

boor, *n.* patán, rústico *m.*

boorish, *a.* villano.

boost, 1. *n.* alza; ayuda *f.* **2.** *v.* levantar, alzar; fomentar.

booster, *n.* fomentador *m.*

boot, *n.* bota *f.*

bootblack, *n.* limpiabotas *m.*

booth, *n.* cabaña; casilla *f.*

booty, *n.* botín *m.*

border, 1. *n.* borde *m.*; frontera *f.* **2.** *v.* **b. on,** lindar con.

borderline, 1. *a.* marginal. **2.** *n.* margen *m.*

bore, 1. *n.* lata *f.*; persona pesada. **2.** *v.* aburrir, fastidiar; (mech.) taladrar.

boredom, *n.* aburrimiento *m.*

boric acid, *n.* ácido bórico *m.*

boring, *a.* aburrido, pesado.

born, *a.* nacido. **be born,** nacer.

borrow, *v.* pedir prestado.

bosom, *v.* seno, pecho *m.*

boss, *n.* jefe, patrón *m.*

botany, *n.* botánica *f.*

both, *pron. & a.* ambos, los dos.

bother, 1. *n.* molestia *f.* **2.** *v.* molestar, incomodar.

bothersome, *a.* molesto.

bottle, 1. *n.* botella *f.* **2.** *v.* embotellar.

bottom, *n.* fondo *m.*

boudoir, *n.* tocador *m.*

bough, *n.* rama *f.*

boulder, *n.* canto rodado.

boulevard, *n.* bulevar *m.*

bounce, 1. *n.* brinco *m.* **2.** *v.* brincar; hacer saltar.

bound, 1. *n.* salto *m.* **2.** *v.* limitar.

boundary, *n.* límite, lindero *m.*

bouquet, *n.* ramillete de flores.

bourgeois, *a. & n.* burgués.

bout, *n.* encuentro; combate *m.*

bow, 1. *n.* saludo *m.*; (of ship) proa *f.*; (archery) arco *m.*; (ribbon) lazo *m.* **2.** *v.* saludar, inclinar.

bowels, *n.* intestinos *m.pl.*; entrañas *f.pl.*

bowl, 1. *n.* vasija *f.*; platón *m.* **2.** *v.* jugar a los bolos. **b. over,** derribar.

bowlegged, *a.* perniabierto.

bowling, *n.* bolos *m.pl.*

box, 1. *n.* caja *f.*; (theat.) palco *m.* **2.** *v.* (pug.) boxear.

boxcar, *n.* vagón *m.*

boxer, *n.* boxeador, pugilista *m.*

boxing, *n.* boxeo *m.*

box office, *n.* taquilla *f.*

boy, *n.* muchacho, chico *m.*

boycott, 1. *n.* boicoteo *m.* **2.** *v.* boicotear.

boyhood, *n.* muchachez *f.*

boyish, *a.* pueril.

boyishly, *adv.* puerilmente.

brace, 1. *n.* grapón *m.*; *pl.* tirantes *m.pl.* **2.** *v.* reforzar.

bracelet, *n.* brazalete *m.*, pulsera *f.*

bracket, *n.* ménsula *f.*

brag, *v.* jactarse.

braggart, *a.* jactancioso. **2.** *n.* jaque *m.*

braid, 1. *n.* trenza *f.* **2.** *v.* trenzar.

brain, *n.* cerebro, seso *m.*

brainy, *a.* sesudo, inteligente.

brake, 1. *n.* freno *m.* **2.** *v.* frenar.

bran, *n.* salvado *m.*

branch, *n.* ramo *m.*; (of tree) rama *f.*

brand, *n.* marca *f.*

brandish, *v.* blandir.

brand-new, *a.* enteramente nuevo.

brandy, *n.* aguardiente, coñac *m.*

brash, *a.* impetuoso.

brass, *n.* bronce, latón *m.*

brassière, *n.* corpiño, sostén *m.*

brat, *n.* mocoso *m.*

bravado, *n.* bravata *f.*

brave, *a.* valiente.

bravery, *n.* valor *m.*

brawl, 1. *n.* alboroto *m.* **2.** *v.* alborotar.

brawn, *n.* músculo *m.*

bray, *v.* rebuznar.

brazen, *a.* desvergonzado.

Brazil, *n.* Brasil *m.*

Brazilian, *a. & n.* brasileño -ña.

breach, *n.* rotura, infracción *f.*

bread, *n.* pan *m.*

breadth, *n.* anchura *f.*

break, 1. *n.* rotura; pausa *f.* **2.** *v.* quebrar, romper.

breakable, *a.* rompible, frágil.

breakage, *n.* rotura *f.*, destrozo *m.*

breakfast, 1. *n.* desayuno, almuerzo *m.* **2.** *v.* desayunarse, almorzar.

breakneck, *a.* rápido, precipitado, atropellado.

breast, *n.* pecho, seno *m.*

breath, *n.* aliento; soplo *m.*

breathe, *v.* respirar.

breathless, *a.* desalentado.

breathlessly, *adv.* jadeantemente, intensamente.

bred, *a.* criado; educado.

breeches, *n.pl.* calzones; pantalones, *m.pl.*

breed, 1. *n.* raza *f.* **2.** *v.* engendrar; criar.

breeder, *n.* criador *m.*

breeding, *n.* cría *f.*

breeze, *n.* brisa *f.*

breezy, *a.:* **it is b.,** hace brisa.

brevity, *n.* brevedad *f.*

brew, *v.* fraguar, elaborar.

brewer, *n.* cervecero *m.*

brewery, *n.* cervecería *f.*

bribe, 1. *n.* soborno, cohecho *m.* **2.** *v.* sobornar, cohechar.

briber, *n.* sobornador *m.*

bribery, *n.* soborno, cohecho *m.*

brick, *n.* ladrillo *m.*

bricklayer, *n.* albañil *m.*

bridal, *a.* nupcial.

bride, *n.* novia *f.*

bridegroom, *n.* novio *m.*

bridesmaid, *n.* madrina de boda.

bridge, *n.* puente *m.*

bridged, *a.* conectado.

bridgehead, *n.* (*mil.*) cabeza de puente.

bridle, *n.* brida *f.*

brief, *a.* breve.

briefcase, *n.* maletín *m.*

briefly, *adv.* brevemente.

briefness, *n.* brevedad *f.*

brier, *n.* zarza *f.*

brig, *n.* bergantín *m.*

brigade, *n.* brigada *f.*

bright, *a.* claro, brillante.

brighten, *v.* abrillantar; alegrar.

brightness, *n.* resplandor *m.*

brilliance, *n.* brillantez *f.*

brilliant, *a.* brillante.

brim, *n.* borde *m.*; (of hat) ala *f.*

brine, *n.* salmuera *f.*

bring, *v.* traer. **b. about,** efectuar, llevar a cabo.

brink, *n.* borde *m.*

briny, *a.* salado.

brisk, *a.* vivo; enérgico.

briskly, *adv.* vivamente.

briskness, *n.* viveza *f.*

bristle, *n.* cerda *f.*

bristly, *a.* hirsuto.

Britain, *n.* **Great B.,** Gran Bretaña *f.*

British, *a.* británico.

British Empire, imperio británico.

British Isles, islas británicas.

Briton, *n.* inglés *m.*

brittle, *a.* quebradizo, frágil.

broad, *a.* ancho.

broadcast, 1. *n.* radiodifusión *m.* **2.** *v.* radiodifundir.

broadcaster, *n.* locutor *m.*

broadcloth, *n.* paño fino.

broaden, *v.* ensanchar.

broadly, *adv.* ampliamente.

broadminded, *a.* tolerante, liberal.

brocade, *n.* brocado *m.*

brocaded, *a.* espolinado.

broil, *v.* asar.

broiler, n. parilla f.
broken, a. roto, quebrado.
broken-hearted, a. angustiado.
broker, n. corredor, cambista m.
brokerage, n. corretaje m.
bronchial, a. bronquial.
bronchitis, n. bronquitis f.
bronze, n. bronce m.
brooch, n. broche m.
brood, 1. n. cría, progenie f. **2.** v. empollar; cobijar.
brook, n. arroyo m., quebrada f.
broom, n. escoba f.
broomstick, n. palo de escoba.
broth, n. caldo m.
brothel, n. burdel m.
brother, n. hermano m.
brotherhood, n. fraternidad f.
brother-in-law, n. cuñado m.
brotherly, a. fraternal.
brow, n. ceja; frente f.
brown, a. pardo, moreno.
browse, v. ramonear.
bruise, 1. n. contusión f. **2.** v. magullar.
brunette, a. & n. moreno -na, trigueño -ña.
brush, 1. n. cepillo m.; brocha f. **2.** v. cepillar.
brushwood, n. matorral m.
brusque, a. brusco.
brusquely, adv. bruscamente.
brutal, a. brutal.
brutality, n. brutalidad f.
brutalize, v. embrutecer.
brute, n. bruto m., bestia f.
bubble, n. ampolla f.
bucket, n. cubo m.
buckle, n. hebilla f.
buckram, n. bucarán m.
bucksaw, n. sierra de bastidor.
buckshot, n. posta f.
buckwheat, n. trigo sarraceno.
bud, 1. n. brote m. **2.** v. brotar.
budding, a. en capullo.
budge, v. moverse.
budget, n. presupuesto m.
buffalo, n. búfalo m.

buffer, n. parachoques m.
buffet, n. bufet m.; (furniture) aparador m.
buffoon, n. bufón m.
bug, n. insecto m.
bugle, n. clarín m.; corneta f.
build, v. construir.
builder, n. constructor m.
building, n. edificio m.
bulb, n. bulbo m.; (of lamp) bombilla, ampolla f.
bulge, 1. n. abultamiento m. **2.** v. abultar.
bulk, n. masa f.; grueso m.; mayoría f.
bulkhead, n. frontón m.
bulky, a. grueso, abultado.
bull, n. toro m.
bulldog, n. perro de presa.
bullet, n. bala f.
bulletin, n. boletín m.
bulletproof, a. a prueba de bala.
bullfight, n. corrida de toros.
bullfighter, n. torero m.
bullfinch, n. pinzón real m.
bully, 1. n. rufián m. **2.** v. bravear.
bulwark, n. baluarte m.
bum, n. holgazán m.
bump, 1. n. golpe, choque m. **2.** v. **b. into,** chocar contra.
bumper, n. parachoques m.
bun, n. bollo m.
bunch, n. racimo; montón m.
bundle, 1. n. bulto m. **2.** v. **b. up,** abrigar.
bungalow, n. casa de un solo piso.
bungle, v. estropear.
bunion, n. juanete m.
bunk, n. litera f.
bunny, n. conejito m.
bunting, n. lanilla, banderas f.
buoy, n. boya f.
buoyant, a. boyante; vivaz.
burden, 1. n. carga f. **2.** v. cargar.
burdensome, a. gravoso.
bureau, n. (furniture) cómoda f.; departamento m.
burglar, n. ladrón m.
burglarize, v. robar.
burglary, n. robo m.
burial, n. entierro m.
burlap, n. arpillera f.
burly, a. corpulento.

burn, v. quemar; arder.
burner, n. mechero m.
burning, a. ardiente.
burnish, v. pulir; acicalar.
burrow, v. minar; horadar.
burst, v. reventar.
bury, v. enterrar.
bus, n. autobús m.
bush, n. arbusto m.
bushy, a. espeso; peludo.
business, n. negocios m.pl.; comercio m.
businesslike, a. directo.
businessman, n. comerciante m.
businesswoman, n. mujer de negocios.
bust, n. busto; pecho m.
bustle, n. bullicio m.; animación f.
busy, a. ocupado, atareado.
busybody, n. entremetido m.
but, conj. pero; sino.
butcher, n. carnicero m.
butchery, n. carnicería; matanza f.
butler, n. mayordomo m.
butt, n. punta f.; cabo extremo m.
butter, n. manteca, mantequilla f.

buttercup, n. ranúnculo m.
butterfat, n. mantequilla f.
butterfly, n. mariposa f.
buttermilk, n. suero (de leche) m.
button, n. botón m.
buttonhole, n. ojal m.
buttress, n. sostén; refuerzo m.
buxom, a. regordete.
buy, v. comprar.
buyer, n. comprador -ra.
buzz, 1. n. zumbido m. **2.** v. zumbar.
buzzard, n. gallinazo m.
buzzer, n. zumbador m.
buzz saw, n. sierra circular f.
by, prep. por; (near) cerca de, al lado de; (time) para.
by-and-by, adv. pronto; luego.
bygone, a. pasado.
by-law, n. estatuto, reglamento m.
by-pass, n. desvío m.
by-product, n. producto accesorio m.
bystander, n. espectador; mirón m.
byway, n. camino desviado m.

C

cab, n. coche de alquiler.
cabaret, n. cabaret m.
cabbage, n. repollo m.
cabin, n. cabaña f.
cabinet, n. gabinete; ministerio m.
cabinetmaker, n. ebanista m.
cable, n. cable m.
cablegram, n. cablegrama m.
cache, n. escondite m.
cackle, 1. n. charla f., cacareo m. **2.** v. cacarear.
cacophony, n. cacofonía f.
cactus, n. cacto m.
cad, n. persona vil.

cadaver, n. cadáver m.
cadaverous, a. cadavérico.
cadence, n. cadencia f.
cadet, n. cadete m.
cadmium, n. cadmio m.
cadre, n. núcleo; (mil.) cuadro m.
café, n. café, cantina f.
cafeteria, n. cafetería f.
caffeine, n. cafeína f.
cage, 1. n. jaula f. **2.** v. enjaular.
caisson, n. arcón m.; (mil.) furgón m.
cajole, v. lisonjear; adular.
cake, n. torta f.; bizcocho m.

calamitous, a. calamitoso.

calamity, n. calamidad f.

calcify, v. calcificar.

calcium, n. calcio m.

calculable, a. calculable.

calculate, v. calcular.

calculating, a. interesado.

calculation, n. calculación f.; cálculo m.

calculus, n. cálculo m.

caldron, n. caldera f.

calendar, n. calendario m.

calf, n. ternero m.

calfskin, n. piel de becerro.

caliber, n. calibre m.

calico, n. percal m.

caliper, n. calibrador m.

calisthenics, n. calistenia, gimnasia f.

calk, v. calafatear; rellenar.

calker, n. calafate m.

call, 1. n. llamada. 2. v. llamar.

calligraphy, n. caligrafía f.

calling, n. vocación f.

calling card, n. tarjeta (de visita) f.

callously, adv. insensiblemente.

callow, a. sin experiencia.

callus, n. callo m.

calm, 1. a. tranquilo, calmado. 2. n. calma f. 3. v. calmar.

calmly, adv. serenamente.

calmness, n. calma f.

caloric, a. calórico.

calorie, n. caloría f.

calorimeter, n. calorímetro m.

calumniate, v. calumniar.

calumny, n. calumnia f.

Calvary, n. Calvario m.

calve, v. parir la (vaca).

calyx, n. cáliz m.

camaraderie, n. compañerismo m., compadrería f.

cambric, n. batista f.

camel, n. camello m.

camellia, n. camelia f.

camel's hair, n. piel de camello.

cameo, n. cameo m.

camera, n. cámara f.

camouflage, n. camuflaje m.

camouflaging, n. simulacro, disfraz m.

camp, 1. n. campamento m. 2. v. acampar.

campaign, n. campaña f.

camper, n. acampado m.

campfire, n. fogata de campamento.

camphor, n. alcanfor m.

camphor ball, n. bola de alcanfor.

campus, n. campo de colegio (o universidad) m.

can, v. (be able) poder.

can, 1. n. lata f. 2. v. conservar en latas.

Canada, n. Canadá m.

Canadian, a. & n. canadiense.

canal, n. canal m.

canalize, v. canalizar.

canard, n. embuste m.

canary, n. canario m.

cancel, v. cancelar.

cancellation, n. cancelación f.

cancer, n. cáncer m.

candelabrum, n. candelabro m.

candid, a. cándido, sincero.

candidacy, n. candidatura f.

candidate, n. candidato -ta.

candidly, adv. candidamente.

candidness, n. candidez; sinceridad f.

candied, a. garapiñado.

candle, n. vela f.

candlestick, n. candelero m.

candor, n. candor m.; sinceridad f.

candy, n. dulces m.pl.

cane, n. caña f.; (for walking) bastón m.

canine, a. canino.

canister, n. frasco m.; lata f.

canker, n. llaga; úlcera f.

cankerworm, n. oruga f.

canned, a. envasado.

canner, n. envasador m.

cannery, n. fábrica de conservas alimenticias f.

cannibal, n. caníbal m.

cannon, n. cañón m.

cannonade, n. cañoneo m.

cannoneer, n. cañonero m.

canny, a. sagaz; prudente.

canoe, n. canoa f.

canon, *n.* canon *m.*; (*rel.*) canónigo *m.*

canonical, *a.* canónico.

canonize, *v.* canonizar.

canopy, *n.* dosel *m.*

cant, *n.* hipocresía *f.*

cantaloupe, *n.* melón *m.*

canteen, 1. *n.* medio galope *m.* **2.** *v.* galopar.

cantonment, *n.* (*mil.*) acuartelamiento *m.*

canvas, *n.* lona *f.*

canyon, *n.* cañón, desfiladero *m.*

cap, 1. *n.* tapa *f.*; (headwear) gorro *m.* **2.** *v.* tapar.

capability, *n.* capacidad *f.*

capable, *a.* capaz.

capably, *adv.* hábilmente.

capacious, *a.* espacioso.

capacity, *n.* capacidad *f.*

cape, *n.* capa *f.*, (geography) cabo *m.*

caper, *n.* zapateta *f.*; (*bot.*) alcaparra *f.*

capillary, *a.* capilar.

capital, *n.* capital *m.*; (govt.) capital *f.*

capitalism, *n.* capitalismo *m.*

capitalist, *n.* capitalista *m.*

capitalistic, *a.* capitalista.

capitalization, *n.* capitalización *f.*

capitalize, *v.* capitalizar.

capitulate, *v.* capitular.

capon, *n.* capón *m.*

caprice, *n.* capricho *m.*

capricious, *a.* caprichoso.

capriciously, *adv.* caprichosamente.

capriciousness, *n.* capricho *m.*

capsize, *v.* zozobrar, volcar.

capsule, *n.* cápsula *f.*

captain, *n.* capitán *m.*

caption, *n.* título *m.*; (motion pictures) subtítulo *m.*

captious, *a.* capcioso.

captivate, *v.* cautivar.

captivating, *a.* encantador.

captive, *n.* cautivo -va, prisionero -ra.

captivity, *n.* cautividad *f.*

captor, *n.* apresador *m.*

capture, 1. *n.* captura *f.* **2.** *v.* capturar.

car, *n.* coche, carro *m.*; (of train) vagón, coche *m.* **baggage c.,** vagón de equipajes. **parlor c.,** coche salón.

carafe, *n.* garrafa *f.*

caramel, *n.* caramelo *m.*

carat, *n.* quilate *m.*

caravan, *n.* caravana *f.*

caraway, *n.* alcaravea *f.*

carbide, *n.* carburo *m.*

carbine, *n.* carabina *f.*

carbohydrate, *n.* hidrato de carbono.

carbon, *n.* carbón *m.*

carbon dioxide, anhídrido carbónico.

carbon monoxide, monóxido de carbono.

carbon paper, *n.* papel carbón *m.*

carbuncle, *n.* carbunclo *m.*

carburetor, *n.* carburador *m.*

card, *n.* tarjeta *f.* **playing c.,** naipe *m.*

cardboard, *n.* cartón *m.*

cardiac, *a.* cardíaco.

cardigan, *n.* chaqueta de punto.

cardinal, 1. *a.* cardinal. **2.** *n.* cardenal *m.*

care, 1. *n.* cuidado *m.* **2.** *v.* **c. for,** cuidar.

careen, *v.* carenar; echarse de costado.

career, *n.* carrera *f.*

carefree, *a.* descuidado.

careful, *a.* cuidadoso. **be c.,** tener cuidado.

carefully, *adv.* cuidadosamente.

carefulness, *n.* esmero; cuidado *m.*; cautela *f.*

careless, *a.* descuidado.

carelessly, *adv.* descuidadamente; negligentemente.

carelessness, *n.* descuido *m.*

caress, 1. *n.* caricia *f.* **2.** *v.* acariciar.

caretaker, *n.* guardián *m.*

cargo, *n.* carga *f.*

caricature, *n.* caricatura *f.*

caries, *n.* caries *f.*

carload, *a.* furgonada, vagonada.

carnal, *a.* carnal.

carnation, *n.* clavel *m.*

carnival, *n.* carnaval *f.*

carnivorous, *a.* carnívoro.

carol, n. villancico m.

carouse, v. parrandear.

carpenter, n. carpintero m.

carpet, n. alfombra f.

carpeting, n. alfombrado m.

carriage, n. carruaje; (bearing) porte m.

carrier, n. portador -ra.

carrier pigeon, n. paloma mensajera.

carrot, n. zanahoria f.

carrousel, n. volantín m.

carry, v. llevar, cargar. **c. out,** cumplir, llevar a cabo.

cart, n. carreta f.

cartage, n. acarreo, carretaje m.

cartel, n. cartel m.

cartilage, n. cartílago m.

carton, n. caja de cartón.

cartoon, n. caricatura f.

cartoonist, n. caricaturista m.

cartridge, n. cartucho m.

carve, v. esculpir; (meat) trinchar.

carver, n. tallador; grabador m.

carving, n. entalladura f.; arte de trinchar. **c. knife,** trinchante m.

cascade, n. cascada f.

case, n. caso m.; (box) caja f. **in any c.,** sea como sea.

cash, 1. n. dinero contante. **2.** v. efectuar, cambiar.

cashier, n. cajero -ra.

cashmere, n. casimir m.

casino, n. casino m.

cask, n. barril m.

casket, n. ataúd m.

casserole, n. cacerola f.

cast, 1. n. (theat.) reparto de papeles. **2.** v. echar; (theat.) repartir.

castanet, n. castañuela f.

castaway, n. náufrago m.

caste, n. casta f.

caster, n. tirador m.

castigate, v. castigar.

Castilian, a. castellano.

cast iron, n. hierro colado m.

castle, n. castillo m.

castoff, n. descartado.

casual, a. casual.

casually, adv. casualmente.

casualness, n. casualidad f.

casualty, n. víctima f.; (military) baja f.

cat, n. gato -ta.

cataclysm, n. cataclismo m.

catacomb, n. catacumba f.

catalogue, n. catálogo m.

catapult, n. catapulta f.

cataract, n. catarata f.

catarrh, n. catarro m.

catastrophe, n. catástrofe m.

catch, v. alcanzar, atrapar, coger.

catchy, a. contagioso.

catechism, n. catequismo m.

catechize, v. catequizar.

categorical, a. categórico.

category, n. categoría f.

cater, v. abastecer; proveer. **c. to,** complacer.

caterpillar, n. gusano m.

catgut, n. cuerda (de tripa).

catharsis, n. purga f.

cathartic, 1. a. catártico; purgante. **2.** n. purgante m.

cathedral, n. catedral f.

cathode, n. cátodo m.

Catholic, 1. a. católico. **2.** n. católico -ca.

Catholicism, n. catolicismo m.

cat nap, n. siesta corta f.

catsup, n. salsa de tomate.

cattle, n. ganado m.

cattleman, n. ganadero m.

cauliflower, n. coliflor m.

causation, n. causalidad f.

cause, n. causa f.

causeway, n. calzada f.; terraplén m.

caustic, a. cáustico.

cauterize, v. cauterizar.

cautery, n. cauterio m.

caution, n. cautela f.

cautious, a. cauteloso.

cavalcade, n. cabalgata f.

cavalier, n. caballero m.

cavalry, n. caballería f.

cave, cavern, n. caverna f.

cave-in, n. hundimiento m.

caviar, n. caviar m.

cavity, n. hueco m.

cayman, n. caimán m.

cease, v. cesar.

ceaseless, a. incesante.

cedar, n. cedro m.

cede, v. ceder.

ceiling, n. cielo m.

celebrant, n. celebrante m.

celebrate, v. celebrar.

celebration, n. celebración f.

celebrity, n. persona célebre.

celerity, n. celeridad; prontitud f.

celery, n. apio m.

celestial, a. celeste.

celibacy, n. celibato m.

celibate, a. & n. célibe m.

cell, n. celda f.; (biol.) célula f.

cellar, n. sótano m.

cellist, a. celista m.

cello, n. violoncelo m.

cellophane, n. celofán m.

cellular, a. celular.

celluloid, n. celuloide m.

cellulose, 1. a. celuloso. **2.** n. celulosa f.

Celtic, a. céltico.

cement, n. cemento m.

cemetery, n. cementerio m.; campo santo m.

censor, n. censor m.

censorious, a. severo; crítico.

censorship, n. censura f.

censure, 1. n. censura f. **2.** v. censurar.

census, n. censo m.

cent, n. centavo m., céntimo m.

centenary, a. & n. centenario m.

centennial, a. & n. centenario m.

center, n. centro m.

centerpiece, n. centro de mesa.

centigrade, a. centígrado.

centigrade thermometer, termómetro centígrado.

central, a. central.

Central American, a. & n. centroamericano -na.

centralize, v. centralizar.

century, n. siglo m.

century plant, n. maguey f.

ceramic, a. cerámico.

ceramics, n. cerámica f.

cereal, n. cereal m.

cerebral, a. cerebral.

ceremonial, a. ceremonial.

ceremonious, a. ceremonioso.

ceremony, ceremonia f.

certain, a. cierto, seguro.

certainly, adv. sin duda, seguramente.

certainty, n. certeza f.

certificate, n. certificado m.

certification, n. certificación f.

certified, a. certificado.

certify, v. certificar.

certitude, n. certeza f.

cessation, n. cesación f., discontinuación f.

cession, n. cesión f.

chafe, v. irritar.

chafing dish, n. escalfador m.

chagrin, n. disgusto m.

chain, 1. n. cadena f. **2.** v. encadenar.

chair, n. silla f.

chairman, n. presidente m.

chalk, n. tiza f.

challenge, 1. n. desafío m. **2.** v. desafiar.

challenger, n. desafiador m.

chamber, n. cámara f.

chamberlain, n. camarero m.

chambermaid, n. camarera f.

chameleon, n. camaleón m.

chamois, n. gamuza f.

champagne, n. champán m., champaña f.

champion, 1. n. campeón m. **2.** v. defender.

championship, n. campeonato m.

chance, n. oportunidad, ocasión f. **by c.,** por casualidad, por acaso. **take a c.,** aventurarse.

chancel, n. antealtar m.

chancellery, n. cancillería f.

chancellor, n. canciller m.

chandelier, n. araña de luces.

change, 1. n. cambio m.; (from a bill) moneda f. **2.** v. cambiar.

changeability, n. mutabilidad f.

changeable, a. variable, inconstante.

changer, n. cambiador m.

channel, 1. n. canal m. **2.** v. encauzar.

chant, 1. n. canto llano m. **2.** v. cantar.

chaos, n. caos m.

chaotic, a. caótico.

chap, 1. n. (coll.) tipo m. **2.** v. rajar.

chapel, n. capilla f.

chaperon, n. dueña f.

chaplain, n. capellán m.

chapter, n. capítulo m.

char, v. carbonizar.

character, n. carácter m.

characteristic, 1. a. característico. **2.** n. característica f.

characterization, n. caracterización f.

characterize, v. caracterizar.

charcoal, n. carbón de leña.

charge, 1. n. acusación f.; ataque m. **2.** v. cargar; acusar; atacar.

chariot, n. carroza f.

charitable, a. caritativo.

charitableness, n. caridad f.

charitably, adv. caritativamente.

charity, n. caridad f.; (alms) limosna f.

charlatan, n. charlatán -na f.

charlatanism, n. charlatanería f.

charm, 1. n. encanto m.; (witchcraft) hechizo m. **2.** v. encantar; hechizar.

charming, a. encantador.

charred, a. carbonizado.

chart, n. mapa m.

charter, 1. n. carta f. **2.** v. alquilar.

chase, 1. n. caza f. **2.** v. cazar; perseguir.

chaser, n. perseguidor m.

chasm, n. abismo m.

chassis, n. chasis m.

chaste, a. casto.

chasten, v. corregir, castigar.

chastise, v. castigar.

chastisement, n. castigo m.

chastity, n. castidad, pureza f.

chat, 1. n. plática, charla f. **2.** v. platicar, charlar.

chateau, n. castillo m.

chattels, n.pl. bienes m.

chatter, 1. v. cotorrear; (teeth) rechinar. **2.** n. cotorreo m.

chatterbox, n. charlador m.

chauffeur, n. chofer m.

cheap, a. barato.

cheapen, v. rebajar, menospreciar.

cheaply, adv. barato.

cheapness, n. baratura f.

cheat, v. engañar.

cheater, n. engañador m.

check, 1. n. verificación f.; (bank) cheque m.; (restaurant) cuenta f.; (chess) jaque m. **2.** v. verificar.

checkers, n. juego de damas.

checkmate, v. dar mate.

cheek, n. mejilla f.

cheer, 1. n. alegría f.; aplauso m. **2.** v. alegrar; aplaudir.

cheerful, a. alegre.

cheerfully, adv. alegremente.

cheerfulness, n. alegría f.

cheerless, a. triste.

cheery, a. alegre.

cheese, n. queso m. **cottage c.,** requesón m.

chef, n. cocinero en jefe.

chemical, 1. a. químico. **2.** n. reactivo m.

chemically, adv. químicamente.

chemist, n. químico m.

chemistry, n. química f.

chenille, n. felpilla f.

cherish, v. apreciar.

cherry, n. cereza f.

cherub, n. querubín m.

chess, n. ajedrez m.

chest, n. arca f.; (physiology) pecho m.

chestnut, n. castaña f.

chevron, n. sardineta f.

chew, v. mascar, masticar.

chewer, n. mascador m.

chic, a. elegante, paquete.

chicanery, n. trampería f.

chick, n. pollito m.

chicken, n. pollo m., gallina f.

chicken-hearted, a. cobarde.

chicken pox, n. viruelas locas f.

chicle, n. chicle m.

chicory, n. achicoria f.

chide, v. regañar, reprender.

chief, 1. a. principal. **2.** n. jefe m.

chiefly, adv. principalmente, mayormente.

chieftain, n. caudillo m.; (Indian c.) cacique m.

chiffon, n. chifón m.

chilblain, n. sabañón m.

child, n. niño -ña; hijo -ja.

childbirth, n. parto m.

childhood, n. niñez f.

childish, a. pueril.

childishness, n. puerilidad f.

childless, a. sin hijos.

childlike, a. infantil.

Chilean, a. & n. chileno -na.

chili, n. chile ají m.

chill, 1. n. frío; escalofrío m. 2. v. enfriar.

chilliness, n. frialdad f.

chilly, a. frío; friolento.

chimes, n. juego de campanas.

chimney, n. chimenea f.

chimpanzee, n. chimpancé m.

chin, n. barba f.

china, n. loza f.

chinchilla, n. chinchilla f.

Chinese, a. & n. chino -na.

chink, n. grieta f.

chintz, n. zaraza f.

chip, 1. n. astilla f. 2. v. astillar.

chiropodist, n. pedicuro m.

chiropractor, n. quiropráctico m.

chirp, 1. n. chirrido m. 2. v. chirriar, piar.

chisel, 1. n. cincel m. 2. v. cincelar, talar.

chivalrous, a. caballeroso.

chivalry, n. caballería f.

chive, n. cebollino m.

chloride, n. cloruro m.

chlorine, n. cloro m.

chloroform, n. cloroformo m.

chlorophyll, n. clorófila f.

chock-full, a. repleto, colmado.

chocolate, n. chocolate m.

choice, 1. a. selecto, escogido. 2. n. selección f.; escogimiento m.

choir, n. coro m.

choke, v. sofocar, ahogar.

cholera, n. cólera f.

choleric, a. colérico, irascible.

choose, v. elegir, escoger.

chop, 1. n. chuleta, costilla f. 2. v. tajar; cortar.

chopper, n. tajador m.

choppy, a. agitado.

choral, a. coral.

chord, n. cuerda f.

chore, n. tarea f., quehacer m.

choreography, n. coreografía f.

chorister, n. corista m.

chorus, n. coro m.

christen, v. bautizar.

Christendom, n. cristiandad f.

Christian, a. & n. cristiano -na.

Christianity, n. cristianismo m.

Christmas, n. navidad, pascua f. **Merry C.,** felices pascuas. **C. Eve,** nochebuena f.

chromatic, a. cromático.

chromium, n. cromo m.

chromosome, n. cromosoma m.

chronic, a. crónico.

chronicle, n. crónica f.

chronological, a. cronológico.

chronology, n. cronología f.

chrysalis, n. crisálida f.

chrysanthemum, n. crisantemo m.

chubby, a. regordete.

chuck, v. (cluck) cloquear; (throw) echar, tirar.

chuckle, v. reír entre dientes.

chum, n. amigo m.; compinche m.

chummy, a. íntimo.

chunk, n. trozo m.

chunky, a. fornido, trabado.

church, n. iglesia f.

churchman, n. eclesiástico m.

churchyard, n. cementerio m.

churn, 1. n. mantequera f. 2. v. agitar, revolver.

chute, n. conducto m.; canal f.

cicada, n. cigarra, chicharra f.

cider, n. sidra f.

cigar, n. cigarro, puro m.

cigarette, n. cigarrillo, pitillo m. **c. case,** cigarrillera f.

cinchona, n. cinchona f.

cinder, n. ceniza f.

cinema, *n.* cine *m.*

cinnamon, *n.* canela *f.*

cipher, *n.* cifra *f.*

circle, *n.* círculo *m.*

circuit, *n.* circuito *m.*

circuitous, *a.* tortuoso.

circuitously, *adv.* tortuosamente.

circular, *a.* circular, redondo.

circularize, *v.* hacer circular.

circulate, *v.* circular.

circulation, *n.* circulación *f.*

circulator, *n.* diseminador *m.*

circulatory, *a.* circulatorio.

circumcise, *v.* circuncidar.

circumcision, *n.* circuncisión *f.*

circumference, *n.* circunferencia *f.*

circumlocution, *n.* circunlocución *f.*

circumscribe, *v.* circunscribir; limitar.

circumspect, *a.* discreto.

circumstance, *n.* circunstancia *f.*

circumstantial, *a.* circunstancial, indirecto.

circumstantially, *adv.* minuciosamente.

circumvent, *v.* evadir, evitar.

circumvention, *n.* trampa *f.*; estratagema *f.*

circus, *n.* circo *m.*

cirrhosis, *n.* cirrosis *f.*

cistern, *n.* cisterna *f.*

citadel, *n.* ciudadela *f.*

citation, *n.* citación *f.*

cite, *v.* citar.

citizen, *n.* ciudadano -na.

citizenship, *n.* ciudadanía *f.*

citric, *a.* cítrico.

city, *n.* ciudad *f.*

civic, *a.* cívico.

civics, *n.* ciencia del gobierno civil.

civil, *a.* civil; cortés.

civilian, *a. & n.* civil *m.*

civility, *n.* cortesía *f.*

civilization, *n.* civilización *f.*

civilize, *v.* civilizar.

civil service, *n.* servicio civil oficial *m.*

civil war, *n.* guerra civil *f.*

clabber, **1.** *n.* cuajo *m.* **2.** *v.* cuajarse.

clad, *a.* vestido.

claim, **1.** *n.* demanda; pretensión *f.* **2.** *v.* demandar, reclamar.

claimant, *n.* reclamante *m.*

clairvoyance, *n.* clarividencia *f.*

clairvoyant, *a.* clarividente.

clam, *n.* almeja *f.*

clamber, *v.* trepar.

clamor, **1.** *n.* clamor *m.* **2.** *v.* clamar.

clamorous, *a.* clamoroso.

clamp, **1.** *n.* prensa de sujeción *f.* **2.** *v.* asegurar, sujetar.

clan, *n.* tribu *f.*

clandestine, *a.* clandestino.

clandestinely, *adv.* clandestinamente.

clangor, *n.* estruendo *m.*, estrépito *m.*

clannish, *a.* unido; exclusivista.

clap, *v.* aplaudir.

clapboard, *n.* chilla *f.*

claque, *n.* claque *f.*

claret, *n.* clarete *m.*

clarification, *n.* clarificación *f.*

clarify, *v.* clarificar.

clarinet, *n.* clarinete *m.*

clarinetist, *n.* clarinero *m.*

clarity, *n.* claridad *f.*

clash, **1.** *n.* choque *m.* **2.** *v.* chocar.

clasp, **1.** *n.* broche *m.* **2.** *v.* abrochar.

class, *n.* clase *f.*

classic, classical, *a.* clásico.

classicism, *n.* clasicismo *m.*

classifiable, *a.* clasificable, calificable.

classification, *n.* clasificación *f.*

classify, *v.* clasificar.

classmate, *n.* compañero de clase.

classroom, *n.* sala de clase.

clatter, **1.** *n.* alboroto *m.* **2.** *v.* alborotar.

clause, *n.* cláusula *f.*

claustrophobia, *n.* claustrofobia *f.*

claw, *n.* garra *f.*

clay, *n.* arcilla *f.*; barro *m.*

clean, 1. *a.* limpio. **2.** *v.* limpiar.

cleaner, *n.* limpiador -ra.

cleanliness, *n.* limpieza *f.*

cleanse, *v.* limpiar, purificar.

cleanser, *n.* limpiador *m.*, purificador *m.*

clear, *a.* claro.

clearance, *n.* espacio libre. **c. sale,** venta de liquidación.

clearing, *n.* despejo *m.*; desmonte *m.*

clearly, *adv.* claramente, evidentemente.

clearness, *n.* claridad *f.*

cleavage, *n.* resquebradura *f.*

cleaver, *n.* partidor *m.*, hacha *f.*

clef, *n.* clave, llave *f.*

clemency, *n.* clemencia *f.*

clench, *v.* agarrar.

clergy, *n.* clero *m.*

clergyman, *n.* clérigo *m.*

clerical, *a.* clerical. **c. work,** trabajo de dependientes.

clericalism, *n.* clericalismo *m.*

clerk, *n.* dependiente, escribiente *m.*

clerkship, *n.* escribanía *f.*, secretaría *f.*

clever, *a.* diestro, hábil.

cleverly, *adv.* diestramente, hábilmente.

cleverness, *n.* destreza *f.*

cliché, *n.* cliché *m.*

client, *n.* cliente *m.*

clientele, *n.* clientela *f.*

cliff, *n.* precipicio, risco *m.*

climate, *n.* clima *m.*

climatic, *a.* climático.

climax, *n.* colmo *m.*, culminación *f.*

climb, *v.* escalar; subir.

climber, *n.* trepador *m.*, escalador *m.*; (bot.) enredadera *f.*

clinch, *v.* afirmar.

cling, *v.* pegarse.

clinic, *n.* clínica *f.*

clinical, *a.* clínico.

clinically, *adv.* clínicamente.

clip, 1. *n.* grapa *f.* **paper c.,** gancho *m.* **2.** *v.* prender; (shear) trasquilar.

clipper, *n.* recortador *m.*; (aer.) clíper *m.*

clipping, *n.* recorte *m.*

clique, *n.* camarilla *f.*, compadraje *m.*

cloak, *n.* capa *f.*, manto *m.*

clock, *n.* reloj *m.* **alarm c.,** despertador *m.*

clod, *n.* terrón *m.*; césped *m.*

clog, *v.* obstruir.

cloister, *n.* claustro *m.*

close, 1. *a.* cercano. **2.** *adv.* cerca. **c. to,** cerca de. **3.** *v.* cerrar; tapar.

closely, *adv.* (near) de cerca; (tight) estrechamente; (care) cuidadosamente.

closeness, *n.* contigüidad *f.*, apretamiento *m.*; (airless) falta de ventilación *f.*

closet, *n.* gabinete *m.* **clothes c.,** ropero *m.*

clot, 1. *n.* coagulación *f.* **2.** *v.* coagularse.

cloth, *n.* paño *m.*; tela *f.*

clothe, *v.* vestir.

clothes, clothing, *n.* ropa *f.*

clothing, *n.* vestidos *m.*, ropa *f.*

cloud, *n.* nube *f.*

cloudburst, *n.* chaparrón *m.*

cloudiness, *n.* nebulosidad *f.*; obscuridad *f.*

cloudless, *a.* despejado, sin nubes.

cloudy, *a.* nublado.

clove, *n.* clavo *m.*

clover, *n.* trébol *m.*

clown, *n.* bufón *m.*

clownish, *a.* grosero; bufonesco.

cloy, *v.* saciar.

club, 1. *n.* porra *f.*; (social) círculo, club *m.*; (cards) basto *m.* **2.** *v.* golpear con una porra.

clubfoot, *n.* pateta *m.*, pie zambo *m.*

clue, *n.* seña, pista *f.*

clump, *n.* grupo *m.*, masa *f.*

clumsiness, *n.* tosquedad *f.*, desmaña *f.*

clumsy, *a.* torpe, desmañado.

cluster, 1. *n.* grupo *m.*; (fruit) racimo *m.* **2.** *v.* agrupar.

clutch, 1. *n.* (auto.) embrague *m.* **2.** *v.* agarrar.

clutter, 1. *n.* confusión *f.* **2.** *v.* poner en desorden.

coach, 1. *n.* coche, vagón *m.*;

coche ordinario; (sports) entrenador *m.* 2. *v.* entrenar.

coachman, *n.* cochero *m.*

coagulate, *v.* coagular.

coagulation, *n.* coagulación *f.*

coal, *n.* carbón *m.*

coalesce, *v.* unirse, soldarse.

coalition, *n.* coalición *f.*

coal oil, *n.* petróleo *m.*

coal tar, *n.* alquitrán *m.*

coarse, *a.* grosero, burdo; (material) tosco, grueso.

coarsen, *v.* vulgarizar.

coarseness, *n.* grosería; tosquedad *f.*

coast, 1. *n.* costa *f.*, litoral *m.* 2. *v.* deslizarse.

coastal, *a.* costanero.

coast guard, *n.* costanero *m.*

coat, 1. *n.* saco *m.*, chaqueta *f.*; (paint) capa *f.* 2. *v.* cubrir.

coat of arms, *n.* escudo *m.*

coax, *v.* instar.

cobalt, *n.* cobalto *m.*

cobbler, *n.* zapatero *m.*

cobblestone, *n.* guijarro *m.*

cobra, *n.* cobra *f.*

cobweb, *n.* telaraña *f.*

cocaine, *n.* cocaína *f.*

cock, *n.* (rooster) gallo *m.*; (water, etc.) llave *f.*; (gun) martillo *m.*

cockfight, *n.* riña de gallos *f.*

cockpit, *n.* gallera *f.*; reñidero de gallos *m.*

cockroach, *n.* cucaracha *f.*

cocktail, *n.* coctel *m.*

cocky, *a.* confiado, atrevido.

cocoa, *n.* cacao *m.*

coconut, *n.* coco *m.*

cocoon, *n.* capullo *m.*

cod, *n.* bacalao *m.*

code, *n.* código *m.*; clave *f.*

codeine, *n.* codeína *f.*

codfish, *n.* bacalao *m.*

codify, *v.* compilar.

coeducation, *n.* coeducación *f.*

coequal, *a.* mutuamente igual.

coerce, *v.* forzar.

coercion, *n.* coerción *f.*

coercive, *a.* coercitivo.

coexist, *v.* coexistir.

coffee, *n.* café *m.* c. plantation, cafetal *m.*

coffer, *n.* cofre *m.*

coffin, *n.* ataúd *m.*

cog, *n.* diente de rueda *m.*

cogent, *a.* convincente.

cogitate, *v.* pensar, reflexionar.

cognizance, *n.* conocimiento *m.*, comprensión *f.*

cognizant, *a.* conocedor, informado.

cogwheel, *n.* rueda dentada *f.*

cohere, *v.* pegarse.

coherent, *a.* coherente.

cohesion, *n.* cohesión *f.*

cohesive, *a.* cohesivo.

cohort, *n.* cohorte *f.*

coiffure, *n.* peinado, tocado *m.*

coil, 1. *n.* rollo *m.*; (nautical) adujada *f.* 2. *v.* enrollar.

coin, *n.* moneda *f.*

coinage, *n.* sistema monetario *f.*

coincide, *v.* coincidir.

coincidence, *n.* coincidencia; casualidad *f.*

coincident, *a.* coincidente.

coincidental, *a.* coincidental.

coincidentally, *adv.* coincidentalmente, al mismo tiempo.

colander, *n.* colador *m.*

cold, *a.* & *n.* frío *m.*; (med.) resfriado *m.* to be c., tener frío; (weather) hacer frío.

coldly, *adv.* fríamente.

coldness, *n.* frialdad *f.*

collaborate, *v.* colaborar.

collaboration, *n.* colaboración *f.*

collaborator, *n.* colaborador *m.*

collapse, 1. *n.* desplome *m.*; (med.) colapso *m.* 2. *v.* desplomarse.

collar, *n.* cuello *m.*

collarbone, *n.* clavícula *f.*

collate, *v.* comparar.

collateral, 1. *a.* colateral. 2. *n.* garantía *f.*

collation, *n.* comparación *f.*; (food) colación *f.*, merienda *f.*

colleague, *n.* colega *m.* & *f.*

collect, v. cobrar; recoger; coleccionar.

collection, n. colección f.

collective, a. colectivo.

collectively, adv. colectivamente, en masa.

collector, n. colector -ra; coleccionista m. & f.

college, n. colegio m.; universidad f.

collegiate, n. colegiado m.

collide, v. chocar.

collision, n. choque m.

colloquial, a. familiar.

colloquially, adv. familiarmente.

colloquy, n. conversación f., coloquio m.

collusion, n. colusión f., connivencia f.

Colombian, a. & n. colombiano -na.

colon, n. colon m.; (punctuation) dos puntos.

colonel, n. coronel m.

colonial, a. colonial.

colonist, n. colono m.

colonization, n. colonización f.

colonize, v. colonizar.

colony, n. colonia f.

color, 1. n. color; colorido m. **2.** v. colorar; colorir.

coloration, n. colorido m.

colored, a. de color.

colorful, a. vívido.

colorless, a. descolorido, sin color.

colossal, a. colosal.

colt, n. potro m.

column, n. columna f.

coma, n. coma f.

comb, 1. n. peine m. **2.** v. peinar.

combat, 1. n. combate m. **2.** v. combatir.

combatant, n. combatiente m.

combative, a. combativo.

combination, n. combinación f.

combine, v. combinar.

combustible, a. & n. combustible m.

combustion, n. combustión f.

come, v. venir. **c. back,** volver. **c. in,** entrar. **c.**

out, salir. **c. up,** subir. **c. upon,** encontrarse con.

comedian, n. cómico -ca.

comedienne, n. cómica f., actriz f.

comedy, n. comedia f.

comet, n. cometa m.

comfort, 1. n. confort m.; solaz m. **2.** v. confortar; solazar.

comfortable, a. cómodo.

comfortably, adv. cómodamente.

comforter, n. colcha f.

comfortingly, adv. confortantemente.

comfortless, a. sin consuelo; sin comodidades.

comic, comical, a. cómico.

coming, 1. n. venida f., llegada f. **2.** a. próximo, que viene, entrante.

comma, n. coma f.

command, 1. n. mando m. **2.** v. mandar.

commandeer, v. reclutar forzosamente, expropiar.

commander, n. comandante m.

commander in chief, n. generalísimo, jefe supremo.

commandment, n. mandato; mandamiento m.

commemorate, v. conmemorar.

commemoration, n. conmemoración f.

commemorative, a. conmemorativo.

commence, v. comenzar, principiar.

commencement, n. comienzo m.; graduación f.

commend, v. encomendar.

commendable, a. recomendable.

commendably, adv. loablemente.

commendation, n. recomendación f.

commensurate, a. proporcionado.

comment, 1. n. comento m. **2.** v. comentar.

commentary, n. comentario m.

commentator, n. comentador -ra.

commerce, n. comercio m.

commercial, a. comercial.

commercialism, n. comercialismo m.

commercialize, v. mercantilizar, explotar.

commercially, a. & adv. comercial.

commiserate, v. compadecerse.

commissary, n. comisario m.

commission, 1. n. comisión f. **2.** v. comisionar.

commissioner, n. comisionista m. & f.

commit, v. cometer.

commitment, n. compromiso m.

committee, n. comité m.

commodious, a. cómodo.

commodity, n. mercadería f.

common, a. común; ordinario.

commonly, adv. comúnmente, vulgarmente.

commonplace, a. trivial, banal.

commonwealth, n. estado m.; nación f.

commotion, n. tumulto m.

communal, a. comunal, público.

commune, 1. n. distrito municipal m.; comuna f. **2.** v. conversar.

communicable, a. comunicativo.

communicate, v. comunicar.

communication, n. comunicación f.

communicative, a. comunicativo.

communion, n. comunión f. **take c.,** comulgar.

communiqué, n. comunicación f.

communism, n. comunismo m.

communist, n. comunista m. & f.

communistic, a. comunístico.

community, n. comunidad f.

commutation, n. conmutación f.

compact, I. a. compacto. **2.**

n. pacto m.; (lady's) polvera f.

companion, n. compañero -ra.

companionable, a. sociable.

companionship, n. compañerismo m.

company, n. compañía f.

comparable, a. comparable.

comparative, a. comparativo.

comparatively, a. relativamente.

compare, v. comparar.

comparison, n. comparación f.

compartment, n. compartimiento m.

compass, n. compás m.; (nautical) brújula f.

compassion, n. compasión f.

compassionate, a. compasivo.

compassionately, adv. compasivamente.

compatible, a. compatible.

compatriot, n. compatriota m. & f.

compel, v. obligar.

compensate, v. compensar.

compensation, n. compensación f.

compensatory, a. compensatorio.

compete, v. competir.

competence, n. competencia f.

competent, a. competente, capaz.

competently, adv. competentemente.

competition, n. concurrencia f.; concurso m.

competitive, a. competidor.

competitor, n. competidor -ra.

compile, v. compilar.

complacency, n. complacencia f.

complacent, a. complaciente.

complacently, adv. complacientemente.

complain, v. quejarse.

complaint, n. queja f.

complement, n. complemento m.

complete, 1. *a.* completo. **2.** *v.* completar.

completely, *adv.* completamente, enteramente.

completeness, *n.* integridad *f.*

completion, *n.* terminación *f.*

complex, *a.* complejo.

complexion, *n.* tez *f.*

complexity, *n.* complejidad *f.*

compliance, *n.* consentimiento *m.* **in c. with,** de acuerdo con.

compliant, *a.* dócil; complaciente.

complicate, *v.* complicar.

complicated, *a.* complicado.

complication, *n.* complicación *f.*

complicity, *n.* complicidad *f.*

compliment, 1. *n.* flor *f.* **2.** *v.* felicitar; echar flores.

complimentary, *a.* galante, obsequioso, regalado.

comply, *v.* cumplir.

component, *a.* & *n.* componente *m.*

comport, *v.* portarse.

compose, *v.* componer.

composed, *a.* tranquilo; (made up) compuesto.

composer, *n.* compositor -ra.

composite, *a.* compuesto.

composition, *n.* composición *f.*

composure, *n.* serenidad *f.*, calma *f.*

compote, *n.* compota *f.*

compound, *a.* & *n.* compuesto *m.*

comprehend, *v.* comprender.

comprehensible, *a.* comprensible.

comprehension, *n.* comprensión *f.*

comprehensive, *a.* comprensivo.

compress, 1. *n.* cabezal *m.* **2.** *v.* comprimir.

compressed, *a.* comprimido.

compression, *n.* compresión *f.*

compressor, *n.* compresor *m.*

comprise, *v.* comprender; abarcar.

compromise, 1. *n.* compromiso *m.* **2.** *v.* comprometer.

compromiser, *n.* compromisario *m.*

compulsion, *n.* compulsión *f.*

compulsive, *a.* compulsivo.

compulsory, *a.* obligatorio.

compunction, *n.* compunción *f.*; escrúpulo *m.*

computation, *n.* computación *f.*

compute, *v.* computar, calcular.

comrade, *n.* camarada *m.* & *f.*; compañero -ra.

comradeship, *n.* camaradería *f.*

concave, *a.* cóncavo.

conceal, *v.* ocultar, esconder.

concealment, *n.* ocultación *f.*

concede, *v.* conceder.

conceit, *n.* amor propio; engreimiento *m.*

conceited, *a.* engreído.

conceivably, *a.* concebible, imaginable.

conceivable, *a.* concebible.

conceive, *v.* concebir.

concentrate, *v.* concentrar.

concentration, *n.* concentración *f.*

concept, *n.* concepto *m.*

conception, *n.* concepción *f.*; concepto *m.*

concern, 1. *n.* interés *m.*; inquietud *f.*; (com.) negocio *m.* **2.** *v.* concernir.

concerning, *prep.* respecto a.

concert, *n.* concierto *m.*

concerted, *a.* convenido.

concession, *n.* concesión *f.*

conciliate, *v.* conciliar.

conciliation, *n.* conciliación *f.*

conciliator, *n.* conciliador *m.*

conciliatory, *a.* conciliatorio.

concise, *a.* conciso.

concisely, *adv.* concisamente.

conciseness, *n.* concisión *f.*

conclave, *n.* conclave *m.*

conclude, *v.* concluir.

conclusion, *n.* conclusión *f.*

conclusive, *a.* conclusivo, decisivo.

conclusively, *adv.* concluyentemente.

concoct, v. confeccionar.
concomitant, n. & a. concomitante.
concord, n. concordia f.
concordat, n. concordato m.
concourse, n. concurso m.; confluencia f.
concrete, a. concreto.
concretely, adv. concretamente.
concubine, n. concubina, amiga f.
concur, v. concurrir.
concurrence, n. concurrencia f.; casualidad f.
concurrent, a. concurrente.
concussion, n. concusión f.; (c. of the brain) conmoción cerebral f.
condemn, v. condenar.
condemnable, a. culpable, condenable.
condemnation, n. condenación f.
condensation, n. condensación f.
condense, v. condensar.
condenser, n. condensador m.
condescend, v. condescender.
condescension, n. condescendencia f.
condiment, n. condimento m.
condition, 1. n. condición f.; estado m. 2. v. acondicionar.
conditional, a. condicional.
conditionally, adv. condicionalmente.
condole, v. condolerse.
condolence, n. pésame m.
condone, v. condonar.
conducive, a. conducente.
conduct, 1. n. conducta f. 2. v. conducir.
conductivity, n. conductividad f.
conductor, n. conductor m.
conduit, n. caño m., canal f.; conducto m.
cone, n. cono m. **ice-cream c.,** barquillo de helado.
confection, n. confitura f.
confectioner, n. confitero m.
confectionery, n. dulcería f.
confederacy, n. federación f.
confederate, a. & n. confederado m.

confederation, n. confederación f.
confer, v. conferenciar; conferir.
conference, n. conferencia f.; congreso m.
confess, v. confesar.
confession, n. confesión f.
confessional, 1. n. confesionario m. 2. a. confesional.
confessor, n. confesor m.
confetti, n. confetti m.
confidant, confidante, n. confidente m. & f.
confide, v. confiar.
confidence, n. confianza f.
confident, a. confiado; cierto.
confidential, a. confidencial.
confidentially, adv. confidencialmente, en secreto.
confidently, adv. confiadamente.
confine, 1. n. confín m. 2. v. confinar; encerrar.
confirm, v. confirmar.
confirmation, n. confirmación f.
confiscate, v. confiscar.
confiscation, n. confiscación f.
conflagration, n. incendio m.
conflict, 1. n. conflicto m. 2. v. oponerse; estar en conflicto.
conform, v. conformar.
conformation, n. conformación f.
conformer, n. conformista m. & f
conformist, n. conformista m. & f.
conformity, n. conformidad f.
confound, v. confundir.
confront, v. confrontar.
confuse, v. confundir.
confusion, n. confusión f.
congeal, v. congelar, helar.
congealment, n. congelación f.
congenial, a. congenial.
congenital, a. congénito.
congenitally, adv. congenitalmente.
congestion, n. congestión f.
conglomerate, 1. v. conglomerar. 2. a. conglomerado.

conglomeration, n. conglomeración f.

congratulate, v. felicitar.

congratulation, n. felicitación f.

congratulatory, a. congratulatorio.

congregate, v. congregar.

congregation, n. congregación f.

congress, n. congreso m.

conic, 1. n. cónica f. **2.** a. cónico.

conjecture, 1. n. conjetura f. **2.** v. conjeturar.

conjugal, a. conyugal, matrimonial.

conjugate, v. conjugar.

conjugation, n. conjugación f.

conjunction, n. conjunción f.

conjunctive, 1. n. (gram.) conjunción f. **2.** a. conjuntivo.

conjunctivitis, n. conjuntivitis f.

conjure, v. conjurar.

connect, v. juntar; relacionar.

connection, n. conexión f.

connivance, n. consentimiento m.

connive, v. disimular.

connoisseur, n. perito -ta.

connotation, n. connotación f.

connote, v. connotar.

connubial, a. conyugal.

conquer, v. conquistar.

conquerable, a. conquistable, vencible.

conqueror, n. conquistador m.

conquest, 1. n. conquista f.

conscience, n. conciencia f.

conscientious, a. concienzudo.

conscientiously, adv. escrupulosamente.

conscious, a. consciente.

consciously, adv. con conocimiento.

consciousness, n. conciencia f.

conscript, 1. n. conscripto m., recluta m. **2.** v. reclutar, alistar.

conscription, n. conscripción f., alistamiento m.

consecrate, v. consagrar.

consecration, n. consagración f.

consecutive, a. consecutivo, seguido.

consecutively, adv. consecutivamente, de seguida.

consensus, n. consenso m., acuerdo general m.

consent, 1. n. consentimiento m. **2.** v. consentir.

consequence, n. consecuencia f.

consequent, a. consiguiente.

consequential, a. importante.

consequently, adv. por lo tanto, por consiguiente.

conservation, n. conservación f.

conservatism, n. conservatismo m.

conservative, a. conservador, conservativo.

conservatory, n. (plants) invernáculo m.; (educ.) conservatorio m.

conserve, v. conservar.

consider, v. considerar.

considerable, a. considerable.

considerably, adv. considerablemente.

considerate, a. considerado.

considerately, adv. consideradamente.

consideration, n. consideración f.

considering, prep. visto que, en vista de.

consign, v. consignar.

consignment, n. consignación f., envío m.

consist, v. consistir.

consistency, n. consistencia f.

consistent, a. consistente.

consolation, n. consolación f.

console, v. consolar.

consolidate, v. consolidar.

consommé, n. caldo m.

consonant, n. consonante f.

consort, 1. n. conyuge m. & f.; socio. **2.** v. asociarse.

conspicuous, a. conspicuo.

conspicuously, *adv.* visiblemente, llamativamente.

conspicuousness, *n.* visibilidad *f.*; evidencia *f.*; fama *f.*

conspiracy, *n.* conspiración *f.*; complot *m.*

conspirator, *n.* conspirador -ra.

conspire, *v.* conspirar.

conspirer, *n.* conspirante *m. & f.*

constancy, *n.* constancia *f.*, lealtad *f.*

constant, *a.* constante.

constantly, *adv.* constantemente, de continuo.

constellation, *n.* constelación *f.*

consternation, *n.* consternación *f.*

constipation, *n.* constipación *f.*

constituency, *n.* distrito electoral *m.*

constituent, 1. *a.* constituyente. **2.** *n.* elector *m.*

constitute, *v.* constituir.

constitution, *n.* constitución *f.*

constitutional, *a.* constitucional.

constrain, *v.* constreñir.

constraint, *n.* constreñimiento *m.*, compulsión *f.*

constrict, *v.* apretar, estrechar.

construct, *v.* construir.

construction, *n.* construcción *f.*

constructive, *a.* constructivo.

constructively, *adv.* constructivamente; por deducción.

constructor, *n.* constructor *m.*

construe, *v.* interpretar.

consul, *n.* cónsul *m.*

consular, *n.* consulado *m.*

consulate, *n.* consulado *m.*

consult, *v.* consultar.

consultant, *n.* consultante *m. & f.*

consultation, *n.* consulta *f.*

consume, *v.* consumir.

consumer, *n.* consumidor -ra.

consummation, *n.* consumación *f.*

consumption, *n.* consumo *m.*

consumptive, 1. *n.* tísico *m.* **2.** *a.* consuntivo.

contact, 1. *n.* contacto *m.* **2.** *v.* ponerse en contacto con.

contagion, *n.* contagio *m.*

contagious, *a.* contagioso.

contain, *v.* contener.

container, *n.* envase *m.*

contaminate, *v.* contaminar.

contemplate, *v.* contemplar.

contemplation, *n.* contemplación *f.*

contemplative, *a.* contemplativo.

contemporary, *n. & a.* contemporáneo -nea.

contempt, *n.* desprecio *m.*

contemptible, *a.* vil, despreciable.

contemptuous, *a.* desdeñoso.

contemptuously, *adv.* desdeñosamente.

contend, *v.* contender; competir.

contender, *n.* competidor *m.*

content, 1. *a.* contento. **2.** *n.* contenido. **3.** *v.* contentar.

contented, *a.* contento.

contention, *n.* contención *f.*

contentment, *n.* contentamiento *m.*

contest, 1. *n.* concurso *m.* **2.** *v.* disputar.

contestable, *a.* contestable.

context, *n.* contexto *m.*

contiguous, *a.* contiguo.

continence, *n.* continencia *f.*, castidad *f.*

continent, *n.* continente *m.*

continental, *a.* continental.

contingency, *n.* eventualidad *f.*, casualidad *f.*

contingent, *a.* contingente.

continual, *a.* continuo.

continuation, *n.* continuación *f.*

continue, *v.* continuar.

continuity, *n.* continuidad *f.*

continuous, *a.* continuo.

continuously, *adv.* continualmente.

contour, *n.* contorno *m.*

contraband, *n.* contrabando *m.*

contract, 1. *n.* contrato *m.* **2.** *v.* contraer.

contraction, *n.* contracción *f.*

contractor, *n.* contratista *m.*

contradict, *v.* contradecir.

contradiction, *n.* contradicción *f.*

contradictory, *a.* contradictorio, opuesto.

contralto, *n.* contralto *m.*

contrary, *a. & n.* contrario *m.*

contrast, 1. *n.* contraste *m.* **2.** *v.* contrastar.

contribute, *v.* contribuir.

contribution, *n.* contribución *f.*

contributive, contributory, *a.* contribuyente.

contributor, *n.* contribuidor *m.*

contrite, *a.* contrito.

contrition, *n.* contrición *f.*

contrivance, *n.* aparato *m.*; estratagema *f.*

contrive, *v.* inventar, tramar; darse maña.

control, 1. *n.* control *m.* **2.** *v.* controlar.

controllable, *a.* controlable, dominable.

controller, *n.* interventor *m.*, contralor *m.*

controversial, *a.* contencioso.

controversy, *n.* controversia *f.*

contusion, *n.* contusión *f.*

convalesce, *v.* convalecer.

convalescence, *n.* convalecencio *f.*

convalescent, *n.* convaleciente *m. & f.*

convene, *v.* juntarse; convocar.

convenience, *n.* comodidad *f.*

convenient, *a.* cómodo. **to be c.,** convenir.

conveniently, *adv.* cómodamente.

convent, *n.* convento *m.*

convention, *n.* convención *f.*

conventional, *a.* convencional.

conventionally, *adv.* convencionalmente.

converge, *v.* convergir.

convergence, *n.* convergencia *f.*

convergent, *a.* convergente.

conversant, *a.* versado; entendido (de).

conversation, *n.* conversación; plática *f.*

conversational, *a.* de conversación.

conversationalist, *n.* conversador *m.*

converse, *v.* conversar.

conversely, *adv.* a la inversa.

convert, 1. *n.* convertido *m.* **2.** *v.* convertir.

converter, *n.* convertidor *m.*

convertible, *a.* convertible.

convex, *a.* convexo.

convey, *v.* transportar; comunicar.

conveyance, *n.* transporte; vehículo *m.*

conveyor, *n.* conductor *m.*; (mech.) transportador *m.*

convict, 1. *n.* reo *m.* **2.** *v.* probar de culpa.

conviction, *n.* convicción *f.*

convince, *v.* convencer.

convincing, *a.* convincente.

convivial, *a.* convival.

convocation, *n.* convocación; asamblea *f.*

convoke, *v.* convocar, citar.

convoy, *n.* convoy *m.*; escolta *f.*

convulse, *v.* convulsionar; agitar violentamente.

convulsion, *n.* convulsión *f.*

convulsive, *a.* convulsivo.

cook, 1. *n.* cocinero -ra. **2.** *v.* cocinar, cocer.

cookbook, *n.* libro de cocina *m.*

cooky, *n.* galleta dulce *f.*

cool, 1. *a.* fresco. **2.** *v.* refrescar.

cooler, *n.* enfriadera *f.*

coolness, *n.* frescura *f.*

coop, 1. *n.* jaula *f.* **chicken c.,** gallinero *m.* **2.** *v.* enjaular.

coöperate, *v.* cooperar.

coöperation, *n.* cooperación *f.*

coöperative, *a.* cooperativo.

coöperatively, *adv.* cooperativamente.

coördinate, *v.* coordinar.

coördination, *n.* coordinación *f.*

coördinator, *n.* coordinador *m.*

cope, *v.* contender. **c. with,** superar, hacer frente a.

copious, *a.* copioso, abundante.

copiously, *adv.* copiosamente.

copiousness, *n.* copia *f.*, abundancia *f.*

copper, *n.* cobre *m.*

copy, **1.** *n.* copia *f.*; ejemplar *m.* **2.** *v.* copiar.

copyist, *n.* copista *m. & f.*

copyright, *n.* derechos de propiedad literaria *m.pl.*

coquetry, *n.* coquetería *f.*

coquette, *n.* coqueta.

coral, *n.* coral *m.*

cord, *n.* cuerda *f.*

cordial, *a.* cordial.

cordiality, *n.* cordialidad *f.*

cordially, *adv.* cordialmente.

cordovan, *n.* cordobán *m.*

corduroy, *n.* pana *f.*

core, *n.* corazón; centro *m.*

cork, *n.* corcho *m.*

corkscrew, *n.* tirabuzón *m.*

corn, *n.* maíz *m.*

cornea, *n.* córnea *f.*

corner, *n.* rincón *m.*; (of street) esquina *f.*

cornet, *n.* corneta *f.*

cornetist, *n.* cornetín *m.*

cornice, *n.* cornisa *f.*

cornstarch, *n.* maicena *f.*

corollary, *n.* corolario *m.*

coronary, *a.* coronario.

coronation, *n.* coronación *f.*

corporal, **1.** *a.* corpóreo. **2.** *n.* cabo *m.*

corporate, *a.* corporativo.

corporation, *n.* corporación *f.*

corps, *n.* cuerpo *m.*

corpse, *n.* cadáver *m.*

corpulent, *a.* corpulento.

corpuscle, *n.* corpúsculo *m.*

corral, **1.** *n.* corral *m.* **2.** *v.* acorralar.

correct, **1.** *a.* correcto. **2.** *v.* corregir.

correction, *n.* corrección; enmienda *f.*

corrective, *n. & a.* correctivo.

correctly, *adv.* correctamente.

correctness, *n.* exactitud *f.*

correlate, *v.* correlacionar.

correlation, *n.* correlación *f.*

correspond, *v.* corresponder.

correspondence, *n.* correspondencia *f.*

correspondent, *a.* correspondiente.

corresponding, *a.* correspondiente.

corridor, *n.* corredor, pasillo *m.*

corroborate, *v.* corroborar.

corroboration, *n.* corroboración *f.*

corroborative, *a.* corroborante.

corrode, *v.* corroer.

corrosion, *n.* corrosión *f.*

corrugate, *v.* arrugar; ondular.

corrupt, **1.** *a.* corrompido. **2.** *v.* corromper.

corruptible, *a.* corruptible.

corruption, *n.* corrupción *f.*

corruptive, *a.* corruptivo.

corset, *n.* corsé *m.*, (girdle) faja *f.*

cortege, *n.* comitiva *f.*, séquito *m.*

corvette, *n.* corbeta *f.*

cosmetic, *a. & n.* cosmético.

cosmic, *a.* cósmico.

cosmopolitan, *a. & n.* cosmopolita *m. & f.*

cosmos, *n.* cosmos *m.*

cost, **1.** *n.* coste *m.*; costa *f.* **2.** *v.* costar.

Costa Rican, *a. & n.* costarricense *m. & f.*

costly, *a.* costoso, caro.

costume, *n.* traje; disfraz *m.*

cot, *n.* catre *m.*

coterie, *n.* camarilla *f.*

cotillion, *n.* cotillón *m.*

cottage, *n.* casita *f.*

cottage cheese, *n.* requesón *m.*

cotton, *n.* algodón *m.*

cottonseed, n. semilla del algodón f.
couch. n. sofá m.
cougar, n. cuguar m.
cough, 1. n. tos f. **2.** v. toser.
council, n. consejo, concilio m.
counsel, 1. n. consejo; (law) abogado. **2.** v. aconsejar.
to keep one's c., no decir nada.
counselor, n. consejero; (legal) abogado m.
count, 1. n. cuenta f.; (title) conde m. **2.** v. contar.
countenance, 1. n. aspecto m.; cara f. **2.** v. aprobar.
counter, 1. adv. **c. to,** contra, en contra de. **2.** n. mostrador m.
counteract, v. contrariar.
counteraction, n. oposición f.
counterbalance, 1. n. contrapeso m. **2.** v. contrapesar.
counterfeit, 1. a. falsificado. **2.** v. falsear.
countermand, v. contramandar.
counteroffensive, n. contraofensiva f.
counterpart, n. contraparte f.
countess, n. condesa f.
countless, a. innumerable.
country, n. campo m.; (political) país m.; (homeland) patria f.
countryman, n. paisano m. **fellow c.,** compatriota m.
countryside, n. campo, paisaje m.
county, n. condado m.
coupé, n. cupé m.
couple, 1. n. par m. **2.** v. unir.
coupon, n. cupón, talón m.
courage, n. valor m.
courageous, a. valiente.
course, n. curso m. **of c.,** por supuesto, desde luego.
court, 1. n. corte f.; cortejo m.; (of law) tribunal m. **2.** v. cortejar.
courteous, a. cortés.
courtesy, n. cortesía f.
courthouse, n. palacio de justicia m., tribunal m.

courtier, n. cortesano m.
courtly, a. cortés, galante.
courtroom, n. sala de justicia f.
courtship, n. corte f.
courtyard, n. patio m.
cousin, n. primo -ma.
covenant, n. contrato, convenio m.
cover, 1. n. cubierta, tapa f. **2.** v. cubrir, tapar.
covet, v. ambicionar, suspirar por.
covetous, a. codicioso.
cow, n. vaca f.
coward, n. cobarde m. & f.
cowardice, n. cobardía f.
cowardly, a. cobarde.
cowboy, n. vaquero, gaucho m.
cower, v. agacharse.
cowhide, n. cuero m.
coy, a. recatado, modesto.
coyote, n. coyote m.
cozy, a. cómodo y agradable.
crab, n. cangrejo m.
crab apple, n. manzana silvestre f.
crack, 1. n. hendedura f.; (noise) crujido m. **2.** v. hender; crujir.
cracker, n. galleta f.
cradle, n. cuna f.
craft, n. arte m.
craftsman, n. artesano m.
craftsmanship, n. mano de obra f.
crafty, a. ladino.
crag, n. despeñadero m.
cram, v. rellenar, hartar.
cramp, n. calambre m.
cranberry, n. arándano m.
crane, 1. n. (bird) grulla f.; (mech.) grúa f.
cranium, n. cráneo m.
crank, n. (mech.) manivela f.
cranky, a. chiflado, caprichoso.
crash, 1. n. choque; estallido m. **2.** v. estallar.
crate, n. canasto m.
crater, n. cráter m.
crave, v. descar; anhelar.
craven, a. cobarde.
craving, n. sed m., anhelo m.
crawl, v. andar a gatas, arrastrarse.
crayon, n. creyón; lápiz m.

crazy, a. loco.

creak, v. crujir.

creaky, a. crujidero.

cream, n. crema f.

creamery, n. lechería f.

crease, 1. n. pliegue m. 2. v. plegar.

create, v. crear.

creation, n. creación f.

creative, a. creativo, creador.

creator, n. criador -ra.

creature, n. criatura f.

credence, n. creencia f.

credentials, n. credenciales f.pl.

credibility, n. credibilidad f.

credible, a. creíble.

credit, 1. n. crédito m. on c. al fiado. 2. v. (com.) abonar.

creditable, a. fidedigno.

creditor, n. acreedor -ra.

credo, n. credo m.

credulity, n. credulidad f.

credulous, a. crédulo.

creed, n. credo m.

creek, n. riachuelo m.

creep, v. gatear.

cremate, v. cremar.

crematory, n. crematorio m.

creosote, n. creosota f.

crepe, n. crespón m.

crescent, n. & n. creciente f.

crest, n. cresta; cima f.; (heraldry) timbre m.

cretonne, n. cretona f.

crevice, n. grieta f.

crew, n. tripulación f.

crib, n. pesebre m.; camita de niño.

cricket, n. grillo m.

crime, n. crimen m.

criminal, a. & n. criminal.

criminologist, n. criminologo m.

criminology, n. criminología f.

crimson, a. & n. carmesí m.

cringe, v. encogerse, temblar.

cripple, 1. n. lisiado -da. 2. v. estropear, lisiar.

crisis, n. crisis f.

crisp, a. crespo; fresco.

crispness, n. encrespadura f.

crisscross, a. entrelazado.

criterion, n. criterio m.

critic, n. crítico m.

critical, a. crítico.

criticism, n. crítica; censura f.

criticize, v. criticar; censurar.

critique, n. crítica f.

croak, 1. n. graznido m. 2. v. graznar.

crochet, 1. n. crochet m. 2. v. hacer crochet.

crock, n. cazuela f.; olla de barro.

crockery, n. loza f.

crocodile, n. cocodrilo m.

crony, n. compinche m.

crooked, a. encorvado; deshonesto.

croon, v. canturrear.

crop, n. cosecha f.

croquet, n. juego de croquet m.

croquette, n. croqueta f.

cross, 1. a. enojado, mal humorado. 2. n. cruz f. 3. v. cruzar, atravesar.

crossbreed, 1. n. mestizo m. 2. v. cruzar.

cross-examine, v. interrogar.

cross-eyed, a. bisco.

cross-fertilization, n. alogamia f.

crossing, crossroads, n. cruce m.

cross section, n. corte transversal m.

crotch, n. bifurcación f.; (anat.) bragadura f.

crouch, v. agacharse.

croup, n. (med.) crup m.

croupier, n. crupié m.

crow, n. cuervo m.

crowd, 1. n. muchedumbre f.; tropel m. 2. v. apretar.

crowded, a. lleno de gente.

crown, 1. n. corona f. 2. v. coronar.

crown prince, n. príncipe heredero m.

crucial, a. crucial.

crucible, n. crisol m.

crucifix, n. crucifijo m.

crucifixion, n. crucifixión f.

crucify, v. crucificar.

crude, a. crudo; (oil) bruto.

crudeness, n. crudeza f.

cruel, a. cruel.

cruelty, n. crueldad f.

cruet, n. vinagrera f.

cruise, 1. n. viaje por mar. 2. v. navegar.

cruiser, n. crucero m.

crumb, n. miga; migaja f.

crumble, v. desmigajar; desmoronar.

crumple, v. arrugar; encogerse.

crusade, n. cruzada f.

crusader, n. cruzado m.

crush, v. aplastar.

crust, n. costra f.

crustacean, n. crustáceo m.

crutch, n. muleta f.

cry, 1. n. grito m. **2.** v. gritar; (weep) llorar.

crypt, n. gruta f., cripta f.

cryptic, a. secreto.

cryptography, n. criptografía f.

crystal, n. cristal m.

crystalline, a. cristalino, transparente.

crystallize, v. cristalizar.

cub, n. cachorro m.

Cuban, n. & a. cubano -na.

cube, n. cubo m.

cubic, a. cúbico.

cubicle, n. cubículo m.

cubic measure, n. medida de capacidad f.

cubism, n. cubismo m.

cuckoo, n. cuco m.

cucumber, n. pepino m.

cuddle, v. abrazar.

cudgel, n. palo m.

cue, n. apunte m.; (billiards) taco m.

cuff, n. puño de camisa. **c. links,** gemelos.

cuisine, n. arte culinario f.

culinary, a. culinario.

culminate, v. culminar.

culmination, n. culminación f.

culpable, a. culpable.

culprit, n. criminal; delincuente m.

cult, n. culto m.

cultivate, v. cultivar.

cultivated, a. cultivado.

cultivation, n. cultivo m.; cultivación f.

cultivator, n. cultivador m.

cultural, a. cultural.

culture, n. cultura f.

cultured, a. culto.

cumbersome, a. pesado, incómodo.

cumulative, a. acumulativo.

cunning, 1. a. astuto. **2.** n. astucia f.

cup, n. taza, jícara f.

cupboard, n. armario, aparador m.

cupidity, n. avaricia f.

curable, a. curable.

curator, n. guardián m.

curb, 1. n. freno m. **2.** v. refrenar.

curd, n. cuajada f.

curdle, v. cuajarse, coagularse.

cure, 1. n. remedio m. **2.** v. curar, sanar.

curfew, n. toque de queda m.

curio, n. objeto curioso.

curiosity, n. curiosidad f.

curious, a. curioso.

curl, 1. n. rizo m. **2.** v. rizar.

curly, a. rizado.

currant, n. grosella f.

currency, n. circulación f.; dinero m.

current, a. & n. corriente f.

currently, adv. corrientemente.

curriculum, n. plan de estudio m.

curse, 1. n. maldición f. **2.** v. maldecir.

cursory, a. sumario.

curt, a. brusco.

curtail, v. reducir; restringir.

curtain, n. cortina f.; (theat.) telón m.

curtsy, 1. n. reverencia f. **2.** v. hacer una reverencia.

curvature, n. curvatura f.

curve, 1. n. curva f. **2.** v. encorvar.

cushion, n. cojín m.; almohada f.

cuspidor, n. escupidera f.

custard, n. flan m.; natillas f. pl.

custodian, n. custodio m.

custody, n. custodia f.

custom, n. costumbre f.

customary, a. acostumbrado, usual.

customer, n. cliente m. & f.

customhouse, customs, n. aduana f.

cut, 1. n. corte m.; cortada f.; tajada f.; (printing) grabado m. **2.** v. cortar; tajar.

cute, *a.* mono, lindo.
cut glass, *n.* cristal tallado *m.*
cuticle, *n.* cutícula *f.*
cutlery, *n.* cuchillería *f.*
cutlet, *n.* coteleta, chuleta *f.*
cutter, *n.* cortador -ra; (naut.) cúter *m.*
cutthroat, *n.* asesino *m.*
cycle, *n.* ciclo *m.*
cyclist, *n.* ciclista *m. & f.*

cyclone, *n.* ciclón, huracán *m.*
cyclotron, *n.* ciclotrón *m.*
cylinder, *n.* cilindro *m.*
cylindrical, *a.* cilíndrico.
cymbal, *n.* címbalo *m.*
cynic, *n.* cínico *m.*
cynical, *a.* cínico.
cynicism, *n.* cinismo *m.*
cypress, *n.* ciprés *m.* **c. nut,** piñuela *f.*
cyst, *n.* quiste *m.*

D

dad, *n.* papa *m.*, papito *m.*
daffodil, *n.* narciso *m.*
dagger, *n.* puñal *m.*
dahlia, *n.* dalia *f.*
daily, *a.* diario, cotidiano.
daintiness, *n.* delicadeza *f.*
dainty, *a.* delicado.
dairy, *n.* lechería, quesería *f.*
dais, *n.* tablado *m.*
daisy, *n.* margarita *f.*
dale, *n.* valle *m.*
dally, *v.* holgar; perder el tiempo.
dam, *n.* presa *f.*; dique *m.*
damage, 1. *n.* daño *m.* **2.** *v.* dañar.
damask, *n.* damasco *m.*
damn, *v.* condenar.
damnation, *n.* condenación *f.*
damp, *a.* húmedo.
dampen, *v.* humedecer.
dampness, *n.* humedad *f.*
damsel, *n.* doncella *f.*
dance, 1. *n.* baile *m.*; danza *f.* **2.** *v.* bailar.
dancer, *n.* bailador -ra; (professional) bailarín -na.
dancing, *n.* baile *m.*
dandelion, *n.* amargón *m.*
dandruff, *n.* caspa *f.*
dandy, *n.* petimetre *m.*
danger, *n.* peligro *m.*
dangerous, *a.* peligroso.
dangle, *v.* colgar.

Danish, *a. & n.* danés -sa; dinamarqués -sa.
dapper, *a.* gallardo.
dare, *v.* atreverse, osar.
daredevil, *n.* atrevido *m.*, -da *f.*
daring. 1. *a.* atrevido. **2.** *n.* osadía *f.*
dark, 1. *a.* obscuro; moreno. **2.** *n.* obscuridad *f.*
darken, *v.* obscurecer.
darkness, *n.* obscuridad *f.*
darkroom, *n.* cámara obscura
darling, *a. & n.* querido, amado.
darn, *v.* zurcir.
darning needle, *n.* agujar de zurcir *m.*
dart, *n.* dardo *m.*
dash, *n.* arranque *m.*; (punctuation) guión *m.*
data, *n.* datos *m.*
date, *n.* fecha *f.*; (engagement) cita *f.*; (fruit) dátil *m.*
daughter, *n.* hija *f.*
daughter-in-law, *n.* nuera *f.*
daunt, *v.* intimidar.
dauntless, *a.* intrépido.
davenport, *n.* sofá *m.*
dawn, 1. *n.* alba, madrugada *f.* **2.** *v.* amanecer.
day, *n.* día *m.* **good d.,** buenos días.

daybreak, *n.* alba, madruga-da *f.*

daydream, *n.* fantasía *f.*

daylight, *n.* luz del día.

daze, *v.* aturdir.

dazzle, *v.* deslumbrar.

deacon, *n.* diácono *m.*

dead, *a.* muerto.

deaden, *v.* amortecer.

deadline, *n.* límite absoluto *m.*

deadlock, *n.* paro *m.*

deadly, *a.* mortal.

deaf, *a.* sordo.

deafen, *v.* ensordecer.

deaf-mute, *n.* sordomudo *m.*

deafness, *n.* sordera *f.*

deal, 1. *n.* trato *m.*; negocia-ción *f.* **a great d., a good d.,** mucho. 2. *v.* tratar; negociar.

dealer, *n.* comerciante *m.*, (at cards) tallador -ra.

dean, *n.* decano *m.*

dear, *a.* querido; caro.

dearth, *n.* escasez *m.*

death, *n.* muerte *f.*

deathless, *a.* inmortal.

debacle, *n.* desastre *m.*

debase, *v.* degradar.

debatable, *a.* discutible.

debate, 1. *n.* debate *m.* 2. *v.* disputar, deliberar.

debauch, *v.* corromper.

debilitate, *v.* debilitar.

debit, *n.* débito *m.*

debonair, *a.* cortés; alegre, vivo.

debris, *n.* escombros *m.pl.*

debt, *n.* deuda *f.*

debtor, *n.* deudor -ra.

debunk, *v.* traer a la realidad.

debut, *n.* debut, estreno *m.*

debutante, *n.* debutante *f.*

decade, *n.* década *f.*

decadence, *n.* decadencia *f.*

decadent, *a.* decadente.

decalcomania, *n.* calcomanía *f.*

decanter, *n.* garrafa *f.*

decapitate, *v.* descabezar.

decay, 1. *n.* descaecimiento *m.*; (dent.) caries *f.* 2. *v.* decaer; (dent.) cariarse.

deceased, *a.* muerto, difunto.

deceit, *n.* engaño *m.*

deceitful, *a.* engañoso.

deceive, *v.* engañar.

December, *n.* diciembre *m.*

decency, *n.* decencia *f.*; decoro *m.*

decent, *a.* decente.

decentralize, *v.* descentrali-zar.

deception, *n.* decepción *f.*

deceptive, *a.* deceptivo.

decide, *v.* decidir.

decimal, *a.* decimal.

decipher, *v.* descifrar.

decision, *n.* decisión *f.*

decisive, *a.* decisivo.

deck, *n.* cubierta *f.*

declamation, *n.* declama-ción *f.*

declaration, *n.* declaración *f.*

declarative, *a.* declarativo.

declare, *v.* declarar.

declension, *n.* declinación *f.*

decline, 1. *n.* decadencia *f.* 2. *v.* decaer; negarse; (gram.) declinar.

decompose, *v.* descomponer.

decorate, *v.* decorar, adornar.

decoration, *n.* decoración *f.*

decorative, *a.* decorativo.

decorator, *n.* decorador *m.*

decorous, *a.* correcto.

decorum, *n.* decoro *m.*

decrease, *v.* disminuir.

decree, *n.* decreto *m.*

decrepit, *a.* decrépito.

decry, *v.* descreditar.

dedicate, *v.* dedicar; con-sagrar.

dedication, *n.* dedicación; dedicatoria *f.*

deduce, deduct, *v.* deducir.

deduction, *n.* rebaja *f.*

deductive, *a.* deductivo.

deed, *n.* acción; hazaña *f.*

deem, *v.* estimar.

deep, *a.* hondo, profundo.

deepen, *v.* profundizar, ahon-dar.

deeply, *adv.* profundamente.

deer, *n.* venado, ciervo *m.*

deface, *v.* mutilar.

defamation, *n.* calumnia *f.*

defame, *v.* difamar.

default, 1. *n.* defecto *m.* 2. *v.* faltar.

defeat, 1. *n.* derrota *f.* 2. *v.* derrotar.

defect, *n.* defecto *m.*

defective, *a.* defectivo.

defend, v. defender.

defendant, n. acusado -da.

defender, n. defensor -ra.

defense, n. defensa f.

defensive, a. defensivo.

defer, v. aplazar; diferir.

deference, n. deferencia f.

defiance, n. desafío m.

defiant, a. desafiador.

deficiency, n. defecto m.

deficient, a. deficiente.

deficit, n. déficit, descubierto m.

defile, 1. n. desfiladero m. **2.** v. profanar.

define, v. definir.

definite, a. exacto; definitivo.

definitely, adv. definidamente.

definition, n. definición f.

definitive, a. definitivo.

deflation, n. desinflación f.

deflect, v. desviar.

deform, v. deformar.

deformity, n. deformidad f.

defraud, v. defraudar.

defray, v. costear.

deft, a. diestro.

defy, v. desafiar.

degenerate, 1. a. degenerado. **2.** v. degenerar.

degeneration, n. degeneración f.

degradation, n. degradación f.

degrade, v. degradar.

degree, n. grado m.

deign, v. condescender.

deity, n. deidad f.

dejected, a. abatido.

dejection, n. tristeza f.

delay, 1. n. retardo m., demora f. **2.** v. tardar, demorar.

delegate, 1. n. delegado -da. **2.** v. delegar.

delegation, n. delegación f.

delete, v. suprimir.

deliberate, 1. a. premeditado. **2.** v. deliberar.

deliberately, adv. deliberadamente.

deliberation, n. deliberación f.

deliberative, a. deliberativo.

delicacy, n. delicadeza f.

delicate, a. delicado.

delicious, a. delicioso.

delight, n. deleite m.

delightful, a. deleitoso.

delinquency, n. delincuencia f.

delinquent, a. & n. delincuente.

delirious, a. delirante.

deliver, v. entregar.

deliverance, n. liberación; salvación f.

delivery, n. entrega f.; (med.) parto m.

delude, v. engañar.

deluge, n. inundación f.

delusion, n. decepción f.; engaño m.

delve, v. cavar, sondear.

demagogue, n. demagogo m.

demand, 1. n. demanda f. **2.** v. demandar; exigir.

demarcation, n. demarcación f.

demeanor, n. conducta f.

demented, a. demente, loco.

demilitarize, v. desmilitarizar.

demobilize, v. desmovilizar.

democracy, n. democracia f.

democrat, n. demócrata m. & f.

democratic, a. democrático.

demolish, v. demoler.

demon, n. demonio m.

demonstrate, v. demostrar.

demonstration, n. demostración f.

demonstrative, a. demostrativo.

demoralize, v. desmoralizar.

demure, a. modesto, serio.

den, n. caverna f.; retrete m.

denature, v. alterar.

denial, n. negación f.

Denmark, n. Dinamarca f.

denomination, n. denominación; secta f.

denote, v. denotar.

denounce, v. denunciar.

dense, a. denso, espeso; estúpido.

density, n. densidad f.

dent, 1. n. abolladura f. **2.** v. abollar.

dental, a. dental.

dentist, n. dentista m.

dentistry, n. odontología f.

denture, n. dentadura f.

denunciation, *n.* denunciación *f.*

deny, *v.* negar, rehusar.

deodorant, *n.* desodorante *m.*

depart, *v.* partir; irse, marcharse.

department, *n.* departamento *m.*

departmental, *a.* departamental.

departure, *n.* salida; desviación *f.*

depend, *v.* depender.

dependability, *n.* confiabilidad *f.*

dependable, *a.* confiable.

dependence, *n.* dependencia *f.*

dependent, *a. & n.* dependiente *m.*

depict, *v.* pintar; representar.

deplete, *v.* agotar.

deplorable, *a.* deplorable.

deplore, *v.* deplorar.

deport, *v.* deportar.

deportation, *n.* deportación *f.*

deportment, *n.* conducta *f.*

depose, *v.* deponer.

deposit, 1. *n.* depósito *m.* 2. *v.* depositar.

depositor, *n.* depositante *m. & f.*

depot, *n.* depósito *m.*; (r.r.) estación *f.*

depravity, *n.* depravación *f.*

deprecate, *v.* deprecar.

depreciate, *v.* depreciar.

depreciation, *n.* depreciación *f.*

depredation, *n.* depredación *f.*

depress, *v.* deprimir; desanimar.

depression, *n.* depresión *f.*

deprive, *v.* privar.

depth, *n.* profundidad, hondura *f.*

depth charge, *n.* carga de profundidad *f.*

deputy, *n.* diputado *m.*

deride, *v.* burlar.

derision, *n.* burla *f.*

derivation, *n.* derivación *f.*

derivative, *a.* derivativo.

derive, *v.* derivar.

derogatory, *a.* derogatorio.

derrick, *n.* grúa *f.*

descend, *v.* descender, bajar.

descendant, *n.* descendiente *m. & f.*

descent, *n.* descenso *m.*; origen *m.*

describe, *v.* describir.

description, *n.* descripción *f.*

descriptive, *a.* descriptivo.

desecrate, *v.* profanar.

desert, 1. *n.* desierto *m.* 2. *v.* abandonar.

deserter, *n.* desertor *m.*

desertion, *n.* deserción *f.*

deserve, *v.* merecer.

design, 1. *n.* diseño *m.* 2. *v.* diseñar.

designate, *v.* señalar, apuntar.

designation, *n.* designación *f.*

designer, *n.* diseñador -ra; (technical) proyectista *m. & f.*

desirability, *n.* conveniencia *f.*

desirable, *a.* deseable.

desire, 1. *n.* deseo *m.* 2. *v.* desear.

desirous, *a.* deseoso.

desist, *v.* desistir.

desk, *n.* escritorio *m.*

desolate, 1. *a.* desolado. 2. *v.* desolar.

desolation, *n.* desolación, ruina *f.*

despair, 1. *n.* desesperación *f.* 2. *v.* desesperar.

despatch, dispatch, 1. *n.* despacho *m.*; prontitud *f.* 2. *v.* despachar.

desperado, *n.* bandido *m.*

desperate, *a.* desesperado.

desperation, *n.* desesperación *f.*

despicable, *a.* vil.

despise, *v.* despreciar.

despite, *prep.* a pesar de.

despondent, *a.* abatido; desanimado.

despot, *n.* déspota *m.*

despotic, *a.* despótico.

dessert, *n.* postre *m.*

destination, *n.* destinación *f.*

destine, *v.* destinar.

destiny, *n.* destino *m.*

destitute, *a.* destituido.

destitution, n. destitución f.

destroy, v. destrozar, destruir.

destroyer, n. destruidor m.; (nav.) destróyer m.

destruction, n. destrucción f.

destructive, a. destructivo.

desultory, a. inconexo; casual.

detach, v. separar, desprender.

detachment, n. (military) destacamento m.

detail, 1. n. detalle m. **2.** v. detallar.

detain, v. detener.

detect, v. descubrir.

detection, n. detección f.

detective, n. detective m.

detention, n. detención; cautividad f.

deter, v. disuadir.

detergent, n. & a. detergente m.

deteriorate, v. deteriorar.

deterioration, n. deterioración f.

determination, n. determinación f.

determine, v. determinar.

detest, v. detestar.

detonate, v. detonar.

detour, n. desvío m.

detract, v. disminuir.

detriment, n. detrimento m., daño m.

detrimental, a. dañoso.

devaluate, v. depreciar.

devastate, v. devastar.

develop, v. desarrollar; (phot.) revelar.

development, n. desarrollo m.

deviate, v. desviar.

deviation, n. desviación f.

device, n. aparato; artificio m.

devil, n. diablo, demonio m.

devious, a. desviado.

devise, v. inventar.

devoid, a. desprovisto.

devote, v. dedicar, consagrar.

devoted, a. devoto.

devotee, n. aficionado m.

devotion, n. devoción f.

devour, v. devorar.

devout, a. devoto.

dew, n. rocío, sereno m.

dexterity, n. destreza f.

dexterous, a. diestro.

diabetes, n. diabetes f.

diabolic, a. diabólico.

diadem, n. diadema f.

diagnose, v. diagnosticar.

diagnosis, n. diagnóstico m.

diagonal, n. diagonal f.

diagram, n. diagrama m.

dial, n. cuadrante m., carátula f.

dialect, n. dialecto m.

dialogue, n. diálogo m.

diameter, n. diámetro m.

diamond, n. diamante, brillante m.

diaper, n. pañal m.

diarrhea, n. diarrea f.

diary, n. diario m.

diathermy, n. diatermia f.

dice, n. dados m.pl.

dictate, 1. n. dictamen m. **2.** v. dictar.

dictation, n. dictado m.

dictator, n. dictador m.

dictatorship, n. dictadura f.

diction, n. dicción f.

dictionary, n. diccionario m.

die, 1. n. matriz f.; (game) dado m. **2.** v. morir.

diet, n. dieta f.

dietary, a. dietético.

dietitian, n. dietista m. & f.

differ, v. diferir.

difference, n. diferencia f. **to make no d.,** no importar.

different, a. diferente, distinto.

differential, n. diferencial f.

differentiate, v. diferenciar.

difficult, a. difícil.

difficulty, n. dificultad f.

diffident, a. tímido.

diffuse, v. difundir.

diffusion, n. difusión f.

dig, v. cavar.

digest, 1. n. extracto m. **2.** v. digerir.

digestible, a. digerible.

digestion, n. digestión f.

digestive, a. digestivo.

digitalis, n. digital f.

dignified, a. digno.

dignify, v. dignificar.

dignitary, n. dignitario m.

dignity, n. dignidad f.

digress, v. divagar.

digression, n. digresión f.
dike, n. dique m.
dilapidated, a. dilapidado.
dilapidation, n. dilapidación f.
dilate, v. dilatar.
dilatory, a. dilatorio.
dilemma, n. dilema m.
dilettante, n. diletante m. & f.
diligence, n. diligencia f.
diligent, a. diligente, aplicado.
dilute, v. diluir.
dim, 1. a. oscuro. **2.** v. oscurecer.
dimension, n. dimensión f.
diminish, v. disminuir.
diminution, n. disminución f.
diminutive, a. diminutivo.
dimness, n. oscuridad f.
dimple, n. hoyuelo m.
din, n. alboroto m.
dine, v. comer, cenar.
diner, n. coche comedor m.
dingy, a. deslucido, deslustrado.
dinner, n. comida, cena f.
dinosaur, n. dinosauro m.
diocese, n. diócesis m.
dip, v. sumergir, hundir.
diphtheria, n. difteria f.
diploma, n. diploma m.
diplomacy, n. diplomacia f.
diplomat, n. diplomático m.
diplomatic, a. diplomático.
dipper, n. cucharón m.
dire, a. horrendo.
direct, 1. a. directo. **2.** v. dirigir.
direction, n. dirección f.
directive, n. directivo m.
directly, adv. directamente.
director, n. director -ra.
directory, n. directorio m., guía f.
dirigible, n. dirigible m.
dirt, n. basura f.; (earth) tierra f.
dirty, a. sucio.
disability, n. inhabilidad f.; invalidez m.
disable, v. incapacitar.
disabuse, v. desengañar.
disadvantage, n. desventaja f.

disagree, v. desconvenir; disentir.
disagreeable, a. desagradable.
disagreement, n. desacuerdo m.
disappear, v. desaparecer.
disappearance, n. desaparición f.
disappoint, v. disgustar, desilusionar.
disappointment, n. disgusto m., desilusión f.
disapproval, n. desaprobación f.
disapprove, v. desaprobar.
disarm, v. desarmar.
disarmament, n. desarme m.
disarrange, v. desordenar; desarreglar.
disaster, n. desastre m.
disastrous, a. desastroso.
disavow, v. repudiar.
disavowal, n. repudiación f.
disband, v. dispersarse.
disbelieve, v. descreer.
disburse, v. desembolsar, pagar.
discard, v. descartar.
discern, v. discernir.
discerning, a. discernidor, perspicaz.
discernment, n. discernimiento m.
discharge, v. descargar; despedir.
disciple, n. discípulo m.
disciplinary, a. disciplinario.
discipline, n. disciplina f.
disclaim, v. repudiar.
disclaimer, n. negador m.
disclose, v. revelar.
disclosure, n. descubrimiento m.
discolor, v. descolorar.
discomfort, n. incomodidad f.
disconcert, v. desconcertar.
disconnect, v. desunir; desconectar.
disconnected, a. desunido.
disconsolate, a. desconsolado.
discontent, n. descontento m.
discontented, a. descontento.

discontinue, v. descontinuar.

discord, n. discordia f.

discordant, a. disonante.

discount, n. descuento m.

discourage, v. desalentar, desanimar.

discouragement, n. desaliento, desánimo m.

discourse, n. discurso m.

discourteous, a. descortés.

discourtesy, n. descortesía f.

discover, v. descubrir.

discoverer, n. descubridor -ra.

discovery, n. descubrimiento m.

discreet, a. discreto.

discrepancy, n. discrepancia f.

discretion, n. discreción f.

discriminate, v. distinguir; diferenciar parcialmente.

discrimination, n. discernimiento m.; discriminación f.

discuss, v. discutir.

discussion, n. discusión f.

disdain, 1. n. desdén m. **2.** v. desdeñar.

disdainful, a. desdeñoso.

disease, n. enfermedad f., mal m.

disembark, v. desembarcar.

disentangle, v. desenredar.

disfigure, v. desfigurar.

disgrace, 1. n. vergüenza; deshonra f. **2.** v. deshonrar.

disgraceful, a. vergonzoso.

disguise, 1. n. disfraz m. **2.** v. disfrazar.

disgust, 1. n. fastidio m. **2.** v. fastidiar.

dish, n. plato m.

dishearten, v. desanimar, descorazonar.

dishonest, a. deshonesto.

dishonesty, n. deshonestidad f.

dishonor, 1. n. deshonra f. **2.** v. deshonrar.

dishonorable, a. deshonroso.

disillusion, 1. n. desengaño m. **2.** v. desengañar.

disinfect, v. desinfectar.

disinfectant, n. desinfectante n.

disinherit, v. desheredar.

disintegrate, v. desintegrar.

disinterested, a. desinteresado.

disk, n. disco m.

dislike, 1. n. antipatía f. **2.** v. no gustar de.

dislocate, v. dislocar.

dislodge, v. desalojar.

disloyal, a. desleal; infiel.

disloyalty, n. deslealtad f.

dismal, a. lúgubre.

dismantle, v. desmantelar.

dismay, 1. n. consternación f. **2.** v. consternar.

dismiss, v. despedir.

dismissal, n. despedida f.

dismount, v. apearse.

disobedience, n. desobediencia f.

disobedient, a. desobediente.

disobey, v. desobedecer.

disorder, n. desorden m.

disorderly, a. desarreglado, desordenado.

disown, v. repudiar.

dispassionate, a. desapasionado; templado.

dispatch, 1. n. despacho m. **2.** v. despachar.

dispel, v. dispersar.

dispensary, n. dispensario m.

dispensation, n. dispensación f.

dispense, v. dispensar.

dispersal, n. dispersión f.

disperse, v. dispersar.

displace, v. dislocar.

display, 1. n. despliegue m., exhibición f. **2.** v. desplegar, exhibir.

displease, v. disgustar; ofender.

displeasure, n. disgusto, sinsabor m.

disposable, a. disponible.

disposal, n. disposición f.

dispose, v. disponer.

disposition, n. disposición f.; índole f., genio m.

dispossess, v. desposeer.

disproportionate, a. desproporcionado.

disprove, v. confutar.

dispute, 1. n. disputa f. **2.** v. disputar.

disqualify, v. inhabilitar.

disregard, 1. n. desatención f. **2.** v. desatender.

disrepair, n. descompostura f.

disreputable, a. desacreditado.

disrespect, n. falta de respeto.

disrespectful, a. irrespetuoso.

disrobe, v. desvestir.

disrupt, v. romper; desbaratar.

dissatisfaction, n. descontento m.

dissatisfy, v. descontentar.

dissect, v. disecar.

dissemble, v. disimular.

disseminate, v. diseminar.

dissension, n. disensión f.

dissent, 1. n. disensión f. **2.** v. disentir.

dissertation, n. disertación f.

dissimilar, a. desemejante.

dissipate, v. disipar.

dissipation, n. disipación f.; libertinaje m.

dissolute, a. disoluto.

dissolution, n. disolución f.

dissolve, v. disolver; derretirse.

dissonant, a. disonante.

dissuade, v. disuadir.

distance, n. distancia f. **at a d.,** in the d., a lo lejos.

distant, a. distante, lejano.

distaste, n. disgusto, sinsabor m.

distasteful, a. desagradable.

distill, v. destilar.

distillation, n. destilación f.

distillery, n. destilería f.

distinct, a. distinto.

distinctive, a. distintivo; característico.

distinctly, adv. distintamente.

distinction, n. distinción f.

distinguish, v. distinguir.

distinguished, a. distinguido.

distort, v. falsear; torcer.

distract, v. distraer.

distraction, n. distracción f.

distraught, a. aturrullado; demente.

distress, 1. n. dolor m. **2.** v. afligir.

distribute, v. distribuir.

distribution, n. distribución f.; reparto m.

distributor, n. distribuidor -ra.

district, n. distrito m.

distrust, 1. n. desconfianza f. **2.** v. desconfiar.

distrustful, a. desconfiado; sospechoso.

disturb, v. incomodar; inquietar.

disturbance, n. disturbio m.

ditch, n. zanja f.; foso m.

divan, n. diván m.

dive, 1. n. clavado m.; (coll.) leonera f. **2.** v. echar un clavado; bucear.

diver, n. buzo m.

diverge, v. divergir.

divergence, n. divergencia f.

divergent, a. divergente.

diverse, a. diverso.

diversion, n. diversión f.; pasatiempo m.

diversity, n. diversidad f.

divert, v. desviar; divertir.

divest, v. desnudar, despojar.

divide, v. dividir.

dividend, n. dividendo m.

divine, a. divino.

divinity, n. divinidad f.

division, n. división f.

divorce, 1. n. divorcio m. **2.** v. divorciar.

divorcee, n. divorciada f.

divulge, v. divulgar; revelar.

dizziness, n. vértigo, mareo m.

dizzy, a. mareado.

do, v. hacer.

docile, a. dócil.

dock, 1. n. muelle m. **dry d.,** astillero m. **2.** v. entrar en muelle.

doctor, n. médico m.; doctor -ra.

doctrine, n. doctrina f.

document, n. documento m.

documentary, a. documental.

documentation, n. documentación f.

dodge, 1. n. evasión f. **2.** v. evadir.

doe, n. gama f.

dog, n. perro m.

dogma, n. dogma m.

dogmatic, a. dogmático.

dogmatism, n. dogmatismo m.

doily, n. servilletita f.

doleful, a. triste.

doll, n. muñeca f.

dollar, n. dólar m.

dolorous, a. lastimoso.

dolphin, n. delfín m.

domain, n. dominio m.

dome, n. domo m.

domestic, a. doméstico.

domesticate, v. domesticar.

domicile, n. domicilio m.

dominance, n. dominación f.

dominant, a. dominante.

dominate, v. dominar.

domination, n. dominación f.

domineer, v. dominar.

domineering, a. tiránico, mandón.

dominion, n. dominio; territorio m.

domino, n. dominó m.

donate, v. donar; contribuir.

donation, n. donación f.

donkey, n. asno, burro m.

doom, 1. n. perdición, ruina f. 2. v. perder, ruinar.

door, n. puerta f.

doorman, n. portero m.

doorway, n. entrada f.

dope, n. narcótico m.

dormant, a. durmiente.

dormitory, n. dormitorio m.

dosage, n. dosificación f.

dose, n. dosis f.

dot, n. punto m.

double, 1. a. doble. 2. v. duplicar.

double-breasted, a. cruzado.

double-cross, v. traicionar.

doubly, adv. doblemente.

doubt, 1. n. duda f. 2. v. dudar.

doubtful, a. dudoso, incierto

doubtless, 1. a. indudable. 2. adv. sin duda.

dough, n. pasta, masa f.

doughnut, n. buñuelo m.

dove, n. paloma f.

dowager, n. viuda f.

down, 1. adv. abajo. 2. prep. **d. the street,** etc. calle abajo, etc.

downcast, a. cabizbajo.

downfall, n. ruina, perdición f.

downhearted, a. descorazonado.

downpour, n. chaparrón m.

downright, a. absoluto, completo.

downstairs, 1. adv. abajo. 2. n. primer piso.

downtown, adv. al centro, en el centro.

downward, 1. a. descendente. 2. adv. hacia abajo.

dowry, n. dote m.

doze, v. dormitar.

dozen, n. docena f.

draft, 1. n. dibujo m.; (com.) giro m.; (mil.) conscripción f. 2. v. dibujar; (mil.) reclutar.

draftee, n. conscripto m.

drag, v. arrastrar.

dragon, n. dragón m.

drain, 1. n. desaguadero m. 2. v. desaguar.

drainage, n. drenaje m.

drama, n. drama m.

dramatic, a. dramático.

dramatics, n. dramática f.

dramatist, n. dramaturgo m.

dramatize, v. dramatizar.

drape, n. cortina f.

drapery, n. colgaduras f.pl.; ropaje m.

drastic, a. drástico.

draw, v. dibujar; atraer. **d. up,** formular.

drawback, n. desventaja f.

drawer, n. cajón m.

drawing, n. dibujo m.; rifa f.

dread, 1. n. terror m. 2. v. temer.

dreadful, a. terrible.

dreadfully, adv. horrendamente.

dream, 1. n. sueño, ensueño m. 2. v. soñar.

dreamer, n. soñador -ra; visionario -ia.

dreamy, a. soñador, contemplativo.

dreary, a. monótono y pesado.

dredge, 1. n. rastra f. 2. v. rastrear.

dregs, n. sedimento m.

drench, v. mojar.

dress, 1. *n.* vestido; traje *m.* **2.** *v.* vestir.

dresser, *n.* (furn.) tocador.

dressing, *n.* (med.) curación *f.*; (cookery) condimento, relleno *m.*

dressing gown, *n.* batá *f.*

dressmaker, *n.* modista *m. & f.*

drift, 1. *n.* tendencia *f.*; (nautical) deriva *f.* **2.** *v.* (nautical) derivar; (snow) amontonarse.

drill, 1. *n.* ejercicio *m.*; (mech.) taladro *m.* **2.** *v.* (mech.) taladrar.

drink, 1. *n.* bebida *f.* **2.** *v.* beber, tomar.

drinkable, *a.* potable, bebible.

drip, *v.* gotear.

drive, 1. paseo *m.* **2.** *v.* impeler; (auto) guiar, conducir.

driver, *n.* chofer *m.*

driveway, *n.* entrada para coches.

drizzle, 1. *n.* llovizna *f.* **2.** *v.* lloviznar.

dromedary, *n.* dromedario *m.*

droop, *v.* inclinarse.

drop, 1. *n.* gota *f.* **2.** *v.* soltar; dejar caer.

dropper, *n.* cuentagotas *m.*

dropsy, *n.* hidropesía *f.*

drought, *n.* seca, sequía *f.*

drove, *n.* manada *f.*

drown, *v.* ahogar.

drowse, *v.* adormecer.

drowsiness, *n.* somnolencia *f.*

drowsy, *a.* soñoliento.

drudge, *n.* ganapán *m.*

drudgery, *n.* trabajo penoso.

drug, 1. *n.* droga *f.* **2.** *v.* narcotizar.

druggist, *n.* farmacéutico, boticario *m.*

drugstore, *n.* farmacia, botica, droguería *f.*

drum, *n.* tambor *m.*

drummer, *n.* tambor *m.*

drumstick, *n.* palillo *m.*; (leg) pierna *f.*

drunk, *a. & n.* borracho.

drunkard, *n.* borrachón *m.*

drunken, *a.* borracho; ebrio.

drunkenness, *n.* embriaguez *f.*

dry, 1. *a.* seco, árido. **2.** *v.* secar.

dry cell, *n.* pila seca *f.*

dry-cleaner, *n.* tintorero *m.*

dryness, *n.* sequedad *f.*

dual, *a.* doble.

dubious, *a.* dudoso.

duchess, *n.* duquesa *f.*

duck, 1. *n.* pato *m.* **2.** *v.* zabullir; (avoid) esquivar.

duct, *n.* canal *m.*

due, 1. *a.* debido; (com.) vencido. **2. dues,** *n.* cuota *f.*

duel, *n.* duelo *m.*

duelist, *n.* duelista *f.*

duet, *n.* dúo *m.*

duke, *n.* duque *m.*

dull, *a.* apagado, desteñido; sin punta; (figurative) pesado, soso.

dullness, *n.* estupidez; pesadez *f.*; deslustre *m.*

duly, *adv.* debidamente.

dumb, *a.* mudo; (coll.) estúpido.

dumbwaiter, *n.* montaplatos *m.*

dumfound, *v.* confundir.

dummy, *n.* figurón *m.*

dump, 1. *n.* depósito *m.* **2.** *v.* descargar.

dune, *n.* duna *f.*

dungeon, *n.* calabozo *m.*

dunk, *v.* mojar.

dupe, *v.* engañar.

duplicate, 1. *a. & n.* duplicado *m.* **2.** *v.* duplicar.

duplication, *n.* duplicación *f.*

duplicity, *n.* duplicidad *f.*

durability, *n.* durabilidad *f.*

durable, *a.* durable, duradero.

duration, *n.* duración *f.*

duress, *n.* compulsión *m.*; encierro *m.*

during, *prep.* durante.

dusk, *n.* crepúsculo *m.*

dusky, *a.* oscuro; moreno.

dust, 1. *n.* polvo *m.* **2.** *v.* polvorear; despolvorear.

dusty, *a.* empolvado.

Dutch, *a.* holandés -sa.

dutiful, *a.* respetuoso.

dutifully, *adv.* respetuosamente, obedientemente.

duty, *n.* deber *m.*; (com.) derechos *m.pl.*

dwarf, **1.** *n.* enano -na. **2.** *v.* achicar.

dwell, *v.* habitar, residir. **d. on**, espaciarse en.

dwelling, *n.* morada, casa *f.*

dwindle, *v.* disminuirse.

dye, **1.** *n.* tintura *f.* **2.** *v.* teñir.

dyer, *n.* tintorero -ra.

dynamic, *a.* dinámico.

dynamite, *n.* dinamita *f.*

dynamo, *n.* dínamo *m.*

dynasty, *n.* dinastía *f.*

dysentery, *n.* disentería *f.*

dyspepsia, *n.* dispepsia *f.*

E

each, **1.** *a.* cada. **2.** *pron.* cada uno -na. **e. other**, el uno al otro.

eager, *a.* ansioso.

eagerly, *adv.* ansiosamente.

eagerness, *n.* ansia *f.*

eagle, *n.* águila *f.*

ear, *n.* oído *m.*; (outer) oreja *f.*; (of corn) mazorca *f.*

earache, *n.* dolor de oído *m.*

earl, *n.* conde *m.*

early, *a. & adv.* temprano.

earn, *v.* ganar.

earnest, *a.* serio.

earnestly, *adv.* seriamente.

earnings, *n.* ganancias *f.pl.*; (com.) ingresos *m.pl.*

earphone, *n.* auricular *m.*

earring, *n.* pendiente, arete *m.*

earth, *n.* tierra *f.*

earthquake, *n.* terremoto *m.*

ease, **1.** *n.* reposo *m.*; facilidad *f.* **2.** *v.* aliviar.

easel, *n.* caballete *m.*

easily, *adv.* fácilmente.

east, *n.* oriente, este *m.*

Easter, *n.* Pascua Florida.

eastern, *a.* oriental.

eastward, *adv.* hacia el este.

easy, *a.* fácil.

eat, *v.* comer.

eaves, *n.* socarrén *m.*

ebb, **1.** *n.* menguante *f.* **2.** *v.* menguar.

ebony, *n.* ébano *m.*

eccentric, *a.* excéntrico.

eccentricity, *n.* excentricidad *f.*

ecclesiastic, *a. & n.* eclesiástico *m.*

ecclesiastical, *a.* eclesiástico.

echelon, *n.* escalón *m.*

echo, *n.* eco *m.*

eclipse, **1.** *n.* eclipse *m.* **2.** *v.* eclipsar.

economic, *a.* económico.

economical, *a.* económico.

economics, *n.* economía política.

economist, *n.* economista *m.*

economize, *v.* economizar.

economy, *n.* economía *f.*

ecstasy, *n.* éxtasis *m.*

Ecuadorian, *a. & n.* ecuatoriano -na.

eczema, *n.* eczema *f.*

eddy, **1.** *n.* remolino *m.* **2.** *v.* remolinar.

edge, **1.** *n.* filo; borde *m.* **2.** *v.* **e. one's way**, abrirse paso.

edible, *a.* comestible.

edict, *n.* edicto *m.*

edifice, *n.* edificio *m.*

edify, *v.* edificar.

edition, *n.* edición *f.*

editor, *n.* redactor *m.*

editorial, *n.* editorial *m.* **e. staff**, redacción *f.*

educate, *v.* educar.

education, *n.* instrucción; enseñanza *f.*

educational, *a.* educativo.

educator, *n.* educador, pedagogo *m.*

eel, *n.* anguila *f.*

efface, *v.* tachar.

effect, 1. *n.* efecto *m.* **in e.,** en vigor. **2.** *v.* efectuar, realizar.

effective, *a.* eficaz; efectivo; en vigor.

effectively, *adv.* eficazmente.

effectiveness, *n.* efectividad *f.*

effectual, *a.* eficaz.

effeminate, *a.* afeminado.

efficacy, *n.* eficacia *f.*

efficiency, *n.* eficiencia *f.*

efficient, *a.* eficaz.

efficiently, *adv.* eficazmente.

effigy, *n.* efigie *f.*

effort, *n.* esfuerzo *m.*

effrontery, *n.* impudencia *f.*

effusive, *a.* expansivo.

egg, *n.* huevo *m.* **fried e.,** huevo frito. **soft-boiled e.,** h. pasado por agua. **scrambled eggs,** huevos revueltos.

eggplant, *n.* berenjena *f.*

egoism, egotism, *n.* egoísmo *m.*

egoist, egotist, *n.* egoísta *m. & f.*

egotism, *n.* egotismo *m.*

egotist, *n.* egotista *m.*

Egypt, *n.* Egipto *m.*

Egyptian, *a. & n.* egipcio *f.* -ia.

eight, *a. & pron.* ocho.

eighteen, *a. & pron.* dieciocho.

eighth, *a.* octavo.

eightieth, *n.* octogésimo *m.*

eighty, *a. & pron.* ochenta.

either, 1. *a. & pron.* cualquiera de los dos. **2.** *adv.* tampoco. **3.** *conj.* **either ... or,** o ... o.

ejaculate, *v.* exclamar.

eject, *v.* expeler.

ejection, *n.* expulsión *f.*

elaborate, 1. *a.* elaborado. **2.** *v.* elaborar; ampliar.

elapse, *v.* transcurrir; pasar.

elastic, *a. & n.* elástico *m.*

elasticity, *n.* elasticidad *f.*

elate, *v.* exaltar.

elation, *n.* exaltación *f.*

elbow, *n.* codo *m.*

elder, 1. *a.* mayor. **2.** *n.* anciano *m.*

elderly, *a.* de edad.

eldest, *a.* mayor.

elect, *v.* elegir.

election, *n.* elección *f.*

elective, *a.* electivo.

electorate, *n.* electorado *m.*

electric, electrical, *a.* eléctrico.

electrician, *n.* electricista *m.*

electricity, *n.* electricidad *f.*

electrocute, *v.* electrocutar.

electrode, *n.* electrodo *m.*

electrolysis, *n.* electrólisis *f.*

electron, *n.* electrón *m.*

electronics, *n.* electrónica *f.*

elegance, *n.* elegancia *f.*

elegant, *a.* elegante.

elegy, *n.* elegía *f.*

element, *n.* elemento *m.*

elemental, *a.* elemental.

elementary, *a.* elemental.

elephant, *n.* elefante *m.*

elevate, *v.* elevar.

elevation, *n.* elevación *f.*

elevator, *n.* ascensor *m.*

eleven, *a. & pron.* once.

eleventh, *a.* undécimo.

elf, *n.* duende *m.*

elicit, *v.* sacar; despertar.

eligibility, *n.* elegibilidad *f.*

eligible, *a.* elegible.

eliminate, *v.* eliminar.

elimination, *n.* eliminación *f.*

elixir, *n.* elixir *m.*

elk, *n.* alce *m.*, anta *f.*

elm, *n.* olmo *m.*

elocution, *n.* elocución *f.*

elongate, *v.* alargar.

elope, *v.* fugarse.

eloquence, *n.* elocuencia *f.*

eloquent, *a.* elocuente.

eloquently, *adv.* elocuentemente.

else, *adv.* más. **someone e.,** otra persona. **something e.,** otra cosa. **or e.,** de otro modo.

elsewhere, *adv.* en otra parte.

elucidate, *v.* elucidar.

elude, *v.* eludir.

elusive, *a.* evasivo.

emaciated, *a.* enflaquecido.

emanate, *v.* emanar.

emancipate, *v.* emancipar.

emancipation, *n.* emancipación *f.*

emancipator, *n.* libertador *m.*

embalm, *v.* embalsamar.

embankment, n. malecón, dique m.

embargo, n. embargo m.

embark, v. embarcar.

embarrass, v. avergonzar; turbar.

embarrassing, a. penoso, vergonzoso.

embarrassment, n. turbación; vergüenza f.

embassy, n. embajada f.

embellish, v. hermosear, embellecer.

embellishment, n. embellecimiento m.

embezzle, v. apropiarse dinero ilícitamente.

emblem, n. emblema m.

embody, v. incorporar.

embrace, 1. n. abrazo m. **2.** v. abrazar.

embroider, v. bordar.

embroidery, n. bordado m.

embryo, n. embrión m.

embryonic, a. embrionario.

emerald, n. esmeralda f.

emerge, v. salir.

emergency, n. emergencia f.

emergent, a. emergente.

emery, n. esmeril m.

emetic, n. emético m.

emigrant, a. & n. emigrante m. & f.

emigrate, v. emigrar.

emigration, n. emigración f.

eminence, n. altura; eminencia f.

eminent, a. eminente.

emissary, n. emisario m.

emit, v. emitir.

emolument, n. emolumento m.

emotion, n. emoción f.

emotional, a. sensible.

emperor, n. emperador m.

emphasis, n. énfasis m. or f.

emphasize, v. acentuar, recalcar.

emphatic, a. enfático.

empire, n. imperio m.

empirical, a. empírico.

employ, v. emplear.

employee, n. empleado -da.

employer, n. patrón -ona.

employment, n. empleo m.

empower, v. autorizar.

emptiness, n. vaciedad; futilidad f.

empty, 1. a. vacío. **2.** v. vaciar.

emulate, v. emular.

emulsion, n. emulsión f.

enable, v. capacitar; permitir.

enact, v. promulgar, decretar.

enactment, n. ley f., estatuto m.

enamel, 1. n. esmalte m. **2.** v. esmaltar.

enamored, a. enamorado.

enchant, v. encantar.

enchantment, n. encanto m.

encircle, v. circundar.

enclose, v. encerrar. **enclosed,** (in letter) adjunto.

enclosure, n. recinto m.; (in letter) incluso m.

encompass, v. circundar.

encounter, 1. n. encuentro m. **2.** v. encontrar.

encourage, v. animar.

encouragement, n. estímulo m.

encroach, v. usurpar; meterse.

encyclical, n. encíclica f.

encyclopedia, n. enciclopedia f.

end, 1. n. fin, término, cabo; extremo; (aim) propósito m. **2.** v. acabar; terminar.

endanger, v. poner en peligro.

endear, v. hacer querer.

endeavor, 1. n. esfuerzo. **2.** v. esforzarse.

ending, n. conclusión f.

endless, a. sin fin.

endorse, v. endosar; apoyar.

endorsement, n. endoso m.

endow, v. dotar, fundar.

endowment, n. dotación f., fundación f.

endurance, n. resistencia f.

endure, v. soportar, resistir, aguantar.

enema, n. enema; lavativa f.

enemy, n. enemigo -ga.

energetic, a. enérgico.

energy, n. energía f.

enervate, v. enervar.

enervation, n. enervación f.

enfold, v. envolver.

enforce, v. ejecutar.

enforcement, n. ejecución f.

engage, v. emplear; ocupar.

engaged (to marry) comprometido.

engagement, *n.* combate; compromiso; contrato *m.*; cita *f.*

engine, *n.* máquina *f.* (railroad) locomotora *f.*

engineer, *n.* ingeniero; maquinista *m.*

engineering, *n.* ingeniería *f.*

England, *n.* Inglaterra *f.*

English, *a. & n.* inglés *m.*

Englishman, *n.* inglés *m.*

Englishwoman, *n.* inglesa *f.*

engrave, *v.* grabar.

engraver, *n.* grabador *m.*

engraving, *n.* grabado *m.*

engross, *v.* absorber.

enhance, *v.* aumentar en valor; realzar.

enigma, *n.* enigma *m.*

enigmatic, *a.* enigmático.

enjoy, *v.* gozar de; disfrutar de. **e. oneself,** divertirse.

enjoyable, *a.* agradable.

enjoyment, *n.* goce *m.*

enlarge, *v.* agrandar; ampliar.

enlargement, *n.* ensanchamiento *m.*, ampliación *f.*

enlarger, *n.* amplificador *m.*

enlighten, *v.* informar.

enlightenment, *n.* esclarecimiento *m.*; cultura *f.*

enlist, *v.* reclutar; alistarse.

enlistment, *n.* alistamiento *m.*

enliven, *v.* avivar.

enmesh, *v.* entrampar.

enmity, *n.* enemistad *f.*

enormity, *n.* enormidad *f.*

enormous, *a.* enorme.

enough, *a. & adv.* bastante. **to be e.,** bastar.

enrage, *v.* enfurecer.

enrich, *v.* enriquecer.

enroll, *v.* registrar; matricularse.

enrollment, *n.* matriculación *f.*

ensign, *n.* bandera *f.*; (naval) sub-teniente *m.*

enslave, *v.* esclavizar.

ensue, *v.* seguir, resultar.

entail, *v.* envolver.

entangle, *v.* enredar.

enter, *v.* entrar.

enterprise, *n.* empresa *f.*

enterprising, *a.* emprendedor.

entertain, *v.* entretener; divertir.

entertainment, *n.* entretenimiento *m.*; diversión *f.*

enthrall, *v.* esclavizar.

enthusiasm, *n.* entusiasmo *m.*

enthusiast, *n.* entusiasta *m. & f.*

enthusiastic, *a.* entusiasmado.

entice, *v.* inducir.

entire, *a.* entero.

entirely, *adv.* enteramente.

entirety, *n.* totalidad *f.*

entitle, *v.* autorizar; (book) titular.

entity, *n.* entidad *f.*

entrails, *n.* entrañas *f.pl.*

entrance, *n.* entrada *f.*

entrant, *n.* competidor *m.*

entreat, *v.* rogar, suplicar.

entreaty, *n.* ruego *m.*, súplica *f.*

entrench, *v.* atrincherar.

entrust, *v.* confiar.

entry, *n.* entrada *f.*; (com.) partida *f.*

enumerate, *v.* enumerar.

enumeration, *n.* enumeración *f.*

enunciate, *v.* enunciar.

enunciation, *n.* enunciación *f.*

envelop, *v.* envolver.

envelope, *n.* sobre *m.*, cubierta *f.*

enviable, *a.* envidiable.

envious, *a.* envidioso.

environment, *n.* ambiente *m.*

environs, *n.* alrededores *m.*

envoy, *n.* enviado *m.*

envy, 1. *n.* envidia *f.* **2.** *v.* envidiar.

eon, *n.* eón *m.*

ephemeral, *a.* efímero.

epic, 1. *a.* épico. **2.** *n.* epopeya *f.*

epicure, *n.* epicúreo *m.*

epidemic, 1. *a.* epidémico. **2.** *n.* epidemia *f.*

epidermis, *n.* epidermis *f.*

epigram, *n.* epigrama *f.*

epilepsy, *n.* epilepsia *f.*

epilogue, *n.* epílogo *m.*

episode, n. episodio m.

epistle, n. epístola f.

epitaph, n. epitafio m.

epithet, n. epíteto m.

epitome, n. epítome m.

epoch, n. época, era f.

equal, 1. a. & n. igual m. **2.** v. igualar; equivaler.

equality, n. igualdad f.

equalize, v. igualar.

equanimity, n. ecuanimidad f.

equate, v. igualar.

equation, n. ecuación f.

equator, n. ecuador m.

equatorial, n. & a. ecuatorial f.

equestrian, 1. n. jinete m. **2.** a. ecuestre.

equilibrium, n. equilibrio m.

equinox, n. equinoccio m.

equip, v. equipar.

equipment, n. equipo m.

equitable, a. equitativo.

equity, n. equidad, justicia f.

equivalent, a. & n. equivalente m.

equivocal, a. equívoco, ambiguo.

era, n. era, época, edad f.

eradicate, v. extirpar.

erase, v. borrar.

eraser, n. borrador m.

erasure, n. borradura f.

erect, 1. a. derecho, erguido. **2.** v. erigir.

erection, erectness, n. erección f.

ermine, n. armiño m.

erode, v. corroer.

erosion, n. erosión f.

erotic, a. erótico.

err, v. equivocarse.

errand, n. encargo, recado m.

errant, a. errante.

erratic, a. errático.

erroneous, a. erróneo.

error, n. error m.

erudite, a. erudito.

erudition, n. erudición f.

eruption, n. erupción, irrupción f.

escalator, n. escalera mecánica f.

escapade, n. escapada; correría f.

escape, 1. n. fuga, huída f.

fire e., escalera de salvamento. **2.** v. escapar; fugarse.

eschew, v. evadir.

escort, 1. n. escolta f. **2.** v. escoltar.

escrow, n. plica f.

escutcheon, n. escudo de armas m.

esophagus, n. esófago m.

esoteric, a. esotérico.

especially, adv. especialmente.

espionage, n. espionaje m.

essay, n. ensayo m.

essayist, n. ensayista.

essence, n. esencia f.; perfume m.

essential, a. esencial.

essentially, adv. esencialmente.

establish, v. establecer.

establishment, n. establecimiento m.

estate, n. estado m.; hacienda f.; bienes m.pl.

esteem, 1. n. estima f. **2.** v. estimar.

estimable, a. estimable.

estimate, 1. n. cálculo; presupuesto m. **2.** v. estimar.

estimation, n. estimación f.; cálculo m.

estrange, v. extrañar; enajenar.

estuary, n. estuario m.

etching, n. grabado al agua fuerte.

eternal, a. eterno.

eternity, n. eternidad f.

ether, n. éter m.

ethereal, a. etéreo.

ethical, a. ético.

ethics, n. ética f.

etiquette, n. etiqueta f.

etymology, n. etimología f.

eucalyptus, n. eucalipto m.

eugenic, a. eugenésico.

eugenics, n. eugenesia f.

eulogize, v. elogiar.

eulogy, n. elogio m.

eunuch, n. eunuco m.

euphonious, a. eufónico.

Europe, n. Europa f.

European, a. & n. europeo -pea.

euthanasia, n. eutanasia f.

evacuate, v. evacuar.

evade, v. evadir.
evaluate, v. avaluar.
evaluation, n. valoración f.
evangelist, n. evangelista m.
evaporate, v. evaporarse.
evaporation, n. evaporación f.
evasion, n. evasión f.
evasive, a. evasivo.
eve, n. víspera f.
even, 1. a. llano; igual. **2.** adv. aun; hasta. **not e.,** ni siquiera.
evening, n. noche, tarde f. **good e.,** buenas noches.
evenness, n. uniformidad f.
event, n. acontecimiento, suceso m.
eventful, a. memorable.
eventual, a. eventual.
ever, adv. alguna vez; (after not) nunca. **e. since,** desde que.
everlasting, a. eterno.
every, a. cada, todos los.
everybody, pron. todo el mundo; cada uno.
everyday, a. ordinario, de cada día.
everyone, pron. cada uno; cada cual; todos.
everything, pron. todo m.
everywhere, adv. por todas partes, en todas partes.
evict, v. expulsar.
eviction, n. evicción f.
evidence, n. evidencia f.
evident, a. evidente.
evidently, adv. evidentemente.
evil, 1. a. malo; maligno. **2.** n. mal m.
evince, v. revelar.
evoke, v. evocar.
evolution, n. evolución f.
evolve, v. desenvolver; desarrollar.
ewe, n. oveja f.
exact, 1. a. exacto. **2.** v. exigir.
exacting, a. exigente.
exactly, adv. exactamente.
exaggerate, v. exagerar.
exaggeration, n. exageración f.
exalt, v. exaltar.
exaltation, n. exaltación f.

examination, n. examen m.; (legal) interrogatorio m.
examine, v. examinar.
example, n. ejemplo m.
exasperate, v. exasperar.
exasperation, n. exasperación f.
excavate, v. excavar, cavar.
exceed, v. exceder.
exceedingly, adv. sumamente, extremadamente.
excel, v. sobresalir.
excellence, n. excelencia f.
Excellency, n. (title) Excelencia f.
excellent, a. excelente.
except, 1. prep. salvo, excepto. **2.** v. exceptuar.
exception, n. excepción f.
exceptional, a. excepcional.
excerpt, n. extracto.
excess, n. exceso m.
excessive, a. excesivo.
exchange, 1. n. cambio; canje m. **stock e.,** bolsa f. **telephone e.,** central telefónica. **2.** v. cambiar, canjear.
exchangeable, a. cambiable.
excise, 1. n. sisa f. **2.** v. extirpar.
excite, v. agitar; provocar; emocionar.
excitement, n. agitación, conmoción f.
exciting, a. emocionante.
exclaim, v. exclamar.
exclamation, n. exclamación f.
exclamation point or mark, n. punto de admiración m.
exclude, v. excluir.
exclusion, n. exclusión f.
exclusive, a. exclusivo.
excommunicate, v. excomulgar, descomulgar.
excommunication, n. excomunión f.
excrement, n. excremento m.
excruciating, a. penosísimo.
exculpate, v. justificar.
excursion, n. excursión; jira f.
excuse, 1. n. excusa f. **2.** v. excusar, perdonar; dispensar; disculpar.

execrable, *a.* execrable.
execute, *v.* ejecutar.
execution, *n.* ejecución *f.*
executioner, *n.* verdugo *m.*
executive, *a. & n.* ejecutivo *m.*
executor, *n.* testamentario *m.*
exemplary, *a.* ejemplar.
exemplify, *v.* ejemplificar.
exempt, 1. *a.* exento. 2. *v.* exentar.
exercise, 1. *n.* ejercicio *m.* 2. *v.* ejercitar.
exert, *v.* esforzar.
exertion, *n.* esfuerzo *m.*
exhale, *v.* exhalar.
exhaust, 1. *n.* (auto.) escape *m.* 2. *v.* agotar.
exhaustion, *n.* agotamiento *m.*
exhaustive, *a.* agotador.
exhibit, 1. *n.* exhibición, exposición *f.* 2. *v.* exhibir.
exhibition, *n.* exhibición *f.*
exhilarate, *v.* alegrar; estimular.
exhort, *v.* exhortar.
exhortation, *n.* exhortación *f.*
exhume, *v.* exhumar.
exigency, *n.* exigencia *f.*, urgencia *f.*
exile, 1. *n.* destierro *m.*, (person) desterrado *m.* 2. *v.* desterrar.
exist, *v.* existir.
existence, *n.* existencia *f.*
existent, *a.* existente.
exit, *n.* salida *f.*
exodus, *n.* éxodo *m.*
exonerate, *v.* exonerar.
exorbitant, *a.* exorbitante.
exorcise, *v.* exorcizar.
exotic, *a.* exótico.
expand, *v.* dilatar; ensanchar.
expanse, *n.* espacio *m.*; extensión *f.*
expansion, *n.* expansión *f.*
expansive, *a.* expansivo.
expatiate, *v.* espaciarse.
expatriate, 1. *n. & a.* expatriado *m.* 2. *v.* expatriar.
expect, *v.* esperar; contar con.
expectancy, *n.* expectación *f.*
expectation, *n.* esperanza *f.*
expectorate, *v.* expectorar.

expediency, *n.* conveniencia *f.*
expedient, 1. *a.* oportuno. 2. *n.* expediente *m.*
expedite, *v.* acelerar, despachar.
expedition, *n.* expedición *f.*
expel, *v.* expeler, expulsar.
expend, *v.* desembolsar, expender.
expenditure, *n.* desembolso, gasto *m.*
expense, *n.* gasto *m.*; costa *f.*
expensive, *a.* caro, costoso.
expensively, *adv.* costosamente.
experience, 1. *n.* experiencia *f.* 2. *v.* experimentar.
experienced, *a.* experimentado, perito.
experiment, 1. *n.* experimento *m.* 2. *v.* experimentar.
experimental, *a.* experimental.
expert, *a. & n.* experto *m.*
expiate, *v.* expiar.
expiration, *n.* expiración *f.*
expire, *v.* expirar; (com.) vencerse.
explain, *v.* explicar.
explanation, *n.* explicación *f.*
explanatory, *a.* explicativo.
expletive, 1. *n.* interjección *f.* 2. *a.* expletivo.
explicit, *a.* explícito, claro.
explode, *v.* estallar, volar; refutar.
exploit, 1. *n.* hazaña *f.* 2. *v.* explotar.
exploitation, *n.* explotación *f.*
exploration, *n.* exploración *f.*
exploratory, *a.* exploratorio.
explore, *v.* explorar.
explorer, *n.* explorador *m.*
explosion, *n.* explosión *f.*
explosive, *a.* explosivo.
export, 1. *n.* exportación *f.* 2. *v.* exportar.
exportation, *n.* exportación *f.*
expose, *v.* exponer; descubrir.
exposition, *n.* exposición *f.*
expository, *a.* expositivo.
expostulate, *v.* altercar.

exposure, *n.* exposición *f.*

expound, *v.* exponer, explicar.

express, 1. *a. & n.* expreso *m.* **e. company,** compañía de porteo. **2.** *v.* expresar.

expression, *n.* expresión *f.*

expressive, *a.* expresivo.

expressly, *adv.* expresamente.

expressman, *n.* empresario de expresos *m.*

expropriate, *v.* expropriar.

expulsion, *n.* expulsión *f.*

expunge, *v.* borrar, expurgar.

expurgate, *v.* expurgar.

exquisite, *a.* exquisito.

extemporaneous, *a.* improvisado.

extend, *v.* extender.

extension, *n.* extensión *f.*

extensive, *a.* extenso.

extensively, *adv.* por extenso.

extent, *n.* extensión *f.*; grado *m.* **to a certain e.,** hasta cierto punto.

extenuate, *v.* extenuar.

exterior, *a. & n.* exterior *m.*

exterminate, *v.* exterminar.

extermination, *n.* exterminio *m.*

external, *a.* externo, exterior.

extinct, *a.* extinto.

extinction, *n.* extinción *f.*

extinguish, *v.* extinguir, apagar.

extol, *v.* alabar.

extort, *v.* exigir dinero sin derecho.

extortion, *n.* extorsión *f.*

extra, 1. *a.* extraordinario; adicional. **2.** *n.* (jour.) extra *m.*

exract, 1. *n.* extracto *m.* **2.** *v.* extraer.

extraction, *n.* extracción *f.*

extraneous, *a.* extraño; ajeno.

extraordinary, *a.* extraordinario.

extravagance, *n.* extravagancia *f.*

extravagant, *a.* extravagante.

extreme, *a. & n.* extremo *m.*

extremity, *n.* extremidad *f.*

extricate, *v.* desenredar.

exuberant, *a.* exuberante.

exude, *v.* exudar.

exult, *v.* regocijarse.

exultant, *a.* triunfante.

eye, 1. *n.* ojo *m.* **2.** *v.* ojear.

eyeball, *n.* globo del ojo.

eyebrow, *n.* ceja *f.*

eyeglasses, *n.* lentes *m.*

eyelash, *n.* pestaña *f.*

eyelid, *n.* párpado *m.*

eyesight, *n.* vista *f.*

F

fable, *n.* fábula; ficción *f.*

fabric, *n.* tejido *m.*, tela *f.*

fabricate, *v.* fabricar.

fabulous, *a.* fabuloso.

façade, *n.* fachada *f.*

face, 1. *n.* cara *f.* **to make faces,** hacer muecas. **2.** encararse con. **f. the street,** dar a la calle.

facet, *n.* faceta *f.*

facetious, *a.* chistoso.

facial, 1. *n.* masaje facial *m.* **2.** *a.* facial.

facile, *a.* fácil.

facilitate, *v.* facilitar.

facility, *n.* facilidad *f.*

facsimile, *n.* facsímile *m.*

fact, *n.* hecho *m.* **in f.,** en realidad.

faction, *n.* facción *f.*

factor, *n.* factor *m.*

factory, *n.* fábrica *f.*

factual, *a.* verdadero.

faculty, *n.* facultad *f.*

fad, *n.* boga; novedad *f.*

fade, v. desteñirse; (flowers) marchitarse.

fail, 1. n. **without f.,** sin falla. **2.** v. fallar; fracasar. **not to f. to,** no dejar de.

failure, n. fracaso m.

faint, 1. a. débil; vago; pálido. **2.** n. desmayo m. **3.** v. desmayarse.

faintly, adv. débilmente; indistintamente.

fair, 1. a. razonable, justo; (hair) rubio; (weather) bueno. **2.** n. feria f.

fairly, adv. imparcialmente; regularmente; claramente; bellamente.

fairness, n. justicia f.

fairy, n. hada f., duende m.

faith, n. fe; confianza f.

faithful, a. fiel.

fake, 1. a. falso; postizo. **2.** n. imitación; estafa f. **3.** v. imitar; fingir.

faker, n. imitador m.; farsante m.

falcon, n. halcón m.

fall, 1. n. caída; catarata f.; (season) otoño m.; (in price) baja f. **2.** v. caer; bajar. **f. asleep,** dormirse; **f. in love,** enamorarse.

fallacious, a. falaz.

fallacy, n. falacia f.

fallible, a. falible.

fallow, a. sin cultivar.

false, a. falso; postizo.

falsehood, n. falsedad; mentira f.

falseness, n. falsedad, perfidia f.

falsetto, n. falsete m.

falsification, n. falsificación f.

falsify, v. falsificar.

falter, v. vacilar; (in speech) tartamudear.

fame, n. fama f.

familiar, 1. a. familiar; conocido. **to be f. with,** estar familiarizado con.

familiarity, n. familiaridad f.

familiarize, v. familiarizar.

family, n. familia f.; especie naje m.

famine, n. hambre; carestía f.

famished, a. muerto de hambre.

famous, a. famoso, célebre.

fan, n. abanico; ventilador m. (sports) aficionado -da.

fanatic, a. & n. fanático -ca.

fanatical, a. fanático.

fanaticism, n. fanatismo m.

fanciful, a. caprichoso; fantástico.

fancy, 1. a. fino, elegante. **f. goods,** novedades f.pl. **2.** n. fantasía f.; capricho m. **3.** v. imaginar.

fanfare, n. fanfarria f.

fang, n. colmillo m.

fantastic, a. fantástico.

fantasy, n. fantasía f.

far, 1. a. lejano, distante. **2.** adv. lejos. **how f.,** a qué distancia. **as f. as,** hasta. **so f., thus f.,** hasta aquí.

farce, n. farsa f.

fare, n. pasaje m.

farewell, 1. n. despedida f. **to say f.** despedirse. **2.** interj. ¡adiós!

far-fetched, a. forzado.

farm, 1. n. granja; hacienda f. **2.** v. cultivar, labrar la tierra.

farmer, n. labrador, agricultor m.

farmhouse, n. hacienda, alquería f.

farming, n. agricultura f.; cultivo m.

fascinate, v. fascinar, embelesar.

fascination, n. fascinación f.

fascism, n. fascismo m.

fashion, 1. n. moda; costumbre; guisa f. **2.** v. formar.

fashionable, a. de moda, en boga.

fast, 1. a. rápido, veloz; (watch) adelantado; (color) firme. **2.** adv. ligero, de prisa. **3.** n. ayuno m. **4.** v. ayunar.

fasten, v. afirmar, atar; fijar.

fastener, n. asegurador m.

fastidious, a. melindroso.

fat, 1. a. gordo. **2.** n. grasa, manteca f.

fatal, *a.* fatal.

fatality, *n.* fatalidad *f.*

fatally, *adv.* fatalmente.

fate, *n.* destino *m.*; suerte *f.*

fateful, *a.* fatal; ominoso.

father, *n.* padre *m.*

fatherhood, *n.* paternidad *f.*

father-in-law, *n.* suegro *m.*

fatherland, *n.* patria *f.*

fatherly, 1. *a.* paternal. 2. *adv.* paternalmente.

fathom, 1. *n.* braza *f.* 2. *v.* sondar; (fig.) penetrar en.

fatigue, 1. *n.* fatiga *f.*, cansancio *m.* 2. *v.* fatigar, cansar.

fatten, *v.* engordar, cebar.

faucet, *n.* grifo *m.*, llave *f.*

fault, *n.* culpa *f.*; defecto *m.* **at f.,** culpable.

faultless, *a.* sin tacha, perfecto.

faultlessly, *adv.* perfectamente.

faulty, *a.* defectuoso, imperfecto.

favor, 1. *n.* favor *m.* 2. *v.* favorecer.

favorable, *a.* favorable.

favorite, *a. & n.* favorito -ta.

favoritism, *n.* favoritismo *m.*

fawn, 1. *n.* cervato *m.* 2. *v.* halagar, adular.

faze, *v.* desconcertar.

fear, 1. *n.* miedo, temor *m.* 2. *v.* temer.

fearful, *a.* temeroso, medroso.

fearless, *a.* intrépido; sin temor.

fearlessness, *n.* intrepidez *f.*

feasible, *a.* factible.

feast, *n.* banquete *m.*; fiesta *f.*

feat, *n.* hazaña *f.*; hecho *m.*

feather, *n.* pluma *f.*

feature, 1. *n.* facción *f.*; rasgo *m.*; (movies) película principal. 2. *v.* presentar como atracción especial.

February, *n.* febrero *m.*

federal, *a.* federal.

federation, *n.* confederación, federación *f.*

fee, *n.* honorarios *m. pl.*

feeble, *a.* débil.

feeble-minded, *a.* necio.

feebleness, *a.* debilidad *f.*

feed, 1. *n.* pasto *m.* 2. *v.* alimentar; dar de comer. **fed up with,** harto de.

feel, 1. *n.* sensación *f.* 2. *v.* sentir; palpar. **f. like,** tener ganas de.

feeling, *n.* sensación; sensibilidad *f.*

feign, *v.* fingir.

felicitate, *v.* felicitar.

felicitous, *a.* feliz.

felicity, *n.* felicidad *f.*, dicha *f.*

feline, *a.* felino.

fellow, *n.* compañero; socio *m.*; (coll.) tipo *m.*

fellowship, *n.* compañía; (for study) beca *f.*

felon, *n.* reo *m.*, felón *m.*

felony, *n.* felonía *f.*

felt, *n.* fieltro *m.*

female, *a. & n.* hembra *f.*

feminine, *a.* femenino.

fence, 1. *n.* cerca *f.* 2. *v.* cercar.

fender, *n.* guardabarros *m.*

ferment, 1. *n.* fermento *m.*; (fig) agitación *f.* 2. *v.* fermentar.

fermentation, *n.* fermentación *f.*

fern, *n.* helecho *m.*

ferocious, *a.* feroz; fiero.

ferociously, *adv.* ferozmente.

ferocity, *n.* ferocidad, fiereza *f.*

ferry, *n.* transbordador *m.*, barca de transporte.

fertile, *a.* fecundo; (land) fértil.

fertility, *n.* fertilidad *f.*

fertilization, *n.* fertilización *f.*

fertilize, *v.* fertilizar, abonar.

fertilizer, *n.* abono *m.*

fervency, *n.* ardor *m.*

fervent, *a.* ferviente.

fervently, *adv.* fervorosamente.

fervid, *a.* férvido.

fervor, *n.* fervor *m.*

fester, *v.* ulcerarse.

festival, *n.* fiesta *f.*

festive, *a.* festivo.

festivity, n. festividad f.

festoon, 1. n. festón m. **2.** v. festonear.

fetch, v. ir por; traer.

fete, 1. n. fiesta f. **2.** v. festejar.

fetid, a. fétido.

fetish, n. fetiche m.

fetter, 1. n. grillete m. **2.** v. engrillar.

fetus, n. feto m.

feud, n. riña f.; feudo m.

feudal, a. feudal.

feudalism, n. feudalismo m.

fever, n. fiebre f.

feverish, a. febril.

feverishly, adv. febrilmente.

few, a. pocos. **a f.,** algunos, unos cuantos.

fiancé, fiancée, n. novio -via.

fiasco, n. fiasco m.

fiat, n. fiat m., orden f.

fib, 1. n. mentira f. **2.** v. mentir.

fiber, n. fibra f

fibrous, a. fibroso.

fickle, a. caprichoso.

fickleness, n. inconstancia f.

fiction, n. ficción f.; (literature) novelas f.pl.

fictitious, a. ficticio.

fidelity, n. fidelidad f.

fidget, v. inquietar.

field, n. campo m.

fiend, n. demonio m.

fiendish, a. diabólico, malvado.

fierce, a. fiero, feroz.

fiery, a. ardiente.

fiesta, n. fiesta f.

fife, n. pífano m.

fifteen, a. & pron. quince.

fifteenth, n. & a. décimoquinto.

fifth, a. quinto.

fifty, a. & pron. cincuenta.

fig, n. higo m. **f. tree,** higuera f.

fight, 1. n. lucha, pelea f. **2.** v. luchar, pelear.

fighter, n. peleador -ra, luchador -ra.

figment, n. invención f.

figurative, a. metafórico.

figuratively, adv. figuradamente.

figure, 1. n. figura; cifra f. **2.** v. figurar; calcular.

filament, n. filamento m.

file, 1. n. archivo m.; (instrument) lima f.; (row) fila f. **2.** v. archivar; limar.

filial, a. filial.

filigree, n. filigrana f.

fill, v. llenar.

fillet, n. filete m.

filling, n. relleno m.; (dental) empastadura f. **f. station,** bomba f.

film, 1. n. película f., film m. **2.** v. filmar.

filter, 1. n. filtro m. **2.** v. filtrar.

filth, n. suciedad, mugre f.

filthy, a. sucio.

fin, n. aleta f.

final, 1. a. final, último. **2.** n. examen final. **finals,** (sports) final f.

finalist, n. finalista.

finally, adv. finalmente.

finances, n. recursos, fondos m.pl.

financial, a. financiero.

financier, n. financiero m.

find, 1. n. hallazgo m. **2.** v. hallar; encontrar. **f. out,** averiguar, enterarse, saber.

fine, 1. a. fino; bueno. **2.** adv. muy bien. **3.** n. multa f. **4.** v. multar.

finery, n. gala f., adorno m.

finesse, 1. n. artificio m. **2.** v. valerse de artificio.

finger, n. dedo m.

finger bowl, m. enjuagatorio m.

fingernail, n. uña f.

fingerprint, 1. n. impresión digital f. **2.** v. tomar las impresiones digitales.

finicky, a. melindroso.

finish, 1. conclusión f. **2.** v. acabar, terminar.

finished, a. acabado.

finite, a. finito.

fir, n. abeto m.

fire, 1. n. fuego; incendio m. **2.** v. disparar, tirar; (coll.) despedir.

firearm, n. arma de fuego.

firecracker, n. triquitraque

m., buscapiés *m.*, petardo *m.*

fire engine, *n.* bomba de incendios *f.*

fire escape, *n.* escalera de incendios *f.*

fire extinguisher, *n.* mata-fuego *m.*

firefly, *n.* luciérnaga *f.*

fireman, *n.* bombero *m.*; (railway) fogonero *m.*

fireplace, *n.* hogar, fogón *m.*

fireproof, *a.* incombustible.

fireside, *n.* hogar *m.* fogón *m.*

fireworks, *n.* fuegos artificiales.

firm, 1. *a.* firme. **2.** *n.* casa de comercio.

firmness, *n.* firmeza *f.*

first, *a. & adv.* primero. **at f.,** al principio.

first aid, *n.* primeros auxilios *m.*

first-class, *a.* de primera clase.

fiscal, *a.* fiscal.

fish, 1. *n.* (food) pescado *m.*; (alive) pez *m.* **2.** *v.* pescar.

fisherman, *n.* pescador *m.*

fishhook, *n.* anzuelo *m.*

fishing, *n.* pesca *f.* **to go f.,** ir de pesca.

fishmonger, *n.* pescadero *m.*

fission, *n.* fisura *f.*

fissure, *n.* grieta *f.*, quebradura *f.*

fist, *n.* puño *m.*

fit, 1. *a.* capaz; justo. **2.** *n.* corte, talle *m.*; (med.) convulsión *f.* **3.** *v.* caber; quedar Lien, sentar bien.

fitful, *a.* espasmódico; caprichoso.

fitness, *n.* aptitud; conveniencia *f.*

fitting, 1. *a.* conveniente. **to be f.,** convenir. **2.** *n.* ajuste *m.*

five, *a. & pron.* cinco.

fix, 1. *n.* apuro *m.* **2.** *v.* fijar; arreglar; componer, reparar.

fixation, *n.* fijación *f.*; fijeza *f.*

fixed, *a.* fijo.

fixture, *n.* instalación; guarnición *f.*

flabby, *a.* flojo.

flaccid, *a.* flojo; flácido.

flag, *n.* bandera *f.*

flagellant, *n. & a.* flagelante *m.*

flagon, *n.* frasco *m.*

flagrant, *a.* flagrante.

flagrantly, *adv.* notoriamente.

flair, *n.* afición *f.*

flake, 1. *n.* lámina *f.*; copo de nieve. **2.** *v.* romperse en láminas.

flamboyant, *a.* flamante, llamativo.

flame, 1. *n.* llama *f.* **2.** *v.* llamear.

flaming, *a.* llameante. flamante.

flamingo, *n.* flamenco *m.*

flank, 1. *n.* ijada *f.*; (military) flanco *m.* **2.** *v.* flanquear.

flannel, *n.* franela *f.*

flap, 1. *n.* cartera *f.* **2.** *v.* aletear; sacudirse.

flare, 1. *n.* llamarada *f.* **2.** *v.* brillar; (fig.) enojarse.

flash, 1. *n.* resplandor *m.*; (lightning) rayo, relámpago *m.*; (fig.) instante *m.* **2.** *v.* brillar.

flashlight, *n.* linterna eléctrica.

flashy, *a.* resplandeciente; ostentoso.

flask, *n.* frasco *m.*

flat, 1. *a.* llano; (tire) desinflado. **2.** *n.* llanura *f.*; apartamento *m.*

flatness, *n.* llanura *f.*

flatten, *v.* aplastar, allanar; abatir.

flatter, *v.* adular, lisonjear.

flatterer, *n.* lisonjero -ra. zalamero -ra.

flattery, *n.* adulación, lisonja *f.*

flaunt, *v.* ostentar.

flavor, 1. *n.* sabor *m.* **2.** *v.* sazonar.

flavoring, *n.* condimento *m.*

flaw, *n.* defecto *m.*

flax, *n.* lino *m.*

flay, *v.* despellejar; excoriar.

flea, *n.* pulga *f.*

fleck, 1. *n.* mancha *f.* **2.** *v.* varetear.

flee, v. huir.

fleece, 1. n. vellón m. **2.** v. esquilar.

fleet, 1. a. veloz. **2.** n. flota f.

fleeting, a. fugaz, pasajero.

flesh, n. carne f.

fleshy, a. gordo; carnoso.

flex, 1. n. doblez f. **2.** v. doblar.

flexibility, n. flexibilidad f.

flexible, a. flexible.

flier, n. aviador -ra.

flight, n. vuelo m.; fuga f.

flimsy, a. débil.

flinch, v. acobardarse.

fling, v. lanzar.

flint, n. pedernal m.

flip, v. lanzar.

flippant, a. impertinente.

flippantly, adv. impertinentemente.

flirt, 1. n. coqueta f. **2.** v. coquetear, flirtear.

flirtation, n. coqueteo m.

float, v. flotar.

flock, 1. n. rebaño m. **2.** v. congregarse.

flog, v. azotar.

flood, 1. n. inundación f. **2.** v. inundar.

floor, 1. n. suelo, piso m. **2.** v. derribar.

floral, a. floral.

florid, a. florido.

florist, n. florista m. & f.

flounce, 1. n. (sew.) volante m. **2.** v. pernear.

flounder, n. rodaballo m.

flour, n. harina f.

flourish, 1. n. floreo m. **2.** v. florecer; prosperar; blandir.

flow, 1. n. flujo m. **2.** v. fluir.

flower, 1. n. flor f. **2.** v. florecer.

flowerpot, n. maceta de flores f.

flowery, a. florido.

fluctuate, v. fluctuar.

fluctuation, n. fluctuación f.

flue, n. humero m.

fluency, n. fluidez f.

fluent, a. fluente.

fluffy, a. velloso.

fluid, a. & n. flúido m.

fluidity, n. fluidez f.

fluoroscope, n. fluoroscopio m.

flurry, n. agitación f.

flush, 1. a. bien provisto. **2.** n. sonrojo m. **3.** v. limpiar con un chorro de agua; sonrojarse.

flute, n. flauta f.

flutter, 1. n. agitación f. **2.** v. agitarse.

flux, n. flujo m.

fly, 1. n. mosca f. **2.** v. volar.

foam, 1. n. espuma f. **2.** v. espumar.

focal, a. focal.

focus, 1. n. enfoque m. **2.** v. enfocar.

fodder, n. forraje m.

foe, n. adversario -ria, enemigo -ga.

fog, n. niebla f.

foggy, a. brumoso.

foil, v. frustrar.

foist, v. emponer.

fold, 1. n. pliegue m. **2.** v. doblar, plegar.

folder, n. circular m.; (for filing) carpeta f.

foliage, n. follaje m.

folio, n. infolio; folio m.

folklore, n. folklore m.

folks, n. gente, familia f.

follicle, n. folículo m.

follow, v. seguir.

follower, n. partidario -ria.

folly, n. locura f.

foment, v. fomentar.

fond, a. cariñoso, tierno. **be f. of,** ser aficionado a.

fondle, v. acariciar.

fondly, adv. tiernamente.

fondness, n. afición f.; cariño m.

food, n. alimento m.; comida f.

foodstuffs, n.pl. comestibles, víveres m.pl.

fool, 1. n. tonto -ta; bobo -ba; bufón -ona. **2.** v. engañar.

foolhardy, a. temerario.

foolish, a. bobo, tonto, majadero.

foolproof, a. seguro.

foot, n. pie m.

footage, n. longitud en pies.

football, n. fútbol, balompié m.

foothold, n. posición establecida.

footing, n. base f., fundamento m.

footlights, n.pl. luces del proscenio.

footnote, n. nota al pie de una página.

footprint, n. huella f.

footstep, n. paso m.

footstool, n. escabuelo m., banqueta f.

fop, n. petimetre m.

for, 1. prep. para; por. **as f.**, en cuanto a. **what f.,** ¿para qué? 2. conj. porque, pues.

forage, 1. n. forraje m. 2. v. forrajear.

foray, n. correría f.

forbear, v. cesar; abstenerse.

forbearance, n. paciencia f.

forbid, v. prohibir.

forbidding, a. repugnante.

force, 1. n. fuerza f. 2. v. forzar.

forceful, a. fuerte; enérgico.

forcible, a. fuerte; enérgico.

ford, 1. n. vado m. 2. v. vadear.

fore, 1. a. delantero. 2. n. delantera f.

fore and aft, de popa a proa.

forearm, n. antebrazo m.

forebears, n.pl. antepasados m.pl.

forebode, v. presagiar.

foreboding, n. presentimiento m.

forecast, 1. n. pronóstico m.; profecía f. 2. v. pronosticar.

forecastle, n. (naut.) castillo de proa.

forefather, n. antepasado m.

forefinger, n. índice m.

forego, v. renunciar.

foregone, a. predeterminado.

foreground, n. primer plano.

forehead, n. frente f.

foreign, a. extranjero.

foreigner, n. extranjero -ra; forastero -ra.

foreleg, n. pierna delantera.

foreman, n. capataz m.

foremost, 1. a. primero. 2. adv. en primer lugar.

forenoon, n. mañana f.

forensic, a. forense.

forerunner, n. precursor -ra.

foresee, v. prever.

foreshadow, v. prefigurar, anunciar.

foresight, n. previsión f.

forest, n. bosque m.; selva f.

forestall, v. anticipar; prevenir.

forester, n. silvicultor; guardamonte m.

forestry, n. silvicultura f.

foretell, v. predecir.

forever, adv. por siempre, para siempre.

forevermore, adv. siempre.

forewarn, v. advertir, avisar.

foreword, n. prefacio m.

forfeit, 1. n. prenda, multa f. 2. v. perder.

forfeiture, n. decomiso m., multa f.

forgather, v. reunirse.

forge, 1. n. fragua f. 2. forjar; falsear.

forger, n. forjador; falsificador m.

forgery, n. falsificación f.

forget, v. olvidar.

forgetful, a. olvidadizo.

forgive, v. perdonar.

forgiveness, n. perdón m.

fork, 1. n. tenedor m.; bifurcación f. 2. v. bifurcarse.

forlorn, a. triste.

form, 1. n. forma f.; (document) formulario m. 2. v. formar.

formal, a. formal; ceremonioso. **f. dance**, baile de etiqueta. **f. dress**, traje de etiqueta.

formality, n. formalidad f.

formally, adv. formalmente.

format, n. formato m.

formation, n. formación f.

formative, a. formativo.

former, a. anterior; antiguo. **the f.**, aquél.

formerly, adv. antiguamente.

formidable, a. formidable.

formless, a. sin forma.

formula, n. fórmula f.

formulate, v. formular.

formulation, n. formulación f.; expresión f.

forsake, v. abandonar.

fort, n. fortaleza f.; fuerte m.

forte, a. & adv. (mus.) forte, fuerte.

forth, adv. adelante. back and f., de aquí allá. and so f., etcétera.

forthcoming, a. futuro, próximo.

forthright, a. franco.

forthwith, adv. inmediatamente.

fortification, n. fortificación f.

fortify, v. fortificar.

fortissimo, a. & adv. (mus.) fortísimo.

fortitude, n. fortaleza; fortitud f.

fortnight, n. quincena f.

fortress, n. fuerte m., fortaleza f.

fortuitous, a. fortuito.

fortunate, a. afortunado.

fortune, n. fortuna; suerte f.

fortuneteller, n. sortílego, adivino m.

forty, a. & pron. cuarenta.

forum, n. foro m.

forward, 1. a. delantero; atrevido. 2. adv. adelante. 3. v. transmitir, reexpedir.

foster, 1. a. f. child, hijo adoptivo. 2. v. fomentar, criar.

foul, a. sucio; impuro.

found, v. fundar.

foundation, n. fundación f.; (of building) cimientos m.pl.

founder, 1. n. fundador -ra. 2. v. irse a pique.

foundry, n. fundición f.

fountain, n. fuente f.

four, a. & pron. cuatro.

fourteen, a. & pron. catorce.

fourth, a. & n. cuarto m.

fowl, n. ave f.

fox, n. zorro -rra.

fox trot, n. foxtrot m.

foxy, a. astuto.

foyer, n. salón de entrada.

fracas, n. riña f.

fraction, n. fracción f.

fracture, 1. n. fractura, rotura f. 2. v. fracturar, romper.

fragile, a. frágil.

fragment, n. fragmento, trozo m.

fragmentary, a. fragmentario.

fragrance, n. fragancia f.

fragrant, a. fragante.

frail, a. débil, frágil.

frailty, n. debilidad, fragilidad f.

frame, 1. n. marco; armazón; cuadro, cuerpo m. 2. v. fabricar; formar; encuadrar.

frame-up, n. (colloq.) conspiración f.

framework, n. armazón m.

France, n. Francia f.

franchise, n. franquicia f.

frank, 1. a. franco. 2. n. carta franca. 3. v. franquear.

frankfurter, n. salchicha f.

frankly, adv. francamente.

frankness, n. franqueza f.

frantic, a. frenético.

fraternal, a. fraternal.

fraternity, n. fraternidad f.

fraternization, n. fraternización f.

fraternize, v. confraternizar.

fratricide, n. fratricida m. & f.

fraud, n. fraude m.

fraudulent, a. fraudulento.

fraudulently, adv. fraudulentamente.

fraught, a. cargado.

freak, n. rareza f.

freckle, n. peca f.

free, 1. a. libre; gratis. 2. v. libertar, librar.

freedom, n. libertad f.

freeze, v. helar, congelar.

freezer, n. heladora f.

freight, 1. n. carga f.; flete m. 2. v. cargar; fletar.

freighter, n. (naut.) fletador m.

French, a. & n. francés m.

Frenchman, n. francés m.

frenzied, a. frenético.

frenzy, n. frenesí m.

frequency, n. frecuencia f.

frequency modulation, modulación de frequencia.

frequent, a. frecuente.

frequently, adv. frecuentemente.

fresco, n. pintura al fresco.

fresh, *a.* fresco. **f. water**, agua dulce.

freshen, *v.* refrescar.

freshness, *n.* frescura *f.*

fret, *v.* quejarse, irritarse.

fretful, *a.* irritable.

fretfully, *adv.* de mala gana.

fretfulness, *n.* mal humor.

friar, *n.* fraile *m.*

fricassee, *n.* fricasé *m.*

friction, *n.* fricción *f.*

Friday, *n.* viernes *m.* **Good F.**, Viernes Santo.

fried, *a.* frito.

friend, *n.* amigo -ga.

friendless, *a.* sin amigos.

friendliness, *n.* amistad *f.*

friendly, *a.* amistoso.

friendship, *n.* amistad *f.*

fright, *n.* susto *m.*

frighten, *v.* asustar, espantar.

frightful, *a.* espantoso.

frigid, *a.* frígido, frío.

frill, *n.* (*sew.*) lechuga *f.*

fringe, *n.* fleco; borde *m.*

frisky, *a.* retozón.

fritter, *n.* fritura *f.*

frivolity, *n.* frivolidad *f.*

frivolous, *a.* frívolo.

frivolousness, *n.* frivolidad *f.*

frock, *n.* vestido de mujer. **f. coat**, levita *f.*

frog, *n.* rana *f.*

frolic, **1.** *n.* retozo *m.* **2.** *v.* retozar.

from, *prep.* de; desde.

front, *n.* frente; (of building) fachada *f.* **in f. of**, delante de.

frontal, *a.* frental.

frontier, *n.* frontera *f.*

frost, *n.* helada, escarcha *f.*

frosty, *a.* helado.

froth, *n.* espuma *f.*

frown, **1.** *n.* ceño *m.* **2.** *v.* fruncir el entrecejo.

frowzy, *a.* desaliñado.

frozen, *a.* helado; congelado.

fructify, *v.* fructificar.

frugal, *a.* frugal.

frugality, *n.* frugalidad *f.*

fruit, *n.* fruta *f.*; (benefits) frutos *m.pl.* **f. tree**, árbol frutal.

fruitful, *a.* productivo.

fruition, *n.* fruición *f.*

fruitless, *a.* inútil, vano.

frustrate, *v.* frustrar.

frustration, *n.* frustración *f.*

fry, *v.* freír.

fuel, *n.* combustible *m.*

fugitive, *a. & n.* fugitivo -va.

fugue, *n.* (*mus.*) fuga *f.*

fulcrum, *n.* fulcro *m.*

fulfill, *v.* cumplir.

fulfillment, *n.* cumplimiento *m.*; realización *f.*

full, *a.* lleno; completo; pleno.

fullness, *n.* plenitud *f.*

fulminate, *v.* volar; fulminar.

fulmination, *n.* fulminación, detonación *f.*

fumble, *v.* chapucear.

fume, **1.** *n.* humo *m.* **2.** *v.* humear.

fumigate, *v.* fumigar.

fumigator, *n.* fumigador *m.*

fun, *n.* diversión *f.* **to make f. of**, burlarse de. **to have f.**, divertirse.

function, **1.** *n.* función *f.* **2.** *v.* funcionar.

functional, *a.* funcional.

fund, *n.* fondo *m.*

fundamental, *a.* fundamental.

funeral, *n.* funeral *m.*

fungus, *n.* hongo *m.*

funnel, *n.* embudo *m.*; (of ship) chimenea *f.*

funny, *a.* divertido, gracioso. **to be f.**, tener gracia.

fur, *n.* piel *f.*

furious, *a.* furioso.

furlough, *n.* permiso *m.*

furnace, *n.* horno *m.*

furnish, *v.* surtir, proveer; (a house) amueblar.

furniture, *n.* muebles *m.pl.*

furrow, **1.** *n.* surco *m.* **2.** *v.* surcar.

further, **1.** *a. & adv.* más. **2.** *v.* adelantar, fomentar.

furthermore, *adv.* además.

fury, *n.* furor *m.*; furia *f.*

fuse, **1.** *n.* fusible *m.* **2.** *v.* fundir.

fuss, **1.** *n.* alboroto *m.* **2.** *v.* preocuparse por pequeñeces.

fussy, *a.* melindroso.

futile, *a.* fútil.

future, **1.** *a.* futuro. **2.** *n.* porvenir *m.*

G

gaiety, *n.* alegría *f.*

gain, 1. *n.* ganancia *f.* **2.** *v.* ganar.

gait, *n.* paso *m.*

gale, *n.* ventarrón *m.*

gall, *n.* hiel *f.*; (fig.) amargura *f.*; descaro *m.*

gallant, 1. *a.* galante. **2.** *n.* galán *m.*

gallery, *n.* galería *f.*; (theater) paraíso *m.*

gallon, *n.* galón *m.*

gallop, 1. *n.* galope *m.* **2.** *v.* galopar.

gallows, *n.* horca *f.*

gamble, 1. *n.* riesgo *m.* **2.** *v.* jugar; aventurar.

game, *n.* juego *m.*; (match) partida *f.*; (hunting) caza *f.*

gang, *n.* cuadrilla; pandilla *f.*

gangster, *n.* rufián *m.*

gap, *n.* raja *f.*

gape, *v.* boquear.

garage, *n.* garaje *m.*

garbage, *n.* basura *f.*

garden, *n.* jardín *m.*; (vegetable) huerta *f.*

gardener, *n.* jardinero -ra.

gargle, 1. *n.* gárgara *f.* **2.** *v.* gargarizar.

garland, *n.* guirnalda *f.*

garlic, *n.* ajo *m.*

garment, *n.* prenda de vestir.

garrison, *n.* guarnición *f.*

garter, *n.* liga *f.*; ataderas *f.pl.*

gas, *n.* gas *m.*

gasoline, *n.* gasolina *f.*

gasp, 1. *n.* boqueada *f.* **2.** *v.* boquear.

gate, *n.* puerta; entrada *f.*

gather, *v.* recoger; inferir; reunir.

gaudy, *a.* brillante; llamativo.

gauge, 1. *a.* manómetro, indicador *m.* **2.** *v.* medir; estimar.

gaunt, *a.* flaco.

gauze, *n.* gasa *f.*

gay, *a.* alegre.

gaze, 1. *n.* mirada *f.* **2.** *v.* mirar con fijeza.

gear, *n.* engranaje *m.* **in g.,** en juego.

gem, *n.* joya *f.*

gender, *n.* género *m.*

general, *a.* & *n.* general *m.*

generality, *n.* generalidad *f.*

generalize, *v.* generalizar.

generation, *n.* generación *f.*

generator, *n.* generador *m.*

generosity, *n.* generosidad *f.*

generous, *a.* generoso.

genial, *a.* genial.

genius, *n.* genio *m.*

gentle, *a.* suave; manso; benigno.

gentleman, *n.* señor, caballero *m.*

gentleness, *n.* suavidad *f.*

genuine, *a.* genuino.

genuineness, *n.* pureza *f.*

geographical, *a.* geográfico.

geography, *n.* geografía *f.*

geometric, *a.* geométrico.

geranium, *n.* geranio *f.*

germ, *n.* germen; microbio *m.*

German, *a.* & *n.* alemán -mana.

Germany, *n.* Alemania *f.*

gesticulate, *v.* gesticular.

gesture, 1. *n.* gesto *m.* **2.** *v.* gesticular, hacer gestos.

get, *v.* obtener; conseguir; (become) ponerse. **go and g.,** ir a buscar; **g. away,** irse; escaparse; **g. together,** reunirse; **g. on,** subir; **g. off,** bajar; **g. up,** levantarse; **g. there,** llegar.

ghastly, *a.* pálido; espantoso.

ghost, *n.* espectro, fantasma *m.*

giant, *n.* gigante *m.*

gift, *n.* regalo, don; talento *m.*

gild, *v.* dorar.

gin, *n.* ginebra *f.*

ginger, *n.* jengibre *m.*

gingerbread, *n.* pan de jengibre.

gingham, *n.* guinga *f.*

gird, *v.* ceñir.

girdle, *n.* faja *f.*

girl, *n.* muchacha, niña, chica *f.*

give, *v.* dar; regalar. **g. back,** devolver. **g. up,** rendirse; renunciar.

giver, *n.* dador -ra; donador -ra.

glacier, *n.* ventisquero *m.*

glad, *a.* alegre, contento. **to be g.,** alegrarse.

gladly, *adv.* con mucho gusto.

gladness, *n.* alegría *f.*; placer *m.*

glamor, *n.* encanto *m.*; elegancia *f.*

glamorous, *a.* encantador, elegante.

glance, 1. *n.* vistazo *m.*, ojeada *f.* **2.** *v.* ojear.

gland, *n.* glándula *f.*

glare, 1. *n.* reflejo; brillo *m.* **2.** *v.* deslumbrar; echar miradas indignadas.

glass, *n.* vidrio; vaso *m.*; **(eyeglasses),** lentes, anteojos *m.pl.*

gleam, 1. *n.* fulgor *m.* **2.** *v.* fulgurar.

glee, *n.* alegría *f.*; júbilo *m.*

glide, *v.* deslizarse.

glimpse, 1. *n.* vistazo *m.* *v.* ojear.

glisten, 1. *n.* brillo *m.* **2.** *v.* brillar.

glitter, 1. *n.* resplandor *m.* **2.** *v.* brillar.

globe, *n.* globo; orbe *m.*

gloom, *n.* oscuridad; tristeza *f.*

gloomy, *a.* oscuro; sombrío, triste.

glorify, *v.* glorificar.

glorious, *a.* glorioso.

glory, *n.* gloria, fama *f.*

glossary, *n.* glosario *m.*

glove, *n.* guante *m.*

glow, 1. *n.* fulgor *m.* **2.** *v.* relucir; arder.

glue, 1. *n.* cola *f.* **2.** *v.* encolar, pegar.

glum, *a.* de mal humor.

glutton, *n.* glotón -ona.

gnaw, *v.* roer.

go, *v.* ir, irse. **g. away,** irse, marcharse. **g. back,** volver,

regresar. **g. down,** bajar. **g. in,** entrar. **g. on,** seguir. **g. out,** salir. **g. up,** subir.

goal, *n.* meta *f.*; objeto *m.*

goat, *n.* cabra *f.*

goblet, *n.* copa *f.*

God, *n.* Dios *m.*

gold, *n.* oro *m.*

golden, *a.* áureo.

good, 1. *a.* bueno. **2.** *n.* bienes *m.pl.*; (com.) géneros *m.pl.*

good-bye, 1. *n.* adiós *m.* **2.** *interj.* ¡adiós!, ¡hasta la vista!, ¡hasta luego! **to say g. to,** despedirse de.

goodness, *n.* bondad *f.*

goose, *n.* ganso *m.*

gooseberry, *n.* uva crespa *f.*

gooseneck, *n.* cuello de cisne *m.*

goose step, *n.* paso de ganso *m.*

gore, 1. *n.* sangre *f.* **2.** *v.* acornear.

gorge, 1. *n.* gorja *f.* **2.** *v.* engullir.

gorgeous, *a.* magnífico; precioso.

gorilla, *n.* gorila *f.*

gory, *a.* sangriento.

gosling, *n.* gansarón *m.*

gospel, *n.* evangelio *m.*

gossamer, 1. *n.* telaraña *f.* **2.** *a.* delgado.

gossip, 1. *n.* chisme *m.* **2.** *v.* chismear.

Gothic, *a.* gótico.

gouge, 1. *n.* gubia *f.* **2.** *v.* escoplear.

gourd, *n.* calabaza *f.*

gourmand, *n.* glotón *m.*

gourmet, *a.* gastrónomo -ma.

govern, *v.* gobernar.

governess, *n.* aya, institutriz *f.*

government, *n.* gobierno *m.*

governmental, *a.* gubernamental.

governor, *n.* gobernador *m.*

governorship, *n.* gobernatura *f.*

gown, *n.* vestido *m.* **dressing g.,** bata *f.*

grab, *v.* agarrar, arrebatar.

grace, *n.* gracia; gentileza; merced *f.*

graceful, *a.* agraciado.

graceless, a. réprobo.

gracious, a. gentil, cortés.

grackle, n. grajo m.

grade, 1. n. grado; nivel m.; pendiente; nota; calidad f. **2.** v. graduar.

grade crossing, n. paso a nivel m.

gradual, a. gradual.

gradually, adv. gradualmente.

graduate, 1. n. graduado -da, diplomado -da. **2.** v. graduar; diplomarse.

graft, 1. n. injerto m.; soborno público. **2.** v. injertar.

graham, a. centeno; acemita.

grail, n. grial m.

grain, n. grano; cereal m.

grain alcohol, n. alcohol de madera m.

gram, n. gramo m.

grammar, n. gramática f.

grammarian, n. gramático m.

grammar school, n. escuela elemental f.

grammatical, a. gramatical.

gramophone, n. gramófono m.

granary, n. granero m.

grand, a. grande, ilustre; estupendo.

grandchild, n. nieto -ta.

granddaughter, n. nieta f.

grandee, n. noble m.

grandeur, n. grandeza f.

grandfather, n. abuelo m.

grandiloquent, a. grandílocuo.

grandiose, a. grandioso.

grand jury, n. gran jurado m.

grandly, adv. grandiosamente.

grandmother, n. abuela f.

grand opera, n. ópera grande f.

grandparents, n. abuelos m.pl.

grandson, n. nieto m.

grandstand, n. andanada f., tribuna f.

grange, n. granja f.

granger, n. labriego m.

granite, n. granito m.

granny, n. abuelita f.

grant, 1. n. concesión; subvención f. **2.** v. otorgar; conceder; conferir. **take for granted,** tomar por cierto.

granular, a. granular.

granulate, v. granular.

granulation, n. granulación f.

granule, n. gránulo m.

grape, n. uva f.

grapefruit, n. toronja f.

grapeshot, n. metralla f.

grapevine, n. vid; parra f.

graph, n. gráfia f.

graphic, a. gráfico.

graphite, n. grafito m.

graphology, n. grafología f.

grapple, v. agarrar.

grasp, 1. n. puño; poder; conocimiento m. **2.** v. empuñar agarrar; comprender.

grasping, a. codicioso.

grass, n. hierba f.

grasshopper, n. saltamontes m.

grassy, a. herboso.

grate, n. reja f.

grateful, a. agradecido.

gratify, v. satisfacer.

grating, 1. n. enrejado m. **2.** a. discordante.

gratis, adv. & a. gratis.

gratitude, n. agradecimiento m.

gratuitous, adv. gratismente.

gratuity, n. propina f.

grave, 1. a. grave. **2.** n. sepultura; tumba f.

gravel, n. cascajo m.

gravely, adv. gravemente.

gravestone, n. lápida sepulcral f.

graveyard, n. cementerio m.

gravitate, v. gravitar.

gravitation, n. gravitación f.

gravity, n. gravedad; seriedad f.

gravure, n. grabado m.

gravy, n. salsa f.

gray, a. gris; (hair) cano.

grayish, a. pardusco.

gray matter, n. substancia gris f.

graze, v. rozar; (cattle) pastar.

grazing, a. pastando.

grease, 1. *n.* grasa *f.* **2.** *v.* engrasar.

greasy, *a.* grasiento.

great, *a.* grande, ilustre; estupendo.

Great Dane, *n.* mastín danés *m.*

greatness, *n.* grandeza *f.*

Greece, *n.* Grecia *f.*

greed, greediness, *n.* codicia, voracidad *f.*

greedy, *a.* voraz.

Greek, *a.* & *n.* griego -ga.

green, *a.* & *n.* verde *m.*

greens, *n.* verduras *f.pl.*

greenery, *n.* verdor *f.*

greenhouse, *n.* invernáculo *m.*

greet, *v.* saludar.

greeting, *n.* saludo *m.*

gregarious, *a.* gregario.

grenade, *n.* granada; bomba *f.*

greyhound, *n.* galgo *m.*

grid, *n.* parrilla *f.*

griddle, *n.* tortera *f.*

griddlecake, *n.* tortita de harina *f.*

gridiron, *n.* parrilla *f.*, campo de fútbol *m.*

grief, *n.* dolor *m.*; pena *f.*

grievance, *n.* pesar; agravio *m.*

grieve, *v.* afligir.

grievous, *a.* penoso.

grill, 1. *n.* parrilla *f.* **2.** *v.* asar a la parrilla.

grillroom, *n.* restaurante de servicio rápido *m.*

grim, *a.* ceñudo.

grimace, 1. *n.* mueca *f.* **2.** *v.* hacer muecas.

grime, *n.* mugre *f.*

grimy, *a.* sucio; mugroso.

grin, 1. *n.* sonrisa *f.* **2.** *v.* sonreír.

grind, *v.* moler; afilar.

grindstone, *n.* esmeriladora *f.*

gringo, *n.* gringo; yanqui *m.*

grip, 1. *n.* maleta *f.* **2.** *v.* agarrar.

gripe, *v.* agarrar. **2.** *n.* asimiento *m.*, opresión *f.*

grippe, *n.* gripe *f.*

grisly, *a.* espantoso.

grist, *n.* molienda *f.*

gristle, *n.* cartílago *m.*

grit, *n.* arena *f.*, entereza *f.*

grizzled, *a.* tordillo.

groan, 1. *n.* gemido *m.* **2.** *v.* gemir.

grocer, *n.* abacero *m.*

grocery, *n.* tienda de comestibles, bodega *f.*

grog, *n.* brebaje *m.*

groggy, *a.* medio borracho; vacilante.

groin, *n.* ingle *f.*

groom, *n.* (of horses) establero; (at wedding) novio *m.*

groove, 1. *n.* estría *f.* **2.** *v.* acanalar.

grope, *v.* tentar; andar a tientas.

gross, 1. *a.* grueso; grosero. **2.** *n.* gruesa *f.*

grossly, *adv.* groseramente.

grossness, *n.* grosería *f.*

grotesque, *a.* grotesco.

grotto, *n.* gruta *f.*

grouch, *n.* gruñón; descontento *m.*

ground, *n.* tierra *f.*; terreno; suelo; campo; fundamento *m.*

ground hog, *n.* marmota *f.*

groundless, *a.* infundado.

groundwork, *n.* base *f.*, fundamento *m.*

group, 1. *n.* grupo *m.* **2.** *v.* agrupar.

grouse, *n.* chachalaca *f.*

grove, *n.* arboleda *f.*

grovel, *v.* rebajarse; envilecerse.

grow, *v.* crecer; cultivar.

growl, 1. *n.* gruñido *m.* **2.** *v.* gruñir.

grown, *a.* crecido; desarrollado.

grownup, *n.* adulto *m.*

growth, *n.* crecimiento; vegetación *f.*; (med.) tumor *m.*

grub, *n.* gorgojo *m.*, larva *f.*

grubby, *a.* guasarapiento.

grudge, *n.* rencor *m.* **bear a g.,** guardar rencor.

gruel, *n.* atole *m.* **2.** *v.* estropear.

gruesome, *a.* horripilante.

gruff, *a.* ceñudo.

grumble, *v.* quejarse.

grumpy, *a.* gruñón; quejoso.

grunt, *v.* gruñir.

guarantee, 1. *n.* garantía *f.* **2.** *v.* garantizar.

guarantor, *n.* fiador *m.*

guaranty, *n.* garantía *f.*

guard, 1. *n.* guardia *m.* or *f.* **2.** *v.* vigilar.

guarded, *a.* cauteloso.

guardhouse, *n.* prisión militar *f.*

guardian, *n.* guardián *m.*

guardianship, *n.* tutela *f.*

guardsman, *n.* centinela *m.*

guava, *n.* guayaba *f.*

gubernatorial, *a.* gubernativo.

guerrilla, *n.* guerrillero *m.*

guess, 1. *n.* conjetura *f.* **2.** *v.* adivinar; (coll.) creer.

guesswork, *n.* conjetura *f.*

guest, *n.* huésped *m.* & *f.*

guffaw, *n.* risotada *f.*

guidance, *n.* dirección *f.*

guide, 1. *n.* guía *m.* & *f.* **2.** *v.* guiar.

guidebook, *n.* guía *f.*

guidepost, *n.* poste indicador *m.*

guild, *n.* gremio *m.*

guile, *n.* engaño *m.*

guillotine, 1. *n.* guillotina *f.* **2.** *v.* guillotinar.

guilt, *n.* culpa *f.*

guiltily, *adv.* culpablemente.

guiltless, *a.* inocente.

guilty, *a.* culpable.

guinea fowl, *n.* gallina de Guinea *f.*

guinea pig, *n.* cobayo *m.*

guise, *n.* modo *m.*

guitar, *n.* guitarra *f.*

gulch, *n.* quebrada *f.*

gulf, *n.* golfo *m.*

gull, *n.* gaviota *f.*

gullet, *n.* esófago *m.*, zanja *f.*

gullible, *a.* crédulo.

gully, *n.* barranca *f.*

gulp, 1. *n.* trago *m.* **2.** *v.* tragar.

gum, 1. *n.* goma *f.*; (anatomy) encía *f.* **chewing g.**, chicle *m.* **2.** *v.* engomar.

gumbo, *n.* quimbombó *m.*

gummy, *a.* gomoso.

gun, *n.* fusil *m.*; cañón *m.*

gunboat, *n.* cañonero *m.*

gunman, *n.* bandido *m.*

gunner, *n.* artillero *m.*

gunpowder, *n.* pólvora *f.*

gunshot, *n.* escopetazo *m.*

gunwale, *n.* borda *f.*

gurgle, 1. *n.* gorgoteo *m.* **2.** *v.* gorgotear.

gush, 1. *n.* chorro *m.* **2.** *v.* brotar, chorrear.

gusher, *n.* pozo de chorro de petróleo *m.*

gust, *n.* soplo *m.*; ráfaga *f.*

gustatory, *a.* del sentido del gusto.

gusto, *n.* gusto; placer *m.*

gusty, *a.* borrascoso.

gut, *n.* intestino *m.*, tripa *f.*

gutter, *n.* canal; zanja *f.*

guttural, *a.* gutural.

guy, *n.* tipo *m.*

guzzle, *v.* engullir; tragar.

gym, *n.* gimnasio *m.*

gymnasium, *n.* gimnasio *m.*

gymnast, *n.* gimnasta *m.*

gymnastic, *a.* gimnástico.

gymnastics, *n.* gimnasia *f.*

gynecology, *n.* ginecología *f.*

gypsum, *n.* yeso *m.*

Gypsy, *a.* & *n.* gitano -na.

gyrate, *v.* girar.

gyroscope, *n.* giroscopio *m.*

H

habeas corpus, *n.* habeas corpus *m.*

haberdasher, *n.* camisero *m.*

haberdashery, *n.* camisería *f.*

habiliment, *n.* vestuario *m.*

habit, *n.* costumbre *f.*; hábito *m.* **be in the h. of**, estar acostumbrado a; soler.

habitable, *a.* habitable.

habitat, n. habitación f.; ambiente m.

habitation, n. habitación f.

habitual, a. habitual.

habituate, v. habituar.

habitué, n. parroquiano m.

hack, 1. n. coche de alquiler. **2.** v. tajar.

hackneyed, a. trillado.

hacksaw, n. sierra para cortar metal f.

haddock, n. merluza f.

haft, n. mango m.

hag, n. bruja f.

haggard, a. trasnochado.

haggle, v. regatear.

hail, 1. n. granizo; (greeting) saludo m. **2.** v. granizar; saludar.

Hail Mary, n. Ave María f.

hailstone, n. piedra de granizo f.

hailstorm, n. granizada f.

hair, n. pelo; cabello m.

haircut, n. corte de pelo.

hairdo, n. peinado m.

hairdresser, n. peluquero m.

hairpin, n. horquilla f.; gancho m.

hair's-breadth, n. ancho de un pelo m.

hairy, a. peludo.

halcyon, 1. n. alcedón m. **2.** a. tranquilo.

hale, a. sano.

half, 1. a. medio. **2.** n. mitad f.

half-and-half, a. mitad y mitad.

half-baked, a. medio crudo.

half-breed, n. mestizo m.

half brother, n. medio hermano m.

half-hearted, a. sin entusiasmo.

half-mast, a. & n. media asta m.

halfpenny, n. medio penique m.

halfway, adv. a medio camino.

half-wit, n. bobo m.

halibut, n. hipogloso m.

hall, n. corredor m.; (for assembling) sala f. **city h.,** ayuntamiento m.

hallmark, n. marca del contraste m.

hallow, v. consagrar.

Halloween, n. víspera de Todos los Santos f.

hallucination, n. alucinación f.

hallway, n. pasadizo m.

halo, n. halo m.; corona f.

halt, 1. v. cojo. **2.** n. parada f. **3.** v. parar. **4.** interj. ¡alto!

halter, n. cabestro m.

halve, v. dividir en dos partes.

halyard, n. driza f.

ham, n. jamón m.

hamburger, n. albóndiga f.

hamlet, n. aldea f.

hammer, 1. n. martillo m. **2.** v. martillar.

hammock, n. hamaca f.

hamper, 1. n. canasta f., cesto m.

hamstring, 1. n. tendón de la corva m. **2.** v. desjarretar.

hand, 1. mano f. **on the other h.,** en cambio. **2.** v. pasar. **h. over,** entregar.

handbag, n. cartera f.

handball, n. pelota f.

handbook, n. manual m.

handcuff, n. esposas f.

handful, n. puñado m.

handicap, n. desventaja f.

handicraft, n. artífice m.

handiwork, n. artefacto m.

handkerchief, n. pañuelo m.

handle, 1. n. mango m. **2.** v. manejar.

handmade, n. hecho a mano m.

handmaid, n. criada de mano f.

hand organ, n. organillo m.

handsome, a. guapo; hermoso.

hand-to-hand, adv. de mano a mano.

handwriting, n. escritura f.

handy, a. diestro; útil; a la mano.

hang, v. colgar; ahorcar.

hangar, n. hangar m.

hangdog, a. & n. camastrón m.

hanger, n. colgador, gancho m.

hanger-on, n. dependiente; mogollón m.

hanging, 1. *n.* ahorcadura *f.* **2.** *a.* colgante.

hangman, *n.* verdugo *m.*

hangnail, *n.* padrastro *m.*

hang out, *v.* enarbolar.

hank, *n.* madeja *f.*

hanker, *v.* ansiar; apetecer.

haphazard, *a.* casual.

happen, *v.* acontecer, suceder, pasar.

happening, *n.* acontecimiento *m.*

happiness, *n.* felicidad; dicha *f.*

happy, *a.* feliz; contento; dichoso.

happy-go-lucky, *a.* & *n.* descuidado *m.*

harakiri, *n.* harakiri (suicidio japonés) *m.*

harangue, 1. *n.* arenga *f.* **2.** *v.* arengar.

harass, *v.* acosar; atormentar.

harbinger, *n.* presagio *m.*

harbor, 1. *n.* puerto; albergue *m.* **2.** *v.* abrigar.

hard, 1. *a.* duro; difícil. **2.** *adv.* mucho.

hard coal, *n.* antracita *f.*

harden, *v.* endurecer.

hard-headed, *a.* terco.

hard-hearted, *a.* empedernido.

hardiness, *n.* vigor *m.*

hardly, *adv.* apenas.

hardness, *n.* dureza; dificultad *f.*

hardship, *n.* penalidad *f.*; trabajo *m.*

hardware, *n.* ferretería *f.*

hardwood, *n.* madera dura *f.*

hardy, *a.* fuerte, robusto.

hare, *n.* liebre *f.*

harebrained, *a.* tolondro.

harelip, 1. *n.* labio leporino *m.* **2.** *a.* labihendido.

harem, *n.* harén *m.*

hark, *v.* escuchar; atender.

Harlequin, *n.* arlequín *m.*

harlot, *n.* ramera *f.*

harm, 1. *n.* mal, daño; perjuicio *m.* **2.** *v.* dañar.

harmful, *a.* dañoso.

harmless, *a.* inocente.

harmonic, *n.* armónico *m.*

harmonica, *n.* armónica *f.*

harmonious, *a.* armonioso.

harmonize, *v.* armonizar.

harmony, *n.* armonía *f.*

harness, *n.* arnés *m.*

harp, *n.* arpa *f.*

harpoon, *n.* arpón *m.*

harridan, *n.* vieja regañona *f.*

harrow, 1. *n.* rastro *m.*; grada *f.* **2.** *v.* gradar.

harry, *v.* acosar.

harsh, *a.* áspero.

harshness, *n.* aspereza *f.*

harvest, 1. *n.* cosecha *f.* **2.** *v.* cosechar.

hash, *n.* picadillo *m.*

hashish, *n.* haxis *m.*

hasn't, *v.* no tiene (neg. + tener).

hassock, *n.* cojín *m.*

haste, *n.* prisa *f.*

hasten, *v.* apresurarse, darse prisa.

hasty, *a.* apresurado.

hat, *n.* sombrero *m.*

hatch, 1. *n.* (nautical) cuartel *m.* **2.** *v.* incubar; (fig.) tramar.

hatchery, *n.* criadero *m.*

hatchet, *n.* hacha pequeña.

hate, 1. *n.* odio *m.* **2.** *v.* odiar, detestar.

hateful, *a.* detestable.

hatred, *n.* odio *m.*

haughtiness, *n.* arrogancia *f.*

haughty, *a.* altivo.

haul, 1. *n.* (fishery) redada *f.* **2.** *v.* tirar, halar.

haunch, *n.* anca *f.*

haunt, 1. *n.* lugar frecuentado. **2.** *v.* frecuentar, andar por.

have, *v.* tener; haber.

haven, *n.* puerto; asilo *m.*

haven't, *v.* no tiene (neg. + tener).

havoc, *n.* ruina *f.*

hawk, *n.* halcón *m.*

hawker, *n.* buhonero *m.*

hawser, *n.* cable *m.*

hawthorn, *n.* espino *m.*

hay, *n.* heno *m.*

hay fever, *n.* catarro anual de la nariz *m.*; alergia nasal.

hayfield, n. henar m.

hayloft, n. henil m.

haystack, n. hacina de heno f.

hazard, 1. n. azar m. **2.** v. aventurar.

hazardous, a. peligroso.

haze, n. niebla f.

hazel, n. avellano m.

hazy, a. brumoso.

he, pron. él m.

head, 1. n. cabeza f.; jefe m. **2.** v. dirigir; encabezar.

headache, n. dolor de cabeza.

headband, n. venda para cabeza f.

headfirst, adv. de cabeza.

headgear, n. tocado m.

headlight, n. linterna delantera f., farol de tope m.

headline, n. encabezado m.

headlong, a. precipitoso.

head-on, adv. de frente.

headquarters, n. jefatura f.; (military) cuartel general.

headstone, n. lápida mortuoria f.

headstrong, a. terco.

headwaters, n. cabeceras f.

headway, n. avance m., progreso m.

headwork, n. trabajo mental m.

heady, a. impetuoso.

heal, v. curar, sanar.

health, n. salud f.

healthful, a. saludable.

healthy, a. sano; salubre.

heap, n. montón m.

hear, v. oír. **h. from,** tener noticias de. **h. about, h. of,** oír hablar de.

hearing, n. oído m.

hearsay, n. rumor m.

hearse, n. ataúd m.

heart, n. corazón; ánimo m. **by h.,** de memoria.

heartache, n. angustia f.

heartbreak, n. angustia f.; pesar m.

heartbroken, a. acongojado.

heartburn, n. acedía f.

heartfelt, a. sentido.

hearth, n. hogar m., chimenea f.

heartless, a. empedernido.

heartsick, a. desconsolado.

heart-stricken, a. afligido.

heart-to-heart, adv. franco; sincero.

hearty, a. cordial; vigoroso.

heat, 1. n. calor; ardor m.; calefacción f. **2.** v. calentar.

heated, a. acalorado.

heater, n. calentador m.

heath, n. matorral m.

heathen, a. & n. pagano -na.

heather, n. brezo m.

heatstroke, n. insolación f.

heat wave, n. onda de calor.

heave, v. tirar.

heaven, n. cielo m.

heavenly, a. divino.

heavy, a. pesado; oneroso.

Hebrew, a. & n. hebreo -ea.

hectic, a. turbulento.

hedge, n. seto m.

hedgehog, n. erizo m.

hedonism, n. hedonismo m.

heed, 1. n. cuidado m. **2.** v. atender.

heedless, a. desatento; incauto.

heel, n. talón m.; (of shoe) tacón m.

heifer, n. novilla f.

height, n. altura f.

heighten, v. elevar; exaltar.

heinous, a. nefando.

heir, heiress, n. heredero -ra.

helicopter, n. helicóptero m.

heliotrope, n. heliotropo m.

helium, n. helio m.

hell, n. infierno m.

Hellenism, n. helenismo m.

hellish, a. infernal.

hello, interj. ¡hola!; (on telephone) aló; bueno.

helm, n. timón m.

helmet, n. yelmo, casco m.

helmsman, n. timonero m.

help, 1. n. ayuda f. **help!** ¡socorro! **2.** v. ayudar. **h. oneself,** servirse. **can't help (but),** no poder menos de.

helper, n. ayudante m.

helpful, a. útil; servicial.

helpfulness, n. utilidad f.

helpless, a. imposibilitado.

hem, 1. *n.* ribete *m.* **2.** *v.* ribetear.

hemisphere, *n.* hemisferio *m.*

hemlock, *n.* abeto *m.*

hemoglobin, *n.* hemoglobina *f.*

hemophilia, *n.* hemofilia *f.*

hemorrhage, *n.* hemorragia *f.*

hemorrhoid, *n.* hemorroides *f.pl.*

hemp, *n.* cáñamo *m.*

hemstitch, 1. *n.* vainica *f.* **2.** *v.* hacer una vainica.

hen, *n.* gallina *f.*

hence, *adv.* por lo tanto.

henceforth, *adv.* de aquí en adelante.

henchman, *n.* paniaguado *m.*

henna, *n.* alheña *f.*

her, 1. *a.* su. **2.** *pron.* ella; la; le.

herald, *n.* heraldo *m.*

heraldic, *a.* heráldico.

heraldry, *n.* heráldica *f.*

herb, *n.* yerba, hierba *f.*

herbaceous, *a.* herbáceo.

herbarium, *n.* herbario *m.*

herd, 1. *n.* hato, rebaño *m.* **2.** *v.* reunir en hatos.

here, *adv.* aquí; acá.

hereafter, *adv.* en lo futuro.

hereby, *adv.* por éstas, por la presente.

hereditary, *a.* hereditario.

heredity, *n.* herencia *f.*

herein, *adv.* aquí dentro; incluso.

heresy, *n.* herejía *f.*

heretic, 1. *a.* herético. **2.** *n.* hereje *m. & f.*

heretical, *a.* herético.

heretofore, *adv.* hasta ahora.

herewith, *adv.* con esto, adjunto.

heritage, *n.* herencia *f.*

hermetic, *a.* hermético.

hermit, *n.* ermitaño *m.*

hernia, *n.* hernia *f.*

hero, *n.* héroe *m.*

heroic, *a.* heroico.

heroically, *adv.* heroicamente.

heroin, *n.* heroína *f.*

heroine, *n.* heroína *f.*

heroism, *n.* heroísmo *m.*

heron, *n.* garza *f.*

herring, *n.* arenque *m.*

hers, *pron.* suyo, de ella.

herself, *pron.* sí, sí misma; se. **she h.,** ella misma. **with h.,** consigo.

hesitancy, *n.* hesitación *f.*

hesitant, *a.* indeciso.

hesitate, *v.* vacilar.

hesitation, *n.* duda; vacilación *f.*

heterogeneous, *a.* heterogéneo.

hexagon, *n.* hexágono *m.*

hibernate, *v.* invernar.

hibernation, *n.* invernada *f.*

hibiscus, *n.* hibisco *m.*

hiccup, 1. *n.* hipo *m.* **2.** *v.* tener hipo.

hickory, *n.* nogal americano *m.*

hidden, *a.* oculto; escondido.

hide, 1. *n.* cuero *m.*; piel *f.* **2.** *v.* esconder; ocultar.

hideous, *a.* horrible.

hide-out, *n.* escondite *m.*

hierarchy, *n.* jerarquía *f.*

high, *a.* alto, elevado; (in price) caro.

highbrow, *n.* erudito *m.*

highly, *adv.* altamente; sumamente.

high school, *n.* escuela secundaria *f.*

highway, *n.* carretera *f.*; camino real *m.*

hike, *n.* caminata *f.*

hilarious, *a.* alegre, bullicioso.

hilariousness, hilarity, *n.* hilaridad *f.*

hill, *n.* colina *f.*; cerro *m.*; **down h.,** cuesta abajo. **up h.,** cuesta arriba.

hilt, *n.* puño *m.* **up to the h.,** a fondo.

him, *pron.* él; lo; le.

himself, *pron.* sí, sí mismo; se. **he h.,** él mismo. **with h.,** consigo.

hinder, *v.* impedir.

hindmost, *a.* último.

hindquarter, *n.* cuarto trasero *m.*

hindrance, *n.* obstáculo *m.*

hinge, 1. *n.* gozne *m.* **2.** *v.*

engoznar. **h. on,** depender de.

hint, 1. *n.* insinuación *f.*; indicio *m.* **2.** *v.* insinuar.

hip, *n.* cadera *f.*

hippopotamus, *n.* hipopótamo *m.*

hire, *v.* alquilar.

his, 1. *a.* su. **2.** *pron.* suyo, de él.

hiss, *v.* silbar, sisear.

historian, *n.* historiador *m.*

historic, historical, *a.* histórico.

history, *n.* historia *f.*

histrionic, *a.* histriónico.

hit, 1. *n.* golpe *m.*; (coll.) éxito *m.* **2.** *v.* golpear, dar.

hitch, *v.* amarrar; enganchar.

hither, *adv.* acá, hacia acá.

hitherto, *adv.* hasta ahora.

hive, *n.* colmena *f.*

hives, *n.* urticaria *f.*

hoard, 1. *n.* acumulación *f.* **2.** *v.* acaparar; atesorar.

hoarse, *a.* ronco.

hoax, 1. *n.* engaño *m.* **2.** *v.* engañar.

hobby, *n.* afición *f.*, pasatiempo *m.*

hobgoblin, *n.* trasgo *m.*

hobnob, *v.* tener intimidad.

hobo, *n.* vagabundo *m.*

hockey, *n.* hockey *m.* **ice-h.,** hockey sobre hielo.

hod, *n.* esparavel *m.*

hodgepodge, *n.* baturillo *m.*; mezcolanza *f.*

hoe, 1. *n.* azada *f.* **2.** *v.* cultivar con azada.

hog, *n.* cerdo, puerco *m.*

hoist, 1. *n.* grúa *f.*, elevador *m.* **2.** *v.* elevar, enarbolar.

hold, 1. *n.* presa *f.*; agarro *m.*; (nautical) bodega *f.* **to get h. of,** conseguir, apoderarse de. **2.** *v.* tener; detener; sujetar; celebrar.

holder, *n.* tenedor *m.* **cigarette h.,** boquilla *f.*

holdup, *n.* salteamiento *m.*

hole, *n.* agujero; hoyo; hueco *m.*

holiday, *n.* día de fiesta.

holiness, *n.* santidad *f.*

Holland, *n.* Holanda *f.*

hollow, 1. *a.* hueco. **2.** *n.*

cavidad *f.* **3.** *v.* ahuecar; excavar.

holly, *n.* acebo *m.*

hollyhock, *n.* malva real *f.*

holocaust, *n.* holocausto *m.*

holster, *n.* pistolera *f.*

holy, *a.* santo.

holy day, *n.* disanto *m.*

Holy See, *n.* Santa Sede *f.*

Holy Spirit, *n.* Espíritu Santo *m.*

Holy Week, *n.* Semana Santa *f.*

homage, *n.* homenaje *m.*

home, *n.* casa, morada *f.*; hogar *m.* **at h.,** en casa. **to go h.,** ir a casa.

homeland, *n.* patria *f.*

homely, *a.* feo; casero.

home rule, *n.* autonomía *f.*

homesick, *a.* nostálgico.

homespun, *a.* casero; tocho.

homeward, *adv.* hacia casa.

homicide, *n.* homicida *m. & f.*

homily, *n.* homilía *f.*

homogeneous, *a.* homogéneo.

homogenize, *v.* homogenizar.

homosexual, *n. & a.* homosexual *m.*

Honduras, *n.* Honduras *f.*

hone, 1. *n.* piedra de afilar *f.* **2.** *v.* afilar.

honest, *a.* honrado, honesto; sincero.

honestly, *adv.* honradamente; de veras.

honesty, *n.* honradez, honestidad *f.*

honey, *n.* miel *f.*

honeybee, *n.* abeja obrera *f.*

honeymoon, *n.* luna de miel.

honeysuckle, *n.* madreselva *f.*

honor, 1. *n.* honra *f.*; honor *m.* **2.** *v.* honrar.

honorable, *a.* honorable; ilustre.

honorary, *a.* honorario.

hood, *n.* capota; capucha *f.*; (auto.) cubierta del motor.

hoodlum, *n.* pillo *m.*, rufián *m.*

hoof, *n.* pezuña *f.*

hook, 1. *n.* gancho *m.* **2.** *v.* enganchar.

hoop, n. cerco m.

hop. 1. n. salto m. **2.** v. saltar.

hope. 1. n. esperanza f. **2.** v. esperar.

hopeful, a. lleno de esperanzas.

hopeless, a. desesperado; sin remedio.

horde, n. horda f.

horehound, n. marrubio m.

horizon, n. horizonte m.

horizontal, a. horizontal.

hormone, n. hormón m.

horn, n. cuerno m.; (music) trompa f.; (auto.) bocina f.

hornet, n. avispón m.

horny, a. córneo; calloso.

horoscope, n. horóscopo m.

horrendous, a. horrendo.

horrible, a. horrible.

horrid, a. horrible.

horrify, v. horrorizar.

horror, n. horror m.

horse, n. caballo m. **to ride a h.,** cabalgar.

horseback, n. **on h.,** a caballo. **to ride h.,** montar a caballo.

horsefly, n. tábano m.

horsehair, n. pelo de caballo m.; tela de crin f.

horseman, n. jinete m.

horsemanship, n. manejo m., equitación f.

horsepower, n. caballo de fuerza m.

horseradish, n. rábano picante m.

horseshoe, n. herradura f.

hortatory, a. exhortatorio.

horticulture, n. horticultura f.

hose, n. medias f.pl.; (garden) manguera f.

hosiery, n. calcetería f.

hospitable, a. hospitalario.

hospital, n. hospital m.

hospitality, n. hospitalidad f.

hospitalization, n. hospitalización f.

hospitalize, v. hospitalizar.

host, n. anfitrión m., dueño de la casa; (religion) hostia f.

hostage, n. rehén m.

hostel, n. hostería f.

hostelry, n. fonda f., parador m.

hostess, n. anfitriona f., dueña de la casa.

hostile, a. hostil.

hostility, n. hostilidad f.

hot, a. caliente; (sauce) picante. **to be h.,** tener calor; (weather) hacer calor.

hotbed, n. estercolero m. (fig.) foco m.

hotel, n. hotel m.

hot-headed, a. turbulente, alborotadizo.

hothouse, n. invernáculo m.

hound. 1. n. sabueso m. **2.** v. perseguir; seguir la pista.

hour, n. hora f.

hourglass, n. reloj de arena m.

hourly. 1. a. por horas. **2.** adv. a cada hora.

house. 1. casa f.; (theater) público m. **2.** v. alojar, albergar.

housefly, n. mosca ordinaria f.

household, n. familia; casa f.

housekeeper, n. ama de llaves.

housemaid, n. criada f., sirvienta f.

housewife, n. ama de casa.

housework, n. tareas domésticas f.

hovel, n. choza f.

hover, v. revolotear.

how, adv. cómo. **h. much,** cuánto. **h. many,** cuántos. **h. far,** a qué distancia.

however, adv. como quiera; sin embargo.

howl. 1. n. aullido m. **2.** v. aullar.

hub, n. centro m.; eje m. **h. of a wheel,** cubo de la rueda m.

hubbub, n. alborota f., bulla f.

hue, n. matiz; color m.

hug. 1. n. abrazo m. **2.** v. abrazar.

huge, a. enorme.

hulk, n. casco de buque m.

hull. 1. n. cáscara f.; (nav.) casco m. **2.** v. decascarar.

hum, 1. *n.* zumbido *m.* **2.** *v.* tararear; zumbar.

human, *a. & n.* humano -na.

humane, *a.* humano, humanitario.

humanism, *n.* humanidad *f.*; benevolencia *f.*

humanitarian, *a.* humanitario.

humanity, *n.* humanidad *f.*

humanly, *a.* humanamente.

humble, *a.* humilde.

humbug, *n.* farsa *f.*, embaucador *m.*

humdrum, *a.* monótono.

humid, *a.* húmedo.

humidity, *n.* humedad *f.*

humiliate, *v.* humillar.

humiliation, *n.* mortificación *f.*; bochorno *m.*

humility, *n.* humildad *f.*

humor, 1. *n.* humor; capricho *m.* **2.** *v.* complacer.

humorist, *n.* humorista *m.*

humorous, *a.* divertido.

hump, *n.* joroba *f.*

humpback, *n.* jorobado *m.*

humus, *n.* humus *m.*

hunch, *n.* giba *f.*; (idea) corazonada *f.*

hunchback, *n.* jorobado *m.*

hundred, 1. *a. & pron.* cien, ciento. **200,** doscientos. **300,** trescientos. **400,** cuatrocientos. **500,** quinientos. **600,** seiscientos. **700,** setecientos. **800,** ochocientos. **900,** novecientos. **2.** *n.* centenar *m.*

hundredth, *n. & a.* centésimo *m.*

Hungarian, *a. & n.* húngaro -ra.

Hungary, Hungría *f.*

hunger, *n.* hambre *f.*

hungry, *a.* hambriento. **to be h.,** tener hambre.

hunt, 1. *n.* caza *f.* **2.** *v.* cazar. **h. up,** buscar.

hunter, *n.* cazador *m.*

hunting, *n.* caza *f.* **to go h.,** ir de caza.

hurdle, *n.* zarzo *m.*, valla *f.*; dificultad *f.*

hurl, *v.* arrojar.

hurricane, *n.* huracán *m.*

hurry, 1. *n.* prisa *f.* **to be**

in a h., tener prisa. **2.** *v.* apresurar; darse prisa.

hurt, 1. *n.* daño, perjuicio *m.* **2.** *v.* dañar; lastimar; doler; ofender.

hurtful, *a.* perjudicial, dañino.

hurtle, *v.* lanzar.

husband, *n.* marido, esposo *m.*

husk, 1. *n.* cáscara *f.* **2.** *v.* descascarar.

husky, *a.* fornido.

hustle, *v.* empujar.

hut, *n.* choza *f.*

hyacinth, *n.* jacinto *m.*

hybrid, *a.* híbrido.

hydrangea, *n.* hortensia *f.*

hydraulic, *a.* hidráulico.

hydroelectric, *a.* hidroeléctrico.

hydrogen, *n.* hidrógeno *m.*

hydrophobia, *n.* hidrofobia *f.*

hydroplane, *n.* hidroavión *m.*

hydrotherapy, *n.* hidroterapia *f.*

hyena, *n.* hiena *f.*

hygiene, *n.* higiene *f.*

hygienic, *a.* higiénico.

hymn, *n.* himno *m.*

hymnal, *n.* himnario *m.*

hypercritical, *a.* hipercrítico.

hyphen, *n.* guión *m.*

hyphenate, *v.* separar con guión.

hypnosis, *n.* hipnosis *f.*

hypnotic, *a.* hipnótico.

hypnotism, *n.* hipnotismo *m.*

hypnotize, *v.* hipnotizar.

hypochondria, *n.* hipocondría *f.*

hypochondriac, *n. & a.* hipocondríaco *m.*

hypocrisy, *n.* hipocresía *f.*

hypocrite, *n.* hipócrita *m. & f.*

hypocritical, *a.* hipócrita.

hypodermic, *a.* hipodérmico.

hypotenuse, *n.* hipotenusa *f.*

hypothesis, *n.* hipótesis *f.*

hypothetical, *a.* hipotético.

hysteria, hysterics, *n.* histeria *f.*

hysterical, *a.* histérico.

I

I, *pron.* yo.
iambic, *a.* yámbico.
ice, *n.* hielo *m.*
iceberg, *n.* iceberg *m.*
icebox, *n.* refrigerador *m.*
ice cream, *n.* helado, mantecado *m.*; **i.-c. cone,** barquillo de helado.
ice skate, *n.* patín de cuchilla *m.*
icon, *n.* icón *m.*
icy, *a.* helado; indiferente.
idea, *n.* idea *f.*
ideal, *a.* ideal.
idealism, *n.* idealismo *m.*
idealist, *n.* idealista *m. & f.*
idealistic, *a.* idealista.
idealize, *v.* idealizar.
ideally, *adv.* idealmente.
identical, *a.* idéntico.
identifiable, *a.* identificable.
identification, *n.* identificación *f.* **i. papers,** cédula de identidad *f.*
identify, *v.* identificar.
identity, *n.* identidad *f.*
ideology, *n.* ideología *f.*
idiocy, *n.* idiotez *f.*
idiom, *n.* modismo *m.*; idioma *m.*
idiot, *n.* idiota *m. & f.*
idiotic, *a.* idiota, tonto.
idle, *a.* desocupado; perezoso.
idleness, *n.* ociosidad, pereza *f.*
idol, *n.* ídolo *m.*
idolatry, *n.* idolatría *f.*
idolize, *v.* idolatrar.
idyl, *n.* idilio *m.*
idyllic, *a.* idílico.
if, *conj.* si. **even if,** aunque.
ignite, *v.* encender.
ignition, *n.* ignición *f.*
ignoble, *a.* innoble, indigno.
ignominious, *a.* ignominioso.
ignoramus, *n.* ignorante *m.*
ignorance, *n.* ignorancia *f.*
ignorant, *a.* ignorante. **to be i. of,** ignorar.
ignore, *v.* desconocer, pasar por alto.

ill, *a.* enfermo, malo.
illegal, *a.* ilegal.
illegible, *a.* ilegible.
illegibly, *a.* ilegiblemente.
illegitimacy, *n.* ilegitimidad *f.*
illegitimate, *a.* ilegítimo; desautorizado.
illicit, *a.* ilícito.
illiteracy, *n.* analfabetismo *m.*
illiterate, *a. & n.* analfabeto-ta.
illness, *n.* enfermedad, maldad *f.*
illogical, *a.* ilógico.
illuminate, *v.* iluminar.
illumination, *n.* iluminación *f.*
illusion, *n.* ilusión *f.*; ensueño *m.*
illusive, *a.* ilusivo.
illustrate, *v.* ilustrar; ejemplificar.
illustration, *n.* ilustración *f.*; ejemplo; grabado *m.*
illustrative, *a.* ilustrativo.
illustrious, *a.* ilustre.
ill will, *n.* malevolencia *f.*
image, *n.* imagen, estatua *f.*
imagery, *n.* imaginación *f.*
imaginable, *a.* imaginable.
imaginary, *a.* imaginario.
imagination, *n.* imaginación *f.*
imaginative, *a.* imaginativo.
imagine, *v.* imaginarse, figurarse.
imbecile, *n. & a.* imbécil *m.*
imitate, *v.* imitar.
imitation, *n.* imitación *f.*
imitative, *a.* imitativo.
immaculate, *a.* inmaculado.
immanent, *a.* inmanente.
immaterial, *a.* inmaterial; sin importancia.
immature, *a.* inmaturo.
immediate, *a.* inmediato.
immediately, *adv.* inmediatamente.
immense, *a.* inmenso.
immerse, *v.* sumergir.

immigrant, n. & a. inmigrante m.

immigrate, v. inmigrar.

imminent, a. inminente.

immobile, a. inmóvil.

immoderate, a. inmoderado.

immodest, a. inmodesto; atrevido.

immoral, a. inmoral.

immorality, n. inmoralidad f.

immorally, adv. licenciosamente.

immortal, a. inmortal.

immortality, n. inmortalidad f.

immortalize, v. inmortalizar.

immune, a. inmune.

immunity, n. inmunidad f.

immunize, v. inmunizar.

impact, n. impacto m.

impair, v. empeorar, perjudicar.

impale, v. empalar.

impart, v. impartir, comunicar.

impartial, a. imparcial.

impatience, n. impaciencia f.

impatient, a. impaciente.

impede, v. impedir, estorbar.

impediment, n. impedimento m.

impel, v. impeler.

impenetrable, a. impenetrable.

impenitent, n. & a. impenitente m.

imperative, a. imperativo.

imperceptible, a. imperceptible.

imperfect, a. imperfecto.

imperfection, n. imperfección f.

imperial, a. imperial.

imperialism, n. imperialismo m.

imperious, a. imperioso.

impersonal, a. impersonal.

impersonate, v. personificar; imitar.

impersonation, n. personificación f.; imitación f.

impertinence, n. impertinencia f.

impervious, a. impermeable.

impetuous, a. impetuoso.

impetus, n. impetú m., impulso m.

impinge, v. tropezar; infringir.

implacable, a. implacable.

implant, v. implantar; inculcar.

implement, n. herramienta f.

implicate, v. implicar; embrollar.

implication, n. inferencia f.; complicidad f.

implicit, a. implícito.

implied, a. implícito.

implore, v. implorar.

imply, v. significar; dar a entender.

impolite, a. descortés.

import, 1. n. importación f. **2.** v. importar.

importance, n. importancia f.

important, a. importante.

importation, n. importación f.

importune, v. importunar.

impose, v. imponer.

imposition, n. imposición f.

impossibility, n. imposibilidad f.

impossible, a. imposible.

impotence, n. impotencia f.

impotent, a. impotente.

impregnable, a. impregnable.

impregnate, v. impregnar; fecundizar.

impresario, n. empresario m.

impress, v. impresionar.

impression, n. impresión f.

impressive, a. imponente.

imprison, v. encarcelar.

imprisonment, n. prisión, encarcelación f.

improbable, a. improbable.

impromptu, a. extemporáneo.

improper, a. impropio.

improve, v. mejorar; progresar.

improvement, n. mejoramiento; progreso m.

improvise, v. improvisar.

impudent, a. descarada.

impugn, v. impugnar.

impulse, n. impulso m.

impulsive, a. impulsivo.

impunity, *n.* impunidad *f.*
impure, *a.* impuro.
impurity, *n.* impureza *f.*; deshonestidad *f.*
impute, *v.* imputar.
in, 1. *prep.* en; dentro de. **2.** *adv.* adentro.
inadvertent, *a.* inadvertido.
inalienable, *a.* inalienable.
inane, *a.* mentecato.
inaugural, *a.* inaugural.
inaugurate, *v.* inaugurar.
inauguration, *n.* inauguración *f.*
Inca, *n.* inca *m.*
incandescent, *a.* incandescente.
incantation, *n.* encantación *f.*, conjuro *m.*
incapacitate, *v.* incapacitar.
incarcerate, *v.* encarcelar.
incarnate, *a.* encarnado; personificado.
incarnation, *n.* encarnación *f.*
incendiary, *a.* incendiario.
incense, 1. *n.* incienso *m.* **2.** *v.* indignar.
incentive, *n.* incentivo *m.*
inception, *n.* comienzo *m.*
incessant, *a.* incesante.
incest, *n.* incesto *m.*
inch, *n.* pulgada *f.*
incidence, *n.* incidencia *f.*
incident, *n.* incidente *m.*
incidental, *a.* incidental.
incidentally, *adv.* incidentalmente; entre paréntesis.
incinerator, *n.* incinerador *m.*
incipient, *a.* incipiente.
incision, *n.* incisión *f.*; cortadura *f.*
incisive, *a.* incisivo; mordaz.
incisor, *n.* incisivo *m.*
incite, *v.* incitar, instigar.
inclination, *n.* inclinación *f.*; declive *m.*
incline, 1. *n.* pendiente *m.* **2.** *v.* inclinar.
inclose, *v.* incluir.
include, *v.* incluir.
including, *prep.* incluso.
inclusive, *a.* inclusivo.
incognito, *n., a. & adv.* incógnito *m.*
income, *n.* renta *f.*; ingresos *m.pl.*

incomparable, *a.* incomparable.
inconvenience, 1. *n.* incomodidad *f.* **2.** *v.* incomodar.
inconvenient, *a.* incómodo.
incorporate, *v.* incoporar; dar cuerpo.
incorrigible, *a.* incorregible.
increase, *v.* crecer; aumentar.
incredible, *a.* increíble.
incredulity, *n.* incredulidad *f.*
incredulous, *a.* incrédulo.
increment, *n.* incremento *m.*, aumento *m.*
incriminate, *v.* incriminar.
incrimination, *n.* incriminación *f.*
incrust, *v.* incrustar.
incubator, *n.* incubadora *f.*
inculcate, *v.* inculcar.
incumbency, *m.* incumbencia *f.*
incumbent, *a.* obligatorio; colocado sobre.
incur, *v.* incurrir.
incurable, *a.* incurable.
indebted, *a.* obligado; adeudado.
indeed, *adv.* verdaderamente, de veras. **no i.,** de ninguna manera.
indefatigable, *a.* incansable.
indefinite, *a.* indefinido.
indefinitely, *adv.* indefinidamente.
indelible, *a.* indeleble.
indemnify, *v.* indemnizar.
indemnity, *n.* indemnización *f.*
indent, 1. *n.* diente *f.*, mella *f.* **2.** *v.* indentar, mellar.
indentation, *n.* indentación *f.*
independence, *n.* independencia *f.*
independent, *a.* independiente.
index, *n.* índice *m.*; (of book) tabla *f.*
India, *n.* India *f.*
Indian, *a. & n.* indio -dia.
indicate, *v.* indicar.
indication, *n.* indicación *f.*
indicative, *a. & n.* indicativo *m.*
indict, *v.* encausar.

indictment, *n.* (law) sumaria *m.*; denuncia *f.*

indifference, *n.* indiferencia *f.*

indifferent, *a.* indiferente.

indigenous, *a.* indígena.

indigent, *a.* indigente, pobre.

indigestion, *n.* indigestión *f.*

indignant, *a.* indignado.

indignation, *n.* indignación *f.*

indignity, *n.* indignidad *f.*

indirect, *a.* indirecto.

indiscreet, *a.* indiscreto.

indiscretion, *n.* indiscreción *f.*

indiscriminate, *a.* promiscuo.

indispensable, *a.* indispensable.

indisposed, *a.* indispuesto.

individual, *a. & n.* individuo *m.*

individuality, *n.* individualidad *f.*

individually, *adv.* individualmente.

indivisible, *a.* indivisible.

indoctrinate, *v.* doctrinar, enseñar.

indolent, *a.* indolente.

indoor, *a.* interior. **indoors**, *adv.* en casa; bajo techo.

indorse, *v.* endosar.

induce, *v.* inducir, persuadir.

induct, *v.* instalar, iniciar.

induction, *n.* introducción *f.*; instalación *f.*

inductive, *a.* inductivo; introductor.

indulge, *v.* favorecer. **i. in**, entregarse a.

indulgence, *n.* indulgencia *f.*

indulgent, *a.* indulgente.

industrial, *a.* industrial.

industrialist, *n.* industrial *m.*

industrious, *a.* industrioso, trabajador.

industry, *n.* industria *f.*

ineligible, *a.* inelegible.

inept, *a.* inepto.

inert, *a.* inerte.

inertia, *n.* inercia *f.*

inevitable, *a.* inevitable.

inexplicable, *a.* inexplicable.

infallible, *a.* infalible.

infamous, *a.* infame.

infamy, *n.* infamia *f.*

infancy, *n.* infancia *f.*

infant, *n.* nene *m.*; criatura *f.*

infantile, *a.* infantil.

infantry, *n.* infantería *f.*

infatuated, *a.* infatuado.

infect, *v.* infectar.

infection, *n.* infección *f.*

infectious, *a.* infeccioso.

infer, *v.* inferir.

inference, *n.* inferencia *f.*

inferior, *a.* inferior.

infernal, *a.* infernal.

inferno, *n.* infierno *m.*

infest, *v.* infestar.

infidel, 1. *n.* infiel *m.*; pagano *m.* 2. *a.* infiel.

infidelity, *n.* infidelidad *f.*

infiltrate, *v.* infiltrar.

infinite, *a.* infinito.

infinitesimal, *a.* infinitesimal.

infinitive, *n. & a.* infinitivo *m.*

infinity, *n.* infinidad *f.*

infirm, *a.* enfermizo.

infirmary, *n.* hospital *m.*, enfermería *f.*

infirmity, *n.* enfermedad *f.*

inflame, *v.* inflamar.

inflammable, *a.* inflamable.

inflammation, *n.* inflamación *f.*

inflammatory, *a.* inflamante; (med.) inflamatorio.

inflate, *v.* inflar.

inflation, *n.* inflación *f.*

inflection, *n.* inflexión *f.*; (of the voice) modulación de la voz *f.*

inflict, *v.* infligir.

infliction, *n.* imposición *f.*

influence, 1. *n.* influencia *f.* 2. *v.* influir en.

influential, *a.* influyente.

influenza, *n.* gripe *f.*

inform, *v.* informar. **i. oneself**, enterarse.

informal, *a.* informal.

information, *n.* informaciones *f.pl.*

infringe, *v.* infringir.

infuriate, *v.* enfurecer.

ingenious, *a.* ingenioso.

ingenuity, *n.* ingeniosidad; destreza *f.*

ingredient, n. ingrediente m.

inhabit, v. habitar.

inhabitant, n. habitante m. & f.

inhale, v. inhalar.

inherent, a. inherente.

inherit, v. heredar.

inheritance, n. herencia f.

inhibit, v. inhibir.

inhibition, n. inhibición f.

inhuman, a. inhumano.

inimical, a. hostil.

inimitable, a. inimitable.

iniquity, n. iniquidad f.

initial, a. & n. inicial f.

initiate, v. iniciar.

initiation, n. iniciación f.

initiative, n. iniciativa f.

inject, v. inyectar.

injection, n. inyección f.

injunction, n. mandato m.; (law) embargo m.

injure, v. herir; lastimar; ofender.

injurious, a. perjudicial.

injury, n. herida; afrenta f. perjuicio m.

injustice, n. injusticia f.

ink, n. tinta f.

inland, 1. a. interior. 2. adv. tierra adentro.

inlet, n. entrada f.; ensenada f.; estuario m.

inmate, n. residente m.; (of a prison) preso m.

inn, n. posada f.; mesón m.

inner, a. interior. **i. tube,** cámara de aire.

innocence, n. inocencia f.

innocent, a. inocente.

innocuous, a. innocuo.

innovation, n. innovación f.

innuendo, n. insinuación f.

innumerable, a. innumerable.

inoculate, v. inocular.

inoculation, n. inoculación f.

inquest, n. indagación f.

inquire, v. preguntar; inquirir.

inquiry, n. pregunta; investigación f.

inquisition, n. escudriñamiento m.; (ch.) inquisición f.

insane, a. loco. **to go i.,**

perder la razón; volverse loco.

insanity, n. locura f.; demencia f.

inscribe, v. inscribir.

inscription, n. inscripción; dedicatoria f.

insect, n. insecto m.

insecticide, n. & a. insecticida f.

inseparable, a. inseparable.

insert, v. insertar, meter.

insertion, n. cosa insertada f.

inside, 1. a. & n. interior m. **2.** adv. adentro, por dentro. **i. out,** al revés. **3.** prep. dentro de.

insidious, a. insidioso.

insight, n. perspicacia f.; comprensión f.

insignia, n. insignias f.pl.

insignificance, n. insignificancia f.

insignificant, a. insignificante.

insinuate, v. insinuar.

insinuation, n. insinuación f.

insipid, a. insípido.

insist, v. insistir.

insistence, n. insistencia f.

insistent, a. insistente.

insolence, n. insolencia f.

insolent, a. insolente.

insomnia, n. insomnio m.

inspect, v. inspeccionar, examinar.

inspection, n. inspección f.

inspector, n. inspector m.

inspiration, n. inspiración f.

inspire, v. inspirar.

install, v. instalar.

installation, n. instalación f.

installment, n. plazo m.

instance, n. ocasión f. **for i.,** por ejemplo.

instant, a. & n. instante m.

instantaneous, a. instantáneo.

instantly, adv. al instante.

instead, adv. en lugar de eso. **i. of,** en vez de, en lugar de.

instigate, v. instigar.

instill, v. instilar.

instinct, n. instinto m.

instinctive, a. instintivo.

institute, 1. *n.* instituto *m.* 2. *v.* instituir.

institution, *n.* institución *f.*

instruct, *v.* instruir.

instruction, *n.* instrucción *f.*

instructive, *a.* instructivo.

instructor, *n.* instructor *m.*

instrument, *n.* instrumento *m.*

instrumental, *a.* instrumental.

insufficient, *a.* insuficiente.

insular, *a.* insular; estrecho de miras.

insulate, *v.* aislar.

insulation, *n.* aislamiento *m.*

insulator, *n.* aislador *m.*

insulin, *n.* insulina *f.*

insult, 1. *n.* insulto *m.* 2. *v.* insultar.

insuperable, *a.* insuperable.

insurance, *n.* seguro *m.*

insure, *v.* asegurar.

insurgent, *a.* & *n.* insurgente *m.*

insurrection, *n.* insurrección *f.*

intact, *a.* intacto.

intangible, *a.* intangible, impalpable.

integral, *a.* íntegro.

integrate, *v.* integrar.

integrity, *n.* integridad *f.*

intellect, *n.* intelecto *m.*

intellectual, *a.* & *n.* intelectual *m.* & *f.*

intelligence, *n.* inteligencia *f.*

intelligent, *a.* inteligente.

intelligible, *a.* inteligible.

intend, *v.* pensar; intentar; destinar.

intense, *a.* intenso.

intensify, *v.* intensificar.

intensity, *n.* intensidad *f.*

intensive, *a.* intensivo.

intent, *n.* intento *m.*

intention, *n.* intención *f.*

intentional, *a.* intencional.

intercede, *v.* interceder.

intercept, *v.* interceptar; detener.

intercourse, *n.* tráfico *m.*: comunicación *f.*; coito *m.*

interest, 1. *n.* interés *m.* 2. *v.* interesar.

interesting, *a.* interesante.

interfere, *v.* meterse; intervenir. **i. with,** estorbar.

interference, *n.* intervención *f.*; obstáculo *m.*

interior, *a.* interior.

interject, *v.* interponer; intervenir.

interjection, *n.* interjección *f.*; interposición *f.*

interlude, *n.* intervalo *m.*; (theater) intermedio *m.*; (music) interludio *m.*

intermediary, *n.* intermediario *m.*

intermediate, *a.* intermedio.

interment, *n.* entierro *m.*

intermission, *n.* intermisión *f.*; (theater) entreacto *m.*

intermittent, *a.* intermitente.

intern, 1. *n.* interno *m.* 2. *v.* internar.

internal, *a.* interno.

international, *a.* internacional.

internationalism, *n.* internacionalismo *m.*

interne, *n.* practicante de hospital *m.*

interpose, *v.* interponer.

interpret, *v.* interpretar.

interpretation, *n.* interpretación *f.*

interpreter, *n.* intérprete *m.* & *f.*

interrogate, *v.* interrogar.

interrogation, *n.* interrogación; pregunta *f.*

interrogative, *a.* interrogativo.

interrupt, *v.* interrumpir.

interruption, *n.* interrupción *f.*

intersect, *v.* cortar.

intersection, *n.* intersección *f.*; (street) bocacalle *f.*

intersperse, *v.* entremezclar.

interval, *n.* intervalo *m.*

intervene, *v.* intervenir.

intervention, *n.* intervención *f.*

interview, 1. *n.* entrevista *f.* 2. *v.* entrevistar.

intestine, *n.* intestino *m.*

intimacy, *n.* intimidad; familiaridad *f.*

intimate, 1. *a.* íntimo, familiar. **2.** *n.* amigo íntimo. **3.** *v.* insinuar.

intimidate, *v.* intimidar.

intimidation, *n.* intimidación *f.*

into, *prep.* en, dentro de.

intonation, *n.* entonación *f.*

intone, *v.* entonar.

intoxicate, *v.* embriagar.

intoxication, *n.* embriaguez *f.*

intravenous, *a.* intravenoso.

intrepid, *a.* intrépido.

intricacy, *n.* intrincación *f.*; enredo *m.*

intricate, *a.* intrincado; complejo.

intrigue, 1. *n.* intriga *f.* **2.** *v.* intrigar.

intrinsic, *a.* intrínseco.

introduce, *v.* introducir; (a person) presentar.

introduction, *n.* presentación; introducción *f.*

introductory, *a.* introductivo.

introvert, *n. & a.* introverso *m.*

intrude, *v.* entremeterse.

intruder, *n.* intruso -sa.

intuition, *n.* intuición *f.*

intuitive, *a.* intuitivo.

inundate, *v.* inundir.

invade, *v.* invadir.

invader, *n.* invasor *m.*

invalid, *a. & n.* inválido -da.

invariable, *a.* invariable.

invasion, *n.* invasión *f.*

invective, 1. *n.* invectiva *f.* **2.** *a.* ultrajante.

inveigle, *v.* seducir.

invent, *v.* inventar.

invention, *n.* invención *f.*

inventive, *a.* inventivo.

inventor, *n.* inventor *m.*

inventory, *n.* inventario *m.*

invertebrate, *n. & a.* invertebrado *m.*

invest, *v.* investir; (com.) invertir.

investigate, *v.* investigar.

investigation, *n.* investigación *f.*

investment, *n.* inversión *f.*

inveterate, *a.* inveterado.

invidious, *a.* difamatorio.

invigorate, *v.* vigorizar, fortificar.

invincible, *a.* invencible.

invisible, *a.* invisible.

invitation, *n.* invitación *f.*

invite, *v.* invitar, convidar.

invocation, *n.* invocación *f.*

invoice, *n.* factura *f.*

invoke, *v.* invocar.

involuntary, *a.* involuntario.

involve, *v.* envolver; implicar.

involved, *a.* complicado.

invulnerable, *a.* invulnerable.

inward, *adv.* hacia adentro.

inwardly, *adv.* interiormente.

iodine, *n.* iodo *m.*

irate, *a.* encolerizado.

Ireland, *n.* Irlanda *f.*

iris, *n.* (anatomy) iris *m.*; (botany) flor de lis *f.*

Irish, *a.* irlandés.

irk, *v.* fastidiar.

iron, 1. *n.* hierro *m.*; (appliance) plancha *f.* **2.** *v.* planchar.

ironical, *a.* irónico.

irony, *n.* ironía *f.*

irrational, *a.* irracional; ilógico.

irregular, *a.* irregular.

irregularity, *n.* irregularidad *f.*

irrelevant, *a.* ajeno.

irresistible, *a.* irresistible.

irresponsible, *a.* irresponsable.

irreverent, *a.* irreverente.

irrevocable, *a.* irrevocable.

irrigate, *v.* regar; (med.) irrigar.

irrigation, *n.* riego *m.*

irritability, *n.* irritabilidad *f.*

irritable, *a.* irritable.

irritant, *n. & a.* irritante *m.*

irritate, *v.* irritar.

irritation, *n.* irritación *f.*

island, *n.* isla *f.*

isolate, *v.* aislar.

isolation, *n.* aislamiento *m.*

isosceles, *a.* isósceles.

issuance, *n.* emisión *f.*; publicación *f.*

issue, 1. *n.* emisión; edición; progenie *f.*; número *m.*;

punto en disputa. **2.** *v.* emitir; publicar.

isthmus, *n.* istmo *m.*

it, *pron.* ello; él, ella; lo, la.

Italian, *a. & n.* italiano -na.

Italy, *n.* Italia *f.*

itch, 1. *n.* picazón *f.* **2.** *v.* picar.

item, *n.* artículo; detalle *m.*;

inserción *f.*; (com.) renglón *m.*

itemize, *v.* detallar.

itinerant, 1. *n.* viandante *m.* **2.** *a.* ambulante.

itinerary, *n.* itinerario *m.*

its, *a.* su.

itself, *pron.* sí; se.

ivory, *n.* marfil *m.*

ivy, *n.* hiedra *f.*

J

jab, 1. *n.* pinchazo *m.* **2.** *v.* pinchar.

jack, *n.* (for lifting) gato *m.*; (cards) sota *f.*

jackal, *n.* chacal *m.*

jackass, *n.* asno *m.*

jacket, *n.* chaqueta *f.*; saco *m.*

jack-of-all-trades, *n.* estuche *m.*

jade, *n.* (horse) rocín *m.*; (woman) picarona *f.*; (min.) jade *m.*

jaded, *a.* rendido.

jagged, *a.* mellado.

jaguar, *n.* jaguar *m.*

jail, *n.* cárcel *f.*

jailer, *n.* carcelero *m.*

jam, 1. *n.* conserva *f.*; apretura *f.* **2.** *v.* apiñar, apretar; trabar.

janitor, *n.* portero *m.*

January, *n.* enero *m.*

Japan, *n.* Japón *m.*

Japanese, *a. & n.* japonés -esa.

jar, 1. *n.* jarro *m.* **2.** *v.* chocar; agitar.

jargon, *n.* jerga *f.*

jasmine, *n.* jazmín *m.*

jaundice, *n.* ictericia *f.*

jaunt, *n.* paseata *f.*

javelin, *n.* jabalina *f.*

jaw, *n.* quijada *f.*

jay, *n.* grajo *m.*

jazz, *n.* jazz *m.*

jealous, *a.* celoso. **to be j.,** tener celos.

jealousy, *n.* celos *m.pl.*

jeer, 1. *n.* burla *f.*, mofa *f.* **2.** *v.* burlar, mofar.

jelly, *n.* jalea *f.*

jellyfish, *n.* aguamar *m.*

jeopardize, *v.* arriesgar.

jeopardy, *n.* riesgo *m.*

jerk, 1. *n.* sacudida *f.* **2.** *v.* sacudir.

jerky, *a.* espasmódico.

Jerusalem, *n.* Jerusalén *m.*

jest, 1. *n.* broma *f.* **2.** *v.* bromear.

jester, *n.* bufón *m.*; burlón *m.*

Jesuit, 1. *n.* jesuíta *m.* **2.** *a.* jesuítico.

Jesus Christ, *n.* Jesucristo *m.*

jet, *n.* chorro *m.*; (gas) mechero *m.*

jetsam, *n.* echazón *f.*

jettison, *v.* echar mercancías al mar.

jetty, *n.* muelle *m.*

Jew, *n.* judío -día.

jewel, *n.* joya *f.*

jeweler, *n.* joyero *m.*

jewelry, *n.* joyería *f.* **j. store,** joyería *f.*

Jewish, *a.* judío.

jib, *n.* (naut.) foque *m.*

jiffy, *n.* instante *m.*

jig, *n.* jiga *f.* **j-saw,** sierra de vaivén *f.*

jilt, *v.* dar calabazas.

jingle, 1. *n.* retintín *m.*; rima pueril *f.* **2.** *v.* retiñir.

jinx, 1. n. aojo m. **2.** v. aojar.
jittery, a. nervioso.
job, n. empleo m.
jobber, n. destajista m., remendero m.
jockey, n. jockey m.
jocular, a. jocoso.
jog, 1. n. empujoncito m. **2.** v. empujar; estimular. **to j. along,** ir a un trote corto.
join, v. juntar; unir.
joiner, n. ebanista m.
joint, n. juntura f.
jointly, adv. conjuntamente.
joke, 1. n. broma, chanza f.; chiste m. **2.** v. bromear.
joker, n. bromista m. & f.
jolly, a. alegre, jovial.
jolt, 1. n. sacudido m. **2.** v. sacudir.
jonquil, n. junquillo m.
jostle, v. rempujar.
journal, n. diario m.; revista f.
journalism, n. periodismo m.
journalist, n. periodista m. & f.
journey, 1. n. viaje m.; jornada f. **2.** v. viajar.
journeyman, n. jornalero m., oficial m.
jovial, a. jovial.
jowl, n. carrillo m.
joy, n. alegría f.
joyful, joyous, a. alegre, gozoso.
jubilant, a. jubiloso.
jubilee, n. jubileo m.
Judaism, n. judaísmo m.
judge, 1. n. juez m. **2.** v. juzgar.
judgment, n. juicio m.

judicial, a. judicial.
judiciary, a. judiciario.
judicious, a. juicioso.
jug, n. jarro m.
juggle, v. escamotear.
juice, n. jugo, zumo m.
juicy, a. jugoso.
July, n. julio m.
jumble, 1. n. revoltillo m. **2.** v. arrebujar, revolver.
jump, 1. n. salto m. **2.** v. saltar, brincar.
junction, n. confluencia f.
juncture, n. junta f.; (r.r.) empalme m.
June, n. junio m.
jungle, n. selva f.
junior, a. menor; más joven. **Jr.,** hijo.
juniper, n. enebro m.
junk, n. basura f.
junket, 1. n. leche cuajado f. **2.** v. festejar.
jurisdiction, n. jurisdicción f.
jurisprudence, n. jurisprudencia f.
jurist, n. jurista m.
juror, n. jurado m.
jury, n. jurado m.
just, 1. a. justo; exacto. **2.** adv. exactamente; (only) sólo. **j. now,** ahora mismo. **to have j.,** acabar de.
justice, n. justicia f.; (person) juez m.
justifiable, a. justificable.
justification, n. justificación f.
justify, v. justificar.
jut, v. sobresalir.
jute, n. yute m.
juvenile, a. juvenil.

K

kaleidoscope, n. calidoscopio m.
kangaroo, n. canguro m.
karakul, n. caracul m.
karat, n. quilate m.
keel, 1. n. quilla f. **2.** v. to k. over, volcarse.
keen, a. agudo; penetrante.

keep, *v.* mantener, retener; guardar; preservar. **k. on,** seguir, continuar.

keeper, *n.* guardián *m.*

keepsake, *n.* recuerdo *m.*

keg, *n.* barrilito *m.*

kennel, *n.* perrera *f.*

kerchief, *n.* pañuelo *m.*

kernel, *n.* pepita *f.*; grano *m.*

kerosene, *n.* kerosén *m.*

ketchup, *n.* salsa de tomate *f.*

kettle, *n.* caldera, olla *f.*

kettledrum, *n.* timpano *m.*

key, *n.* llave *f.*; (music) clave *f.*; (piano) tecla *f.*

keyhole, *n.* bocallave *f.*

khaki, *a.* caqui.

kick, 1. *n.* patada *f.* **2.** *v.* patear; (coll.) quejarse.

kid, 1. *n.* cabrito *m.*; (coll.) niño -ña, chico -ca. **2.** *v.* (coll.) bromear.

kidnap, *v.* secuestrar.

kidnaper, *n.* secuestrador *m.*

kidney, *n.* riñón *m.*

kidney bean, *n.* frijol *m.*

kill, *v.* matar.

killer, *n.* matador *m.*

kiln, *n.* horno *m.*

kilogram, *n.* kilogramo *m.*

kilometer, *n.* kilómetro *m.*

kilowatt, *n.* kilovatio *m.*

kin, *n.* parentesco *m.*; parientes *m.pl.*

kind, 1. *a.* bondadoso, amable. **2.** *n.* género *m.*; clase *f.* **k. of,** algo, un poco.

kindergarten, *n.* kindergarten *m.*

kindle, *v.* encender.

kindling, *n.* encendimiento *m.* **k.-wood,** leña menuda *f.*

kindly, *a.* bondadoso.

kindness, *n.* bondad *f.*

kindred, *n.* parentesco *m.*

kinetic, *a.* cinético.

king, *n.* rey *m.*

kingdom, *n.* reino *m.*

kink, *n.* retorcimiento *m.*

kiosk, *n.* kiosco *m.*

kiss, 1. *n.* beso *m.* **2.** *v.* besar.

kitchen, *n.* cocina *f.*

kite, *n.* cometa *f.*

kitten, *n.* gatito -ta.

kleptomania, *n.* cleptomanía *f.*

kleptomaniac, *n.* cleptómano *m.*

knack, *n.* don *m.*, destreza *f.*

knapsack, *n.* alforja *f.*

knead, *v.* amasar.

knee, *n.* rodilla *f.*

kneecap, *n.* rodillera *f.*

kneel, *v.* arrodillarse.

knickers, *n.* calzón corto *m.*, pantalones *m.*

knife, *n.* cuchillo *m.*

knight, *n.* caballero *m.*; (chess) caballo *m.*

knit, *v.* tejer.

knob, *n.* tirador *m.*

knock, 1. *n.* golpe *m.*; llamada *f.* **2.** *v.* golpear; tocar, llamar.

knot, 1. *n.* nudo; lazo *m.* **2.** *v.* anudar.

knotty, *a.* nudoso.

know, *v.* saber; (a person) conocer.

knowledge, *n.* conocimiento, saber *m.*

knuckle, *n.* nudillo *m.* **k. bone,** jarrete *m.* **to k. under,** ceder a.

Korea, *n.* Corea *f.*

L

label, 1. *n.* rótulo *m.* **2.** *v.* rotular; designar.

labor, 1. *n.* trabajo *m.*; la clase obrera. **2.** *v.* trabajar.

laboratory, *n.* laboratorio *m.*

laborer, trabajador, obrero *m.*

laborious, *a.* laborioso, difícil.

labor union, *n.* gremio obrero *m.*

labyrinth, *n.* laberinto *m.*

lace, 1. *n.* encaje *m.*; (of shoe) lazo *m.* **2.** *v.* amarrar.

lacerate, *v.* lacerar, lastimar.

laceration, *n.* laceración *f.*; desgarro *m.*

lack, 1. *n.* falta *f.* **2.** faltar, carecer.

lackadaisical, *a.* indiferente; soñador.

laconic, *a.* lacónico.

lacquer, 1. *n.* laca *f.*, barniz *m.* **2.** *v.* laquear, barnizar.

lactic, *a.* láctico.

lactose, *n.* lactosa *f.*

ladder, *n.* escalera *f.*

ladle, 1. *n.* cucharón *m.* **2.** *v.* servir con cucharón.

lady, *n.* señora, dama *f.*

ladybug, *n.* mariquita *f.*

lag, 1. *n.* retraso *m.* **2.** *v.* quedarse atrás.

lagoon, *n.* laguna *f.*

laity, *n.* laicidad *f.*

lake, *n.* lago *m.*

lamb, *n.* cordero *m.*

lame, 1. *a.* cojo; estropeado. **2.** *v.* estropear.

lament, 1. *n.* lamento *m.* **2.** *v.* lamentar.

lamentable, *a.* lamentable.

lamentation, *n.* lamento *m.*; lamentación *f.*

laminate, *v.* laminado.

lamp, *n.* lámpara *f.*

lampoon, 1. *n.* pasquín *m.* **2.** *v.* pasquinar.

lance, 1. lanza *f.* **2.** *v.* (med.) abrir.

land, 1. *n.* país *m.*; tierra *f.* **native l.,** patria *f.* **2.** *v.* desembarcar; (plane) aterrizar.

landholder, *n.* hacendado *m.*

landing, *n.* (of stairs) descanso *m.*; (ship) desembarcadero *m.*; (airplane) aterrizaje *m.*

landlady, landlord, *n.* propietario -ria.

landmark, *n.* mojón *m.*, señal *f.*; rasgo sobresaliente *m.*

landscape, *n.* paisaje *m.*

landslide, *n.* derrumbe *m.*

lane, *n.* senda *f.*

language, *n.* lengua *f.*, idioma; lenguaje *m.*

languid, *a.* lánguido.

languish, *v.* languidecer.

languor, *n.* languidez *f.*

lanolin, *n.* lanolina *f.*

lantern, *n.* linterna *f.*; farol *m.*

lap, 1. *n.* regazo *m.*; falda *f.* **2.** *v.* lamer.

lapel, *n.* solapa *f.*

lapse, 1. *n.* lapso *m.* **2.** *v.* pasar; decaer; caer en error.

larceny, *n.* ratería *f.*

lard, *n.* manteca *f.*

large, *a.* grande.

largely, *adv.* ampliamente; mayormente; muy.

largo, *n. & a.* (mus.) largo *m.*

lariat, *n.* lazo *m.*

lark, *n.* (bird) alondra *f.*

larva, *n.* larva *f.*

laryngitis, *n.* laringitis *f.*

larynx, *n.* laringe *f.*

lascivious, *a.* lascivo.

lash, 1. *n.* azote, latigazo *m.* **2.** *v.* azotar.

lass, *n.* doncella *f.*

lassitude, *n.* lasitud *f.*

lasso, 1. *n.* lazo *m.* **2.** *v.* enlazar.

last, 1. *a.* pasado; (final) último. **at l.,** por fin. **2.** *v.* durar.

lasting, *a.* duradero.

latch, *n.* aldaba *f.*

late, 1. *a.* tardío; (deceased) difunto. **to be l.,** llegar tarde. **2.** *adv.* tarde.

lately, *adv.* recientemente.

latent, *a.* latente.

lateral, *a.* lateral.

lather, 1. *n.* espuma de jabón. **2.** *v.* enjabonar.

Latin, *n.* latín *m.*

Latin America, *n.* Hispanoamérica, América Latina *f.*

Latin American, *a. & n.* hispanoamericano -na.

latitude, *n.* latitud *f.*

latrine, *n.* letrina *f.*

latter, *a.* posterior. **the l.,** éste.

lattice, *n.* celosía *f.*

laud, *v.* loar.

laudable, *a.* laudable.

laudanum, *n.* láudano *m.*

laudatory, *a.* laudatorio.

laugh, 1. *n.* risa, risotada *f.*
2. *v.* reír. **l. at,** reírse de.

laughable, *a.* risible.

laughter, *n.* risa *f.*

launch, 1. *n.* (nautical) lancha *f.* **2.** *v.* lanzar.

launder, *v.* lavar y planchar la ropa.

laundry, *n.* lavandería *f.*

laundryman, *n.* lavandero *m.*

laureate, *n. & a.* laureado *m.*

laurel, *n.* laureado.

lava, *n.* lava *f.*

lavatory, *n.* lavatorio *m.*

lavender, *n.* lavándula *f.*

lavish, 1. *a.* pródigo. **2.** *v.* prodigar.

law, *n.* ley *f.*; derecho *m.*

lawful, *a.* legal.

lawless, *a.* sin ley.

lawn, *n.* césped; prado *m.*

lawsuit, *n.* pleito *m.*

lawyer, *n.* abogado *m.*

lax, *a.* flojo, laxo.

laxative, *n.* purgante *m.*

laxity, *n.* laxidad *f.*; flojedad *f.*

lay, 1. *a.* secular. **2.** *v.* poner.

layer, *n.* capa *f.*

layman, *n.* lego, seglar *m.*

lazy, *a.* perezoso.

lead, 1. *n.* plomo *m.*; (theat.) papel principal. **to take the l.,** tomar la delantera. **2.** *v.* conducir; dirigir.

leaden, *a.* plomizo; pesado; abatido.

leader, *n.* líder; jefe; director *m.*

leadership, *n.* dirección *f.*

leaf, *n.* hoja *f.*

leaflet, *n.* (bot.) hojilla *f.*; folleto *m.*

league, *n.* liga; (measure) legua *f.*

leak, 1. *n.* escape; goteo *m.* **2.** *v.* gotear; (nautical) hacer agua.

leakage, *n.* goteo *m.*, escape *m.*, pérdida *f.*

leaky, *a.* llovedizo, resquebrajado.

lean, 1. *a.* flaco, magro. **2.** *v.* apoyarse, arrimarse.

leap, 1. *n.* salto *m.* **2.** *v.* saltar.

leap year, *n.* año bisiesto *m.*

learn, *v.* aprender; saber.

learned, *a.* erudito.

learning, *n.* erudición *f.*, instrucción *f.*

lease, 1. *n.* arriendo *m.* **2.** *v.* arrendar.

leash, 1. *n.* correa *f.* **2.** *v.* atraillar.

least, *a.* menor; mínimo. **the l.,** lo menos. **at l.,** por lo menos.

leather, *n.* cuero *m.*

leathery, *a.* coriáceo.

leave, 1. *n.* licencia *f.* **to take l.,** despedirse. **2.** *v.* dejar; (depart) salir, irse. **l. out,** omitir.

leaven, 1. *n.* levadura *f.* **2.** *v.* fermentar, imbuir.

lecherous, *a.* lujurioso.

lecture, *n.* conferencia *f.*

lecturer, *n.* conferencista *m.*; catedrático *m.*

ledge, *n.* borde, *m.*; capa *f.*

ledger, *n.* libro mayor *m.*

lee, *n.* sotavento *m.*

leech, *n.* sanguijuela *f.*

leek, *n.* porro *m.*

leer, *v.* mirar de soslayo.

leeward, *a.* sotavento.

left, *a.* izquierdo. **the l.,** la izquierda. **to be left,** quedarse.

leftist, *n.* izquierdista *m. & f.*

leg, *n.* pierna *f.*

legacy, *n.* legado *m.*, herencia *f.*

legal, *a.* legal.

legalize, *v.* legalizar.

legation, *n.* legación, embajada *f.*

legend, *n.* leyenda *f.*

legendary, *a.* legendario.

legible, *a.* legible.

legion, *n.* legión *f.*

legislate, *v.* legislar.

legislation, *n.* legislación *f.*

legislator, *n.* legislador *m.*

legislature, *n.* legislatura *f.*

legitimate, *a.* legítimo.

legume, *n.* legumbre *f.*

leisure, *n.* desocupación *f.*; horas libres.

leisurely, 1. *a.* deliberado. **2.** *adv.* despacio.

lemon, n. limón m.
lemonade, n. limonada f.
lend, v. prestar.
length, n. largo m.; duración f.
lengthen, v. alargar.
lengthwise, adv. a lo largo.
lengthy, a. largo.
lenient, a. indulgente.
lens, n. lente m. or f.
Lent, n. cuaresma f.
Lenten, a. cuaresmal.
lentil, n. lenteja f.
leopard, n. leopardo m.
leper, n. leproso m.
leprosy, n. lepra.
lesion, n. lesión f.
less, a. & adv. menos.
lessen, v. disminuir.
lesser, a. menor; más pequeño.
lesson, n. lección f.
lest, conj. para que no.
let, v. dejar; permitir; arrendar.
lethal, a. letal.
lethargic, a. letárgico.
lethargy, n. letargo m.
letter, n. carta; (of alphabet) letra f.
letterhead, n. membrete m.
lettuce, n. lechuga f.
leukemia, n. leucemia f.
levee, n. recepción f.
level, 1. a. llano, nivelado. **2.** n. nivel m.; llanura f. **3.** v. allanar; nivelar.
lever, n. palanca f.
levity, n. levedad f.
levy, 1. n. leva f. **2.** v. imponer.
lewd, a. lascivo.
lexicon, n. léxico m.
liability, n. riesgo m.; obligación f.
liable, a. sujeto; responsable.
liaison, n. vinculación f.; enlace m.; concubinaje m.
liar, n. embustero -ra.
libel, 1. n. libelo m. **2.** v. difamar.
libelous, a. difamatorio.
liberal, a. liberal; generoso.
liberalism, n. liberalismo m.
liberality, n. liberalidad f.
liberate, v. libertar.
liberty, n. libertad f.
libidinous, a. libidinoso.

librarian, n. bibliotecario m.
library, n. biblioteca f.
libretto, n. libreto m.
license, n. licencia f.; permiso m.
licentious, a. licencioso.
lick, v. lamer.
licorice, n. regaliz m.
lid, n. tapa f.
lie, 1. n. mentira f. **2.** v. mentir. **l. down,** acostarse, echarse.
lieutenant, n. teniente m.
life, n. vida f.
lifeboat, n. bote salvavidas m.
life buoy, n. buya f.
life insurance, n. seguro de vida m.
lifeless, a. sin vida.
life preserver, n. salvavidas m.
lift, v. levantar, alzar, elevar.
ligament, n. ligamento m.
ligature, n. ligadura f.
light, 1. a. ligero; liviano; (in color) claro. **2.** n. luz; candela f. **3.** v. encender; iluminar.
lighten, v. aligerar; aclarar; iluminar.
lighter, n. encendedor m.
lighthouse, n. faro m.
lightness, n. ligereza; agilidad f.
lightning, n. relámpago m.
like, 1. a. semejante. **2.** prep. como. **3.** v. **I like . . .**, me gusta, me gustan . . . **I should like,** quisiera.
likeable, a. simpático, agradable.
likelihood, n. probabilidad f.
likely, a. probable; verosímil.
liken, v. comparar; asemejar.
likeness, n. semejanza f.
likewise, adv. igualmente.
lilac, n. lila f.
lilt, 1. n. cadencia alegre f. **2.** v. cantar alegremente.
lily, n. lirio m.
lily of the valley, n. muguete m.
limb, n. rama f.
limber, a. flexible. **to l. up,** ponerse flexible.
limbo, n. limbo m.

lime, *n.* cal *f.*; (fruit) limon-cito *m.*, lima *f.*

limestone, *n.* piedra caliza *f.*

limewater, *n.* agua de cal *f.*

limit, 1. *n.* límite *m.* **2.** *v.* limitar.

limitation, *n.* limitación *f.*

limitless, *a.* ilimitado.

limousine, *n.* limousine *f.*

limp, 1. *n.* cojera *f.* **2.** *a.* flojo. **3.** *v.* cojear.

limpid, *a.* límpido.

line, 1. *n.* línea; fila; raya *f.*; (of print) renglón *m.* **2.** *v.* forrar; rayar.

lineage, *n.* linaje *m.*

lineal, *a.* lineal.

linear, *a.* linear, longitudinal.

linen, *n.* lienzo, lino *m.*; ropa blanca.

liner, *n.* vapor *m.*

linger, *v.* demorarse.

lingerie, *n.* ropa blanca *f.*

linguist, *n.* lingüista *m. & f.*

linguistic, *a.* lingüístico.

liniment, *n.* linimento *f.*

lining, *n.* forro *m.*

link, 1. *n.* eslabón; vínculo *m.* **2.** *v.* vincular.

linoleum, *n.* linóleo *m.*

linseed, *n.* linaza *f.*; simiente de lino *f.*

lint, *n.* hilacha *f.*

lion, *n.* león *m.*

lip, *n.* labio *m.*

lipstick, *n.* lápiz de labios.

liqueur, *n.* cordial *m.*

liquid, *a. & n.* líquido *m.*

liquidate, *v.* liquidar.

liquidation, *n.* liquidación *f.*

liquor, *n.* licor *m.*

lisp, 1. *n.* ceceo *m.* **2.** *v.* cecear.

list, 1. *n.* lista *f.* **2.** *v.* registrar.

listen (to), *v.* escuchar.

listless, *a.* indiferente.

litany, *n.* letanía *f.*

liter, *n.* litro *m.*

literal, *a.* literal.

literary, *a.* literario.

literate, *a.* literato.

literature, *n.* literatura *f.*

litigant, *n. & a.* litigante *m.*

litigation, *n.* litigio, pleito *m.*

litter, 1. *n.* litera *f.*; cama de

paja. **2.** *v.* poner en desorden.

little, *a.* pequeño; (quantity) poco.

liturgical, *a.* litúrgico.

liturgy, *n.* liturgia *f.*

live, 1. *a.* vivo. **2.** *v.* vivir.

livelihood, *n.* subsistencia *f.*

lively, *a.* vivo; rápido; animado.

liver, *n.* hígado *m.*

livery, *n.* librea *f.*

livestock, *n.* ganadería *f.*

livid, *a.* lívido.

living, 1. *a.* vivo. **2.** *n.* sustento *m.* **to earn (make) a living,** ganarse la vida.

lizard, *n.* lagarto *m.*, lagartija *f.*

llama, *n.* llama *f.*

load, 1. *n.* carga *f.* **2.** *v.* cargar.

loaf, 1. *n.* pan *m.* **2.** *v.* holgazanear.

loam, *n.* marga *f.*

loan, 1. *n.* préstamo *m.* **2.** *v.* prestar.

loathe, *v.* aborrecer, detestar.

lobby, *n.* vestíbulo *m.*

lobe, *n.* lóbulo *m.*

lobster, *n.* langosta *f.*

local, *a.* local.

locale, *n.* localidad *f.*

locality, *n.* localidad *f.*, lugar *m.*

localize, *v.* localizar.

locate, *v.* situar; hallar.

location, *n.* sitio *m.*; posición *f.*

lock, 1. *n.* cerradura *f.*; *n.pl.* cabellos *m.pl.* **2.** *v.* cerrar con llave.

locker, *n.* cajón *m.*; ropero *m.*

locket, *n.* guardapelo *m.*, medallón *m.*

lockjaw, *n.* trismo *m.*

locksmith, *n.* cerrajero *m.*

locomotive, *n.* locomotora *f.*

locust, *n.* cigarra *f.*, saltamontes *m.*

locution, *n.* locución *f.*

lode, *n.* filón *m.*, vena *f.*

lodge, 1. *n.* logia; (inn) posada *f.* **2.** *v.* fijar; alojar, morar.

lodger, *n.* inquilino *m.*

lodging, *n.* posada *f.*

loft, *n.* piso *m.*, sobrado *m.*

lofty, a. alto; altivo.

log, n. tronco de árbol; (nautical) barquilla f.

loge, n. palco m.

logic, n. lógica f.

logical, a. lógico.

loin, n. lomo m.

loiter, v. haraganear.

lone, a. solitario.

loneliness, n. soledad f.; tristeza f.

lonely, lonesome, a. solo y triste.

lonesome, a. solitario; triste.

long, 1. a. largo. **a l. time,** mucho tiempo. 2. adv. mucho tiempo. **how l.,** cuánto tiempo. **no longer,** ya no. 3. v. **l. for,** anhelar.

longevity, n. longevidad f.

longing, n. anhelo m.

longitude, n. longitud m.

look, 1. n. mirada f.; aspecto m. 2. v. parecer; mirar. **l. at,** mirar. **l. for,** buscar. **l. like,** parecerse a. **l. out!** ¡cuidado! **l. up,** buscar; ir a ver, venir a ver.

looking glass, n. espejo m.

loom, 1. n. telar m. 2. v. asomar.

loop, n. vuelta f.

loophole, n. abertura f., mirador m.

loose, a. suelto; flojo.

loosen, v. soltar; aflojar.

loot, 1. n. botín m., saqueo m. 2. v. saquear.

lopsided, a. desequilibrado.

loquacious, a. locuaz.

lord, n. señor m.; (Brit. title) lord m.

lordship, n. señorío m.

lose, v. perder.

loss, n. pérdida f.

lost, a. perdido.

lot, n. suerte f.; **building l.,** solar m. **a lot (of), lots of,** mucho.

lotion, n. loción f.

lottery, n. lotería f.

loud, 1. a. fuerte; ruidoso. 2. adv. alto.

loud-speaker, n. altavoz m.

lounge, n. sofá m.; salón de fumar m.

louse, n. piojo m.

love, 1. n. amor m. **in l.,** enamorado. **to fall in l.,** enamorarse. 2. v. querer; amar; adorar.

lovely, a. hermoso.

lover, n. amante m.

low, a. bajo; vil.

lower, v. bajar; (in price) rebajar.

lowly, a. humilde.

loyal, a. leal, fiel.

loyalist, n. lealista m. & f.

loyalty, n. lealtad f.

lozenge, n. pastilla f.

lubricant, n. lubricante m.

lubricate, v. engrasar, lubricar.

lucid, a. claro, lúcido.

luck, suerte; fortuna f.

lucky, a. afortunado. **to be l.,** tener suerte.

lucrative, a. lucrativo.

ludicrous, a. ridículo.

luggage, n. equipaje m.

lukewarm, a. tibio.

lull, 1. n. momento de calma. 2. v. calmar.

lullaby, n. arrullo m.

lumbago, n. lumbago m.

lumber, n. madera f.

luminous, a. luminoso.

lump, n. protuberancia f.; (of sugar) terrón m.

lunacy, n. locura f.

lunar, a. lunar.

lunatic, a. & n. loco -ca.

lunch, luncheon, 1. n. merienda f., almuerzo m. 2. v. merendar, almorzar.

lung, n. pulmón m.

lunge, 1. n. estocada f. 2. v. dar una estocada.

lure, v. atraer.

lurid, a. rojizo; fantástico.

lurk, v. esconderse; espiar.

luscious, a. sabroso, delicioso.

lust, n. sensualidad; codicia f.

luster, n. lustre m.

lustful, a. sensual, lascivo.

lusty, a. vigoroso.

lute, n. laúd m.

Lutheran, n. & a. luterano m.

luxuriant, a. exuberante, frondoso.

luxurious, *a.* lujoso.
luxury, *n.* lujo *m.*
lying, *a.* mentiroso.
lymph, *n.* linfa *f.*

lynch, *v.* linchar.
lyre, *n.* lira *f.*
lyric, *a.* lírico.
lyricism, *n.* lirismo *m.*

M

macabre, *a.* macabre.
macaroni, *n.* macarrones *m.*
machine, *n.* máquina *f.*
machine gun, *n.* ametralladora *f.*
machinery, *n.* maquinaria *f.*
machinist, *n.* maquinista, mecánico *m.*
mackerel, *n.* escombro *m.*
mad, *a.* loco; furioso.
madam, *n.* señora *f.*
magazine, *n.* revista *f.*
magic, 1. *a.* mágico. **2.** *n.* magia *f.*
magician, *n.* mágico *m.*
magistrate, *n.* magistrado *m.*
magnanimous, *a.* magnánimo.
magnate, *n.* magnate *m.*
magnesium, *n.* magnesio *m.*
magnet, *n.* imán *m.*
magnetic, *a.* magnético.
magnificence, *n.* magnificencia *f.*
magnificent, *a.* magnífico.
magnify, *v.* magnificar.
magnitude, *n.* magnitud *f.*
mahogany, *n.* caoba *f.*
maid, *n.* criada *f.* **old m.,** solterona *f.*
maiden, *a.* soltero.
mail, 1. *n.* correo *m.* **air m.,** correo aéreo. **by return m.,** a vuelta de correo. **2.** *v.* echar al correo.
mailbox, *n.* buzón *m.*
mailman, *n.* cartero *m.*
maim, *v.* multilar.
main, *a.* principal.
mainland, *n.* continente *m.*
maintain, *v.* mantener; sostener.
maintenance, *n.* mantenimiento; sustento *m.*; conservación *f.*
maize, *n.* maíz *m.*
majestic, *a.* majestuoso.
majesty, *n.* majestad *f.*
major, 1. *a.* mayor. **2.** *n.* (mil.) comandante *m.*; (study) especialidad *f.*
majority, *n.* mayoría *f.*
make, 1. *n.* marca *f.* **2.** *v.* hacer; fabricar; (earn) ganar.
maker, *n.* fabricante *m.*
makeshift, *a.* provisional.
make-up, *n.* cosméticos *m. pl.*
malady, *n.* mal *m.*, enfermedad *f.*
malaria, *n.* paludismo *m.*
male, *a.* & *n.* macho *m.*
malevolent, *a.* malévolo.
malice, *n.* malicia *f.*
malicious, *a.* malicioso.
malign, 1. *v.* difamar. **2.** *a.* maligno.
malignant, *a.* maligno.
malnutrition, *n.* desnutrición *f.*
malt, *n.* malta *f.* & *f.*
mammal, *n.* mamífero *m.*
man, *n.* hombre; varón *m.*
manage, *v.* manejar; dirigir; administrar; arreglárselas. **m. to,** lograr.
management, *n.* dirección, administración *f.*
manager, *n.* director *m.*
mandate, *n.* mandato *m.*
mandatory, *a.* obligatorio.
mandolin, *n.* mandolina *f.*
mane, *n.* crines *f.*
maneuver, 1. *n.* maniobra *f.* **2.** *v.* maniobrar.

manganese, *n.* manganeso *m.*

manger, *n.* pesebre *m.*

mangle, 1. *n.* planchadora mecánica. **2.** *v.* mutilar.

manhood, *n.* virilidad *f.*

mania, *n.* manía *f.*

maniac, *a. & n.* maniático *m.*

manicure, *n.* manicuro *m.*

manifest, 1. *a. & n.* manifiesto *m.* **2.** *v.* manifestar.

manifesto, *n.* manifiesto *m.*

manifold, 1. *a.* muchos. **2.** *n.* (auto.) tubo múltiple.

manipulate, *v.* manipular.

mankind, *n.* humanidad *f.*

manly, *a.* varonil.

manner, *n.* manera *f.*, modo *m.* **manners,** modales *m. pl.*

mannerism, *n.* manerismo *m.*

mansion, *n.* mansión *f.*

mantel, *n.* manto de chimenea.

mantle, *n.* manto *m.*

manual, *a. & n.* manual *m.*

manufacture, *v.* fabricar.

manufacturer, *n.* fabricante *m.*

manufacturing, *n.* fabricación *f.*

manure, *n.* abono, estiércol *m.*

manuscript, *n.* manuscrito *m.*

many, *a.* muchos. **how m., so m.,** tantos. **too m.,** demasiados, cuántos. **as m. as,** tantos como.

map, *n.* mapa *m.*

maple, *n.* arce *m.*

mar, *v.* estropear; desfigurar.

marble, *n.* mármol *m.*

march, 1. *n.* marcha *f.* **2.** *v.* marchar.

mare, *n.* yegua *f.*

margarine, *n.* margarina *f.*

margin, *n.* margen *m. or f.*

marine, 1. *a.* marino. **2.** *n.* soldado de marina.

mariner, *n.* marinero *m.*

marionette, *n.* marioneta *f.*

marital, *a.* marital.

maritime, *a.* marítimo.

mark, 1. *n.* marca *f.* **2.** *v.* marcar.

market, *n.* mercado *m.* **meat**

m., carnicería *f.* **stock m.,** bolsa *f.*

marmalade, *n.* mermelada *f.*

maroon, *a. & n.* color rojo oscuro.

marquis, *n.* marqués *m.*

marriage, *n.* matrimonio *m.*

married, *a.* casado. **to get m.,** casarse.

marrow, *n.* médula *f.*; substancia *f.*

marry, *v.* casarse con; casar.

marsh, *n.* pantano *m.*

marshal, *n.* mariscal *m.*

marshmallow, *n.* malvavisco *m.*; bombón de altea *m.*

martial, *a.* marcial. **m. law,** gobierno militar.

martyr, *n.* mártir *m. & f.*

martyrdom, *n.* martirio *m.*

marvel, 1. *n.* maravilla *f.* **2.** *v.* maravillarse.

marvelous, *a.* maravilloso.

mascot, *n.* mascota *f.*

masculine, *a.* masculino.

mash, *v.* majar. **mashed potatoes,** puré de papas *m.*

mask, *n.* máscara *f.*

mason, *n.* albañil *m.*

masquerade, *n.* mascarada *f.*

mass, *n.* masa *f.*; (rel.) misa *f.* **to say m.,** cantar misa. **m. production,** producción en serie.

massacre, 1. *n.* carnicería, matanza *f.* **2.** *v.* matar atrozmente, destrozar.

massage, 1. *n.* masaje *m.*; soba *f.* **2.** *v.* sobar.

masseur, *n.* masajista *m. & f.*

massive, *a.* macizo, sólido.

mast, *n.* palo, árbol *m.*

master, 1. *n.* amo; maestro *m.* **2.** *v.* domar, dominar.

masterpiece, *n.* obra maestra.

mastery, *n.* maestría *f.*

mat, 1. *n.* estera; palleta *f.* **2.** *v.* enredar.

match, 1. *n.* igual *m.*; fósforo *m.*; (sport) partida, contienda *f.*; (marriage) noviazgo; casamiento. **2.** *v.* ser igual a; igualar.

mate, 1. *n.* consorte *m. & f.*;

compañero -ra. **2.** *v.* igualar; casar.

material, *a.* & *n.* material *m.* **raw materials,** materias primas.

materialism, *n.* materialismo *m.*

materialize, *v.* materializar.

maternal, *a.* materno.

maternity, *n.* maternidad *f.*

mathematical, *a.* matemático.

mathematics, *n.* matemáticas *f. pl.*

matinee, *n.* matiné *m.*

matrimony, *n.* matrimonio *m.*

matron, *n.* matrona; directora *f.*

matter, *n.* materia *f.;* asunto *m.;* **what's the m.?,** ¿qué pasa? **2.** *v.* importar.

mattress, *n.* colchón *m.*

mature, 1. *a.* maduro. **2.** *v.* madurar.

maturity, *n.* madurez *f.*

maudlin, *a.* sentimental en exceso; peneque.

maul, *v.* maltratar a golpes.

maxim, *n.* máxima *f.*

maximum, *a.* & *n.* máximo.

may, *v.* poder.

May, *n.* mayo *m.*

maybe, *adv.* quizá, quizás, tal vez.

mayonnaise, *n.* mayonesa *f.*

mayor, *n.* alcalde *m.*

maze, *n.* laberinto *m.*

me, *pron.* mí; me. **with me,** conmigo.

meadow, *n.* prado *m.;* vega *f.*

meager, *a.* magro; pobre.

meal, *n.* comida; (flour) harina *f.*

mean, 1. *a.* bajo; malo. **2.** *n.* medio (see also **means**). **3.** *v.* significar; querer decir.

meaning, *n.* sentido, significado *m.*

means, *n. pl.* medios, recursos. **by all m.,** sin falta. **by no m.,** de ningún modo. **by m. of,** por medio de.

meanwhile, *adv.* mientras tanto.

measles, *n.* sarampión *m.*

measure, 1. *n.* medida *f.;*

(music) compás *m.* **2.** *v.* medir.

measurement, *n.* medida, dimensión *f.*

meat, *n.* carne *f.*

mechanic, *n.* mecánico *m.*

mechanical, *a.* mecánico.

mechanism, *n.* mecanismo *m.*

mechanize, *v.* mecanizar.

medal, *n.* medalla *f.*

meddle, *v.* meterse, entremeterse.

mediate, *v.* mediar.

medical, *a.* médico.

medicine, *n.* medicina *f.*

medieval, *a.* medioeval.

mediocre, *a.* mediocre.

mediocrity, *n.* mediocridad *f.*

meditate, *v.* meditar.

meditation, *n.* meditación *f.*

Mediterranean, *n.* Mediterráneo *m.*

medium, 1. *a.* mediano, medio. **2.** *n.* medio *m.*

medley, *n.* mezcla *f.,* ensalada *f.*

meek, *a.* manso; humilde.

meekness, *n.* modestia; humildad *f.*

meet, 1. *a.* propio. **2.** *n.* concurso *m.* **3.** *v.* encontrar; reunirse; conocer.

meeting, *n.* reunión *f.;* mitin, *m.*

megaphone, *n.* megáfono *m.*

melancholy, 1. *a.* melancólico. **2.** *n.* melancolía *f.*

mellow, *a.* suave; blando; maduro.

melodious, *a.* melodioso.

melodrama, *n.* melodrama *m.*

melody, *n.* melodía *f.*

melon, *n.* melón *m.*

melt, *v.* derretir.

member, *n.* socio -ia; miembro *m.*

membership, *n.* membrecía *f.*

membrane, *n.* membrana *f.*

memento, *n.* recuerdo *m.*

memoir, *n.* memoria *f.*

memorable, *a.* memorable.

memorandum, *n.* memorándum, volante *m.*

memorial, 1. *a.* conmemorativo. **2.** *n.* memorial *m.*

memorize, *v.* aprender de memoria.

memory, *n.* memoria *f.*; recuerdo *m.*

menace, 1. *n.* amenaza *f.* **2.** *v.* amenazar.

mend, *v.* reparar, remendar.

menial, 1. *a.* servil. **2.** *n.* sirviente *m.*

menopause, *n.* menopausia *f.*

menstruation. *n.* menstruación *f.*

mental, *a.* mental.

mentality, *n.* mentalidad *f.*

menthol, *n.* mentol *m.*

mention, 1. *n.* mención *f.* **2.** *v.* mencionar.

menu, *n.* menú *m.*, lista *f.*

mercantile, *a.* mercantil.

mercenary, *a. & n.* mercenario -ria.

merchandise, *n.* mercancía *f.*

merchant, 1. *a.* mercante. **2.** *n.* comerciante *m.*

merciful, *a.* misericordioso, compasivo.

merciless, *a.* cruel, inhumano.

mercury, *n.* mercurio *m.*

mercy, *n.* misericordia; merced *f.*

mere, *a.* mero, puro.

merely, *adv.* solamente; simplemente.

merge, *v.* unir, combinar.

merger, *n.* consolidación, fusión *f.*

meringue, *n.* merengue *m.*

merit, 1. *n.* mérito *m.* **2.** *v.* merecer.

meritorious, *a.* meritorio.

mermaid, *n.* sirena *f.*

merriment, *n.* regocijo *m.*

merry, *a.* alegre, festivo.

merry-go-round, *n.* caballitos *m.*

mesh, *n.* malla *f.*

mess, 1. *n.* lío *m.*; confusión *f.*; (mil.) salón comedor, rancho *m.* **2.** *v.* **m. up,** ensuciar; enredar.

message, *n.* mensaje, recado *m.*

messenger, *n.* mensajero -ra.

messy, *a.* confuso, desarreglado.

metabolism, *n.* metabolismo *m.*

metal, *n.* metal *m.*

metallic, *a.* metálico.

metaphysics, *n.* metafísica *f.*

meteor, *n.* meteoro *m.*

meteorology, *n.* meteorología *f.*

meter, *n.* medidor; (measure) metro *m.*

method. *n.* método *m.*

meticulous, *a.* meticuloso.

metric, *a.* métrico.

metropolis, *n.* metrópoli *f.*

metropolitan, *a.* metropolitano.

Mexican, *a. & n.* mexicano -na.

Mexico, *n.* México *m.*

mezzanine, *n.* entresuelo *m.*

microbe, *n.* microbio *m.*

microfilm, *n.* microfilm *m.*

microphone, *n.* micrófono *m.*

microscope, *n.* microscopio *m.*

microscopic, *a.* microscópico.

mid, *a.* medio.

middle, 1. *a. & n.* medio *m.* **in the m. of,** en medio de, a mediados de.

middle-aged, *a.* de edad madura.

midget, *n.* enano -na.

midnight, *n.* medianoche *f.*

midwife, *n.* partera *f.*

might, *n.* poder *m.*, fuerza *f.*

mighty, *a.* poderoso.

migraine, *n.* migraña *f.*; jaqueca *f.*

migrate, *v.* emigrar.

migration, *n.* emigración *f.*

migratory, *a.* migratorio.

mild, *a.* moderado, suave; templado.

mildew, *n.* añublo *m.*, moho *m.*

mile, *n.* milla *f.*

militant, *a.* militante.

militarism, *n.* militarismo *m.*

military, *a.* militar.

militia, *n.* milicia *f.*

milk, 1. *n.* leche *f.* **2.** *v.* ordeñar.

milkman, *n.* lechero *m.*

milky, *a.* lácteo; lechoso.

mill, 1. *n.* molino *m.*; fábrica
f. **2.** *v.* moler.

miller, *n.* molinero *m.*

millimeter, *n.* milímetro *m.*

milliner, *n.* modista *m.* & *f.*

millinery, *n.* sombrerería *f.*

million, *n.* millón *m.*

millionaire, *n.* millonario
-ria.

mimic, 1. *n.* mimo *m.* **2.** *v.*
imitar.

mind, 1. *n.* mente; opinión *f.*
2. *v.* obedecer. **never m.,**
no se ocupe.

mindful, *a.* atento.

mine, 1. *pron.* mío. **2.** *v.*
mina *f.* **3.** *v.* minar.

miner, *n.* minero *m.*

mineral, *a.* & *n.* mineral *m.*

mine sweeper, *n.* dragaminas *f.*

mingle, *v.* mezclar.

miniature, *n.* miniatura *f.*

minimize, *v.* menospreciar.

minimum, *a.* & *n.* mínimo
m.

mining, *n.* minería *f.*

minister, 1. *n.* ministro *m.*
(rel.) pastor *m.* **2.** *v.* minis-
trar.

ministry, *n.* ministerio *m.*

mink, *n.* visón *m.*; (fur) piel
de visón *m.*

minor, 1. *a.* menor. **2.** *n.*
menor de edad.

minority, *n.* minoría *f.*

minstrel, *n.* juglar *m.*

mint, 1. *n.* menta *f.*; casa de
moneda. **2.** *v.* acuñar.

minus, *prep.* menos.

minute, 1. *a.* minucioso. **2.**
minuto, momento *m.*

miracle, *n.* milagro *m.*

miraculous, *a.* milagroso.

mirage, *n.* miraje *m.*

mire, *n.* lodo *m.*

mirror, *n.* espejo *m.*

mirth, *n.* alegría; risa *f.*

misbehave, *v.* portarse mal.

miscellaneous, *a.* misceláneo.

mischief, *n.* travesura, diablura *f.*

mischievous, *a.* travieso,
dañino.

miser, *n.* avaro -ra.

miserable, *a.* miserable; infeliz.

miserly, *a.* avariento, tacaño.

misfortune, *n.* desgracia *f.*,
infortunio, revés *m.*

misgiving, *n.* recelo *m.*, desconfianza *f.*

mishap, *n.* desgracia *f.*, contratiempo *m.*

mislead, *v.* extraviar, despis-
tar; pervertir.

misplaced, *a.* extraviado.

mispronounce, *v.* pronunciar mal.

miss, 1. *n.* señorita *f.* **2.** *v.*
perder; echar de menos.
extrañar. **be missing,** faltar.

missile, *n.* proyectil *m.*

mission, *n.* misión; comisión
f.

missionary, *n.* misionero -ra.

mist, *n.* niebla, bruma *f.*

mistake, 1. *n.* equivocación
f.; error *m.* **to make a m.,**
equivocarse.

mistaken, *a.* equivocado.

mister, *n.* señor *m.*

mistletoe, *n.* muérdago *m.*

mistreat, *v.* maltratar.

mistress, *n.* ama; señora;
concubina *f.*

mistrust, *v.* desconfiar; sospechar.

misty, *a.* nebuloso, brumoso.

misunderstand, *v.* entender
mal.

misuse, *v.* maltratar; abusar.

mite, *n.* pizca *f.*, blanca *f.*

mitten, *n.* mitón, confor-
tante *m.*

mix, *v.* mezclar. **m. up,** confundir.

mixture, *n.* mezcla, mixtura
f.

mix-up, *n.* confusión *f.*

moan, 1. *n.* quejido, gemido
m. **2.** *v.* gemir.

mob, *n.* muchedumbre *f.*;
gentío *m.*

mobilization, *n.* movilización *f.*

mobilize, *v.* movilizar.

mock, *v.* burlar.

mockery, n. burla f.

mode, n. modo m.

model, 1. n. modelo m. **2.** v. modelar.

moderate, 1. a. moderado. **2.** v. moderar.

moderation, n. moderación; sobriedad f.

modern, a. moderno.

modernize, v. modernizar.

modest, a. modesto.

modesty, n. modestia f.

modify, v. modificar.

modulate, v. modular.

moist, a. húmedo.

moisten, v. humedecer.

moisture, n. humedad f.

molar, n. molar m.

molasses, n. molaza f.

mold, 1. n. molde; moho m. **2.** v. moldar, formar; enmohecerse.

moldy, a. mohoso.

mole, n. lunar m.; (animal) topo m.

molecule, n. molécula f.

molest, v. molestar.

mollify, v. molificar.

moment, n. momento m.

momentary, a. momentáneo.

momentous, a. importante.

monarch, n. monarca m.

monarchy, n. monarquía f.

monastery, n. monasterio m.

Monday, n. lunes m.

monetary, a. monetario.

money, n. dinero m. **m. order,** giro postal.

mongrel, 1. n. mestizo m. **2.** a. mestizo, cruzado.

monitor, n. amonestador m.

monk, n. monje m.

monkey, n. mono -na.

monocle, n. monóculo m.

monologue, n. monólogo m.

monopolize, v. monopolizar.

monopoly, n. monopolio m.

monosyllable, n. monosílabo m.

monotone, n. monotonía f.

monotonous, a. monótono.

monotony, n. monotonía f.

monsoon, n. monzón m.

monster, n. monstruo m.

monstrosity, n. monstruosidad f.

monstrous, a. monstruoso.

month, n. mes m.

monthly, a. mensual.

monument, n. monumento m.

monumental, a. monumental.

mood, n. humor m.; (grammar) modo m.

moody, a. caprichoso, taciturno.

moon, n. luna f.

moonlight, n. luz de la luna.

moor, 1. n. páramo m. **2.** v. anclar.

mop, 1. n. estropajo m. **2.** v. fregar.

moral, 1. a. moral. **2.** n. moraleja f. **morals,** moralidad f.

morale, n. espíritu m.

moralist, n. moralista m. & f.

morality, n. moralidad, ética f.

morbid, a. mórbido.

more, a. & adv. más. **m. and m.,** cada vez más.

moreover, adv. además.

morgue, n. necrocomio m.

morning, n. mañana f. **good m.,** buenos días.

morose, a. malhumorado.

morphine, n. morfina f.

morsel, n. bocado m.

mortal, a. & n. mortal m.

mortality, n. mortalidad f.

mortar, n. mortero m.

mortgage, 1. n. hipoteca f. **2.** v. hipotecar.

mortify, v. mortificar.

mosaic, n. & a. mosaico m.

mosquito, n. mosquito m.

moss, n. musgo m.

most, 1. a. más. **2.** adv. más; sumamente. **3.** pron. **m. of,** la mayor parte de.

mostly, adv. principalmente; en su mayor parte.

moth, n. polilla f.

mother, n. madre f.

mother-in-law, n. suegra f.

motif, n. tema m.

motion, 1. n. moción f.; movimiento m. **2.** v. hacer señas.

motionless, a. inmóvil.

motion picture, n. película f.

motivate, v. motivar.

motive, n. motivo m.
motor, n. motor m.
motorboat, n. bote de gasolina.
motorcycle, n. motocicleta f.
motorist, n. motorista m. & f.
motto, n. lema m.
mound, n. terrón; montón m.
mount, 1. n. monte m.; (horse) montura f. 2. v. montar; subir.
mountain, n. montaña f.
mountaineer, n. montañés m.
mountainous, a. montañoso.
mourn, v. lamentar, llorar; llevar luto.
mournful, a. triste.
mourning, n. luto; lamento m.
mouse, n. ratón, ratoncito m.
mouth, n. boca f.; (of river) desembocadura f.
movable, a. movible, movedizo.
move, 1. n. movimiento m.; mudanza f. 2. v. mover; mudarse; emocionar, conmover. **m. away**, quitar; alejarse; mudarse.
movement, n. movimiento m.
movie, n. película f. **m. theater, movies**, cine m.
moving, a. conmovedor; persuasivo.
mow, v. guadañar, segar.
Mr., title. Señor (Sr.)
Mrs., title. Señora (Sra.)
much, a. & adv. mucho. **how m.**, cuánto. **so m.**, tanto. **too m.**, demasiado. **as m. as**, tanto como.
mucilage, n. mucílago m.
mucous, a. mucoso.
mucous membrane, n. mucosa f.
mud, n. fango, lodo m.
muddy, 1. a. lodoso; turbio. 2. v. ensuciar; enturbiar.
muff, n. manguito m.
muffin, n. panecillo m.
mug, n. cubilete m.
mulatto, n. mulato m.
mule, n. mula f.

multiple, a. múltiple.
multiplication, n. multiplicación f.
multiplicity, n. multiplicidad f.
multiply, v. multiplicar.
multitude, n. multitud f.
mummy, n. momia f.
mumps, n. poperas f.pl.
municipal, a. municipal.
munificent, a. munífico.
munition, n. municiones m.
mural, a. & n. mural m.
murder, 1. n. asesinato; homicidio m. 2. v. asesinar.
murderer, n. asesino -na.
murmur, 1. n. murmullo m. 2. v. murmurar.
muscle, n. músculo m.
muscular, a. muscular.
muse, 1. n. musa f. 2. v. meditar.
museum, n. museo m.
mushroom, n. seta f., hongo m.
music, n. música f.
musical, a. musical; melodioso.
musician, n. músico m.
muslin, n. muselina f., percal m.
must, v. deber; tener que.
mustache, n. bigotes m.pl.
mustard, n. mostaza f.
muster, 1. n. (mil.) revista f. 2. v. agregar.
mute, a. & n. mudo m.
mutilate, v. mutilar.
mutiny, 1. n. motín m. 2. amotinarse.
mutter, v. refunfuñar, gruñir.
mutton, n. carnero m.
mutual, a. mutuo.
muzzle, 1. n. hocico m.; bozal m. 2. v. embozar.
my, a. mi.
myriad, n. miríada f.
myrtle, n. mirto m.
myself, pron. mí, mí mismo; me. **I m.**, yo mismo.
mysterious, a. misterioso.
mystery, n. misterio m.
mystic, a. místico.
mystify, v. confundir.
myth, n. mito m.
mythical, a. mítico.
mythology, n. mitología f.

N

nag. 1. *n.* jaca *f.* **2.** *v.* regañar; sermonear.

nail. 1. *n.* clavo *m.*; (finger) uña *f.* **2.** *v.* clavar.

naïve, *a.* ingenuo.

naked, *a.* desnudo.

name, 1. *n.* nombre *m.*; reputación *f.* **2.** *v.* nombrar, mencionar.

namely, *adv.* a saber; es decir.

namesake, *n.* tocayo *m.*

nap, *n.* siesta *f.* **to take a n.,** echar una siesta.

naphtha, *n.* nafta *f.*

napkin, *n.* servilleta *f.*

narcissus, *n.* narciso *m.*

narcotic, *a. & n.* narcótico *m.*

narrate, *v.* narrar.

narrative, 1. *a.* narrativo. **2.** *n.* cuento, relato *m.*

narrow, *a.* estrecho, angosto. **n.-minded,** intolerante.

nasal, *a.* nasal.

nasty, *a.* desagradable; antipático.

nation, *n.* nación *f.*

national, *a.* nacional.

nationalism, *n.* nacionalismo.

nationality, *n.* nacionalidad *f.*

nationalization, *n.* nacionalización *f.*

nationalize, *v.* nacionalizar.

native, 1. *a.* nativo. **2.** *n.* natural; indígena *m & f.*

nativity, *n.* natividad *f.*

natural, *a.* natural.

naturalist, *n.* naturalista *m.*

naturalize, *v.* naturalizar.

naturalness, *n.* naturalidad *f.*

nature, *n.* naturaleza *f.*; índole *f.*; humor *m.*

naughty, *a.* travieso, desobediente.

nausea, *n.* náusea *f.*

nauseous, *a.* nauseoso.

nautical, *a.* náutico.

naval, *a.* naval.

nave, *n.* nave *f.*

navel, *n.* ombligo *m.*

navigable, *a.* navegable.

navigate, *v.* navegar.

navigation, *n.* navegación *f.*

navigator, *n.* navegante *m.*

navy, *n.* marina *f.*

near, 1. *a.* cercano, próximo. **2.** *adv.* cerca. **3.** *prep.* cerca de.

nearby, 1. *a.* cercano. **2.** *adv.* cerca.

nearly, *adv.* casi.

near-sighted, *a.* corto de vista.

neat, *a.* aseado; ordenado.

neatness, *n.* aseo *m.*

nebulous, *a.* nebuloso.

necessary, *a.* necesario.

necessity, *n.* necesidad *f.*

neck, *n.* cuello *m.*

necklace, *n.* collar *m.*

necktie, *n.* corbata *f.*

nectar, *n.* néctar *m.*

need. 1. *n.* necesidad; (poverty) pobreza *f.* **2.** *v.* necesitar.

needle, *n.* aguja *f.*

needless, *a.* innecesario, inútil.

needy, *a.* indigente, necesitado, pobre.

nefarious, *a.* nefario.

negative, 1. *a.* negativo. **2.** *n.* negativa *f.*

neglect, 1. *n.* negligencia *f.*; descuido *m.* **2.** *v.* descuidar.

negligee, *n.* negligee *m.*, bata de casa *f.*

negligent, *a.* negligente, descuidado.

negligible, *a.* insignificante.

negotiate, *v.* negociar.

negotiation, *n.* negociación *f.*

Negro, *n.* negro -ra.

neighbor, *n.* vecino -na.

neighborhood, *n.* vecindad *f.*

neither. 1. *a. & pron.* ninguno de los dos. **2.** *adv.* tampoco. **3.** *conj.* **neither . . . nor,** ni . . . ni.

neon, *n.* neón n.   **n. light,** tubo neón *m.*

nephew, *n.* sobrino *m.*

nerve, *n.* nervio *m.*; (coll.) audacia *f.*

nervous, *a.* nervioso.

nest, *n.* nido *m.*

net, 1. *a.* neto. **2.** *n.* red; **hair n.,** albanega *f.* **3.** redar; (com.) ganar.

netting, *n.* red *m.*; obra de malla *f.*

network, *n.* (radio) red radiodifusora.

neuralgia, *n.* neuralgia *f.*

neurology, *n.* neurología *f.*

neurotic, *a.* neurótico.

neutral, *a.* neutral.

neutrality, *n.* neutralidad *f.*

never, *adv.* nunca, jamás; **n. mind,** no importa.

nevertheless, *adv.* no obstante, sin embargo.

new, *a.* nuevo.

news, *n.* noticias *f.pl.*

newsboy, *n.* vendedor de periódicos.

newspaper, *n.* periódico *m.*

New Testament, *n.* Nuevo Testamento *m.*

new year, *n.* año nuevo *m.*

next, 1. *a.* próximo; siguiente; contiguo. **2.** *adv.* luego, después. **n. door,** al lado. **n. to,** al lado de.

nibble, *v.* picar.

nice, *a.* simpático, agradable; amable; hermoso; exacto.

nick, *n.* muesca *f.*, picadura *f.* **in the n. of time,** apunto.

nickel, *n.* níquel *m.*

nickname, 1. *n.* apodo, mote *m.* **2.** *v.* apodar.

nicotine, *n.* nicotina *f.*

niece, *n.* sobrina *f.*

niggardly, *a.* mezquino.

night, *n.* noche *f.* **good n.,** buenas noches. **last n.,** anoche. **n. club,** cabaret *m.*

night club, *n.* cabaret *m.*

nightgown, *n.* camisa de dormir.

nightingale, *n.* ruiseñor *m.*

nightly, *adv.* todas las noches.

nightmare, *n.* pesadilla *f.*

nimble, *a.* ágil.

nine, *a. & pron.* nueve.

nineteen, *a. & pron.* diecinueve.

ninety, *a. & pron.* noventa.

ninth, *a.* noveno.

nipple, *n.* teta *f.*; pezón *m.*

nitrogen, *n.* nitrógeno *m.*

no, 1. *a.* ninguno. **no one,** nadie. **2.** *adv.* no.

nobility, *n.* nobleza *f.*

noble, *a. & n.* noble *m.*

nobleman, *n.* noble *m.*

nobody, *pron.* nadie.

nocturnal, *a.* nocturno.

nocturne, *n.* nocturno *m.*

nod, 1. *n.* seña con la cabeza. **2.** *v.* inclinar la cabeza; (doze) dormitar.

noise, *n.* ruido *m.*

noiseless, *a.* silencioso.

noisy, *a.* ruidoso.

nominal, *a.* nominal.

nominate, *v.* nombrar.

nomination, *n.* nombramiento *m.*, nominación *f.*

nominee, *n.* nombrado *m.*

nonchalant, *a.* indiferente.

noncombatant, *n.* no combatiente *m.*

noncommittal, *a.* evasivo; reservado.

nondescript, *a.* difícil de describir.

none, *pron.* ninguno.

nonentity, *n.* nulidad *f.*

nonpartisan, *a.* sin afiliación.

nonsense, *n.* tontería *f.*

noodle, *n.* fideo *m.*

noon, *n.* mediodía *m.*

noose, *n.* lazo corredizo *m.*; dogal *m.*

nor, *conj.* ni.

normal, *a.* normal.

north, *n.* norte *m.*

North America, *n.* Norte América *f.*

North American, *a. & n.* norteamericano -na.

northeast, *n.* nordeste *m.*

northern, *a.* septentrional.

North Pole, *n.* polo norte *m.*

northwest, *n.* noroeste *m.*

Norway, *n.* Noruega *f.*

Norwegian, *a. & n.* noruego -ga.

nose, *n.* nariz *f.*

nostalgia, *n.* nostalgia *f.*

nostril, *n.* ventana de la nariz; (pl.) narices.

not, *adv.* no. **n. at all,** de ninguna manera. **n. even,** ni siquiera.

notable, *a.* notable.

notary, *n.* notario *m.*

notation, *a.* notación *f.*

notch, *n.* muesca *f.*; corte *m.*

note, 1. *n.* nota *f.*; apunte *m.* **2.** *v.* notar.

notebook, *n.* libreta *f.*, cuaderno *m.*

noted, *a.* célebre.

noteworthy, *a.* notable.

nothing, *pron.* nada.

notice, 1. *n.* aviso *m.*; noticia *f.* **2.** *v.* observar, fijarse en.

noticeable, *a.* notable.

notification, *n.* notificación *f.*

notify, *v.* notificar.

notion, *n.* noción; idea *f.*; (pl.) novedades *f.pl.*

notoriety, *n.* notoriedad *f.*

notorious, *a.* notorio.

noun, *n.* nombre, sustantivo *m.*

nourish, *v.* nutrir, alimentar.

nourishment, *n.* nutrimento, alimento *m.*

novel, 1. *a.* nuevo, original. **2.** *n.* novela *f.*

novelist, *n.* novelista *m. & f.*

novelty, *n.* novedad *f.*

November, *n.* noviembre *m.*

novena, *n.* novena *f.*

novice, *n.* novicio -cia, novato -ta.

Novocaine, *n.* novocaína *f.*

now, *adv.* ahora. **n. and then,** de vez en cuando. **by n.,** ya. **from n. on,** de ahora en adelante. **just n.,** ahorita. **right n.,** ahora mismo.

nowhere, *adv.* en ninguna parte.

nozzle, *n.* boquilla *f.*

nuance, *n.* matiz *m.*

nucleus, *n.* núcleo *m.*

nude, *a.* desnudo.

nuisance, *n.* molestia *f.*

nullify, *v.* anular.

number, 1. *n.* número *m.*; cifra *f.* **license n.,** matrícula *f.* **2.** *v.* numerar, contar.

numerical, *a.* numérico.

numerous, *a.* numeroso.

nun, *n.* monja *f.*

nuptial, *a.* nupcial.

nurse, 1. *n.* enfermera *f.*; (child's) ama, niñera *f.* **2.** *v.* criar, alimentar, amamantar; cuidar.

nursery, *n.* cuarto destinado a los niños; (agr.) plantel, criadero *m.*

nurture, *v.* nutrir.

nut, *n.* nuez *f.*; (mech.) tuerca *f.*

nutrition, *n.* nutrición *f.*

nutritious, *a.* nutritivo.

nylon, *n.* nilón *m.*

nymph, *n.* ninfa *f.*

O

oak, *n.* roble *m.*

oar, *n.* remo *m.*

oasis, *n.* oasis *m.*

oat, *n.* avena *f.*

oath, *n.* juramento *m.*

oatmeal, *n.* harina de avena *f.*

obedience, *n.* obediencia *f.*

obedient, *a.* obediente.

obese, *a.* obeso, gordo.

obey, *v.* obedecer.

obituary, *n.* obituario *m.*

object, 1. *n.* objeto *m.*; (grammar) complemento *m.* **2.** *v.* oponerse; objetar.

objection, *n.* objeción *f.*

objectionable, *a.* censurable.

objective, *a. & n.* objetivo
m.

obligation, *n.* obligación *f.*

obligatory, *a.* obligatorio.

oblige, *v.* obligar; complacer.

oblique, *a.* oblicuo.

obliterate, *v.* borrar; destruir.

oblivion, *n.* olvido *m.*

oblong, *a.* oblongo.

obnoxious, *a.* ofensivo, odioso.

obscene, *a.* obsceno, indecente.

obscure, 1. *a.* obscuro. **2.**
v. obscurecer.

observance, *n.* observancia;
ceremonia *f.*

observation, *n.* observación
f.

observatory, *n.* observatorio
m.

observe, *v.* observar; celebrar.

observer, *n.* observador -ra.

obsession, *n.* obsesión *f.*

obsolete, *a.* anticuado.

obstacle, *n.* obstáculo *m.*

obstetrician, *n.* obstétrico
m.

obstinate, *a.* obstinado, terco.

obstruct, *v.* obstruir, impedir.

obstruction, *n.* obstrucción
f.

obtain, *v.* obtener, conseguir.

obtuse, *a.* obtuso.

obviate, *v.* obviar.

obvious, *a.* evidente, obvio.

occasion, 1. *n.* ocasión *f.* **2.**
v. ocasionar.

occasional, *a.* ocasional.

occult, *a.* oculto.

occupant, *n.* ocupante *m.*;
inquilino -na.

occupation, *n.* ocupación *f.*;
empleo *m.*

occupy, *v.* ocupar; emplear.

occur, *v.* ocurrir.

occurrence, *n.* ocurrencia *f.*

ocean, *n.* océano *m.*

o'clock, it's one o., es la
una. **it's two o.,** son las
dos, etc. **at . . . o.,** a las . . .

octagon, *n.* octágono *m.*

octave, *n.* octava *f.*

October, *n.* octubre *m.*

octopus, *n.* pulpo *m.*

oculist, *n.* oculista *m.*

odd, *a.* impar; suelto; raro.

odious, *a.* odioso.

odor, *n.* olor *m.*; fragancia *f.*

of, *prep.* de.

off, *prep.* (see under verb:
stop off, take off, etc.)

offend, *v.* ofender.

offender, *n.* ofensor -ra; delincuente *m.*

offense, *n.* ofensa *f.*; crimen
m.

offensive, 1. *a.* ofensivo. **2.**
n. ofensiva *f.*

offer, 1. *n.* oferta *f.* **2.** *v.*
ofrecer.

offering, *n.* oferta *f.*

office, *n.* oficina *f.*; despacho
m.; oficio, cargo *m.*

officer, *n.* oficial *m.* **police
o.,** agente de policía.

official, 1. *a.* oficial. **2.** *n.*
oficial, funcionario *m.*

officiate, *v.* oficiar.

officious, *a.* oficioso.

offspring, *n.* hijos *m.pl.*; progenie *f.*

often, *adv.* muchas veces, a
menudo. **how o.,** con qué
frecuencia.

oil, 1. *n.* aceite; óleo; petróleo
m. **2.** *v.* aceitar; engrasar.

oily, *a.* aceitoso.

ointment, *n.* ungüento *m.*

old, *a.* viejo; antiguo. **o.
man, o. woman,** viejo -ja.

old-fashioned, *a.* fuera de
moda.

Old Testament, *n.* Antiguo
Testamento *m.*

olive, *n.* aceituna, oliva *f.*

omelet, *n.* tortilla de huevos.

omen, *n.* agüero *m.*

ominous, *a.* ominoso, siniestro.

omission, *n.* omisión *f.*;
olvido *m.*

omit, *v.* omitir.

omnibus, *n.* ómnibus *m.*

omnipotent, *a.* omnipotente.

on, *prep.* en, sobre, encima
de. **2.** *adv.* adelante.

once, *adv.* una vez. **at o.,**
en seguida. **o. in a while,**
de vez en cuando.

one, *a. & pron.* uno.

oneself, *pron.* sí mismo; se. **with o.,** consigo.

onion, *n.* cebolla *f.*

only, 1. *a.* único, solo. **2.** *adv.* sólo, solamente.

onward, *adv.* adelante.

opal, *n.* ópalo *m.*

opaque, *a.* opaco.

open, 1. *a.* abierto; franco. **o. air,** aire libre. **2.** *v.* abrir.

opening, *n.* abertura *f.*

opera, *n.* ópera *f.* **o. glasses,** anteojos de ópera; gemelos *m.pl.*

operate, *v.* operar.

operation, *n.* operación *f.* **to have an o.,** operarse, ser operado.

operative, *a.* eficaz, operativo.

operator, *n.* operario -ria. **elevator o.,** ascensorista *m. & f.* **telephone o.,** telefonista *m. & f.*

operetta, *n.* opereta *f.*

ophthalmic, *a.* oftálmico.

opinion, *n.* opinión *f.*

opponent, *n.* antagonista *m. & f.*

opportunism, *n.* oportunismo *m.*

opportunity, *n.* ocasión, oportunidad *f.*

oppose, *v.* oponer.

opposite, 1. *a.* opuesto, contrario. **2.** *prep.* al frente de. **3.** *n.* contrario *m.*

opposition, *n.* oposición *f.*

oppress, *v.* oprimir.

oppression, *n.* opresión *f.*

oppressive, *a.* opresivo.

optic, *a.* óptico.

optician, *n.* óptico *m.*

optics, *n.* óptica *f.*

optimism, *n.* optimismo *m.*

optimistic, *a.* optimista.

option, *n.* opción, elección *f.*

optional, *a.* discrecional, facultativo.

optometry, *n.* optometría *f.*

opulent, *a.* opulento.

or, *conj.* o, (before o-, ho-) u.

oracle, *n.* oráculo *m.*

oral, *a.* oral, vocal.

orange, *n.* naranja *f.*

oration, *n.* discurso *m.*; oración *f.*

orator, *n.* orador *m.*

oratory, *n.* elocuencia *f.*; (church) oratorio *m.*

orbit, *n.* órbita *f.*

orchard, *n.* huerto *m.*

orchestra, *n.* orquesta *f.* **o. seat,** butaca *f.*

orchid, *n.* orquídea *f.*

ordain, *v.* ordenar.

ordeal, *n.* prueba *f.*

order, 1. *n.* orden, *m. o. clase f.*; (com.) pedido *m.* **in o. that,** para que. **2.** *v.* ordenar; mandar; pedir.

orderly, *a.* ordenado.

ordinance, *n.* ordenanza *f.*

ordinary, *a.* ordinario.

ordination, *n.* ordenación *f.*

ore, *n.* mineral *m.*

organ, *n.* órgano *m.*

organdy, *n.* organdí *m.*

organic, *a.* orgánico.

organism, *n.* organismo *m.*

organist, *n.* organista *m. & f.*

organization, *n.* organización *f.*

organize, *v.* organizar.

orgy, *n.* orgía *f.*

orient, 1. *n.* oriente *m.* **2.** *v.* orientar.

Oriental, *a.* oriental.

orientation, *n.* orientación *f.*

origin, *n.* origen *m.*

original, *a. & n.* original *m.*

originality, *n.* originalidad *f.*

ornament, 1. *n.* ornamento *m.* **2.** *v.* ornamentar.

ornamental, *a.* ornamental, decorativo.

ornate, *a.* ornado.

ornithology, *n.* ornitología *f.*

orphan, *a. & n.* huérfano -na.

orphanage, *n.* orfanato *m.*

orthodox, *a.* ortodoxo.

ostentation, *n.* ostentación *f.*

ostentatious, *a.* ostentoso.

ostrich, *n.* avestruz *m.*

other, *a. & pron.* otro. **every o. day,** un día sí otro no.

otherwise, *adv.* de otra manera.

ought, *v.* deber.

ounce, *n.* onza *f.*

our, ours, *a. & pron.* nuestro.

ourselves, *pron.* nosotros mismos; nos.

oust, *v.* desalojar.

ouster, *n.* desahucio *m.*

out, 1. *adv.* fuera, afuera. **out of,** fuera de. **2.** *prep.* por.

outbreak, *n.* erupción *f.*

outcast, *n.* paria *m. & f.*

outcome, *n.* resultado *m.*

outdoors, *adv.* fuera de casa; al aire libre.

outer, *a.* exterior, externo.

outfit, 1. *n.* equipo; traje *m.* **2.** *v.* equipar.

outgrowth, *n.* resultado *m.*

outing, *n.* paseo *m.*

outlaw, 1. *n.* bandido *m.* **2.** *v.* proscribir.

outlet, *n.* salida *f.*

outline, 1. *n.* contorno; esbozo *m.*; silueta *f.* **2.** *v.* esbozar.

outlive, *v.* sobrevivir.

out-of-date, *a.* pasado.

outpost, *n.* puesto avanzado.

output, *n.* capacidad *f.*

outrage, 1. *n.* ultraje *m.*; atrocidad *f.* **2.** *v.* ultrajar.

outrageous, *a.* atroz.

outrun, *v.* exceder.

outside, 1. *a. & n.* exterior *m.* **2.** *adv.* afuera, por fuera. **3.** *prep.* fuera de.

outskirt, *n.* borde *m.*

outward, *adv.* hacia afuera.

outwardly, *adv.* exteriormente.

oval, 1. *a.* oval, ovalado. **2.** *n.* óvalo *m.*

ovary, *n.* ovario *m.*

ovation, *n.* ovación *f.*

oven, *n.* horno *m.*

over, 1. *prep.* sobre, encima de; por. **2.** *adv.* **o. here,** aquí. **o. there,** allí, por allí. **to be o.,** estar terminado.

overcoat, *n.* abrigo, sobretodo *m.*

overcome, *v.* superar, vencer.

overdue, *a.* retrasado.

overflow, 1. *n.* inundación *f.* **2.** *v.* inundar.

overhaul, *v.* repasar.

overhead, *adv.* arriba, en lo alto.

overlook, *v.* pasar por alto.

overnight, *adv.* **to stay** or **stop o.,** pasar la noche.

overpower, *v.* vencer.

overrule, *v.* predominar.

overrun, *v.* invadir.

oversee, *v.* superentender.

oversight, *n.* equivocación *f.*

overt, *a.* abierto.

overtake, *v.* alcanzar.

overthrow, 1. *n.* trastorno *m.* **2.** *v.* trastornar.

overture, *n.* obertura *f.*

overturn, *v.* trastornar.

overweight, *a.* demasiado pesado.

overwhelm, *v.* abrumar.

overwork, *v.* trabajar demasiado.

owe, *v.* deber. **owing to,** debido a.

owl, *n.* lechuza *f.*

own, 1. *a.* propio. **2.** *v.* poseer.

owner, *n.* dueño -ña.

ox, *n.* buey *m.*

oxygen, *n.* oxígeno *m.*

oxygen tent, *n.* tienda de oxígeno *f.*

oyster, *n.* ostra *f.*

P

pace, 1. *n.* paso *m.* **2.** *v.* pasearse. **p. off,** medir a pasos.

pacific, *a.* pacífico.

pacifier, *n.* pacificador *m.*; (baby p.) chupete *m.*

pacifism, *n.* pacifismo *m.*

pacifist, *n.* pacifista *m. & f.*

pacify, v. pacificar.

pack, 1. n. fardo; paquete m.; (animals) muta f. p. of cards, baraja f. 2. v. empaquetear; (baggage) empacar.

package, n. paquete, bulto m.

pact, n. pacto m.

pad, 1. n. colchoncillo m. p. of paper, bloc de papel. 2. v. rellenar.

paddle, 1. n. canalete m. 2. v. remar.

padlock, n. candado m.

pagan, a. & n. pagano -na.

page, n. página f.; (boy) paje m.

pageant, n. espectáculo m.; procesión f.

pail, n. cubo m.

pain, 1. n. dolor m. to take pains, esmerarse.

painful, a. doloroso; penoso.

paint, 1. n. pintura f. 2. v. pintar.

painter, n. pintor -ra.

painting, n. pintura f.; cuadro m.

pair, 1. n. par m.; pareja f. 2. v. parear. p. off, emparejarse.

pajamas, n. pijama m.

palace, n. palacio m.

palatable, a. sabroso, agradable.

palate, n. paladar m.

palatial, a. palaciego, suntuoso.

pale, a. pálido. to turn pale, palidecer.

paleness, n. palidez f.

palette, n. paleta f.

pallbearer, n. andero m.

pallid, a. pálido.

palm, n. palma f. p. tree, palmera f.

palpitate, v. palpitar.

paltry, a. miserable.

pamper, v. mimar.

pamphlet, n. folleto m.

pan, n. cacerola f.

panacea, n. panacea f.

Pan-American, a. panamericano.

pane, n. hoja f., cuadro m.

panel, n. tablero m.

pang, n. dolor; remordimiento m.

panic, n. pánico m.

panorama, n. panorama m.

pant, v. jadear.

panther, n. pantera f.

pantomime, n. pantomima f.; mímica f.

pantry, n. despensa f.

pants, n. pantalones m.pl.

papal, a. papal.

paper, n. papel; periódico: artículo m.

paper hanger, n. empapelador m.

par, n. paridad f.; (com.) par f.

parable, n. parábola f.

parachute, n. paracaídas m.

parade, 1. n. desfile m., procesión f. 2. v. desfilar.

paradise, n. paraíso m.

paradox, n. paradoja f.

paraffin, n. parafina f.

paragraph, n. párrafo m.

parakeet, n. perico m.

parallel, 1. a. paralelo. 2. v. correr parejas con.

paralysis, n. parálisis f.

paralyze, v. paralizar.

paramount, a. supremo.

paraphrase, 1. n. paráfrasis f. 2. v. parafrasear.

parasite, n. parásito m.

parcel, n. paquete m. p. of land, lote de terreno.

parchment, n. pergamino m.

pardon, 1. n. perdón m. 2. v. perdonar.

pare, v. pelar.

parentage, n. origen m.; extracción f.

parenthesis, n. paréntesis m.

parents, n. padres m.pl.

parish, n. parroquia f.

Parisian, a. & n. parisiense m. & f.

park, 1. n. parque m. 2. v. estacionar.

parkway, n. bulevar m.

parley, n. conferencia f.; (mil.) parlamento m.

parliament, n. parlamento m.

parliamentary, a. parlamentario.

parlor, n. sala f., salón m.

parochial, a. parroquial.

parody, 1. *n.* parodia *f.* **2.** *v.* parodiar.

parole, 1. *n.* palabra *f.*; (mil.) santo y seña. **2.** *v.* poner en libertad bajo palabra.

paroxysm, *n.* paroxismo *m.*

parrot, *n.* loro, papagayo *m.*

parsimony, *n.* parsimonia *f.*

parsley, *n.* perejil *m.*

parson, *n.* párroco *m.*

part, 1. *n.* parte *f.*; (theater) papel *m.* **2.** *v.* separar(se) partirse. **p. with,** desprenderse de.

partake, *v.* tomar parte.

partial, *a.* parcial.

participant, *n.* participante *m. & f.*

participate, *v.* participar.

participation, *n.* participación *f.*

participle, *n.* participio *m.*

particle, *n.* partícula *f.*

particular, *a. & n.* particular *m.*

parting, *n.* despedida *f.*

partisan, *a. & n.* partidario -ria.

partition, *n.* tabique *m.*

partly, *adv.* en parte.

partner, *n.* socio -cia; compañero -ra.

partridge, *n.* perdiz *f.*

party, *n.* tertulia, fiesta, *f.*; grupo *m.*; (political) partido *m.*

pass, 1. *n.* pase; (mountain) paso *m.* **2.** *v.* pasar. **p. away,** fallecer.

passable, *a.* transitable; regular.

passage, *n.* pasaje; (corridor) pasillo *m.*

passé, *a.* anticuado.

passenger, *n.* pasajero -ra.

passer-by, *n.* transeúnte *m. & f.*

passion, *n.* pasión *f.*

passionate, *a.* apasionado.

passive, *a.* pasivo.

passport, *n.* pasaporte *m.*

past, 1. *a. & n.* pasado *m.* **2.** *prep.* más allá de; después de.

paste, 1. *n.* pasta *f.* **2.** *v.* empastar; pegar.

pasteurize *v.* pasteurizar.

pastime, *n.* pasatiempo *m.*; diversión *f.*

pastor, *n.* pastor *m.*

pastry, *n.* pastelería *f.*

pasture, 1. *n.* pasto *m.*; pradera *f.* **2.** *v.* pastar.

pat, 1. *n.* golpecillo *m.* **to stand p.,** mantenerse firme. **2.** *v.* dar golpecitos.

patch, 1. *n.* remiendo *m.* **2.** *v.* remendar.

patent, 1. *a. & n.* patente *f.* **2.** *v.* patentar.

patent leather, *n.* charol *m.*

paternal, *a.* paterno, paternal.

paternity, *n.* paternidad *f.*

path, *n.* senda *f.*

pathetic, *a.* patético.

pathology, *n.* patología *f.*

pathos, *n.* rasgo conmovedor *m.*

patience, *n.* paciencia *f.*

patient, 1. *a.* paciente. **2.** *n.* enfermo, paciente *m.*

patio, *n.* patio *m.*

patriarch, *n.* patriarca *m.*

patriot, *n.* patriota *m.*

patriotic, *a.* patriótico.

patriotism, *n.* patriotismo *m.*

patrol, 1. *n.* patrulla *f.* **2.** *v.* patrullar.

patrolman, *n.* vigilante *m.*; patrullador *m.*

patron, *n.* patrón *m.*

patronize, *v.* condescender; patrocinar; ser cliente de.

pattern, *n.* modelo *m.*

pauper, *n.* indigente *m. & f.*

pause, 1. *n.* pausa *f.* **2.** *v.* pausar.

pave, *v.* pavimentar. **p. the way,** preparar el camino.

pavement, *n.* pavimento *m.*

pavilion, *n.* pabellón *m.*

paw, 1. *n.* pata *f.* **2.** *v.* patear.

pawn, 1. *n.* prenda *f.*; (chess) peón de ajedrez *m.* **2.** *v.* empeñar.

pay, 1. *n.* pago; sueldo, salario *m.* **2.** *v.* pagar. **p. back,** pagar; vengarse de.

payment, *n.* pago *m.*; recompensa *f.*

pea, *n.* guisante *m.*

peace, *n.* paz *f.*

peaceable, a. pacífico.

peaceful, a. tranquilo.

peach, n. durazno, melocotón m.

peacock, n. pavo real m.

peak, n. pico, cumbre; máximo m.

peal, n. repique; estruendo m. **p. of laughter,** risotada f.

peanut, n. maní, cacahuete m.

pear, n. pera f.

pearl, n. perla f.

peasant, n. campesino -na.

pebble, n. guija f.

peck, 1. n. picotazo m. 2. v. picotear.

peculiar, a. peculiar.

pecuniary, a. pecuniario.

pedagogue, n. pedagogo m.

pedagogy, n. pedagogía f.

pedal, n. pedal m.

pedant, n. pedante m.

peddler, n. buhonero m.

pedestal, n. pedestal m.

pedestrian, n. peatón -na.

pediatrician, n. pediatra m. & f.

pedigree, n. genealogía f.

peek, 1. n. atisbo m. 2. v. atisbar.

peel, 1. n. corteza f.; (fruit) pellejo m. 2. v. descortezar; pelar.

peep, n. ojeada f.

peer, 1. n. par m. 2. v. mirar fijamente.

peg, n. clavija; estaquilla f.; gancho m.

pelt, 1. n. pellejo m. 2. v. apedrear; (rain) caer con fuerza.

pelvis, n. pelvis f.

pen, n. pluma f.; corral m. **fountain p.,** pluma fuente.

penalty, n. pena; multa f.; castigo m.

penance, n. penitencia f. **to do p.,** penar.

penchant, n. propensión f.

pencil, n. lápiz m.

pending, a. pendiente. **to be p.,** pender.

penetrate, v. penetrar.

penetration, n. penetración f.

penicillin, n. penicilina f.

peninsula, n. península f.

penitent, n. & a. penitente m.

penknife, n. cortaplumas f.

penniless, a. indigente.

penny, n. penique m.

pension, n. pensión f.

pensive, a. pensativo.

penury, n. penuria f.

people, 1. n. gente f.; (of a nation) pueblo m. 2. v. poblar.

pepper, n. pimienta f.; (veg.) pimiento m.

per, prep. por.

perambulator, n. cochecillo de niño m.

perceive, v. percibir.

percent, adv. por ciento.

percentage, n. porcentaje m.

perceptible, a. perceptible.

perception, n. percepción f.

perch, n. percha f.; (fish) perca f.

perdition, n. perdición f.

peremptory, a. perentorio, terminante.

perennial, a. perenne.

perfect, 1. a. perfecto. 2. v. perfeccionar.

perfection, n. perfección f.

perforation, n. perforación f.

perform, v. hacer; ejecutar; (theater) representar.

performance, n. ejecución f.; (theater) representación f.

perfume, 1. n. perfume m.; fragancia f. 2. v. perfumar.

perfunctory, a. perfunctorio, superficial.

perhaps, adv. quizá, quizás, tal vez.

peril, n. peligro m.

perilous, a. peligroso.

perimeter, n. perímetro m.

period, n. período m.; (punctuation) punto m.

periodic, a. periódico.

periodical, n. revista f.

periphery, n. periferia f.

perish, v. perecer.

perishable, a. perecedero.

perjury, n. perjurio m.

permanent, a. permanente. **p. wave,** ondulado permanente.

permeate, v. penetrar.

permissible, a. permisible.

permission, *n.* permiso *m.*

permit, 1. *n.* permiso *m.* **2.** *v.* permitir.

pernicious, *a.* pernicioso.

perpendicular, *n. & a.* perpendicular *m.*

perpetrate, *v.* perpetrar.

perpetual, *a.* perpetuo.

perplex, *v.* confundir.

perplexity, *n.* perplejidad *f.*

persecute, *v.* perseguir.

persecution, *n.* persecución *f.*

perseverance, *n.* perseverancia *f.*

persevere, *v.* perseverar.

persist, *v.* persistir.

persistent, *a.* persistente.

person, *n.* persona *f.*

personage, *n.* personaje *m.*

personal, *a.* personal.

personality, *n.* personalidad *f.*

personnel, *n.* personal *m.*

perspective, *n.* perspectiva *f.*

perspiration, *n.* sudor *m.*

perspire, *v.* sudar.

persuade, *v.* persuadir.

persuasive, *a.* persuasivo.

pertain, *v.* pertenecer.

pertinent, *a.* pertinente.

perturb, *v.* perturbar.

peruse, *v.* leer con cuidado.

pervade, *v.* penetrar; llenar.

perverse, *a.* perverso.

perversion, *n.* perversión *f.*

pessimism, *n.* pesimismo *m.*

pestilence, *n.* pestilencia *f.*

pet, 1. *n.* favorito -ta. **2.** *v.* mimar.

petal, *n.* pétalo *m.*

petition, 1. *n.* petición, súplica *f.* **2.** *v.* pedir, suplicar.

petrify, *v.* petrificar.

petroleum, *n.* petróleo *m.*

petticoat, *n.* enagua *f.*

petty, *a.* mezquino, insignificante.

petulant, *a.* quisquilloso.

pew, *n.* banco de iglesia *m.*

pewter, *n.* peltre *m.*

phantom, *n.* espectro, fantasma *m.*

pharmacist, *n.* farmacéutico, boticario *m.*

pharmacy, *n.* farmacia, botica *f.*

phase, *n.* fase *f.*

pheasant, *n.* faisán *m.*

phenomenal, *a.* fenomenal.

phenomenon, *n.* fenómeno *m.*

philanthropy, *n.* filantropía *f.*

philately, *n.* filatelia *f.*

philosopher, *n.* filósofo *m.*

philosophical, *a.* filosófico.

philosophy, *n.* filosofía *f.*

phlegm, *n.* flema *f.*; frialdad de ánimo *f.*

phobia, *n.* fobia *f.*

phonetic, *a.* fonético.

phonograph, *n.* fonógrafo *m.*

phosphorus, *n.* fósforo *m.*

photoelectric, *a.* fotoeléctrico.

photogenic, *a.* fotogénico.

photograph, 1. *n.* fotografía *f.* **2.** *v.* fotografiar; retratar.

photography, *n.* fotografía *f.*

Photostat, *n.* fotocopia *f.*

phrase, 1. *n.* frase *f.* **2.** *v.* expresar.

physical, *a.* físico.

physician, *n.* médico *m.*

physics, *n.* física *f.*

physiology, *n.* fisiología *f.*

physiotherapy, *n.* fisioterapia *f.*

physique, *n.* físico *m.*

pianist, *n.* pianista *m. & f.*

piano, *n.* piano *m.*

picayune, *a.* insignificante.

piccolo, *n.* flautín *m.*

pick, 1. *n.* pico *m.* **2.** *v.* escoger. **p. up,** recoger.

picket, *n.* piquete *m.*

pickle, 1. *n.* salmuera *f.*; encurtido *m.* **2.** *v.* escabechar.

pickpocket, *n.* cortabolsas *m. & f.*

picnic, *n.* picnic *m.*

picture, 1. *n.* cuadro; retrato *m.*; fotografía *f.*; (movie) película *f.* **2.** *v.* imaginarse.

picturesque, *a.* pintoresco.

pie, *n.* pastel *m.*

piece, *n.* pedazo *m.*; pieza *f.*

pier, *n.* muelle *m.*

pierce, *v.* perforar; pinchar; traspasar.

piety, *n.* piedad *f.*

pig, *n.* puerco, cerdo, lechón *m.*

pigeon, *n.* paloma *f.*

pigeonhole, *n.* casilla *f.*

pigment, *n.* pigmento *m.*

pile, 1. *n.* pila *f.*; montón *m.*; *pl.* (med.) hemorroides *f.pl.* **2.** *v.* amontonar.

pilfer, *v.* ratear.

pilgrim, *n.* peregrino -na, romero -ra.

pilgrimage, *n.* romería *f.*

pill, *n.* píldora *f.*

pillage, 1. *n.* pillaje *m.* **2.** *v.* pillar.

pillar, *n.* columna *f.*

pillow, *n.* almohada *f.*

pillowcase, *n.* funda de almohada *f.*

pilot, 1. *n.* piloto *m.* **2.** *v.* pilotear.

pimple, *n.* grano *m.*

pin, 1. *n.* alfiler; broche *m.*; (mech.) clavija *f.* **2.** *v.* prender. **p. up,** fijar.

pinch, 1. *n.* pellizco *m.* **2.** *v.* pellizcar.

pine, 1. *n.* pino *m.* **2.** *v.* **p. away,** languidecer. **p. for,** anhelar.

pineapple, *n.* piña, ananá *m.*

pink, *a.* rosado.

pinnacle, *n.* pináculo *m.*; cumbre *f.*

pint, *n.* pinta *f.*

pioneer, *n.* pionero -ra.

pious, *a.* piadoso.

pipe, *n.* pipa *f.*; tubo; (of organ) cañón *m.*

piper, *n.* flautista *m. & f.*

piquant, *a.* picante.

pirate, *n.* pirata *m.*

pistol, *n.* pistola *f.*

piston, *n.* pistón *m.*

pit, *n.* hoyo *m.*; (fruit) hueso *m.*

pitch, 1. *n.* brea *f.*; grado de inclinación; (music) tono *m.* **2.** *v.* lanzar; (ship) cabecear.

pitchblende, *n.* pechblenda *f.*

pitcher, *n.* cántaro *m.*; (baseball) lanzador *m.*

pitchfork, *n.* horca *f.*; tridente *m.*

pitfall, *n.* trampa *f.*, hoya cubierta *f.*

pitiful, *a.* lastimoso.

pitiless, *a.* cruel.

pity, 1. *n.* compasión, piedad *f.* **to be a p.,** ser lástima. **2.** *v.* compadecer.

pivot, 1. *n.* espiga *f.*, pivote *m.*; punto de partido *m.* **2.** *v.* girar sobre un pivote.

placard, 1. *n.* cartel *m.* **2.** *v.* f jar carteles.

placate, *v.* aplacar.

place, 1. *n.* lugar, sitio, puesto *m.* **2.** *v.* colocar, poner.

placid, *a.* plácido.

plagiarism, *n.* plagio *m.*

plague, 1. *n.* plaga, peste *f.* **2.** *v.* atormentar.

plain, 1. *a.* sencillo; puro; evidente. **2.** *n.* llano *m.*

plaintiff, *n.* demandador -ra.

plan, 1. *n.* plan, propósito *m.* **2.** *v.* planear; pensar. **p. on,** contar con.

plane, 1. *n.* plano; (tool) cepillo *m.* **2.** *v.* allanar; acepillar.

planet, *n.* planeta *m.*

planetarium, *n.* planetario *m.*

plank, *n.* tablón *m.*

plant, 1. *n.* mata, planta *f.* **2.** *v.* sembrar, plantar.

plantation, *n.* plantación *f.* **coffee p.,** cafetal *m.*

planter, *n.* plantador; hacendado *m.*

plasma, *n.* plasma *m.*

plaster, 1. *n.* yeso; emplasto *m.* **2.** *v.* enyesar; emplastar.

plastic, *a.* plástico.

plate, 1. *n.* plato *m.*; plancha de metal. **2.** *v.* planchear.

plateau, *n.* meseta *f.*

platform, *n.* plataforma *f.*

platinum, *n.* platino *m.*

platitude, *n.* perogrullada *f.*

platter, *n.* fuente *f.*; platel *m.*

plaudit, *n.* aplauso *m.*

plausible, *a.* plausible.

play, 1. *n.* juego *m.*; (theater) pieza *f.* **2.** *v.* jugar; (music) tocar; (theater) representar. **p. a part,** hacer un papel.

player, *n.* jugador -ra; (music) músico *m.*; (theater) actor *m.*, actriz *f.*

playful, *a.* juguetón.

playground, *n.* campo de deportes; patio de recreo.

playmate, *n.* compañero -ra de juego.

playwright, *n.* dramaturgo *m.*

plea, *n.* ruego *m.*; súplica *f.*; (legal) declaración *f.*

plead, *v.* suplicar; declararse. **p. a case,** defender un pleito.

pleasant, *a.* agradable.

please, 1. *v.* gustar, agradar. **Pleased to meet you,** Mucho gusto en conocer a Vd. **2.** *adv.* por favor. **Please...** Haga el favor de ..., Tenga la bondad de ..., Sírvase ...

pleasure, *n.* gusto, placer *m.*

pleat, 1. *n.* pliegue *m.* **2.** *v.* plegar.

plebiscite, *n.* plebiscito *m.*

pledge, 1. *n.* empeño *m.* **2.** *v.* empeñar.

plentiful, *a.* abundante.

plenty, *n.* abundancia *f.* **p. of,** bastante. **p. more,** mucho más.

pleurisy, *n.* pleuritis *f.*

pliable, pliant, *a.* flexible.

pliers, *n.pl.* alicates *m.pl.*

plight, *n.* apuro, aprieto *m.*

plot, 1. *n.* conspiración *f.*; (of a story) trama; (of land) parcela *f.* **2.** *v.* conspirar; tramar.

plow, 1. *n.* arado *m.* **2.** *v.* arar.

pluck, 1. *n.* valor *m.* **2.** *v.* arrancar; desplumar.

plug, 1. *n.* tapón; (elec.) enchufe *m.* **spark p.,** bujía *f.* **2.** *v.* tapar.

plum, *n.* ciruela *f.*

plumage, *n.* plumaje *m.*

plumber, *n.* plomero *m.*

plume, *n.* pluma *f.*

plump, *a.* regordete.

plunder, 1. *n.* botín *m.*; despojos *m.pl.* **2.** *v.* saquear.

plunge, *v.* zambullir; precipitar.

plural, *a. & n.* plural *m.*

plus, *prep.* más.

plutocrat, *n.* plutócrata *m. & f.*

pneumatic, *a.* neumático.

pneumonia, *n.* pulmonía *f.*

poach, *v.* (eggs) escalfar; invadir; cazar en vedado.

pocket, 1. *n.* bolsillo *m.* **2.** *v.* embolsar.

pocketbook, *n.* cartera *f.*

podiatry, *n.* podiatría *f.*

poem, *n.* poema *m.*

poet, *n.* poeta *m.*

poetic, *a.* poético.

poetry, *n.* poesía *f.*

poignant, *a.* conmovedor.

point, 1. *n.* punta *f.*; punto *m.* **2.** *v.* apuntar. **p. out,** señalar.

pointed, *a.* puntiagudo; directo.

pointless, *a.* inútil.

poise, 1. *n.* equilibrio *m.*; serenidad *f.* **2.** *v.* equilibrar; estar suspendido.

poison, 1. *n.* veneno *m.* **2.** *v.* envenenar.

poisonous, *a.* venenoso.

poke, 1. *n.* empuje *m.*, hurgonada *f.* **2.** *v.* picar; haronear.

Poland, *n.* Polonia *f.*

polar, *a.* polar.

pole, *n.* palo; (geog.) polo *m.*

police, *n.* policía *f.*

policeman, *n.* policía *m.*

policy, *n.* política *f.* **insurance p.,** póliza de seguro.

Polish, *a. & n.* polaco *m.*

polish, 1. *n.* lustre *m.* **2.** *v.* pulir, lustrar.

polite, *a.* cortés.

politic, political, *a.* político.

politician, *n.* político *m.*

politics, *n.* política *f.*

poll, *n.* encuesta *f.*; (pl.) urnas *f.pl.*

pollen, *n.* polen *m.*

pollute, *v.* contaminar.

polo, *n.* polo *m.*

polygamy, *n.* poligamia *f.*

polygon, *n.* polígono *m.*

pomp, *n.* pompa *f.*

pompous, *a.* pomposo.

poncho, *n.* poncho *m.*

pond, *n.* charca *f.*

ponder, *v.* ponderar, meditar.

ponderous, *a.* ponderoso, pesado.

pontiff, *n.* pontífice *m.*

pontoon, *n.* pontón *m.*

pony, *n.* caballito *m.*

pool, *n.* charco *m.* **swimming p.,** piscina *f.*

poor, *a.* pobre; (not good) malo.

pop, *n.* chasquido *m.*

popcorn, *n.* maíz tostado *m.*

pope, *n.* papa *m.*

popular, *a.* popular.

popularity, *n.* popularidad *f.*

population, *n.* población *f.*

porcelain, *n.* porcelana *f.*

porch, *n.* pórtico *m.*; galería *f.*

pore, *n.* poro *m.*

pork, *n.* carne de puerco.

pornography, *n.* pornografía *f.*

porous, *a.* poroso, esponjoso.

port, *n.* puerto; (naut.) babor *m.* **p. wine,** oporto *m.*

portable, *a.* portátil.

portal, *n.* portal *m.*

portend, *v.* pronosticar.

portent, *n.* presagio *m.*, portento *m.*

porter, *n.* portero *m.*

portfolio, *n.* cartera *f.*

porthole, *n.* porta *f.*

portion, *n.* porción *f.*

portly, *a.* corpulento.

portrait, *n.* retrato *m.*

portray, *v.* pintar.

Portugal, *n.* Portugal *m.*

Portuguese, *a. & n.* portugués -sa.

pose, 1. *n.* postura; actitud *f.* **2.** *v.* posar. **p. as,** pretender ser.

position, *n.* posición *f.*

positive, *a.* positivo.

possess, *v.* poseer.

possession, *n.* posesión *f.*

possessive, *a.* posesorio.

possibility, *n.* posibilidad *f.*

possible, *a.* posible.

post, 1. *n.* poste; puesto *m.* **2.** *v.* fijar; situar; echar al correo.

postage, *n.* porte de correo. **p. stamp,** sello *m.*

postal, *a.* postal.

post card, tarjeta postal.

poster, *n.* cartel, letrero *m.*

posterior, *a.* posterior.

posterity, *n.* posteridad *f.*

postgraduate, *a.* postgraduado.

postmark, *n.* matasellos *m.*

post office, casa de correos.

postpone, *v.* posponer, aplazar.

postscript, *n.* posdata *f.*

posture, *n.* postura *f.*

pot, *n.* olla, marmita *f.* **flower p.,** tiesto *m.*

potassium, *n.* potasio *m.*

potato, *n.* patata, papa *f.* **sweet p.,** batata *f.*

potent, *a.* potente, poderoso.

potential, *a. & n.* potencial *f.*

potion, *n.* poción *f.*, pócima *f.*

pottery, *n.* alfarería *f.*

pouch, *n.* saco *m.*; bolsa *f.*

poultry, *n.* aves de corral.

pound, 1. *n.* libra *f.* **2.** *v.* golpear.

pour, *v.* echar; verter; llover a cántaros.

poverty, *n.* pobreza *f.*

powder, 1. *n.* polvo *m.*; (gun) pólvora *f.* **2.** *v.* empolvar; pulverizar.

power, *n.* poder *m.*; potencia *f.*

powerful, *a.* poderoso, fuerte.

powerless, *a.* impotente.

practical, *a.* práctico.

practically, *adv.* casi; prácticamente.

practice, 1. práctica; costumbre; clientela *f.* **2.** *v.* practicar; ejercer.

practiced, *a.* experto.

practitioner, *n.* practicante *m.*

pragmatic, *a.* pragmática.

prairie, *n.* llanura; (Arg.) pampa *f.*

praise, 1. *n.* alabanza *f.* **2.** *v.* alabar.

prank, *n.* travesura *f.*

pray, *v.* rezar; *(beg) rogar.*

prayer, *n.* oración; súplica *f.*; ruego *m.*

preach, *v.* predicar; sermonear.

preacher, *n.* predicador *m.*

preamble, *n.* preámbulo *m.*

precarious, *a.* precario.

precaution, *n.* precaución *f.*

precede, *v.* preceder, anteceder.

precedent, *a. & n.* precedente *m.*

precept, *n.* precepto *m.*

precinct, *n.* recinto *m.*

precious, *a.* precioso.

precipice, *n.* precipicio *m.*

precipitate, *v.* precipitar.

precise, *a.* preciso, exacto.

precision, *n.* precisión *f.*

preclude, *v.* evitar.

precocious, *a.* precoz.

predatory, *a.* de rapiña, rapaz.

predecessor, *n.* predecesor, antecesor *m.*

predicament, *n.* dificultad *f.*; apuro *m.*

predict, *v.* pronosticar, predecir.

predilection, *n.* predilección *f.*

predispose, *v.* predisponer.

predominant, *a.* predominante.

prefabricate, *n.* fabricar de antemano.

preface, *n.* prefacio *m.*

prefer, *v.* preferir.

preferable, *a.* preferible.

preference, *n.* preferencia *f.*

prefix, 1. *n.* prefijo *m.* **2.** *v.* prefijar.

pregnant, *a.* preñada.

prehistoric, *a.* prehistórico.

prejudice, *n.* prejuicio *m.*

prejudiced, *a.* prejuiciado.

preliminary, *a.* preliminar.

prelude, *n.* preludio *m.*

premature, *a.* prematuro.

premeditate, *v.* premeditar.

premier, *n.* primer ministro.

première, *n.* estreno *m.*

premise, *n.* premisa *f.*

premium, *n.* premio *m.*

premonition *n.* presentimiento *m.*

prenatal, *a.* prenatal.

preparation, *n.* preparativo *m.*; preparación *f.*

preparatory, *a.* preparatorio. **p. to,** antes de.

prepare, *v.* preparar.

preponderant, *a.* preponderante.

preposition, *n.* preposición *f.*

preposterous, *a.* prepóstero, absurdo.

prerequisite, *n.* requisito previo.

prerogative, *n.* prerrogativa *f.*

prescribe, *v.* prescribir; (med.) recetar.

prescription, *n.* prescripción; (med.) receta *f.*

presence, *n.* presencia *f.*; porte *m.*

present, 1. *a.* presente. **to be present at,** asistir a. **2.** *n.* presente; (gift) regalo *m.* **at p.,** ahora. **for the p.,** por ahora. **3.** *v.* presentar.

presentable, *a.* presentable.

presentation, *n.* presentación; introducción *f.*; (theater) representación *f.*

presently, *adv.* luego; dentro de poco.

preservative, *a. & v.* preservativo *m.*

preserve, 1. *n.* conserva *f.*; (hunting) vedado *m.* **2.** *v.* preservar.

preside, *v.* presidir.

presidency, *n.* presidencia *f.*

president, *n.* presidente -ta.

press, 1. *n.* prensa *f.* **2.** *v.* apretar; urgir; (clothes) planchar.

pressing, *a.* urgente.

pressure, *n.* presión *f.*

pressure cooker, *n.* cocina de presión *f.*

prestige, *n.* prestigio *m.*

presume, *v.* presumir; suponer.

presumptuous, *a.* presuntuoso.

presuppose, *v.* presuponer.

pretend, *v.* fingir. **p. to the throne,** aspirar al trono.

pretense, *n.* pretensión *f.*; fingimiento *m.*

pretension, *n.* pretensión *f.*

pretentious, *a.* presumido.

pretext, *n.* pretexto *m.*

pretty, 1. *a.* bonito, lindo. **2.** *adv.* bastante.

prevail, *v.* prevalecer.

prevailing, prevalent, *a.* predominante.

prevent, *v.* impedir; evitar.

prevention, *n.* prevención *f.*

preventive, *a.* preventivo.

preview, *n.* vista previa *f.*

previous, *a.* anterior, previo.

prey, *n.* presa *f.*

price, *n.* precio *m.*

priceless, *a.* sin precio.

prick, 1. *n.* punzada *f.* **2.** *v.* punzar.

pride, *n.* orgullo *m.*

priest, *n.* sacerdote, cura *m.*

prim, *a.* severamente modesto.

primary, *a.* primario, principal.

prime, 1. *a.* primero. **2.** *n.* flor *f.* **3.** *v.* alistar.

prime minister, *n.* primer ministro *m.*

primitive, *a.* primitivo.

prince, *n.* príncipe *m.*

princess, *n.* princesa *f.*

principal, 1. *a.* principal. **2.** *n.* principal; director *m.*

principle, *n.* principio *m.*

print, 1. *n.* letra *f.*; (art) grabado *m.* **2.** *v.* imprimir, estampar.

printing, *n.* imprenta *f.*

printing press, *n.* prensa *f.*

priority, *n.* prioridad, precedencia *f.*

prism, *n.* prisma *f.*

prison, *n.* prisión, cárcel *f.*

prisoner, *n.* prisionero, preso *m.*

privacy, *n.* soledad *f.*

private, 1. *a.* particular. **2.** *n.* soldado raso. **in p.,** en particular.

privation, *n.* privación *f.*

privet, *n.* ligustro *m.*

privilege, *n.* privilegio *m.*

privy, *n.* letrina *f.*

prize, 1. *n.* premio *m.* **2.** *v.* apreciar, estimar.

probability, *n.* probabilidad *f.*

probable, *a.* probable.

probate, *a.* testamentario.

probation, *n.* prueba *f.*; probación *f.*; libertad condicional *f.*

probe, 1. *n.* indagación *f.* **2.** *v.* indagar; tentar.

probity, *n.* probidad *f.*

problem, *n.* problema *m.*

procedure, *n.* procedimiento *m.*

proceed, *v.* proceder; proseguir.

process, *n.* proceso *m.*

procession, *n.* procesión *f.*

proclaim, *v.* proclamar, anunciar.

proclamation, *n.* proclamación *f.*; decreto *m.*

procrastinate, *v.* dilatar.

procure, *v.* obtener, procurar.

prodigal, *n. & a.* pródigo *m.*

prodigy, *n.* prodigio *m.*

produce, *v.* producir.

product, *n.* producto *m.*

production, *n.* producción *f.*

productive, *a.* productivo.

profane, 1. *a.* profano. **2.** *v.* profanar.

profanity, *n.* profanidad *f.*

profess, *v.* profesar; declarar.

profession, *n.* profesión *f.*

professional, *a. & n.* profesional *m.*

professor, *n.* profesor -ra; catedrático *m.*

proficient, *a.* experto, proficiente.

profile, *n.* perfil *m.*

profit, 1. *n.* provecho *m.*; ventaja *f.*; (com.) ganancia *f.* **2.** *v.* aprovechar; beneficiar.

profitable, *a.* provechoso, ventajoso, lucrativo.

profiteer, 1. *n.* explotador *m.* **2.** *v.* explotar.

profound, *a.* profundo, hondo.

profuse, *a.* pródigo, profuso.

prognosis, *n.* pronóstico *m.*

program, *n.* programa *m.*

progress, 1. *n.* progresos *m. pl.* **in p.,** en marcha. **2.** *v.* progresar; marchar.

progressive, *a.* progresivo; progresista.

prohibit, *v.* prohibir.

prohibition, *n.* prohibición *f.*

prohibitive, *a.* prohibitivo.

project, 1. *n.* proyecto *m.* **2.** *v.* proyectar.

projectile, *n.* proyectil *m.*

projection, *n.* proyección *f.*

projector, *n.* proyector *m.*

prolific, *a.* prolífico.

prologue, *n.* prólogo *m.*

prolong, *v.* prolongar.

prominent, *a.* prominente; eminente.

promiscuous, *a.* promiscuo.

promise, 1. *n.* promesa *f.* **2.** *v.* prometer.

promote, *v.* fomentar; estimular; adelantar.

promotion, *n.* promoción *f.*; adelanto *m.*

prompt, 1. *a.* pronto; puntual. **2.** *v.* impulsar; (theater) apuntar.

promulgate, *v.* promulgar.

pronoun, *n.* pronombre *m.*

pronounce, *v.* pronunciar.

pronunciation, *n.* pronunciación *f.*

proof, *n.* prueba *f.*

proofread, *v.* corregir pruebas.

prop, 1. *n.* apoyo, *m.* **2.** *v.* sostener.

propaganda, *n.* propaganda *f.*

propagate, *v.* propagar.

propel, *v.* propulsar.

propeller, *n.* hélice *f.*

propensity, *n.* tendencia *f.*

proper, *a.* propio; correcto.

property, *n.* propiedad *f.*

prophecy, *n.* profecía *f.*

prophesy, *v.* predecir, profetizar.

prophet, *n.* profeta *m.*

prophetic, *a.* profético.

propitious, *a.* propicio.

proponent, *n. & v.* proponente *m.*

proportion, *n.* proporción *f.*

proportionate, *a.* proporcionado.

proposal, *n.* propuesta; oferta *f.*; (marriage) declaración *f.*

propose, *v.* proponer; pensar; declararse.

proposition, *n.* proposición *f.*

proprietor, *n.* propietario, dueño *m.*

propriety, *n.* corrección *f.,* decoro *m.*

prosaic, *a.* prosaico.

proscribe, *v.* proscribir.

prose, *n.* prosa *f.*

prosecute, *v.* acusar, procesar.

prospect, *n.* perspectiva; esperanza *f.*

prospective, *a.* anticipado, presunto.

prosper, *v.* prosperar.

prosperity, *n.* prosperidad *f.*

prosperous, *a.* próspero.

prostitute, 1. *n.* prostituta *f.*

2. *v.* prostituir. **3.** *a.* prostituido.

prostrate, 1. *a.* postrado. **2.** *v.* postrar.

protect, *v.* proteger; amparar.

protection, *n.* protección *f.*; amparo *m.*

protective, *a.* protector.

protector, *n.* protector *m.*

protégé, *n.* protegido -da.

protein, *n.* proteína *f.*

protest, 1. *n.* protesta *f.* **2.** *v.* protestar.

Protestant, *a. & n.* protestante *m.*

protocol, *n.* protocolo *m.*

proton, *n.* protón *m.*

protract, *v.* alargar, demorar.

protrude, *v.* salir fuera.

protuberance, *n.* protuberancia *f.*

proud, *a.* orgulloso.

prove, *v.* comprobar.

proverb, *n.* proverbio, refrán *m.*

provide, *v.* proporcionar; proveer.

provided, *conj.* con tal que.

providence, *n.* providencia *f.*

province, *n.* provincia *f.*

provincial, 1. *a.* provincial. **2.** *n.* provinciano -na.

provision, 1. *n.* provisión *f.*; (pl.) comestibles *m.pl.* **2.** *v.* abastecer.

provocation, *n.* provocación *f.*

provoke, *v.* provocar.

prowess, *n.* proeza *f.*

prowl, *v.* rondar.

proximity, *n.* proximidad *f.*

proxy, *n.* delegado *m.* **by p.,** mediante apoderado.

prudence, *n.* prudencia *f.*

prudent, *a.* prudente, cauteloso.

prune, *n.* ciruela pasa.

pry, *v.* atisbar; curiosear; (mech.) alzaprimar.

psalm, *n.* salmo *m.*

pseudonym, *n.* seudónimo *m.*

psychiatrist, *n.* psiquiatra *m.*

psychiatry, *n.* psiquiatría *f.*

psychoanalysis, n. psicoanálisis m. or f.

psychological, a. psicológico.

psychology, n. psicología f.

psychosis, n. psicosis.

ptomaine, n. tomaína f.

public, a. & n. público m.

publication, n. publicación;
revista f.

publicity, n. publicidad f.

publish, v. publicar.

publisher, n. editor m.

pudding, n. pudín m.

puddle, n. charco, lodazal m.

Puerto Rico, n. Puerto Rico
m.

Puerto Rican, a. & n. puertorriqueño -ña.

puff, 1. n. soplo m.; (of
smoke) bocanada f. **pow-
der p.,** polvera f. 2. v.
jadear; echar bocanadas. **p.
up,** hinchar; (fig.) engreír.

pugnacious, a. pugnaz.

pull, 1. n. tirón m.; (coll.)
influencia f. 2. v. tirar;
halar.

pulley, n. polla f., motón m.

pulmonary, a. pulmonar.

pulp, n. pulpa; (of fruit)
carne f.

pulpit, n. púlpito m.

pulsate, v. pulsar.

pulse, n. pulso m.

pump, 1. n. bomba f. 2. v.
bombear. **p. up,** inflar.

pumpkin, n. calabaza f.

pun, n. juego de palabras.

punch, 1. n. puñetazo m.; (mech.)
punzón m.; (beverage) ponche
m. 2. v. dar puñetazos;
punzar.

punctual, a. puntual.

punctuate, v. puntuar.

puncture, 1. n. pinchazo m.,
perforación f. 2. v. pinchar,
perforar.

pungent, a. picante, pungen-
te.

punish, v. castigar.

punishment, n. castigo m.

punitive, a. punitivo.

puny, a. encanijado.

pupil, n. alumno -na; (anat.)
pupila f.

puppet, n. muñeco m.

puppy, n. perrito m.

purchase, 1. n. compra f. 2.
v. comprar.

pure, a. puro.

purée, n. puré m.

purge, v. purgar.

purify, v. purificar.

puritanical, a. puritano.

purity, n. pureza f.

purple, 1. a. purpúreo. 2.
n. púrpura f.

purport, 1. n. significación f.
2. v. significar.

purpose, n. propósito m. **on
p.,** de propósito.

purse, n. bolsa f.

pursue, v. perseguir.

pursuit, n. caza; busca; ocupación f. **p. plane,** caza m.

push, 1. n. empuje; impulso
m. 2. v. empujar.

put, v. poner, colocar. **p.
away,** guardar. **p. in,** meter. **p. off,** dejar. **p. on,**
ponerse. **p. out,** apagar.
p. up with, aguantar.

putrid, a. podrido.

puzzle, 1. n. enigma; rompecabezas m. 2. v. dejar per-
plejo. **p. out,** descifrar.

pyramid, n. pirámide f.

pyromania, n. piromanía f.

Q

quadrangle, n. cuadrángulo
m.

quadruped, a. & n. cuadrú-
pedo m.

quail, 1. n. codorniz f. 2. v.
descorazonarse.

quaint, a. arcaico y curioso.

quake, 1. *n.* temblor *m.* **2.** *v.* temblar.
qualification, *n.* requisito *m.*; (pl.) preparaciones.
qualified, *a.* calificado, competente; preparado.
qualify, *v.* calificar, modificar; llenar los requisitos.
quality, *n.* calidad *f.*
quandary, *n.* incertidumbre *f.*
quantity, *n.* cantidad *f.*
quarantine, *n.* cuarentena *f.*
quarrel, 1. *n.* riña, disputa *f.* **2.** reñir, disputar.
quarry, *n.* cantera; (hunting) presa *f.*
quarter, *n.* cuarto *m.*; (pl.) vivienda *f.*
quarterly, 1. *a.* trimestral. **2.** *adv.* por cuartos.
quartet, *n.* cuarteto *m.*
quartz, *n.* cuarzo *m.*
quaver, *v.* temblar.
queen, *n.* reina *f.*; (chess) dama *f.*
queer, *a.* extraño, raro.
quell, *v.* reprimir.
quench, *v.* apagar.
query, 1. *n.* pregunta *f.* **2.** *v.* preguntar.
quest, *n.* busca *f.*
question, 1. *n.* pregunta; cuestión *f.* **q. mark,** signo

de interrogación. **2.** *v.* preguntar; interrogar; dudar.
questionable, *a.* dudoso.
questionnaire, *n.* cuestionario *m.*
quick, *a.* rápido.
quicken, *v.* acelerar.
quicksand, *n.* arena movediza.
quiet, 1. *a.* quieto, tranquilo; callado. **to be q., keep q.,** callarse. **2.** *n.* calma; quietud *f.* **3.** *v.* tranquilizar. **q. down,** callarse; calmarse.
quilt, *n.* colcha *f.*
quinine, *n.* quinina *f.*
quintet, *n.* (*mus.*) quinteto *m.*
quip, 1. *n.* pulla *f.* **2.** *v.* echar pullas.
quit, *v.* dejar; renunciar a. **q. doing** (etc.), dejar de hacer (etc.).
quite, *adv.* bastante; completamente. **not q.,** no precisamente; no completamente.
quiver, 1. *n.* aljaba *f.*; temblor *m.* **2.** *v.* temblar.
quixotic, *a.* quijotesco.
quorum, *n.* quórum *m.*
quota, *n.* cuota *f.*
quotation, *n.* citación; (com.) cotización *f.* **q. marks,** comillas *f.pl.*
quote, *v.* citar; (com.) cotizar.

R

rabbi, *n.* rabí, rabino *m.*
rabbit, *n.* conejo *m.*
rabble, *n.* canalla *f.*
rabid, *a.* rabioso.
rabies, *n.* hidrofobia *f.*
race, 1. *n.* raza; carrera *f.* **2.** *v.* echar una carrera; correr de prisa.
rack, 1. *n.* (cooking) pesebre *m.*; (clothing) colgador *m.* **2.** *v.* atormentar.
racket, *n.* (noise) ruido *m.*;

(tennis) raqueta *f.*; (graft) fraude organizado.
radar, *n.* radar *m.*
radiance, *n.* brillo *m.*
radiant, *a.* radiante.
radiate, *v.* irradiar.
radiation, *n.* irradiación *f.*
radiator, *n.* calorífero *m.*; (auto.) radiador *m.*
radical, *a. & n.* radical *m.*
radio, *n.* radio *m. or f.* **r.**

station, estación radiodifusora.

radioactive, *a.* radioactivo.

radish, *n.* rábano *m.*

radium, *n.* radio *m.*

radius, *n.* radio *m.*

raffle, 1. *n.* rifa, lotería *f.* **2.** *v.* rifar.

raft, *n.* balsa *f.*

rafter, *n.* viga *f.*

rag, *n.* trapo *m.*

ragamuffin, *n.* galopín *m.*

rage, 1. *n.* rabia *f.* **2.** *v.* rabiar.

ragged, *a.* andrajoso; desigual.

raid, *n.* (military) correría *f.*

rail, *n.* baranda *f.*; carril *m.* **by r.,** por ferrocarril.

railroad, *n.* ferrocarril *m.*

rain, 1. *n.* lluvia *f.* **2.** *v.* llover.

rainbow, *n.* arco iris *m.*

raincoat, *n.* impermeable *m.*

rainfall, *n.* precipitación *f.*

rainy, *a.* lluvioso.

raise, 1. *n.* aumento *m.* **2.** *v.* levantar, alzar; criar.

raisin, *n.* pasa *f.*

rake, 1. *n.* rastro *m.* **2.** *v.* rastrillar.

rally, 1. *n.* reunión *f.* **2.** *v.* reunirse.

ram, *n.* carnero *m.*

ramble, *v.* vagar.

ramp, *n.* rampa *f.*

rampart, *n.* terraplén *m.*

ranch, *n.* rancho *m.*

rancid, *a.* rancio.

rancor, *n.* rencor *m.*

random, *a.* fortuito. **at r.,** a la ventura.

range, 1. *n.* extensión *f.*; alcance *m.*; estufa; sierra *f.*; terreno de pasto. **2.** *v.* recorrer; extenderse.

rank, 1. *a.* espeso; rancio. **2.** *n.* fila *f.*; grado, rango *m.* **3.** *v.* clasificar.

ransack, *v.* saquear.

ransom, 1. *n.* rescate *m.* **2.** *v.* rescatar.

rap, 1. *n.* golpecito *m.* **2.** *v.* golpear.

rapid, *a.* rápido.

rapport, *n.* armonía *f.*

rapture, *n.* éxtasis *m.*

rare, *a.* raro.

rascal, *n.* pícaro, bribón *m.*

rash, 1. *a.* temerario. **2.** *n.* erupción *f.*

raspberry, *n.* frambuesa *f.*

rat, *n.* rata *f.*

rate, 1. *n.* velocidad; tasa *f.*; precio *m.*; (of exchange; of interest) tipo *m.* **at any r.,** de todos modos. **2.** *v.* valuar.

rather, *adv.* bastante; más bien, mejor dicho.

ratify, *v.* ratificar.

ratio, *n.* razón; proporción *f.*

ration, 1. *n.* ración *f.* **2.** *v.* racionar.

rational, *a.* racional.

rattle, 1. *n.* ruido *m.*; matraca *f.* **r. snake,** culebra de cascabel. **2.** *v.* matraquear; rechinar.

raucous, *a.* ronco.

ravage, *v.* pillar; destruir; asolar.

rave, *v.* delirar; entusiasmarse.

ravel, *v.* deshilar.

raven, *n.* cuervo *m.*

ravenous, *a.* voraz.

raw, *a.* crudo; verde.

ray, *n.* rayo *m.*

rayon, *n.* rayón *m.*

razor, *n.* navaja de afeitar. **r. blade,** hoja de afeitar.

reach, 1. *n.* alcance *m.* **2.** *v.* alcanzar.

react, *v.* reaccionar.

reaction, *n.* reacción *f.*

reactionary, 1. *a.* reaccionario. **2.** *n.* (*pol.*) retrógrado *m.*

read, *v.* leer.

reader, *n.* lector *m.*; libro de lectura.

readily, *adv.* fácilmente.

reading, *n.* lectura *f.*

ready, *a.* listo, preparado; dispuesto.

real, *a.* verdadero; real.

realist, *n.* realista *m. & f.*

reality, *n.* realidad *f.*

realization, *n.* comprensión; realización *f.*

realize, *v.* darse cuenta de; realizar.

really, *adv.* de veras; en realidad.

realm, *n.* reino; dominio *m.*

reap, v. segar, cosechar.

rear, 1. a. posterior. **2.** n. parte posterior. **3.** v. criar; levantar.

reason, 1. n. razón; causa f.; motivo m. **2.** v. razonar.

reasonable, a. razonable.

reassure, v. calmar, tranquilizar.

rebate, n. rebaja f.

rebel, 1. n. rebelde m. & f. **2.** v. rebelarse.

rebellion, n. rebelión f.

rebellious, a. rebelde.

rebirth, n. renacimiento m.

rebound, v. repercutir; resaltar.

rebuff, 1. n. repulsa f. **2.** v. rechazar.

rebuke, 1. n. reprensión f. **2.** v. reprender.

rebuttal, n. refutación f.

recalcitrant, a. recalcitrante.

recall, 1. n. recordar; acordarse de; hacer volver.

recapitulate, v. recapitular.

recede, v. retroceder.

receipt, n. recibo m.; (com. pl.) ingresos m.pl.

receive, v. recibir.

receiver, n. receptor m.

recent, a. reciente.

recently, adv. recién.

receptacle, n. receptáculo m.

reception, n. acogida; recepción f.

receptionist, n. recepcionista m. & f.

receptive, a. receptivo.

recess, n. nicho; retiro recreo m.

recipe, n. receta f.

recipient, n. receptor, recipiente m.

reciprocate, v. corresponder; reciprocar.

recite, v. recitar.

reckless, a. descuidado; imprudente.

reckon, v. contar; calcular.

reclaim, v. reformar; (legal) reclamar.

recline, v. reclinar; recostar.

recognition, n. reconocimiento m.

recognize, v. reconocer.

recoil, 1. n. culatada f. **2.** v. recular.

recollect, v. recordar, acordarse de.

recommend, v. recomendar.

recommendation, n. recomendación f.

recompense, 1. n. recompensa f. **2.** v. recompensar.

reconcile, v. reconciliar.

recondition, v. reacondicionar.

reconsider, v. considerar de nuevo.

reconstruct, v. reconstruir.

record, 1. n. registro; (sports) record m. **phonograph r.,** disco m. **2.** v. registrar.

recount, v. relatar; contar.

recover, v. recobrar; restablecerse.

recovery, n. recobro m.; recuperación f.

recruit, 1. n. recluta m. **2.** v. reclutar.

rectangle, n. rectángulo m.

rectify, v. rectificar.

recuperate, v. recuperar.

recur, v. recurrir.

red, a. rojo; colorado.

redeem, v. redimir, rescatar.

redemption, n. redención f.

reduce, v. reducir.

reduction, n. reducción f.

reed, n. caña f., (S.A.) bejuco m.

reef, n. arrecife, escollo m.

reel, n. aspa f.; carrete m. **2.** v. aspar.

refer, v. referir.

referee, n. árbitro m.

reference, n. referencia f.

refill, 1. n. relleno m. **2.** v. rellenar.

refine, v. refinar.

refinement, n. refinamiento m.; cultura f.

reflect, v. reflejar; reflexionar.

reflection, n. reflejo m.; reflexión f.

reflex, a. reflejo.

reform, 1. n. reforma f. **2.** v. reformar.

reformation, n. reformación f.

refractory, a. refractorio.

refrain, 1. n. estribillo m. **2.** v. abstenerse.

refresh, v. refrescar.

refreshment, n. refresco m.

refrigerator, n. refrigerador m.

refuge, n. refugio m.

refugee, n. refugiado -da.

refund, 1. n. reembolso m. **2.** v. reembolsar.

refusal, n. negativa f.

refuse, 1. n. basura f. **2.** v. negarse, rehusar.

refute, v. refutar.

regain, v. recobrar.

regal, a. real.

regard, 1. n. aprecio; respeto m. **with r. to,** con respecto a. **2.** v. considerar; estimar.

regarding, prep. en cuanto a, acerca de.

regardless (of), a pesar de.

regent, n. regente m.

regime, n. régimen m.

regiment, 1. n. regimiento m. **2.** v. regimentar.

region, n. región f.

register, 1. n. registro m. **cash r.** caja registradora. **2.** v. registrar; matricularse; (a letter) certificar.

registration, n. registro m.; matrícula f.

regret, 1. n. pena f. **2.** v. sentir, lamentar.

regular, a. regular; ordinario.

regularity, n. regularidad f.

regulate, v. regular.

regulation, n. regulación f.

regulator, n. regulador m.

rehabilitate, v. rehabilitar.

rehearse, v. repasar; (theater) ensayar.

reign, 1. n. reino, reinado m. **2.** v. reinar.

reimburse, v. reembolsar.

rein, 1. n. rienda f. **2.** v. refrenar.

reincarnation, n. reencarnación f.

reindeer, n. reno m.

reinforce, v. reforzar.

reinforcement, n. refuerzo m.; armadura f.

reiterate, v. reiterar.

reject, v. rechazar.

rejoice, v. regocijarse.

rejoin, v. reunirse con; replicar.

rejuvenate, v. rejuvenecer.

relapse, 1. n. recaída f. **2.** v. recaer.

relate, v. relatar, contar; relacionar.

relation, n. relación f.; pariente m. & f.

relative, 1. a. relativo. **2.** n. pariente m. & f.

relativity, n. relatividad f.

relax, v. descansar; relajar.

relay, 1. n. relevo m. **2.** v. retransmitir.

release, 1. n. liberación f. **2.** v. soltar.

relent, v. ceder.

relevant, a. pertinente.

reliability, n. veracidad f.

reliable, a. responsable; digno de confianza.

relic, n. reliquia f.

relief, n. alivio; (sculpture) relieve m.

relieve, v. aliviar.

religion, n. religión f.

religious, a. religioso.

relinquish, v. abandonar.

relish, 1. n. sabor; condimento m. **2.** v. saborear.

reluctant, a. renuente.

rely, v. **r. on,** confiar en; contar con; depender de.

remain, 1. n. (pl.) restos m.pl. **2.** v. quedar, permanecer.

remainder, n. resto m.

remark, 1. n. observación f. **2.** v. observar.

remarkable, a. notable.

remedial, a. reparador.

remedy, 1. n. remedio m. **2.** v. remediar.

remember, v. acordarse de, recordar.

remembrance, n. recuerdo m.

remind, v. **r. of,** recordar.

reminisce, v. pensar en o hablar de cosas pasadas.

remiss, a. remiso; flojo.

remit, v. remitir.

remorse, n. remordimiento m.

remote, a. remoto.

removal, n. alejamiento m.; eliminación f.

remove, v. quitar; remover.

renaissance, n. renacimiento m.

rend, v. hacer pedazos; separar.

render, v. dar; rendir; (theater) interpretar.

rendezvous, n. cita f.

rendition, n. interpretación, rendición f.

renege, v. renunciar.

renew, v. renovar.

renewal, n. renovación; (com.) prórroga f.

renounce, v. renunciar a.

renovate, v. renovar.

renown, n. renombre m., fama f.

rent, 1. n. alquiler m. **2.** v. arrendar, alquilar.

repair, 1. n. reparo m. **2.** v. reparar.

repatriate, v. repatriar.

repay, v. pagar; devolver.

repeat, v. repetir.

repel, v. repeler, repulsar.

repent, v. arrepentirse.

repentance, n. arrepentimiento m.

repercussion, n. repercusión f.

repertoire, n. repertorio m.

repetition, n. repetición f.

replace, v. reemplazar.

replenish, v. rellenar; surtir de nuevo.

reply, 1. n. respuesta f. **2.** v. replicar; contestar.

report, 1. n. informe m. **2.** v. informar, contar; denunciar; presentarse.

reporter, n. repórter. reportero m.

repose, 1. n. reposo m. **2.** v. reposar; reclinar.

reprehensible, a. reprensible.

represent, v. representar.

representation, n. representación f.

representative, 1. a. representativo. **2.** n. representante m.

repress, v. reprimir.

reprimand, 1. n. regaño m. **2.** v. regañar.

reprisal, n. represalia f.

reproach, 1. n. reproche m. **2.** v. reprochar.

reproduce, v. reproducir.

reproduction, n. reproducción f.

reproof, n. censura f.

reprove, v. censurar, regañar.

reptile, n. reptil m.

republic, n. república f.

republican, a. & n. republicano -na.

repudiate, v. repudiar.

repulsive, a. repulsivo, repugnante.

reputation, n. reputación; fama f.

repute, 1. n. reputación f. **2.** v. reputar.

request, 1. n. súplica f., ruego m. **2.** v. pedir; rogar, suplicar.

require, v. requerir; exigir.

requirement, n. requisito m.

requisite, 1. a. necesario. **2.** n. requisito m.

requisition, n. requisición f.

rescind, v. rescindir, anular.

rescue, 1. n. rescate m. **2.** v. rescatar.

research, n. investigación f.

resemble, v. parecerse a, asemejarse a.

resent, v. resentirse de.

reservation, n. reservación f.

reserve, 1. n. reserva f. **2.** v. reservar.

reservoir, n. depósito; tanque m.

reside, v. residir, morar.

residence, n. residencia, morada f.

resident, n. residente m. & f.

residue, n. residuo m.

resign, v. dimitir; resignar.

resignation, n. dimisión; resignación f.

resist, v. resistir.

resistance, n. resistencia f.

resolute, a. resuelto.

resolution, n. resolución f.

resolve, v. resolver.

resonant, a. resonante.

resort, 1. n. recurso; expediente m. **summer r.,** lugar de veraneo. **2.** v. acudir, recurrir.

resound, v. resonar.

resource, n. recurso m.

respect, 1. n. respeto m. **with r. to,** con respecto a. **2.** v. respetar.

respectable, a. respetable.

respectful, a. respetuoso.

respective, a. respectivo.

respiration, n. respiración f.

respite, n. pausa, tregua f.

respond, v. responder.

response, n. respuesta f.

responsibility, n. responsabilidad f.

responsible, a. responsable.

responsive, a. respondiente, sensible.

rest, 1. n. descanso; reposo m.; (music) pausa f. **the r.,** el resto, lo demás, los demás. **2.** v. descansar; recostar.

restaurant, n. restaurante m.

restful, a. tranquilo.

restitution, n. restitución f.

restless, a. inquieto.

restoration, n. restauración f.

restore, v. restaurar.

restrain, v. refrenar.

restraint, n. limitación, restricción f.

restrict, v. restringir, limitar.

result, 1. n. resultado m. **2.** v. resultar.

resume, v. reasumir; empezar de nuevo.

resurgent, a. resurgente.

resurrect, v. resucitar.

retail, n. **at r.,** al por menor.

retain, v. retener.

retaliate, v. vengarse.

retard, v. retardar.

retention, n. retención f.

reticent, a. reticente.

retire, v. retirar.

retort, 1. n. réplica; (chemical) retorta f. **2.** v. replicar.

retreat, 1. n. retiro m.; (military) retirada, retreta f. **2.** v. retirarse.

retribution, n. retribución f.

retrieve, v. recobrar.

return, 1. n. vuelta f., regreso; retorno m. **by r. mail,** a vuelta de correo. **2.** v. volver, regresar; devolver.

reunion, n. reunión f.

reveal, v. revelar.

revelation, n. revelación f.

revenge, n. venganza f. **to get r.,** vengarse.

revenue, n. renta f.

revere, v. reverenciar, venerar.

reverence, 1. n. reverencia f. **2.** v. reverenciar.

reverend, 1. a. reverendo. **2.** n. pastor m.

reverent, a. reverente.

reverse, 1. a. inverso. **2.** n. revés, inverso m. **3.** v. invertir; revocar.

revert, v. revertir.

review, 1. n. repaso m.; revista f. **2.** v. repasar; revistar.

revise, v. revisar.

revision, n. revisión f.

revival, n. reavivamiento m.

revive, v. avivar; revivir.

revoke, v. revocar.

revolt, 1. n. rebelión f. **2.** v. rebelarse.

revolution, n. revolución f.

revolutionary, a. & n. revolucionario -ria.

revolve, v. girar; dar vueltas.

revolver, n. revólver m.

reward, 1. n. pago m.; recompensa f. **2.** v. recompensar.

rhetoric, n. retórica f.

rheumatism, n. reumatismo m.

rhinoceros, n. rinoceronte m.

rhyme, 1. n. rima f. **2.** v. rimar.

rhythm, n. ritmo m.

rhythmical, a. rítmico.

rib, n. costilla f.

ribbon, n. cinta f.

rice, n. arroz m.

rich, a. rico.

rid, v. librar. **get r. of,** deshacerse de, quitarse.

riddle, n. enigma f.; rompecabezas m.

ride, 1. n. paseo (a caballo o en coche) m. **2.** v. cabalgar; ir en coche.

ridge, n. cerro m.; arruga f.; (of a roof) caballete m.

ridicule, 1. n. ridículo m. **2.** v. ridiculizar.

ridiculous, a. ridículo.

rifle, 1. n. fusil m. **2.** v. robar.

rig, 1. n. aparejo m. **2.** v. aparejar.

right, 1. a. derecho; correcto. **to be r.,** tener razón. **2.** adv. bien, correctamente. **r. here,** etc., aquí mismo, etc.

all r., está bien, muy bien.
3. *n.* derecho *m.*; justicia *f.*
to the r., a la derecha. **4.**
v. corregir; enderezar.
righteous, *a.* justo.
rigid, *a.* rígido.
rigor, *n.* rigor *m.*
rigorous, *a.* riguroso.
rim, *n.* margen *m.* or *f.*;
borde *m.*
ring, **1.** *n.* anillo *m.*; sortija
f.; círculo; campaneo *m.* **2.**
v. cercar; sonar; tocar.
rinse, *v.* enjuagar, lavar.
riot, **1.** *n.* motín; alboroto *m.*
rip, **1.** *n.* rasgadura *f.* **2.** *v.*
rasgar; descoser.
ripe, *a.* maduro.
ripen, *v.* madurar.
ripple, **1.** *n.* onda *f.* **2.** *v.*
ondear.
rise, **1.** *n.* subida *f.* **2.** *v.*
ascender; levantarse; (moon)
salir.
risk, **1.** *n.* riesgo *m.* **2.** *v.*
arriesgar.
rite, *n.* rito *m.*
ritual, *a. & n.* ritual *m.*
rival, *n.* rival *m. & f.*
rivalry, *n.* rivalidad *f.*
river, *n.* río *m.*
rivet, **1.** *n.* remache, roblón
m. **2.** *v.* remachar, roblar.
road, *n.* camino *m.*; carretera
f.
roam, *v.* vagar.
roar, **1.** *n.* rugido, bramido *m.*
2. *v.* rugir, bramar.
roast, **1.** *n.* asado *m.* **2.** *v.*
asar.
rob, *v.* robar.
robber, *n.* ladrón -na.
robbery, *n.* robo *m.*
robe, *n.* manto *m.*
robin, *n.* petirrojo *m.*
robust, *a.* robusto.
rock, **1.** *n.* roca *f.* **2.** *v.*
mecer; oscilar.
rocker, *n.* mecedora *f.*
rocket, *n.* cohete *m.*
rocky, *a.* pedregoso.
rod, *n.* varilla *f.*
rodent, *n.* roedor *m.*
rogue, *n.* bribón, pícaro *m.*
roguish, *a.* pícaro.
role, *n.* papel *m.*
toll, **1.** rollo *m.*; lista *f.*;
panecillo *m.* **to call the r.**,

pasar lista. **2.** *v.* rodar. **r.
up**, enrollar.
roller, *n.* rodillo, cilindro *m.*
Roman, *a. & n.* romano -na.
romance, **1.** *a.* románico.
2. *n.* romance *m.*; amorío *m.*
romantic, *a.* romántico.
romp, *v.* retozar; jugar.
roof, **1.** *n.* techo *m.* **2.** *v.*
techar.
room, **1.** *n.* cuarto *m.*, habitación *f.*; lugar *m.* **2.** *v.*
alojarse.
roommate, *n.* compañero
-ra de cuarto.
rooster, *n.* gallo *m.*
root, *n.* raíz *f.* **to take r.**,
arraigar.
rope, *n.* cuerda, soga *f.*
rose, *n.* rosa *f.*
rosy, *a.* róseo, rosado.
rot, **1.** *n.* putrefacción *f.* **2.**
pudrirse.
rotary, *a.* giratorio; rotativo.
rotate, *v.* girar; alternar.
rotation, *n.* rotación *f.*
rotten, *a.* podrido.
rouge, *n.* colorete *m.*
rough, *a.* áspero; rudo; grosero; aproximado.
round, **1.** *a.* redondo. **r. trip**,
viaje de ida y vuelta. **2.** *n.*
ronda *f.*; (boxing) asalto *m.*
rouse, *v.* despertar.
rout, **1.** *n.* derrota *f.* **2.** *v.*
derrotar.
route, *n.* ruta, vía *f.*
routine, **1.** *a.* rutinario. **2.**
n. rutina *f.*
rove, *v.* vagar.
rover, *n.* vagabundo -da.
row, **1.** *n.* fila; pelea *f.* **2.** *v.*
(nautical) remar.
rowboat, *n.* bote de remos.
rowdy, *a.* alborotoso.
royal, *a.* real.
royalty, *n.* realeza *f.*; (pl.)
regalías *f. pl.*
rub, *v.* frotar. **r. against**,
rozar. **r. out**, borrar.
rubber, *n.* goma *f.*; caucho
m.; (pl.) chanclos *m. pl.*,
zapatos de goma.
rubbish, *n.* basura *f.*; (nonsense) tonterías *f. pl.*
ruby, *n.* rubí *m.*
rudder, *n.* timón *m.*
ruddy, *a.* colorado.

rude, a. rudo; grosero; descortés.

rudiment, n. rudimento m.

rue, v. deplorar; lamentar.

ruffian, n. rufián, bandolero m.

ruffle, 1. n. volante fruncido. **2.** v. fruncir; irritar.

rug, n. alfombra f.

rugged, a. áspero; robusto.

ruin, 1. n. ruina f. **2.** v. arruinar.

ruinous, a. ruinoso.

rule, 1. n. regla f. **as a r.,** por regla general. **2.** v. gobernar; mandar; rayar.

ruler, n. gobernante; soberano m.; regla f.

rum, n. ron m.

rumble, v. retumbar.

rumor, n. rumor m.

run, v. correr; hacer correr.

r. away, escaparse. **r. into,** chocar con.

runner, n. corredor -ra; mensajero -ra.

rupture, 1. n. rotura; hernia f. **2.** v. reventar.

rural, a. rural, campestre.

rush, 1. n. prisa f.; (bot.) junco m. **2.** v. ir de prisa.

Russia, n. Rusia f.

Russian, a. & n. ruso -sa.

rust, 1. n. herrumbre f. **2.** v. aherrumbrarse.

rustic, a. rústico.

rustle, 1. n. susurro m. **2.** v. susurrar.

rusty, a. mohoso.

rut, n. surco m.

ruthless, a. cruel, inhumano.

rye, n. centeno m.

S

saber, n. sable m.

sable, n. cebellina f.

sabotage, n. sabotaje m.

sachet, n. perfumador m.

sack, 1. n. saco m. **2.** v. (military) saquear.

sacred, a. sagrado, santo.

sacrifice, 1. n. sacrificio m. **2.** v. sacrificar.

sacrilege, n. sacrilegio m.

sad, a. triste.

saddle, 1. n. silla de montar. **2.** v. ensillar.

safe, 1. a. seguro; salvo. **2.** n. caja de caudales.

safeguard, 1. n. salvaguardia m. **2.** v. proteger, poner a salvo.

safety, n. seguridad, protección f.

safety pin, n. imperdible m.

sage, 1. a. sabio, sagaz. **2.** n. sabio m.; (botany) salvia f.

sail, 1. n. vela f.; paseo por mar. **2.** v. navegar; embarcarse.

sailboat, n. barco de vela.

sailor, n. marinero m.

saint, n. santo -ta.

sake, n. **for the s. of,** por; por el bien de.

salad, 1. n. ensalada f. **s. bowl,** ensaladera f.

salary, n. sueldo, salario m.

sale, n. venta f.

salesman, n. vendedor m.; viajante de comercio.

saliva, n. saliva f.

salmon, n. salmón m.

salt, 1. a. salado. **2.** n. sal f. **3.** v. salar.

salute, 1. n. saludo m. **2.** v. saludar.

salvage, v. salvar; recobrar.

salvation, n. salvación f.; redención f.

salve, n. emplasto, ungüento m.

same, a. & pron. mismo. **it's all the s.,** lo mismo da.

sample, 1. *n.* muestra *f.* **2.** *v.* probar.

sanatorium, *n.* sanatorio *m.*

sanctify, *v.* santificar.

sanction, 1. *n.* sanción *f.* **2.** *v.* sancionar.

sanctity, *n.* santidad *f.*

sanctuary, *n.* santuario, asilo *m.*

sand, *n.* arena *f.*

sandal, *n.* sandalia *f.*

sandwich, *n.* sandwich *m.*

sandy, *a.* arenoso; (color) rufo.

sane, *a.* cuerdo; sano.

sanitary, *a.* higiénico, sanitario.

sanitation, *n.* saneamiento *m.*

sanity, *n.* cordura *f.*

sap, 1. *n.* savia *f.*; (coll.) estúpido, bobo *m.* **2.** *v.* agotar.

sapphire, *n.* zafiro *m.*

sarcasm, *n.* sarcasmo *m.*

sardine, *n.* sardina *f.*

sash, *n.* cinta *f.*

satellite, *n.* satélite *m.*

satin, *n.* raso *m.*

satire, *n.* sátira *f.*

satisfaction, *n.* satisfacción *f.*; recompensa *f.*

satisfactory, *a.* satisfactorio.

satisfy, *v.* satisfacer. **be satisfied that . . . ,** estar convencido de que.

saturate, *v.* saturar.

Saturday, *n.* sábado *m.*

sauce, *n.* salsa; compota *f.*

saucer, *n.* platillo *m.*

saucy, *a.* descarado, insolente.

sausage, *n.* salchicha *f.*

savage, *a. & n.* salvaje *m.*

save, 1. *v.* salvar; guardar; ahorrar, economizar. **2.** *prep.* salvo, excepto.

savings, *n.* ahorros *m.pl.*

savior, *n.* salvador *m.*

savor, 1. *n.* sabor *m.* **2.** *v.* saborear.

savory, *a.* sabroso.

saw, 1. *n.* sierra *f.* **2.** *v.* aserrar.

say, *v.* decir; recitar.

saying, *n.* dicho, refrán *m.*

scaffold, *n.* andamio; (gallows) patíbulo *m.*

scald, *v.* escaldar.

scale, 1. *n.* escala; (of fish) escama *f.*; (pl.) balanza *f.* **2.** *v.* escalar; escamar.

scalp, 1. *n.* pericráneo *m.* **2.** *v.* escalpar.

scan, *v.* hojear, repasar; (poetry) escandir.

scandal, *n.* escándalo *m.*

scant, *a.* escaso.

scar, *n.* cicatriz *f.*

scarce, *a.* escaso; raro.

scarcely, *adv. & conj.* apenas.

scare, 1. *n.* susto *m.* **2.** *v.* asustar. **s. away,** espantar.

scarf, *n.* pañueleta, bufanda *f.*

scarlet, *n.* escarlata *f.*

scatter, *v.* esparcir; dispersar.

scavenger, *n.* basurero *m.*

scene, *n.* vista *f.*, paisaje *m.*; (theater) escena *f.* **behind the scenes,** bajo cuerda.

scenery, *n.* paisaje *m.*; (theater) decorado *m.*

scent, 1. *n.* olor, perfume; (sense) olfato *m.* **2.** *v.* perfumar; (fig.) sospechar.

schedule, 1. *n.* programa, horario *m.* **2.** *v.* fijar la hora para.

scheme, 1. *n.* proyecto, esquema *m.* **2.** *v.* intrigar.

scholar, *n.* erudito; becado -da.

scholarship, *n.* beca; erudición *f.*

school, 1. *n.* escuela *f.*; colegio *m.*; (of fish) banco *m.* **2.** *v.* enseñar.

sciatica, *n.* ciática *f.*

science, *n.* ciencia *f.*

scientific, *a.* científico.

scientist, *n.* científico -ca.

scissors, *n.* tijeras *f.pl.*

scoff, *v.* mofarse, burlarse.

scold, *v.* regañar.

scoop, 1. *n.* cucharón *m.*; cucharada *f.* **2.** *v.* **s. out,** recoger, sacar.

scope, *n.* alcance; campo *m.*

scorch, *v.* chamuscar.

score, 1. *n.* tantos *m.pl.*; (music) partitura *f.* **2.** *v.* marcar, hacer tantos.

scorn, 1. *n.* desprecio *m.* **2.** *v.* despreciar.

scornful, a. desdeñoso.

Scotch, a. escocés.

Scotland, n. Escocia f.

scour, v. fregar, estregar.

scourge, n. azote m.; plaga f.

scout, 1. n. explorador m. 2. v. explorar, reconocer.

scramble, 1. n. rebatiña f. 2. v. bregar. scrambled eggs, huevos revueltos.

scrap, 1. n. migaja f.; pedacito m.; (coll.) riña f. s. metal, hierro viejo. s. paper, papel borrador. 2. v. desechar; (coll.) reñir.

scrape, 1. n. lío, apuro m. 2. v. rascar; (feet) restregar.

scratch, 1. n. rasguño m. 2. v. rasguñar; rayar.

scream, 1. n. grito, chillido m. 2. v. gritar, chillar.

screen, n. biombo m.; (for window) tela metálica; (movie) pantalla f.

screw, 1. n. tornillo m. 2. v. atornillar.

screwdriver, n. destornillador m.

scribble, v. hacer garabatos.

scroll, n. rúbrica f.; rollo de papel.

scrub, v. fregar, estregar.

scruple, n. escrúpulo m.

scrupulous, a. escrupuloso.

sculptor, n. escultor m.

sculpture, 1. n. escultura f. 2. v. esculpir.

scythe, n. guadaña f.

sea, n. mar m. or f.

seal, 1. n. sello m.; (animal) foca f. 2. v. sellar.

seam, n. costura f.

seaport, n. puerto de mar.

search, 1. n. registro m. in s. of, en busca de. 2. v. registrar. s. for, buscar.

seasick, a. mareado. to get s., marearse.

season, 1. n. estación f.; sazón, temporada f. 2. v. sazonar.

seasoning, n. condimento m.

seat, 1. n. asiento m.; residencia, sede f.; (theater) localidad f. 2. v. sentar. be seated, sentarse.

second, 1. a. & n. segundo m. 2. v. apoyar, segundar.

secondary, a. secundario.

secret, a. & n. secreto m.

secretary, n. secretario -ria; (govt.) ministro m.; (furniture) papelera f.

sect, n. secta f.; partido m.

section, n. sección, parte f.

sectional, a. regional, local.

secular, a. secular.

secure, 1. a. seguro. 2. v. asegurar; obtener, conseguir; (financial) garantizar.

security, n. seguridad; garantía f.

sedative, a. & n. sedativo m.

seduce, v. seducir.

see, v. ver; comprender. s. off, despedirse de. s. to, encargarse de.

seed, 1. n. semilla f. 2. v. sembrar.

seek, v. buscar. s. to, tratar de.

seem, v. parecer.

seep, v. colarse.

segment, n. segmento m.

segregate, v. segregar.

seize, v. agarrar; apoderarse de.

seldom, adv. rara vez.

select, 1. a. escogido, selecto. 2. v. elegir, seleccionar.

selection, n. selección f.

selective, a. escogedor.

selfish, a. egoísta.

selfishness, n. egoísmo m.

sell, v. vender.

semester, n. semestre m.

semicircle, n. semicírculo m.

senate, n. senado m.

senator, n. senador -ra.

send, v. mandar, enviar; (a wire) poner. s. away, despedir. s. back, devolver. s. for, mandar buscar. s. off, expedir. s. word, mandar recado.

senile, a. senil.

senior, a. mayor; más viejo. Sr., padre.

sensation, n. sensación f.

sensational, a. sensacional.

sense, 1. n. sentido; juicio m. 2. v. percibir; sospechar.

sensible, a. sensato, razonable.

sensitive, a. sensible; sensitivo.

sensual, a. sensual.

sentence, 1. n. frase; (gram.) oración; (legal) sentencia f. **2.** v. condenar.

sentiment, n. sentimiento m.

sentimental, a. sentimental.

separate, 1. a. separado; suelto. **2.** v. separar, dividir.

separation, n. separación f.

September, n. septiembre m.

sequence, n. serie f. **in s.,** seguidos.

serenade, 1. n. serenata f. **2.** v. dar serenata a.

serene, a. sereno; tranquilo.

sergeant, n. sargento m.

serial, a. en serie, de serie.

series, n. serie f.

serious, a. serio; grave.

sermon, n. sermón m.

serpent, n. serpiente f.

servant, n. criado -da; servidor -ra.

serve, v. servir.

service, 1. n. servicio m. **at the s. of,** a las órdenes de. **to be of s.,** servir; ser útil. **2.** v. (auto.) reparar.

session, n. sesión f.

set. 1. a. fijo. **2.** n. colección f.; (of a game) juego; (mech.) aparato; (theat.) decorado m. **3.** v. poner, colocar; fijar; (sun) ponerse. **s. forth,** exponer. **s. off, s. out,** salir. **s. up,** instalar; establecer.

settle, v. solucionar; arreglar; establecerse.

settlement, n. caserío; arreglo; acuerdo m.

settler, n. poblador -ra.

seven, a. & pron. siete.

seventeen, a. & pron. diecisiete.

seventh, a. séptimo.

seventy, a. & pron. setenta.

sever, v. desunir; romper.

several, a. & pron. varios.

severe, a. severo; grave.

severity, n. severidad f.

sew, v. coser.

sewer, n. cloaca f.

sex, n. sexo m.

sexton, n. sacristán m.

sexual, a. sexual.

shabby, a. haraposo, desalineado.

shade, 1. n. sombra f.; tinte m.; (window) transparente m. **2.** v. sombrear.

shadow, n. sombra f.

shady, a. sombroso; sospechoso.

shaft, n. columna; (mech.) asta f.

shake, v. sacudir; agitar; temblar. **s. hands with,** dar la mano a.

shallow, a. poco hondo; superficial.

shame, 1. n. vergüenza f. **to be a s.,** ser una lástima. **2.** v. avergonzar.

shameful, a. vergonzoso.

shampoo, n. champú m.

shape, 1. n. forma f.; estado m. **2.** v. formar.

share, 1. n. parte; (stock) acción f. **2.** v. compartir.

shark, n. tiburón m.

sharp, a. agudo; (blade) afilado.

sharpen, v. aguzar; afilar.

shatter, v. estrellar; hacer pedazos.

shave, 1. n afeitada f. **2.** v. afeitarse.

shawl, n. rebozo, chal m.

she, pron. ella f.

sheaf, n. gavilla f.

shear, v. cizallar.

shears, n. cizallas f.pl.

sheath, n. vaina f.

shed, 1. n. cobertizo m. **2.** v. arrojar, quitarse.

sheep, n. oveja f.

sheet, n. sábana f.; (of paper) hoja f.

shelf, n. estante m., repisa f.

shell, 1. n. cáscara; (sea) concha f.; (military) proyectil m. **2.** v. desgranar; bombardear.

shellac, n. laca f.

shelter, 1. n. albergue; refugio m. **2.** v. albergar; amparar.

shepherd, n. pastor m.

sherry, n. jerez m.

shield, 1. n. escudo m. **2.** v. amparar.

shift, 1. n. cambio; (work) turno m. **2.** v. cambiar, mudar. **s. for oneself,** arreglárselas.

shine, 1. n. brillo, lustre m. **2.** v. brillar; (shoes) lustrar.

shiny, a. brillante, lustroso.

ship, 1. n. barco m., nave f. **2.** v. embarcar; (com.) enviar.

shipment, n. envío, embarque m.

shirk, v. faltar a.

shirt, n. camisa f.

shiver, 1. n. temblor m. **2.** v. temblar.

shock, 1. n. choque m. **2.** v. chocar.

shoe, n. zapato m.

shoelace, n. lazo m.; cordón de zapato.

shoemaker, n. zapatero m.

shoot, v. tirar; (gun) disparar. **s. away, s. off,** salir disparado.

shop, n. tienda f.

shopping, n. **to go s.,** hacer compras, ir de compras.

shore, n. orilla; playa f.

short, a. corto; breve; (in stature) pequeño, bajo. **a s. time,** poco tiempo. **in s.,** en suma.

shortage, n. escasez; falta f.

shorten, v. acortar, abreviar.

shortly, adv. en breve, dentro de poco.

shorts, n. calzoncillos m.pl.

shot, n. tiro; disparo m.

shoulder, 1. n. hombro m. **2.** v. asumir; cargar con.

shout, 1. n. grito. **2.** v. gritar.

shove, 1. n. empujón m. **2.** v. empujar.

shovel, 1. n. pala f. **2.** v. traspalar.

show, 1. n. ostentación f.; (theater) función f.; espectáculo m. **2.** v. enseñar, mostrar; verse. **s. up,** destacarse; (coll.) asomar.

shower, n. chubasco m.; (bath) ducha f.

shrapnel, n. metralla f.

shrewd, a. astuto.

shriek, 1 n. chillido m. **2.** v. chillar.

shrill, a. chillón, agudo.

shrimp, n. camarón m.

shrine, n. santuario m.

shrink, v. encogerse, contraerse. **s. from,** huir de.

shroud, 1. n. mortaja f. **2.** v. (fig.) ocultar.

shrub, n. arbusto m.

shudder, 1. n. estremecimiento m. **2.** v. estremecerse.

shun, v. evitar, huir de.

shut, v. cerrar. **s. in,** encerrar. **s. up,** (coll.) callarse.

shutter, n. persiana f.

shy, a. tímido, vergonzoso.

sick, a. enfermo. **s. of,** aburrido de, cansado de.

sickness, n. enfermedad f.

side, 1. n. lado; partido m.; parte f.; (anatomy) costado m. **2.** v. **s. with,** ponerse del lado de.

sidewalk, n. acera, vereda f.

siege, n. asedio m.

sieve, n. cedazo m.

sift, v. cerner.

sigh, 1. n. suspiro m. **2.** v. suspirar.

sight, 1. n. vista f.; punto de interés. **to lose s. of,** perder de vista. **2.** v. divisar.

sign, 1. n. letrero; señal, seña f. **2.** v. firmar. **s. up,** inscribirse.

signal, 1. n. señal f. **2.** v. hacer señales.

signature, n. firma f.

significance, n. significación f.

significant, a. significativo.

signify, v. significar.

silence, 1. n. silencio m. **2.** v. hacer callar.

silent, a. silencioso; callado.

silk, n. seda f.

silken, silky, a. sedoso.

sill, n. umbral de puerta m., solera f.

silly, a. necio, tonto.

silo, n. silo m.

silver, n. plata f.

silverware, n. artículos de plata.

similar, a. semejante, parecido.

similarity, n. semejanza f.

simple, a. sencillo, simple.

simplicity, n. sencillez f.

simplify, v. simplificar.

simulate, v. simular.

simultaneous, *a.* simultáneo.

sin, 1. *n.* pecado *m.* 2. *v.* pecar.

since, 1. *adv.* desde entonces. 2. *prep.* desde. 3. *conj.* desde que; puesto que.

sincere, *a.* sincero.

sincerely, *adv.* sinceramente.

sincerity, *n.* sinceridad *f.*

sinew, *n.* tendón *m.*

sinful, *a.* pecador.

sing, *v.* cantar.

singe, *v.* chamuscar.

singer, *n.* cantante *m.* & *f.*

single, *a.* solo; (room) sencillo; (unmarried) soltero.

singular, *a.* & *n.* singular *m.*

sinister, *a.* siniestro.

sink, 1. *n.* fregadero *m.* 2. *v.* hundir; (fig.) abatir.

sinner, *n.* pecador -ra.

sinuous, *a.* sinuoso.

sinus, *n.* seno; hueco *m.*

sip, 1. *n.* sorbo *m.* 2. *v.* sorber.

siphon, *n.* sifón *m.*

sir, *title.* señor.

siren, *n.* sirena *f.*

sirloin, *n.* solomillo *n.*

sisal, *n.* henequén *m.*

sister, *n.* hermana *f.*

sister-in-law, *n.* cuñada *f.*

sit, *v.* sentarse; posar. **be sitting**, estar sentado. **sit down**, sentarse. **s. up**, incorporarse; quedar levantado.

site, *n.* sitio, local *m.*

sitting, *n.* sesión *f.*

situate, *v.* situar.

situation, *n.* situación *f.*

six, *a.* & *pron.* seis.

sixteen, *a.* & *pron.* dieciséis.

sixth, *a.* sexto.

sixty, *a.* & *pron.* sesenta.

size, 1. *n.* tamaño *f.*; (of shoe, etc.) número *m.*

sizing, *n.* aderezo *m.*

skate, 1. *n.* patín *m.* 2. *v.* patinar.

skein, *n.* madeja *f.*

skeleton, *n.* esqueleto *m.*

skeptic, *n.* escéptico -ca.

skeptical, *a.* escéptico.

sketch, 1. *n.* esbozo *m.* 2. *v.* esbozar.

ski, 1. *n.* esquí *m.* 2. *v.* esquiar.

skid, 1. *v.* resbalar. 2. *n.* varadera *f.*

skill, *n.* destreza, habilidad *f.*

skillful, *a.* diestro, hábil.

skim, *v.* rasar; (milk) desnatar. **s. over**, **s. through**, hojear.

skin, 1. *n.* piel; (of fruit) corteza *f.* 2. *v.* desollar.

skip, 1. *n.* brinco *m.* 2. *v.* brincar. **s. over**, pasar por alto.

skirmish, *n.* escaramuza *f.*

skirt, *n.* falda *f.*

skull, *n.* cráneo *m.*

skunk, *n.* zorrillo *m.*

sky, *n.* cielo *m.*

skylight, *n.* tragaluz *m.*

skyscraper, *n.* rascacielos *m.*

slab, *n.* tabla *f.*

slack, *a.* flojo; descuidado.

slacken, *v.* relajar.

slacks, *n.* pantalones flojos.

slam, 1. *n.* portazo *m.* 2. *v.* cerrar de golpe.

slander, 1. *n.* calumnia *f.* 2. *v.* calumniar.

slang, *n.* jerga *f.*

slant, 1. *n.* sesgo *m.* 2. *v.* sesgar.

slap, 1. *n.* bofetada, palmada *f.* 2. *v.* dar una bofetada.

slash, 1. *n.* cuchillada *f.* 2. *v.* acuchillar.

slat, 1. *n.* tablilla *f.* 2. *v.* lanzar.

slate, 1. *n.* pizarra *f.*; lista de candidatos. 2. *v.* destinar.

slaughter, 1. *n.* matanza *f.* 2. *v.* matar.

slave, *n.* esclavo -va.

slavery, *n.* esclavitud *f.*

Slavic, *a.* eslavo.

slay, *v.* matar, asesinar.

sled, *n.* trineo *m.*

sleek, *a.* liso.

sleep, 1. *n.* sueño *m.* **to get much s.**, dormir mucho. 2. *v.* dormir.

sleeper, **sleeping car**, *n.* coche cama.

sleepy, *a.* soñoliento. **to be s.**, tener sueño.

sleet, 1. *n.* cellisca *f.* 2. *v.* cellisquear.

sleeve, *n.* manga *f.*

sleigh, n. trineo m.

slender, a. delgado.

slice, 1. n. rebanada; (of meat) tajada f. **2.** v. rebanar; tajar.

slide, v. resbalar, deslizarse.

slide rule, n. regla de cálculo f.

slight, 1. n. desaire m. **2.** a. pequeño; leve. **3.** v. desairar.

slim, a. delgado.

slime, n. lama f.

sling, 1. n. honda f.; (med.) cabestrillo m. **2.** v. tirar.

slink, v. escabullirse.

slip, 1. n. imprudencia; (garment) combinación f.; (of paper) trozo m.; ficha f. **2.** v. resbalar; deslizar. **s. up,** equivocarse.

slipper, n. chinela f.

slippery, a. resbaloso.

slit, 1. n. abertura f. **2.** v. cortar.

slogan, n. lema m.

slope, 1. n. declive m. **2.** v. inclinarse.

sloppy, a. desaliñado, chapucero.

slot, n. ranura f.

slot machine, n. máquina de servicio automático f.

slouch, 1. n. patán m. **2.** v. estar gacho.

slovenly, a. desaliñado.

slow, 1. a. lento; (watch) atrasado. **2.** v. **s. down, s. up,** retardar; ir más despacio.

slowly, adv. despacio.

slowness, n. lentitud f.

sluggish, a. perezoso, inactivo.

slum, n. barrio bajo m.

slumber, v. dormitar.

slur, 1. n. estigma m. **2.** v. menospreciar.

slush, n. fango m.

sly, a. taimado. **on the s.,** a hurtadillas.

smack, 1. n. manotada f. v. manotear.

small, a. pequeño.

smallpox, n. viruela f.

smart, 1. a. listo; elegante. **2.** v. escocer.

smash, v. aplastar; hacer pedazos.

smear, 1. n. mancha; difamación f. **2.** v. manchar; difamar.

smell, 1. n. olor; (sense) olfato m. **2.** v. oler.

smelt, 1. n. eperlano m. **2.** v. fundir.

smile, 1. n. sonrisa f. **2.** v. sonreír.

smite, v. afligir; apenar.

smock, n. camisa de mujer f.

smoke, 1. n. humo m. **2.** v. fumar; (food) ahumar.

smokestack, n. chimenea f.

smolder, v. arder sin llama.

smooth, 1. a. liso; suave; tranquilo. **2.** v. alisar.

smother, v. sofocar.

smug, a. presumido.

smuggle, v. pasar de contrabando.

snack, n. bocadillo m.

snag, n. nudo m., obstáculo m.

snail, n. caracol m.

snake, n. culebra, serpiente f.

snap, 1. n. trueno m. **2.** v. tronar, romper.

snapshot, n. instantánea f.

snare, n. trampa f.

snarl, 1. n. gruñido m. **2.** v. gruñir; (hair) enredar.

snatch, v. arrebatar.

sneak, v. ir, entrar, salir (etc.) a hurtadillas.

sneaker, n. sujeto ruín m.

sneer, 1. n. mofa f. **2.** v. mofarse.

sneeze, 1. n. estornudo m. **2.** v. estornudar.

snicker, n. risita m.

snob, n. esnob m.

snore, 1. n. ronquido m. **2.** v. roncar.

snow, 1. n. nieve f. **2.** v. nevar.

snowdrift, n. ventisquero m.

snub, v. desairar.

snug, a. abrigado y cómodo.

so, 1. adv. así; (also) también. **so as to,** para. **so that,** para que. **so...as,** tan... como. **so...that,** tan... que. **2.** conj. así es que.

soak, v. empapar.

soap, 1. *n.* jabón *m.* **2.** *v.* enjabonar.

soar, *v.* remontarse.

sob, 1. *n.* sollozo *m.* **2.** *v.* sollozar.

sober, *a.* sobrio; pensativo.

sociable, *a.* sociable.

social, 1. *a.* social. **2.** *n.* tertulia *f.*

socialism, *n.* socialismo *m.*

socialist, *a. & n.* socialista *m.*

society, *n.* sociedad; compañía *f.*

sociology, *n.* sociología *f.*

sock, 1. *n.* calcetín; puñetazo *m.* **2.** *v.* dar un puñetazo a.

socket, *n.* cuenca *f.*; (elec.) enchufe *m.*

sod, *n.* césped *m.*

soda, *n.* soda; (chem.) sosa *f.*

sodium, *n.* sodio *m.*

sofa, *n.* sofá *m.*

soft, *a.* blando; fino; suave.

soft drink, *n.* bebida no alcohólica *f.*

soften, *v.* ablandar; suavizar.

soil, 1. *n.* suelo *m.*; tierra *f.* **2.** *v.* ensuciar.

sojourn, *n.* morada *f.*, estancia *f.*

solace, 1. *n.* solaz *m.* **2.** *v.* solazar.

solar, *a.* solar.

solar system, *n.* sistema solar *m.*

solder, 1. *v.* soldar. **2.** *n.* soldadura *f.*

soldier, *n.* soldado *m.*

sole, 1. *n.* suela; (of foot) planta *f.*; (fish) lenguado *m.* **2.** *a.* único.

solemn, *a.* solemne.

solemnity, *n.* solemnidad *f.*

solicit, *v.* solicitar.

solicitous, *a.* solícito.

solid, *a. & n.* sólido *m.*

solidify, *v.* solidificar.

solidity, *n.* solidez *f.*

solitary, *a.* solitario.

solitude, *n.* soledad *f.*

solo, *n.* solo *m.*

soloist, *n.* solista *m.*

soluble, *a.* soluble.

solution, *n.* solución *f.*

solve, *v.* solucionar; resolver.

solvent, *a.* solvente.

somber, *a.* sombrío.

some, *a. & pron.* algo (de),

un poco (de); alguno; (pl.) algunos, unos.

somebody, someone, *pron.* alguien.

somehow, *adv.* de algún modo.

someone, *n.* alguien o alguno.

somersault, *n.* salto mortal *m.*

something, *pron.* algo, alguna cosa.

sometime, *adv.* alguna vez.

sometimes, *adv.* a veces, algunas veces.

somewhat, *adv.* algo, un poco.

somewhere, *adv.* en (or a) alguna parte.

son, *n.* hijo *m.*

song, *n.* canción *f.*

son-in-law, *n.* yerno *m.*

soon, *adv.* pronto. **as s. as possible,** cuanto antes. **sooner or later,** tarde o temprano. **no sooner . . . than,** apenas . . . cuando.

soot, *n.* hollín *m.*

soothe, *v.* calmar.

soothingly, *adv.* tiernamente.

sophisticated, *a.* sofisticado.

sophomore, *n.* estudiante de segundo año *m.*

soprano, *n.* soprano *m. & f.*

sorcery, *n.* encantamiento *m.*

sordid, *a.* sórdido.

sore, 1. *n.* llaga *f.* **2.** *a.* lastimado; (coll.) enojado. **to be s.,** doler.

sorority, *n.* hermandad de mujeres *f.*

sorrow, *n.* pesar, dolor *m.*, aflicción *f.*

sorrowful, *a.* doloroso; afligido.

sorry, *a.* **to be s.,** sentir, lamentar. **to be s. for,** compadecer.

sort, 1. *n.* tipo *m.*; clase, especie *f.* **s. of,** algo, un poco. **2.** *v.* clasificar.

soul, *n.* alma *f.*

sound, 1. *a.* sano; razonable; firme. **2.** *n.* sonido *m.* **3.** *v.* sonar; parecer.

soup, *n.* sopa *f.*

sour, *a.* agrio; ácido; rancio.

source, *n.* fuente; causa *f.*

south, *n.* sur *m.*

South America, *n.* Sud América, América del Sur.

South American, *a. & n.* sudamericano -na.

southeast, *n.* sudeste *m.*

southern, *a.* meridional.

South Pole, *n.* polo sur *m.*

southwest, *n.* sudoeste *m.*

souvenir, *n.* recuerdo *m.*

sovereign, *n.* soberano *m.*

sovereignty, *n.* soberanía *f.*

Soviet Russia, *n.* Rusia Soviética *f.*

sow, 1. *n.* puerca *f.* **2.** *v.* sembrar.

space, 1. *n.* espacio *m.* **2.** *v.* espaciar.

spacious, *a.* espacioso.

spade, 1. *n.* laya; (cards) espada *f.* **2.** *v.* layar.

spaghetti *n.* fideo *m.*

Spain, *n.* España *f.*

span, 1. *n.* tramo *m.* **2.** *v.* extenderse sobre.

Spaniard, *n.* español -la.

Spanish, *a. & n.* español *m.*

spank, *v.* pegar.

spanking, *n.* tunda, zumba *f.*

spar, *v.* altercar.

spare, 1. *a.* de repuesto. **2.** *v.* perdonar; ahorrar; prestar. **have . . . to s.,** tener . . . de sobra.

spark, *n.* chispa *f.*

sparkle, 1. *n.* destello *m.* **2.** *v.* chispear. **sparkling wine,** vino espumoso.

spark plug, *n.* bujía *f.*

sparrow, *n.* gorrión *m.*

sparse, *a.* esparcido.

spasm, *n.* espasmo *m.*

spasmodic, *a.* espasmódico.

spatter, *v.* salpicar; manchar.

speak, *v.* hablar.

speaker, *n.* conferencista *m. & f.*

spear, *n.* lanza *f.*

special, *a.* especial. **s. delivery,** entrega inmediata, entrega urgente.

specialist, *n.* especialista *m. & f.*

speciality, *n.* especialidad *f*

species, *n.* especie *f.*

specific, *a.* específico.

specify, *v.* especificar.

specimen, *n.* espécimen *m.*; muestra *f.*

spectacle, *n.* espectáculo *m.*; (pl.) lentes, anteojos *m.pl.*

spectacular, *a.* espectacular, aparatoso.

spectator, *n.* espectador -ra.

spectrum, *n.* espectro *m.*

speculate, *v.* especular.

speculation, *n.* especulación *f.*

speech, *n.* habla *f.*; lenguaje; discurso *m.* **part of s.,** parte de la oración.

speechless, *a.* mudo.

speed, 1. *n.* velocidad; rapidez *f.* **2.** *v.* **s. up,** acelerar, apresurar.

speedometer, *n.* velocímetro *m.*

speedy, *a.* veloz, rápido.

spell, 1. *n.* hechizo; rato; (med.) ataque *m.* **2.** *v.* escribir; relevar.

spelling, *n.* ortografía *f.*

spend, *v.* gastar; (time) pasar.

spendthrift, *n.* pródigo; manirroto *m.*

sphere, *n.* esfera *f.*

spice, 1. *n.* especia *f.* **2.** *v.* especiar.

spider, *n.* araña *f.*

spike, *n.* alcayata *f.*

spill, *v.* derramar.

spillway, *n.* vertedero *m.*

spin, *v.* hilar; girar.

spinach, *n.* espinaca *f.*

spine, *n.* espinazo *m.*

spinet, *n.* espineta *f.*

spinster, *n.* solterona *f.*

spiral, *a. & n.* espiral *m.*

spire, *n.* caracol *m.*, espira *f.*

spirit, *n.* espíritu; ánimo *m.*

spiritual, *a.* espiritual.

spiritualism, *n.* espiritismo *m.*

spit, *v.* escupir.

spite, *n.* despecho *m.* **in s. of,** a pesar de.

splash, 1. *n.* salpicadura *f.* **2.** *v.* salpicar.

splendid, *a.* espléndido.

splendor, *n.* esplendor *m.*

splice, 1. *v.* empalmar. **2.** *n.* empalme *m.*

splint, *n.* tablilla *f.*

splinter, 1. *n.* astilla *f.* **2.** *v.* astillar.

split, 1. *n.* división *f.* **2.** *v.* dividir, romper en dos.

splurge, 1. *v.* fachendear. **2.** *n.* fachenda *f.*

spoil, 1. *n.* (pl.) botín *m.* **2.** *v.* echar a perder; (a child) mimar.

spoke, *n.* rayo (de rueda) *m.*

spokesman, *n.* interlocutor *m.*

sponge, *n.* esponja *f.*

sponsor, 1. *n.* patrocinador *m.* **2.** *v.* patrocinar; costear.

spontaneity, *n.* espontaneidad *f.*

spontaneous, *a.* espontáneo.

spool, *n.* carrete *m.*

spoon, *n.* cuchara *f.*

spoonful, *n.* cucharada *f.*

sporadic, *a.* esporádico.

sport, *n.* deporte *m.*

sportsman, 1, *a.* deportivo. **2.** *n.* deportista *f.*

spot, 1. *n.* mancha *f.*; lugar, punto *m.* **2.** *v.* distinguir.

spouse, *n.* esposo (o esposa) *m.* or *f.*

spout, 1. *n.* chorro; (of teapot) pico *m.* **2.** *v.* correr a chorro.

sprain, 1. *n.* torcedura *f.* **2.** *v.* torcerse.

sprawl, *v.* tenderse.

spray, 1. *n.* rociada *f.* **2.** *v.* rociar.

spread, 1. *n.* propagación; extensión; (for bed) colcha *f.* **2.** *v.* propagar; extender.

spree, *n.* parranda *f.*

sprig, *n.* ramita *f.*

sprightly, *a.* garboso.

spring, 1. *n.* resorte, muelle *m.*; (season) primavera *f.*; (of water) manantial *m.*

springboard, *n.* trampolín *m.*

sprinkle, *v.* rociar; (rain) lloviznar.

sprint, *n.* carrera *f.*

sprout, *n.* retoño *m.*

spry, *a.* ágil.

spun, *a.* hilado.

spur, 1. *n.* espuela *f.* **on the s. of the moment,** sin pensarlo. **2.** *v.* espolear.

spurious, *a.* espurio.

spurn, *v.* rechazar, despreciar.

spurt, 1. *n.* chorro *m.*; esfuerzo supremo. **2.** *v.* salir en chorro.

spy, 1. espía *m. & f.* **2.** *v.* espiar.

squabble, 1. *n.* riña *f.* **2.** *v.* reñir.

squad, *n.* escuadra *f.*

squadron, *n.* escuadrón *m.*

squalid, *a.* escuálido.

squall, *n.* borrasca *f.*

squalor, *n.* escualidez *f.*

squander, *v.* malgastar.

square, 1. *a.* cuadrado. **2.** *n.* cuadrado *m.*; plaza *f.*

square dance, *n.* contradanza *f.*

squat, *v.* agacharse.

squeak, 1. *n.* chirrido *m.* **2.** *v.* chirriar.

squeamish, *a.* escrupuloso.

squeeze, 1. *n.* apretón *m.* **2.** *v.* apretar; (fruit) exprimir.

squirrel, *n.* ardilla *f.*

squirt, 1. *n.* chisguete *m.* **2.** *v.* jeringar.

stab, 1. *n.* puñalada *f.* **2.** *v.* apuñalar.

stability, *n.* estabilidad *f.*

stabilize, *v.* estabilizar.

stable, 1. *a.* estable, equilibrado. **2.** *n.* caballeriza *f.*

stack, 1. *n.* pila *f.* **2.** *v.* apilar.

stadium, *n.* estadio *m.*

staff, *n.* personal *m.* **editorial s.,** cuerpo de redacción. **general s.,** estado mayor.

stag, *n.* ciervo *m.*

stage, 1. *n.* etapa *f.*; (theat.) escena *f.* **2.** *v.* representar.

stagger, *v.* tambalear.

stagnant, *a.* estancado.

stagnate, *v.* estancarse.

stain, 1. *n.* mancha *f.* **2.** *v.* manchar.

staircase, stairs, *n.* escalera *f.*

stake, *n.* estaca *f.*; (bet) apuesta *f.* **at s.,** en juego; en peligro.

stale, *a.* rancio.

stalemate, *n.* estancación *f.*, tablas.

stalk, n. caña f.; (of flower) tallo m.

stall, 1. n. tenderete; (for horse) pesebre m. 2. v. demorar; (motor) atascar.

stallion, n. garañón m.

stalwart, a. fornido.

stamina, n. vigor m.

stammer, v. tartamudear.

stamp, 1. n. sello m., estampilla f. 2. v. sellar.

stampede, n. estampida f.

stand, 1. n. puesto m.; posición; (speaker's) tribuna; (furn.) mesita f. 2. v. estar; estar de pie; aguantar. **s. up**, pararse, levantarse.

standard, 1. a. normal, corriente. 2. n. norma f. **s. of living**, nivel de vida.

standardize, v. uniformar.

standing, a. fijo; establecido.

standpoint, n. punto de vista m.

staple, n. materia prima f.

star, n. estrella f.

starboard, n. estribor m.

starch, 1. n. almidón m.; (in diet) fécula f. 2. v. almidonar.

stare, v. mirar fijamente.

stark, 1. a. severo. 2. adv. completamente.

start, 1. n. susto; principio m. 2. v. comenzar, empezar; salir; poner en marcha; causar.

startle, v. asustar.

starvation, n. hambre f.

starve, v. morir de hambre.

state, 1. n. estado m. 2. v. declarar, decir.

statement, n. declaración f.

stateroom, n. camarote m.

statesman, n. estadista m.

static, 1. a. estático. 2. n. estática f.

station, n. estación f.

stationary, a. estacionario, fijo.

stationery, n. papel de escribir.

statistics, n. estadística f.

statue, n. estatua f.

stature, n. estatura f.

status, n. estado legal m.

statute, n. ley f.

staunch, a. fiel, constante.

stay, 1. n. estancia; visita f. 2. v. quedar, permanecer; parar, alojarse. **s. away**, ausentarse. **s. up**, velar.

steadfast, a. inmutable.

steady, 1. a. firme; permanente; regular. 2. v. sostener.

steak, n. biftec, bistec m.

steal, 1. n. plagio m. 2. v. robar. **s. away**, escabullirse.

stealth, n. cautela.

steam, n. vapor m.

steamboat, steamer, steamship, n. vapor m.

steel, 1. n. acero m. 2. v. **s. oneself**, fortalecerse.

steep, a. escarpado, empinado.

steeple, n. campanario m.

steer, 1. n. buey m. 2. v. guiar, manejar.

stellar, a. astral.

stem, 1. n. tallo m. 2. v. parar. **s. from**, emanar de.

stencil, 1. n. estarcidor. 2. v. estarcir.

stenographer, n. estenógrafo -fa.

stenography, n. taquigrafía f.

step, 1. n. paso m.; medida f.; (stairs) escalón m. 2. v. pisar. **s. back**, retirarse.

stepladder, n. escalera de mano f.

stereotype, 1. n. estereotipo. 2. v. estereotipar.

sterile, a. estéril.

sterilize, v. esterilizar.

sterling, a. esterlina, genuino.

stern, 1. n. popa f. 2. a. duro, severo.

stethoscope, n. estetoscopio m.

stevedore, n. estibador m.

stew, 1. n. guisado m. 2. v. estofar.

steward, stewardess, n. camarero -ra.

stick, 1. n. palo, bastón m. 2. v. pegar; (put) poner, meter.

sticky, a. pegajoso.

stiff, a. tieso; duro.

stiffness, n. tiesura f.

stifle, v. sofocar; (fig.) suprimir.

stigma, n. estigma m.

still, 1. a. quieto; silencioso. **to keep s.,** callarse. 2. adv. todavía, aún; no obstante. 3. n. alambique m.

stillborn, n. & a. nacido muerto m.

still life, n. naturaleza muerta f.

stillness, n. silencio m.

stilted, a. altisonante.

stimulant, a. & n. estimulante m.

stimulate, v. estimular.

stimulus, n. estímulo m.

sting, 1. n. picadura f. 2. v. picar.

stingy, a. tacaño.

stipulate, v. estipular.

stir, 1. n. conmoción f. 2. v. mover. **s. up,** conmover; suscitar.

stitch, 1. n. puntada f. 2. v. coser.

stock, n. surtido m.; raza f.; (finance) acciones f.pl. **in s.,** en existencia. **to take s. in,** tener fe en.

stock exchange, n. bolsa f.

stockholder, n. corredor de bolsa m.

stocking, n. media f.

stockyard, n. corral de ganado m.

stodgy, a. pesado.

stoical, a. estoico.

stole, n. estola f.

stolid, a. impasible.

stomach, n. estómago m.

stone, n. piedra f.

stool, n. banquillo m.

stoop, v. encorvarse; (fig.) rebajarse.

stop, 1. n. parada f. **to put a s. to,** poner fin a. 2. v. parar; suspender; detener; impedir. **s. doing** (etc.). dejar de hacer (etc.).

stopgap, n. subterfugio m.

storage, n. almacenaje m.

store, 1. n. tienda; provisión f. **department s.,** almacén m. 2. v. guardar; almacenar.

storm, n. tempestad, tormenta f.

stormy, a. tempestuoso.

story, n. cuento; relato m.; historia f. **short s.,** cuento.

stout, a. corpulento.

stove, n. hornilla; estufa f.

straight, 1. a. recto; derecho. 2. adv. directamente.

straighten, v. enderezar. **s. out,** poner en orden.

straightforward, a. recto, sincero.

strain, 1. n. tensión f. 2. v. colar.

strainer, n. colador m.

strait, n. estrecho m.

strand, 1. n. hilo m. 2. v. **be stranded,** encallarse.

strange, a. extraño; raro.

stranger, n. extranjero -ra, forastero -ra; desconocido -da.

strangle, v. estrangular.

strap, n. correa f.

stratagem, n. estratagema f.

strategic, a. estratégico.

strategy, n. estrategia f.

stratosphere, n. estratosfera f.

straw, n. paja f.

strawberry, n. fresa f.

stray, 1. a. vagabundo. 2. v. extraviarse.

streak, 1. n. racha; raya f.; lado m. 2. v. rayar.

stream, n. corriente f.

street, n. calle f.

streetcar, n. tranvía m.

strength, n. fuerza f.

strengthen, v. reforzar.

strenuous, a. estrenuo.

streptococcus, n. estreptococo m.

stress, 1. n. tensión f.; énfasis m. 2. v. recalcar; acentuar.

stretch, 1. n. trecho m. **at one s.,** de un tirón. 2. v. tender; extender; estirarse.

stretcher, n. camilla f.

strew, v. esparcir.

stricken, a. agobiado.

strict, a. estricto; severo.

stride, 1. n. tranco m.; (fig., pl.) progresos. 2. v. andar a trancos.

strife, n. contienda f.

strike, 1. n. huelga f. 2. v.

pegar; chocar con; (clock) dar.

string, n. cuerda f.: cordel m.

string bean, n. habichuela f.

stringent, a. estricto.

strip, 1. n. tira f. **2.** despojar; desnudarse.

stripe, n. raya f.; (mil.) galón m.

strive, v. esforzarse.

stroke, n. golpe m.; (swim.) brazada f.; (med.) ataque m.

s. of luck, suerte f.

stroll, 1. n. paseo m. **2.** v. pasearse.

stroller, n. vagabundo m.

strong, a. fuerte.

stronghold, n. fortificación f.

structure, n. estructura f.

struggle, 1. n. lucha f. **2.** v. luchar.

strut, 1. n. pavonada f. **2.** v. pavonear.

stub, 1. n. cabo; (ticket) talón m. **2.** v. **s. one's toe on,** tropezar con.

stubborn, a. testarudo.

stucco, 1. n. estuco. **2.** v. estucar.

student, n. alumno -na, estudiante -ta.

studio, n. estudio m.

studious, a. aplicado; estudioso.

study, 1. n. estudio m. **2.** v. estudiar.

stuff, 1. n. cosas f.pl. **2.** v. llenar; rellenar.

stuffing, n. relleno m.

stumble, v. tropezar.

stump, n. tronco m.

stun, v. aturdir.

stunt, 1. n. suerte f. **2.** v. impedir crecimiento.

stupendous, a. estupendo.

stupid, a. estúpido.

stupidity, n. estupidez f.

stupor, n. estupor m.

sturdy, a. robusto.

stutter, 1. v. tartamudear. **2.** n. tartamudeo m.

sty, n. pocilga f.

style, n. estilo m.; moda f.

stylish, a. elegante; a la moda.

suave, a. afable, suave.

subconscious, a. subconsciente.

subdue, v. dominar.

subject, 1. a. sujeto. **2.** n. tema m.; (of study) materia f.; (pol.) súbdito -ta; (gram.) sujeto m. **3.** v. someter.

subjugate, v. sojuzgar, subjugar.

subjunctive, a. & n. subjuntivo m.

sublimate, v. sublimar.

sublime, a. sublime.

submarine, a. & n. submarino m.

submerge, v. sumergir.

submission, f. sumisión f.

submit, v. someter.

subnormal, a. subnormal.

subordinate, 1. a. & n. subordinado -da. **2.** v. subordinar.

subscribe, v. aprobar; abonarse.

subscription, n. abono m.

subsequent, a. subsiguiente.

subservient, a. servicial.

subside, v. apaciguarse.

subsidy, n. subvención f.

substance, n. substancia f.

substantial, a. substancial; considerable.

substitute, 1. a. substitutivo. **2.** n. substituto m. **3.** v. substituir.

substitution, n. substitución f.

subterfuge, n. subterfugio m.

subtle, a. sutil.

subtract, v. substraer.

suburb, n. suburbio m.; (pl.) afueras f.pl.

subversive, a. subversivo.

subway, n. metro m.

succeed, v. lograr, tener éxito; (in office) suceder a.

success, n. éxito m.

successful, a. próspero; afortunado.

succession, n. sucesión f.

successive, a. sucesivo.

successor, n. sucesor -ra; heredero -ra.

succor, 1. n. socorro m. **2.** v. socorrer.

succumb, v. sucumbir.

such, a. tal.

suck, v. chupar.

suction, n. succión f.

sudden, a. repentino, súbito.
all of a s., de repente.

suds, n. jabonaduras f.

sue, v. demandar.

suffer, v. sufrir; padecer.

suffice, v. bastar.

sufficient, a. suficiente.

suffocate, v. sofocar.

sugar, n. azúcar m.

suggest, v. sugerir.

suggestion, n. sugerencia f.

suicide, n. suicidio m.; (person) suicida m. & f. **to commit s.,** suicidarse.

suit, 1. n. traje; (cards) palo; (law) pleito m. **2.** v. convenir a.

suitable, a. apropiado; que conviene.

suitcase, n. maleta f.

suite, n. serie f., séquito m.

suitor, n. pretendiente m.

sullen, a. hosco.

sum, 1. n. suma f. **2.** v. **s. up,** resumir.

summarize, v. resumir.

summary, n. resumen m.

summer, n. verano m.

summon, v. llamar; (law) citar.

summons, n. citación f.

sumptuous, a. suntuoso.

sun, 1. n. sol m. **2.** v. tomar el sol.

sunburn, n. quemadura de sol.

sunburned, a. quemado por el sol.

Sunday, n. domingo m.

sunken, a. hundido.

sunny, a. asoleado. **s. day,** día de sol. **to be s.,** (weather) hacer sol.

sunshine, n. luz del sol.

superb, a. soberbio.

superficial, a. superficial.

superfluous, a. superfluo.

superhuman, a. sobrehumano.

superintendent, n. superintendente m.; (of building) conserje m.; (of school) director general.

superior, a. & n. superior m.

superiority, n. superioridad f.

superlative, a. superlativo.

supernatural, a. sobrenatural.

supersede, v. reemplazar.

superstition, n. superstición f.

superstitious, a. supersticioso.

supervise, v. supervisar.

supper, n. cena f.

supplement, 1. n. suplemento m. **2.** v. suplementar.

supply, 1. n. provisión f.; (com.) surtido m.; (econ.) existencia f. **2.** v. suplir; proporcionar.

support, 1. n. sustento; apoyo m. **2.** v. mantener; apoyar.

suppose, v. suponer. **be supposed to,** deber.

suppress, v. suprimir.

suppression, n. supresión f.

supreme, a. supremo.

sure, a. seguro, cierto. **for s.,** con seguridad. **to make s.,** asegurarse.

surety, n. garantía f.

surf, n. marejada f.

surface, n. superficie f.

surge, v. surgir.

surgeon, n. cirujano m.

surgery, n. cirujía f.

surmise, 1. n. conjetura f. **2.** v. suponer.

surmount, v. vencer.

surname, n. apellido m.

surpass, v. superar.

surplus, a. & n. sobrante m.

surprise, 1. n. sorpresa. **2.** v. sorprender. **I am surprised . . . ,** me extraña . . .

surrender, 1. n. rendición f. **2.** v. rendir.

surround, v. rodear, circundar.

surveillance, n. vigilancia f.

survey, 1. n. examen, estudio m. **2.** v. examinar, estudiar; (land) medir.

survival, n. supervivencia f.

survive, v. sobrevivir.

susceptible, a. susceptible.

suspect, v. sospechar.

suspend, v. suspender.

suspense, n. incertidumbre f. **in s.,** en suspenso.

suspension, n. suspensión f.

suspension bridge, *n.* puente colgante *m.*

suspicion, *n.* sospecha *f.*

suspicious, *a.* sospechoso.

sustain, *v.* sustentar; mantener.

swallow, 1. *n.* trago *m.;* (bird) golondrina *f.* **2.** *v.* tragar.

swamp, 1. *n.* pantano *m.* **2.** *v.* (fig.) abrumar.

swan, *n.* cisne *m.*

swap, 1. *n.* trueque *m.* **2.** *v.* cambalachear.

swarm, *n.* enjambre *m.*

sway, 1. *n.* predominio *m.* **2.** *v.* bambolearse; (fig.) influir en.

swear, *v.* jurar. **s. off,** renunciar a.

sweat, 1. sudor *m.* **2.** *v.* sudar.

sweater, *n.* suéter *m.*

Swede, *n.* sueco -ca.

Sweden, *n.* Suecia *f.*

Swedish, *a.* sueco.

sweep, *v.* barrer.

sweet, 1. *a.* dulce; amable, simpático. **2.** *n.* (pl.) dulces *m.pl.*

sweetheart, *n.* amante *m.*

sweetness, *n.* dulzura *f.*

swell, 1. *a.* (coll.) estupendo, excelente. **2.** *n.* (mar.) oleada *f.* **3.** *v.* hincharse; aumentar.

swelter, *v.* sofocar.

swift, *a.* rápido, veloz.

swim, 1. *n.* nadada *f.* **2.** *v.* nadar.

swindle, 1. *n.* estafa *f.* **2.** *v.* estafar.

swine, *n.* puercos *m.pl.*

swing, 1. *n.* columpio *m.* **in full s.,** en plena actividad. **2.** *v.* mecer; balancear.

swirl, 1. *n.* remolino *m.* **2.** *v.* arremolinar.

Swiss, *a. & n.* suizo -za.

switch, 1. *n.* varilla *f.;* (elec.) llave *f.,* conmutador *m.;* (railr.) cambiavía *m.* **2.** *v.* cambiar; trocar.

switchboard, *n.* cuadro conmutador *m.*

Switzerland, *n.* Suiza *f.*

sword, *n.* espada *f.*

syllable, *n.* sílaba *f.*

symbol, *n.* símbolo *m.*

sympathetic, *a.* **to be s.,** tener simpatía.

sympathy, *n.* lástima; condolencia *f.*

symphony, *n.* sinfonía *f.*

symptom, *n.* síntoma *m.*

synchronize, *v.* sincronizar.

syndicate, *n.* sindicato *m.*

synonym, *n.* sinónimo *m.*

synthetic, *a.* sintético.

syringe, *n.* jeringa *f.*

syrup, *n.* almíbar; (cough) jarabe *m.*

system, *n.* sistema *m.*

systematic, *a.* sistemático.

T

tabernacle, *n.* tabernáculo *m.*

table, *n.* mesa; (math.) tabla *f.*

tablespoon, *n.* cuchara *f.*

tablespoonful, *n.* cucharada *f.*

tablet, *n.* tableta; (med.) pastilla *f.*

tack, *n.* tachuela *f.*

tact, *n.* tacto *m.*

tag, *n.* etiqueta *f.,* rótulo *m.*

tail, *n.* cola *f.,* rabo *m.*

tailor, *n.* sastre *m.*

take, *v.* tomar; llevar. **t. away,** quitar. **t. off,** quitarse. **t. out,** sacar. **t. long,** tardar mucho.

tale, *n.* cuento *m.*

talent, *n.* talento *m.*

talk, 1. *n.* plática, habla *f.;* discurso *m.* **2.** *v.* hablar.

talkative, *a.* locuaz.

tall, *a.* alto.

tame, 1. *a.* manso, domesticado. **2.** *v.* domesticar.

tamper, *v.* **t. with,** entremeterse en.

tan, 1. *a.* color de arena. **2.** *v.* curtir; tostar.

tangible, *a.* tangible.

tangle, 1. *n.* enredo *m.* **2.** *v.* enredar.

tank, *n.* tanque *m.*

tap, 1. *n.* golpe ligero. **2.** *v.* golpear ligeramente; decentar.

tape, *n.* cinta *f.*

tapestry, *n.* tapiz *m.*; tapicería *f.*

tar, 1. *n.* brea *f.* **2.** *v.* embrear.

target, *n.* blanco *m.*

tarnish, 1. *n.* deslustre *m.* **2.** *v.* deslustrar.

task, *n.* tarea *f.*

taste, 1. *n.* gusto; sabor *m.* **2.** *v.* gustar; probar. **t. of,** saber a.

tasty, *a.* sabroso.

taut, *a.* tieso.

tavern, *n.* taberna *f.*

tax, 1. *n.* impuesto *m.* **2.** *v.* imponer impuestos.

taxi, *n.* taxi, taxímetro *m.*

tea, *n.* té *m.*

teach, *v.* enseñar.

teacher, *n.* maestro -tra, profesor -ra.

team, *n.* equipo *m.*; pareja *f.*

tear, 1. *n.* rasgón *m.*; lágrima *f.* **2.** *v.* rasgar, lacerar; separar.

tease, *v.* atormentar; embromar.

teaspoon, *n.* cucharita *f.*

technical, *a.* técnico.

technique, *n.* técnica *f.*

tedious, *a.* tedioso.

telegram, *n.* telegrama *m.*

telegraph, 1. *n.* telégrafo *m.* **2.** *v.* telegrafiar.

telephone, 1. *n.* teléfono *m.* **t. book,** directorio telefónico. **2.** *v.* telefonear; llamar por teléfono.

telescope, 1. *n.* telescopio *m.* **2.** *v.* enchufar.

television, *n.* televisión *f.*

tell, *v.* decir; contar; distinguir.

temper, 1. *n.* temperamento, genio *m.* **2.** *v.* templar.

temperament, *n.* temperamento *m.*

temperamental, *a.* sensible, emocional.

temperance, *n.* moderación; sobriedad *f.*

temperate, *a.* templado.

temperature, *n.* temperatura *f.*

tempest, *n.* tempestad *f.*

tempestuous, *a.* tempestuoso.

temple, *n.* templo *m.*

temporary, *a.* temporal, temporario.

tempt, *v.* tentar.

temptation, *n.* tentación *f.*

ten, *a., & pron.* diez.

tenant, *n.* inquilino -na.

tend, *v.* tender. **t. to,** atender.

tendency, *n.* tendencia *f.*

tender, 1. *a.* tierno. **2.** *v.* ofrecer.

tenderness, *n.* ternura *f.*

tennis, *n.* tenis *m.*

tenor, *n.* tenor *m.*

tense, 1. *a.* tenso. **2.** *n.* tiempo *m.*

tent, *n.* tienda, carpa *f.*

tenth, *a.* décimo.

term, 1. *n.* término; plazo *m.* **2.** *v.* llamar.

terrace, *n.* terraza *f.*

terrible, *a.* terrible, espantoso.

territory, *n.* territorio *m.*

terror, *n.* terror, espanto *m.*

test, 1. *n.* prueba *f.*; examen *m.* **2.** *v.* probar, examinar.

testament, *n.* testamento *m.*

testify, *v.* atestiguar, testificar.

testimony, *n.* testimonio *m.*

text, *n.* texto; tema *m.*

textile, 1. *a.* textil. **2.** *n.* tejido *m.*

texture, *n.* textura *f.*; tejido *m.*

than, *conj.* que; de.

thank, *v.* agradecer, dar gracias; **thanks, th. you,** gracias.

thankful, *a.* agradecido; grato.

that, 1. *a.* ese, aquel. **2.**

dem. pron. ése, aquél; eso, aquello. **3.** *rel. pron. & conj.* que.

the, *art.* el, la, los, las; lo.

theater, *n.* teatro *m.*

theft, *n.* robo *m.*

their, *a.* su.

theirs, *pron.* suyo, de ellos.

them, *pron.* ellos, ellas; los, las; les.

theme, *n.* tema *m.*; (mus.) motivo *m.*

themselves, *pron.* sí, sí mismos -as. **they th.,** ellos mismos, ellas mismas. **with th.,** consigo.

then, *adv.* entonces, después; pues.

thence, *adv.* de allí.

theology, *n.* teología *f.*

theory, *n.* teoría *f.*

there, *adv.* allí, allá, ahí. **there is, there are,** hay.

therefore, *adv.* por lo tanto, por consiguiente.

thermometer, *n.* termómetro *m.*

they, *pron.* ellos, ellas.

thick, *a.* espeso, grueso, denso; torpe.

thicken, *v.* espesar, condensar.

thief, *n.* ladrón -na.

thigh, *n.* muslo *m.*

thimble, *n.* dedal *m.*

thin, **1.** *a.* delgado; raro; claro; escaso. **2.** *v.* enrarecer; adelgazar.

thing, *n.* cosa *f.*

think, *v.* pensar; creer.

thinker, *n.* pensador -ra.

third, *a.* tercero.

thirst, *n.* sed *f.*

thirsty, *a.* sediento. **to be th.,** tener sed.

thirteen, *a. & pron.* trece.

thirty, *a. & pron.* treinta.

this, **1.** *a.* este. **2.** *pron.* éste; esto.

thorough, *a.* completo; cuidadoso.

though, **1.** *adv.* sin embargo. **2.** *conj.* aunque. **as th.,** como si.

thought, *n.* pensamiento *m.*

thoughtful, *a.* pensativo; considerado.

thousand, *a. & pron.* mil.

thread, *n.* hilo *m.*; (of screw) rosca *f.*

threat, *n.* amenaza *f.*

threaten, *v.* amenazar.

three, *a. & pron.* tres.

thrift, *n.* economía, frugalidad, *f.*

thrill, **1.** *n.* emoción *f.* **2.** *v.* emocionar.

thrive, *v.* prosperar.

throat, *n.* garganta *f.*

throne, *n.* trono *m.*

through, **1.** *prep.* por; a través de; por medio de. **2.** *a.* continuo. **th. train,** tren directo. **to be th.,** haber terminado.

throughout, **1.** *prep.* por todo, durante todo. **2.** *adv.* en todas partes; completamente.

throw, **1.** *n.* tiro *m.* **2.** *v.* tirar, lanzar. **th. away,** arrojar. **th. out,** echar.

thrust, **1.** *n.* lanzada *f.* **2.** *v.* empujar.

thumb, *n.* pulgar *m.*

thunder, **1.** *n.* trueno *m.* **2.** *v.* tronar.

Thursday, *n.* jueves *m.*

thus, *adv.* así, de este modo.

thwart, *v.* frustrar.

ticket, **1.** *n.* billete, boleto *m.* **t. window,** taquilla *f.* **round trip t.,** billete de ida y vuelta.

tickle, **1.** *n.* cosquilla *f.* **2.** *v.* hacer cosquillas a.

ticklish, *a.* cosquilloso.

tide, *n.* marea *f.*

tidy, **1.** *a.* limpio, ordenado. **2.** *v.* poner en orden.

tie, **1.** *n.* corbata *f.*; lazo; (game) empate *m.* **2.** *v.* atar; anudar.

tier, *n.* hilera *f.*

tiger, *n.* tigre *m.*

tight, *a.* apretado; tacaño.

tighten, *v.* estrechar, apretar.

tile, *n.* teja *f.*, azulejo *m.*

till, **1.** *prep.* hasta. **2.** *conj.* hasta que. **3.** *n.* cajón *m.* **4.** *v.* cultivar, labrar.

tilt, **1.** *n.* inclinación; justa *f.* **2.** *v.* inclinar; justar.

timber, *n.* madera *f.*; (beam) madero *m.*

time, *n.* tiempo *m.*; vez *f.*; (of day) hora *f.*

timetable, *n.* horario, itinerario *m.*

timid, *a.* tímido.

timidity, *n.* timidez *f.*

tin, *n.* estaño *m.*; hojalata *f.* **t. can,** lata *f.*

tint, 1. *n.* tinte *m.* **2.** *v.* teñir.

tiny, *a.* chiquito, pequeñito.

tip, 1. *n.* punta; propina *f.* **2.** *v.* inclinar; dar propina a.

tire, 1. *n.* llanta, goma *f.*, neumático *m.* **2.** *v.* cansar.

tired, *a.* cansado.

tissue, *n.* tejido *m.* **t. paper,** papel de seda.

title, 1. *n.* título *m.* **2.** *v.* titular.

to, *prep.* a; para.

toast, 1. *n.* tostada *f.*; (drink) brindis *m.* **2.** *v.* tostar; brindar por.

tobacco, *n.* tabaco *m.*

today, *adv.* hoy.

toe, *n.* dedo del pie.

together, 1. *a.* juntos. **2.** *adv.* juntamente.

toil, 1. *n.* trabajo *m.* **2.** *v.* afanarse.

toilet, *n.* tocado; excusado, retrete *m.* **t. paper,** papel higiénico.

token, *n.* señal *f.*

tolerance, *n.* tolerancia *f.*

tolerate, *v.* tolerar.

tomato, *n.* tomate *m.*

tomb, *n.* tumba *f.*

tomorrow, *adv.* mañana. **day after t.,** pasado mañana.

ton, *n.* tonelada *f.*

tone, *n.* tono *m.*

tongue, *n.* lengua *f.*

tonic, *a.* tónico *m.*

tonight, *adv.* esta noche.

tonsil, *n.* amígdala *f.*

too, *adv.* también; demasiado. **t. much,** demasiado. **t. many,** demasiados.

tool, *n.* herramienta *f.*

tooth, *n.* diente *m.*; (back) muela *f.*

toothache, *n.* dolor de muela.

toothbrush, *n.* cepillo de dientes.

top, 1. *n.* parte de arriba. **2.** *v.* cubrir; sobrepasar.

topic, *n.* tópico *m.*

topical, *a.* tópico.

torch, *n.* antorcha *f.*

torment, 1. *n.* tormento *m.* **2.** *v.* atormentar.

torrent, *n.* torrente *m.*

torture, 1. *n.* tortura *f.* **2.** *v.* torturar.

toss, *v.* tirar; agitar.

total, 1. *a.* total, entero. **2.** *n.* total *m.*

totalitarian, *a.* totalitario.

touch, 1. *n.* tacto *m.* **in t.,** en comunicación. **2.** *v.* tocar; conmover.

tough, *a.* tosco; tieso; fuerte.

tour, 1. *n.* viaje *m.*, jira *f.* **2.** *v.* viajar.

tourist, *n.* turista *m. & f.*

tournament, *n.* torneo *m.*

tow, 1. *n.* remolque *m.* **2.** *v.* remolcar.

toward, *prep.* hacia.

towel, *n.* toalla *f.*

tower, *n.* torre *f.*

town, *n.* pueblo *m.*

toy, 1. *n.* juguete *m.* **2.** *v.* jugar.

trace, 1. *n.* vestigio; rastro *m.* **2.** *v.* trazar; rastrear; investigar.

track, 1. *n.* huella, pista *f.* **race 1.** *n.* hipódromo *m.* **2.** *v.* rastrear.

tract, *n.* trecho, tracto; tratado *m.*

tractor, *n.* tractor *m.*

trade, 1. *n.* comercio, negocio; oficio; canje *f.* **2.** *v.* comerciar, negociar; cambiar.

trader, *n.* comerciante *m.*

tradition, *n.* tradición *f.*

traditional, *a.* tradicional.

traffic, 1. *n.* tráfico *m.* **2** *v* traficar.

tragedy, *n.* tragedia *f.*

tragic, *a.* trágico.

trail, 1. *n.* sendero; rastro *m.* **2.** *v.* rastrear; arrastrar.

train, 1. *n.* tren *m.* **2.** *v.* enseñar; disciplinar; (sport) entrenarse.

traitor, *n.* traidor *m.*

tramp, 1. *n.* caminata *f.*; vagabundo *m.* **2.** *v.* patear.

tranquil, *a.* tranquilo.

tranquillity, *n.* tranquilidad *f.*

transaction, *n.* transacción *f.*

transfer, 1. *n.* traslado *m.*; boleto de transbordo. **2.** *v.* trasladar, transferir.

transform, *v.* transformar.

transfusion, *n.* transfusión *f.*

transition, *n.* transición *f.*

translate, *v.* traducir.

translation, *n.* traducción *f.*

transmit, *v.* transmitir.

transparent, *a.* transparente.

transport, 1. *n.* transporte *m.*, transportación *f.* **2.** *v.* transportar.

transportation, *n.* transporte *m.*

trap, 1. *n.* trampa *f.* **2.** *v.* atrapar.

trash, *n.* desecho *m.*; basura *f.*

travel, 1. *n.* tráfico *m.*; (pl.) viajes *m.pl.* **2.** *v.* viajar.

traveler, *n.* viajero -ra.

tray, *n.* bandeja *f.*

tread, 1. *n.* pisada *f.*; (of a tire) cubierta *f.* **2.** *v.* pisar.

treason, *n.* traición *f.*

treasure, *n.* tesoro *m.*

treasurer, *n.* tesorero -ra.

treasury, *n.* tesorería *f.*

treat, *v.* tratar; convidar.

treatment, *n.* trato, tratamiento *m.*

treaty, *n.* tratado, pacto *m.*

tree, *n.* árbol *m.*

tremble, *v.* temblar.

tremendous, *a.* tremendo.

trench, *n.* foso *m.*; (mil.) trinchera *f.*

trend, 1. *n.* tendencia *f.* **2.** *v.* tender.

trespass, *v.* traspasar; violar.

trial, *n.* prueba *f.*; (leg.) proceso, juicio *m.*

triangle, *n.* triángulo *m.*

tribulation, *n.* tribulación *f.*

tributary, *a. & n.* tributario *m.*

tribute, *n.* tributo *m.*

trick, 1. *n.* engaño *m.*; maña *f.*; (cards) baza *f.* **2.** *v.* engañar.

trifle, 1. *n.* pequeñez *f.* **2.** *v.* juguetear.

trigger, *n.* gatillo *m.*

trim, 1. *a.* ajustado, acicalado. **2.** *n.* adorno *m.* **3.** *v.* adornar; ajustar; cortar un poco.

trinket, *n.* bagatela, chuchería *f.*

trip, 1. *n.* viaje *m.* **2.** *v.* tropezar.

triple, 1. *a.* triple. **2.** *v.* triplicar.

trite, *a.* banal.

triumph, 1. *n.* triunfo *m.* **2.** *v.* triunfar.

triumphant, *a.* triunfante.

trivial, *a.* trivial.

trolley, *n.* tranvía *m.*

troop, *n.* tropa *f.*

trophy, *n.* trofeo *m.*

tropical, *a.* trópico.

tropics, *n.* trópico *m.*

trot, 1. *n.* trote *m.* **2.** *v.* trotar.

trouble, 1. *n.* apuro *m.*; congoja; aflicción *f.* **2.** *v.* molestar; afligir.

troublesome, *a.* penoso, molesto.

trough, *n.* artesa *f.*

trousers, *n.* pantalones, calzones *m.pl.*

trout, *n.* trucha *f.*

truce, *n.* tregua *f.*

truck, *n.* camión *m.*

true, *a.* verdadero; cierto, verdad.

trumpet, *n.* trompeta, trompa *f.*

trunk, *n.* baúl *m.*; (of a tree) tronco *m.*

trust, 1. *n.* confianza *f.* **2.** *v.* confiar.

trustworthy, *a.* digno de confianza.

truth, *n.* verdad *f.*

truthful, *a.* veraz.

try, 1. *n.* prueba *f.*; ensayo *m.* **2.** *v.* tratar; probar; ensayar; (leg.) juzgar. **t. on,** probarse.

tub, *n.* tina *f.*

tube, *n.* tubo *m.*

tuberculosis, *n.* tuberculosis, tisis *f.*

tuck, 1. *n.* recogido *m.* **2.** *v.* recoger.

Tuesday, n. martes m.

tug, 1. n. tirada f.; (boat) remolcador m. **2.** v. tirar.

tuition, n. matrícula, colegiatura f.

tumble, 1. caída f. **2.** v. caer, tumbar; voltear.

tumult, n. tumulto, alboroto m.

tune, 1. n. tono m.; melodía, canción f. **2.** v. templar.

tunnel, n. túnel m.

turf, n. césped m.

Turkey, n. Turquía f.

Turkish, a. turco.

turmoil, n. disturbio m.

turn, 1. n. vuelta f.; giro; turno m. **2.** v. volver, tornear, girar; transformar. **t. around,** volverse. **t. on,** encender; abrir. **t. off, t. out,** apagar.

turnip, n. nabo m.

turret, n. torrecilla f.

turtle, n. tortuga f.

tutor, 1. n. tutor m. **2.** v. enseñar.

twelve, a. & pron. doce.

twenty, a. & pron. veinte.

twice, adv. dos veces.

twig, n. varita, ramita f.; vástago m.

twilight, n. crepúsculo m.

twin, n. gemelo -la.

twine, 1. n. guita f. **2.** v. torcer.

twinkle, v. centellear.

twist, v. torcer.

two, a. & pron. dos.

type, 1. n. tipo m. **2.** v. escribir a máquina.

typewriter, n. máquina de escribir.

typhoid fever, fiebre tifoidea.

typical, a. típico.

typist, n. mecanógrafo -fa.

tyranny, n. tiranía f.

tyrant, n. tirano m.

U

udder, n. ubre f.

ugly, a. feo.

ulcer, n. úlcera f.

ulterior, a. ulterior.

ultimate, a. último.

umbrella, n. paraguas m. **sun u.,** quitasol m.

umpire, n. árbitro m.

unable, a. incapaz. **to be u.,** no poder.

unanimous, a. unánime.

uncertain, a. incierto, inseguro.

uncle, n. tío m.

unconscious, a. inconsciente; desmayado.

uncover, v. descubrir.

under, 1. adv. debajo, abajo. **2.** prep. bajo, debajo de.

underestimate, v. menospreciar, subestimar.

undergo, v. sufrir.

underground, a. subterráneo.

underline, v. subrayar.

underneath, 1. adv. por debajo. **2.** prep. debajo de.

undershirt, n. camiseta f.

understand, v. entender, comprender.

undertake, v. emprender.

underwear, n. ropa interior.

undo, v. deshacer; desatar.

undress, v. desnudar, desvestir.

uneasy, a. inquieto.

uneven, a. desigual.

unexpected, a. inesperado.

unfair, a. injusto.

unfit, a. incapáz; inadecuado.

unfold, v. desplegar; revelar.

unforgettable, a. inolvidable.

unfortunate, *a.* desafortunado, desgraciado.

unhappy, *a.* infeliz.

uniform, *a. & n.* uniforme *m.*

unify, *v.* unificar.

union, *n.* unión *f.* **labor u.**, sindicato de obreros.

unique, *a.* único.

unit, *n.* unidad *f.*

unite, *v.* unir.

unity, *n.* unidad *f.*

universal, *a.* universal.

universe, *n.* universo *m.*

university, *n.* universidad *f.*

unless, *conj.* a menos que, si no es que.

unlike, *a.* disímil.

unload, *v.* descargar.

unlock, *v.* abrir.

untie, *v.* desatar, soltar.

until, **1.** *prep.* hasta. **2.** *conj.* hasta que.

unusual, *a.* raro, inusitado.

up, **1.** *adv.* arriba. **2.** *prep.* **u. the street**, *etc.* calle arriba, etc.

uphold, *v.* apoyar, defender.

upholster, *v.* entapizar.

upon, *prep.* sobre, encima de.

upper, *a.* superior.

upright, *a.* derecho, recto.

uproar, *n.* alboroto, tumulto *m.*

upset, **1.** *n.* trastorno *m.* **2.** *v.* trastornar.

upward, *adv.* hacia arriba.

urge, **1.** deseo *m.* **2.** *v.* instar.

urgency, *n.* urgencia *f.*

urgent, *a.* urgente. **to be u.**, urgir.

us, *pron.* nosotros -as; nos.

use, **1.** *n.* uso *m.* **2.** *v.* usar, emplear. **u. up**, gastar, agotar. **be used to**, ser acostumbrado a.

useful, *a.* útil.

useless, *a.* inútil.

usher, **1.** *n.* acomodador *m.* **2.** *v.* introducir.

usual, *a.* usual.

utensil, *n.* utensilio *m.*

utmost, *a.* sumo, extremo.

utter, **1.** *a.* completo. **2.** *v.* proferir; dar.

utterance, *n.* expresión *f.*

V

vacancy, *n.* vacante *f.*

vacant, *a.* desocupado, libre.

vacation, *n.* vacaciones *f.pl.*

vaccinate, *v.* vacunar.

vacuum, *n.* vacuo, vacío *m.* **v. cleaner**, aspirador *m.*

vagrant, *n.* vagabundo.

vague, *a.* vago.

vain, *a.* vano; vanidoso. **in v.**, en vano.

valiant, *a.* valiente.

valid, *a.* válido.

valley, *n.* valle *m.*

valor, *n.* valor *m.*, valentía *f.*

valuable, *a.* precioso. **to be v.**, valer mucho.

value, **1.** *n.* valor, importe *m.* **2.** *v.* valorar; estimar.

vandal, *n.* vándalo *m.*

vanish, *v.* desaparecer.

vanity, *n.* vanidad *f.* **v. case**, polvera *f.*

vanquish, *v.* vencer.

vapor, *n.* vapor *m.*

variation, *n.* variación *f.*

variety, *n.* variedad *f.*

various, *a.* varios, diversos.

varnish, **1.** *n.* barniz *m.* **2.** *v.* barnizar.

vary, *v.* variar; cambiar.

vase, *n.* vaso, jarrón *m.*

vassal, *n.* vasallo *m.*

vast, *a.* vasto.

vat, *n.* tina *f.*, tanque *m.*

vault, *n.* bóveda *f.*

vegetable, **1.** *a. & n.* vegetal *m.*; (pl.) legumbres, verduras *f.pl.*

vehement, *a.* vehemente.

vehicle, *n.* vehículo *m.*

veil, **1.** *n.* velo *m.* **2.** *v.* velar.

vein, *n.* vena *f.*

velocity, *n.* velocidad *f.*

velvet, *n.* terciopelo *m.*

vengeance, *n.* venganza *f.*

vent, *n.* apertura *f.*

ventilate, *v.* ventilar.

venture, *n.* ventura *f.*

verb, *n.* verbo *m.*

verbose, *a.* verboso.

verdict, *n.* veredicto, fallo *m.*

verge, *n.* borde *m.*

verify, *v.* verificar.

versatile, *a.* versátil.

verse, *n.* verso *m.*

version, *n.* versión *f.*

vertical, *a.* vertical.

very, 1. *a.* mismo. **2.** *adv.* muy.

vessel, *n.* vasija *f.*; barco *m.*

vest, *n.* chaleco *m.*

veteran, *a. & n.* veterano -na.

veto, *n.* veto *m.*

vex, *v.* molestar.

via, *prep.* por la vía de; por.

viaduct, *n.* viaducto *m.*

vibrate, *v.* vibrar.

vibration, *n.* vibración *f.*

vice, *n.* vicio *m.*

vicinity, *n.* vecindad *f.*

vicious, *a.* vicioso.

victim, *n.* víctima *f.*

victor, *n.* vencedor *m.*

victorious, *a.* victorioso.

victory, *n.* victoria *f.*

view, 1. *n.* vista. **2.** *v.* ver.

vigil, *n.* vigilia, vela *f.*

vigilant, *a.* vigilante.

vigor, *n.* vigor *m.*

vile, *a.* vil, bajo.

village, *n.* aldea *f.*

villain, *n.* malvado *m.*

vindicate, *v.* vindicar.

vine, *n.* parra, vid *f.*

vinegar, *n.* vinagre *m.*

vintage, *n.* vendimia *f.*

violate, *v.* violar.

violation, *n.* violación *f.*

violence, *n.* violencia *f.*

violent, *a.* violento.

violin, *n.* violín *m.*

virgin, *n.* virgen *f.*

virile, *a.* viril.

virtual, *a.* virtual.

virtue, *n.* virtud *f.*

virtuous, *a.* virtuoso.

virus, *n.* virus *m.*

visa, *n.* visa *f.*

visible, *a.* visible.

vision, *n.* visión *f.*

visit, 1. *n.* visita *f.* **2.** *v.* visitar.

visitor, *n.* visitante *m. & f.*

visual, *a.* visual.

vital, *a.* vital.

vitality, *n.* vitalidad *f.*

vitamin, *n.* vitamina *f.*

vivacious, *a.* vivaz.

vivid, *a.* vivo; gráfico.

vocabulary, *n.* vocabulario *m.*

vocal, *a.* vocal.

vogue, *n.* boga; moda *f.*

voice, 1. *n.* voz *f.* **2.** *v.* expresar.

void, 1. *a.* vacío. **2.** *n.* vacío *m.* **3.** *v.* invalidar.

volume, *n.* volumen, tomo *m.*

voluntary, *a.* voluntario.

volunteer, 1. *n.* voluntario *m.* **2.** *v.* ofrecerse.

vomit, *v.* vomitar.

vote, 1. *n.* voto *m.* **2.** *v.* votar.

voter, *n.* votante *m. & f.*

vouch, *v.* **v. for,** garantizar.

vow, 1. *n.* voto *m.* **2.** *v.* jurar.

vowel, *n.* vocal *f.*

voyage, *n.* viaje *m.*

vulgar, *a.* vulgar; común.

vulnerable, *a.* vulnerable.

W

wade, *v.* vadear.

wag, *v.* menear.

wage, 1. *n.* (pl.) sueldo, salario *m.* **2.** *v.* **w. war,** hacer guerra.

wagon, *n.* carreta *f.*

wail, 1. *n.* lamento, gemido *m.* **2.** *v.* lamentar, gemir.

waist, *n.* cintura *f.*

wait, 1. *n.* espera *f.* **2.** *v.*

esperar. **w. for,** esperar. **w. on,** atender.

waiter, waitress, *n.* camarero -ra.

wake, *v.* **w. up,** despertar.

walk, 1. *n.* paseo *m.*; vuelta; caminata *f.*; modo de andar. **2.** *v.* andar; caminar; ir a pie.

wall, *n.* pared; (outdoor) tapia; muralla *f.*

wallet, *n.* cartera *f.*

walnut, *n.* nuez *f.*

waltz, *n.* vals *m.*

wander, *v.* vagar.

want, 1. *n.* necesidad *f.* **2.** *v.* querer.

war, *n.* guerra *f.*

ward, 1. *n.* (pol.) barrio *m.*; (hosp.) cuadra *f.* **2.** *v.* **w. off,** parar.

wares, *n.* mercancías *f.pl.*

warlike, *a.* belicoso.

warm, 1. *a.* caliente; (fig.) caluroso. **to be w.,** tener calor; (weather) hacer calor. **2.** *v.* calentar.

warmth, *n.* calor *m.*

warn, *v.* advertir.

warp, *v.* alabear.

warrant, *v.* justificar.

warrior, *n.* guerrero *m.*

warship, *n.* navío de guerra.

wash, *v.* lavar.

wasp, *n.* avispa *f.*

waste, 1. *n.* gasto *m.*; desechos *m.pl.* **2.** *v.* gastar, perder.

watch, 1. *n.* reloj *m.*; (mil.) guardia *f.* **2.** *v.* observar, mirar. **w. for,** esperar. **w. out for,** tener cuidado con. **w. over,** guardar; velar por.

watchful, *a.* desvelado.

watchmaker, *n.* relojero *m.*

watchman, *n.* sereno *m.*

water, 1. *n.* agua *f.* **w. color,** acuarela *f.* **2.** *v.* aguar.

waterfall, *n.* catarata *f.*

waterproof, *a.* impermeable.

wave, 1. *n.* onda; ola *f.* **2.** *v.* ondear; agitar; hacer señas.

waver, *v.* vacilar.

wax, 1. *n.* cera *f.* **2.** *v.* encerar.

way, *n.* camino; modo *m.*; manera *f.* **in a w.,** hasta

cierto punto. **a long w.,** muy lejos. **by the w.,** a propósito. **this w.,** por aquí. **that w.,** por allí. **which w.,** por dónde.

we, *pron.* nosotros -as.

weak, *a.* débil.

weaken, *v.* debilitar.

weakness, *n.* debilidad *f.*

wealth, *n.* riqueza *f.*

wealthy, *a.* rico.

weapon, *n.* arma *f.*

wear, 1. *n.* uso, desgaste *m.*; (clothes) ropa *f.* **2.** *v.* usar, llevar. **w. out,** gastar; cansar.

weary, *a.* cansado, rendido.

weather, *n.* tiempo *m.*

weave, *v.* tejer.

weaver, *n.* tejedor -ra.

web, *n.* tela *f.*

wedding, *n.* boda *f.*

wedge, *n.* cuña *f.*

Wednesday, *n.* miércoles *m.*

weed, *n.* maleza *f.*

week, *n.* semana *f.* **w. end,** fin de semana.

weekday, *n.* día de trabajo.

weekly, *a.* semanal.

weep, *v.* llorar.

weigh, *v.* pesar.

weight, *n.* peso *m.*

weird, *a.* misterioso, sobrenatural.

welcome, 1. *a.* bienvenido. **you're w.,** de nada, no hay de qué. **2.** *n.* acogida, bienvenida *f.* **3.** *v.* acoger, recibir bien.

welfare, *n.* bienestar *m.*

well, 1. *a.* sano, bueno. **2.** *adv.* bien; pues. **3.** *n.* pozo *m.*

well-known, *a.* bien conocido.

west, *n.* oeste, occidente *m.*

western, *a.* occidental.

westward, *adv.* hacia el oeste.

wet, 1. *a.* mojado. **to get w.,** mojarse. **2.** *v.* mojar.

whale, *n.* ballena *f.*

what, 1. *a.* qué; cuál. **2.** *interrog. pron.*, qué. **3.** *rel. pron.* lo que.

whatever, 1. *a.* cualquier. **2.** *pron.* lo que; todo lo que.

wheat, *n.* trigo *m.*

wheel, *n.* rueda *f.* **steering w.,** volante *m.*

when, 1. *adv.* cuándo. **2.** *conj.* cuando.

whenever, *conj.* siempre que, cuando quiera que.

where, 1. *adv.* dónde, adónde. **2.** *conj.* donde.

wherever, *conj.* dondequiera que, adondequiera que.

whether, *conj.* si.

which, 1. *a.* qué. **2.** *interrog. pron.* cuál. **3.** *rel. pron.* que; el cual; lo cual.

whichever, *a. & pron.* cualquiera que.

while, 1. *conj.* mientras; mientras que. **2.** *n.* rato *m.* **to be worth w.,** valer la pena.

whip, 1. *n.* látigo *m.* **2.** *v.* azotar.

whirl, *v.* girar.

whirlpool, *n.* vórtice *m.*

whirlwind, *n.* torbellino *m.*

whisk broom, *n.* escobilla *f.*

whisker, *n.* bigote *m.*

whiskey, *n.* whisky *m.*

whisper, 1. *n.* cuchicheo *m.* **2.** *v.* cuchichear.

whistle, 1. *n.* pito *m.*; silbido *m.* **2.** *v.* silbar *m.*

white, 1. *a.* blanco. **2.** *n.* (of egg) clara *f.*

who, whom, 1. *interrog. pron.* quién. **2.** *rel. pron.* que; quien.

whoever, whomever, *pron.* quienquiera que.

whole, 1. *a.* entero. **the wh.,** todo el. **2.** *n.* totalidad *f.* **on the wh.,** por lo general.

wholesale, *n.* **at wh.,** al por mayor.

wholesome, *a.* sano, saludable.

wholly, *adv.* enteramente.

whose, 1. *interrog. adj.* de quién. **2.** *rel. adj.* cuyo.

why, *adv.* por qué; para qué.

wicked, *a.* malo, malvado.

wickedness, *n.* maldad *f.*

wide, 1. *a.* ancho; extenso. **2.** *adv.* **w. open,** abierto de par en par.

widen, *v.* ensanchar; extender.

widespread, *a.* extenso.

widow, *n.* viuda *f.*

widower, *n.* viudo *m.*

width, *n.* anchura *f.*

wield, *v.* manejar, empuñar.

wife, *n.* esposa, señora, mujer *f.*

wig, *n.* peluca *f.*

wild, *a.* salvaje; bárbaro.

wilderness, *n.* desierto *m.*

will, 1. *n.* voluntad *f.*; testamento *m.* **2.** *v.* querer; determinar; (leg.) legar.

willful, *a.* voluntarioso; premeditado.

willing, *a.* **to be w.,** estar dispuesto.

willingly, *adv.* de buena gana.

wilt, *v.* marchitar.

win, *v.* ganar.

wind, 1. *n.* viento *m.* **2.** *v.* torcer; dar cuerda a.

window, *n.* ventana; (of car) ventanilla *f.*

windy, *a.* ventoso. **to be w.,** (weather) hacer viento.

wine, *n.* vino *m.*

wing, *n.* ala *f.*; (theat.) bastidor *m.*

wink, 1. *n.* guiño *m.* **2.** *v.* guiñar.

winner, *n.* ganador -ra.

winter, *n.* invierno *m.*

wipe, *v.* limpiar; (dry) secar. **w. out,** destruir.

wire, 1. *n.* alambre; hilo; telegrama *m.* **2.** *v.* telegrafiar.

wireless, *n.* telégrafo sin hilos.

wisdom, *n.* juicio *m.*; sabiduría *f.*

wise, *a.* sensato, juicioso; sabio.

wish, 1. *n.* deseo; voto *m.* **2.** *v.* desear; querer.

wit, *n.* ingenio *m.*, sal *f.*

witch, *n.* bruja *f.*

with, *prep.* con.

withdraw, *v.* retirar.

wither, *v.* marchitar.

withhold, *v.* retener, suspender.

within, 1. *adv.* dentro, por dentro. **2.** *prep.* dentro de; en.

without, 1. adv. fuera, por fuera. **2.** prep. sin.

witness, 1. n. testigo; testimonio m. **2.** v. presenciar; atestar.

witty, a. ingenioso, gracioso.

wizard, n. hechicero m.

woe, n. dolor m., pena f.

wolf, n. lobo m.

woman, n. mujer f.

womb, n. entrañas f.pl., matriz f.

wonder, 1. n. maravilla; admiración f. **for a w.,** por milagro. **no w.,** no es extraño. **2.** v. preguntarse; maravillarse.

wonderful, a. maravilloso; estupendo.

woo, v. cortejar.

wood, n. madera; (for fire) leña f.

wooden, a. de madera.

wool, n. lana f.

woolen, a. de lana.

word, 1. n. palabra f. **the words** (of a song), la letra. **2.** v. expresar.

work, 1. n. trabajo m.; (of art) obra f. **2.** v. trabajar; obrar; funcionar.

worker, n. trabajador -ra; obrero -ra.

workman, n. obrero m.

world, n. mundo m. **w. war,** guerra mundial.

worldly, a. mundano.

world-wide, a. mundial.

worm, n. gusano m.

worn, a. usado. **w. out,** gastado, cansado, rendido.

worry, 1. n. preocupación f. **2.** v. preocupar.

worse, a. peor. **to get w.,** empeorar.

worship, 1. n. adoración f. **2.** v. adorar.

worst, a. peor.

worth, 1. a. to be w., valer. **2.** n. valor m.

worthless, a. sin valor.

worthy, a. digno.

wound, 1. n. herida f. **2.** v. herir.

wrap, 1. n. (pl.) abrigos m.pl. **2.** n. envolver.

wrapping, n. cubierta f.

wrath, n. ira, cólera f.

wreath, n. guirnalda; corona f.

wreck, 1. n. ruina f.; accidente m. **2.** v. destrozar, arruinar.

wrench, n. llave f. **monkey w.,** llave inglesa.

wrestle, v. luchar.

wretched, a. miserable.

wring, v. retorcer.

wrinkle, 1. n. arruga f. **2.** v. arrugar.

wrist, n. muñeca f. **w. watch,** reloj de pulsera.

write, v. escribir. **w. down,** apuntar.

writer, n. escritor -ra.

writhe, v. contorcerse.

wrong, 1. a. equivocado; incorrecto. **to be w.,** equivocarse; no tener razón. **2.** adv. mal, incorrectamente. **3.** n. agravio m. **right and w.,** el bien y el mal. **4.** v. agraviar, ofender.

X, Y, Z

x-ray, n. rayo X m.

xylophone, n. xilófono m.

yacht, n. yate m.

yard, n. patio, corral m.; (meas.) yarda f.

yarn, n. hilo.

yawn, 1. n. bostezo m. **2.** v. bostezar.

year, n. año m.

yearly, a. anual.

yearn, v. anhelar.

yell, 1. n. grito m. **2.** v. gritar.

yellow, *a.* amarillo.
yes, *adv.* sí.
yesterday, *adv.* ayer.
yet, *adv.* todavía, aún.
yield, *v.* producir; ceder.
yoke, *n.* yugo *m.*
yolk, *n.* yema *f.*
you, *pron.* usted, (pl.) ustedes; lo, la, los, las; le, les; (familiar) tú, (pl.) vosotros -as; ti; te, (pl.) os. **with y.,** contigo.
young, *a.* joven.
your, *a.* su; (familiar) tu; (pl.) vuestro.
yours, *pron.* suyo; (familiar) tuyo; (pl.) vuestro.

yourself, -selves, *pron.* sí; se; (familiar) ti; te. **with y.,** consigo; contigo. **you y.,** usted mismo, ustedes mismos; tú mismo, vosotros mismos.
youth, *n.* juventud *f.*; (person) joven *m.*
youthful, *a.* juvenil.
zeal, *n.* celo, fervor *m.*
zealous, *a.* celoso, fervoroso.
zero, *n.* cero *m.*
zest, *n.* gusto *m.*
zone, *n.* zona *f.*
zoo, *n.* jardín zoológico.

Useful Phrases

Good day, Good morning.—Buenos días.
Good afternoon.—Buenas tardes.
Good night, Good evening.—Buenas noches.
Hello.—¡Hola!
See you later.—Hasta luego.
Goodbye.—¡Adiós!
How are you?—¿Cómo está usted?
I am fine, thank you.—Estoy bien, gracias.
I am pleased to meet you.—Mucho gusto en conocerle.
Thank you very much.—Muchas gracias.
You're welcome.—De nada.
Please.—Por favor.
Good luck.—¡Buena suerte!
To your health.—¡Salud!

Please help me.—Ayúdeme, por favor.
I don't know.—No sé.
I don't understand.—No entiendo.
Do you understand?—¿Entiende usted?
I don't speak Spanish.—No hablo español.
Do you speak English?—¿Habla usted inglés?
How do you say . . . in Spanish?—¿Cómo se dice . . . en
   español?
Speak slowly, please.—Hable despacio, por favor.
Please repeat.—Repita, por favor.
I don't like it.—No me gusta.

What is your name?—¿Cómo se llama usted?
My name is . . .—Me llamo . . .
I am an American.—Soy norteamericano.

How is the weather?—¿Qué tiempo hace?
It's cold (hot) today.—Hace frío (calor) hoy.
What time is it?—¿Qué hora es?

How much is it?—¿Cuánto es?
It is too much.—Es demasiado.
What do you wish?—¿Qué desea usted?
I want to buy . . .—Quiero comprar . . .

I am hungry.—Tengo hambre.
I am thirsty.—Tengo sed.
Where is there a restaurant?—¿Dónde hay un restaurante?
The bill, please.—La cuenta, por favor.
Where is there a hotel?—¿Dónde hay un hotel?
Where is the post office?—¿Dónde está el correo?

Take me to. . . .—Lléveme a . . .
I believe I am ill.—Creo que estoy enfermo.
Please call a doctor.—Por favor, llame al médico.
I want to send a telegram.—Quiero poner un telegrama.
As soon as possible.—Cuanto antes.

Round trip—Ida y vuelta.
Where can I change my money?—¿Dónde puedo cambiar mi dinero?
Can you accept my check?—¿Puede aceptar usted mi cheque?
What is the postage?—¿Cuánto es el franqueo?

Right away.—¡Pronto!
Help.—¡Socorro!
Come in.—¡Pase usted!
Pardon me.—Dispense usted.
Stop.—¡Pare!
Look out.—¡Cuidado!
Hurry.—¡De prisa!
Go on.—¡Siga!
To (on, at) the right—A la derecha.
To (on, at) the left—A la izquierda.
Straight ahead—Adelante.

Signs

Caution—Precaución	No admittance—Prohibida la entrada
Danger—Peligro	One way—una vía
Exit—Salida	Women—Señoras, Mujeres, Damas
Entrance—Entrada	
Stop—Alto	Men—Señores, Hombres, Caballeros
Closed—Cerrado	
Open—Abierto	Ladies' Room—El cuarto de damas
Slow—Despacio	
No smoking—Prohibido fumar	Men's Room—El servicio